# 2A Renegade

The Modern Argument for the Second
Amendment

J. P. Rothe

Gunsmoke Publishing

Book Cover by Mark Karis

Book Edited by Daniel J. Tortora

First edition 2025

# Contents

# Introduction

*The Second Amendment isn't about duck hunting. It's about our right to protect ourselves from all enemies, foreign and domestic, including our own government.*

—Clint Smith

*Political correctness is tyranny with manners.*

—Charlton Heston

In 21st-century America, the relevance and necessity of the Second Amendment has never been more pronounced. As we navigate an era marked by increasing lawlessness, record-breaking crime rates in major cities, social unrest, and riots on college campuses, the importance of the right to keep and bear arms becomes unmistakably clear. International conflicts further compound this sense of instability, driving people to seek means of protection and self-reliance. It is no surprise that Americans are purchasing firearms more than at any other time in history.

For many, the decision to own a gun is a new and exciting venture. Countless individuals who previously never considered gun ownership are now embracing their Second Amendment rights, realizing the critical role these rights play in ensuring personal safety and security. This widespread awakening is a response to the undeniable reality that the systems meant to protect us are increasingly strained or ineffective. The disconnect between on-the-ground realities and the narratives perpetuated by media and political figures has driven a surge in gun ownership, as people take personal responsibility for their safety.

Reflecting on my own journey, I find a sense of camaraderie with the many Americans who have recently come to understand and appreciate the Second Amendment. While my awakening occurred several years ago, it is heartening to see so many others now recognizing the importance of this fundamental right. The trend is unmistakable: Despite what mainstream media might suggest, public sentiment is shifting towards a more pro-gun stance. People from diverse backgrounds and for various reasons are now seeing the value in owning firearms, united by a common desire to protect themselves and their loved ones.

As we dive into this exploration of the Second Amendment, it is important to acknowledge that every individual's journey to embracing gun ownership is unique. However, the overarching theme remains consistent: In times of uncertainty and danger, the ability to defend oneself is paramount.

I, too, once found myself on the side of advocating stricter gun control. Growing up, I had no exposure to gun culture, leaving me more susceptible to anti-gun narratives. The news media bombarded me with stories of gun violence, painting a grim picture of a society plagued by senseless shootings and tragedies. Like many others, the solution lay in stricter regulations and even outright bans on certain types of firearms.

However, my perspective began to shift when I embarked on a journey of education and self-discovery. I decided to delve deeper into the issue, seeking to understand the historical context of the Second Amendment and the reasons behind its enshrinement in our Constitution. As I learned more about firearms and their role in American history, I came to realize that the debate over gun rights was not just about weapons; it was about fundamental principles of liberty and democracy.

The turning point came when I confronted my own misconceptions about guns and the people who owned them. I had never interacted with gun owners or taken the time to understand their perspective. But as I engaged in conversations with responsible gun owners and enthusiasts, I gained a newfound appreciation for their passion and commitment to the Second Amendment. I learned that for many Americans, gun ownership is not just a hobby or a right; it is a deeply held belief rooted in a desire to protect themselves, their loved ones, and their way of life.

This book is the culmination of my journey from being ignorant about guns to recognizing the importance of an armed population in safeguarding against tyranny. It is a testament to the power of education and open-mindedness in shaping our beliefs and perspectives. Through careful examination of history, legal precedents, and contemporary debates, I aim to shed light on the true meaning and significance of the Second Amendment.

In the pages ahead, we'll dive headfirst into the roots of the Second Amendment, uncovering its purpose, power, and enduring relevance. We'll break down how firearms play a vital role in self-defense, revisit the haunting lessons of tyrannies past, and tackle the tough—but necessary—questions about balancing public safety with personal liberty. Along the way, we'll expose the influence of media and academia in twisting the national conversation, debunk the myths that muddy the waters, and make the unapologetic case that an armed citizenry is a free citizenry. Above all, this journey is a bold reaffirmation of the Second Amendment—not as a relic of the past, but as a living safeguard against tyranny, oppression, and the slow erosion of freedom.

I am not a seasoned historian, nor am I particularly interested in or savvy with the trends of 2020s modernity. By profession, I am a project manager for an environmental consulting firm, holding a master's degree in environmental science and chemistry. My daily work involves extensive writing, primarily scientific reports and environmental studies based on my investigations and research, which has honed my ability to express knowledge and ideas clearly and effectively. While environmental work is my day job, the Second Amendment is my passion. Through this book, I blend my skills in research and writing with my deep-seated interest in America's right to bear arms.

Before we begin, I want to stress that this book is not for the faint of heart. For those expecting a carefully balanced debate that tiptoes around both sides of the issue—look elsewhere. This book doesn't pretend to be neutral. It takes a firm, unapologetic stance in defense of the Second Amendment, because the stakes are too high for lukewarm half-measures. That said, if you're someone who's undecided, uncertain, or simply curious—someone willing to challenge their assumptions and engage with hard truths—then welcome. This book invites open minds, not closed hearts. It isn't about appeasing everyone—it's about making the strongest case for liberty, personal responsibility, and the right to defend both.

In a landscape where anti-gun narratives dominate our mainstream institutions and where most people are fed misleading information on this critical issue, this book aims to provide the much-needed counterbalance. It serves as a corrective to the one-sided views propagated by the mainstream media, academia, and political elites, offering a robust defense of the fundamental right the Second Amendment provides.

Also, while it may appear that I frequently insert my personal opinions and experiences throughout this book, these viewpoints are grounded in historical evidence—both recent and ancient—and supported by statistical facts and common sense. Many, myself included, initially struggled to accept the historical truth surrounding contentious issues. However, my intention is not to cater to people's sensibilities but to challenge the prevailing narratives about a topic that is often misunderstood or overlooked in mainstream discourse. This book aims to provoke thoughtful consideration and foster a deeper understanding of the importance of the Second Amendment and its far-reaching implications, and to do that effectively, it blends elements of history, philosophy, personal narrative, and editorial commentary.

I've also structured this book so that readers can approach it however they prefer—whether flipping to the topics that interest them most or reading it straight through from cover to cover. Reading the pages ahead requires an open mind and a willingness to critically examine deeply held beliefs. Each chapter stands on its own, covering a distinct aspect of the Second Amendment without requiring prior knowledge from earlier sections. Whether you're a seasoned advocate, someone newly exploring the issue, or just curious about one particular facet, you'll be able to dive right in without feeling lost. My goal is to create a book that's as engaging as it is informative, providing readers with both a deeper understanding and an appreciation for the complexities, history, and enduring relevance of the Second Amendment.

The detailed information presented herein is part of a larger, enduring argument in defense of the Second Amendment. While I strive to keep this book updated with the most up-to-date information, it is important to acknowledge that laws, narratives, and events related to the Second Amendment evolve rapidly. It is impossible to cover every new law, rumor, or news article regarding the changing landscape of gun rights. Should any significant rulings or changes occur within the American landscape, they will be addressed in future editions of this book, if warranted.

As an amateur historian and Second Amendment guru, I sincerely hope this book serves as a catalyst for anyone who might be on the fence about the Second Amendment, inspiring them to embark on a similar journey of discovery and understanding as I have, along with many others. I am not an expert on firearms or firearms law, nor am I claiming to be. The purpose of this book is to provide a nearly complete and comprehensive volume about Second Amendment history, laws, issues, and the like. However, I want to pass on what I have learned on my long journey into the world of the Second Amendment. Through extensive research and personal exploration, I have uncovered fascinating insights and critical perspectives that I believe are essential for understanding this pivotal element of American liberty. This book reflects that journey, aiming to inform, provoke thought, and contribute to the ongoing dialogue about one of the most fundamental rights enshrined in our Constitution.

The future of our freedom in the United States, and indeed around the world, depends on preserving our Second Amendment rights. To achieve this, we must work to expand our Second Amendment community by engaging with others and changing minds, one person at a time. Only by cultivating a stronger understanding and respect for these rights can we secure them for generations to come. May this book be one more step toward that goal.

—J. P. Rothe

# Chapter 1

## From Ignorance to Advocacy

*The only true wisdom is in knowing you know nothing.*
—Socrates

*Nothing in the world is more dangerous than sincere ignorance and conscientious stupidity.*
—Martin Luther King Jr.

*The trouble with our liberal friends is not that they're ignorant; it's just that they know so much that isn't so.*
—Ronald Reagan

The journey from being anti-gun to pro-Second Amendment is a transformative experience for many, often sparked by personal encounters, increasing awareness of the real-world implications of gun ownership, or a deeper understanding of constitutional rights. This shift in perspective mirrors my own journey; as the more I learned, the more I became a fervent advocate for the Second Amendment.

My personal awakening from ignorance to advocacy was not marked by any extraordinary events; rather, it was a gradual and eye-opening process. As I delved deeper into the complexities of the Second Amendment and gun rights, my perspective underwent a dramatic transformation. My journey from skepticism to becoming an enthusiastic advocate for gun rights and the Second Amendment mirrors the experiences of many others who kept an open mind and evolved in their views.

Growing up in a small suburban town in New Jersey, just a stone's throw from the George Washington Bridge and the bustling city of Manhattan, my childhood was, in many ways, quintessentially American. Our household did not have guns, and I didn't think much about them one way or another. My grandfather served in the Army, but the only gun he owned was his father's 12-gauge hunting shotgun, which he kept tucked away in the attic, out of sight and out of mind. I was never exposed to it. My father, a paratrooper and sniper in the Army, owned several firearms. However, due to his frequent absences and limited presence in my life, I never had any exposure to them either.

I was an average American kid, really, who enjoyed the usual suburban pastimes. Cap guns, toy guns, and water pistols were staples of my playtime arsenal. I even made homemade slingshots, using them to shoot at cardboard targets propped up against my grandparents' aluminum shed, or at groundhogs, squirrels, and other critters—though I never actually hit any of them. My friends and I, along with the neighborhood kids, spent endless hours playing cops and robbers with toy guns, or cowboys and Indians with cap guns and toy bows and arrows. We roamed freely through backyards and fields, our imaginations transforming our surroundings into vast frontiers and bustling cityscapes.

In those days, there were no busybody Karens or hysterical liberal parents in the neighborhood to throw a hissy fit over our games using toy guns. Everyone understood it was just innocent fun, a part of growing up. Those were good times, filled with laughter and a sense of freedom that seems harder to come by these days.

My love for action-packed video games was no secret either. I spent countless hours on my NES, battling through games like *Contra*, *Mega Man*, *Duck Hunt*, and *Wild Gunman*, all of which featured guns and shooting. These games were a thrilling escape and a big part of my childhood. During summer camp, I discovered the joy of shooting BB guns and practicing archery, activities I looked forward to every year.

As I moved into high school, my exposure to firearms was limited. Occasionally, I would join friends for some shotgun shooting in the woods. Yet, guns still were not a big part of my life. They were just another activity that I felt neutral about—nothing to fear, nothing to idolize.

However, as I entered college and ventured into the wider world, my perspective began to shift. My college experience was relatively typical for the time, characterized by the usual academic and social challenges. While there was a certain level of ideological indoctrination on campus, as has been the case nationwide since at least the 1960s, it was not as pervasive or extreme as it seems to be today. Professors certainly had their biases, and some pushed radical viewpoints, but the atmosphere still allowed for a range of ideas and healthy debate. We could still focus on our studies, make lifelong friends, and engage in activities without feeling constantly bombarded by a singular ideological agenda. However, the political debates around gun ownership and the portrayal of certain types of weapons in the media at the time started to influence me. The constant barrage of anti-gun rhetoric painted a picture of firearms as something inherently dangerous and undesirable. I absorbed these narratives, forming a bias against guns and developing a certain level of fear towards them. The idea of owning a gun seemed alien, even a bit frightening.

Unfortunately, my ignorance towards guns persisted well into my thirties, even as my philosophical and political views began to shift in other areas. I regretfully voted for Barack Obama in 2008, but it did not take long for his radical views to become evident, despite the mainstream media's efforts to shield him. Shortly after the passage of Obamacare, I received a letter informing me that my excellent healthcare plan was no longer compliant with the new regulations and would not be available for renewal. My company was forced to find a new healthcare plan, which turned out to be both inferior and significantly more expensive. I felt duped. Since then, my healthcare coverage has deteriorated and become even more costly. I have not voted for a Democrat candidate for president since that time. However, my bias against guns remained intact a bit longer; that change would come a little later in 2016.

In April 2016, my spouse and I purchased a contemporary-style house built in 1988, set on two acres of land in a rural area of upstate New York. The house, with its numerous large windows, offered picturesque views of the woods surrounding us but also left us feeling vulnerable, especially given the lengthy response times for law enforcement in such a remote location. It was suggested to me that we consider getting a gun for protection. Initially, I was very uncomfortable with the idea. I had never really seen myself as a gun owner and felt intimidated by the thought of having firearms in the house. While I was not opposed to gun ownership in principle, I simply never envisioned myself as someone who would want or need a gun. However, it was pointed out to me that we were essentially sitting ducks and needed something for our safety in case of an emergency. After several discussions and some time to ponder, I agreed to explore the idea further.

After deciding to get a gun, I embarked on a comprehensive journey to educate myself on firearm ownership. Questions flooded my mind: Which gun should I choose? What is the process to acquire one? Do I need a permit? How will I learn to use it safely and effectively, and who will guide me through this learning process? The entire endeavor seemed overwhelming.

I quickly discovered that obtaining a handgun in New York is exceedingly challenging. The permit process is not only daunting and expensive but also incredibly time-consuming, often taking up to a year to complete. I was taken aback by the state's stringent gun control laws, especially since the media had portrayed gun acquisition as straightforward and easily accessible to anyone at any time. This realization sparked a broader questioning of the media narratives I had previously accepted. What other misconceptions had I been led to believe? Although I had heard of the Second Amendment, I began to question my understanding of its true significance. As such, my expedition of discovery and education began.

I soon found myself grappling with misconceptions and misunderstandings surrounding firearms and the Second Amendment. Unlike some, I was not necessarily against the idea of people owning guns, but I was intimidated by the idea of owning a gun. Like many others, I had been influenced by media portrayals and societal norms that painted a one-dimensional picture of guns as instruments of violence and chaos. The prevailing narrative in mainstream media outlets reinforced these perceptions, often sensationalizing stories of gun violence while downplaying instances of lawful self-defense or responsible gun ownership. I was initially apprehensive about firearms and saw little reason for myself to own one. However, as I delved deeper into the complexities of the issue, I began to realize the importance of questioning preconceived notions and seeking a more nuanced understanding.

Something that immediately stood out to me was the hypocrisy among political and cultural elites who advocate strict gun control. It struck me as contradictory that those who push for disarmament measures for the general population often rely on armed protection for themselves and their families. This observation prompted me to further research the issue, questioning the motives behind such advocacy and exploring the principles underlying the Second Amendment. I sought to understand the practical implications of gun ownership, the role of firearms in self-defense, and the broader cultural and historical context of the Second Amendment. Through conversations with gun owners and advocates, I gained valuable insights into the importance of individual liberties and the need to safeguard the right to bear arms.

My transformation began with a simple question: *Why* is the right to bear arms enshrined in our Constitution? This question served as a catalyst for deeper exploration, leading me to confront my own ignorance and biases. The words of the Second Amendment struck me as powerful and timeless, but their true meaning remained elusive. What did it mean to speak of "a well regulated Militia" in the context of a free society? As I pondered these questions, I realized that the language of the Second Amendment conveyed a deeper significance than I had initially grasped and so, I sought out diverse perspectives and sources of information to better understand the complexities of gun rights and the Second Amendment.

My epiphany about the true linguistic meaning of the Second Amendment came from watching Bill Whittle's videos. One particularly enlightening resource was his video "Your Second Amendment," which offered a detailed analysis of the amendment's language and meaning. Whittle, a renowned commentator and advocate for gun rights, provided valuable insights into the grammatical structure and syntax of the amendment, shedding light on its true significance. Free from legal jargon and lawyerly spin, his explanations helped me understand and appreciate the Second Amendment in a new way.

In the video, Whittle breaks down the language of the Second Amendment, emphasizing the importance of understanding the sentence structure and the placement of key clauses. He highlights the often-overlooked significance of the prefatory clause, "A well regulated Militia, being necessary to the security of a free State," and its relationship to the operative clause, "the right of the people to keep and bear Arms, shall not be infringed."

Whittle's analysis underscores the foundational importance of the Second Amendment in preserving individual liberties and safeguarding against government tyranny. By dissecting the language of the amendment, he clarifies its true intent and dispels common misconceptions about its meaning. Here is an excerpt from Whittle's analysis:

> *The Second Amendment does not say, 'The people shall have the right to form a well-regulated militia.' It says, 'Because a well-regulated militia is one of the nice things an armed population can provide, it isn't the only thing and it's not the reason to arm the people. In addition, the right to the people isn't even granted by the Constitution; its existence is assumed, and it says that the government cannot infringe upon that preexisting right. It is not a hunting right. It is not a sporting right. It is not even a self-defense right. It's the right to be armed for the purpose of defending freedom.'*

In other words, the prefatory clause, "A well regulated Militia, being necessary to the security of a free State," underscores the Founding Fathers' recognition of the essential role of an armed citizenry in maintaining the security and sovereignty of the nation. However, the operative clause, "the right of the people to keep and bear Arms, shall not be infringed," extends beyond the context of militia service, affirming the individual's inherent right to possess and carry firearms for personal defense and the defense of liberty.

In another one of his videos, "Number One with a Bullet," Bill Whittle challenges the common belief that the United States' high gun ownership (120.5 guns per 100 residents) correlates with the highest murder rate globally. He presents data showing that although Americans own more guns per capita than any other country, nations with stricter gun control laws like Honduras and Venezuela experience much higher murder rates. Whittle observes that those cities in the US with the highest gun ownership, such as Plano, Texas, have some of the lowest murder rates, while cities with strict gun control laws, like Chicago, have some of the highest. He also points to countries like Switzerland and Finland, where high gun ownership coincides with low gun violence. Whittle criticizes the media for conflating gun ownership with gun violence and misusing statistics, such as including suicides in gun violence figures. His analysis emphasizes the need for a nuanced understanding of gun violence, suggesting that responsible gun ownership, effective law enforcement, and socioeconomic policies can coexist with low crime rates, thereby supporting the preservation of gun rights in the US.

Amidst my desire towards better understanding the Second Amendment, a pivotal moment occurred when we all witnessed the tragic events of the Orlando mass shooting on June 12, 2016. The senseless loss of life left me reeling, but it also sparked a new line of inquiry. As I pondered the aftermath of the attack, I could not shake the thought: What if a Good Samaritan in that club had been carrying a gun? Could they have stopped the shooter more quickly? My initial reaction would probably have been that it is not smart to carry a concealed firearm inside a crowded club, especially where alcohol and, in some cases, illegal drug use is involved. The risk of an argument or fight escalating into a shooting is certainly higher. However, this risk is not unique to clubs; it can happen anywhere. So, what is the solution? What about having a licensed armed security guard? If no guns are allowed, in the event of a shooting, everyone would be helpless. We need to consider what's worse: a shooter coming in and murdering dozens of helpless, unarmed people, or allowing the carrying of firearms with the remote possibility of misuse? As with anything, it is a trade-off, not necessarily a definitive solution.

Thinking through all the scenarios and possibilities challenged my preconceived notions and opened my mind to the idea that good guys with guns could be used to stop bad guys with guns. It dawned on me that making it difficult for law-abiding citizens to carry guns reduces the likelihood of stopping a public shooting. Criminals do not follow gun laws, leaving people vulnerable. When seconds count, the police are minutes away, as this shooting clearly demonstrated.

I encountered a wealth of information that challenged my assumptions and expanded my understanding of the role of guns in society. I read dozens of books and case studies about the Second Amendment, listened to podcasts, watched documentaries and historical videos, and paid closer attention to the political debates surrounding the Second Amendment and gun control. The more I learned, the more I realized that my previously indifferent and negative attitude toward guns did not hold up to the pro-Second Amendment arguments and statistics that I encountered. It was during this time that I made a decision that would mark a significant turning point in my journey: I decided to purchase my first gun.

But which one to choose? My options were limited by strict regulations. Initially, I wanted to buy a pistol—something basic that I could easily access in case of an emergency. However, I quickly learned that in New York, I would not even be allowed to handle a pistol without a handgun license.

I had a couple of options: I could get an on-premises-only permit, which would limit me to keeping the firearm at home, or I could apply for an unrestricted concealed carry license. This license would allow me not only to purchase and keep a firearm at home but also to carry it concealed outside the home in most places. The process for obtaining a concealed carry license, however, seemed daunting and time-consuming, potentially taking up to a year to complete. Given my desire to acquire a firearm promptly, I realized that pursuing this option would not satisfy my immediate needs.

My other option was to purchase either a rifle or a shotgun, which did not require a permit to buy, keep, or take outside the home. After considering my choices, I ultimately decided on an AR-15 style rifle chambered in 5.56. Not only did it look cool, but I also did not need to wait for an extensive licensing process, provided I passed the standard background check. This decision allowed me to quickly obtain a firearm for self-defense and recreational purposes while planning to eventually obtain my concealed carry license in the future. Having the AR-15 at home gave me a sense of security and the ability to practice shooting and become more familiar with firearm handling in the meantime.

Walking into the gun store for the first time, I felt a mix of excitement and apprehension. I knew almost nothing about the various kinds of rifle models or manufacturers to choose from, and it was obvious to anyone who saw me that I was new to this. I was afraid of looking stupid and clueless, so I clung to the printout of the kind of rifle I wanted—an AR-15–style rifle. The sales associate, who turned out to be a retired law enforcement officer, noticed my unease and offered to help. I was upfront about my lack of knowledge, admitting that I knew almost nothing about which rifle to buy. To my relief, he patiently answered my questions and guided me through the options available.

As we discussed the various models, I was surprised to learn about New York State's restrictions on cosmetic features. I had not realized that if a rifle had a removable magazine, it could not have the "cool" features I wanted, such as a pistol grip, muzzle brake, and adjustable stock. This meant the rifle would look strange and less functional to me. However, the salesman explained that if the magazine was fixed in place and couldn't be removed, I could have all the other features I desired. This came with a trade-off: Reloading the firearm would be more challenging, as it would have to be done either manually through the ejection port or by disassembling the rifle and separating the upper from the lower.

Being new to firearms, I was not thrilled about the idea of making my learning process more difficult. But ultimately, I chose the fixed magazine option because it allowed me to have the features I wanted. Despite the added challenge of loading the magazine manually, which is not easy and can be prone to jams and misfeeds, I felt more comfortable with this setup. The salesman's guidance was invaluable, and although I knew the learning curve would be steeper, I was excited to start practicing and to become proficient with my new rifle.

Soon after acquiring my rifle, I took the time to educate myself on how to correctly operate it, safely shoot it, and take it apart. I spent hours examining its distinct parts and learning their functions until I felt confident enough to use it correctly. Once I was ready, I booked some time at the gun range for my first genuine experience with live fire.

Having never been to a range before, I did not know what to expect. The media depicted gun ranges as dirty and dangerous, but my experience was the complete opposite. The range was modern and pristinely clean, with a welcoming atmosphere. The woman at the front desk was friendly and helpful, and the customers browsing the store were from all walks of life—a diverse crowd, very different from the stereotype portrayed in the media. After purchasing a box of 55 grain 5.56 NATO ammunition and a few paper targets, I watched the required safety video to ensure I was fully prepared. I made sure I had my hearing protection ready before entering the firing range.

The excitement of finally getting to shoot my rifle was mixed with nerves about making a fool of myself. As I stepped onto the range, surrounded by seasoned shooters, I couldn't help but feel a sense of intimidation. I worried about appearing inexperienced and foolish in front of others. However, the environment was far from intimidating. The other shooters were focused on their own practice, and the range officers were attentive and ready to assist if needed. As I reminded myself of the basic gun safety rules, loaded my rifle and took aim at my paper target, something remarkable happened. With each pull of the trigger, I felt a surge of exhilaration and empowerment. It was a moment of realization—I was no longer just a bystander in the debate over gun rights; I was an active participant, embracing my newfound role as a responsible gun owner.

Although my experience at the gun range was very positive, my rifle did jam a few times due to the inconvenience of the fixed magazine loading mechanism. Not knowing what to do, I had to ask for help. I came clean to the range officer, admitting that I was new and unsure how to resolve the issue since my magazine could not be removed. Aside from those embarrassing moments, I had a lot of fun. The seed was planted, and I could not wait to go back.

After my first trip to the gun range with my newly acquired firearm, my journey into the world of shooting truly began to take shape. Eager to improve, I immersed myself in studying shooting techniques, learning the intricacies of my rifle, and frequenting the range to hone my skills. With each visit, I became more confident and precise, transforming my initial curiosity into disciplined practice.

As I learned more about the configuration options of my AR-style rifle, I was pleasantly surprised to realize it was the Lego set of the gun world. The modularity of the platform allowed me to swap factory parts for new, cooler-looking upgrades, reconfiguring my rifle to better suit my preferences. I experimented with various scopes and red dots, eventually finding the perfect setup that enhanced my accuracy and comfort. Taking apart and reassembling my rifle became second nature, and I learned how to replace factory-grade parts with custom accessories, making the firearm uniquely mine.

The result of these efforts was a sleek, lightweight rifle that not only looked impressive but felt incredibly comfortable to shoot. My journey didn't stop there; the excitement of customization led me to purchase another rifle, which I also upgraded to meet my specifications. Over the years, my knowledge of rifle building expanded, and so did my collection of firearms. Each new addition was a canvas for customization, allowing me to create personalized weapons that reflected my style and preferences.

As I was learning more about shooting, going to the range, and customizing my firearms, I also started the process of getting my concealed carry permit for New York. The process was long and grueling, taking me about a year to complete. It was tedious; I had to take a pistol safety class, attend several interviews with the county sheriff's office, file a mountain of paperwork, and obtain references. Additionally, I had to write letters to judges and endure long waiting periods.

Finally, when I received my license in the mail, I discovered that I still was not allowed to take possession of the pistol I had chosen until I filed more paperwork and paid additional fees to get the pistol information added to my license. It took another six weeks to two months for the paperwork to be processed and for my updated license to be mailed to me. Every single handgun purchase is required to go through this same lengthy procedure.

Despite the challenges and frustrations, obtaining my concealed carry permit was a significant milestone in my journey. This arduous process taught me patience and perseverance and reinforced the importance of being well-informed and prepared.

After obtaining my unrestricted concealed carry license for the state of New York, I initially thought I could carry my gun into other states. I quickly learned that this was not the case. Some states do not recognize another state's firearms permit, and carrying a gun across state lines without the appropriate permit can lead to prosecution for illegal firearms possession. This realization was frustrating and didn't make much sense to me. If I'm legally able to conceal carry in a strict state like New York, why can't I cross into New Jersey and have my permit recognized there?

However, I also discovered that most of the states around the nation have reciprocity agreements and recognize New York's license. Despite this, none of the states surrounding me, aside from Pennsylvania and Vermont, would permit me to bring my handguns into their territory for recreational shooting or travel. This meant I had to find another solution if I wanted the freedom to carry my firearm more broadly.

After extensive research, I realized that obtaining nonresident concealed carry permits for Florida and New Hampshire would allow me to carry my firearm in more than three-quarters of all states. The process of obtaining these permits was surprisingly straightforward. I filled out a form, submitted a photo, and sent them a copy of my New York license, and within a few weeks, after they conducted a background check, I received my concealed carry licenses from both states. More recently, I was invited to attend a class by a friend of mine (who happens to be a firearms instructor) who was conducting a Utah concealed carry permit course. I took the class, filled out the paperwork, and submitted it to the state of Utah.

With the combination of my New York, Florida, New Hampshire, and Utah firearms licenses, I am now eligible to conceal carry in over 40 states. This experience taught me a lot about the complexities and variations in gun laws across the United States, and it underscored the importance of doing thorough research and ensuring compliance with all applicable regulations. Despite the initial hurdles, I now have a greater sense of security and freedom when traveling across the country.

As my knowledge of firearms and the Second Amendment grew, naturally, so too did my firearms collection. As such, I often encountered people who would roll their eyes and ask why I needed a gun like that, or why I needed more than one kind of gun. These questions didn't bother me because of the questions themselves, but because of the snarky, disapproving tone in which they were asked. Surprisingly, I was well prepared for their criticisms and sarcasm because, to an extent, I once shared some of their biases against guns. Having once held their perspectives allowed me to anticipate and debunk their arguments effectively. The only way to respond to such a silly question is to look them in the eye and say,

"Because I can and it's my right." When confronted with statements like "I don't think anyone should be allowed to own a gun like that," my response was simple and firm: "Well, we can."

I don't need to justify my right to own whatever gun I want to anyone. Their self-righteous attitude is baffling, especially when considering that they likely own or enjoy things they don't necessarily need. Using their logic, countless personal choices would come under unnecessary scrutiny. *Need* doesn't enter the equation when exercising a constitutional right. The *right* to bear arms is fundamental, and need is irrelevant. When you point out a few facts or ask them follow-up questions about the specific guns and restrictions they want banned, they often can't provide details and concede they don't know much about guns. This realization usually causes them to let their guard down, at least the ones humble enough to admit their lack of knowledge.

One of the interesting things during my journey into becoming a Second Amendment advocate was making new friends and losing longtime ones. For much of my life, my circle of friends consisted mostly of individuals who did not view the Second Amendment or firearms positively. Whenever the topic came up, it became clear that their opinions were shaped more by media talking points than by any substantial understanding of the issues. Their hostility was obvious, and discussions often got a little heated. Over time, this created a rift, and we drifted apart amicably. It was a shame to see those friendships fade, but I realized that if something as fundamental as a belief in the Second Amendment could be the catalyst for the end of our friendship, then perhaps those relationships had run their course.

However, as the cliché goes, when one door closes, another one opens. As I delved deeper into the world of firearms and Second Amendment advocacy, I met many wonderful people who shared my newfound passion. Some of these individuals became close friends. Our shared interest in firearms and shooting sports created a strong bond, and I found myself surrounded by a community that was supportive, knowledgeable, and enthusiastic. These new friendships have enriched my life in ways I hadn't anticipated, providing camaraderie and a sense of belonging that I truly value.

Despite my evolution into a staunch advocate for the Second Amendment, I will admit that my proficiency lies more in the academic and philosophical realms than in my skills as a shooter. Even now, after all these years, I still need to improve my shooting and tactical skills. I am not an expert, but merely an enthusiast who is constantly learning. Unfortunately, the challenging part, for myself and likely many others in my shoes, is balancing these pursuits with a busy schedule. I work a lot and write extensively, which limits my available time for practice. And the price of ammunition remains high, making it costly to replenish what I use at the range. These factors combine to make it difficult to consistently work on my shooting proficiency, but I remain committed to finding ways to improve and grow in this area.

## The Journeys of Others, Including Yours

If you're holding this book, there's a good chance you're curious. Maybe you've found yourself questioning some long-held beliefs, or perhaps you've stumbled across information that doesn't quite fit the narrative you've always heard. That's perfectly okay. In fact, it's more than okay—it's healthy. It can feel a little intimidating to dive into unfamiliar territory, especially when it comes to something as emotionally charged and politically tangled as the Second Amendment and gun rights. If you're starting to question your stance on the Second Amendment or gun control, believe me—you're not alone. I've been right where you are. You are one among millions of Americans who, in just the last few years, have experienced what I'd call an awakening. Regular people, just like you and me, have begun to take a hard look at these issues and realized that maybe what they've been told doesn't quite hold water.

I started out skeptical, hesitant, and frankly, not knowing much about firearms beyond what I'd absorbed from media soundbites and popular culture. But over time, my perspective shifted as I asked tough questions and followed where the answers led me. And guess what? I'm not some outlier. Many people—ordinary folks like you and me—have walked this same path, discovering that there's a lot more to this issue than meets the eye.

As a matter of fact, plenty of well-known people—many you'd probably never expect—have embraced their Second Amendment rights. Take Dave Rubin, for example. He started out as an anti-gun advocate while working as a commentator for the left-wing outlet The Young Turks Network. Back then, he echoed some of the same arguments I used to believe. But, like me—and like so many others—he had a change of heart. Today, Rubin is a supporter of gun rights, has left the gun control circus of California behind, and now calls gun-friendly Florida home—complete with a firearm of his own. Stories like his, and mine, are becoming more common, and they prove that it's okay to question, rethink, and ultimately change where you stand.

Another well-known figure who underwent such a transformation is Dana Loesch, a former anti-gun advocate who became a leading spokesperson for the National Rifle Association (NRA). Loesch's journey began as a liberal journalist who initially supported stricter gun control measures. However, after becoming a mother and experiencing a home invasion, her perspective shifted dramatically. Loesch realized the importance of self-defense and the inadequacies of relying solely on law enforcement for protection. Her deep dive into the Second Amendment and gun rights led her to become one of the most vocal proponents of gun ownership and self-defense, advocating for the rights of law-abiding citizens to protect themselves and their families.

There are even celebrities who exercise their Second Amendment rights. Angelina Jolie has a gun collection and even has a private shooting range at one of her homes. Her ex, Brad Pitt, has talked about owning guns and teaching his kids firearm safety. Keanu Reeves is not just a Hollywood action star; he's also an avid shooter and has trained extensively with firearms. And then there's Kurt Russell, who's been unapologetic about his support for gun rights and has openly discussed being a gun owner.

The journeys of ordinary citizens are just as compelling. Take the story of Sarah McKinley, a young widow in Oklahoma who defended her home and infant son from intruders with a shotgun. Initially, McKinley had no strong opinions about gun ownership, but after the death of her husband and the subsequent break in, she quickly realized the importance of having the means to protect her family. Her harrowing experience, widely publicized, resonated with many and highlighted the critical role firearms play in self-defense.

Similarly, Maj Toure, founder of the Black Guns Matter movement, transformed from a skeptic of gun ownership to a fervent Second Amendment advocate. Growing up in Philadelphia, Toure was exposed to the dangers of urban violence and initially believed that fewer guns on the streets would lead to safer communities. However, as he educated himself about gun laws, the history of gun control, and the importance of self-defense, his views evolved. Toure now travels the country educating urban communities about gun rights, safety, and responsible ownership, advocating for empowerment through knowledge and self-defense.

The point is, gun ownership doesn't fit into a single stereotype. It cuts across demographics, politics, professions, and personalities, and includes people from all walks of life who recognize the value in protecting themselves and their loved ones.

Like many, I began with a limited understanding of the Second Amendment, influenced by media narratives and societal norms that often portrayed guns negatively. However, the more I researched the topic, the more I recognized the importance of the right to keep and bear arms. Personal research, discussions with knowledgeable individuals, and a deeper appreciation for constitutional rights all contributed to my evolving viewpoint. My journey, much like those of many others, was marked by a growing awareness of the realities of self-defense and the critical role the Second Amendment plays in safeguarding individual freedoms. Understanding the stories of others who have made this transition underscores the significance of the Second Amendment and the diverse reasons people have come to support it. Whether through personal experience, increased knowledge, or a deeper understanding of constitutional principles, the shift from anti-gun to pro-Second Amendment reflects a broader recognition of the importance of self-defense and the preservation of liberty.

As I moved forward along this path, the complexities and significance of the Second Amendment became increasingly clear. In the chapters ahead, I will share everything I have learned about this fundamental right, exploring its rich history, its crucial role in safeguarding liberty, and the myriad ways it continues to impact our society today. We will explore the historical context, legal interpretations, and contemporary relevance of this essential constitutional provision. We will examine the atrocities committed against disarmed populations by their own governments, highlighting the dire consequences of civilian disarmament. Additionally, we will discuss the issue of gun control, debunking the untruths, manipulated statistics, and fallacies promoted by advocates in the media. We will also contrast the elitist attitudes toward gun ownership with the views of the general public, revealing a vast difference in perspectives, and we will uncover the truth behind the rhetoric and understand the enduring importance of the right to keep and bear arms. Drawing on extensive research and personal experiences, I hope to provide a comprehensive understanding of why the Second Amendment remains a vital part of American identity and freedom. Ultimately, this book aims to inspire and empower more people to educate themselves and actively engage in exercising their Second Amendment rights.

# Chapter 2

## The Birth of a Right

*No free man shall ever be debarred the use of arms.*
—Thomas Jefferson

*To disarm the people ... was the best and most effectual way to enslave them.*
—George Mason

The Second Amendment of the United States Constitution is a cornerstone of American liberty, representing a fundamental right that predates the very founding of the nation. Rooted deeply in the principles of natural law, the right to keep and bear arms is recognized not merely as a legal construct but as an inherent, God-given right essential for the preservation of life, liberty, and the pursuit of happiness. The concept of natural law is the belief that certain rights are inherent to all human beings, bestowed not by governments or human institutions, but by a higher power: God. This idea, deeply influenced by Enlightenment thinkers like John Locke, was central to the philosophy of America's Founding Fathers. They believed that individual rights are derived from God and intrinsic to human nature and cannot be granted or taken away by any government, as they are woven into the very fabric of existence. For the Founders, natural law provided a moral framework that transcended human legislation, ensuring that individual rights would remain protected regardless of political changes.

By tracing the historical foundations of the Second Amendment, this chapter will reveal the enduring significance of this right in safeguarding individual freedom and preventing tyranny. Through an exploration of the past, we will gain a deeper appreciation for the timeless principles that continue to underpin the right to keep and bear arms in modern America. We will explore how the Founding Fathers, in their wisdom, foresaw the evolution of weaponry and made it clear through their various writings that the Second Amendment's protections extend to arms not yet imagined in their time. By examining their foresight, we will see how the principles enshrined in the Second Amendment remain relevant and robust in the face of modern advancements.

## English Common Law and the Right to Bear Arms

The history of the Second Amendment finds its roots in the ancient legal traditions of English common law. Dating back to the Magna Carta in 1215, English common law recognized the fundamental right of individuals to possess arms for self-defense and the defense of the realm. This principle was further codified in the English Bill of Rights of 1689, which affirmed the "ancient right of Englishmen" to keep and bear arms.

Throughout history, several cases and statutes reinforced this right. The Assize of Arms of 1181 required English freemen to arm themselves for the defense of the kingdom. This mandate ensured that the realm could call upon a ready and armed populace in times of need. The Statute of Winchester in 1285 further reinforced this requirement, mandating that all able-bodied men maintain arms according to their social status and wealth.

During the tumultuous period of the English Civil War in the mid-17th century, the disarmament of political opponents by the monarchy highlighted the necessity of an armed populace to resist tyranny. The conflict between King Charles I and Parliament over the control of the military underscored the importance of an armed citizenry as a check on monarchical power. The eventual victory of Parliament and the subsequent establishment of a constitutional monarchy reaffirmed the principle that the people, through their representatives, should have control over the military and the means of defense.

The concept of the right to bear arms was deeply intertwined with notions of individual liberty and resistance to tyranny. English subjects viewed the possession of arms as essential to safeguarding their freedoms against arbitrary government intrusion and oppression. This tradition of armed self-defense would later play a pivotal role in shaping American attitudes towards gun ownership and the Second Amendment.

## Militias in the Early Colonies

As English colonists settled in America, they brought with them these cherished principles of the right to bear arms. In the colonies, where threats from Native American tribes, hostile European powers, and internal unrest were ever-present, the need for an armed populace became even more pronounced. Colonists organized local militias to defend their communities and maintain public order, reflecting the English tradition of citizen-soldiers bearing arms in defense of their liberties.

Militias played a multifaceted role in colonial society, serving as both a defensive force against external threats and a means of maintaining internal order. Militiamen were expected to undergo regular training and drilling to ensure readiness for potential conflicts. They were also tasked with enforcing local laws, apprehending criminals, and responding to emergencies, such as fires and natural disasters.

The structure and organization of militias varied from colony to colony, but they typically operated under the authority of colonial governments and were subject to civilian control. Militia officers were often drawn from the local community and elected by their peers, reflecting the democratic principles that underpinned colonial society. One of the most significant contributions of militias in the early colonies was their role in defending against attacks by Native American tribes and hostile European powers. During conflicts such as King Philip's War in New England and the French and Indian War, militias played a crucial role in protecting colonial settlements and securing the frontier. These militias, composed of farmers, tradesmen, and other local inhabitants, demonstrated the practical necessity of an armed populace capable of rapid mobilization.

The experiences of colonial militias during times of crisis would have a lasting impact on American attitudes towards firearms and the importance of an armed citizenry. The concept of the citizen-soldier, ready to take up arms in defense of home and country, became deeply ingrained in the American psyche and would later influence the drafting of the Second Amendment.

## The Revolutionary War and the Right to Bear Arms

The American Revolution marked a turning point in the history of the right to bear arms, as armed colonists revolted against British oppression and asserted their independence. The conflict not only demonstrated the importance of an armed populace in resisting tyranny; it also solidified the concept of individual gun ownership as a fundamental right.

The American Revolution was fueled by the British attempts to disarm the colonists, a fact that underscores the foundational importance of the Second Amendment. While the Boston Tea Party and the broader tax revolt played essential roles in igniting the revolution, the direct catalyst for armed conflict was the British efforts to seize colonial arms. Understanding this context requires a deep dive into the events leading up to the Boston Massacre, the subsequent British policies, and the eventual outbreak of hostilities.

In the years leading up to the Boston Massacre in 1770, tensions between the American colonists and the British government had been escalating steadily. The root of these tensions lay in the Parliament's efforts to exert greater political and economic control over the colonies. One of the most contentious issues was the series of taxes and trade restrictions imposed by the British, which the colonists saw as unfair and oppressive. These measures included the Stamp Act of 1765 and the Townshend Acts of 1767, which levied taxes on everyday items such as paper, glass, and tea. The colonists viewed these acts as violations of their rights, as they were implemented without their consent or representation in Parliament.

As resentment grew, so did the spirit of resistance among the colonists. The British responded by increasing their military presence in the colonies, particularly in Boston, which was a hotbed of revolutionary activity. In 1768, the British government sent several regiments of troops to Boston to enforce the new laws and maintain order. This military occupation further inflamed tensions, as the presence of armed soldiers on the streets was a constant reminder of British authority and the colonists' lack of autonomy.

A critical aspect of the British strategy to maintain control was to regulate and, in some cases, confiscate the arms of the colonists. The British sought to disarm the population to prevent any potential uprising and to ensure that any resistance could be swiftly and effectively crushed. Mandates were imposed to restrict the ownership and carrying of firearms, and British troops conducted searches and seizures to confiscate weapons. This disarmament effort was deeply resented by the colonists, who saw it as a direct attack on their rights and freedoms.

The situation reached a boiling point on the night of March 5, 1770. A confrontation between a group of colonists and British soldiers stationed outside the Customs House in Boston quickly escalated into violence. The colonists, angry and emboldened by the presence of the troops, began to taunt and harass the soldiers, throwing snowballs, rocks, and other objects. In the chaos and confusion, the soldiers opened fire on the crowd, killing five colonists and wounding several others. This event, which became known as the Boston Massacre, shocked and galvanized the colonies, fueling further outrage against British rule.

The Boston Massacre highlighted the deep-seated animosity between the colonists and the British authorities, and it underscored the lengths to which the British were willing to go to maintain control. This episode united the colonies against a common enemy and set the stage for the revolutionary conflict that would ultimately lead to American independence.

The situation escalated further with the passage of the Tea Act in 1773, which granted the British East India Company a monopoly on the tea trade in the colonies and allowed it to sell surplus tea directly to the colonists at reduced prices, bypassing colonial merchants. While this act made tea cheaper, it was seen as a ploy to get the colonists to accept British taxation policies. The monopoly threatened local businesses and further eroded the principle of self-governance. In response, colonial resistance groups, such as the Sons of Liberty, mobilized to oppose the Act. Their anger reached a boiling point on the night of December 16, 1773, when a group of colonists disguised as Mohawk Indians boarded three British ships docked in Boston Harbor and dumped 342 chests of tea into the water. This act of defiance, known as the Boston Tea Party, was a powerful statement against British tyranny and galvanized the colonies, setting the stage for the revolutionary struggle that would soon follow.

In the aftermath of the Boston Tea Party, the British government enacted the Coercive Acts (known as the Intolerable Acts in the colonies) in 1774, which were designed to punish Massachusetts and deter other colonies from similar rebellious acts. These laws included the closing of Boston Harbor and the revocation of Massachusetts' charter, which effectively placed the colony under direct British control. The colonial response was one of increased unity and defiance, with the formation of the First Continental Congress and the establishment of local militias prepared to resist British aggression.

The British attempt to disarm the colonists came to a head in 1775. General Thomas Gage, the British military governor of Massachusetts, received orders to suppress the growing rebellion by confiscating arms and munitions held by the colonial militias. On April 18, 1775, Gage dispatched a force to seize a stockpile of colonial arms stored at Concord. Paul Revere and other riders famously warned the countryside of the British advance, allowing the colonial militias to mobilize.

The following day, April 19, 1775, marked the Battles of Lexington and Concord, the first military engagements of the American Revolution. At Lexington, a small group of colonial militiamen faced off against the British troops. Although the colonists were initially overwhelmed, the confrontation set the stage for a broader resistance. As the British troops continued to Concord, they encountered a larger and more organized force of militiamen. The ensuing battle forced the British to retreat to Boston, suffering significant casualties along the way. This clash demonstrated the colonists' willingness to take up arms to defend their rights and property, solidifying the move towards full-scale rebellion.

The attempt to confiscate arms was a direct attack on the colonists' ability to defend themselves and their liberties. This event underscored the importance of an armed populace in resisting tyranny, a principle that would later be enshrined in the Second Amendment. The right to bear arms was seen not merely as a means of self-defense but as a safeguard against government overreach and oppression.

The colonial response to British disarmament efforts was rooted in a broader philosophical and practical tradition of self-defense and resistance to tyranny.

The writings of Enlightenment thinkers, such as John Locke, who argued for the natural rights of individuals to life, liberty, and property, heavily influenced the colonial mindset. Locke's assertion that people had the right to resist unjust government provided an intellectual foundation for the armed resistance that characterized the early stages of the revolution. This legacy of armed resistance against tyranny became a cornerstone of American political thought and was codified in the Second Amendment to the United States Constitution.

From the outset of hostilities, armed colonists played a central role in the struggle for independence. Militias, composed of ordinary citizens armed with muskets and rifles, mobilized to confront British regulars and loyalist forces. The Battles of Lexington and Concord in April 1775, often referred to as the "shot heard 'round the world," ignited the Revolutionary War and underscored the readiness of American colonists to defend their liberties with force of arms.

In the aftermath of Lexington and Concord, the Continental Congress convened to coordinate the colonies' response to British aggression. Recognizing the need for a unified effort, the Congress established the Continental Army in June 1775, appointing George Washington as its commander-in-chief. Despite early setbacks and logistical challenges, the Continental Army engaged British forces in several significant battles, including the Siege of Boston, which ultimately forced the British to evacuate the city in March 1776. These military actions solidified the resolve of the colonists and highlighted the necessity of a formal declaration of independence.

As the war progressed, it became increasingly clear that reconciliation with Britain was unlikely. The British government responded to the colonial uprising with punitive measures, blockading American ports and authorizing the seizure of American ships. These actions further alienated the colonists and reinforced the perception that their rights and liberties were under direct threat from a tyrannical government.

In June 1776, the Continental Congress appointed a committee to draft a formal declaration of independence. The task fell primarily to Thomas Jefferson, who penned a document that eloquently outlined the philosophical and practical reasons for breaking away from British rule. The Declaration of Independence emphasized the colonists' right to alter or abolish a government that became destructive to their unalienable rights, a principle that directly supported the armed resistance that had already begun. It articulated a vision of a government based on the consent of the governed, where the protection of life, liberty, and the pursuit of happiness were paramount.

On July 2, 1776, the Continental Congress voted in favor of independence, and two days later, on July 4, it formally adopted the Declaration of Independence. This document was sent to the British Crown as a proverbial middle finger, symbolizing the colonists' rejection of British authority and their determination to forge a new nation. The Declaration enumerated the colonies' grievances, including the imposition of taxes without consent, the dissolution of colonial legislatures, and the quartering of British troops in American homes. It condemned King George III for his abuses of power and declared that the colonies were free and independent states.

The boldness of the Declaration of Independence cannot be overstated. It was a direct challenge to the most powerful empire of the time, asserting that the colonies had the right and the duty to throw off a government that no longer protected their rights. By declaring their independence, the colonists were not only affirming their desire for self-governance but also justifying their armed resistance against British forces. The document resonated deeply with the colonists and galvanized support for the revolutionary cause. The Declaration of Independence was more than a mere statement of separation; it was a revolutionary manifesto that laid the foundation for a new nation built on the principles of equality, individual rights, and democratic governance. It marked a definitive break from a past of colonial subjugation and a bold step toward an uncertain future of self-determination. The document continues to influence democratic movements worldwide, symbolizing the universal struggle for freedom and justice.

Throughout the long and arduous conflict in the months and years following the Declaration, the Revolutionary War raged on, and the colonies faced numerous hardships and battles as they fought to secure their independence. Citizen militias continued to serve as the backbone of the American cause, fighting alongside Continental Army units led by commanders such as George Washington. The war also benefited from contributions by figures such as the Minutemen, a specialized militia force renowned for their rapid response capabilities. These citizen-soldiers were pivotal during early engagements and exemplified the principle of an armed populace ready to defend their rights at a moment's notice. The contributions of militia forces were instrumental in securing key victories such as the Battle of Saratoga in 1777, which convinced France to enter the war on the side of the American colonies, and the ultimate triumph at Yorktown in 1781, where British General Cornwallis surrendered to American and French forces. Throughout these struggles, the principles articulated in the Declaration of Independence served as a guiding light, inspiring the colonists to persevere in their quest for liberty.

The experiences of the Revolutionary War left an indelible mark on American attitudes towards firearms and the right to bear arms. For many colonists, the war served as a reaffirmation of the importance of individual gun ownership in safeguarding liberty and resisting government tyranny. The right to bear arms was no longer seen as a mere privilege granted by the state but as an inherent and inalienable right derived from natural law.

As the Revolutionary War drew to a close and the fledgling United States sought to establish a new system of government, the question of individual rights and liberties loomed large. The Articles of Confederation, adopted during the war and ratified in 1781, served as the first constitution of the United States. This document established a confederation of sovereign states with a weak central government, reflecting the colonists' fear of centralized authority after their experience with British rule. Under the Articles, Congress had limited powers, including conducting foreign affairs, maintaining armed forces, and issuing currency. However, it lacked the authority to levy taxes, regulate commerce, or enforce laws directly on the states or individuals.

The weaknesses of the Articles of Confederation became apparent soon after the war. The lack of a traditional federal government led to financial instability, as Congress could not raise revenue or pay off war debts effectively. Each state retained significant independence, often pursuing its own interests at the expense of national unity. Interstate commerce suffered from conflicting state regulations and tariffs, and foreign policy was hampered by the inability to present a united front.

## The Constitutional Convention and Ratification of the Second Amendment

Recognizing these issues, delegates convened the Constitutional Convention in 1787 to address the inadequacies of the Articles. The result was the drafting of a new Constitution, which created a different federal government with the power to tax, regulate commerce, and enforce laws. Importantly, the Constitution set the United States up as a republic, not a democracy. In a republic, representatives are elected to make decisions on behalf of the people, whereas in a pure democracy, decisions are made directly by the people through majority rule. This distinction was crucial as the Framers sought to protect individual rights and prevent the tyranny of the majority, ensuring a more stable and balanced system of governance. Of note: When the Constitution granted the federal government the power to tax, it did so with the intention of levying taxes on items like tariffs and excise taxes, not on individual incomes. This original framework aimed to fund the government without placing a direct burden on individual citizens. It was only with the ratification of the Sixteenth Amendment in 1913 that the federal government gained the authority to impose an income tax, fundamentally changing the scope of federal taxation power.

The new Constitution also established a system of checks and balances among three branches of government—executive, legislative, and judicial—to prevent any single entity from gaining too much power. Additionally, it sought to limit the power of the federal government by explicitly sharing power with the states and the people. The Tenth Amendment, in particular, states that any powers not explicitly granted to the federal government by the Constitution are reserved to the states or the people. This framework ensured a balance of power, preventing federal overreach and protecting the rights and autonomy of state governments and individuals. This new framework created a more cohesive and effective national government.

The Second Amendment to the United States Constitution, enshrining the right of the people to keep and bear arms, emerged from a complex historical and political landscape. In the aftermath of the Revolutionary War, the Founding Fathers grappled with the question of how best to secure the liberties won through armed struggle. The experiences of the war underscored the importance of an armed populace in resisting tyranny and defending against external threats. Against this backdrop, the Framers of the Constitution sought to strike a delicate balance between individual rights and collective security.

The drafting of the Constitution sparked intense discussions over the inclusion of a Bill of Rights to protect the rights of citizens from government intrusion. Anti-Federalists, wary of the powers granted to the federal government under the proposed Constitution, argued for the inclusion of explicit guarantees of individual liberties. One of the primary concerns raised by Anti-Federalists was the absence of a specific provision protecting the right to bear arms. They feared that without such a safeguard, the federal government could potentially disarm the populace and infringe upon their liberties. Several state ratifying conventions, such as those in Virginia and New York, conditioned their acceptance of the Constitution on the inclusion of a Bill of Rights. In response to these concerns, the Framers of the Constitution debated the need for an amendment explicitly affirming the right to bear arms. These debates ultimately led to the adoption of the Bill of Rights, including the Second Amendment.

Also central to the debates over the Second Amendment was the concept of the militia, a cornerstone of American defense and governance in the early years of the republic. The Founding Fathers viewed the militia as a bulwark against standing armies and a means of preserving the sovereignty of the states. The inclusion of the Second Amendment was in part a recognition of the importance of maintaining a well-regulated militia composed of armed citizens.

On December 15, 1791, the Bill of Rights, comprising the first ten amendments to the Constitution, was ratified by the requisite number of states. Among these amendments was the Second Amendment, which read, "A well regulated Militia, being necessary to the security of a free State, the right of the people to keep and bear Arms, shall not be infringed."

The Second Amendment reflected the Founding Fathers' recognition of the importance of an armed citizenry in preserving liberty and deterring tyranny. It enshrined the right of individuals to possess and carry firearms for self-defense, defense of the community, and as a check against government overreach.

## The Founding Fathers' Views on the Second Amendment

The Founding Fathers viewed the Second Amendment as a recognition of a preexisting natural law and God-given right to self-defense, a right which predates the Constitution itself.

Thomas Jefferson articulated this belief by stating, "No free man shall ever be debarred the use of arms" in his draft of the Virginia Constitution. Jefferson, influenced by the Enlightenment thinker John Locke, who argued that self-defense was a fundamental natural right, believed that the ability to bear arms was integral to personal and collective security.

The Founding Fathers also intended for this right to be an individual right, which would extend beyond mere participation in a militia, although they encouraged the formation of militias composed of armed citizens. Samuel Adams declared, "The Constitution shall never be construed to prevent the people of the United States who are peaceable citizens from keeping their own arms." Patrick Henry, during the Virginia Ratifying Convention, stressed the importance of individual armament, stating, "The great object is that every man be armed. Everyone who is able might have a gun."

In drafting the Second Amendment, the Founding Fathers were influenced by their experiences under British rule, where the disarmament of citizens was a strategy used to exert control and suppress resistance. Their intention was to prevent such tyranny by ensuring that the people retained the means to defend their freedoms. Richard Henry Lee succinctly captured this sentiment by asserting, "To preserve liberty, it is essential that the whole body of people always possess arms, and be taught alike, especially when young, how to use them."

The Federalist Papers, a series of essays written by Alexander Hamilton, James Madison, and John Jay, played a critical role in shaping public opinion and garnering support for the ratification of the Constitution. Among the topics addressed in the Federalist Papers were the principles of republican government, the separation of powers, and the protection of individual rights.

In Federalist No. 29, Alexander Hamilton articulated the necessity of a well-regulated militia as a safeguard against external threats and internal insurrections. Hamilton emphasized the importance of a militia composed of citizens armed with their own weapons, capable of resisting foreign invasion and domestic tyranny. He wrote:

> *If circumstances should at any time oblige the government to form an army of any magnitude, that army can never be formidable to the liberties of the people while there is a large body of citizens, little if at all inferior to them in discipline and the use of arms, who stand ready to defend their own rights and those of their fellow-citizens.*

He continued: "But though the scheme of disciplining the whole nation must be abandoned as mischievous or impracticable; yet it is a matter of the utmost importance that a well-digested plan should, as soon as possible, be adopted for the proper establishment of the militia."

James Madison, often regarded as the "Father of the Constitution," argued that a well-armed citizenry would serve as a bulwark against potential government overreach and ensure that the federal government remained accountable to the people.

He wrote: "Americans have the right and advantage of being armed—unlike the citizens of other countries whose governments are afraid to trust the people with arms." He explained what made America exceptional, in Federalist No. 46:

> *Besides the advantage of being armed, which the Americans possess over the people of almost every other nation, the existence of subordinate governments, to which the people are attached and by which the militia officers are appointed, forms a barrier against the enterprises of ambition, more insurmountable than any which a simple government of any form can admit of.*

Likewise, Samuel Adams stated during the Massachusetts ratifying convention in 1788, "The Constitution shall never be construed to prevent the people of the United States who are peaceable citizens from keeping their own arms." Richard

Henry Lee is also on record stating "To preserve liberty, it is essential that the whole body of people always possess arms, and be taught alike, especially when young, how to use them."

President George Washington stated in his first annual address on January 8, 1790, "A free people ought not only to be armed but disciplined; to which end a uniform and well-digested plan is requisite." Thomas Jefferson likewise agreed: "The laws that forbid the carrying of arms are laws of such a nature. They disarm only those who are neither inclined nor determined to commit crimes."

Unfortunately, following its ratification in 1791, the Second Amendment was met with varying interpretations and applications. While many viewed it as affirming an individual right to bear arms for self-defense and the defense of the community independent of militia service, others emphasized the collective nature of the right, focusing on the role of the militia in ensuring the security of a free state. These differing interpretations would continue to shape debates over gun rights and gun control in the centuries to come.

Those who do not appreciate the concept of the Second Amendment often argue, "That's not what the Founding Fathers really meant," as if they possess the unique ability to delve into the minds of individuals who lived nearly 250 years ago. This claim is not only presumptuous but also flawed. The notion that one can preemptively interpret the intentions of the Founding Fathers, bypassing the clear and plain language they used, is both ridiculous and evasive. Such arguments ignore the historical context and the straightforward way the Second Amendment was written.

What anti-Second Amendment advocates fail to grasp is that the true measure of the Founding Fathers' intentions lies in the words they explicitly chose. The Second Amendment is written in plain English, leaving little room for misinterpretation. The Founding Fathers were meticulous in their language, ensuring their intentions were clear and unambiguous. To dismiss their written words in favor of speculative mind reading is to undermine the very foundation of constitutional law. The words and writings of the Founding Fathers are our most reliable sources for understanding their intentions, and they should be respected as such. What matters is what they wrote down, and that written word is what governs us. Therefore, the only thing that holds weight is the clear, unambiguous language of the Second Amendment as it stands.

Ultimately, the genesis of the Second Amendment reflects the Founding Fathers' commitment to preserving individual liberty and civic duty in the new American republic. As the nation grappled with governance and the protection of rights, the Second Amendment emerged as a foundational element of the constitutional framework, embodying the enduring values of freedom, self-reliance, and the right of the people to defend their liberties. Reflecting on the Federalist Papers and the insights they provide into the Founding Fathers' views on the Second Amendment, it becomes clear that their vision encompassed not only the firearms technology of their era but also the potential for advancements in the future. The Founders understood the importance of preserving the right to bear arms in all its forms, from flintlock muskets to modern firearms, as a safeguard against tyranny and a bulwark of individual liberty.

## The Founding Fathers on Gun Ownership

George Washington's views on firearms ownership among the civilian population were deeply influenced by his experiences during the war. He firmly believed that an armed populace was essential to the preservation of liberty. Washington recognized that a free society required not only the protection of individual rights but also the ability of its citizens to defend those rights if necessary. He often emphasized the importance of a well-regulated militia, composed of ordinary citizens who were ready and able to bear arms in defense of their country. He saw the armed citizenry capable of self-organizing as a crucial check against government overreach, ensuring that power remained with the people rather than becoming concentrated in the hands of a few.

George Washington owned a notable collection of personal firearms that reflected both his status and his practical needs as a military leader and landowner. Among his most prized possessions were a pair of flintlock pistols given to him by the Marquis de Lafayette, a gift that symbolized the close bond between the two men and their shared commitment to the cause of liberty. These pistols were elegantly crafted and highly functional, a blend of artistry and utility that Washington valued. He also owned a Brown Bess musket, the standard British infantry weapon of the time, which was known for its reliability in battle. Washington's firearms were not just tools of war; they represented his personal commitment to the principles he fought for.

One of Jefferson's lesser known but intriguing possessions was a Girardoni air rifle, an advanced weapon for its time, capable of firing multiple rounds without reloading. This rifle, which Jefferson acquired in the late 18th century, was a remarkable piece of technology that symbolized his forward-thinking approach to firearms. Jefferson valued the rifle not only for its engineering but also for what it represented—a tool for personal defense and a deterrent against tyranny. Jefferson's ownership of such a sophisticated weapon underlined his belief that citizens should have access to arms that would enable them to effectively defend their rights.

Jefferson's view on firearms ownership extended to his vision of a free, self-governing society. Like Washington, he believed that a well-armed populace was a necessary check against government overreach, preventing the accumulation of too much power in the hands of the few. This belief was a driving force behind his support for the Second Amendment. Jefferson was concerned about the potential for government corruption and the dangers posed by standing armies. To him, an armed citizenry was the ultimate safeguard of democracy, ensuring that the government remained accountable to the people.

Benjamin Franklin, known for his wit, wisdom, and significant contributions to the founding of the United States, was also a proponent of the right to bear arms. While Franklin is often remembered for his contributions to diplomacy, science, technology, and political theory, his views on the importance of an armed populace were equally important. Franklin's thoughts on firearms were shaped by both his experiences and his philosophical beliefs.

During the French and Indian War, Franklin helped organize a militia in Pennsylvania, recognizing that self-defense was not just a right but a civic duty. Franklin understood that a well-armed citizenry was essential for the protection of both individuals and the community at large. He famously said, "Those who would give up essential Liberty, to purchase a little temporary Safety, deserve neither Liberty nor Safety." This quote, though often cited in different contexts, can be interpreted as a defense of the right to bear arms, as it underscores Franklin's belief that liberty and security are intertwined, and that an armed populace is a key component of both. Moreover, Franklin owned a variety of firearms, including muskets and pistols, which he kept at his Philadelphia home. These weapons were not just for show; they were practical tools for defense in a time when the young nation was still vulnerable.

John Adams, the second President of the United States and a key figure in the American Revolution, had a firm belief in the importance of an armed populace. Adams owned a flintlock musket, a standard weapon of the time, which he kept for both hunting and defense. This musket was a symbol of Adams' belief in the right of individuals to bear arms, a right he viewed as essential to the protection of liberty.

While Adams is often remembered for his legal acumen and his role in drafting the Massachusetts Constitution, his views on firearms were equally influential. Adams was particularly concerned with the idea of self-defense, both on a personal and national level. He believed that the right to bear arms was not just a matter of personal security, but a necessary condition for the maintenance of a free society. Adams once stated, "To suppose arms in the hands of citizens, to be used at individual discretion . . . is to demolish every constitution, and lay the laws prostrate, so that liberty can no longer be enjoyed." While this statement might be interpreted as cautioning against misuse, it also underscores Adams' belief in the responsible exercise of the right to bear arms—to secure liberty against tyranny.

John Adams's cousin, Samuel Adams, owned several firearms, including a flintlock musket that he used during the early conflicts of the Revolutionary War. This musket was a practical tool for Adams, who argued that "The Constitution shall never be construed to prevent the people of the United States who are peaceable citizens from keeping their own arms." This statement reflected his deep conviction that the right to bear arms was essential to the preservation of liberty and that any attempt to infringe upon this right would be an affront to the principles of the American Revolution.

John Hancock, best known for his bold signature on the Declaration of Independence, was also a gun owner and a strong advocate for the right to bear arms. Hancock, who helped to organize and fund the Massachusetts militia, believed that the militia, composed of ordinary citizens, was the best defense against both foreign threats and domestic tyranny. Hancock viewed the British effort to disarm the colonists as an attempt to strip them of their most basic rights. He once remarked, "Resistance to tyranny becomes the Christian and social duty of each individual. . . . Continue steadfast, and with a proper sense of your dependence on God, nobly defend those rights which heaven gave, and no man ought to take from us." As this quote reveals, Hancock believed that the right to bear arms was a God-given right, essential to the defense of liberty. His support for the Second Amendment was rooted in his conviction that an armed populace prepared to defend their freedoms was the best guarantee of liberty, and that any attempt to disarm the people would be a direct threat to their rights.

Patrick Henry, renowned for his fiery oratory and his famous declaration, "Give me liberty, or give me death!" was also a passionate advocate for the right to bear arms. Henry owned a variety of firearms, including a smoothbore musket that he used for both hunting and defense. In his speeches and writings, Henry argued that the militia, composed of ordinary citizens, was the most natural and effective defense against tyranny. He famously declared, "The great object is that every man be armed. Everyone who is able may have a gun." For Henry, the right to bear arms was not just a privilege, but a fundamental and essential right.

James Madison played a critical role in the drafting of the Bill of Rights, including the Second Amendment. Madison's views on the right to bear arms were shaped by his deep understanding of political philosophy and his belief in the necessity of an armed populace as a check on government power. Madison owned several firearms, including a pair of flintlock pistols that he kept for personal defense. He once wrote, "The advantage of being armed, which the Americans possess over the people of almost every other nation . . . forms a barrier against the enterprises of ambition." For Madison, the right to bear arms was a crucial safeguard against tyranny and a key component of the American system of government.

The Founders' belief in an armed citizenry wasn't rooted in nostalgia—it was forward-looking, even as weapons evolved alongside the young Republic. The Founders recognized that while the tools of self-defense and warfare would inevitably change, the core principle—that the people must retain the means to resist tyranny—would remain constant.

## The Founders on Advancements in Firearms Technology

The evolution of firearms technology spans centuries, reflecting humanity's ceaseless quest for innovation and improvement. From the early days of flint-lock muskets to the innovative firearms of the modern era, each advancement has left an indelible mark on history and reshaped the dynamics of warfare and self-defense.

During the late 18th century, flintlock muskets emerged as the standard infantry weapon of the day. These muzzle-loaded firearms, ignited by a flint striking against a steel plate, played a pivotal role in conflicts like the American Revolutionary War. Despite their rudimentary design, flintlock muskets symbolized the dawn of a new era in firearms technology.

The introduction of rifled barrels in the early 19th century represented a significant leap forward in accuracy and range. Rifling, spiral grooves inside the barrel, imparted spin to the projectile, greatly enhancing its stability and precision. Rifled firearms, such as the Springfield Model 1861 rifle, became the backbone of military arsenals and shaped the outcome of conflicts like the American Civil War.

In the mid-19th century, Samuel Colt's invention of the revolver revolutionized handgun design. Revolvers, with their multiple chambers in a rotating cylinder, offered rapid successive firing without the need for frequent reloading. This innovation transformed handguns into formidable weapons for soldiers, law enforcement officers, and civilians alike, establishing Colt as a pioneering figure in firearms history.

The late 19th and early 20th centuries witnessed the rise of bolt-action rifles as the standard infantry weapon. Firearms like the Mauser and Lee–Enfield offered superior accuracy, reliability, and rate of fire compared to their predecessors, became synonymous with military might, and shaped the tactics and strategies of armies around the world.

By the turn of the 20th century, semi-automatic firearms had emerged as the next frontier in firearms technology. These weapons, capable of firing a single round with each pull of the trigger, represented a significant advancement in rate of fire and ease of use. Semi-automatic firearms became indispensable tools for military, law enforcement, and civilian users alike, setting the stage for further innovations to come.

The early 20th century also saw the advent of fully automatic firearms, transforming the nature of warfare and military tactics. Submachine guns and machine guns, capable of continuous fire if the trigger was held down, revolutionized the battlefield and gave rise to new strategies and doctrines. These weapons became synonymous with firepower and influenced the outcome of conflicts worldwide.

Today, firearms technology continues to push the boundaries of what is possible. Advancements in materials, manufacturing processes, and electronic components have led to the development of highly sophisticated firearms with enhanced performance and usability. Modern firearms incorporate features such as polymer frames, modular designs, and electronic sights, reflecting the ongoing pursuit of innovation and excellence in the field of firearms engineering.

Critics of the Second Amendment often argue that the Founding Fathers could not have anticipated the technological advancements in firearms that have occurred since the late 18th century. They assert that the Second Amendment only applies to the firearms of the Founders' era and does not encompass modern firearms. However, this argument overlooks the Founders' foresight and understanding of human nature.

At the time of the Second Amendment's ratification in 1791, flintlock muskets and rifles were the standard infantry arms of the day, representing the pinnacle of military technology. But firearms technology had already advanced considerably since the Revolutionary War.

The Founding Fathers understood that technology would continue to evolve and that future generations would confront new challenges and threats. They crafted the Second Amendment knowing that the right to bear arms must adapt to changing circumstances and advancements in firearms technology. They understood that limiting the scope of the Second Amendment to the firearms of their era would undermine its purpose as a safeguard against tyranny.

Moreover, the absence of any specific limitations on the types of arms protected by the Second Amendment underscores the Founders' intention to preserve the broadest possible scope of individual firearms ownership. If the Founders had intended to restrict the right to bear arms to a specific type or category of firearms, they could have done so explicitly. Instead, they chose to safeguard the right to possess and carry arms in defense of liberty without imposing arbitrary restrictions.

If the Founders intended to limit the right to bear arms to specific weapons, they could have explicitly done so in the Second Amendment. If they had believed technological advancements in weaponry should be off-limits to the general population, they had every opportunity to clarify that, yet they chose not to. Instead, they used the broad term "arms," indicating an understanding that weaponry would evolve, just as speech and the press have evolved under the First Amendment. They did not limit the right to bear arms to only swords or flintlock muskets or hunting rifles, nor did they impose restrictions on firepower, ammunition capacity, or the number of weapons one could own. Their silence on such limitations speaks volumes, affirming their intent that the right to keep and bear arms remains unrestricted by technological advances.

## The Second Amendment's Legacy

The Second Amendment continues to be a cornerstone of American constitutional rights, embodying the enduring principles of self-defense, resistance to oppression, and the preservation of liberty. As the nation grapples with contemporary debates over gun control and individual rights, the historical foundations of the Second Amendment provide essential context and guidance in navigating these complex issues. As such, the Second Amendment's historical foundations highlight the deep-rooted belief in the necessity of an armed citizenry for self-preservation, and to safeguard freedom and ensure the security of a free country.

# Chapter 3

# Locked and Loaded: Guardians of Justice

*Self-defense is a part of the law of nature; nor can it be denied the community, even against the king himself.*

—John Locke

*Homicide is enjoined by the law of nature in cases of necessity, and as when one man attempts to kill another, or presents a weapon, or other dangerous instrument, in order to commit any felonious offense against him.*

—James Wilson

T he right to self-defense is one of the most fundamental human rights, deeply ingrained in the very fabric of our being. This right, which predates any written laws, is an instinct to protect oneself and one's loved ones from harm. Throughout history, various societies have recognized and upheld this principle, but none more explicitly than in the context of the American Second Amendment.

As we saw in chapter 2, Enlightenment philosopher John Locke's theories, which emphasized the individual's right to self-preservation, found a receptive audience among America's Founding Fathers. They believed that an armed populace was not only essential for personal defense but also for safeguarding against tyranny. The Second Amendment thus serves as a testament to their commitment to protecting the right to self-defense.

When discussing the right to self-defense, it is crucial to understand that it extends beyond mere personal protection. It encompasses the right to safeguard one's home, family, and, by extension, community from threats. Firearms have played a pivotal role in this aspect of self-defense, offering individuals a means to effectively protect themselves when threatened. Consider, for example, the increasing number of home invasions in various parts of the country in recent years. In these scenarios, firearms provide a level of security that is unmatched by other forms of self-defense. A woman living alone, an elderly couple, or a family in a remote area all find themselves on an equal footing against potential aggressors when they have access to a firearm for self-defense.

The right to bear arms acts as a powerful equalizer, enabling individuals to protect themselves and their loved ones regardless of physical strength or size. As the following case studies reveal, firearms play an important role in personal safety. By examining these cases, we can better appreciate the practical implications of the Second Amendment and understand why the ability to own and use firearms for self-defense is a fundamental right that deserves to be upheld and respected. From thwarting armed robberies and home invasions to defending against violent assailants, these instances demonstrate the importance of the Second Amendment in ensuring public safety and individual security. The case studies presented here offer a well-rounded representation of the types of firearms-related, self-defense-related incidents that occur across the country, from small towns to major cities. Some of these cases gained national attention, while others remained relatively obscure, but all illustrate the common reality of law-abiding citizens using firearms to protect themselves and others in a variety of circumstances.

## The Sarah McKinley Incident

One notable case that highlights the importance of firearms in self-defense is the widely reported instance of Sarah McKinley, a young mother in Blanchard, Oklahoma. On New Year's Eve in 2011, McKinley was at home with her three-month-old son when two men attempted to break into her house. This incident occurred shortly after the tragic death of her husband from cancer, leaving McKinley alone and vulnerable during a time of profound grief and adjustment to single parenthood.

The intruders had been plotting to rob McKinley, and one of them, Justin Martin, had previously been to her home under the pretense of offering help after her husband's death. Sensing danger, McKinley fortified herself inside her home. She locked the doors, barricaded herself in her bedroom with her infant, and called 911. The dispatcher stayed on the line with her, providing moral support and assuring her that help was on the way. However, knowing that the intruders were breaking through her front door, she realized that law enforcement might not arrive in time to prevent them from entering.

With her child's safety as her utmost priority, McKinley armed herself with a 12-gauge shotgun. She also had a pistol nearby, but she chose the shotgun for its stopping power and ease of use in such a tense situation. As the intruders attempted to force their way in, McKinley warned them that she was armed. Despite the warning, Justin Martin continued his efforts and eventually broke through the door. At that critical moment, McKinley fired her shotgun, fatally wounding Martin. The second intruder, Dustin Stewart, fled the scene upon hearing the gunshot and was later apprehended by the police.

This incident underscores the critical role firearms can play in self-defense situations, particularly for those who might be physically disadvantaged against an intruder. Sarah McKinley's actions were later deemed justifiable by the authorities, who confirmed that she had acted in self-defense to protect herself and her child from immediate danger. The local sheriff supported her actions, stating, "You're allowed to shoot an unauthorized person that is in your home. The law provides you the remedy, and instincts tell you to do that."

The case of Sarah McKinley highlights how firearms can serve as an equalizer, empowering those who might otherwise be defenseless against stronger or more numerous assailants. McKinley's ability to defend herself and her child from a potentially deadly threat reinforces the argument that the right to bear arms is essential for personal protection and self-defense, especially since it took about 14 minutes for help to arrive at the McKinley home after the break-in had occurred, an eternity when your life is in danger.

## The Clackamas Town Center Shooting

Another powerful example of the impact of armed self-defense can be found in the numerous cases where concealed carry permit holders have thwarted potential mass shootings. One such instance occurred during the 2012 Clackamas Town Center shooting in Oregon.

On December 11, 2012, Jacob Tyler Roberts entered the Clackamas Town Center mall, armed with a stolen AR-15 rifle and multiple magazines. Roberts began his shooting spree in the food court area, tragically killing two people and injuring a third. Amidst the chaos, shoppers and employees scrambled for cover, and the situation could have escalated further had it not been for the presence of a concealed carry permit holder, Nick Meli.

Meli, a 22-year-old off-duty security guard, was at the mall with a friend and her baby when the shooting started. He had his Glock pistol with him, legally carried under his concealed carry permit. When Meli heard the gunfire, he quickly moved to a position where he could see the shooter. He drew his firearm and aimed it at Roberts, ready to intervene if necessary.

Although Meli did not fire his weapon, his actions had a psychological impact on the shooter. Realizing that an armed civilian was prepared to confront him, Roberts retreated into a stairwell and took his own life, ending the shooting spree. Meli's presence and readiness to act undoubtedly influenced Roberts' decision to stop his attack, preventing further potential casualties.

This incident at the Clackamas Town Center underscores the potential lifesaving impact of armed self-defense. It demonstrates that responsible, armed citizens can play a vital role in protecting public safety and stopping violent threats.

Moreover, this case highlights the importance of concealed carry permits and the ability of trained individuals to respond effectively in critical situations. Critics often argue that the presence of more guns in public spaces increases the risk of violence, but incidents like the Clackamas Town Center shooting show that armed civilians can act as a force for good, providing a critical line of defense when law enforcement is not immediately available.

The presence of a responsible, armed citizen like Nick Meli can make all the difference in such critical moments, reinforcing the argument that the right to carry firearms for self-defense is a fundamental and necessary component of American society.

## The Boiling Springs Self-Defense Case

In Boiling Springs, South Carolina, a concealed carry permit holder named Aaron Guyton stopped a potential massacre in 2012. This incident occurred at the Blue Ridge Baptist Church, where congregants were attending a Sunday service. The church, like many places of worship, was a serene environment where the community gathered to find solace and spiritual connection. However, this peace was abruptly shattered when a gunman, intent on causing harm, entered the church.

The gunman, identified as Jesse Gates, an individual with a history of violent behavior, burst into the church with a shotgun. His intentions were clear and malevolent. Panic spread among the congregants as they realized the imminent threat. However, amidst the chaos, churchgoer Aaron Guyton, who had a concealed carry permit, drew his weapon and confronted the attacker. Jesse Smith and Leland Powers, who were also in the church at the time, held the gunman down while Aaron Guyton held a gun on him until deputies arrived. Guyton's quick thinking and decisive action prevented what could have been a tragic mass shooting. No one was injured, and the churchgoers were spared from what could have been a horrific event.

This incident highlights several critical points about the role of armed citizens in public safety. First, it underscores the importance of the Second Amendment and the right to bear arms for self-defense. In this case, the immediate threat was neutralized without a single shot being fired, demonstrating the deterrent effect that an armed citizen can have.

Second, the incident at the Blue Ridge Baptist Church emphasizes the need for responsible gun ownership and training. Guyton, Smith, and Powers were able to respond effectively because they were prepared and had the necessary skills to handle a firearm safely and responsibly. Guyton's actions reflect the positive impact that well-trained, law-abiding gun owners can have in protecting their communities.

Third, this event challenges the narrative often propagated by gun control advocates that more guns lead to more violence. On the contrary, responsible gun ownership can be a crucial element in ensuring public safety. In environments where law enforcement may not be able to respond immediately, armed citizens can provide a critical line of defense.

The media's coverage of such incidents is also noteworthy. While some outlets reported on Guyton's heroism, these stories often receive less attention than those involving gun violence perpetrated by criminals. It is essential to highlight these positive examples to provide a balanced perspective on gun ownership and its role in self-defense.

## The Nashville Gas Station Robbery

In the early morning hours of July 8, 2023, an incident at the Clarksville Pike gas station in Nashville, Tennessee, highlighted the critical role of armed self-defense. The gas station clerk, 20, was threatened as a man, 25, walked in brandishing a handgun, demanding money. When the clerk refused, the man jumped over the counter, tackling and attacking the clerk. However, the clerk, prepared and aware of the right to self-defense, drew his legally owned firearm from his shirt pocket, and shot the robber as he landed on him. Although the robber was shot, he continued to attack the clerk and a struggle ensued. The clerk fired additional shots at the robber, who died from the gunshot wounds. The clerk then called the authorities after the incident. The clerk's swift response neutralized the threat before authorities could arrive.

This incident underscores several important aspects of the debate surrounding gun rights and self-defense. In the absence of immediate law enforcement, the clerk's firearm was the critical tool that ensured his safety. This scenario is a real-world example of why many advocate for the right to carry firearms. The ability to respond to threats in real time, before law enforcement can intervene, is a powerful argument in favor of preserving and protecting Second Amendment rights.

Moreover, this case challenges the narrative that firearms in the hands of civilians invariably leads to increased violence. On the contrary, the clerk's actions in Nashville demonstrate that responsible gun ownership can directly contribute to the safety and security of individuals and communities.

## The Dothan Traffic Light Incident

In Dothan, Alabama, on the evening of July 12, 2023, an incident unfolded that demonstrated the critical role of responsible armed citizens in stopping violent attacks. At a busy traffic light, a man armed with a knife menacingly approached a car driven by his ex-girlfriend, who was the mother of his children, and her male acquaintance. The situation escalated quickly as the armed man ignored repeated warnings to back off. The aggressor's intentions were clearly threatening, as he continued to advance despite the visible distress and verbal attempts to dissuade him.

The male acquaintance, recognizing the imminent danger, took decisive action to protect both himself and the woman. As the aggressor closed in, brandishing the knife with clear intent to harm, the woman's acquaintance drew his legally owned firearm. In a matter of moments, the confrontation reached its peak. Despite the life-threatening circumstances, the woman's male acquaintance maintained composure and issued a final warning to the knife-wielding man. The aggressor, undeterred, continued his advance.

Faced with no other options and in a bid to prevent what could have been a fatal attack, the male companion fired his weapon, wounding the woman's ex. The single shot was enough to neutralize the threat, causing the aggressor to fall and cease his advance. Bystanders who witnessed the incident quickly called emergency services. Police and medical personnel arrived on the scene shortly thereafter. The aggressor was taken to a nearby hospital where he received treatment for his injuries.

This incident at the Dothan traffic light demonstrates how quickly a situation can escalate into violence and how important it is to be prepared to defend oneself and others. The male companion's actions exemplify the principle that good guys with guns can effectively stop violent attacks and prevent greater harm.

Law enforcement officials reviewed the incident and confirmed that the male companion acted in self-defense. The local police chief praised the actions taken, noting that the armed citizen's intervention was justified given the immediate threat posed by the knife-wielding aggressor.

Witnesses later spoke to local news outlets, describing the fear and tension they felt as the events unfolded. Many expressed relief that the situation was resolved without loss of life, crediting the male companion's quick and decisive response. This case also sparked discussions within the community about the importance of self-defense and the role of firearms in personal protection.

The Dothan incident adds to the growing body of evidence that armed citizens can play a vital role in stopping violent crimes.

## The Philadelphia Home Invasion

In Philadelphia, Pennsylvania, on the evening of July 16, 2023, a terrifying incident occurred that showcased the importance of self-defense and the bravery of a woman protecting her home. As she returned to her German-town apartment, she was confronted with a terrifying sight: Four intruders had broken into her home. Faced with an immediate threat to her safety and the sanctity of her living space, she had to act swiftly and decisively.

The woman, whose name was not immediately released to protect her privacy, quickly assessed the situation. The intruders, startled by her unexpected return, likely anticipated an easy robbery. However, they did not account for her preparedness and resolve. Armed with a firearm she legally owned, the woman did not hesitate to defend herself. She issued a warning to the intruders, hoping they would leave peacefully, but when they continued to advance, she was forced to act.

In the ensuing confrontation, the woman fired her weapon, injuring two of the burglars. The sudden and forceful response caught the intruders off guard. The wounded burglars fell to the ground, incapacitated, while the remaining two, realizing the peril they faced, fled the scene in a panic. The gunshots alerted neighbors, who promptly called the police.

When law enforcement arrived, they found the woman unharmed but understandably shaken. The two injured intruders were taken into custody and transported to a nearby hospital for treatment of their non-life-threatening injuries. The other two burglars remained at large but were the subject of an intensive police search.

The local authorities praised the woman's bravery and quick thinking. Police officials confirmed that she acted within her rights to protect herself and her home, emphasizing that her actions likely prevented a much more dangerous outcome. The woman's decision to use her firearm in self-defense not only safeguarded her life but also sent a clear message to would-be criminals about the risks of home invasion.

Community reactions to the incident were mixed but largely supportive of the woman's right to defend her home. Many residents expressed relief that she was able to protect herself and prevent the situation from escalating further. Discussions around the event also touched on broader themes of self-defense and public safety, with some advocating for greater awareness and training in responsible firearm use.

This incident highlights the critical role that firearms can play in self-defense, especially in situations where the police may not be able to respond immediately. The woman's ability to protect herself from multiple attackers underscores the importance of responsible gun ownership and the need for individuals to have the means to defend themselves when faced with imminent danger. This Philadelphia case also serves as another compelling example of how armed citizens can effectively deter crime and protect their lives and property. The woman's courageous actions ensured her safety and highlighted the vital role of self-defense in maintaining personal security in the face of danger.

## The Sand Springs Domestic Assault

In Sand Springs, Oklahoma, on the night of March 2, 2023, an incident unfolded that vividly illustrates the critical role of firearms in protecting vulnerable individuals, particularly single women escaping abusive relationships. A woman, seeking refuge from her abusive ex-boyfriend, had moved in with her uncle, hoping to find safety and a fresh start. Unfortunately, her ex-boyfriend, driven by a sinister determination, tracked her down and broke into the home, intent on causing harm.

The ex-boyfriend's violent intentions became immediately clear as he forced his way into the house and assaulted the woman. The situation was dire, with the woman once again finding herself at the mercy of her abuser. However, this time she was not alone. Her uncle, understanding the threat and prepared to defend his niece, intervened decisively. Armed with a firearm, the uncle confronted the assailant, aiming to stop the attack and protect his family.

As the assailant continued his assault, the uncle was left with no choice but to use his weapon. He shot the ex-boyfriend in the face, a critical move that instantly ended the threat. The assailant was incapacitated, and the woman was saved from further harm. The assailant fled the scene and was treated at the local hospital, after which he faced charges related to the assault. The prompt and decisive action of her uncle not only protected her in that moment but also served as a powerful deterrent against future attempts by the abuser or anyone else who might wish to do harm.

The reaction from the community and law enforcement was supportive of the uncle's actions. Authorities confirmed that he acted in self-defense and within his rights to protect his niece. This response underscores the legal and moral justification for using a firearm in such dire circumstances.

This incident also highlights several vital points about self-defense and the protection of vulnerable individuals. Single women, especially those escaping abusive relationships, often find themselves in precarious situations. Abusers can be relentless in their pursuit, and the threat of violence is ever-present. In such scenarios, the ability to defend oneself or be defended by a trusted individual is crucial.

Firearms act as an equalizer in these situations. The uncle's use of a firearm in Sand Springs exemplifies how a gun can be the decisive factor in stopping an attack and ensuring the safety of the victim. The ability to protect oneself and loved ones from imminent danger is a fundamental aspect of safety and security.

## The Attempted Liquor Store Robbery, Norco, California

On August 2, 2022, at 2:47 AM, a harrowing incident unfolded in Southern California that underscored the importance of the Second Amendment and the right to self-defense. In the quiet town of Norco, an elderly liquor store owner found himself face-to-face with a life-threatening situation when armed intruders attempted to rob his store. The intruders, carrying rifles, stormed into the store with the clear intent to overpower and possibly harm anyone who stood in their way. But what they did not anticipate was that the store owner, despite his age, was prepared to defend himself and his livelihood.

As the intruders were about to enter the store, the owner, Craig Cope, an 80-year-old man, saw the intruders on the surveillance monitors and quickly assessed the situation and recognized the imminent danger. Acting swiftly, he hid behind the counter, reached for his own legally owned rifle, and fired at the armed men. His quick and decisive action struck one of the intruders in the shoulder, causing the would-be robbers to panic and flee the scene. The surveillance footage of the incident, later released to the public, showed the moment the intruders realized they were not in control and scrambled to escape, leaving behind their plans and a wounded accomplice. It was later discovered that the vehicle and firearms used in the crime by the assailants had been stolen.

In the aftermath of the incident, the store owner spoke to the media about what had transpired. He recounted how he had no choice but to defend himself when faced with the threat of armed intruders. "They were here to take my life and my property," he told reporters, emphasizing the fear and uncertainty he felt in those critical moments. The man also expressed relief that he was able to protect himself and his store, and he urged others to consider the importance of being prepared for such situations.

The incident quickly gained national attention, with news outlets across the country picking up the story of the brave liquor store owner who defended his life and livelihood against armed intruders. As the video footage of the attempted robbery and Craig's courageous response went viral, support for him poured in from all corners of the nation. Locally, the community rallied around Craig, praising him for his quick thinking and bravery. Neighbors, customers, and fellow business owners expressed their gratitude and relief, recognizing that his actions not only saved his own life but also sent a strong message to criminals. The public at large echoed this sentiment, with many hailing Craig as a hero for standing his ground and exercising his right to self-defense. His story resonated with countless Americans who saw in Craig's actions the embodiment of the fundamental right to protect oneself and one's property, reaffirming the importance of the Second Amendment in safeguarding those rights.

The actions of the Norco liquor store owner were a clear demonstration of the fundamental right to self-defense. In a situation where seconds counted and the police were not present, his ability to defend himself with a firearm was the only thing that stood between him and potentially fatal harm. His actions not only saved his life but also likely prevented further harm to others in the community.

## The Mesquite Jewelry Store Robbery

In Mesquite, Texas, on November 2, 2023, a jewelry store owner found himself in a life-threatening situation as armed thieves attempted to rob his store. The incident unfolded in the late afternoon when two thieves entered the jewelry store with clear intentions: to steal valuable merchandise. The store owner, who had previously experienced an armed robbery, was prepared for such an eventuality. He swiftly retrieved his firearm, ready to defend his property and himself.

As the thieves began to loot the store, one of them brandished a weapon. The store owner, understanding the immediate threat to his life and the lives of any customers or employees present, decided to act. He fired at the armed robber, engaging in a tense exchange of gunfire. The sounds of the shots echoed through the store, creating a chaotic and perilous scene.

Despite the intense situation, the store owner's resolve and preparedness paid off. Realizing they were facing an armed and determined defender, the thieves decided to flee the scene rather than risk further confrontation. The quick and courageous actions of the store owner not only protected his merchandise but also likely prevented potential harm to himself and others in the store.

Law enforcement officials acknowledged that the store owner acted within his rights to defend himself and his property from an imminent threat. The community's reaction to the incident was one of support and admiration for the store owner's bravery. Local residents and fellow business owners recognized the importance of his actions in maintaining personal and public safety.

This incident highlights the recurring risks faced by business owners, particularly those dealing with valuable goods. For the store owner, this was the second time he had to use his firearm to defend his store, illustrating that criminals often target businesses they perceive as vulnerable. It also shows the necessity for self-defense measures in situations where police response times might not be immediate. The store owner's ability to protect his business with a firearm is a reminder of the practical benefits of Second Amendment rights, particularly in high-risk professions.

The above examples vividly illustrate how law-abiding citizens can use guns to protect themselves and others from imminent threats. From thwarting armed robberies and home invasions to defending against violent assailants, these incidents underscore the critical role that firearms play in ensuring personal and community safety. Despite the significant number of defensive gun uses—estimated to occur between 500,000 and 3 million times annually—the media often downplays, covers up, or fails to report these events. This is largely because such stories do not align with the prevailing gun control narrative that emphasizes the dangers of firearm ownership. Instead, the media tends to focus on gun violence and mass shootings, which, while undeniably tragic, represent a small fraction of overall gun use. By highlighting only the negative aspects of gun ownership, the media skews public perception and policy discussions, neglecting the important fact that guns can and do save lives in the hands of responsible citizens.

Although these case studies highlight the benefits of armed citizens stopping small-scale incidents such as home invasions, burglaries, assaults, and shootings, the right to defend oneself becomes even more critical during periods of widespread social unrest. In such times, the breakdown of societal norms and the absence of reliable law enforcement can leave individuals and communities vulnerable to widespread violence and chaos. The ability to protect one's family, property, and community during these periods is of the utmost importance, illustrating the fundamental necessity of the Second Amendment rights.

In the following discussions, we will explore historical and contemporary examples of societal breakdown and anarchy, focusing on the measures citizens took to defend themselves and their communities. These examples will underscore the importance of self-defense during times of crisis, highlighting how armed citizens have safeguarded their lives and maintained order when conventional systems of protection failed. Through these discussions, we will gain a deeper understanding of the role of firearms in preserving safety and security amid chaos and uncertainty.

## The University of Texas Tower Shooting in 1966

One notable self-defense situation from the 1960s that highlights the role of armed citizens in ending mayhem occurred during the infamous University of Texas tower shooting on August 1, 1966. Charles Whitman, a former Marine, ascended the university's clock tower and began a shooting spree that lasted for 96 minutes, tragically killing 14 people and wounding 31 others.

As the horror unfolded, several professors, students, and others on campus took decisive action. Many of these individuals went to their cars or homes to retrieve their personal firearms, primarily hunting rifles, and returned to the scene to provide suppressive fire against Whitman. These armed citizens played a big role in limiting Whitman's ability to target more victims by forcing him to take cover, thereby reducing his field of fire and slowing the rate of his attacks.

While the police were mobilizing and formulating a plan to neutralize Whitman, the armed citizens on the ground created a chaotic environment for the shooter, effectively pinning him down and allowing law enforcement officers to approach the tower more safely. Eventually, police officers Ramiro Martinez and Houston McCoy made their way to the observation deck and shot Whitman, bringing the horrific event to an end.

This incident underscores the potential for armed citizens to play a vital role in self-defense and public safety during active shooter situations. It is a powerful example of how arms can be instrumental in stopping a violent threat and protecting innocent lives. The quick actions of those who retrieved their firearms to defend their campus helped to mitigate the tragedy and demonstrated the value of responsible gun ownership.

## Firearms and Social Unrest: The Riots of 1968

In 1968, America was rocked by a series of devastating riots that erupted in cities across the nation following the assassination of civil rights leader Dr. Martin Luther King Jr. on April 4th. The grief and anger over King's death sparked widespread unrest, resulting in looting, arson, and violent confrontations with law enforcement. Major cities, such as Washington, DC, Chicago, and Baltimore, were hard hit, with large swaths of these cities left in ruins. The riots were not only a manifestation of sorrow over King's assassination but also an expression of deep-seated frustrations with perceived racial inequality.

During these tumultuous times, many citizens found themselves in a precarious position, with law enforcement stretched thin and unable to protect all neighborhoods effectively. In response, individuals and communities took up arms to defend themselves, their families, and their property. The Second Amendment, which guarantees the right to keep and bear arms, became a crucial element of personal security for many Americans during the chaos. Homeowners and business owners alike armed themselves with firearms, prepared to defend against looters and arsonists who posed immediate threats to their safety and livelihood.

In Washington, DC, neighborhoods saw residents banding together, often standing guard with shotguns and rifles to deter potential attacks on their homes and businesses. In Chicago, similar scenes played out as shop owners and residents took to the rooftops and storefronts, armed and ready to protect their property from the waves of rioters moving through the streets.

These events had a lasting impact on the national conversation about gun rights and gun control. The riots of 1968, along with other tumultuous events of the decade, contributed to the passage of the Gun Control Act of 1968. This federal law aimed to regulate interstate commerce in firearms and restrict certain individuals, such as felons and those with mental illness, from purchasing guns. While intended to address rising concerns about gun violence, the act also sparked ongoing debates about the balance between regulation and the right to self-defense.

The role of the Second Amendment during the 1968 riots highlighted its importance as a safeguard of personal liberty and security, particularly in times when governmental authorities are unable to provide immediate protection. The ability to bear arms provided many Americans with a necessary means of defense during a time of widespread lawlessness and uncertainty, highlighting the enduring importance of this constitutional right. For many, the ability to defend themselves was not just a theoretical right but a real and immediate necessity to ensure their safety and the preservation of their property.

## Firearms and Social Unrest: The Rodney King Riots of 1992

One of the most notable examples of individuals using firearms for self-defense occurred during the Rodney King riots in Los Angeles in 1992. The riots erupted following the acquittal of four police officers who had been videotaped brutally beating Rodney King, an African American man. The verdict shocked and outraged many, leading to days of intense violence, looting, and arson that paralyzed large parts of Los Angeles. Amidst the chaos, the city's residents found themselves under siege, as rioters targeted businesses, homes, and individuals indiscriminately.

In response to the escalating violence, many residents took up arms to defend their homes and businesses. Facing rampant looting and destruction, they formed armed militias to protect their livelihoods. The Los Angeles Police Department (LAPD) was overwhelmed by the sheer scale of the unrest and was often unable to respond to emergency calls, leaving many communities vulnerable. Korean American shop owners, in particular, whose businesses were concentrated in the epicenter of the riots, banded together, armed with rifles, shotguns, and handguns. They patrolled rooftops and storefronts, ready to defend against the lawless mobs.

One of the most memorable images from the riots is that of Korean American shop owners standing guard on rooftops, firearms in hand, vigilantly watching over their properties. This stark visual symbolized the dire necessity of the right to bear arms when law enforcement fails. Their actions were not just about protecting property but also about ensuring personal safety in a situation where the government could not provide security. These brave individuals exemplified the spirit of self-reliance and the critical role that armed self-defense plays in protecting oneself during periods of anarchy.

The chaos of the riots demonstrated how vulnerable communities can become when civil order breaks down and law enforcement is unable to maintain control. For many, the events of those days were a vivid illustration of why the right to keep and bear arms must be protected and respected. In such scenarios, the Second Amendment becomes not just a constitutional right but a vital tool for survival and protection.

## Social Unrest: The Nationwide Summer of 2020 Riots

In 2020, the United States experienced a significant surge in gun ownership amidst widespread social unrest. The turmoil was largely sparked by the killing of George Floyd in Minneapolis on May 25, 2020, which led to nationwide protests against "police brutality" and "systemic racism." While some demonstrations were peaceful, most devolved into violent riots characterized by looting, robberies and smash-and-grabs, murder, and arson. These events played a crucial role in the dramatic increase in gun purchases as Americans sought to protect themselves, their families, and their properties.

Looting became rampant in various cities, with businesses large and small targeted. High-profile incidents included the widespread looting in downtown Chicago, where numerous stores were ransacked, and in New York City, where luxury retailers on Fifth Avenue were hit hard. These incidents created an atmosphere of lawlessness and fear, prompting many to seek means of self-defense.

Alongside looting, there was a notable increase in robberies and smash-and-grab incidents. Organized groups often targeted retail stores, breaking windows to steal goods quickly. These tactics were widely reported in cities such as San Francisco, where high-end stores like Louis Vuitton and Neiman Marcus were heavily looted.

The social unrest saw an uptick in violent crimes, including murders. For instance, in cities like New York, Chicago, and Los Angeles, there were large increases in homicides compared to previous years. This rise in violence further fueled concerns about personal safety.

Arson was another critical component of the unrest. In Minneapolis, the epicenter of the initial protests, entire blocks were set on fire, including the Third Precinct police station. Similar incidents occurred in cities like Kenosha, Wisconsin, and Portland, Oregon, where buildings, vehicles, and other properties were intentionally set ablaze.

The chaotic and unpredictable nature of the unrest led many Americans to reconsider their personal safety and security. As law enforcement struggled to contain the widespread violence and destruction, the public's trust in the ability of the police to protect them waned, driving a surge in gun sales. According to the FBI's National Instant Criminal Background Check System (NICS), there were unprecedented numbers of background checks for gun purchases. In 2020, the FBI conducted over 39.7 million background checks, up from 28.4 million in 2019. This surge was indicative of a broad-based response to the social instability.

The surge in gun ownership spanned various demographics, including women, minorities, and first-time buyers. The National Shooting Sports Foundation (NSSF) reported that approximately 8.4 million people became first-time gun buyers in 2020. Women made up about 40 percent of these new buyers, while large increases were also noted among African American, Asian American, and Hispanic American communities. Many new gun owners were urban residents who previously might not have considered firearm ownership but felt compelled to do so due to the proximity of riots and civil disturbances. Business owners, particularly those in urban areas affected by riots, purchased firearms to defend their property.

As law enforcement struggled to respond swiftly to widespread violence, many Americans felt compelled to take their safety into their own hands. The ongoing unrest, combined with the economic and social strain of the pandemic, created a pervasive sense of instability, driving millions to seek security through firearm ownership. Yet, despite the unprecedented surge in gun ownership starting in 2020, there was no corresponding spike in violent gun crime tied to these new gun owners. This challenges the notion that more firearms inevitably leads to more violence, highlighting the need to focus on the deeper causes of crime rather than simply the number of guns in circulation.

## The Kyle Rittenhouse Case

The case of Kyle Rittenhouse is a prominent example of a citizen defending themselves with a firearm under life-threatening circumstances. On the night of August 25, 2020, Kyle Rittenhouse, a 17-year-old from Antioch, Illinois, traveled to Kenosha, Wisconsin, amidst ongoing protests and riots following the police shooting of Jacob Blake. It is important to note that Rittenhouse lived near the border of Wisconsin, just a stone's throw away from Kenosha. Contrary to many media reports, he did not cross state lines with a rifle. The firearm was already in Kenosha, as he had friends and relatives there. Rittenhouse went to Kenosha to help protect his friend's car dealership, which had been targeted by rioters. In addition, Wisconsin state law permits 16- to 18-year-olds to possess a rifle as long as the rifle's barrel is at least 16 inches in length, making Rittenhouse's actions legal under state law. Unfortunately, that night, Rittenhouse found himself in a series of confrontations that escalated into violence.

The first confrontation involved Joseph Rosenbaum, who chased Rittenhouse into a parking lot and attempted to take his rifle. Rittenhouse fired four shots, killing Rosenbaum. Shortly after, Rittenhouse fled the scene and was pursued by several individuals. One of them, Anthony Huber, struck Rittenhouse with a skateboard and tried to grab his rifle, resulting in Rittenhouse firing a single shot that killed Huber. Gaige Grosskreutz, who was armed with a handgun, approached Rittenhouse, and was shot in the arm when he advanced on him.

The mainstream media's coverage of the Rittenhouse case was marked by significant bias and misinformation. Many outlets painted Rittenhouse as a white supremacist vigilante who crossed state lines with a firearm to incite violence. Despite clear video evidence showing Rittenhouse being attacked and defending himself, these narratives persisted, contributing to widespread public misunderstanding and outrage. In addition, polling and public opinion at the time showed a stark partisan divide in reactions to Kyle Rittenhouse's case. A vast majority of

Democrats believed he was guilty of unlawful possession of a firearm and murder, while an overwhelming number of Republicans saw his actions as justified self-defense. This sharp divide highlights how deeply political biases influence people's perceptions, often leading to snap judgments based on ideology rather than a careful examination of the facts.

Media narratives often omitted key facts, such as Rittenhouse's role in providing medical assistance earlier in the evening and the criminal backgrounds of the individuals involved in the confrontation. The portrayal of Rittenhouse was less about presenting a balanced account and more about fitting a broader political agenda. One common argument against Rittenhouse is that he should not have been present in Kenosha during the riots. However, this point is irrelevant to the legal case and his right to self-defense. Whether or not Rittenhouse should have been there does not negate his right to protect his life when faced with imminent threats. Additionally, the rioters who attacked him should not have been there either, effectively canceling out the argument that Rittenhouse's presence was the primary issue.

The case went to trial in November 2021, where the jury had to decide whether Rittenhouse acted in self-defense or was guilty of intentional homicide and other charges. Throughout the trial, the defense presented clear video evidence showing that Rittenhouse acted in self-defense, responding to direct threats against his life. Witnesses testified about the chaotic environment and the aggressive actions of those who attacked Rittenhouse.

On November 19, 2021, the jury acquitted Rittenhouse on all counts, affirming his claim of self-defense. This verdict was an important moment, reinforcing the legal principle that individuals have the right to defend their lives, even amidst hostile public opinion and media misrepresentation.

This case highlights the necessity of the Second Amendment in ensuring individuals can defend themselves against immediate threats. Moreover, the case underscores the dangers of media bias and misinformation. The slanderous narratives and selective reporting not only misled the public but also fueled political agendas aimed at restricting gun rights. The media's role in shaping public perception can have profound implications for individuals exercising their constitutional rights.

Following his acquittal, Kyle Rittenhouse took legal action against several mainstream media outlets for slander. These lawsuits aim to hold the media accountable for spreading false and damaging narratives about him. This step serves as a reminder of how critical it is to defend oneself with firearms, no matter the media or political backlash. The right to self-defense is paramount, and individuals must be prepared to act in their own defense, regardless of how they may be portrayed by the media.

***

In modern times, the role of firearms in personal protection cannot be overstated. While law enforcement agencies work tirelessly to protect citizens (when not prohibited from doing so by the powers that be), they cannot be everywhere at once. The average police response time for a 911 call varies depending on the city you live in. Response times range from 3 to 15+ minutes. In many emergency situations, every second counts.

In such scenarios, individuals armed with firearms can defend themselves and their loved ones until help arrives. Statistics from the National Crime Victimization Survey suggest that defensive gun use occurs more frequently than many realize, highlighting the significant role that firearms play in personal defense and the prevention of crime.

The stories of armed civilians stopping crimes and defending themselves with firearms serve as powerful testaments to the importance of the Second Amendment. Despite what the media may say, guns are used in far more defensive situations than in the commission of crimes. The narrative that guns are inherently dangerous and have no place in civilian hands ignores the countless instances where firearms have saved lives and prevented tragedies. Every story of a homeowner defending their home or family (such as in the Philadelphia home invasion in 2023) or a bystander stopping a mass shooting (such as in the 2012 Clackamas Town Center shooting) underscores the critical role that armed citizens play in maintaining public safety. The right to defend oneself from criminals or break-ins is a fundamental liberty that hundreds of millions of people throughout the last century and beyond have been denied. This lack of personal protection has led to some of the worst atrocities in history, where unarmed populations have fallen prey to murderous, oppressive regimes and violent criminals.

# Chapter 4

## Unarmed and Persecuted: The Grim Toll of Disarmament

*If I could have gotten 51 votes in the Senate of the United States for an outright ban, picking up every one of them—Mr. and Mrs. America, turn them all in—I would have done it.*

—Dianne Feinstein

*History shows that the first step in any totalitarian movement is disarmament of the citizens. The Second Amendment is our insurance policy against tyranny.*

—Mike Huckabee

*Political power grows out of the barrel of a gun.*

—Mao Zedong

The comic strip featuring a dog sitting in a burning room, drinking coffee and saying, "This is fine," created by artist K. C. Green, has become a widely recognized symbol of apathy and denial in the face of impending disaster. This image poignantly captures a significant segment of contemporary society, both in the United States and globally, who remain indifferent or dismissive towards critical issues, including gun rights and the Second Amendment.

The dog's serene demeanor amidst the chaos in the "This is fine" comic strip is a metaphor for those who remain indifferent to the erosion of their rights. They fail to realize that even if they do not personally own firearms, the right to do so is a crucial check on government power and a fundamental aspect of individual liberty. By ignoring or supporting gun bans, they inadvertently pave the way for greater governmental overreach and potential tyranny, affecting everyone, including themselves.

This comic also resonates with people who choose to disengage from politics or abstain from voting, whether out of apathy or disillusionment. In many democracies, voter turnout is disappointingly low, and political apathy is rampant. Many individuals feel that their vote does not matter, that the system is rigged, or that the issues are too complex or irrelevant to their daily lives. This lack of engagement allows those with more extreme or authoritarian agendas to seize power and implement policies that may infringe on individual freedoms. As the saying goes, evil happens not just because evil people do evil things, but because good people sit back and do nothing.

So how is the "This is fine" comic strip relevant to this discussion? Although gun ownership in the United States is the highest in the world, a substantial portion of the population does not own firearms or has no desire to own them. This group often displays apathy towards the increasing calls for gun control and gun bans. They might perceive these regulations as irrelevant to their lives, believing that since they do not possess guns, the restrictions will not affect them personally.

History, however, has shown us that such complacency can have dire consequences. In the 20th century, tyrannical and genocidal regimes often began their terror reigns with stringent gun control measures. The disarmament of the populace was a common precursor to the widespread atrocities committed by these regimes. Once the population was disarmed, the true extent of the tyranny became apparent, affecting everyone indiscriminately.

The Holocaust, the Armenian Genocide, and the massacres under Stalin's Soviet Union and Mao's China all serve as grim reminders of what can happen when a government, unchallenged by an armed populace, turns tyrannical. The citizens of these nations often did not resist these measures, believing that such laws would not affect them or that the state had their best interests at heart. This dangerous complacency allowed oppressive regimes to gain and consolidate power unopposed.

The 20th century witnessed some of the most horrific tyrannies and genocides in human history. The common origins of the ideology that led to these atrocities go back centuries. Niccolò Machiavelli, an influential Italian Renaissance political philosopher, is renowned for his work *The Prince*, which offers pragmatic advice on political leadership, emphasizing that "the ends justify the means." His ideas, particularly on maintaining control through force and the importance of a well-armed populace for deterring tyranny, have influenced political thought, especially among leftist ideologies that prioritize societal goals over individual morality. Thomas More, an English statesman, presented a vision of an ideal society in his work *Utopia*, where property is communally owned, a concept that has often led to totalitarian regimes enforcing strict control and oppression.

The ideas of Machiavelli and More profoundly influenced Karl Marx and Friedrich Engels's *Communist Manifesto*, which laid the groundwork for communist and socialist movements worldwide. The manifesto calls for the abolition of private property and the centralization of production, echoing More's utopian ideals, but with an emphasis on revolutionary action. A fundamental aspect of communist ideology is the disarmament of the civilian population to prevent resistance and enforce radical changes. This principle has been implemented by various totalitarian regimes in the 20th century, leading to widespread disarmament and suppression of dissent.

In the United States, the radical left of the Democrat Party has long pushed for stricter gun control measures, reflecting the disarmament principles of the *Communist Manifesto*. Advocates argue that reducing firearms in civilian hands will create a safer society, but critics contend this undermines Second Amendment rights and paves the way for increased government control and potential tyranny. The phrase "You can vote your way into socialism, but you have to shoot your way out" underscores the danger of disarming the populace, highlighting the importance of an armed citizenry as a safeguard against authoritarianism. The current push for gun control can be seen as part of a broader ideological struggle, echoing the manifesto's call for state control over violence and suppression of resistance.

From the Ottoman Empire to the Soviet Union, Nazi Germany, Maoist China, Cambodia, Uganda, and beyond, one common thread links these atrocities: the systematic disarmament of the populace before the mass killings began. These governments employed various methods to strip their citizens of the means to defend themselves, paving the way for state-sponsored murder on an unimaginable scale.

This chapter delves into the grim realities of how civilian disarmament has enabled some of history's most oppressive regimes, resulting in a staggering loss of life. The analysis first includes a comparison between the Reign of Terror during the French Revolution and the newly formed United States, showcasing the stark consequences of disarmament. Then, by examining well-known tyrannies of the 20th century and lesser-known genocides, we will highlight critical lessons to prevent history from repeating itself. Additionally, we will contextualize historical disarmament efforts with modern gun control narratives, aiming to debunk common anti-Second Amendment arguments perpetuated by the media, academia, and anti-gun politicians.

## The French Revolution (1789–1799), Including the Reign of Terror (1793–1794)

The landscape of civilian disarmament and tyranny during the French Revolution presents a harrowing tale of unchecked power and mass persecution. In the late 18th century, revolutionary fervor swept through France, toppling the aristocratic class and the monarchy. What began as a movement for liberty and equality quickly developed into the Reign of Terror, a period from 1793 to 1794 during which tens of thousands of perceived enemies of the revolution were executed, primarily by guillotine.

The absence of a constitutional right to bear arms in France drastically differed with the emerging American Republic, which had just ratified the Bill of Rights in 1791, including the Second Amendment that ensured the right to keep and bear arms. In France, strict gun control measures were in place, and civilians were largely barred from owning personal firearms. This lack of arms among the general populace made it easier for the revolutionary government to carry out its brutal purges without much resistance.

During the Reign of Terror, the revolutionary government, led by the Committee of Public Safety and figures like Maximilien Robespierre, exercised absolute power. They conducted mass executions to eliminate supposed threats to the revolution, targeting not only the aristocracy but also political rivals and ordinary citizens accused of counterrevolutionary activities. The Revolutionary Tribunal, established to root out enemies of the state, often conducted trials with little to no evidence, leading to widespread fear and paranoia.

Without the means to defend themselves, the people of France were left vulnerable to the whims of the revolutionaries. Public executions became a spectacle, and the guillotine, a symbol of the revolution's justice, was used with horrifying frequency. Entire families were condemned to death, and neighborhoods lived in constant fear of denunciation and arrest.

Had the French populace been armed, the dynamics of the revolution could have been markedly different. The ability to resist government overreach and defend oneself against unlawful persecution is a cornerstone of the right to bear arms, as envisioned by the American Founding Fathers. In the French Revolution, armed resistance could have provided a check against the excesses of the revolutionary government, potentially saving countless lives.

The lack of armed self-defense contributed to the efficiency with which the Reign of Terror was executed. Revolutionary leaders were able to implement their draconian measures with little fear of armed insurrection. In contrast, the newly formed United States, with its enshrined right to bear arms, provided a framework for its citizens to defend their liberties against any potential tyranny. This right was seen as essential to the preservation of freedom and the prevention of government overreach.

As France descended into chaos and bloodshed, the lack of civilian firearms facilitated the revolutionary government's ability to maintain control through terror. This period in history serves as a poignant reminder of the dangers of disarmament and the critical role that armed self-defense plays in safeguarding against tyranny. While the Reign of Terror remains one of the darkest chapters in French history, it also provides valuable lessons on the importance of protecting the right to bear arms as a fundamental human right.

Moreover, the narrative of the French Revolution's Reign of Terror takes an ironic turn with the execution of Maximilien Robespierre, the architect of the terror. Robespierre, who had sent thousands to their deaths, ultimately lost his head to the guillotine himself on July 28, 1794. This event reveals the inevitable tendency of revolutionary movements to devour their own leaders and followers. The revolution, once begun, often turns on its own proponents, highlighting the perilous and cyclical nature of unchecked power and fanaticism.

By reflecting on the French Revolution, we can better appreciate the protections afforded by the Second Amendment and the necessity of maintaining the right to self-defense to prevent such atrocities from occurring in the future.

## The Armenian Genocide (1915–1917)

The Armenian Genocide, orchestrated by the Ottoman Empire during World War I, serves as one of the earliest examples of state-sponsored mass murder in the 20th century. The Ottoman government began systematically disarming the Armenian population under the pretense of public safety and national security. This disarmament was the initial step in a broader plan to eliminate the Armenian people, as it stripped them of the means to defend themselves against the impending atrocities.

The process of disarming the Armenian population was meticulous and deceptive. The Ottoman authorities ordered the confiscation of weapons from Armenian civilians, often under the guise of temporary security measures due to the ongoing war. Armenians were assured that their weapons would be returned after the war, a promise that was never kept. In some cases, Armenians were required to turn in their weapons and register with local authorities, effectively creating a registry that made it easier for the government to target them later.

One of the key laws implemented was the Tehcir Law, enacted in May 1915. This law authorized the forced relocation of Armenians, ostensibly for their own protection, but in reality, it was a pretext for deportations that led to mass killings.

The Ottoman government used this law to justify the arrest and execution of Armenian leaders, intellectuals, and community figures, further crippling any potential resistance.

With the Armenian population vulnerable and their leadership decimated, the Ottoman authorities began their systematic extermination campaign. Armenian men were often taken away under the guise of military conscription, only to be executed en masse. This tactic served a dual purpose: It removed able-bodied men who could potentially resist and simultaneously terrorized the remaining population.

Women, children, and the elderly were subjected to brutal death marches through the Syrian desert. Deprived of food, water, and shelter, countless Armenians perished from starvation and dehydration. These death marches were orchestrated with the intent to cause maximum suffering and death. Those who survived the initial marches faced further atrocities in concentration camps, where they were often executed or left to die from neglect and disease.

The few who managed to escape the death marches were frequently captured and executed. The use of mass graves was common, as the Ottomans sought to erase the identities and existence of their victims. These graves, often left unmarked, stand as a silent testimony to the scale of the genocide.

The estimated death toll of the Armenian Genocide is over 1.5 million, a staggering number that highlights the effectiveness of the Ottoman Empire's genocidal strategy. The disarmament of the Armenian population was an important component of this strategy. The genocide not only decimated the Armenian population but also served as a grim precursor to the genocidal tactics employed by later totalitarian regimes.

## The Soviet Union (1917–1953)

Under the regimes of Lenin and Stalin, the Soviet Union implemented policies that led to the deaths of millions of its own citizens. The Soviet government enacted strict gun control laws to disarm the populace, ensuring that the state's power could not be challenged. The disarmament was justified under the guise of protecting the revolution and maintaining public order.

The Soviet Union's approach to gun control began with the 1918 decree by the Council of People's Commissars, which mandated the confiscation of all firearms from the civilian population. This decree was followed by further legislation that prohibited private gun ownership, effectively disarming the populace. The regime's focus was gaining absolute control and eliminating any potential resistance to communist rule. By 1929, Stalin had established a totalitarian state where the government exercised complete control over all aspects of life, including the prohibition of firearms.

The disarmament facilitated numerous atrocities, including the forced collectivization of agriculture, which led to the Holodomor—a man-made famine in Ukraine that killed between 3.5 to 7 million people. The Soviet government forcibly confiscated grain and other foodstuffs from Ukrainian peasants, leaving them to starve. Armed resistance to these brutal policies was virtually impossible due to the strict gun control measures.

During the Great Purge (1936–1938), Stalin's regime executed hundreds of thousands of perceived enemies of the state, often through summary executions and mass shootings. The NKVD, the Soviet secret police, carried out these purges with ruthless efficiency. Individuals were arrested on fabricated charges of espionage, sabotage, or counterrevolutionary activities, subjected to show trials, and then executed or sent to the Gulag labor camps. The population had no means to resist these state-sponsored atrocities.

The methods of slaughter were varied and brutal. Victims of the Great Purge were often executed by a single shot to the back of the head, with bodies buried in unmarked mass graves. The NKVD conducted mass shootings in remote areas to conceal the scale of the killings. In the Gulags, millions more perished due to overwork, starvation, disease, and harsh conditions. It is estimated that during Stalin's rule, approximately 20 million people died because of state-sponsored violence, purges, forced labor, and famine.

The disarmament of the Soviet population played a critical role in enabling these atrocities. Without the means to defend themselves, ordinary citizens were no match for the might of the state. The Soviet experience underscores the vital importance of the right to bear arms as a check against government tyranny and as a means of protecting individual liberties. The legacy of Soviet gun control and the subsequent mass killings is a reminder of the potential consequences of disarming a population and the importance of safeguarding the Second Amendment rights in contemporary society.

## Fascist Italy and Benito Mussolini (1922–1943)

The rise of Fascist Italy under Benito Mussolini marked a significant chapter in the history of 20th-century totalitarian regimes. Like other totalitarian regimes of the era, Mussolini's government implemented strict gun control measures to disarm the populace, thereby preventing any potential resistance to his rule.

Benito Mussolini, originally a socialist, founded the Fascist Party in 1919, capitalizing on the political and social unrest in post–World War I Italy. Fascism, derived from the Latin word "fasces" (a bundle of rods bound together around an axe), symbolizes strength through unity and is often associated with authoritarian and national socialist ideologies. This term, deeply rooted in ancient Roman symbolism, was adopted by Mussolini to represent state power and the suppression of opposition.

Mussolini's rise to power was marked by his adept use of propaganda, manipulation of public opinion, and exploitation of the prevailing fear of communism, although fascism and communism are first cousins. By 1922, Mussolini's Fascist Party had grown in influence, leading to the infamous March on Rome, which ultimately resulted in King Victor Emmanuel III inviting Mussolini to form a government.

Once in power, Mussolini quickly moved to consolidate his control over Italy. By 1925, he had established a dictatorship, eliminating political opposition through censorship, intimidation, disarmament, and violence. Mussolini's regime emphasized a totalitarian ideology that glorified the state, promoted national socialism, and demanded absolute loyalty to the leader, or "Il Duce," as Mussolini was known.

A key component of Mussolini's strategy to maintain control over Italy was the disarmament of the civilian population. The Fascist regime implemented stringent gun control measures to prevent any form of armed resistance. In 1931, the Italian government enacted the Public Safety Act, which imposed strict regulations on firearm ownership. Under this law, civilians were required to obtain government permits to possess firearms, and the criteria for obtaining these permits were highly restrictive.

The Fascist regime justified these measures by claiming they were necessary to maintain public order and national security. Mussolini's disarmament of the populace was a deliberate strategy to eliminate any threat to his authoritarian rule, effectively neutralizing the citizens' ability to resist government oppression.

Historically, fascist regimes implemented strict gun control measures to disarm and suppress the populace and eliminating potential resistance. In stark contrast, Second Amendment advocates in the United States champion the right to bear arms precisely to prevent such authoritarian overreach and to safeguard individual liberties. By labeling gun owners as fascists, anti-gun activists inadvertently echo the very tactics of control and suppression employed by the fascist regimes they decry. This mischaracterization not only misrepresents the historical context but also overlooks the fundamental principles of individual freedom and resistance to tyranny that underpin the Second Amendment. Thus, the rhetoric of anti-gun activists ironically aligns more closely with the actions of historical fascists than with the values of those who advocate for the right to bear arms as a protection against such tyranny.

## Nazi Germany (1933–1945)

Nazi Germany's genocide against the Jewish people and other targeted groups is one of the most well-documented atrocities in history. The Nazis, upon coming to power, enacted stringent gun control laws, targeting Jews and political dissidents. These laws facilitated the systematic roundup and extermination of six million Jews, along with millions of others, including Romani people, individuals with disabilities, and political opponents.

Nazism, although diverging from classical Marxism in its nationalistic and racial components, shares a common foundation in the belief of strong centralized control. This reflects its origins in leftist thinking, where the state plays a big role in economic and social life, including stringent gun control. In the early 20th century, many progressives in Europe and the US admired the National Socialists for their collectivist policies, with figures like George Bernard Shaw and H. G. Wells praising their societal restructuring before their full totalitarian brutality was exposed.

Adolf Hitler and the Nazi regime expanded and enforced Weimar Republic gun control laws to disarm potential opponents and minorities, making resistance to their policies far more difficult. One of the key pieces of legislation was the 1938 German Weapons Act. It prohibited Jews and other targeted groups from manufacturing or dealing in firearms and ammunition. The law also required all citizens to register their firearms, creating a detailed registry that the Nazi regime could use to identify and disarm those they considered undesirable or threatening. In addition to the Weapons Act, the Nazi regime enacted the Regulations Against Jews' Possession of Weapons. This regulation forbid Jews from acquiring, possessing, and carrying firearms and other weapons, including truncheons and stabbing weapons.

By disarming the populace, particularly targeted minority groups, the regime removed any means of organized resistance, making it easier to control and eventually exterminate these populations. This systematic disarmament of civilians before and during the Holocaust underscores the critical role that firearm ownership can play in deterring tyranny and protecting vulnerable populations from oppressive regimes.

The Nazis used a combination of legislative measures, propaganda, and brute force to disarm their enemies. The infamous Kristallnacht, or the Night of Broken Glass, marked the beginning of widespread violence against Jews. Thousands of Jewish homes, businesses, and synagogues were destroyed, and many Jews were arrested or killed. Following this pogrom, Jews were further subjected to relentless persecution. The genocide was carried out through a network of concentration and extermination camps where victims were murdered in gas chambers, shot en masse, or worked to death. The Holocaust claimed the lives of 6 million Jews, with the total number of victims of Nazi atrocities reaching up to 17 million, with some estimates as much as 21 million.

It is important to note that the horrors of death camps such as Auschwitz were not hidden away in some remote corner. Auschwitz was surrounded by a tall concrete wall topped and surrounded by with barbed wire, just beyond which lay a suburban neighborhood with single-family homes. The residents lived with a constant smoky haze and the unmistakable smell of burning bodies, as the camp's crematoria operated relentlessly. The vulnerability of the neighborhood's inhabitants, unable to own guns, amplified their fear, knowing they could be the next victims with no means to resist. Would today's proponents of gun control, if they were among the residents just outside Auschwitz hearing the cries and screams, smelling the burning bodies, seeing the raining down of ash and cinder from the crematoria onto the nearby neighborhood, and never seeing people come out, wish they owned a gun at that time? I think we all know the answer to that question. Yes, they would, and their views on gun control would vanish in an instant.

## North Korea (1948–Present)

North Korea, under the rule of the Kim dynasty, remains one of the most oppressive regimes in the world. The government's absolute control over firearms has prevented any form of resistance, allowing the regime to maintain its grip on power through widespread human rights abuses, forced labor camps, and state-sponsored executions. The Kim regime, beginning with Kim Il Sung and continuing through Kim Jong Il and Kim Jong Un, has maintained strict gun control measures as a central component of its strategy to suppress dissent and prevent uprisings.

The North Korean government uses severe penalties and pervasive surveillance to enforce strict gun control. Citizens are forbidden from possessing firearms, and the military and police forces maintain a tight monopoly on all weaponry. The regime's propaganda portrays gun control as essential for national security and social stability, creating a narrative that justifies the extreme measures taken to disarm the populace and render them unable to challenge the regime's authority.

Gun control in North Korea is enforced through a combination of draconian laws and a pervasive surveillance state. The possession of firearms by civilians is punishable by death, and even the slightest suspicion of disobedience can result in severe punishment. The regime employs a vast network of informants who report any signs of dissent or unauthorized weapon possession. This climate of fear ensures that the populace remains compliant and incapable of organizing any form of armed resistance.

Victims of the regime's purges are often executed in public or sent to labor camps where they face death through overwork, starvation, and disease. Public executions serve as a grim reminder of the consequences of defying the state's authority. These executions are designed to instill terror and discourage any thoughts of rebellion among the population. Forced labor camps, known as *kwanliso*, housed hundreds of thousands of political prisoners who endure inhumane conditions, forced labor, and constant abuse.

Reports from defectors and human rights organizations reveal a relentless pattern of oppression that continues in present-day North Korea. The continued existence of such an oppressive state in the modern world underscores the dangers of totalitarianism and the critical role that gun control can play in enabling a regime to maintain power through fear and violence.

North Korea's experience demonstrates the extreme lengths to which a regime will go to disarm its population and the devastating consequences that follow. The international community continues to grapple with the challenge of addressing the human rights abuses in North Korea, but the regime's tight control over information and weaponry makes meaningful intervention difficult.

## Maoist China (1949–1976)

Mao Zedong's regime in China is responsible for the deaths of up to 75 million people through policies such as the Great Leap Forward and the Cultural Revolution. The Chinese Communist Party (CCP) implemented strict gun control measures to disarm the populace, ensuring that resistance to the regime's radical and often disastrous policies was minimal.

Following the communists' victory in 1949, the People's Republic of China launched nationwide campaigns to confiscate firearms, often using propaganda to convince people to voluntarily surrender their weapons. These efforts were supported by the 1951 Regulations on Firearms, which mandated the registration and surrender of all privately owned firearms. Possession of unregistered firearms was met with severe penalties, including imprisonment and execution.

Propaganda was a critical tool in the Chinese Communist Party's strategy to enforce gun control. The regime portrayed disarmament as a necessary step to protect the nation from internal threats and counterrevolutionary elements. Posters, films, and public speeches emphasized the dangers of firearms in private hands and glorified the state's role in maintaining order. The message was clear: Only the government could be trusted with the means of violence, and any dissent or resistance would be ruthlessly crushed.

Once the population was disarmed, Mao Zedong's regime was able to implement its radical policies without much opposition. The Great Leap Forward (1958–1962) aimed to rapidly transform China from an agrarian society into a socialist industrial powerhouse. This policy led to the forced collectivization of agriculture, where millions of farmers were coerced into communal farming projects. The government seized control of land and livestock, disrupting traditional farming practices and leading to a catastrophic decline in food production.

The consequences were devastating. The Great Leap Forward resulted in one of the deadliest famines in human history, with 30 to 45 million people starving to death. The rural population was unable to resist the state's requisitioning of grain and other resources, which were often diverted to urban areas or exported to showcase China's supposed progress. Villagers who attempted to hide food or resist the policies were met with brutal punishment, including public executions, imprisonment, and torture.

The horrors did not end there. In 1966, Mao launched the Cultural Revolution, a decade-long campaign to preserve Communist ideology by purging remnants of capitalist and traditional elements from Chinese society. The Red Guards, radical youth groups loyal to Mao, were given free rein to attack anyone perceived as an enemy of the revolution. Intellectuals, artists, religious figures, and even members of the Communist Party itself were targeted.

During the Cultural Revolution, millions were subjected to public humiliation, arbitrary imprisonment, torture, and execution. Entire families were torn apart as children were encouraged to denounce their parents, and communities were engulfed in a frenzy of violence and suspicion. The sheer scale of the violence and persecution was staggering. Estimates suggest that 1.5 to 3 million people were executed during the Cultural Revolution, with countless others dying from the harsh conditions in labor camps or from the psychological trauma inflicted by the relentless political campaigns. The populace had no means to defend themselves against the atrocities committed by the Red Guards and the military, who acted with impunity. Mao's policies not only decimated the population but also left deep scars on Chinese society.

Mao Zedong's quote, "Political power grows out of the barrel of a gun," encapsulates the essence of how regimes can assert and maintain control through force and the monopolization of violence. By controlling the means of armed force, Mao ensured that the Communist Party could dominate the political landscape, suppress dissent, and implement radical societal changes without substantial opposition. This quote underscores the belief that ultimate authority and governance are inextricably linked to the ability to wield and control military power.

In the context of gun control and population disarmament, Mao's assertion highlights the dangers of a population forbidden to own firearms. Mao's approach to power illustrates how disarming the population was integral to establishing an unchallenged regime that could enforce policies like the Great Leap Forward and the Cultural Revolution, which resulted in millions of deaths through famine, purges, and repressive measures.

Although Mao has been out of power for decades, Communist China still enforces some of the world's strictest gun control laws, leaving its citizens virtually defenseless against government tyranny. For decades, private gun ownership in China has been completely prohibited, with only government forces and a few select individuals allowed access to firearms. This absolute control over weaponry ensures that the state maintains total power over its citizens, ensuring that the population remains obedient to the communist state. Nowhere is this more evident than in the horrific persecution of the Uyghur Muslim minority in Xinjiang, where the Chinese Communist Party (CCP) has orchestrated a campaign of mass internment, forced labor, and genocide. Over a million Uyghurs have been rounded up and placed in "reeducation camps," subjected to brainwashing, forced sterilizations, torture, and relentless government surveillance. With no means to resist, they have become victims of one of the greatest human rights atrocities of the modern era.

The Uyghurs are not only helpless against an authoritarian state that deems them second-class citizens, but they are also exploited for economic gain through forced organ harvesting. Reports from defectors, investigative journalists, and human rights organizations indicate that Uyghur prisoners, along with Falun Gong practitioners and other persecuted groups, are killed for their organs, which are then sold in China's multibillion-dollar transplant industry. Corneas, kidneys, livers, and hearts are forcibly removed from prisoners of conscience, and their bodies are discarded as if they were mere commodities. This level of state-sanctioned brutality is possible because there is no fear of an armed uprising, no Second Amendment equivalent, and no way for the people to fight back.

Unlike present-day China, where strict gun control ensures absolute state dominance, America's protection of the right to keep and bear arms serves as a vital safeguard against political tyranny, reinforcing the principle that true power belongs to the people, not the government alone.

## Communist Cuba (1959–Present)

The tyranny of communist Cuba, which began with Fidel Castro's rise to power in 1959, has led to decades of misery, poverty, and persecution for its citizens. The Cuban Revolution, initially celebrated as a liberation from the Batista dictatorship, quickly turned into a repressive regime that sought to control every aspect of Cuban life, including the disarmament of its people to prevent any form of resistance.

When Fidel Castro and his revolutionary forces overthrew Batista, there was widespread hope for a more just and equitable society. However, Castro's vision for Cuba soon revealed itself to be one of strict communist control. One of his first actions was to implement sweeping gun control laws. The government decreed that only state security forces could possess firearms. This was a strategic move to ensure that no armed resistance could threaten the new regime's hold on power.

The disarmament of the Cuban populace was followed by a wave of brutal repression. Anyone suspected of opposing the new government was subject to arrest, imprisonment, or execution. The infamous trials and executions overseen by Che Guevara were part of this broader campaign to eliminate dissent. Thousands were put to death, and many more were imprisoned in harsh conditions. This climate of fear stifled any potential opposition and solidified the communist regime's control over the island.

As the years passed, the Cuban government maintained its grip on power through constant surveillance, censorship, and persecution of political dissidents. The Cuban people were subjected to severe economic hardships, with widespread poverty and lack of basic necessities becoming the norm. Any attempt to improve one's situation outside the confines of the government's plans was met with harsh penalties. The regime's policies led to economic stagnation, and the island's infrastructure deteriorated.

Fidel Castro, while presenting himself as a champion of the people, amassed significant personal wealth. At the time of his death in 2016, it was estimated that Castro had nearly a billion dollars in his bank account. This wealth was then passed on to his brother Raúl Castro, who continued the same oppressive policies. The irony of a socialist dictator amassing such wealth while his people suffered from extreme poverty highlights the hypocrisy and corruption endemic to the regime.

The revolution that promised equality and prosperity instead delivered decades of suffering and death. The Cuban government's strict control over firearms ensured that the population could not challenge the oppression. The initial promise of liberation turned into a nightmare of surveillance, control, and fear. The gun control laws implemented by the Castro regime were not just about reducing crime but about ensuring that the population could not revolt against the tyranny imposed upon them.

## Che Guevera's Reign of Terror (1959–1967)

Che Guevara is often hailed as a socialist icon and a champion of the people by leftists and academic intellectuals, but the truth of his legacy tells a far darker story. Born Ernesto Guevara in Argentina, he rose to prominence through his role in the Cuban Revolution, which ultimately brought Fidel Castro to power. Guevara's early life was marked by his studies in medicine and his extensive travels across Latin America, where he witnessed widespread poverty. These experiences radicalized him, and he embraced Marxist ideology, becoming determined to ignite revolutionary change across the continent.

Guevara's rise to power began when he joined Fidel Castro's 26th of July Movement, which aimed to overthrow the Cuban dictator Fulgencio Batista. Guevara quickly became one of Castro's most trusted lieutenants, known for his ruthlessness and tactical acumen. After years of guerrilla warfare, Castro's forces succeeded in toppling Batista in 1959, and Guevara was appointed to several key positions in the new Cuban government, including overseeing sham trials and executions of hundreds of Batista's supporters. It was during this time that his darker side became more apparent.

His philosophy was that the ends justified the means, and he believed that revolutionary violence was necessary to achieve the goals of socialism. This led to widespread fear and repression. Guevara's time as a revolutionary leader was characterized by his belief in the necessity of purging society of counterrevolutionaries, which often meant anyone who opposed the new regime.

One of Guevara's most insidious actions was his role in disarming the Cuban population. He argued that firearms should only be in the hands of the revolutionary government and its forces. This move to disarm civilians was a strategic effort to prevent any uprising against the new socialist dictatorship he helped establish. With the population made vulnerable, the government could impose its will without fear of armed rebellion.

Guevara's influence extended beyond Cuba as he sought to export the revolution to other parts of Latin America and Africa. Guevara's attempts to incite uprisings in Bolivia and the Congo failed, leading to further bloodshed. Lacking local support in Bolivia, he was captured and executed in 1967, but he has been immortalized and romanticized as a socialist martyr.

The legacy of Che Guevara is a testament to the dangers of charismatic leaders who advocate civilian disarmament, violent revolution, and authoritarian control. His image as a revolutionary hero is contrasted by the reality of the misery, death, and despair that followed in his wake. The adulation he receives from certain quarters overlooks the oppressive regime he helped create and the countless lives that were destroyed by his policies. Guevara's actions serve as a cautionary tale about the perils of disarming the population and concentrating power in the hands of a few.

## Guatemala (1960–1996)

During the Guatemalan Civil War, the government targeted Indigenous Mayan communities, resulting in the deaths of approximately 200,000 people. The government's gun control measures made it much easier to carry out the genocidal campaign.

The Guatemalan government justified disarmament through anti-communist rhetoric, claiming that Indigenous populations were potential communist sympathizers or insurgents, thus rationalizing their systematic disarmament. This strategy effectively stripped these communities of any means of self-defense, leaving them vulnerable to the military's brutal campaigns.

The gun control measures were part of a broader strategy to exert total control over the population. Laws were enacted that required the registration of firearms, followed by the confiscation of those weapons from individuals deemed a threat to national security. This often meant that any Indigenous person in possession of a firearm could be labeled as an insurgent or sympathizer, leading to immediate and severe consequences.

Once the gun control measures were successfully executed, the Indigenous populations faced relentless and brutal military operations. Government forces, often supported by paramilitary groups, carried out extreme acts of violence in Mayan villages, including mass shootings, arson, and the destruction of entire communities. The intent was clear: to eliminate any resistance and instill fear within the surviving population.

Victims of these brutal campaigns were frequently buried in mass graves, their identities erased and their deaths unacknowledged by the regime. Families of the victims were left without any knowledge of their loved ones' final resting places, adding a layer of psychological torment to the physical violence.

The scale and intensity of the violence against the Mayan communities was unfathomable. Entire villages were wiped out, leaving behind a trail of destruction and trauma. Survivors of the massacres often faced ongoing persecution and intimidation, ensuring that any remaining resistance was thoroughly crushed. This genocidal campaign against the Mayan people of Guatemala illustrates the lethal combination of disarmament and state-sponsored violence.

## Cambodia (1975–1979)

The Khmer Rouge, led by Pol Pot, orchestrated one of the most brutal genocides of the 20th century, resulting in the deaths of approximately two million Cambodians. The regime disarmed the population under the pretense of creating a utopian agrarian society. Without means of self-defense, the Cambodian people were subjected to mass executions, forced labor, and starvation.

It all began shortly after the Khmer Rouge seized power in April 1975. The regime, under the guise of promoting national unity and security, coerced civilians into surrendering their firearms, with the government claiming that this was essential for the reconstruction of Cambodia into a classless agrarian society. This gun confiscation scheme left the population vulnerable to the whims of the Khmer Rouge, who quickly demonstrated their capacity for extreme violence.

The Khmer Rouge used propaganda to promote disarmament, portraying it as a necessary step towards building a peaceful and equitable society. However, the reality was drastically different. Once the population was disarmed, the regime embarked on a series of radical and deadly policies aimed at transforming Cambodia. Intellectuals, professionals, and anyone associated with the former government were targeted for execution. The populace had no means to resist or defend themselves against the regime's brutal tactics.

Victims of the Khmer Rouge were often taken to the infamous Killing Fields, a series of sites across the country where mass executions were carried out. The regime's soldiers used rudimentary tools, such as hoes, axes, and bamboo sticks, to kill their victims in order to save ammunition. These executions were brutal and inhumane, with many victims being bludgeoned to death and buried in shallow mass graves.

In addition to the Killing Fields, the Khmer Rouge established numerous prison camps, the most notorious being Tuol Sleng, also known as S-21, where thousands of Cambodians were subjected to horrific acts of violence. Prisoners were often accused of being enemies of the state and were tortured until they confessed to crimes they did not commit. Afterward, they were executed and buried in mass graves. The methods of torture and execution were grotesque and dehumanizing, designed to instill fear and compliance among the population.

The regime's policies extended beyond mass executions and torture. The Khmer Rouge forced millions of Cambodians into rural labor camps, where they were subjected to grueling work conditions, inadequate food, and rampant disease. The Khmer Rouge's goal was to transform Cambodia into a self-sufficient agrarian society, but the result was widespread suffering and death. Starvation and malnutrition were rampant, as the regime confiscated food supplies and controlled distribution.

The impact of the genocide was devastating. Families were torn apart, communities were destroyed, and the social fabric of Cambodia was irrevocably damaged. The disarmament of the population played a crucial role in enabling the Khmer Rouge to carry out their genocidal policies with little to no resistance. The people of Cambodia were sitting ducks, unable to protect themselves or their loved ones from the atrocities being committed.

The Khmer Rouge's genocide was carried out at an alarming rate, with the regime killing a quarter of Cambodia's entire population in just four years. This rate of killing was faster than that of the Nazis during the Holocaust, underscoring the sheer brutality and efficiency of the Khmer Rouge's methods. The Cambodian genocide is yet another example of the catastrophic consequences of disarmament and the vital need to preserve the right to self-defense in the face of potential oppression.

On a more personal note, someone I know shared a story about a trip he took to Cambodia about 20 years ago, eager to immerse himself in the country's rich history and vibrant culture. Among his many activities, he joined a guided tour through a forested area that was once the site of one of the infamous killing fields and mass graves from the Khmer Rouge era. As they hiked along the trail, he noticed an unsettling sight: scattered white rocks, along with fragments of clothing and shoes protruding from the ground. Intrigued, someone reached down to pick up one of the rocks, but the tour guide quickly intervened, urging them to leave it untouched. These were not rocks; they were bones—the remains of victims buried in mass graves during Pol Pot's brutal regime in the 1970s.

As he delved deeper into the history of what transpired in Cambodia, he became profoundly horrified. The tour took them to a monument filled with thousands of human skulls, shocking reminders of the genocide. These skulls were meticulously arranged as a somber tribute to the countless individuals who were murdered by their own government. Witnessing the physical remnants of such an atrocity, the bones and skulls of victims, brought a chilling reality to the horrors of genocide and the consequences of a disarmed populace unable to defend themselves against tyranny. The bones scattered throughout the trails were once part of someone's loved ones—brutally murdered and buried in mass graves, destined to be forgotten. Walking through these fields, which serve as the final resting place for tens of thousands of innocent people, carries a weight that is almost unbearable and defies comprehension. It is a memory that he says he will carry with him forever, a poignant reminder of the need to remember and learn from history's darkest chapters.

## Uganda (1971–1979)

Under the dictatorship of Idi Amin, Uganda experienced a period of extreme repression and mass murder. Amin's regime targeted ethnic groups and political opponents, resulting in the deaths of an estimated 300,000 people. By implementing stringent gun control laws and systematic disarmament policies, Amin's government effectively neutralized any potential resistance, paving the way for widespread atrocities.

In the early years of his regime, Idi Amin enacted several laws aimed at disarming the civilian population under the guise of maintaining national security and public order. The Public Security Act of 1970 was one such law, which mandated the registration of all firearms and required civilians to surrender unauthorized weapons to the authorities. This legislation was coupled with aggressive propaganda campaigns that painted gun ownership among civilians as a threat to national stability.

Government forces conducted widespread raids on homes and communities, forcibly confiscating firearms and arresting those found in possession of weapons. These operations were often accompanied by severe violence and intimidation, with security forces targeting specific ethnic groups and political dissidents. By disarming these groups, Amin ensured that they had no means to defend themselves against the subsequent waves of violence and repression.

With the population stripped of their guns, Amin's regime carried out its campaign of terror without fear of armed resistance. Mass killings were conducted with impunity, often under the cover of darkness or in remote areas to avoid international scrutiny. Victims were rounded up, taken to isolated locations, and executed en masse. Many were buried in unmarked mass graves, their bodies never recovered, and their families left without closure. Torture was rampant, with political prisoners subjected to unimaginable cruelty in secret detention centers scattered across the country.

One of the most infamous sites of Amin's brutality was the Nakasero State Research Bureau, a notorious torture chamber where countless Ugandans were detained, tortured, and killed. The regime's security forces operated with total impunity, and the lack of firearms among the civilian population meant that there was little to no organized resistance against these state-sponsored atrocities.

Idi Amin was overthrown in 1979 after a coalition of Ugandan exiles and Tanzanian forces invaded Uganda, capturing the capital city of Kampala. Faced with imminent defeat, Amin fled the country and sought refuge in Libya before eventually settling in Saudi Arabia. Despite his brutal regime, which resulted in the deaths of 300,000 people, Amin lived out the remainder of his life in exile, never facing justice or being held accountable for the horrific atrocities committed under his rule. He died in Jeddah, Saudi Arabia, in 2003, leaving behind a legacy of terror and suffering.

## Bosnia (1992–1995)

During the Bosnian War, which lasted from 1992 to 1995, the Serb-dominated Yugoslav People's Army (JNA) and Serb paramilitary forces targeted Bosniak (Bosnian Muslim) and Croat populations in a brutal campaign of ethnic cleansing. The disarmament of these groups played a large role in leaving them vulnerable to mass killings and other atrocities. The most infamous of these was the Srebrenica massacre, where over 8,000 Bosniak men and boys were executed by Serb forces in July 1995.

The chaos and violence of the Bosnian War provided the Serb forces with the opportunity to disarm Bosniak and Croat communities systematically. Often, this was done under the guise of maintaining order or enforcing ceasefires. Well-armed and organized Serb forces would enter villages and towns, demanding that civilians hand over their weapons. Those who complied were left unprotected, while those who resisted were often summarily executed, paving the way for acts of ethnic cleansing. The Serb forces conducted widespread massacres, destroyed homes and cultural sites, and forcibly expelled non-Serb populations from their homes. Entire villages were wiped out, and survivors were often raped and tortured.

The Srebrenica massacre is one of the most harrowing examples of the consequences of disarmament during the Bosnian War. In July 1995, Bosniak men and boys were separated from their families, detained, and systematically executed by Serb forces under the command of General Ratko Mladić. The victims' bodies were buried in mass graves, and many of these graves were later exhumed and moved to cover up the atrocities. The International Criminal Tribunal for the former Yugoslavia (ICTY) later ruled that the Srebrenica massacre was an act of genocide.

Throughout the Bosnian War, the lack of arms among Bosniak and Croat civilians rendered them unable to defend themselves against Serb aggression. The disarmament policies and subsequent atrocities highlight the importance of the right to self-defense and the dangers posed by an imbalance of power during conflicts. The war resulted in the deaths of about 100,000 people, the majority of whom were civilians. Many more were displaced, with entire communities uprooted and destroyed. The Bosnian War left deep scars on the region. The ethnic tensions and memories of atrocities continue to impact the lives of survivors and shape the political landscape of the Balkans.

At the same time the Bosnian catastrophe was unfolding, another tragedy was taking shape in Central Africa. In 1994, Rwanda became the site of one of the most horrifying and rapid genocides in modern history.

## Rwanda (1994)

The Rwandan Genocide is one of the most horrific examples of mass murder in recent history, with approximately 800,000 Tutsis and moderate Hutus killed in just 100 days. The Hutu-led government implemented strict gun control laws aimed at the Tutsi population, leaving them unable to stop the genocide orchestrated by Hutu extremists.

The disarmament of the Tutsi population was a deliberate and calculated move by the Hutu-led government. In the years leading up to the genocide, the Rwandan government enacted laws that restricted the ownership and use of firearms. These measures were justified under the guise of maintaining public order and preventing violence, but in reality, they were aimed at weakening the Tutsi population and making them vulnerable to attack.

One of the key laws implemented was the 1979 decree that required all firearms to be registered with the government. This law allowed the government to identify and target Tutsi individuals who owned guns. Additionally, the government conducted house-to-house searches to confiscate any unregistered firearms. By the time the genocide began, the Tutsi population was disarmed, while Hutu extremists had access to weapons supplied by the government and the military.

The propaganda campaign waged by the Hutu government was a crucial element in the lead-up to the genocide. Through radio broadcasts, newspapers, and public speeches, the government incited hatred and fear against the Tutsi population. Tutsis were dehumanized and labeled as "cockroaches," and the government portrayed them as a threat to national security. This propaganda not only justified the disarmament but also prepared the Hutu population to participate in the violence.

Once the genocide began, the lack of firearms among the Tutsi population meant that they were unable to defend themselves against the well-armed Hutu militias. The Interahamwe, the paramilitary wing of the ruling party, led many of the attacks, using machetes, clubs, and firearms to carry out mass killings. The brutality of the genocide was shocking; entire families were slaughtered, women and girls were subjected to sexual violence, and victims were left to die in the streets or in their homes. The aftermath of the genocide saw the establishment of mass graves, with thousands of bodies buried in unmarked locations.

The disarmament of the Tutsi population and the subsequent genocide highlight the dangers of gun control measures that strip vulnerable populations of their means of self-defense. The Rwandan Genocide was not only a result of ethnic hatred and political manipulation but also a consequence of deliberate disarmament policies. The international community's response was largely one of inaction, and the Tutsi population paid the ultimate price.

## Venezuela (1999–Present)

Venezuela was once one of the richest, most prosperous countries in South America, with vast energy resources, oil reserves, and a bustling economy. However, Venezuela's decline began under Hugo Chávez, who took power in 1999. Chávez implemented sweeping socialist policies that included nationalizing key industries and redistributing wealth. A critical component of his strategy to assume total control was the implementation of stringent gun control laws.

The disarmament of the Venezuelan populace was justified under the guise of reducing crime and ensuring public safety. However, the real motive was to eliminate any potential threats to the government's authority.

In 2012, the Chávez government passed the Control of Arms, Munitions, and Disarmament Law, which banned the commercial sale of firearms and ammunition. Law-abiding citizens were left vulnerable to the whims of the increasingly authoritarian government and criminal elements that operated with impunity. The law also included provisions for the confiscation of privately owned firearms, further weakening the people's ability to defend themselves. By restricting access to firearms, Chávez ensured that the civilian population could not mount any meaningful resistance to his regime.

As the Chávez government tightened its grip on power, the country's economic situation deteriorated. Mismanagement, corruption, and the collapse of oil prices led to a severe economic crisis. The once-prosperous nation, rich in natural resources, descended into poverty. Food and medicine shortages became widespread, and basic services deteriorated. The disarmed population found themselves unable to protect their families or their property from rampant crime and government abuses.

Upon Chávez's death in 2013, Nicolás Maduro assumed power and continued the oppressive policies of his predecessor. Under Maduro, the situation in Venezuela worsened. The government intensified its use of force against political opponents and protestors. In 2014, widespread anti-government protests were met with violent crackdowns. Security forces and pro-government militias, known as *colectivos*, used firearms and other weapons to suppress dissent, while ordinary citizens remained unarmed under the stringent gun control laws. As such, the Maduro regime further entrenched its power by manipulating elections, imprisoning political opponents, and suppressing independent media.

The humanitarian crisis in Venezuela has reached catastrophic levels. Hyperinflation has rendered the national currency nearly worthless, leading to widespread poverty and hunger. The healthcare system has collapsed, resulting in a resurgence of diseases such as malaria and tuberculosis. Millions of Venezuelans have fled the country in search of better living conditions, creating a refugee crisis in neighboring countries. Despite orchestrating Venezuela's socialist transformation, Hugo Chávez amassed immense personal wealth, reportedly having a net worth of nearly a billion dollars at his death, while his people suffered starvation and deprivation under his socialist policies.

The lessons from Venezuela are clear: Disarming a population and taking power away from the people can lead to unimaginable suffering and loss of freedom. The government's oppressive tactics continue into the present-day unabated, and the population remains largely powerless to resist.

## The Russian Invasion of Ukraine (2022–Present)

The Russian invasion of Ukraine in 2022 highlighted the critical role that armed civilians can play in defending their country against an aggressor. As Russian forces advanced, the Ukrainian government took the extraordinary step of distributing arms to its citizens, empowering them to join the fight and defend their homes.

The Ukrainian case underscores a fundamental principle behind the Second Amendment: the right to bear arms as a means of self-defense and protection against tyranny or invasion. In Ukraine, ordinary citizens, equipped with firearms, have been able to support military efforts, defend their communities, and contribute to the overall resilience of the nation. This grassroots defense effort has proved the effectiveness of an armed populace in deterring and resisting a powerful military force. Although Ukraine does not have a Second Amendment enshrined in its constitution, the swift mobilization of armed civilians has been instrumental in slowing down the Russian advance and maintaining resistance in key areas.

The situation in Ukraine has sparked debate in the United States, particularly among advocates of the Second Amendment. Many Americans view the Ukrainian government's decision to arm its civilians as a stark reminder of the importance of the right to bear arms, evidence that the Second Amendment serves not only as a safeguard against domestic tyranny but also to protect the nation from foreign invasion.

At the same time, they also notice the hypocrisy among American politicians who advocate for strict gun control domestically while supporting the arming of Ukrainian civilians. They question why these politicians believe that firearms are essential for Ukrainians to defend their freedom but argue against the same rights for Americans. This perceived double standard raises important questions about the consistency of gun control arguments and the fundamental principles of self-defense and liberty.

## The Invasion of Guyana by Venezuela (2023–Present)

Recently, the territorial dispute between Venezuela and Guyana over the Essequibo region has escalated into a full-blown crisis. Venezuela, under President Nicolás Maduro, has intensified its claims on the oil-rich Essequibo region, culminating in a referendum that purportedly supports its annexation. Despite the low voter turnout and international condemnation, Maduro has pressed forward, leveraging nationalist sentiments and economic desperation to justify the aggression.

The invasion and subsequent military actions have left Guyana in a vulnerable position. Guyana's strict gun laws, which heavily restrict civilian access to firearms, have essentially stripped their ability to defend their homes and communities from the Venezuelan military's incursions. This situation contrasts with the principles underpinning the Second Amendment in the United States, which posits that an armed populace serves as a deterrent to both internal tyranny and external threats.

Since the invasion, reports of atrocities committed by Venezuelan troops have emerged. These include forced displacements, destruction of property, and violence against civilians, particularly in the Amerindian communities of the Essequibo region. The Venezuelan military has been accused of exploiting the region's natural resources, including oil and minerals, often with little regard for the environmental and human impact. This exploitation has led to severe pollution and disruption of local ecosystems, further exacerbating the humanitarian crisis.

The current situation in Guyana highlights yet another example of the dangers of disarmament policies to the civilian population in the face of external aggression.

## Hamas Terrorist Attacks and the Israel–Hamas War (October 7, 2023–Present)

The ongoing conflict between Israel and Hamas has underscored the critical role that armed civilians can play in national defense. This strategy is deeply rooted in the country's history and reflects the importance placed on civilian preparedness in the face of terrorism and invasion.

During times of escalated conflict, such as the recent attacks by Hamas on October 7, 2023, the Israeli government has facilitated the arming of its civilian population. This includes not only easing restrictions on firearm ownership but also providing weapons to citizens, particularly those living in border areas and regions prone to terrorist activity. The rationale is clear: In a country where threats can emerge suddenly and violently, having an armed populace enhances national security and enables quick, localized responses to attacks.

One notable example is the community security model in Israeli settlements and border towns, where residents are often trained and equipped to defend themselves against terrorist incursions. Civilians are seen not just as potential victims but as active participants in the nation's defense.

The importance of an armed civilian population in Israel also draws attention to the broader principles of self-defense and deterrence. Just as the Second Amendment in the United States aims to ensure that citizens can protect themselves and their communities, Israel's policies highlight the practical benefits of civilian armament in a volatile security environment.

This approach, however, has sparked debate and controversy. Some critics argue that increasing the number of firearms in civilian hands can lead to unintended consequences, such as accidental shootings or the escalation of violence. Nevertheless, the Israeli government's stance reflects a calculated decision to balance these risks against the immediate need for self-defense in a nation perpetually on high alert. The effectiveness of this policy in saving lives and preventing larger-scale attacks provides a compelling case for the strategic arming of civilians in similar contexts globally.

\*\*\*

The lessons of disarmed populations and government overreach are not just distant historical warnings; they have played out here at home as well. While the horrors of past tyrannies are often dismissed as foreign problems, the same patterns of control, oppression, and vulnerability have shaped American history. From the disarmament of enslaved people to racist gun laws that empowered groups like the Ku Klux Klan, to the helplessness of unarmed citizens during the 9/11 terrorist attacks, the consequences of restricting firearm access have been profound. More recently, the COVID-19 lockdowns revealed just how quickly governments could strip away basic freedoms, including the right to purchase firearms for self-defense. The dangers of gun control are not just theoretical. They are a real and present threat, proving that an armed populace remains essential in safeguarding individual liberties against both historical injustices and modern-day government overreach.

## Slavery and the Role of the Second Amendment

Slavery is an institution that has been practiced since the dawn of humanity. Despite what some people may believe, slavery is not unique to the history of the United States. Every single civilization throughout every country in the history of the world has practiced slavery in some form or another. However, had the Second Amendment been universally applied during the era of slavery in America, the course of history could have been markedly different. The right to keep and bear arms, as enshrined in the Second Amendment, serves as a fundamental check against tyranny and oppression. If enslaved individuals had possessed the means to defend themselves with firearms, the institution of slavery would likely have faced insurmountable resistance. Armed slaves could have organized effective rebellions and deterred slaveholders through the threat of force, potentially leading to a quicker end to the inhumane practice.

The Founding Fathers, despite their personal involvement in slavery, were complex figures shaped by the context of their times. Many of them, including Thomas Jefferson and George Washington, expressed discomfort with the institution of slavery and hoped for its eventual abolition. They believed that the principles of liberty and equality enshrined in the Constitution and the Bill of Rights would ultimately lead to the end of slavery. The Constitution, although flawed in its initial accommodation of slavery, was designed to be a document that could be changed through the amendment process, capable of evolving toward greater justice and equality. The Founders' foresight in crafting a system that allowed for amendments and change set the stage for the eventual abolition of slavery.

The Southern states' resistance to the immediate abolition of slavery during the Constitutional Convention reflected the deep economic and social entrenchment of the practice. The Founders were pragmatic in their approach, understanding that insisting on the abolition of slavery at that moment would have fractured the fragile union and possibly prevented the creation of the United

States. Instead, they laid the groundwork for a future where the values of liberty and equality could triumph over slavery. The inclusion of the Second Amendment as a safeguard against tyranny was part of this broader vision of a free and just society.

During the antebellum period, some slaves did manage to acquire firearms, and these weapons played a big role in various acts of resistance and rebellion. Armed resistance, though limited, showed the potential power that an armed populace could wield against oppressive forces. The fear of slave insurrections was a constant concern for slaveholders, indicating that the presence of firearms among slaves was a big factor in maintaining a tenuous balance of power. This underscores the importance of the right to bear arms as a means of self-defense and resistance against tyranny.

The ultimate resolution of the question of slavery came through the Civil War (1861–1865), a bloody and protracted conflict that resulted in the deaths of hundreds of thousands of Americans. During the war, the arming of former slaves and free African Americans played a critical role in the Union's victory. The enlistment of Black soldiers, many of whom fought valiantly for their freedom and the preservation of the Union, exemplified the transformative power of armed resistance against oppression. The Second Amendment's principles were put into practice as these individuals took up arms to secure their rights and liberties.

In the aftermath of the Civil War, the Reconstruction Amendments, particularly the Thirteenth, Fourteenth, and Fifteenth Amendments, sought to enshrine the rights of the newly freed slaves and ensure their full integration into American society. The Second Amendment continued to serve as a vital protection for these rights, allowing African Americans to defend themselves against the rampant racial violence and oppression that persisted in the South. Despite the challenges of the Reconstruction era, the availability of firearms provided a measure of security and empowerment for formerly enslaved individuals as they navigated their newfound freedom. The Founding Fathers' vision, though imperfectly realized in their own time, laid the foundation for a nation where the principles of equality and individual rights could ultimately prevail, ending slavery in America.

While the battles for freedom and self-defense have taken many forms throughout American history, the threats to liberty did not end with the past.

In the modern era, they have evolved—from internal oppression to global terrorism—forcing the nation to reevaluate the meaning of security in a post-9/11 world.

## The Second Amendment and the Lessons of 9/11

The tragic events of September 11, 2001, revealed vulnerabilities in America's security infrastructure that extended beyond the immediate threat of terrorism. The terrorists who hijacked four commercial airplanes that day did so without sophisticated weaponry, using simple box cutters to overpower flight crews and passengers. This reality underscores a critical discussion within the context of the Second Amendment: the role of armed defense in preventing such catastrophic events.

On that day, the strict regulations on weapons in the airline industry, designed to ensure safety, paradoxically contributed to the ease with which the terrorists executed their plan. Federal laws and airline policies prohibited passengers from carrying firearms, even those licensed to do so. Consequently, the terrorists faced little resistance as they took control of the planes. The absence of armed individuals capable of responding to the hijackers allowed the terrorists to turn commercial aircraft into deadly weapons, leading to nearly 3,000 deaths and changing the course of American history.

In the aftermath of 9/11, several changes were made to airline security protocols, including the introduction of reinforced cockpit doors and stricter screening processes. However, one critical aspect that remains contentious is the potential role of armed security on flights. The Second Amendment, which enshrines the right to keep and bear arms, offers a perspective on this issue that advocates for a reconsideration of armed defense measures in preventing similar tragedies.

Some say that had there been licensed civilians carrying firearms on those flights, or at least an armed security guard, the outcome might have been different. Armed passengers or security personnel could have provided a critical line of defense, potentially neutralizing the hijackers before they could take control of the aircraft. This argument aligns with the broader principle of the Second

Amendment, which is to empower individuals to defend themselves and others against threats.

Air marshals, trained federal law enforcement officers who carry firearms, have been deployed on flights to enhance security. However, the number of air marshals is limited, and they cannot be present on every flight. Expanding this concept to include either more air marshals or allowing licensed civilians to carry firearms on planes could bolster in-flight security.

Critics of this approach argue that introducing firearms into the highly sensitive environment of a commercial airplane could lead to unintended consequences, such as accidental discharges or the potential for firearms to be seized by hijackers. These concerns are valid and must be addressed through rigorous training and strict protocols. However, the potential benefits of having armed individuals capable of responding to threats cannot be overlooked.

The presence of armed security personnel on flights could act as a powerful deterrent to would-be hijackers. Knowing that they could face immediate and armed resistance, terrorists might be less likely to attempt a hijacking. This deterrent effect is a fundamental aspect of the Second Amendment's intent: to prevent tyranny and violence through the potential for armed defense.

Moreover, the argument for armed defense extends beyond the immediate context of airline security. It underscores a broader principle of self-reliance and preparedness in the face of threats. Just as communities benefit from responsible gun ownership in deterring and responding to crime, so too could the airline industry benefit from a measured and responsible approach to arming individuals who are trained and prepared to defend against hijackings.

While strict gun control measures aim to enhance safety, they often have the opposite effect. In the case of the 9/11 hijackers, the lack of armed resistance on the planes facilitated one of the most devastating attacks in history. Reexamining the role of the Second Amendment in this context opens the door to a discussion on how responsible, armed defense can complement other security measures to prevent future tragedies. Whether through air marshals or licensed civilians, this could enhance our ability to respond to and prevent such catastrophic events. This approach requires careful implementation and rigorous training but aligns with the broader goal of empowering individuals to defend themselves and others against threats.

## The COVID-19 Lockdowns (2020–2022)

During the extended COVID-19 lockdowns, many people across the United States perceived the strict control of movement and business closures in the name of public safety as overreaching and tyrannical. This sentiment was particularly pronounced in states with stringent anti-gun laws, where the shutdown of gun stores was seen as a direct violation of Second Amendment rights. As states and cities imposed lockdown measures, the classification of gun stores as "non-essential" businesses effectively denied citizens access to firearms at a time when personal security concerns were heightened.

The lockdowns were marked by various abuses and inconsistencies that fueled public distrust. Many politicians who were proponents of restrictive measures were caught flouting the very rules they imposed on their constituents. A notable example is California governor Gavin Newsom, who was photographed dining at the exclusive French Laundry restaurant without adhering to social distancing or mask guidelines. Such instances of hypocrisy were not isolated; numerous other political figures were seen violating lockdown protocols, undermining their credibility and the public's willingness to comply with the restrictions.

The dangers of the virus were often exaggerated, with media outlets and public health officials presenting conflicting information. The selective outrage of the media further exacerbated public frustration. Events and gatherings that aligned with certain political agendas were often celebrated or justified, such as the widespread protests and riots during the summer of 2020. Conversely, gatherings of people who opposed the lockdowns or who held different views were criticized and portrayed as dangerous and irresponsible.

The lockdowns and the associated gun store closures were perceived by many as a test of the public's willingness to accept government overreach. The swift and often severe enforcement of these measures suggested an underlying attempt to gauge how much control could be exerted over the population before resistance would emerge.

Despite these provocations, the American populace exhibited considerable restraint. The irony is palpable: While those pushing for disarmament were often involved in or supported violent protests, gun owners, and Second Amendment advocates largely adhered to the law and maintained peace, underscoring their commitment to lawful conduct and responsible gun ownership. As the public observed these actions, the realization that their Second Amendment rights were under threat became more pronounced, reinforcing the need to protect and preserve these freedoms.

## Historical Echoes of Gun Control

The consequences of gun control are not just historical lessons; they are ongoing realities that continue to shape modern policies and debates. The same justifications once used to strip rights from vulnerable populations have been repackaged under the guise of "common sense" gun control. While the rhetoric may have changed, the underlying goal remains the same: to consolidate power by restricting the people's ability to defend themselves. The parallels between past tyrannies and today's gun control efforts are impossible to ignore, and understanding these connections is crucial in recognizing the dangers of disarmament before history repeats itself.

In modern times, similarities can be drawn between contemporary gun control efforts and the disarmament tactics used by tyrannical governments throughout history. Politicians and advocates pushing for stringent gun control measures often employ similar strategies to those used by historical despots: exploiting crime and tragedy to justify disarmament and pushing their agenda during times of crisis. This approach is encapsulated in the statement "Never let a good crisis go to waste," a sentiment historically and contemporarily echoed by those seeking to centralize power at the expense of individual freedoms.

One striking example of this is seen in the aftermath of mass shootings in the United States. After incidents such as the Sandy Hook Elementary School shooting in 2012 and the Parkland, Florida, shooting in 2018, politicians and media figures were quick to use the emotional impact of these tragedies to push for legislation that would significantly restrict the Second Amendment rights of law-abiding citizens. This mirrors the historical tactics used by regimes like the Soviet Union and Nazi Germany, which leveraged societal fears and tragic events to implement sweeping disarmament policies. In both historical and modern contexts, the narrative is the same. Public safety is used as a pretext to justify stripping away individual rights.

In Europe, similar patterns emerge. Countries such as the United Kingdom and Australia implemented stringent gun control measures following mass shootings. The UK's Firearms Act of 1997, passed after the Dunblane school massacre, and Australia's National Firearms Agreement, enacted after the Port Arthur massacre, are prime examples. These laws severely restricted civilian access to firearms, much like the gun control laws enacted by authoritarian regimes in the past. These measures were justified using the same rationale of public safety and crime prevention, despite overwhelming evidence that such policies have a very limited impact on actual crime rates.

Gun control proponents often argue that the atrocities committed by historical tyrannies couldn't happen in modern democratic societies. However, this viewpoint is both naïve and dangerous. The mechanisms of power and control that facilitated past genocides and tyrannies remain relevant today. The disarmament of a populace is a critical step in the centralization of power, as it removes the primary means of resistance against government overreach. By disarming citizens, governments can more easily impose authoritarian measures without fear of significant opposition.

In the United States, proposed measures such as assault weapons bans and universal background checks are frequently cited as necessary to prevent gun violence. However, these proposals often involve broad and sweeping restrictions that would disproportionately affect law-abiding citizens rather than criminals. For example, the 1994 Federal Assault Weapons Ban, which expired in 2004, was ineffective in reducing crime while placing unnecessary burdens on responsible gun owners. The ban targeted specific features of firearms that were largely cosmetic, without addressing the underlying issues of crime and violence.

Similarly, in New York, the SAFE Act (Secure Ammunition and Firearms Enforcement Act) of 2013 imposed some of the strictest gun control measures in the country, including expanded background checks and restrictions on magazine capacities. Critics argue that these measures infringe on Second Amendment rights while doing little to address the root causes of gun violence. Instead, they create legal and logistical hurdles for law-abiding citizens seeking to exercise their right to self-defense.

Proponents of gun control often fail to acknowledge that criminals, by definition, do not obey laws. Thus, restrictive gun laws primarily impact those who are inclined to follow them: law-abiding citizens. Historical examples demonstrate that disarmament leads to increased vulnerability and oppression. The insistence that such atrocities could not occur in modern democratic societies ignores the fundamental dynamics of power and control.

## Red Flag Laws and Their Parallels to Historical Tyrannies

Red flag laws, also known as extreme risk protection orders (ERPOs), have been increasingly adopted across the United States in recent years. These laws allow courts to temporarily remove firearms from individuals deemed to be a danger to themselves or others, based on petitions from family members, law enforcement, or other concerned parties. While the intent behind these laws is to prevent violence and ensure public safety, they have been criticized for bypassing due process and infringing on constitutional rights. The lack of due process is particularly concerning, as it echoes tactics used by totalitarian regimes like the Soviet Union and Nazi Germany, where secret police and arbitrary laws were employed to disarm and silence political dissidents.

In states such as Florida, Colorado, and California, red flag laws have been implemented with varying degrees of rigor. For example, Florida's red flag law, passed in the wake of the Parkland school shooting, allows law enforcement to petition for the temporary removal of firearms from individuals deemed dangerous without their presence in court during the initial hearing. Critics argue that this undermines the principle of due process, as individuals are deprived of their property and rights without a fair opportunity to defend themselves. In some cases, these laws have been used to disarm individuals who have committed no crime, solely based on the subjective judgment of others, leading to potential abuses and miscarriages of justice.

The potential for abuse is a significant concern. There have been instances where red flag laws have been used vindictively, such as in domestic disputes or personal grudges, to disarm individuals without just cause. This misuse of power can lead to innocent people being stripped of their constitutional rights and left susceptible to totalitarianism. The parallels to historical tyrannies are striking. In the Soviet Union, the NKVD (the secret police) had the authority to arrest and disarm anyone deemed a threat to the state without due process. Similarly, the Gestapo in Nazi Germany employed arbitrary laws to disarm and imprison political opponents, Jews, and other targeted groups. These actions facilitated the regimes' control and repression, making it easier to carry out their genocidal policies.

Modern-day red flag laws also draw comparisons to the gun control measures used by these historical totalitarian regimes. The creation of a gun registry, which is often proposed alongside red flag laws, is a tactic that was notoriously used by the Nazis. The 1938 German Weapons Act required the registration of all firearms, making it easier for the Nazi regime to confiscate guns from Jews and other persecuted groups. Today, politicians advocating for a national gun registry in the United States argue that it would help track and prevent illegal gun sales and use. However, critics warn that such a registry could be used to facilitate mass disarmament, just as it was in Nazi Germany, leaving citizens vulnerable to government overreach and potential tyranny.

The implementation of red flag laws and the push for a national gun registry highlight a concerning trend: the erosion of due process and individual rights in the name of public safety. While preventing violence is a noble goal, sacrificing fundamental liberties is a dangerous precedent. As we navigate the complexities of modern gun control, it is imperative to learn from the past and remain vigilant against any measures that could pave the way for future oppression.

## The Fallacy of Dismissing the Deterrent Power of Armed Citizens

Critics of the Second Amendment often argue that the notion of private gun ownership as a deterrent against government tyranny is obsolete. They claim that, given the modern military's advanced weaponry, including nuclear bombs and fighter jets, the idea that civilians with firearms could effectively resist a tyrannical government is unrealistic. However, this argument overlooks several critical factors and fails to appreciate the broader context in which an armed populace operates.

First, the sheer number of armed citizens acts as a deterrent. The United States has more than 400 million firearms in civilian hands. Some estimates put the number as high as 500 million firearms. No matter the exact number, it is substantial compared to the size of the military and law enforcement combined. This vast arsenal in the hands of private citizens makes the prospect of widespread resistance a formidable challenge for any government contemplating tyranny. Historical examples show that well-equipped military forces can struggle against determined insurgents with much less sophisticated weaponry. The American Revolution itself was fought against one of the most powerful armies of its time, yet the armed citizenry was able to prevail through guerrilla tactics and widespread resistance.

Moreover, the argument that modern military technology renders civilian firearms obsolete fails to consider the practicalities of governance and control. The military's advanced weapons are designed for large-scale warfare, not for controlling a dispersed and potentially hostile civilian population. The use of such weaponry against civilians would not only be impractical but would also likely result in significant domestic and international backlash. The logistical, ethical, and political challenges of using advanced military force against one's own population make this scenario highly unlikely. Instead, small arms and guerilla tactics have proven effective in numerous conflicts around the world, demonstrating that the power of an armed populace should not be underestimated.

Another critical point is the attitude and loyalty of the military itself. A large proportion of the US military is composed of individuals who support the Second Amendment and hold strong beliefs in individual liberties. In a hypothetical scenario where the government orders the military to disarm the populace or engage in oppressive actions, it is highly plausible that many service members would refuse to comply. Historical precedents, such as the refusal of soldiers to fire on protesters during the fall of the Soviet Union, illustrate that military personnel are not mere automatons; they have moral and ethical considerations that influence their actions. The loyalty of the military to the Constitution and their oath to defend it against all enemies, foreign and domestic, further supports the notion that they would resist unlawful orders against American citizens.

Furthermore, the argument against the need for semi-automatic weapons and other modern firearms ignores the practical aspects of self-defense and the historical context of the Second Amendment. Semi-automatic weapons provide citizens with the means to defend themselves effectively against multiple threats, be it in situations of home defense, civil unrest, or natural disasters, where law enforcement response may be delayed. The Second Amendment was not designed solely for hunting or sport shooting; it was enshrined to ensure that citizens could defend themselves against tyranny and oppression. This principle remains as relevant today as it was in the 18th century. The ability to possess effective means of self-defense is a cornerstone of individual liberty and a safeguard against potential abuses of power.

## Threats Against the Armed Civilian Population

During his presidency, Joe Biden frequently dismissed the notion that armed civilians could effectively oppose a tyrannical government, mockingly suggesting that the government's possession of F-15s and fighter jets would render civilian resistance futile. This argument is deeply flawed and ignores several crucial aspects.

When politicians like Biden imply that civilian rifles are ineffective against military might, it can be perceived as a veiled threat, suggesting that the government might use such overwhelming force against its own citizens. The implication is not only menacing but also reveals a dangerous misunderstanding of the Second Amendment's purpose. The Second Amendment is not merely about matching the government's firepower but about ensuring that citizens have the means to resist tyranny and oppression.

Firstly, the notion that armed civilians would be entirely helpless against a tyrannical government because of the latter's superior military hardware overlooks the principles of guerrilla warfare and the power of an armed populace. Historical and contemporary examples demonstrate that technologically inferior forces can effectively resist and even defeat more advanced militaries through unconventional tactics, local knowledge, and sheer numbers. The American Revolution itself is a testament to this, where colonial militias, using their rifles, managed to challenge and ultimately defeat the British Army, one of the most powerful military forces of the time.

Additionally, the claim that military equipment like F-15s and bombers could easily suppress an armed citizenry ignores the practical and ethical limitations of such an approach. Using heavy military force against one's own population is not only logistically challenging but would also result in political and social backlash, both domestically and internationally. The prospect of the US government deploying such tactics against its citizens is not only impractical but, as previously mentioned, would also likely lead to widespread condemnation and resistance from within the military itself, as many service members might refuse to turn their weapons on fellow Americans.

Moreover, the sheer number of armed civilians in the United States—estimated to be in the hundreds of millions—presents a formidable challenge to any notion of governmental overreach. Attempting to disarm such a vast and dispersed population would be a logistical nightmare. Civilians significantly outnumber the government and its armed forces, making the idea of complete control through force highly implausible. This overwhelming numerical advantage ensures that civilian ownership of firearms remains a check against tyranny.

Furthermore, the argument that civilian rifles are useless against the government is self-defeating when considering the ongoing efforts to restrict these very firearms. If AR-15s and similar rifles were truly ineffective and inconsequential, there would be little reason for such stringent regulations and bans. The persistent attempts to limit civilian access to these weapons suggest that they do, in fact, pose a potential threat to any would-be tyrannical government, thereby affirming their importance in the hands of the populace.

The rhetorical fallacy that civilian ownership of military-style rifles is futile against a government equipped with advanced military technology not only misrepresents the realities of asymmetric warfare but also dangerously underestimates the power of an armed citizenry. This argument, often framed as a veiled threat, fails to acknowledge the historical and practical evidence that an armed population can effectively resist tyranny.

## The Tyranny Paradox in Modern Times

An interesting paradox arises when considering the anti-gun left's rhetoric against Second Amendment advocates and pro-gun voters. These individuals are often slandered as dangerous and unhinged, supporting politicians who the left deem to be fascist tyrants. The left frequently equates support for pro-Second Amendment candidates with endorsing fascism or Nazism. However, if the left truly believed that a significant portion of the country supported candidates they perceive as tyrannical, why would they advocate for strict gun control laws? This bizarre stance suggests one of two possibilities.

Firstly, the anti-gun left may not genuinely believe the accusations they level against Second Amendment supporters. If they truly believed that half the country supported fascist-like leaders, it would be counterintuitive to push for disarming the populace. Under such dire circumstances, one would expect the left to advocate for maintaining or even expanding gun rights to protect themselves from potential tyranny. The idea of disarming oneself in the face of a perceived tyrannical threat is inherently contradictory. Therefore, the persistent push for gun control indicates that the left may not sincerely believe their own rhetoric, which serves more as a tool for demonizing political opponents rather than reflecting an actual fear of fascism.

By promoting the disarmament of the population, especially those who support the Second Amendment, the anti-gun left could be seeking to force political opposition to bend a knee to their will. Disarming political opponents would grant them a monopoly on force and power, allowing them to implement their agenda without opposition. This perspective suggests that the left's calls for gun control are less about public safety and more about controlling dissenting voices and potential resistance. The disingenuous nature of their anti-gun rhetoric becomes apparent, as it either masks their true intentions or reveals a desire for control over those with differing political views.

Alternatively, the left's aggressive push for gun control could be seen as projection, revealing their own tyrannical tendencies. By accusing Second Amendment supporters of harboring tyrannical tendencies, they deflect attention from their own authoritarian impulses. Their projection serves as a means of distraction, redirecting public scrutiny away from their actions and onto their opponents. This tactic creates a false narrative that demonizes pro-gun advocates while obscuring the left's own potential for oppressive behavior. By disarming the population, particularly those who value the Second Amendment, the left can more easily impose their will, free from the threat of armed resistance.

Historically, disarmament has been a precursor to tyranny. The anti-gun left's push for stricter gun control laws, despite their claims of fearing fascist leaders, raises questions about their true motivations. If they were sincere, they would logically support an armed populace capable of defending against tyranny. Instead, their actions suggest a desire to weaken their political opponents and consolidate control, casting doubt on their professed fears and highlighting a deeper, more manipulative agenda.

The anti-gun left's paradoxical stance on gun control and their demonization of Second Amendment supporters reveals a complex interplay of disingenuous rhetoric and projection. Whether they genuinely disbelieve their own accusations or seek to disarm opponents for greater control, their actions undermine their stated concerns about fascism and tyranny. This paradox exposes the need for a critical examination of their motives and the importance of preserving the right to bear arms as a safeguard against potential oppression.

## Who Wants to Disarm Us?

While societal problems, corruption, and government overreach are not exclusive to any single political ideology, the political left's advocacy for civilian disarmament places them squarely in the camp of those who have historically pursued tyrannical control. This inclination towards disarming the populace mirrors the tactics employed by various totalitarian regimes throughout history, which have sought to neutralize potential resistance by stripping citizens of their means of self-defense.

The political right in the US, despite their own set of issues and occasional lapses into corruption and overreach, generally advocates for an armed society. This fundamental belief in the right to bear arms suggests a commitment to individual liberty and a recognition of the importance of an armed populace in safeguarding against tyranny. The right's stance on gun ownership implies an understanding that a disarmed population is vulnerable to oppression and that the means to resist government overreach is a key aspect of a free society.

The political left's push for gun control, by contrast, raises many concerns about their ultimate intentions. History has shown that disarmament is a common precursor to oppressive regimes. In the 20th century alone, countless examples illustrate how authoritarian governments, from Nazi Germany to the Soviet Union to Maoist China, first took guns away from their citizens before proceeding with widespread atrocities. That the political left in America aligns with these historical precedents by advocating for stringent gun control measures suggests a potential for similar overreach.

This concern is not merely theoretical. In recent years, prominent left-leaning politicians and activists have called for sweeping gun control measures, often using mass shootings and other tragedies as a platform to advance their agenda. While their stated goal is to reduce gun violence, the underlying implication is that an unarmed populace is easier to control. This raises the specter of a government that seeks to centralize power by eliminating the primary means through which citizens can defend their rights.

Moreover, the hypocrisy of many gun control advocates further undermines their credibility. Many of these individuals, while advocating for disarmament of the general populace, live in secure, gated communities, and are protected by private armed security. This double standard suggests that their opposition to gun ownership is not based on principle but on a desire to control who has access to firearms. It is not that they do not believe in the efficacy of guns for protection; rather, they do not want ordinary citizens to possess them.

The political left's support for gun control must be viewed in the context of their broader political agenda. Their policies often involve significant government intervention in the economy, extensive regulatory frameworks, and the centralization of power. An armed populace stands as an impediment to the implementation of such policies, as it provides citizens with the means to resist government overreach. This is why the Second Amendment is a safeguard against tyranny.

In contrast, the political right's support for the Second Amendment indicates a respect for individual autonomy and a recognition of the importance of self-defense. By advocating for the right to bear arms, the right affirms their commitment to protecting citizens from potential government overreach. This fundamental difference in perspective highlights why the right is less likely to engage in the kind of authoritarian practices associated with disarmament.

Ultimately, the American left's advocacy for gun control places them in a historical continuum with other regimes that have sought to disarm their populations. This alignment raises serious concerns about their commitment to individual liberty and the principles of a free society. While the right is not without its flaws, their support for an armed populace suggests a deeper respect for the foundational principles upon which the United States was built. The left's push for disarmament, by contrast, represents a threat to these principles and underscores the importance of maintaining the Second Amendment as a bulwark against tyranny.

## The Defect of the Human Heart

Many people might wonder why anyone living in the United States, one of the freest and most prosperous countries in the world, would want to disarm the population and curtail individual freedoms, especially the fundamental right to self-defense. My theory is that this desire stems from an inherent defect in the human heart, an unchangeable aspect of human nature. It is often said that absolute power corrupts absolutely, and throughout history, there have always been individuals who cannot be content unless they have the power to dictate the lives of others.

Before the founding of the United States, the world was predominantly ruled by kings, emperors, dictators, and oligarchies. The creation of the United States by the Founding Fathers disrupted this age-old system, introducing a radical concept of true individual liberty and self-governance. The freedom enjoyed in the United States is a historical anomaly, the first experiment in extensive personal liberty. However, the desire to control others is deeply ingrained in the human species, and certain individuals, particularly within the political and cultural elite, seem unable to be satisfied unless they can impose their will on the broader population.

This intrinsic urge to control others explains why some individuals are so vehemently opposed to the Second Amendment. The Founding Fathers, recognizing this flaw in human nature, established the Constitution as a safeguard against tyranny and the concentration of power. They understood that some people would always seek to exert control over others, and they designed a system of checks and balances to prevent this. The Second Amendment acts as a powerful check against those who would seek to impose their will on the populace. It ensures that citizens retain the means to defend their liberties against encroachment.

The political and cultural elite often find it deeply troubling that ordinary citizens can live freely and prosperously, without needing to be subjugated or controlled. This sense of autonomy among the masses undermines the unique sense of specialness and privilege that the elite desire for themselves. The hatred directed toward the Second Amendment by these elites stems from its role as a barrier to their ability to dictate how others should live. In essence, the Second Amendment preserves the balance of power between the government and the governed, frustrating those who would prefer a more authoritarian system. As long as this amendment remains in place, it will continue to act as a deterrent against those who seek to undermine the freedoms that make the United States an exceptional experiment in human liberty.

One lesson we should learn from the atrocities outlined in this chapter is that we should all be wary of politicians who advocate for gun control. While it is true that some may have good intentions driven by ignorance or a genuine desire to reduce violence, there are no doubt others who seek to disarm the population to gain more control. The tyrants of the 20th century, such as Adolf Hitler, Vladimir Lenin, Joseph Stalin, and Mao Zedong, were often charismatic, well-spoken, and smooth-talking individuals who used their charm to mask their authoritarian intentions. Their regimes began with promises of safety and order, which quickly turned into brutal oppression once the population's guns were stripped from them. It is crucial to be suspicious of any politicians who, despite appearing pleasant and reasonable on the outside, advocate for policies that aim to disarm law-abiding citizens. Disarmament has historically been a precursor to greater control and oppression by the state. The right to bear arms is a fundamental safeguard against such overreach, ensuring that citizens retain the means to defend their liberties. Advocating gun control can be a slippery slope, leading to the erosion of other constitutional rights and freedoms. Therefore, it is essential to scrutinize the motives behind gun control measures and remain vigilant against any attempts to undermine the Second Amendment, which serves as a critical check on government power.

In chapter 5, we will explore the landmark Supreme Court decisions that have shaped the interpretation of the Second Amendment in modern times. These rulings have been pivotal in defining the scope and limits of gun rights in America, further solidifying the constitutional protections that safeguard our freedoms.

# Chapter 5

# Verdicts and Judgments: The Courts and the Second Amendment

*The Constitution, in part, is the fulfillment of the promise made in the Declaration of Independence. The right to bear arms is a clear and specific provision of our Constitution. It is one of the basic rights of every American.*

—Chief Justice Warren E. Burger

*The Constitution was written to be understood by the voters; its words and phrases were used in their normal and ordinary as distinguished from technical meaning. Normal meaning may of course include an idiomatic meaning, but it excludes secret or technical meanings. . . . We start therefore with a strong presumption that the Second Amendment right is exercised individually and belongs to all Americans.*

—Justice Antonin Scalia

The judicial interpretation of the Second Amendment has evolved significantly over the years, reflecting changes in societal values, legal philosophies, and historical contexts. However, not all early interpretations of the Second

Amendment have been favorable to gun rights. Several Supreme Court cases, especially those between the Civil War and World War II, saw courts and judges interpret the right to bear arms very differently than the pro-gun rulings of recent years.

The transformation in judicial interpretation highlights the dynamic nature of constitutional law, shaped by changing societal norms, evolving legal doctrines, and the personal biases of the judiciary. As we delve into these landmark Supreme Court cases, we will explore the complex interplay between legal interpretations, historical contexts, and the enduring principles enshrined in the Second Amendment. The shift towards originalist judges has played a crucial role in reaffirming the Second Amendment's original intent, ensuring that the right to keep and bear arms remains a fundamental aspect of American liberty. These landmark decisions have clarified, expanded, or sometimes restricted the Second Amendment, reflecting the evolving nature of legal and societal views on gun ownership. This chapter dives into key Supreme Court cases, the judicial reasoning behind the decisions, and the broader implications for Second Amendment jurisprudence.

In the late 19th and early 20th centuries, the Supreme Court often upheld state and local regulations on firearms, interpreting the Second Amendment as applying primarily to federal restrictions rather than state actions. One of the earliest and most notable cases was *United States v. Cruikshank* (1876), where the Court held that the Second Amendment did not apply to the actions of individuals but only to the federal government. This decision emerged from the violent aftermath of the Colfax Massacre, where the Court controversially ruled that the federal government had limited power to protect African Americans from violence by private individuals.

Similarly, in *Presser v. Illinois* (1886), the Supreme Court ruled that the Second Amendment did not prevent states from regulating private militias. The decision emphasized that the right to bear arms was not unlimited and that states could impose restrictions to maintain public order and safety. These early interpretations set a precedent that the Second Amendment was not an absolute barrier to gun control laws enacted at the state level.

The Supreme Court continued this trend in *Miller v. Texas* (1894), which held that the Second Amendment did not apply to the states and reaffirmed the notion that states could regulate firearms without infringing on federally protected rights.

However, the most pivotal case before the modern era was *United States v. Miller* (1939). In this case, the Court upheld the National Firearms Act, ruling that the Second Amendment did not guarantee an individual's right to possess a sawed-off shotgun because it did not have a reasonable relationship with the preservation or efficiency of a well-regulated militia. The decision suggested that the government could regulate firearms that were not directly related to militia service, further complicating the landscape of Second Amendment jurisprudence.

These early rulings were heavily influenced by the personal biases and prejudices of the judges, who were often shaped by the prevalent hostility towards particular groups of people in the 19th and early 20th centuries. This hostility led to interpretations that favored restrictive gun control measures. It wasn't until the latter part of the 20th century, with the appointment of originalist judges, that there was a shift towards preserving the spirit of the original meaning of the Constitution.

The modern era of Second Amendment jurisprudence, marked by decisions such as *District of Columbia v. Heller* (2008) and *McDonald v. City of Chicago* (2010), recognized an individual's right to bear arms for self-defense within the home and extended Second Amendment protections to the states through the Fourteenth Amendment. These rulings represented a shift towards acknowledging broader individual rights to gun ownership, reflecting a deeper appreciation for the historical and cultural significance of firearms in American society.

### *United States v. Cruikshank* (1876)

To understand *United States v. Cruikshank* (1876), one must first grasp the historical context of the Colfax Massacre of 1873. This tragic event unfolded in Colfax, Louisiana, during the fraught Reconstruction era. The massacre was a direct consequence of the intense racial and political tensions that defined this period. White supremacists, organized under the banner of the White League, sought to regain political control and suppress African American civil rights by force. The White League, a paramilitary group, was determined to overthrow the legally elected Republican government, which had gained much African American support.

On April 13, 1873, armed white supremacists attacked the Grant Parish courthouse, where a group of African Americans had gathered to protect Republican officials. The confrontation quickly escalated into violence. The attackers used firearms, and the ensuing battle resulted in the deaths of over 100 African Americans, many of whom were brutally executed after surrendering. This atrocity marked one of the bloodiest instances of racial violence during Reconstruction and highlighted the pervasive threat African Americans faced despite their new-found freedoms.

In response to the massacre, the federal government sought to bring the perpetrators to justice using the Enforcement Act of 1870. This legislation was part of a broader effort by Congress to enforce the Fourteenth Amendment and protect the civil rights of African Americans, particularly in the face of state inaction or complicity in racial violence. The Enforcement Act criminalized conspiracies to deprive citizens of their constitutional rights, aiming to curb the activities of white supremacist groups like the Ku Klux Klan and the White League.

Several members of the white supremacist group responsible for the Colfax Massacre were charged under this act. The federal charges represented an attempt to assert the power of the federal government in safeguarding the rights of African Americans against violent oppression. However, the legal journey that ensued would underscore the limitations of federal authority in this domain and the enduring power of states to regulate their own affairs.

When *United States v. Cruikshank* reached the Supreme Court in 1876, the justices were tasked with interpreting the scope of federal power to protect individual rights under the Constitution. The Court's ruling, delivered by Chief Justice Morrison Waite, would have profound implications.

The Supreme Court concluded that the charges brought under the Enforcement Act of 1870 could not stand because the protections of the Bill of Rights, including the Second Amendment, did not apply to the states. The Court asserted that the Second Amendment's guarantee of the right to bear arms was a restriction solely on federal power, not on state or private actions. In a pivotal statement, the Court declared, "The right to bear arms is not granted by the Constitution; neither is it in any manner dependent upon that instrument for its existence."

This interpretation underscored a narrow view of federal authority, suggesting that the primary responsibility for maintaining public order and protecting individual rights lay with the states. The decision reflected the prevailing judicial philosophy of the time, which favored states' rights and limited federal intervention in state affairs. By ruling that the Second Amendment did not apply to the states, the Supreme Court effectively allowed state governments to regulate the right to bear arms without federal oversight.

The ramifications of the Cruikshank decision were far-reaching and deeply troubling for African Americans in the post–Reconstruction South. This decision weakened the federal government's ability to protect African Americans from racial violence and discrimination.

In the aftermath of *Cruikshank*, Southern states continued to enact and enforce discriminatory laws designed to disarm African Americans and maintain white supremacy. These measures, combined with the inability of the federal government to intervene, left African Americans vulnerable to violence and oppression. The ruling in Cruikshank ignored the broader implications of the Second Amendment as a safeguard against tyranny, particularly the tyranny of oppressive state governments.

In modern times, the ruling is seen as part of a broader pattern of judicial decisions during the Reconstruction era that curtailed federal efforts to protect civil rights, ultimately leading to the establishment of Jim Crow laws and the perpetuation of racial segregation and disenfranchisement.

*United States v. Cruikshank* highlighted the complexities of federalism and the scope of the Second Amendment. The Supreme Court's ruling that the Second Amendment applied only to the federal government and not to the states underscored the notion that the protection of individual rights, including the right to bear arms, was primarily a state responsibility. This interpretation limited the federal government's role in safeguarding these rights and allowed states considerable leeway in regulating firearms. The *Cruikshank* ruling thus shaped the landscape of gun rights and state autonomy, illustrating the challenges of balancing federal oversight with state sovereignty.

## *Presser v. Illinois* (1886)

*Presser v. Illinois* stands as a foundational case in the annals of American legal history, particularly in the context of Second Amendment jurisprudence. The case involved Herman Presser, a member of a private militia, who was convicted under Illinois law for parading with an armed group without a permit. Presser contended that his conviction violated his Second Amendment rights, arguing that the right to keep and bear arms should protect him against state regulations. The Supreme Court's decision in this case, however, reaffirmed a restrictive interpretation of the Second Amendment, emphasizing that it constrained only the federal government, not the states.

The origins of the case lie in the post–Civil War period, a time marked by significant social and political upheaval. The late 19th century saw a rise in private militias and labor unrest, with groups often arming themselves to protect their interests or assert their rights. Herman Presser, a prominent figure in the labor movement, led the Lehr und Wehr Verein, an armed socialist workers' group. In 1879, Presser and approximately 400 members of his militia marched through the streets of Chicago, openly carrying firearms. This act was in direct violation of an Illinois statute that prohibited such parades without a permit from the governor.

Presser was arrested and charged under the Illinois law. He argued that the statute infringed upon his Second Amendment rights to keep and bear arms and his Fourteenth Amendment rights to assemble and engage in activities protected by the Constitution. The case quickly escalated through the courts, ultimately reaching the Supreme Court of the United States.

The Supreme Court's ruling in *Presser v. Illinois* was unequivocal. In a unanimous decision, the Court upheld Presser's conviction, reiterating the position it had established in *United States v. Cruikshank*. The Court declared that the Second Amendment restricted only the federal government and did not apply to state governments. Justice William Woods, writing for the Court, stated, "The Second Amendment declares that it shall not be infringed; but this, as has been seen, means no more than that it shall not be infringed by Congress. This is one of the amendments that has no other effect than to restrict the powers of the national government."

The Court further elaborated that the right to keep and bear arms, as protected by the Second Amendment, was not intended to prevent states from regulating their own militias. The ruling underscored the principle of states' rights, affirming that state governments possessed the authority to impose their own restrictions on militias and the bearing of arms. The decision reinforced the notion that states retained their autonomy in regulating firearms within their borders.

The implications of the *Presser* decision were profound. By affirming that the Second Amendment did not apply to the states, the Supreme Court effectively allowed state governments to enact and enforce their own gun control measures without fear of federal interference. This ruling entrenched the idea that state-level regulations on firearms were permissible, provided they did not conflict with the limited protections afforded by the Second Amendment against federal infringement.

Critics of the *Presser* decision argue that it undermined the fundamental purpose of the Second Amendment as a universal safeguard against tyranny. They contend that the ruling left citizens vulnerable to disparate and potentially oppressive state-level regulations, effectively creating a patchwork of gun laws across the United States. This patchwork approach, they argue, could lead to significant disparities in the protection of individual rights, depending on one's state of residence.

The decision in *Presser v. Illinois*, along with the earlier ruling in *Cruikshank*, established a legal framework that persisted for decades. The Supreme Court's interpretation of the Second Amendment as a restriction solely on federal power remained the prevailing view, influencing subsequent legal decisions and the development of state-level gun control laws. This interpretation allowed states considerable leeway in regulating firearms, resulting in a wide variety of approaches to gun control across the country.

The restrictive interpretation of the Second Amendment established by *Presser* and *Cruikshank* remained largely unchallenged until the mid-20th century. It wasn't until the landmark decision in *District of Columbia v. Heller* (2008) that the Supreme Court reinterpreted the Second Amendment, recognizing an individual's right to possess firearms for self-defense within the home. This decision marked a departure from the collective rights perspective and laid the groundwork for extending Second Amendment protections to the states.

The incorporation of the Second Amendment against the states was ultimately achieved in *McDonald v. City of Chicago* (2010). In this case, the Supreme Court ruled that the Second Amendment applies to the states through the Fourteenth Amendment, ensuring that individual rights to keep and bear arms are protected nationwide. This decision effectively overturned the precedent set by *Presser* and *Cruikshank*, reshaping the legal landscape and affirming the Second Amendment as a fundamental right applicable at all levels of government.

However, the implications of *Presser v. Illinois* continue to resonate in contemporary debates over gun control and Second Amendment rights. The case serves as a historical touchstone, illustrating the complexities and challenges of balancing state autonomy with the protection of individual liberties. It highlights the dynamic nature of constitutional interpretation and the ongoing tension between different levels of government in regulating firearms. The Supreme Court's decision affirmed the authority of states to impose their own gun control measures, reinforcing the principle of states' rights. This ruling, along with other decisions, established a legal framework that allowed for much variation in state-level gun regulations.

## *Miller v. Texas* (1894): A Pivotal Case in State-Level Firearms Regulation

*Miller v. Texas* is an important case in the history of Second Amendment jurisprudence, as it highlights the complex relationship between federal and state powers in regulating firearms. The case revolved around Franklin Miller, who was convicted of carrying a concealed weapon in violation of Texas state law. Miller contended that his conviction infringed upon his Second Amendment rights, arguing that the Constitution protected his right to bear arms against state interference. However, the Supreme Court ultimately rejected Miller's claim, reinforcing the notion that the Second Amendment did not extend its protections to the states.

Franklin Miller's legal troubles began when he was arrested and convicted under a Texas statute that prohibited the carrying of concealed weapons. This law was part of a broader effort by the state to regulate firearms and address concerns about public safety and violence. Miller's defense hinged on the argument that the Texas law violated his Second Amendment rights. His case brought forth a fundamental question about the scope of the Second Amendment and whether it provided a shield against state-level regulations.

The Supreme Court's decision in *Miller v. Texas* was consistent with its earlier rulings in *United States v. Cruikshank* (1876) and *Presser v. Illinois* (1886). In these cases, the Court had already established that the Second Amendment imposed limitations only on the federal government, not on the states. The Court in Miller reiterated this position, stating that the protections afforded by the Second Amendment did not apply to state laws. This decision reinforced the precedent that state governments had the authority to regulate firearms independently of federal oversight.

The Court's ruling was rooted in the interpretation of the Fourteenth Amendment, which had been ratified in 1868 to protect individual rights against state infringements. However, the prevailing judicial interpretation at the time did not extend these protections to the Second Amendment. The Supreme Court maintained that the Second Amendment was intended to limit only the federal government, and that states retained the power to regulate firearms as they saw fit.

The Miller decision was emblematic of the broader legal context of the late 19th and early 20th centuries, during which the Supreme Court took a narrow view of the Bill of Rights' applicability to the states. This era, often referred to as the period of "selective incorporation," saw the Court gradually apply certain protections of the Bill of Rights to the states through the Fourteenth Amendment, but the Second Amendment was not among them.

Critics of the *Miller* decision argue that it failed to protect individual rights against state encroachments and allowed for disparate and potentially oppressive state-level gun control measures. By affirming that the Second Amendment did not apply to the states, the ruling permitted variation in gun laws across the country, leading to a patchwork of regulations that could disadvantage individuals depending on their state of residence.

The implications of *Miller* were far-reaching. It effectively sanctioned state autonomy in firearm regulation, allowing states like Texas to enforce strict laws on concealed carry without fear of federal intervention. This autonomy led to a diverse landscape of gun control measures, where some states imposed rigorous restrictions while others maintained more permissive laws.

The legal landscape established by *Miller v. Texas* remained largely unchanged until the mid-20th century when the Supreme Court began to reassess the scope of the Fourteenth Amendment and its application to the Bill of Rights. This shift culminated in the landmark decision of *District of Columbia v. Heller* (2008) and later *McDonald v. City of Chicago* (2010), which fundamentally—and correctly—altered the interpretation of the Second Amendment and its applicability to the states.

*Miller v. Texas* played a crucial role in shaping the early interpretation of the Second Amendment, emphasizing state authority over firearm regulation, and reinforcing the collective rights perspective. This precedent persisted for over a century, influencing the landscape of gun control in the United States. The Miller decision and its eventual reversal highlight the dynamic nature of constitutional interpretation and the ongoing debate over the balance between individual rights and government regulation. This evolution underscores the complex interplay between federal and state powers, the protection of individual rights, and the enduring significance of the Second Amendment in American law and society.

## United States v. Miller (1939)

*United States v. Miller* stands as one of the most critical and often-debated Supreme Court cases concerning the Second Amendment. This case influenced the interpretation of the right to keep and bear arms, emphasizing the collective rights perspective associated with a well-regulated militia rather than individual gun ownership. The ruling has had a long-lasting impact and has been both criticized and defended by various legal scholars and gun rights advocates.

The origins of *United States v. Miller* lie in the passage of the National Firearms Act (NFA) of 1934, one of the earliest federal attempts to regulate firearms. The NFA was enacted in response to the rampant crime and violence associated with the Prohibition era, particularly the use of firearms like machine guns and sawed-off shotguns by criminal organizations. The act required the registration of certain types of firearms, including short-barreled shotguns, and imposed a tax on their manufacture and transfer.

Jack Miller and Frank Layton were two men who found themselves at the center of this landmark case. Both men were convicted criminals with a history of run-ins with the law. In 1938, they were charged with transporting an unregistered short-barreled shotgun across state lines, in direct violation of the NFA. Miller and Layton argued that the NFA infringed upon their Second Amendment rights, setting the stage for a constitutional showdown.

The case was initially heard in the District Court for the Western District of Arkansas. The court ruled in favor of Miller and Layton, declaring the NFA unconstitutional. The court reasoned that the Second Amendment protected the right to keep and bear arms and that this right was not limited by the type of firearm or its use in a militia context. This decision, however, was quickly appealed by the federal government, bringing the case before the Supreme Court.

The Supreme Court agreed to hear the case, and arguments were presented in March 1939. Notably, Miller and Layton did not have legal representation at the Supreme Court level, and no brief was filed on their behalf. As a result, the federal government's argument, which emphasized the necessity of the NFA for public safety and its alignment with the Second Amendment, went largely unchallenged.

On May 15, 1939, the Supreme Court delivered its decision in *United States v. Miller*. In a unanimous opinion written by Justice James Clark McReynolds, the Court upheld the constitutionality of the NFA, ruling against Miller and Layton. The key aspect of the ruling was the interpretation of the Second Amendment's connection to a "well regulated Militia."

The Court stated, "In the absence of any evidence tending to show that possession or use of a [short-barreled shotgun] at this time has some reasonable relationship to the preservation or efficiency of a well-regulated militia, we cannot say that the Second Amendment guarantees the right to keep and bear such an instrument." This language emphasized that the protection of the right to keep and bear arms was tied to the functionality and relevance of the weapon to a militia context.

The *Miller* decision marked a continued shift towards the collective rights interpretation of the Second Amendment. This interpretation posits that the Amendment was intended to protect the right to bear arms only in the context of service in a state militia, rather than as an individual right to own firearms for personal use. The Supreme Court's ruling suggested that only weapons with a clear and reasonable relationship to the maintenance of a well-regulated militia were protected under the Second Amendment.

The immediate aftermath of the *Miller* decision saw the reaffirmation of the National Firearms Act's constitutionality, leading to continued regulation of certain types of firearms under federal law. The ruling also set a precedent for future cases involving the Second Amendment, shaping the legal landscape for decades to come.

One of the significant effects of the *Miller* decision was the reinforcement of the government's ability to regulate firearms without infringing upon the Second Amendment, provided the regulations were framed within the context of public safety and the militia clause. This interpretation held sway in many subsequent lower court decisions, influencing the development of gun control legislation across the United States.

The *Miller* decision remained the primary precedent in Second Amendment jurisprudence until the landmark *District of Columbia v. Heller* decision in 2008. The *Heller* case, which affirmed an individual's right to possess firearms unconnected with service in a militia, shifted the legal interpretation of the Second Amendment. However, the principles established in *Miller* continued to influence legal thought and policy, particularly in discussions about the types of firearms that could be regulated.

Following the *Miller* decision, both federal and state governments continued to develop and implement gun control measures aimed at curbing gun violence and regulating the types of firearms available to the public. The precedent set by *Miller* provided a constitutional framework that allowed for these regulations, as long as they did not infringe upon the functional necessity of a well-regulated militia.

At the federal level, the Gun Control Act of 1968 and the Firearm Owners Protection Act of 1986 further expanded the regulatory framework established by the NFA. These laws introduced additional controls on the sale, transfer, and possession of firearms, reflecting ongoing concerns about public safety and crime prevention.

State governments also enacted various gun control measures, often tailored to the specific needs and contexts of their jurisdictions. For example, states like California and New York implemented stringent regulations on firearm ownership and use, including background checks, waiting periods, and bans on certain types of firearms and accessories. These state-level laws were influenced by the collective rights interpretation established in *Miller*, allowing for a more restrictive approach to gun control within the framework of the Second Amendment.

Despite the legal precedent set by *Miller*, the collective rights interpretation of the Second Amendment has faced much criticism from gun rights advocates and legal scholars. Critics argue that this interpretation undermines the fundamental purpose of the Second Amendment, which is to ensure individual self-defense and to serve as a check against government tyranny.

Supporters of the individual rights interpretation point to historical evidence, such as the writings of the Founding Fathers and early American legal documents, which emphasize the importance of an armed citizenry. They contend that the Second Amendment was intended to protect the right of individuals to keep and bear arms for lawful purposes, including self-defense, hunting, and resistance to oppression.

*United States v. Miller* influenced the interpretation of the Second Amendment. By emphasizing the connection between the right to bear arms and the functionality of a well-regulated militia, the Supreme Court's ruling established a collective rights interpretation that shaped gun control legislation and legal thought for decades.

That precedent held for nearly seventy years, reinforcing the idea that the Second Amendment protected a collective, not individual, right. But in 2008, the Supreme Court would revisit the issue in *District of Columbia v. Heller*—fundamentally and correctly redefining the modern understanding of the Second Amendment.

## District of Columbia v. Heller (2008)

The 2008 Supreme Court case *District of Columbia v. Heller* stands as a pivotal moment in the interpretation and application of the Second Amendment. This landmark case challenged the constitutionality of Washington, DC's stringent gun control laws, which included a comprehensive handgun ban and a mandate that firearms in homes be kept nonfunctional even during instances of self-defense. The case was brought forth by Dick Heller, who was denied a permit to keep a handgun at his home. This denial prompted Heller to file a lawsuit, arguing that the District's regulations infringed upon his Second Amendment rights.

Prior to the *Heller* decision, the prevailing legal interpretations of the Second Amendment were varied and often contradictory. The Amendment, which reads, "A well regulated Militia, being necessary to the security of a free State, the right of the people to keep and bear Arms, shall not be infringed," had been the subject of intense debate. The key issue was whether the right to bear arms was intended to be an individual right or one that was solely tied to service in a state militia.

The District of Columbia had some of the strictest gun control laws in the nation. The Firearms Control Regulations Act of 1975 effectively banned the possession of handguns by civilians and required that all firearms in homes be kept unloaded and either disassembled or bound by a trigger lock. These regulations were designed to reduce gun violence and accidents but faced criticism for potentially leaving law-abiding citizens defenseless in their own homes.

Dick Heller, who carried a handgun while on duty as a special police officer at the Federal Judicial Center, applied for a permit to keep a handgun at his residence for self-defense. When his application was denied, Heller, along with five other plaintiffs, filed a lawsuit in the United States District Court for the District of Columbia. The plaintiffs argued that the District's laws violated their Second Amendment rights to keep and bear arms for lawful purposes, including self-defense within their homes.

The case, initially dismissed by the District Court for the District of Columbia, was appealed to the United States Court of Appeals for the DC Circuit. The appellate court reversed the lower court's decision, ruling that the Second Amendment protects an individual's right to possess firearms and that the District's handgun ban was unconstitutional. The District of Columbia then appealed to the Supreme Court, which granted certiorari to address the significant constitutional questions presented by the case.

The Supreme Court heard oral arguments on March 18, 2008. The arguments focused on the historical context and original intent of the Second Amendment, the nature of individual versus collective rights, and the practical implications of gun control measures. The case drew widespread attention from legal scholars, historians, and advocacy groups on both sides of the gun control debate. Numerous amicus curiae briefs were filed, providing the Court with extensive historical and legal analyses of the Second Amendment.

On June 26, 2008, the Supreme Court delivered its landmark decision in *District of Columbia v. Heller*. In a 5–4 ruling, the Court held that the Second Amendment protects an individual's right to possess a firearm, unconnected with service in a militia, and to use that firearm for traditionally lawful purposes, such as self-defense within the home. Justice Antonin Scalia authored the majority opinion, which was joined by Chief Justice John Roberts and Justices Anthony Kennedy, Clarence Thomas, and Samuel Alito.

Justice Scalia's opinion meticulously examined the text and historical context of the Second Amendment. He argued that the phrase "the right of the people" was commonly used in the Constitution to refer to individual rights. Scalia emphasized that the Amendment's prefatory clause, "A well regulated Militia, being necessary to the security of a free State," did not limit the operative clause, "the right of the people to keep and bear Arms, shall not be infringed." Instead, the prefatory clause served to explain one of the purposes for the right, which was to ensure the effectiveness of state militias.

Scalia's opinion also delved into the historical understanding of the right to bear arms, tracing its roots back to English common law and the colonial experience. He noted that the right to self-defense was deeply ingrained in American legal traditions and was considered a fundamental natural right. Scalia stated,

"The inherent right of self-defense has been central to the Second Amendment right. The handgun ban amounts to a prohibition of an entire class of 'arms' that is overwhelmingly chosen by American society for that lawful purpose."

The dissenting opinions, authored by Justices John Paul Stevens and Stephen Breyer, argued for a more restrictive interpretation of the Second Amendment. Justice Stevens contended that the Amendment was primarily intended to protect state militias and that it did not guarantee an individual right to possess firearms for personal use. He emphasized the historical context of the Amendment's adoption, arguing that the primary concern was to prevent the federal government from disarming state militias.

Justice Breyer's dissent focused on the practical implications of the majority's decision. He argued that the District's handgun ban was a reasonable regulation aimed at reducing gun violence and that it did not violate the core protections of the Second Amendment. Breyer advocated for a balancing test that would allow courts to weigh the benefits of gun control measures against the potential infringement on individual rights.

The *Heller* decision had immediate and far-reaching implications. It struck down the District of Columbia's handgun ban and the requirement that firearms in homes be kept nonfunctional, setting a precedent that would influence future Second Amendment cases. The ruling was hailed as a monumental victory for gun rights advocates, who saw it as a confirmation of the individual right to bear arms.

In response to the decision, the District of Columbia revised its gun laws to comply with the Supreme Court's ruling while still maintaining certain restrictions. The new regulations included requirements for gun registration, mandatory safety training, and limitations on the types of firearms that could be possessed. These measures faced legal challenges but were upheld by the courts as consistent with the *Heller* decision.

The influence of *Heller* extended beyond the District of Columbia. The ruling provided a foundation for challenging restrictive gun laws in other jurisdictions. The *Heller* decision also influenced public policy and legislative debates on gun control. Advocates for gun rights used the ruling to argue against proposed regulations that they viewed as infringing on Second Amendment protections.

The decision emboldened state legislatures to pass laws expanding gun rights, such as "stand your ground" laws and constitutional carry statutes. Conversely, gun control advocates sought to introduce measures that would comply with the constitutional framework established by *Heller* while addressing concerns about gun violence.

At the federal level, the *Heller* decision prompted discussions about the need for comprehensive gun control legislation that could withstand constitutional scrutiny. Proposals included enhanced background checks, restrictions on certain types of firearms and accessories, and measures to address mental health issues related to gun violence. These debates highlighted the ongoing tension between protecting individual rights and ensuring public safety.

The *Heller* decision marked a notable shift in Second Amendment jurisprudence, establishing a clear precedent for the individual right to bear arms. The ruling has been cited in numerous court cases challenging various gun control measures, shaping the legal landscape for years to come. The decision also reinforced the cultural significance of the Second Amendment in American society, affirming the importance of self-defense and individual liberty.

The broader effect of *Heller* can be seen in the evolving public discourse on gun rights and gun control. The decision has become a touchstone for debates on the balance between constitutional freedoms and regulatory measures. It has influenced the rhetoric of political campaigns, policy proposals, and grassroots movements on both sides of the issue. The ruling underscored the deep-seated value placed on the right to bear arms in American culture and highlighted the complexities of addressing gun violence in a manner that respects constitutional protections.

One of the most significant follow-up cases was *McDonald v. City of Chicago* (2010), in which the Supreme Court held that the Second Amendment applies to the states through the Fourteenth Amendment. The *McDonald* decision extended the protections recognized in *Heller* to state and local governments, ensuring that individuals nationwide could exercise their right to bear arms for self-defense. This ruling closed a major loophole that had allowed cities and states to impose sweeping gun restrictions despite federal recognition of the right.

## *McDonald v. City of Chicago* (2010)

Following the landmark decision in *District of Columbia v. Heller*, which affirmed the Second Amendment right of individuals to keep and bear arms for self-defense within the federal enclave of Washington, DC, the scope of this ruling remained limited to federal jurisdictions. The pivotal question that *McDonald v. City of Chicago* sought to address was whether this right extended to the states through the Fourteenth Amendment. This case arose from the efforts of Otis McDonald and other plaintiffs who challenged Chicago's stringent handgun ban, asserting that it violated their Second Amendment rights.

McDonald, a 76-year-old African American resident of Chicago, sought to own a handgun for personal protection. Living in a high-crime neighborhood, McDonald argued that the city's ban on handguns left him vulnerable and unable to defend himself effectively. Along with other plaintiffs, McDonald brought the case against the city, contending that the Second Amendment should apply to the states through the Due Process Clause or the Privileges or Immunities Clause of the Fourteenth Amendment. Their argument was that self-defense is a fundamental right essential to the American legal tradition and personal liberty.

The Supreme Court's decision in *McDonald v. City of Chicago* was monumental. On June 28, 2010, the Court ruled in a 5–4 decision that the Second Amendment right to keep and bear arms for self-defense is fully applicable to the states through the Fourteenth Amendment. Writing for the majority, Justice Samuel Alito emphasized the historical and traditional importance of the right to self-defense. He stated, "Self-defense is a basic right, recognized by many legal systems from ancient times to the present day, and in *Heller*, we held that individual self-defense is 'the central component' of the Second Amendment right."

Justice Alito's opinion underscored that the Framers of the Constitution and the Fourteenth Amendment intended for fundamental rights, including the right to keep and bear arms, to be protected against infringement by state and local governments. The decision effectively incorporated the Second Amendment against the states, meaning that state and local governments could no longer enact laws that violated the fundamental right to bear arms for self-defense. This ruling was a big victory for gun rights advocates, as it extended the protections recognized in *Heller* to individuals nationwide, ensuring a uniform application of the Second Amendment across all levels of government.

The immediate aftermath of the *McDonald* decision saw a flurry of legal activity as gun rights advocates and state and local governments grappled with the implications of the ruling. In Chicago, the city council quickly moved to revise its gun regulations to comply with the Supreme Court's decision while still maintaining some degree of control over firearms. Chicago introduced new regulations that included strict registration requirements, mandatory training, and restrictions on where firearms could be carried. These measures were soon challenged in court, leading to ongoing legal battles over the extent of permissible gun control under the newly incorporated Second Amendment.

At the federal level, the *McDonald* decision reaffirmed the importance of the Second Amendment and emboldened gun rights advocates to challenge restrictive gun laws across the country. The ruling provided a legal foundation for numerous lawsuits aimed at overturning state and local gun control measures deemed too restrictive. In states with stringent gun laws like California, New York, and Massachusetts, gun rights groups utilized the *McDonald* precedent to argue against bans on certain types of firearms, high-capacity magazines, and restrictive permitting processes.

The *McDonald* ruling also had significant political ramifications. It intensified the national debate over gun control, with advocates on both sides of the issue mobilizing to influence public policy. Gun rights organizations, such as the National Rifle Association (NRA) and the Second Amendment Foundation, used the decision to bolster their campaigns for more permissive gun laws, advocating for "constitutional carry" policies and the elimination of "gun-free zones." Conversely, gun control advocates pushed for legislation that would impose stricter regulations while ostensibly complying with the constitutional protections affirmed by *McDonald*.

States with historically restrictive gun laws faced substantial pressure to amend their regulations. In Illinois, where Chicago is located, the state legislature eventually passed laws that were more permissive regarding concealed carry, marking a shift in response to the *McDonald* ruling. Illinois had been the last state to prohibit concealed carry entirely, but the *McDonald* decision, combined with subsequent court rulings, forced the state to adopt a shall-issue concealed carry permit system in 2013.

Other states took a different approach, attempting to navigate the fine line between complying with the Supreme Court's ruling and maintaining certain restrictions. For instance, states like New York and California enacted laws that imposed rigorous background checks, training requirements, and limitations on the types of firearms and ammunition that could be purchased. These states argued that such measures were necessary to ensure public safety and did not violate the core protections of the Second Amendment as interpreted in *McDonald* and *Heller*.

*McDonald v. City of Chicago* has had lasting implications for the legal landscape surrounding the Second Amendment. It has established a precedent that courts across the country use to evaluate the constitutionality of state and local gun control measures. The ruling has also fostered a broader cultural acceptance of gun rights, particularly in states where firearm ownership is deeply rooted in the local tradition. The *McDonald* ruling, by ensuring the applicability of the Second Amendment at all levels of government, has undeniably strengthened the legal foundation for gun rights advocates, setting the stage for ongoing legal and legislative battles over the right to keep and bear arms in the United States.

## Caetano v. Massachusetts (2016)

In *Caetano v. Massachusetts*, Jaime Caetano was convicted for possessing a stun gun in violation of Massachusetts law. She argued that her conviction violated her Second Amendment rights. The Supreme Court ruled in favor of Caetano, emphasizing that "the Second Amendment extends, prima facie, to all instruments that constitute bearable arms, even those that were not in existence at the time of the founding." The *Caetano* decision expanded the scope of the Second Amendment, affirming that it protects modern weapons used for self-defense. This ruling reinforced the principle that the right to bear arms is not limited to firearms but includes all bearable arms. It also served as a rebuke to lower courts that had attempted to sidestep Heller by narrowly interpreting what qualifies as protected weaponry.

### *New York State Rifle & Pistol Association Inc. v. Bruen* (2022)

One of the most significant Supreme Court cases of recent years was the landmark case *New York State Rifle & Pistol Association Inc. v. Bruen* (2022). *Bruen* challenged New York's stringent concealed carry laws, which required individuals to demonstrate a special need for self-protection to obtain a concealed carry license. The Supreme Court ruled that New York's requirement was unconstitutional, reinforcing the principle that the Second Amendment protects the right to carry firearms for self-defense outside the home. The Court stated, "The constitutional right to bear arms in public for self-defense is not a second-class right, subject to an entirely different body of rules than the other Bill of Rights guarantees."

In the *Bruen* decision, the Supreme Court introduced a "historical test" to determine the constitutionality of gun control measures. According to this test, any proposed gun control law must be consistent with the text, history, and tradition of the Second Amendment. The historical test requires that for a gun control law to be deemed constitutional, it must be shown to be in line with the historical understanding of the right to bear arms as it existed at the time of the Founding. This means that modern restrictions must have analogues in the laws and practices of the late 18th century. If a proposed law does not have a historical precedent, it is likely to be struck down as unconstitutional. The implications of this new standard are far-reaching. By requiring that gun control laws adhere to historical practices, the Court has raised the bar for the enactment of new regulations. This test effectively narrows the scope of permissible gun control measures, ensuring that any restrictions on the right to bear arms are deeply rooted in the nation's history and tradition.

One of the immediate consequences of the *Bruen* decision was the invalidation of New York's "proper cause" requirement for obtaining a concealed carry permit. The Court ruled that this requirement, which allowed state officials to exercise discretion in issuing permits, was inconsistent with the Second Amendment. This ruling forced New York and other states with similar discretionary permitting schemes to revise their laws to comply with the new standard.

The Court emphasized that the Second Amendment is not a "second-class right" and should be treated with the same respect and rigor as other constitutional protections. This ruling echoed the original intent behind the Second Amendment, which was designed to protect the individual's right to self-defense and to serve as a check against tyranny. The Founders understood that an armed populace was essential to maintaining liberty and deterring government oppression. The *Bruen* decision reinforced this principle by emphasizing that any restrictions on this right must be firmly grounded in historical precedent. The *Bruen* decision was indeed a big victory for gun rights advocates, further solidifying individual gun rights and challenging restrictive state laws. This ruling reinforced the Second Amendment's protection of the right to carry firearms in public.

While the *Bruen* decision represents a victory for gun rights advocates, it also sets the stage for ongoing legal battles. States that favor stricter gun control measures will need to navigate the new legal landscape, potentially facing numerous challenges to their existing and proposed laws. This decision will likely lead to increased litigation as courts apply the historical test to a wide range of gun control measures.

## Aftermath of the *Bruen* Decision

The aftermath of this landmark ruling has seen a striking resistance from several states, particularly those with historically strict gun control measures. States like New York, the subject of the *Bruen* decision, have responded to *Bruen* by enacting new laws that aim to circumvent the Supreme Court's ruling, thus continuing their restrictive gun control policies. The state's response was swift and deliberate. Immediately following the Supreme Court's decision in *Bruen*, New York State convened an emergency legislative session to address the implications of the ruling, and lawmakers passed a series of measures designed to maintain strict control over firearm possession and carry rights. Despite the Supreme Court's clear mandate, New York's new laws arguably aimed to undermine the spirit of the *Bruen* decision.

One of the key measures enacted was the imposition of more restrictive and burdensome requirements for obtaining a concealed carry license. The new laws mandated a rigorous application process, including more extensive background checks, mandatory in-person interviews, a two-day firearms safety course, and the requirement for applicants to provide detailed information about their social media accounts and character references. These measures created additional hurdles for law-abiding citizens seeking to exercise their Second Amendment rights.

But that was not all; New York passed a new law requiring a license to purchase semi-automatic rifles and shotguns, a regulation that did not exist before the *Bruen* decision. This new requirement further restricted access to firearms, particularly impacting those who wished to own rifles for self-defense, hunting, or sport shooting. Critics argue that these laws are not only an overreach but also a direct defiance of the Supreme Court's ruling.

New York was not alone in its legislative defiance. Several other states with strict gun control laws followed suit, enacting measures designed to circumvent the *Bruen* decision. California, for instance, introduced legislation to impose additional restrictions on concealed carry permits, including more stringent requirements for training and background checks. The state also sought to expand the list of "sensitive places" where carrying a firearm is prohibited, thereby limiting the areas where law-abiding citizens could legally carry their weapons.

Similarly, New Jersey enacted laws to tighten its already strict gun control regime. The state increased the fees associated with gun permits, implemented mandatory insurance requirements for gun owners, and expanded background check procedures. These measures were seen by many as efforts to deter citizens from pursuing gun ownership and to complicate the process of obtaining a carry permit.

The legislative actions taken by these states have not gone unchallenged. Gun rights organizations and individual plaintiffs have filed numerous lawsuits, arguing that these new laws are unconstitutional and in direct violation of the Supreme Court's ruling in *Bruen*. Plaintiffs argue that the requirements for obtaining a license are overly burdensome and infringe upon their Second Amendment rights. They contend that their state's actions are an attempt to undermine the Supreme Court's decision and maintain restrictive gun control measures by other means. For instance, in New York, several lawsuits have been filed challenging the state's new concealed carry laws. These legal challenges are making their way through the courts, with some cases already resulting in preliminary injunctions against certain provisions of the new laws.

The defiance of the *Bruen* decision by these states highlights a broader tension between state governments and the Supreme Court regarding Second Amendment rights. The actions taken by states like New York, California, and New Jersey suggest a willingness to push back against federal judicial authority in favor of maintaining local control over gun regulation. This resistance raises important questions about the balance of power between state and federal governments and the extent to which states can or should go in regulating firearms.

The legislative responses to the *Bruen* decision are also deeply political. Many of the states that have enacted these new laws are governed by Democratic majorities that traditionally support stricter gun control measures. The defiance of the Supreme Court's ruling can thus be seen as part of a broader ideological battle over gun rights in America.

Public opinion on this issue is sharply divided, although in recent years, it has shifted more in favor of gun rights. Gun control advocates argue that stricter laws are necessary to curb gun violence and enhance public safety. They point to the high rates of gun-related deaths in the United States and argue that more regulation is needed to prevent firearms from falling into the wrong hands. On the other hand, Second Amendment supporters contend that the right to bear arms is a fundamental liberty that should not be infringed. They argue that lawful gun ownership is a critical means of self-defense and a deterrent against tyranny. Criminals, they argue (correctly, I might add), can and will get guns illegally, no matter what gun control laws are passed. The only thing these restrictive laws do is deprive law-abiding citizens from obtaining the means to defend themselves against violent criminals.

In addition to legislative actions, the role of the judiciary cannot be overlooked. In some cases, judges who are perceived to be hostile to the Second Amendment have upheld restrictive gun control measures, citing public safety concerns and the need to regulate firearms more stringently. These decisions often highlight the ongoing judicial debate over the proper scope and application of Second

Amendment rights. Critics of these judicial rulings argue that they reflect a flawed interpretation of the Constitution and an overreach of judicial authority. They contend that such decisions undermine the clear intent of the Supreme Court in cases like *Bruen* and *Heller*, which affirmed the individual right to bear arms for self-defense.

The implications of this ongoing struggle are significant. If the courts ultimately uphold these new state laws, it could signal a shift in how Second Amendment rights are interpreted and enforced, potentially allowing for more restrictive gun control measures at the state level despite federal rulings to the contrary. Conversely, if the courts strike down these laws, it will reinforce the authority of Supreme Court decisions and ensure a more uniform application of Second Amendment rights across the country.

Not all the reactions to the *Bruen* decision have been negative. Numerous lower court cases have been influenced by these landmark Supreme Court rulings, shaping state and local gun laws. These cases have often resulted in the relaxation of restrictive measures and the affirmation of individual rights to bear arms, reflecting the broad influence of the Supreme Court's decisions on Second Amendment jurisprudence. In the wake of the Supreme Court's landmark decision, lower courts across the United States have begun to relax, and even repeal various gun control measures, reflecting the renewed emphasis on Second Amendment rights. The following examples underscore a broader recognition of the fundamental rights enshrined in the Constitution and echo the growing public sentiment favoring gun rights.

In Texas, the Fifth Circuit Court of Appeals struck down a longstanding law that prohibited young adults aged 18–20 from carrying handguns in public. The court ruled that the restriction was inconsistent with the Second Amendment and historical traditions, noting that young adults were considered part of the militia at the time of the founding of the United States and thus were entitled to bear arms. This decision was a notable expansion of Second Amendment protections, ensuring that a broader segment of the population could exercise their right to self-defense.

Meanwhile, in California, the Ninth Circuit Court of Appeals overturned a ban on high-capacity magazines, deeming it unconstitutional. The court argued that the law infringed upon the core Second Amendment right of self-defense, particularly in the home, where citizens might need more than 10 rounds to protect themselves against multiple assailants. This ruling came as a surprise to many, given the Ninth Circuit's historically restrictive stance on gun rights, and marked a pivotal moment in the rollback of stringent gun control measures in the state.

In New York, a federal district court ruled against a provision of the state's SAFE Act that required background checks for ammunition purchases. The court found that this requirement placed an undue burden on lawful gun owners and did not have a historical precedent supporting such regulation. This decision not only aligned with the *Bruen* ruling but also highlighted the court's acknowledgment of the fundamental right to bear arms without excessive governmental interference.

Further south, in Florida, the Eleventh Circuit Court of Appeals invalidated a local ordinance in Miami that banned the open carry of firearms. The court emphasized that the Second Amendment protects the right to bear arms in public for self-defense and that such ordinances must be scrutinized against historical practices. This ruling reinforced the constitutional guarantee that individuals should not be unduly restricted in their ability to carry firearms for protection.

In Colorado, following the *Bruen* decision, a state court overturned a ban on "assault weapons" in Boulder. The judge ruled that the ban, which targeted specific semi-automatic firearms based on their cosmetic features, did not align with the Second Amendment. This decision underscored the principle that gun control measures must be rooted in historical context and cannot arbitrarily infringe upon the rights of gun owners.

Lastly, in Maryland, the Fourth Circuit Court of Appeals ruled against a law that imposed stringent requirements for obtaining a concealed carry permit, including proving a "good and substantial reason" for carrying a handgun. The court found that this requirement violated the Second Amendment by placing an undue burden on citizens seeking to exercise their right to self-defense. This ruling was a big step towards expanding concealed carry rights in a state known for its restrictive gun laws.

These six examples from various states and cities illustrate a nationwide trend towards relaxing and repealing restrictive gun laws in the aftermath of the *Bruen* decision. Lower courts have increasingly recognized the fundamental rights protected by the Second Amendment, ensuring that lawful gun owners can exercise their rights without undue interference. These rulings reflect a growing public sentiment that values the right to bear arms as an essential component of individual liberty and self-defense, echoing the principles laid down by the Founding Fathers and reaffirmed by the Supreme Court.

## *Garland v. Cargill* (2024)

The most recent Supreme Court's decision pertaining to the Second Amendment on June 14, 2024, to overturn the bump stock ban marks a significant victory for Second Amendment rights. This ruling came from the case *Garland v. Cargill*, which challenged the legality of the bump stock ban implemented by the Bureau of Alcohol, Tobacco, Firearms and Explosives (ATF) in 2018.

The bump stock ban was initiated following the tragic mass shooting in Las Vegas in 2017, where the shooter used bump stocks to increase the rate of fire of his semi-automatic rifles, resulting in a devastating loss of life. In response, the ATF reclassified bump stocks as "machine guns" under the National Firearms Act (NFA), thereby making their possession and sale illegal.

The central argument for the ban was that bump stocks allowed semi-automatic rifles to fire at a rate comparable to fully automatic weapons, effectively making them just as dangerous and lethal. Proponents of the ban, including various gun control advocates and some lawmakers, argued that these devices should be regulated under the same stringent laws that apply to machine guns.

Opponents of the ban, however, argued that the ATF overstepped its regulatory authority by redefining bump stocks as machine guns. They contended that bump stocks do not meet the statutory definition of a machine gun, which is a firearm that continues to fire with a single pull of the trigger. Instead, bump stocks require continuous manual input from the shooter to sustain rapid fire, thus maintaining the semi-automatic nature of the firearm. This argument was a key aspect of the case brought before the Supreme Court.

In *Garland v. Cargill*, the plaintiffs argued that the ATF's reclassification was an unconstitutional overreach and violated the Administrative Procedure Act (APA), which governs the process by which federal agencies develop and issue regulations. They asserted that the ATF lacked the authority to reinterpret the law in a manner that effectively created new gun control measures without congressional approval.

The Supreme Court's decision to overturn the bump stock ban was based on several key points. First, the Court agreed with the plaintiffs that the ATF's interpretation of the term "machine gun" was inconsistent with the statutory definition provided by Congress. The Court emphasized that the law must be interpreted as written and that any changes to the definition of machine guns should be made by Congress, not by an executive agency.

Second, the Court highlighted the principle of separation of powers, underscoring that regulatory agencies cannot unilaterally create or modify laws. This decision reinforces the importance of maintaining clear boundaries between the legislative and executive branches of government.

Furthermore, the Court recognized that the ban imposed undue burdens on law-abiding gun owners who had purchased bump stocks legally before the reclassification. Many of these individuals had complied with existing laws and regulations at the time of their purchase, and the retroactive nature of the ban was deemed unfair and punitive.

The ruling in *Garland v. Cargill* is a pivotal moment in the ongoing debate over gun control and the Second Amendment. It reaffirms the necessity of adhering to constitutional principles and ensuring that any regulatory changes involving firearms must be enacted through the proper legislative channels. This decision not only restores the legality of bump stocks but also sets a precedent for future challenges to executive overreach in the realm of gun regulation.

## United States v. Rahimi (2024)

On June 21, 2024, the Supreme Court ruled 8–1 in favor of the government in *United States v. Rahimi*, upholding the constitutionality of laws that temporarily restrict firearm possession for individuals subject to domestic violence restraining orders. This decision reaffirmed the federal prohibition established under a provision of the 1994 Violent Crime Control and Law Enforcement Act, which bars individuals under such restraining orders from possessing firearms.

The case originated when Zackey Rahimi, a Texas man with a history of violent altercations, was found in possession of firearms despite being subject to a domestic violence restraining order. Rahimi challenged the constitutionality of this restriction under the Second Amendment, citing the Supreme Court's 2022 ruling in *Bruen*, which required firearm regulations to be justified by historical precedent. The Fifth Circuit Court of Appeals sided with Rahimi, ruling that the government had failed to provide a sufficiently close historical analogue to justify disarming individuals solely based on a civil restraining order.

In the Supreme Court's decision, Chief Justice John Roberts authored the majority opinion, which was joined by all but Justice Clarence Thomas. Roberts acknowledged the "historic tradition" standard from *Bruen* but rejected the Fifth Circuit's rigid interpretation, emphasizing that courts should not demand an exact "historic twin" for modern laws. Instead, Roberts argued that courts should look at laws that are "relevantly similar" to contemporary regulations. He cited historical English and American laws that prevented individuals who posed a physical threat from misusing firearms, concluding that such restrictions are consistent with the Second Amendment. "When an individual poses an explicit threat of violence to another, the threatening individual may be disarmed," Roberts wrote, affirming the constitutionality of the statute.

Notably, while the majority upheld the law's general constitutionality, they disagreed with the government's argument that Zackey Rahimi could be disarmed simply because he was "not a responsible citizen." The Court declined to endorse this broad interpretation of Second Amendment limitations, signaling that while public safety concerns can justify temporary restrictions on firearm possession, such prohibitions must be narrowly applied within constitutional boundaries.

Justice Clarence Thomas, the lone dissenter, argued that the majority failed to meet the historical standard established in *Bruen* and that the government had not demonstrated a clear historical precedent justifying gun bans based solely on civil restraining orders.

The ruling in *Rahimi* clarifies the *Bruen* decision, reinforcing the government's ability to regulate firearm possession for those deemed a physical threat while maintaining Second Amendment protections. This decision ensures that domestic violence restraining orders remain a valid legal mechanism for temporary firearm restrictions, though it leaves room for future challenges regarding how such laws are applied on a case-by-case basis.

## United States v. Morgan (2024)

In August 2024, US District Judge John Broomes in Kansas dismissed charges against Tamori Morgan, who was accused of illegally possessing a machine gun and a conversion device known as a "Glock switch." Judge Broomes ruled that the federal ban on machine guns was unconstitutional, stating that such weapons are "bearable arms" protected by the Second Amendment. He argued that prosecutors failed to provide historical evidence supporting the ban, as required by the Supreme Court's 2022 decision in *Bruen*. The judge's ruling effectively overturned decades of federal law regulating machine guns, setting a precedent that could challenge other aspects of the NFA and related legislation. This ruling was a departure from previous interpretations of the Second Amendment, which had allowed some restrictions on "dangerous and unusual weapons." This decision also marked a shift in how courts may interpret the Second Amendment moving forward, particularly concerning the regulation of firearms that are classified as "dangerous and unusual."

The implications of this ruling are profound. If upheld, this decision could pave the way for the deregulation of other types of firearms that are currently heavily regulated under the NFA, such as short-barreled rifles, short-barreled shotguns, and suppressors. The ruling suggests that the government's ability to impose categorical bans on certain types of firearms may be severely curtailed, thereby expanding the scope of Second Amendment protections.

Supporters of the ruling argue that it represents a correct interpretation of the Second Amendment and the principles set forth in the *Bruen* decision. They contend that the right to bear arms is a fundamental right that should not be subject to arbitrary or overly restrictive regulations. They also argue that machine guns, like other firearms, can be used for lawful purposes such as self-defense and should therefore be protected under the Second Amendment. Furthermore, proponents of the decision assert that the NFA's restrictions are an outdated response to a bygone era and that modern interpretations of the Second Amendment should reflect the realities of today's society and the original intent of the Founding Fathers.

One of the key arguments in favor of the ruling is that it restores the Second Amendment to its proper place as a safeguard against government overreach. The ruling reinforces the idea that the Constitution does not grant the government the authority to pick and choose which firearms are acceptable for public use. Instead, it affirms that the right to bear arms is a broad and inclusive right that extends to all arms in common use, regardless of how the government may classify them.

Critics of the ruling, on the other hand, argue that allowing the unrestricted ownership of machine guns poses a huge risk to public safety. They contend that machine guns, due to their rapid rate of fire and destructive potential, should be subject to stricter regulations to prevent their misuse. However, supporters of the ruling counter that the mere potential for misuse does not justify a blanket ban on an entire category of firearms. They argue that responsible, law-abiding citizens should not be deprived of their constitutional rights based on the actions of a criminal minority.

The decision has sparked intense reactions from both sides of the gun rights debate. Gun rights advocates have hailed the ruling as a monumental victory for the Second Amendment, viewing it as a long-overdue correction of unconstitutional restrictions. They see it as a vindication of their belief that the right to bear arms should not be infringed and that the government has overstepped its bounds in regulating firearms.

On the other hand, gun control advocates have expressed deep concern over the ruling, warning that it could lead to increased gun violence and make it more difficult to maintain public safety. They fear that the ruling could open the door to the proliferation of highly dangerous weapons, leading to a destabilization of efforts to curb gun violence in the United States. These opponents are likely to push for legislative or judicial responses to counteract the effects of the ruling.

Despite the controversy, the ruling aligns with a growing trend in the judiciary to interpret the Second Amendment more expansively. Following the *Bruen* decision, lower courts have increasingly struck down gun control laws that fail to meet the historical tradition test, signaling a shift toward a more robust protection of gun rights. This trend suggests that the judiciary is moving away from deference to government regulations on firearms and is instead emphasizing the constitutional protections afforded by the Second Amendment.

The ruling is almost certain to be appealed, and it could eventually reach the Supreme Court. If the Supreme Court upholds the ruling, it will solidify the principle that categorical bans on certain types of firearms are unconstitutional unless they can be justified by a historical tradition of regulation. This would represent a significant limitation on the government's ability to regulate firearms and could lead to further challenges against other provisions of the NFA.

Should this ruling stand, it could have sweeping implications for federal and state firearms regulations. The NFA, which has been the cornerstone of federal gun control since its enactment in 1934, could be largely undermined, leading to a reevaluation of other long-standing restrictions. The case could also prompt a broader reconsideration of what constitutes "arms in common use," potentially expanding the range of firearms protected under the Second Amendment.

## Judicial Activism

Activist judges are a blight on the judiciary, operating less like impartial interpreters of the Constitution and more like political operatives in robes. These jurists abandon their duty to apply the law as written and instead impose their personal political beliefs from the bench, often at the expense of individual liberty.

Nowhere is this more evident than in their assault on the Second Amendment. Rather than uphold the clear language of the Second Amendment, which states unequivocally that "the right of the people to keep and bear arms shall not be infringed," activist judges contort the text, invent historical fictions, and cherry-pick selective interpretations to whittle away at one of the most fundamental freedoms in the Bill of Rights. These judges disregard the clear text of the

Constitution in favor of advancing a political agenda that undermines individual rights. Rather than act as referees in legal disputes, they behave as legislators from the bench, reinterpreting or outright ignoring the Framers' intent. This dangerous trend has turned the judiciary into a tool of the radical left, where personal ideology is elevated above constitutional principle.

Among the most notorious examples of this judicial activism are the radical leftist justices currently sitting on the US Supreme Court—Sonia Sotomayor, Ketanji Brown Jackson, and Elena Kagan. Time and again, these justices have shown contempt for the Second Amendment, siding with restrictions that chip away at the rights of law-abiding gun owners. Sotomayor has a long history of ruling against individual gun rights, infamously voting to uphold Chicago's handgun ban in *McDonald*, despite clear precedent from *Heller* affirming that the Second Amendment protects an individual right to keep and bear arms. Kagan and Jackson have followed in lockstep, rubber-stamping anti-gun legislation under the guise of "public safety" while showing a blatant disregard for the plain meaning of the Bill of Rights. Their rulings are less about constitutional interpretation and more about advancing a progressive worldview hostile to personal freedoms.

Former Supreme Court Justice John Paul Stevens embodies the very definition of radical judicial activism, twisting the plain meaning of the Constitution to fit a leftist, anti-Second Amendment narrative. Stevens' dissent in *Heller* and his subsequent public statements reveal a deep disdain for the individual right to keep and bear arms, a right that is clearly stated in the text of the Second Amendment. Stevens argued that the Second Amendment was only meant to apply to state militias, not to individual citizens, ignoring both the language of the amendment and its historical context. His reasoning is a textbook example of judicial activism: prioritizing personal political ideology over the original intent and meaning of the Constitution.

Stevens went even further in 2018, writing an op-ed for *The New York Times* calling for the outright repeal of the Second Amendment. He described it as a "relic of the 18th century" that is no longer relevant to modern America, as if liberty and the right to self-defense have an expiration date. His suggestion that the Second Amendment is obsolete is not just incorrect—it is dangerous. The right to keep and bear arms is a cornerstone of individual liberty, a safeguard against tyranny, and a fundamental check on the power of the state. Stevens' position reeks of contempt for the very principles that underpin the Bill of Rights.

What Stevens conveniently ignores—and what the Supreme Court majority correctly affirmed in *Heller*—is that "the right of the people" unmistakably refers to individual citizens, not government-run militias. The same wording appears in the First and Fourth Amendments, which even Stevens would not dare suggest only apply to state actors. His claim is a radical reimagining of constitutional rights, one that strips away individual sovereignty and hands it to the government under the guise of "public safety." His call to repeal the Second Amendment is not only out of step with constitutional principles but also with the overwhelming majority of Americans who recognize the right to self-defense as non-negotiable. In short, Stevens is not just wrong—he is dangerously wrong, pushing a radical ideological agenda that undermines the liberties of every law-abiding citizen.

As we previously discussed, Supreme Court Decisions are routinely undermined or ignored by lower courts, which are plagued with similar activist judges. Take Judge Robert Lasnik of the US District Court for the Western District of Washington, who infamously blocked the online publication of 3D-printed gun blueprints in *State of Washington v. Defense Distributed*. Despite First and Second Amendment implications, Lasnik decided the public shouldn't have access to this information, treating free speech and the right to bear arms as privileges the state can revoke when it sees fit.

Another glaring example is Judge William Young of the US District Court for the District of Massachusetts, who upheld the state's "assault weapons" ban by absurdly claiming that AR-15s and similar rifles are "weapons of war" undeserving of Second Amendment protection. Young went as far as to cite former Justice Stevens' anti-Second Amendment rhetoric in his ruling, exemplifying how activist judges recycle the same anti-gun talking points while dismissing legal precedent and constitutional protections.

These judges and justices display nothing short of contempt for the Constitution they swore to uphold. Their rulings are not merely legal disagreements; they are ideological crusades aimed at stripping Americans of their fundamental rights. Their hostility toward the Second Amendment is not rooted in law but in an elitist belief that the average citizen cannot be trusted with the means to defend themselves. This brand of activism corrodes the judiciary's credibility and transforms the courts into battlegrounds for political agendas, rather than halls of justice.

## Interpreting vs. Applying

It's deeply disturbing that we even entertain the notion that the Constitution requires constant "interpretation" by judges. What exactly is there to interpret? The document is written in plain language for the people—not for a select priesthood of legal elites to twist and mold at will. The Founders drafted the Constitution to be clear, direct, and binding, yet modern judges have taken it upon themselves to insert their personal ideologies, prejudices, and political agendas into rulings, distorting the original intent of the Framers. Instead of applying the law as written, they bend and warp it to suit the cultural or political narrative of the day.

The Second Amendment is about as clear as it gets: "A well regulated Militia, being necessary to the security of a free State, the right of the people to keep and bear Arms shall not be infringed." It's one simple sentence, written in plain 18th-century English, yet somehow we've been locked in a century-long debate about what it "really" means. The Founders weren't writing riddles. They were crystal clear that the people—meaning individual citizens—have the right to keep and bear arms, and that this right shall not be infringed. But activist judges, politicians, and gun control advocates treat this straightforward mandate like it's encoded in ancient hieroglyphics. Why? Because applying it as written limits government power, and some simply can't stomach that.

That the Second Amendment is still being "debated" is proof of how willing some are to ignore plain language when it doesn't align with their ideology. If judges can twist "shall not be infringed" to mean "shall be infringed, restricted, and regulated into oblivion," then what other rights can they conveniently "reinterpret"? Would they do the same with the First Amendment? Imagine if free speech only applied when convenient or if freedom of religion was "interpreted" as freedom from religion altogether. This isn't a matter of literacy; it's a matter of willful distortion. The problem isn't that they *can't* read it—it's that they *won't*.

It's ironic—and infuriating—that society tolerates this kind of judicial creativity when it comes to something as critical as the Constitution, yet we would never accept that logic elsewhere. Imagine if we decided to "interpret" the tax code based on our personal preferences—maybe we'd all decide paying taxes is optional because that's how we read it. Or what if gun owners collectively "interpreted" restrictive gun laws to mean they don't apply because we don't feel like they should? Gun controllers would have a meltdown, but that's the exact precedent activist judges set every time they sidestep the actual words of the Second Amendment or any other part of the Constitution. The fact is, when judges start interpreting instead of applying, the rule of law crumbles, and what's left is arbitrary, ideological governance disguised as legal authority.

## The Future of Second Amendment Court Rulings

The current composition of the Supreme Court suggests strong support for Second Amendment rights, with a conservative majority likely to favor gun rights in future rulings. This judicial climate, coupled with public opinion favoring gun ownership rights, indicates that the protection and expansion of Second Amendment rights will continue to shape American society.

Recently, in a landmark decision, a federal judge declared New Jersey's ban on AR-15 rifles unconstitutional, citing that the law infringes upon the Second Amendment rights of citizens. This ruling challenged the widespread notion that "assault weapons" bans are legally sound and could have significant implications for similar laws nationwide. The decision emphasizes that the AR-15 and similar firearms, which are commonly owned for self-defense, fall under the protection of the Second Amendment.

The ruling comes as the Supreme Court is potentially poised to take up a case that could have even broader implications for gun rights across the country. If the Supreme Court were to rule against such bans, it could effectively dismantle existing restrictions on these firearms nationwide, reaffirming the constitutional right to own and carry firearms that are commonly used by law-abiding citizens.

This would be a tremendous victory for the Second Amendment and for individual freedoms, ensuring that the rights of citizens to protect themselves with the tools they choose are not arbitrarily restricted by government overreach. The case in New Jersey is a critical step in this ongoing battle.

As we've seen throughout this chapter, landmark Supreme Court cases have played a crucial role in defining and defending the Second Amendment, affirming the fundamental right of Americans to keep and bear arms. These rulings have protected and expanded individual liberties while also prompting ongoing debates about the balance between public safety and constitutional rights.

However, these victories are not guaranteed to be permanent. The composition of the Supreme Court, shaped by presidential appointments, has a lasting effect on the future of gun rights in this country. Elections, therefore, have profound consequences. A shift in the balance of power could easily reverse the pro-Second Amendment gains of recent years if a future anti-gun administration succeeds in packing the court with justices sympathetic to their cause.

Historically, the American left has relied on the Supreme Court to implement policies that were unpopular with the electorate and unlikely to pass through Congress. Today, as the Court moves toward originalist interpretations of the Constitution, including rulings that protect the Second Amendment, there is a growing push to reshape the judiciary to align with certain political agendas. This highlights the critical importance of the judicial branch in upholding fundamental rights, particularly those enshrined in the Second Amendment. Our elected officials play a crucial role in this process: The president nominates justices, and the Senate confirms them. Ensuring that these appointments reflect a commitment to constitutional principles is essential. The Supreme Court serves as a safeguard against the erosion of individual liberties, and vigilance is necessary to prevent judicial activism that could undermine the right to bear arms. Tyranny often begins with the disarmament of the populace, making it even more vital to support a judiciary that upholds, rather than reinterprets, the clear intent of the Constitution.

# Chapter 6

## Control Freaks

*The right of the citizen to keep and bear arms must not be infringed if liberty in America is to survive. We need crime control, not gun control.*

—Ronald Reagan

*To disarm the people is the best and most effective way to enslave them. A government that would deny this right is a government of occupation, not a government of the people.*

—Rand Paul

Freedom is rooted in the ability to exercise one's rights without undue interference or control by the government. The Second Amendment, as enshrined in the Bill of Rights, was intended to protect this freedom by ensuring that citizens retain the means to defend themselves and their liberties. When the government has the authority to dictate what types of firearms individuals may own, it effectively holds the power to disarm the populace, making them vulnerable to potential abuses of power and tyranny. This dynamic erodes the principle of individual sovereignty, reducing citizens to subjects who must seek approval to exercise their constitutionally guaranteed rights.

The Framers of the Constitution understood the dangers of such a power imbalance, having experienced tyranny firsthand. They enshrined the Second

Amendment to prevent the government from gaining the ability to disarm and control the populace. Therefore, any requirement for government permission to own firearms is not just an infringement on a specific right, but a broader assault on the very concept of individual freedom and autonomy that underpins the American republic.

Moreover, the Second Amendment, like all rights enshrined in the United States Constitution, was designed to protect individual rights against the tyranny of the majority. This principle is foundational to Americanism, ensuring that fundamental rights cannot be overridden by fleeting public opinion or political pressures. The Framers of the Constitution, informed by historical abuses of power, sought to create a system where individual liberties are safeguarded against any form of majoritarian rule that might seek to infringe upon them. This protection extends to all the rights in the Bill of Rights, including the right to free speech, religious freedom, and, critically, the right to keep and bear arms.

The Second Amendment, therefore, guarantees that the right to own firearms is not up for debate based on popular sentiment. Even if a supermajority of the population were to oppose certain kinds of guns, they do not have the constitutional authority to strip away the rights of the minority. The purpose of the Bill of Rights is to ensure that certain fundamental rights remain inviolable, regardless of changing societal norms, public opinion, political trends, or the agendas of those in power.

Gun control, by its very nature, stands in direct opposition to the fundamental rights enshrined in the United States Constitution. Despite this clear constitutional mandate, various levels of government have repeatedly sought to impose restrictive measures under the guise of public safety. However, history and evidence suggest that these laws are less about protecting citizens and more about exerting control over them.

The absurdities of gun control laws are numerous and often border on the comical if not for their serious consequences. Consider, for instance, the legislation in New York, where it is illegal to possess a magazine that holds more than seven rounds, despite most standard firearms being designed for magazines of higher capacity. Or California, where the definition of an "assault weapon" includes cosmetic features that have no bearing on the firearm's functionality or lethality. In New Jersey, a man can face prison time for possessing hollow-point ammunition in his home, even if it is legal to purchase it. Such laws are deliberately vague and oppressive, designed to entrap law-abiding citizens rather than target criminals.

These measures, far from enhancing public safety, create a labyrinth of regulations that burden responsible gun owners, making it difficult, if not impossible, for them to comply fully. The result is a landscape where ordinary citizens can be turned into criminals overnight for innocuous actions like possessing a certain type of magazine or failing to register a firearm part that was recently reclassified. This level of control is not about safety; it is about power and the ability to dictate who can and cannot exercise their constitutional rights.

Many times, high-profile tragedies have triggered knee-jerk reactions resulting in gun control legislation that often targets the appearance of firearms, implementing bans on certain features that make guns less attractive or more uncomfortable to handle, without effectively solving the problem of gun violence. For instance, legislation might ban certain stocks, grips, or cosmetic features while failing to address the root causes of crime and violence.

This introduction serves as a prelude to a deeper exploration of the disparate gun laws across the United States, the heavy-handed tactics of the ATF, and the unconstitutional nature of the National Firearms Act. In this chapter, we will compare the most and least restrictive states, highlight the bureaucratic overreach of federal agencies, and argue for the abolition of laws that infringe on the fundamental right to keep and bear arms.

In addition, we will embark on a comprehensive examination of gun control in the United States, scrutinizing the efforts of various state and federal agencies dedicated to regulating firearms. We will also delve into the critical question: Is it really the gun that's the problem, or do we have a more significant issue with criminal activity and mental health? By examining both sides of the debate, we aim to uncover whether the focus on gun control is misplaced and whether addressing criminal behavior and mental health issues could offer more effective solutions. Hint: Yes and yes.

Finally, we will also examine cases where reduced gun control measures have either reduced crime or had no noticeable impact on crime rates. By juxtaposing these scenarios, we aim to shed light on the true efficacy of gun control laws and challenge the often-simplistic narratives presented by gun control advocates. This chapter promises an in-depth exploration of one of the most contentious issues in American public policy, backed by rigorous analysis and real-world examples. Through this discussion, we will underscore the essential truth that true public safety is achieved not through disarmament but through the preservation and respect of constitutional freedoms.

It is a widely held opinion by those of us in the Second Amendment community that those who advocate for strict gun control measures understand such regulations do not effectively reduce crime. The reality is that criminals do not adhere to laws, including those governing firearms. Implementing more stringent gun control laws will not change the fact that there will always be individuals who obtain illegal firearms to commit crimes.

The true motivation behind many gun control advocates and anti-gun politicians lies not in crime reduction but in their inherent desire to exert control. These individuals, who I refer to as "control freaks," can never be content unless they are making others conform to their dictates. Human nature is inherently flawed, and there will always be those who seek to dominate and control others. Gun control is merely one avenue through which these elite individuals can gain more power over a population.

This chapter, aptly named "Control Freaks," delves deep into the true nature of these motivations and the broader implications for our society. We must remain vigilant against such efforts to ensure that our fundamental rights and liberties are preserved against those who would seek to undermine them for their own gain.

## What Is Gun Control?

The term "gun control" refers to the laws, regulations, and policies that are implemented by governments to control the manufacture, sale, possession, and use of firearms by civilians. These measures can include background checks, waiting periods, mandatory registration, restrictions on certain types of firearms, licensing requirements, and limitations on the number of firearms a person can own. Gun control is typically pitched as reducing gun violence, preventing crime, and ensuring public safety by restricting access to firearms for individuals who may pose a threat.

In theory, gun control is designed to reduce the incidence of gun violence and improve public safety. Proponents argue that by restricting access to firearms, particularly for individuals deemed high-risk, gun control can lower the rates of homicides, suicides, and accidental shootings. The underlying assumption is that fewer guns in circulation will lead to fewer opportunities for their misuse. This perspective is often supported by data from countries with stringent gun control laws, which tend to have lower rates of gun-related deaths compared to countries with more permissive gun laws.

Gun control measures vary widely from country to country and even within different regions of the same country. In the United States, federal gun laws set a baseline, but individual states and municipalities can implement additional restrictions. Countries like Australia and the United Kingdom have implemented strict gun control laws, including comprehensive background checks, firearm registration, and, in some cases, outright bans on certain categories of firearms. These laws are enforced by law enforcement agencies, and violations can result in severe penalties, including imprisonment.

While the stated goals of gun control measures sound noble to many, it is essential to consider the broader implications and motivations behind these policies. Gun control ultimately boils down to a method for those in power to exercise control over the population. By disarming citizens, governments can reduce the potential for armed resistance, making it easier to impose their will without fear of significant opposition. This dynamic creates a power imbalance where the state holds a monopoly on force, potentially paving the way for authoritarian rule. As we discussed in previous chapters, history has shown that gun registries and disarmament are frequently precursors to tyranny. This historical context underscores the potential dangers of allowing the government to have a complete record of firearm ownership and the ability to restrict access to arms.

Many gun control advocates are driven by an inherent desire to dictate and restrict the actions of others. This tendency manifests in policies that prioritize regulatory oversight and diminish individual freedoms. By implementing universal background checks and other restrictive measures, they effectively create de facto gun registries, which can be used to track and control lawful gun owners. These measures are often justified under the guise of public safety, but they serve to expand governmental authority and curtail personal liberties.

While the theory behind gun control is centered on reducing violence and enhancing safety, the practice and underlying motivations reveal a more complex and concerning reality. The true nature of gun control is not just about public safety but about the exercise of power by a select few over the many.

Gun control can take many forms, from the seemingly innocuous, such as standard background checks, to the extreme, like outright gun confiscation. Across the United States, various states have implemented a range of gun control measures aimed at reducing gun violence, regulating firearm ownership, and promoting public safety. Heavily regulated states often have more stringent laws, while others maintain more relaxed regulations in line with the Second Amendment. Here, we will explore many of the most common types of gun control measures across the United States.

## Standard Background Checks

Standard background checks are a widely accepted form of gun control required by federal law for all firearm purchases through licensed dealers. These checks involve screening buyers through the National Instant Criminal Background Check System (NICS) to ensure they are not prohibited from owning firearms due to their criminal history, mental health issues, or other disqualifying factors. Proponents argue that background checks are essential for preventing firearms from falling into the hands of individuals who are deemed dangerous or unfit to possess them. They believe that thorough background checks can reduce gun violence and prevent mass shootings by stopping potential perpetrators from acquiring guns legally. However, some critics argue that background checks are not foolproof and often fail to prevent criminals from obtaining firearms through illegal means; most criminals acquire guns through theft, black market transactions, or other illicit methods that bypass the background check system entirely.

Additionally, they argue that background checks can create unnecessary barriers for law-abiding citizens exercising their Second Amendment rights.

A common objection to standard background checks for purchasing firearms stems from the fact that throughout most of US history, such checks were not required. As recently as the 1970s, it was possible to walk into a department store and purchase as much ammunition and as many guns as one could afford, all without a background check. Despite this lack of regulation, mass shootings were not a prevalent issue at that time. It is not the availability of guns that has changed, but rather the breakdown of societal structures. That guns were much easier to obtain back then, but shootings are more common now, despite the implementation of background checks and stricter gun laws, raises important questions about the overall effectiveness of these measures. Focusing solely on gun control may overlook deeper, more systemic issues contributing to the rise in violence.

While standard background checks are widely considered a reasonable requirement, their effectiveness is limited by the ability of determined criminals to circumvent legal channels. The requirement for background checks is, to some, a form of government overreach that infringes on the constitutional right to bear arms. Moreover, these checks can lead to delays and complications for law-abiding citizens seeking to exercise their rights.

## Gun Registration and Universal Background Checks

Gun registration requires firearm owners to record their weapons with the government. This measure aims to track firearm ownership, facilitate law enforcement investigations, and prevent illegal firearm sales and transfers. Advocates believe that registration can help law enforcement trace firearms used in crimes, reduce illegal gun trafficking, and ensure accountability among gun owners. They argue that a comprehensive registry can enhance public safety and aid in criminal investigations. Critics argue that gun registration infringes on privacy rights and can lead to government overreach and eventual confiscation. They contend that registries can be abused by authorities and that criminals are unlikely to comply with registration requirements. Additionally, opponents believe that registration does not effectively prevent crime or reduce gun violence. Gun registration, they say, poses risks to privacy and can pave the way for future confiscation efforts. Historical examples, such as the confiscations following registration in countries like Australia and Canada, fuel concerns about government overreach. The practical benefits of registration are limited, as it does not address the root causes of gun violence and relies on the compliance of individuals who are already law-abiding.

A gun registry is inherently intrusive. It requires gun owners to report their firearms to the government, creating a comprehensive database of who owns what weapons. This level of surveillance is an unacceptable invasion of privacy. Knowing who owns firearms gives the government undue power and control over its citizens, which can lead to abuse and oppression.

The push for universal background checks is often presented as a common-sense measure to ensure that firearms do not end up in the hands of dangerous individuals. However, universal background checks can effectively create a de facto gun registry. Unlike traditional background checks conducted at the point of sale through a Federal Firearms License (FFL) dealer, universal background checks require the documentation of all firearm transfers, including private sales and transfers between individuals. This documentation can easily be compiled into a comprehensive registry of gun ownership.

The gun community is deeply concerned about the implications of universal background checks and gun registries. There is a widespread fear that such measures are merely the first steps toward broader firearm confiscation. History has shown that registries often lead to confiscation, as they provide a roadmap for the government to identify and seize firearms. This fear is not unfounded, given the historical precedents and the rhetoric from some gun control advocates. As discussed in chapter 4, gun registries have been employed by various tyrannical governments throughout history as tools for control—such as Nazi Germany and the Soviet Union—where firearm registration was a precursor to widespread confiscation and the establishment of totalitarian rule.

While the intention behind universal background checks is to prevent prohibited individuals from obtaining firearms, the effectiveness of this measure in reducing crime is debated. Criminals who are determined to acquire firearms often bypass legal channels entirely, obtaining guns through theft, the black market, or straw purchases. Universal background checks primarily affect law-abiding citizens and do little to deter criminals who do not follow the law. Therefore, the practical impact on reducing gun violence may be limited.

Universal background checks and gun registries also raise important constitutional concerns. A registry places an additional burden on gun ownership and is a form of prior restraint, which is at odds with the spirit of the Second Amendment. Moreover, the Fourth Amendment protects against unreasonable searches and seizures. A gun registry, which entails the collection and storage of personal information about gun owners, is an unreasonable intrusion into the private lives of citizens. This data collection without probable cause is a violation of the constitutional protections against unwarranted government surveillance.

While typical background checks are reasonable for ensuring that firearms do not fall into the hands of those who are prohibited from owning them, gun registries and universal background checks pose large risks and constitutional concerns. It is crucial to balance the need for public safety with the protection of individual liberties, ensuring that the fundamental rights enshrined in the Constitution are not eroded by "reasonable sounding" but ultimately harmful policies.

## Background Checks for Private Sales

Background checks for private sales and transfers between individuals falls into a similar category of universal background checks. This measure aims to close the "gun show loophole" and prevent prohibited individuals from obtaining firearms. States like Colorado and Washington have implemented these kinds of background checks.

One of the primary concerns about background checks for private sales is the potential for creating de facto gun registries. Although proponents of these checks argue that the information is not used to create a registry, the systematic collection of transaction data inevitably leads to a repository of gun ownership details. Like the concept of universal background checks, critics fear that this data could be accessed or used in the future to track and monitor lawful gun owners, leading to potential abuses of power and infringements on the right to privacy.

Another issue with background checks for private sales is the potential infringement on individuals' privacy rights. Private firearm transactions between family members, friends, or neighbors typically involve a level of trust and privacy. Mandating background checks for these transfers introduces government oversight into private dealings, which many gun owners view as an unnecessary intrusion. The requirement to involve a third party, such as a licensed dealer, to conduct the check also means sharing personal information with additional entities, further compromising privacy. Even more absurd is the idea that gifting or transferring a firearm to a legal, of-age family member—such as a spouse, parent, or sibling—would require jumping through bureaucratic hoops. Forcing families to seek government approval for something as simple as passing down a hunting rifle or home-defense firearm is not only unnecessary but an outright infringement on personal rights.

The implementation of background checks for private sales can also impose financial and logistical burdens on law-abiding citizens. Conducting a background check through a licensed dealer often comes with hefty fees—amounts vary by state, which can be a financial strain for some individuals. The process requires both parties to coordinate and travel to a dealer, which can be inconvenient and time-consuming. These added steps may discourage legal firearm transfers and create unnecessary obstacles for responsible gun owners who wish to sell or gift firearms within their community.

The expansion of background checks to include private sales raises concerns about potential government overreach. Requiring government approval for private transactions between individuals sets a precedent for increased regulation and control over personal property and can lead to an erosion of individual freedoms and autonomy. Such measures pave the way for further restrictions and regulations that encroach on the rights of gun owners, ultimately undermining the Second Amendment.

Enforcing background checks for private sales presents unique challenges. Unlike transactions through licensed dealers, private sales are often conducted discreetly, making it difficult for authorities to monitor compliance. This creates a situation where responsible gun owners are more likely to adhere to the law, while those intent on circumventing regulations can do so with relative ease.

The uneven enforcement of these laws can lead to selective prosecution and a perception of unfairness, further complicating the issue.

Background checks for private sales also affect gun shows and online firearm sales. Gun shows are often targeted in discussions about the "gun show loophole," where private sellers can sell firearms without conducting background checks. Implementing universal background checks would require all sales at gun shows, even those by private individuals, to go through licensed dealers. Similarly, online sales would necessitate background checks, adding layers of complexity and regulation to these transactions. This might reduce the number of private sellers willing to participate in gun shows or online platforms, limiting the options for buyers and sellers.

While the goal of background checks for private sales is to enhance public safety by preventing prohibited individuals from obtaining firearms, the measure introduces several contentious issues. The potential for de facto gun registries, infringement on privacy rights, financial and logistical burdens, questionable effectiveness in preventing crime, concerns about government overreach, enforcement challenges, and detrimental effects on gun shows and online sales all contribute to the complexity of this policy.

## Background Checks for Ammunition Purchases

Some states, like California and New York, require background checks for ammunition purchases to prevent prohibited individuals from obtaining ammunition (The California requirement went into effect in 2019, while the New York requirement went into effect in 2023.) This measure aims to complement firearm background checks and close potential loopholes that allow prohibited individuals to acquire ammunition even if they cannot legally obtain firearms. Proponents believe that this measure can help prevent gun violence by restricting access to ammunition for those who should not possess it. Critics argue that these checks are burdensome, place unnecessary burdens on law-abiding citizens, and do not effectively prevent crime. They contend that criminals can still obtain ammunition through illegal means, and the added bureaucracy does little to enhance public safety. The practical challenges and limited effectiveness of ammunition background checks make this measure controversial. While the goal is to prevent crime, the implementation can create additional obstacles for responsible gun owners without reducing the risk posed by determined criminals.

## Waiting Periods

Waiting periods mandate a delay between the purchase of a firearm and its actual transfer to the buyer. These delays, which can range from a few days to several weeks, are intended to provide a cooling-off period to prevent impulsive acts of violence and to allow for thorough background checks. Supporters argue that waiting periods can reduce the risk of impulsive shootings, suicides, and domestic violence incidents. By imposing a mandatory delay, proponents believe that individuals may reconsider their actions or resolve conflicts without resorting to gun violence. Critics contend that waiting periods infringe on the rights of law-abiding citizens, particularly those who need immediate protection. They argue that individuals in imminent danger, such as victims of domestic violence, should not be forced to wait to obtain a means of self-defense. Opponents also question the effectiveness of waiting periods in preventing premeditated crimes. The assumption that a waiting period will prevent impulsive actions does not address the underlying issues driving violent behavior. Furthermore, waiting periods can leave individuals vulnerable to threats during the mandatory delay, undermining their ability to defend themselves.

## Limiting Gun Purchases

Some states limit the number of firearms an individual can purchase within a specified time frame, such as one gun per month. These limits aim to prevent stockpiling and trafficking of firearms. States like California and Virginia have implemented purchase limits to reduce gun violence. Limiting gun purchases is intended to prevent individuals from amassing large quantities of firearms that could be used for illegal trafficking or other malicious purposes. Proponents believe that purchase limits can help reduce the risk of firearms falling into the wrong hands. Critics argue that these limits are unnecessary, infringe on Second Amendment rights, and do not effectively prevent crime. They argue that these limits are arbitrary and do not consider the legitimate reasons individuals may have for purchasing multiple firearms. While the so-called intention of purchase limits is to reduce gun trafficking and violence, the practical impact on responsible gun owners can be disproportionate and unjustified.

## Restrictions on Certain Types of Firearms

Some states and countries restrict the ownership of specific types of firearms, such as short-barreled rifles, shotguns, and fully automatic weapons. These restrictions aim to limit access to particularly dangerous weapons. In the United States, the National Firearms Act of 1934 and the Gun Control Act of 1968 regulate these firearms. These laws were established to prevent the misuse of firearms with a high potential for mass casualties. However, critics argue that these restrictions are arbitrary and do not effectively reduce crime.

Restrictions on specific types of firearms are intended to prevent access to weapons perceived as particularly dangerous or unnecessary for civilian use. Proponents believe that limiting access to these firearms can reduce the potential for mass casualties and violent crime. They argue that certain firearms, due to their design and capability, pose a greater risk to public safety and therefore should be subject to stricter controls. For instance, fully automatic weapons can discharge multiple rounds with a single trigger pull, making them potentially more lethal in a short period.

Despite these intentions, critics contend that the restrictions are often arbitrary. They point out that while short-barreled rifles and shotguns are heavily regulated, other firearms with similar capabilities are not. This inconsistency suggests that the criteria for banning certain firearms may not be based on a thorough assessment of their actual danger or potential for misuse. The arbitrary nature of these bans can lead to confusion and frustration among law-abiding gun owners who see little difference between regulated and non-regulated firearms in terms of their functionality and potential for harm.

One of the main arguments against restrictions on specific types of firearms is that they do not effectively prevent crime. Data shows that most gun-related crimes are committed with handguns, which are less regulated than the firearms targeted by these bans. For example, despite the stringent regulations on semi-automatic rifles such as the AR-15 or AK-47s and their variants, their use in crimes is exceedingly rare. This indicates that the focus on banning specific types of firearms may be misplaced and that other measures could be more effective in reducing gun violence.

Furthermore, these firearm restrictions disproportionately affect law-abiding citizens who use these weapons for legal uses, such as hunting, sport shooting, and self-defense. The process of obtaining the necessary permits and complying with regulations can be burdensome and costly. Law-abiding citizens may face lengthy waiting periods, extensive background checks, and expensive fees, all of which can discourage lawful firearm ownership. This regulatory burden can be onerous for individuals who rely on these firearms for recreational or practical purposes.

Bans on certain kinds of guns are not only unconstitutional but also immoral. The Second Amendment explicitly guarantees the right of the people to keep and bear arms. Any attempt to undermine this fundamental right is a direct assault on the Constitution and the principles of individual liberty it enshrines. The ability to defend oneself, one's family, and one's property is a basic human right that should not be infringed by arbitrary regulations. These bans treat law-abiding citizens as potential criminals simply because they wish to exercise their constitutional rights.

Moreover, the argument that certain firearms are "unnecessary" for civilian use is both elitist and condescending. It assumes that the government has the authority to dictate what is and isn't necessary for personal protection and recreation, undermining individuals' right to make that decision for themselves. The morality of self-defense dictates that citizens must have access to effective means of protection, and in many cases, the firearms that are most effective for self-defense are those that are targeted by these bans.

The practical challenges and potential for overreach make these restrictions not only ineffective but dangerous. When the government starts deciding which firearms are permissible, it sets a dangerous precedent that could lead to further erosions of constitutional rights. The incremental nature of gun control measures means that each new regulation brings us closer to a society where the right to bear arms is severely restricted, if not entirely eliminated. This is not only a violation of the Second Amendment but a fundamental threat to personal liberty and security.

## Assault Weapons Bans

"Assault weapons" bans prohibit the sale, manufacture, and possession of certain semi-automatic firearms deemed "assault weapons" based on specific features such as detachable magazines, pistol grips, and folding stocks. Advocates argue that banning assault weapons can reduce the lethality of mass shootings and limit access to firearms designed for military use. They believe that such bans can prevent potential mass shooters from obtaining high-capacity, rapid-fire weapons. Critics argue that assault weapons bans are based on cosmetic features rather than functionality and do not effectively reduce crime. They contend that the term "assault weapon" is often misused and that many of the banned features do not noticeably affect a firearm's lethality. Assault weapons bans are often criticized for targeting firearms based on appearance rather than actual function. The arbitrary nature of these bans can lead to confusion and inconsistent enforcement. From a constitutional perspective, such bans infringe on the right to bear arms and fail to address the root causes of gun violence. Moreover, determined criminals can still obtain similar weapons through illegal channels.

## Magazine Bans and Capacity Limits

A magazine is the cartridge that holds and feeds the ammunition into the firearm. High-capacity magazine bans restrict the sale and possession of magazines that hold more than a specified number of rounds, typically 10. These bans aim to reduce the lethality of mass shootings by limiting the number of rounds a shooter can fire without reloading. Supporters argue that limiting magazine capacity can reduce the potential for mass casualties in shootings by forcing attackers to reload more frequently, providing opportunities for intervention. Critics contend that high-capacity magazine bans do not lower crime rates and infringe on Second Amendment rights. They argue that skilled shooters can quickly reload, and that such restrictions do not deter determined attackers. Additionally, opponents believe that these bans can disadvantage law-abiding citizens in self-defense situations. High-capacity magazine bans, they assert, also impose arbitrary limits on firearm accessories, which can be easily circumvented by criminals.

In addition, many standard capacity magazines have been reclassified as high capacity by various state laws and regulations. This reclassification often targets magazines that hold more than 10 rounds, despite their common use in many popular firearms for self-defense and sporting purposes. This arbitrary redefinition serves to restrict the rights of law-abiding gun owners by imposing limitations on commonly used equipment, which were previously considered standard in firearm design and functionality.

The effectiveness of these bans in preventing crime is questionable, as they do not address the underlying motivations for violent behavior. From a constitutional standpoint, such bans infringe on the right to keep and bear arms and fail to provide noticeable public safety benefits.

## The 2018 Bump Stock Ban

Bump stocks, devices that enable semi-automatic rifles to fire more rapidly, have been at the center of the gun control debate. Following the 2017 Las Vegas shooting, the ATF moved to ban bump stocks in 2018 by classifying them as machine guns under the National Firearms Act. This reclassification sparked constitutional challenges, as bump stocks do not alter a firearm's fundamental operation—each shot still requires a separate trigger pull.

Critics argue that the ATF overstepped its authority, as bump stocks merely enhance the rate of fire without converting semi-automatic rifles into true machine guns. They contend that accessories that do not fundamentally change a firearm's trigger mechanism should not be subject to machine gun regulations. The Supreme Court's 2008 *Heller* decision affirmed the right to own firearms in common use, and bump stocks, legally purchased by thousands before the ban, arguably fall under this protection.

The broader concern is regulatory overreach. If the government can unilaterally reclassify and ban an accessory, it sets a precedent for further restrictions.

Additionally, enforcing the ban has proven difficult, with many bump stocks still in circulation and no clear mechanism for compensating legal owners.

On June 14, 2024, the Supreme Court overturned the ban in *Garland v. Cargill*, ruling it unconstitutional and a case of executive overreach. In response, gun control advocates in the Senate attempted to pass new legislation banning bump stocks but were stalled by the filibuster. As a result, bump stocks remain legal, highlighting both the resilience of Second Amendment protections and the challenges gun control advocates face in navigating legislative hurdles.

## Red Flag Laws

Red flag laws, also known as extreme risk protection orders (ERPOs), allow law enforcement or family members to petition a court to temporarily remove firearms from individuals deemed a danger to themselves or others. These laws aim to prevent suicides and mass shootings by intervening before a crisis occurs. As of April 2025, 21 states and the District of Columbia have implemented red flag laws. While these laws are intended to act as preventive measures, identifying and disarming individuals who exhibit dangerous behavior before they can commit violence, they are not without controversy.

Between 2020 and 2022, red flag laws were invoked roughly 15,000 times nationwide—averaging just under 10 uses per 100,000 adults. Florida stands out as an exception, issuing over 21,000 orders since 2018 and approving petitions at rates of 97 to 99 percent. In contrast, many other states see sporadic use, with some jurisdictions barely aware the laws exist. After the Buffalo shooting in 2022, New York suddenly ramped up enforcement, issuing more red flag orders in three months than it had in the prior three years combined. These numbers tell a story not just of policy, but of inconsistency—where a law's impact depends less on its presence and more on whether anyone bothers to use it.

Critics argue that red flag laws can be abused and infringe on due process rights. The process of petitioning a court to remove someone's firearms typically involves a relatively low standard of evidence, such as "a preponderance of the evidence" or "reasonable suspicion." This can lead to firearm confiscation based on unverified or exaggerated claims. The lack of sufficient safeguards against false accusations means that an embittered ex-spouse, a disgruntled neighbor, or even a political adversary could misuse red flag laws to target an individual unfairly, resulting in the unjust confiscation of legally owned firearms.

The potential for abuse is exacerbated by the fact that red flag laws can bypass traditional legal processes. Firearms are often confiscated without a criminal conviction or proper legal proceedings, leading to what many see as a violation of constitutional rights. Typically, the accused individual is not present to defend themselves during the initial hearing. This ex parte proceeding can lead to a situation where an individual's property is seized without their knowledge or opportunity to contest the allegations. This lack of due process undermines the fundamental legal principle of being presumed innocent until proven guilty.

Furthermore, the implementation of red flag laws can erode trust in the legal system. When individuals see that firearms can be confiscated based on potentially flimsy or malicious accusations, they may become wary of the authorities and legal procedures intended to protect them. This distrust can be particularly damaging in communities where relationships with law enforcement are already strained. The perception that the legal system can be manipulated to unjustly target law-abiding citizens undermines confidence in the rule of law and the fair administration of justice.

In addition to these concerns, red flag laws do not effectively address the root causes of violent behavior. These laws are inherently reactive, relying on the identification and disarmament of individuals after they have already exhibited signs of dangerous behavior. They do little to address the underlying issues that contribute to such behavior, such as mental health problems, substance abuse, or socioeconomic factors. By focusing on the immediate removal of firearms, red flag laws can divert attention and resources away from more comprehensive and proactive measures that could prevent violent behavior from developing in the first place.

The temporary nature of red flag orders also raises questions about their long-term effectiveness. While removing firearms from an individual who poses a threat can prevent immediate harm, it does not necessarily resolve the underlying issues that led to the dangerous behavior. Once the order expires, the individual may still pose a threat, and without adequate support and intervention, the risk of future violence remains.

The use of red flag laws can also be compared to the practices of tyrannical governments and secret police in history, where snitching and baseless accusations were used to suppress dissent and control the populace. This historical parallel highlight the potential dangers of allowing individuals to be disarmed based on accusations that may lack solid evidence or due process. The fear of being unjustly targeted can have a chilling effect on free expression and the willingness to seek help for mental health issues, as individuals may worry that any sign of distress could lead to the loss of their constitutional rights.

While red flag laws are designed to prevent harm by disarming individuals who exhibit dangerous behavior, their implementation raises many concerns about due process, potential abuse, and the overall effectiveness of such measures.

## Safe Storage Laws

Safe storage laws require gun owners to securely store their firearms to prevent unauthorized access, particularly by children. These laws mandate the use of gun safes, trigger locks, and other safety devices. States like Massachusetts and California have implemented safe storage laws to reduce accidental shootings and gun thefts. Safe storage laws aim to enhance safety by ensuring that firearms are stored in a manner that prevents unauthorized access and accidental discharge. Proponents believe that these measures can reduce incidents of accidental shootings, particularly among children, and decrease the likelihood of stolen firearms being used in crimes.

While well-intentioned in theory, safe storage laws are often impractical and unenforceable in real-world scenarios. In the critical moments of a home invasion or break-in, the need to retrieve a firearm from a locked safe or to remove a trigger lock can mean the difference between life and death. Expecting an individual to calmly unlock their firearm or remember the combination under the duress of a potential life-threatening situation ignores the realities of high-stress emergencies. In the event of a break-in, every second counts. The idea of fumbling with keys or combinations while an intruder is already inside the home is not only impractical but potentially fatal. Safe storage laws place the homeowner in a vulnerable position, reducing their ability to respond effectively to a threat.

The purpose of keeping a firearm for home defense is to ensure quick and ready access in case of an emergency. Safe storage laws, by design, compromise this purpose by imposing barriers to immediate access. While the goal of preventing accidental shootings and unauthorized access is important, it must be balanced with the practical need for self-defense.

Moreover, the enforcement of safe storage laws poses significant challenges. Law enforcement agencies would need to conduct inspections to ensure compliance, raising serious concerns about privacy and the potential for governmental overreach. These inspections would likely require a lot of resources, diverting attention and funding away from more pressing public safety concerns. The effectiveness of such laws is also questionable, as criminals who intend to use firearms for illegal activities are unlikely to comply with safe storage requirements, leaving law-abiding citizens at a disadvantage.

Additionally, the assumption that safe storage laws will reduce accidental shootings and unauthorized access is not always supported by evidence. Education and training on responsible gun ownership and safety can be more effective in preventing accidents than rigid storage mandates. Promoting a culture of responsible gun use, where individuals are taught how to safely handle and store firearms, is likely to have a more substantial impact on reducing accidents and unauthorized use.

Safe storage laws vary across the US, with some states imposing strict requirements while others have minimal or no regulations. California and Massachusetts mandate that all firearms be stored in a locked container or with a locking device, regardless of household composition. New Jersey, Oregon, and Washington have similar laws, requiring secure storage if a minor or prohibited person could gain access. Connecticut, New York, Maryland, Illinois, and Colorado enforce safe storage laws specifically when minors or prohibited individuals are present in the home.

Enforcement of safe storage laws is largely reactive, typically triggered by firearm-related incidents rather than proactive inspections. The effectiveness, consistency, and enforcement of these laws is dependent upon local priorities and resources. It's also the inevitable consequence of control-obsessed, anti-gun busybodies who can't stand the idea of anyone making their own decisions—even within the privacy of their own home.

## Age Restrictions

Age restrictions set minimum age requirements for purchasing and possessing firearms. Federal law mandates that individuals must be at least 18 years old to purchase rifles and shotguns and 21 years old to purchase handguns. Some states have implemented stricter age requirements to further limit youth access to firearms. Proponents believe that setting minimum age requirements can reduce accidents, impulsive acts of violence, and youth involvement in crime. Opponents argue that age restrictions do not address the root causes of gun violence and unfairly restrict young adults' rights. Age restrictions aim to prevent firearms from being accessed by younger individuals who may lack the maturity or responsibility to handle them safely. Critics contend that age restrictions are arbitrary and do not consider the individual maturity and responsibility of young adults. They argue that denying legal adults the right to purchase firearms infringes on their constitutional rights and does not effectively prevent crime. The arbitrary nature of age restrictions and their potential infringement on rights make this measure contentious. While the intention is to promote safety, the practical impact on reducing gun violence is debatable, and the restrictions may unfairly limit the rights of responsible young adults.

On a different note, the argument that 18-year-olds should be allowed to exercise their constitutional right to purchase firearms is grounded in the recognition of their status as legal adults. If an 18-year-old can join the military and fight in a war, wielding sophisticated and deadly weaponry, it is inconsistent to deny them the right to buy a firearm upon reaching adulthood. Serving in the military requires a high level of responsibility, discipline, and trust. The same society that entrusts 18-year-olds with the defense of the nation and the lives of their fellow citizens should also trust them to responsibly exercise their Second Amendment rights.

The inconsistency extends to other adult privileges and responsibilities. If 18-year-olds are deemed mature enough to vote, a critical responsibility that shapes the direction of the country, it follows that they should also be considered responsible enough to purchase and own firearms. Voting is a important civic duty that requires sound judgment and an understanding of societal issues. Denying the right to purchase a firearm while allowing the right to vote sends a contradictory message about the maturity and responsibility of young adults. Either society recognizes 18-year-olds as fully legal adults with all the associated rights and responsibilities, or it does not. Picking and choosing which rights they can exercise undermines the coherence of the legal and social framework regarding adulthood.

## Gun-Free Zones

Gun-free zones prohibit firearms in designated areas such as schools, government buildings, and certain public spaces. These zones are established by state and local governments with the intent of enhancing public safety by reducing the presence of firearms in high-risk or sensitive locations. Proponents argue that restricting guns in these areas lowers the likelihood of gun-related violence, prevents potential conflicts from escalating, and fosters a sense of security. They believe that keeping firearms out of certain spaces minimizes opportunities for accidents or impulsive acts of violence.

However, opponents argue that gun-free zones do the opposite of what they intend. They contend that criminals, who by definition do not follow the law, are not deterred by these restrictions. Instead, these zones effectively disarm law-abiding citizens, leaving them defenseless against threats. Critics point out that mass shooters and criminals often deliberately target gun-free zones, knowing they are less likely to face armed resistance. Rather than preventing violence, these zones can create "soft targets" where victims have no means to defend themselves, potentially increasing the risk of harm.

While the goal of gun-free zones is to enhance safety, their effectiveness remains highly debated. Rather than preventing violence, they often create environments where only criminals remain armed, leaving law-abiding citizens vulnerable.

## Mandatory Gun Buybacks

Mandatory gun buybacks are a misleading and coercive government policy in which the state forces individuals to surrender their privately owned firearms, often for a fraction of their true value. Mandatory gun buybacks involve the government "purchasing" firearms from citizens, often at market value, to reduce the number of guns in circulation. Australia implemented a gun buyback program following a mass shooting in 1996, resulting in the confiscation and destruction of over 600,000 firearms. Mandatory gun buybacks aim to reduce the number of firearms in circulation by incentivizing or compelling owners to sell their guns to the government. Proponents believe that reducing the overall number of guns can lower the incidence of gun violence and mass shootings. Critics contend that buybacks do not effectively reduce crime, as criminals are unlikely to participate, and the focus on reducing gun numbers overlooks the behavior and intentions of individuals. Critics argue that buybacks are ineffective, costly, and infringe on property rights.

The term "buyback" itself is a non sequitur, as it implies the government is "buying back" something that was never theirs to begin with. In reality, it is a forced confiscation disguised as a transaction. The key word here is "mandatory," which strips citizens of their voluntary participation and effectively turns it into an act of seizure. This type of policy does not just infringe on Second Amendment rights; it devalues personal property by offering minimal compensation. The notion that the government can dictate the surrender of constitutionally protected items underlines the dangerous implications for individual liberty.

## Licensing Requirements

Licensing requires individuals to obtain a permit to purchase, own, or carry firearms. These permits often involve mandatory background checks, training courses, and other qualifications to ensure that only responsible individuals can own guns. Supporters argue that licensing can promote responsible gun ownership by ensuring that individuals meet specific criteria before acquiring firearms. They believe that mandatory background checks and training can reduce acci-

dents, misuse, and gun-related violence. Critics contend that licensing requirements create unnecessary barriers to exercising Second Amendment rights. They
argue that the process can be overly burdensome, discriminatory, and subject to
bureaucratic delays. Additionally, opponents believe that responsible gun owners should not be penalized for the actions of a few irresponsible individuals.
Licensing requirements are often seen as an infringement on the constitutional
right to bear arms. The process can be time-consuming, expensive, and subject
to arbitrary criteria. Furthermore, licensing does not address the behavior of
criminals who obtain firearms through illegal means.

## Firearm Identification Cards

Firearm identification cards (FIDs) require individuals to obtain a card or permit
to purchase, own, or carry firearms. These cards often involve background checks,
training courses, and other qualifications. States like Massachusetts and Illinois
require FIDs. While proponents believe that FIDs can promote responsible gun
ownership and enhance public safety, opponents argue that these cards create
unnecessary barriers and infringe on personal freedoms.

The process of obtaining a firearm identification card typically involves navigating a complex bureaucratic system. Applicants must undergo extensive background checks, complete mandatory training courses, and meet various qualifications. This process can be time-consuming and confusing, deterring many
law-abiding citizens from pursuing legal firearm ownership. For instance, in states
like Massachusetts, the application process can take several weeks or even months,
involving multiple trips to police stations, training facilities, and other regulatory
offices. The bureaucratic nature of these requirements adds layers of red tape that
can discourage responsible individuals from exercising their Second Amendment
rights.

The financial burden associated with obtaining an FID is another big concern.
Costs can include application fees, fingerprinting fees, training course fees, and
sometimes additional expenses for mandatory safety equipment. For low-income
individuals, these costs—which can amount to several hundred dollars—can be
prohibitive, effectively pricing them out of legal gun ownership.

Critics argue that FIDs infringe on individuals' constitutional rights by imposing preconditions on the exercise of the Second Amendment. The requirement to obtain a permit or card before purchasing, owning, or carrying a firearm introduces a government-controlled gatekeeping mechanism that can be seen as an infringement on the right to bear arms. The process itself, with its multiple steps and approvals, can be viewed as an undue burden that restricts an individual's ability to freely exercise their constitutional rights. This perspective is especially relevant in light of the Supreme Court's decision in *District of Columbia v. Heller*, which affirmed that the Second Amendment protects an individual's right to possess firearms unconnected with service in a militia and to use them for lawful purposes such as self-defense.

The practical implementation of FIDs can also be discriminatory. Studies have shown that marginalized communities, including racial minorities and low-income individuals, face higher barriers to obtaining these permits, making it more difficult for them to protect themselves and their families. Factors such as lack of access to required training facilities, limited financial resources, and potential biases in the approval process contribute to this disparity. Those who may be most in need of self-defense options are the least likely to be able to legally obtain a firearm.

Another critical argument against FIDs is their limited impact on preventing crime. Criminals do not comply with legal requirements for firearm ownership. They are unlikely to go through the process of obtaining an FID and will instead obtain firearms through illegal means. This misalignment means that FIDs do little to address the behavior of criminals, undermining the measure's effectiveness in enhancing public safety.

The practical challenges of implementing and maintaining a system of FIDs are also significant. The administrative burden on law enforcement agencies and other regulatory bodies can be substantial. The need to process applications, conduct background checks, administer training programs, and maintain up-to-date records requires much investment in time, personnel, and technology. This resource allocation can strain public safety budgets and reduce the overall efficiency of law enforcement operations.

While the goal of FIDs is to regulate firearm ownership and promote safety, the measure creates unnecessary obstacles for responsible gun owners without effectively addressing the behavior of criminals.

## Guns as "Public Health Emergencies"

In recent years, the federal government and gun control advocacy groups have rebranded the gun control debate as a "public health emergency," targeting gun ownership and gun violence. The notion that guns constitute a public health crisis is a strategic maneuver employed by various administrative agencies and advocacy groups to regulate firearms through a different lens. This tactic, while ostensibly branded as improving public safety, is fraught with dishonesty and potential dangers. By reclassifying gun violence and gun ownership in general as a public health issue, proponents seek to sidestep traditional legislative processes and impose regulations through health and safety mandates.

This approach has been notably pursued by entities such as the Centers for Disease Control and Prevention (CDC) and other public health organizations. The argument hinges on the idea that gun-related injuries and deaths should be treated similarly to diseases or other public health concerns, thereby justifying a range of restrictive measures. However, this classification is fundamentally flawed and misleading. Unlike infectious diseases, which spread through pathogens, gun violence is a complex social issue with multifaceted causes, including crime, socioeconomic factors, and mental health issues.

The dishonesty of this tactic lies in its oversimplification of the problem. By labeling guns themselves as the crisis, rather than addressing the underlying issues that lead to violence, proponents avoid tackling the real root causes of gun violence. This approach also opens the door to broad and sweeping regulations that infringe upon Second Amendment rights. The focus shifts from addressing criminal behavior and improving community safety to restricting the rights of law-abiding citizens under the guise of public health.

Recent attempts to classify gun violence as a public health crisis have included proposals to fund research into gun violence prevention through health agencies, as well as efforts to impose stricter regulations on gun ownership and usage by framing it as a health emergency. For instance, some states have tried to pass legislation that would enable public health departments to track gun ownership and use, similar to how they monitor contagious diseases. Gun rights advocates see it as a backdoor method to impose gun control without legislative debate.

A notable instance occurred in 2021 when the Biden administration declared gun violence a public health epidemic and directed federal resources toward addressing it. The administration's plan included funding for the CDC to research gun violence as a health issue, attempting to reframe the debate around gun control by leveraging public health narratives. There were also efforts to empower administrative agencies such as the Department of Health and Human Services (HHS) with greater authority to collect data on gun ownership and implement regulations under the pretense of addressing the public health emergency. This move aimed to bypass the legislative gridlock that often stalls gun control measures in Congress, raising alarms about executive overreach and the potential erosion of constitutional rights.

By treating gun ownership as a health issue, it becomes easier to justify invasive and broad-reaching restrictions that would be unacceptable under normal regulatory frameworks. This could lead to mandatory reporting of gun ownership to health agencies, increased scrutiny and surveillance of gun owners, and potentially even confiscation measures in extreme cases.

The dangers of this reclassification are manifold. First and foremost, it undermines the constitutional protections afforded by the Second Amendment. This tactic also sets a concerning precedent for how other rights and freedoms might be restricted in the future. If gun ownership can be redefined as a public health crisis, what other rights might be similarly reclassified to justify greater governmental control? It would only be a matter of time before freedom of speech and opposing viewpoints are similarly reclassified and restricted. This approach would erode trust in the already-tainted public health institutions, which are meant to protect and improve the well-being of citizens, not infringe upon their fundamental rights.

The recent moves by the federal government to reclassify guns as a public health emergency underscore the need for vigilance and advocacy to protect Second Amendment rights from being eroded under the guise of public health. It is crucial to challenge this narrative and promote policies that genuinely enhance public safety without compromising fundamental freedoms.

## Insurance Requirements

Some proposed gun control measures include mandatory liability insurance for gun owners to cover potential damages caused by their firearms. Proponents believe that this measure can incentivize safe gun storage and handling practices while providing a financial safety net for victims.

However, critics argue that insurance requirements are burdensome, expensive, and unlikely to prevent crime. Annual premiums could range from hundreds to thousands of dollars, depending on the coverage required and the perceived risk associated with owning a firearm. These costs could deter law-abiding citizens from owning guns, effectively limiting their Second Amendment rights through financial means. This is particularly problematic for residents of high-crime areas who may need firearms for personal protection but cannot afford the additional financial burden.

Beyond the financial aspect, the implementation of mandatory liability insurance introduces significant bureaucratic hurdles. Gun owners would be required to navigate complex insurance markets, obtain quotes, and purchase policies that meet regulatory standards. This process can be time-consuming and confusing. The requirement to maintain proof of insurance and potentially face penalties for lapses in coverage adds another layer of stress and administrative oversight. The intrusive nature of these requirements can discourage responsible gun ownership by creating unnecessary obstacles.

Critics also argue that mandatory liability insurance is unlikely to have a meaningful impact on crime prevention. Criminals do not adhere to laws, including insurance mandates. Therefore, those most likely to commit gun-related crimes would not be deterred by the requirement to carry liability insurance. Instead, the burden falls on law-abiding citizens who are already inclined to follow the law and practice safe gun ownership. This disconnect means that the policy does little to address the root causes of gun violence or to prevent firearms from falling into the wrong hands.

There are also concerns about the unintended consequences of such a policy. Insurers could impose restrictions or conditions that go beyond state and federal regulations, such as requiring gun owners to invest in expensive safety equipment or limiting the types of firearms that can be insured. These additional requirements could further increase the cost and complexity of owning a firearm, making it even more difficult for ordinary citizens to comply. Insurance companies could deny coverage to individuals deemed high-risk, effectively creating a de facto ban on gun ownership for certain groups.

While the intention behind mandatory liability insurance is to promote responsibility and provide compensation for victims, there are more effective and less burdensome ways to achieve these goals. For example, investing in community-based violence prevention programs, improving mental health services, and enhancing law enforcement capabilities can address the root causes of gun violence more directly. Encouraging voluntary safe storage practices through education and providing financial incentives for the purchase of gun safes and other safety equipment can also promote responsible gun ownership without imposing prohibitive costs.

## Microstamping

Microstamping requires firearms to imprint a unique code on each cartridge case when fired, allowing law enforcement to trace spent casings back to the firearm. California has implemented microstamping requirements to aid in criminal investigations. Microstamping is intended to provide law enforcement with a tool to trace firearms used in crimes by linking spent casings to the guns that fired them. Proponents believe that this technology can help solve crimes and deter illegal gun use. Opponents argue that the technology is unproven, expensive, and easily circumvented. Microstamping technology is unreliable, can be easily tampered with or bypassed, and imposes expensive costs on manufacturers and consumers. Critics contend that the benefits are minimal compared to the practical challenges and expenses involved. The reliability and cost issues associated with microstamping make this measure contentious. While the goal is to aid law enforcement, the practical implementation can be problematic, and the effectiveness in solving crimes is debatable.

## Ballistic Fingerprinting

Ballistic fingerprinting involves creating a database of unique markings on bullets and casings fired from specific firearms. This database can be used to match spent casings to firearms used in crimes. Maryland and New York have implemented ballistic fingerprinting programs to aid in criminal investigations. Ballistic fingerprinting aims to provide law enforcement with a tool to trace firearms used in crimes by linking spent casings to the guns that fired them. Proponents believe that this technology can help solve crimes and deter illegal gun use. Opponents argue that the technology is unreliable, can be easily tampered with or bypassed, and imposes significant costs on manufacturers and consumers. They contend that the benefits are minimal compared to the practical challenges and expenses involved. While the goal of ballistic fingerprinting is to aid law enforcement, its practical implementation can be problematic, and its effectiveness in solving crimes is debatable.

## Smart Gun Technology

Smart gun technology involves firearms equipped with features like biometric readers or RFID chips that restrict use to authorized individuals. New Jersey, for one, has passed laws promoting the development and sale of smart guns. This technology aims to prevent unauthorized access and reduce accidental shootings. However, this technology also raises concerns and potential dangers.

Smart gun technology is intended to enhance firearm safety by ensuring that only authorized users can operate the weapon. Proponents believe that this technology can reduce accidental shootings and prevent firearms from being used by unauthorized individuals, such as children or thieves. Opponents argue that the technology is unreliable, expensive, and infringes on Second Amendment rights. Critics argue that smart gun technology can fail in critical situations. They contend that the added expense and potential for malfunction make this technology impractical for widespread use. And they believe that mandating smart gun technology infringes on Second Amendment rights by imposing unnecessary restrictions on firearm ownership. Reliability concerns, cost, and potential infringement on rights make smart gun technology contentious.

One of the primary concerns is the reliability of smart gun technology in emergency situations. Firearms are often used in high-stress, life-threatening scenarios where every second counts. If a smart gun fails to recognize its authorized user due to a malfunction or a simple technological glitch, it could lead to catastrophic consequences. For instance, biometric readers might fail to recognize a user's fingerprint if their hands are wet, dirty, or injured, potentially preventing the gun from firing when it is most needed.

And not everyone is tech-savvy. Introducing complex technology into firearms could create barriers for some gun owners, particularly older individuals, or those not familiar with digital devices. In a crisis, having to troubleshoot a gun's technology could mean the difference between life and death.

Another major concern is the potential for external control and monitoring. Smart guns could, in theory, be programmed or updated remotely, raising the possibility that regulators or hackers could disable firearms or track their use. Just as cell phones and other smart devices can be monitored and controlled, so too could smart guns, leading to a loss of control for the gun owner.

The risk of hacking is particularly troubling. If smart guns are connected to networks or utilize wireless technology, they could become vulnerable to cyberattacks. Hackers could potentially disable a firearm remotely, rendering it useless in a critical moment. They could also potentially track the firearm's usage, leading to privacy violations.

The cost of smart guns is another factor to consider. Integrating advanced technology into firearms will undoubtedly increase their price, potentially making them less accessible to law-abiding citizens who rely on firearms for personal protection. This could disproportionately affect low-income individuals who may be unable to afford these more expensive, more technologically advanced firearms.

The introduction of smart gun technology could also lead to legislative and regulatory mandates requiring all firearms to incorporate such features. This could ultimately result in a de facto ban on traditional firearms, infringing upon

Second Amendment rights. The fear of such regulations is not unfounded, as there have been numerous legislative attempts to mandate the use of smart gun technology.

While the intention behind smart guns is to enhance safety, the potential dangers and drawbacks of this technology cannot be overlooked. From reliability issues and barriers to use in emergencies to privacy concerns and the risk of hacking, smart guns introduce detrimental risks that could outweigh their benefits. These concerns must be carefully weighed before any widespread adoption or legislative mandates are considered.

***

Gun control measures, from background checks to outright confiscation, are often justified as necessary for reducing gun violence and ensuring public safety. However, the real impact of these policies frequently raises concerns about their effectiveness, constitutional overreach, and potential for abuse. Critics argue that many of these laws are not about safety but about control, creating legal barriers that disproportionately target law-abiding citizens while doing little to deter criminals.

This pattern of overreach is particularly evident in the National Firearms Act (NFA), a foundational piece of gun control legislation that set the stage for modern restrictions and the bureaucratic enforcement power of the ATF. The ATF, acting as an unelected regulatory force, has systematically eroded Second Amendment rights through arbitrary rule changes and heavy-handed enforcement. As we examine the NFA's legacy, the role of the ATF, and the stark contrasts between anti-gun and pro-gun states, it becomes clear how an intricate web of confusing and unconstitutional laws is designed to entrap law-abiding citizens. We will also explore how executive actions have been weaponized to bypass legislative processes, further restricting gun rights through unilateral mandates.

This patchwork of overreach isn't accidental—it's the result of decades of incremental power grabs that began with laws like the National Firearms Act. To understand how we got here, we have to go back to where federal gun control first took root.

## The National Firearms Act: A Major Gun Control Hurdle

The National Firearms Act (NFA) of 1934 represents one of the earliest attempts by the Federal government to regulate firearms in the United States. It was enacted in response to the rampant violence associated with organized crime during the Prohibition era, particularly the use of automatic weapons and other "gangster" firearms. Despite its initial intent, the NFA has been a source of contention and legal challenges ever since, with critics arguing that it imposes unconstitutional burdens on law-abiding citizens and fails to effectively address criminal misuse of firearms.

The NFA was primarily designed to regulate the manufacture, sale, and possession of certain types of firearms deemed particularly dangerous, such as machine guns, short-barreled rifles and shotguns, silencers, and other devices considered "destructive" or "exotic." The Act imposed a tax on the manufacture and transfer of these firearms and required their registration with the federal government. Specifically, it mandated a $200 tax on the manufacture or transfer of these weapons, a significant sum at the time (equivalent to about $4,800 today), intended to dissuade individuals from acquiring them.

From its inception, the NFA faced legal challenges. One of the most notable cases was *United States v. Miller* (1939), where the Supreme Court upheld the NFA's provisions. As discussed in chapter 5, the case involved two men charged and convicted with transporting an unregistered short-barreled shotgun across state lines, which they argued was a violation of their Second Amendment rights. The Court ruled that because the defendants failed to demonstrate that their firearm had any reasonable relationship to the preservation or efficiency of a well-regulated militia, the Second Amendment did not guarantee the right to keep and bear such an instrument. This decision effectively endorsed the NFA's restrictions but also left room for future debate on what constitutes a "militia-useful" weapon.

Critics of the NFA argue that it places unnecessary burdens on law-abiding citizens. The stringent registration requirements and the hefty tax can be prohibitive, especially for those who want to collect or use these firearms legally.

Moreover, the frequent changes in rules and regulations by the Bureau of Alcohol, Tobacco, Firearms and Explosives (ATF), discussed below, have added layers of complexity and confusion. The definition of a "short-barreled rifle" or an "automatic weapon," for instance, has been subject to reinterpretation, leading to legal ambiguities that can trap unsuspecting gun owners.

The arguments against the NFA's constitutionality center on the Second Amendment's protection of the right to bear arms. Opponents claim that the NFA's regulations infringe upon this right by imposing taxes and registration requirements that effectively limit the ability of citizens to own certain firearms. They argue that the Act creates a de facto ban on these weapons for those who cannot afford the taxes or navigate the complex regulatory landscape, thus undermining the Second Amendment.

Furthermore, the arbitrary and vague nature of some NFA regulations has led to legal troubles for individuals. For example, gun owners who unknowingly possess a firearm part that, when combined with another part, could be classified as a restricted item under the NFA, can face severe penalties. This was evident in the case of a man who was arrested for possessing a piece of plastic classified as a machine gun part under the NFA. The absurdity of such regulations highlights the overreach and impracticality of the NFA.

The NFA represents a significant federal effort to regulate firearms, but its implementation has been fraught with controversy and legal challenges. The frequent changes in regulations, the burdensome tax, and the complex registration requirements have placed undue strain on law-abiding citizens, often resulting in legal trouble for minor or unintentional infractions.

Over the years, there have been various efforts to repeal or reform the NFA. Advocacy groups like the National Rifle Association (NRA) and the Gun Owners of America (GOA) have consistently lobbied against the Act, arguing that it is an outdated and unconstitutional measure that punishes law-abiding citizens. Legislative efforts have been made to remove suppressors (silencers) from the NFA's purview, with proponents arguing that these devices are essential for hearing protection and have legitimate sporting uses.

Despite these efforts, the NFA remains in force, due to political resistance and the perception that these types of firearms pose a public safety risk. However, the push for its repeal continues.

## The Bureau of Alcohol, Tobacco, Firearms and Explosives

The Bureau of Alcohol, Tobacco, Firearms and Explosives (ATF) is a federal law enforcement agency within the United States Department of Justice. The ATF is tasked with enforcing federal laws related to alcohol, tobacco, firearms, explosives, and arson. Its primary mission is to protect communities from violent criminals, criminal organizations, illegal use and trafficking of firearms, illegal use and storage of explosives, acts of arson and bombings, acts of terrorism, and the illegal diversion of alcohol and tobacco products.

The ATF has a long and ever-evolving history, rooted in the federal government's desire to regulate and tax certain industries. Originally emerging from the taxation of distilled spirits in 1789, the agency's role expanded during the Civil War when the Office of Internal Revenue was created to enforce excise taxes on alcohol and tobacco. Prohibition in the 1920s saw a surge in federal enforcement, leading to the establishment of the Alcohol Tax Unit (ATU) within the Treasury Department. Over the following decades, its scope continued to grow, culminating in the passage of the Gun Control Act of 1968, which brought firearms under its jurisdiction and led to its renaming as the Alcohol, Tobacco, and Firearms Division (ATF). In 1972, the ATF became a standalone bureau within the Treasury Department, tasked with enforcing federal gun laws alongside its regulatory duties. However, its most notable transformation came in 2003, when it was moved to the Department of Justice under the Homeland Security Act, solidifying its role as a federal law enforcement agency with broad regulatory power over firearms. Over time, the ATF has morphed from a tax-collection agency into a powerful, unelected bureaucracy with a history of overreach, undermining the Second Amendment through arbitrary rule changes, aggressive enforcement tactics, and regulatory expansions that go far beyond its original mandate.

To those unfamiliar with its operations outside of its name, the ATF may seem like a necessary and reasonable federal agency dedicated to protecting communities. However, the ATF has a long history of controversial practices and operations that have raised serious concerns among Second Amendment advocates and civil libertarians. Over the years, the ATF has been accused of harassment, intimidation, and even illegal actions against law-abiding gun owners, gun stores, and firearms manufacturers. These actions have been well documented and perceived as a direct assault on the Second Amendment and individual freedoms, fostering a climate of fear and mistrust.

One of the most alarming aspects of the ATF's operations is its use of harassment and intimidation tactics against gun owners and businesses. Warrantless searches, home raids, and the confiscation of legally owned firearms have become increasingly common. In many instances, these actions are based on vague or dubious suspicions, often resulting in much distress and financial hardship for those targeted.

For example, in recent years, there have been multiple reports of ATF agents conducting warrantless "knock and talk" visits to gun owners' homes. These visits involve agents arriving unannounced and demanding to see firearms and related paperwork, often without presenting a warrant. Such actions raise serious Fourth Amendment concerns, as they circumvent the legal requirement for a warrant based on probable cause.

The ATF has also been involved in high-profile raids and confiscations of firearms from individuals and businesses. One notable case is the raid on Ares Armor in 2014, a California-based company that legally sold unfinished lower receivers, which are not classified as firearms under federal law. Despite the company's compliance with existing regulations, the ATF conducted a raid, seizing customer records and inventory. This heavy-handed approach highlighted the agency's willingness to target businesses operating within the bounds of the law.

Similarly, the ATF's actions against Polymer80, a manufacturer of gun parts, in December 2020, drew widespread condemnation. The ATF raided the company's Nevada facility, seizing inventory and customer records. The raid was based on the ATF's reclassification of certain gun parts as firearms, despite the lack of a clear legal basis for such a designation. This reclassification and subsequent raid underscore the agency's arbitrary and often opaque decision-making process.

The ATF's unconstitutional practices extend to entrapment schemes, where agents encourage individuals to engage in illegal activities and then arrest them. One of the most egregious examples of this was the "Fast and Furious" operation during the Obama years, where the ATF allowed firearms to be sold to known straw purchasers with the intent of tracing the guns to Mexican drug cartels. This operation resulted in the loss of hundreds of firearms, some of which were later used in crimes, including the murder of Border Patrol Agent Brian Terry.

The operation's fallout highlighted the agency's reckless disregard for legal and ethical standards, as well as the dire risks posed to public safety. It also raised questions about the ATF's oversight and accountability, as the operation was conducted with minimal transparency and led to severe consequences.

## How the ATF is Weaponized Against Gun Owners

In recent years, the ATF has come under intense scrutiny and criticism for targeting political opponents and Second Amendment advocates at the behest of the Biden administration's Justice Department. This perceived weaponization of the ATF has sparked outrage among gun owners, firearms enthusiasts, and independent and conservative groups who see these actions as a direct attack on their constitutional rights.

When Democrat Joe Biden took the Oval Office in January 2021, numerous reports have surfaced that the ATF has increasingly focused its enforcement efforts on individuals and entities associated with pro-gun and conservative causes. Gun store owners, YouTubers specializing in firearms content, and outspoken Second Amendment advocates have reported heightened scrutiny and enforcement actions, which many believe are politically motivated. For instance, some prominent YouTubers who promote gun safety and review firearms have claimed that they have been unfairly targeted for minor infractions or technical violations. These actions are an attempt to silence voices that advocate for gun rights and to intimidate others in the community from speaking out.

Gun store owners have also found themselves in the crosshairs of the ATF. Numerous accounts have surfaced of ATF agents conducting surprise inspections and raids, often citing obscure and minor paperwork errors as justification for severe penalties or the revocation of licenses. This aggressive approach has led many to believe that the ATF is using its regulatory power to shut down businesses that legally sell firearms, thereby restricting access to guns through bureaucratic means. A notable case involved a gun store owner in Texas who claimed that the ATF conducted multiple exhaustive inspections within a short period, each time focusing on trivial administrative errors to justify heavy penalties. These actions have been perceived as part of a broader strategy to undermine the gun industry and reduce the availability of firearms to the general public.

The aggressive tactics employed by the ATF have generated widespread outrage among the firearms community and in conservative circles. Many see these actions as an overreach of federal power and a direct assault on the Second Amendment. The backlash has been amplified by some media outlets and pro-gun organizations, who have highlighted these cases to rally opposition against what they view as an authoritarian crackdown on constitutional rights.

This perceived targeting of political opponents by the ATF has further polarized an already divided nation. It has galvanized Second Amendment advocates and gun rights organizations, leading to increased activism and political mobilization against what they see as an oppressive government agenda. The situation has also drawn criticism from legal experts and civil liberties advocates, who argue that the ATF's actions undermine due process and the rule of law by punishing individuals and businesses for minor or technical violations.

There was a case where the ATF conducted a warrantless raid on a homeowner's property. The homeowner, who had legally acquired and registered his firearms, was taken aback when ATF agents arrived unannounced and demanded to inspect his collection without presenting a warrant. This incident underscores the agency's disregard for Fourth Amendment protections against unreasonable searches and seizures.

Another example involved the ATF's crackdown on a small gun shop for minor paperwork errors. Despite the shop owner's long-standing compliance with federal regulations, the ATF shut down his business over trivial infractions.

The ATF also arbitrarily reclassifies certain gun parts as actual firearms. In one instance, an individual was arrested for possessing a piece of plastic that the ATF had recently designated as a machine gun component. The arbitrary nature of such classifications leaves gun owners vulnerable to sudden legal jeopardy. One day you're a law-abiding citizen, and the next you're a felon because the ATF changed their mind about what constitutes a firearm.

The ATF's actions, particularly under the former Biden administration, also have ignited a firestorm of controversy and resistance from those who view them as politically motivated attacks on gun owners and Second Amendment supporters. This has not only intensified the national debate over gun control but also raised serious concerns about the potential misuse of federal power to target political opponents. By employing harassment, intimidation, and entrapment tactics, the agency undermines the constitutional rights of Americans and creates an environment of fear and uncertainty. These practices are not only unconstitutional but also counterproductive. They alienate law-abiding citizens and businesses, pushing gun ownership further underground and fostering distrust in government institutions. The Second Amendment was designed to protect the individual's right to bear arms and defend against tyranny, yet the ATF's actions appear to embody the very tyranny the Amendment seeks to guard against.

Former Congressman Matt Gaetz (R-FL) introduced a bill to dismantle the agency in 2021, citing its long history of targeting law-abiding gun owners instead of criminals. Abolishing the ATF would eliminate an agency that has repeatedly ignored the Constitution and reassign its legitimate functions to other agencies like the FBI and DEA, which already handle firearms-related crimes without the ATF's history of corruption, harassment, and abuse. This move would reduce bureaucratic redundancy while strengthening constitutional protections. Abolishing the ATF sits high on the wish list of most gun owners and Second Amendment advocates, as it would not only remove yet another bureaucratic obstacle but also put an end to the agency's long-standing pattern of overreach and abuse toward law-abiding gun owners.

As we turn our attention to the sharp divide between pro-gun and anti-gun states, the ATF's inconsistent enforcement only highlights how wildly different the Second Amendment is treated depending on where you live. This disparity exposes a deeper constitutional crisis—one where your rights hinge on your zip code. It's a reality that not only undermines equal protection under the law but also reinforces the urgent need to restore nationwide respect for the Second Amendment.

## Pro-Gun vs. Anti-Gun States

In the United States, the divergence in gun laws between states reveals a large contrast in how Second Amendment rights are interpreted and enforced. The comparison between three of the most pro-gun states—where constitutional rights are highly respected—and three of the most anti-gun states—where stringent gun control measures are prevalent—highlights big differences in the legal landscape and the implications for residents.

The pro-gun states often cited as examples of robust Second Amendment protections are Texas, Arizona, and Alaska. These states have embraced constitutional carry laws, which allow individuals to carry firearms without a permit, reflecting a commitment to the fundamental right to bear arms.

Texas is a prime example of a pro-gun state where constitutional carry is the law of the land. In 2021, Texas passed House Bill 1927, which permits residents to carry handguns without a license. This law underscores the state's belief in the right to self-defense and personal freedom. Texas has a strong stand-your-ground law, which allows individuals to use deadly force if they believe it is necessary to protect themselves from a threat without the duty to retreat. The state also protects gun owners from federal overreach through laws like the Second Amendment Protection Act, which restricts state and local law enforcement from enforcing federal gun laws deemed unconstitutional.

Arizona, another pro-gun state, also allows constitutional carry. Since 2010, Arizona residents have been able to carry concealed firearms without a permit. The state has lenient open carry laws and does not require background checks for private gun sales. Arizona's approach to gun laws emphasizes individual responsibility and the belief that an armed populace is a safer populace. The state's commitment to Second Amendment rights is evident in its legislation that prohibits local governments from enacting their own gun control measures, ensuring uniformity and protection of gun rights across the state.

Alaska rounds out this list with its strong constitutional carry law in place since 2003. Alaskans can carry firearms openly or concealed without a permit, reflecting the state's frontier spirit and emphasis on self-reliance. The state also allows non-residents to carry firearms without a permit and does not impose waiting periods for gun purchases. Alaska's laws prioritize the right of individuals to defend themselves and their families in a state where many residents live in remote areas with limited law enforcement presence.

In contrast, three of the most anti-gun states—California, New York, and New Jersey—enforce some of the strictest gun control laws in the nation, often at odds with the constitutional protections upheld in pro-gun states.

California is known for its comprehensive and restrictive gun control measures. The state has banned the sale of assault weapons and large-capacity magazines, requiring existing owners to register these firearms with the state. California imposes a 10-day waiting period for all gun purchases, mandatory background checks for all firearm sales, including private transactions, and strict regulations on concealed carry permits, which are issued on a may-issue basis and subject to local law enforcement discretion. California also has safe storage laws, requiring gun owners to store firearms in locked containers or use trigger locks when not in use. The state's approach reflects a belief that stringent regulations are necessary to prevent gun violence, but critics argue that these measures infringe on the rights of law-abiding citizens.

New York's gun laws are similarly restrictive. In response to the Supreme Court's decision in *New York State Rifle & Pistol Association Inc. v. Bruen*, New York enacted new laws that further tightened gun control. These laws include stringent requirements for obtaining a concealed carry license, such as in-person interviews, detailed disclosure of social media accounts, and character references. New York also bans assault weapons, limits magazine capacities, and mandates background checks for all gun sales. The state's SAFE Act, passed in 2013, introduced measures like mandatory background checks for ammunition purchases and mental health reporting requirements.

New Jersey is another state with the most restrictive gun laws in the country. The state requires permits for both purchasing and carrying firearms, with a complex application process that includes background checks, references, and approval from local law enforcement. New Jersey has banned assault weapons and limits magazine capacities to 10 rounds. The state also enforces stringent storage requirements and has a red flag law that allows firearms to be confiscated from individuals deemed a threat to themselves or others.

The differences between pro-gun and anti-gun states extend beyond regulations to the practical implications for residents. In states like California, New York, and New Jersey, legitimate self-defense with a firearm can result in legal complications and potential imprisonment. Individuals who use a firearm in self-defense may face scrutiny over whether they complied with the state's strict storage laws or whether their firearm met the state's stringent legal requirements. In contrast, residents of pro-gun states like Texas, Arizona, and Alaska enjoy greater legal protections when using firearms for self-defense, reflecting a broader respect for the right to bear arms.

The restrictive gun control measures in anti-gun states are often criticized as unconstitutional, oppressive, and immoral. These laws are seen as infringing on the fundamental right to self-defense, disproportionately affecting law-abiding citizens, while failing to address the root causes of gun violence. The imposition of extensive regulations and the creation of bureaucratic hurdles undermine the constitutional guarantee of the right to bear arms, leading to a form of state overreach that contradicts the principles of individual liberty and personal responsibility.

Moreover, the strict gun control laws in these states can leave residents vulnerable, as they may be unable to defend themselves effectively in dangerous situations. The prohibition of certain firearms and the imposition of restrictive permitting processes mean that individuals are often left without the means to protect themselves and their families. This reality highlights the moral dilemma of disarming citizens and stripping them of their ability to defend their own lives in the face of imminent threats.

The contrast between these pro-gun and anti-gun states illustrates the profound differences in how Second Amendment rights are respected and enforced across the United States. The trend towards greater gun rights in pro-gun states reflects a broader national sentiment that values individual freedoms and the right to self-defense. Conversely, the restrictive measures in anti-gun states highlight ongoing tensions between state regulations and constitutional protections.

## Gun Control Labyrinths

States like California, New York, and New Jersey have some of the most restrictive and convoluted gun laws in the country, creating legal traps that turn law-abiding citizens into criminals overnight. These laws are often poorly publicized, rapidly changing, and inconsistently enforced, making compliance difficult even for the most responsible gun owners.

In California, small business owners like Joseph Roh have found themselves entangled in the state's labyrinth of firearm regulations. Roh, who operated a rifle manufacturing business, was arrested in 2014 for allegedly manufacturing firearms without a license, highlighting how complicated state laws are used to criminalize legitimate business owners.

Similarly, New York's SAFE Act, passed in 2013, has led to numerous arrests for violations that many gun owners did not even realize were illegal. This law bans so-called assault weapons, limits magazine capacity, and requires firearm registration—often without clear public education on compliance. Gregory Dean, a Dutchess County resident, was arrested for having seven rounds in his magazine—a provision later ruled unconstitutional. These cases illustrate how quickly new laws can ensnare otherwise law-abiding citizens.

Another prime example is Shaneen Allen, a Pennsylvania mother arrested in 2013 after voluntarily informing a New Jersey police officer that she had a legally owned, Pennsylvania-permitted firearm in her vehicle. New Jersey did not recognize her permit, and she faced up to 11 years in prison for unlawful possession. Despite no criminal intent, Allen endured months of legal battles before receiving a pardon from Governor Chris Christie.

Even elderly gun owners are not immune. Many longtime, lawful firearm owners unknowingly violate new restrictions. One elderly New Yorker was arrested for possessing a firearm with a magazine capacity exceeding the state's limit—a gun he had legally owned for decades. These cases expose the arbitrary nature of ever-changing gun laws, where citizens are punished for laws they may never have even been informed about.

Beyond individual hardships, these laws raise constitutional and ethical concerns. Critics argue that gun laws in these states are not about public safety but about control, criminalizing law-abiding citizens while failing to curb actual violent crime. Laws passed in response to high-profile shootings or political pressure often lack public awareness campaigns, leading to confusion and unintended legal violations.

Beyond California, New York, and New Jersey, other states have aggressively pursued new gun restrictions. Illinois, Washington, and Colorado have recently enacted laws that gun rights advocates argue violate the Second Amendment and contradict recent Supreme Court rulings favoring gun rights.

In January 2023, Illinois passed a sweeping gun control law banning so-called assault weapons and high-capacity magazines, requiring registration of certain firearms with state police. Critics argue that this law is unconstitutional, as it bans commonly owned firearms and imposes burdensome restrictions in direct conflict with the Supreme Court's rulings in *Heller* and *McDonald*, which affirmed an individual's right to own firearms for self-defense.

Similarly, the State of Washington passed laws in 2023 prohibiting the sale and manufacture of high-capacity magazines, expanding mandatory training requirements, and imposing waiting periods on firearm purchases. Critics argue these measures erect unnecessary barriers to lawful gun ownership and disproportionately burden low-income individuals, preventing them from exercising their Second Amendment rights.

Colorado's 2023 gun laws expanded the state's red flag law, raised the minimum purchase age for all firearms to 21, and imposed a three-day waiting period. The expansion of red flag laws has been controversial, as it allows a broader range of individuals, including teachers and healthcare professionals, to petition for firearm confiscation, raising serious due process concerns. Opponents argue that such laws violate the Fourth Amendment's protections against unreasonable searches and seizures, as firearms can be confiscated without prior notice or a hearing.

In February 2025, the Minnesota Supreme Court issued a bizarre ruling in *State v. Bee*, classifying the interior of a personal vehicle as a "public place" under state law. This ruling stemmed from a 2022 case where Kyaw Be Bee was arrested for carrying a BB gun without a permit after a traffic stop in St. Paul. The court ruled that vehicles on public roads fall under public space regulations, effectively allowing the state to regulate what individuals carry inside their own cars.

Legal experts warn this ruling sets a dangerous precedent by eroding the expectation of privacy in personal vehicles. Critics argue it expands law enforcement authority to conduct warrantless searches and seizures, directly challenging Fourth Amendment protections. Many anticipate the ruling will face federal court challenges, given its far-reaching implications for gun rights and privacy rights nationwide.

These new gun control laws and court rulings are being aggressively challenged in federal courts. The Supreme Court's 2022 *Bruen* decision established that any firearm regulation must be consistent with the historical tradition of gun laws in the United States. Many of the recent restrictions in Illinois, Washington, and Colorado are being contested on the grounds that they fail this historical test.

In Illinois, lawsuits have been filed against the so-called assault weapons ban and magazine capacity limits, arguing they violate *Bruen*'s standard. Similar legal actions are underway in Washington and Colorado, challenging new firearm restrictions as unconstitutional infringements on gun owners' rights.

These legal battles could set critical precedents for the future of gun control. If the courts strike down these laws, it will reinforce the constitutional protections affirmed in *Heller*, *McDonald*, and *Bruen*, limiting states' ability to enact similar measures in the future. But if these laws are upheld, it could embolden other states to impose even more extreme restrictions.

Despite these aggressive state-level gun control efforts, there is growing momentum for pro-gun legislation at the federal level. Donald Trump's 2024 decisive election victory and Republican control of Congress have reignited efforts to expand Second Amendment protections, including national concealed carry reciprocity. President Trump's promise—"Your Second Amendment rights do not end at your state line"—has reassured gun rights advocates that legislative action could soon reverse many of these restrictions.

With a Republican-controlled Congress, the opportunity exists to pass national pro-gun reforms, rolling back excessive regulations and ensuring gun rights are uniformly protected across all states. This is a critical moment for Second Amendment supporters to hold lawmakers accountable and push for legislation that protects law-abiding gun owners from state-level overreach.

## State Responses to Shootings Elsewhere

States that favor gun control often seize on shootings in other states as justification for imposing additional restrictions, regardless of whether the incident is relevant to their own crime patterns or firearm laws. These reactive responses often appear knee-jerk and opportunistic, leading to sweeping gun control measures that fail to address the specific needs or circumstances of the state enacting them. This pattern is common, especially in the aftermath of high-profile shootings, where heightened political and emotional pressure results in rushed legislation rather than well-considered policy.

A prime example is New York's response to the 2012 Sandy Hook shooting in Connecticut. In 2013, New York quietly passed the NY SAFE Act, banning the sale of so-called assault weapons, restricting magazine capacities, and implementing universal background checks, amongst many other regulations. While framed as a public safety measure, the law was a reaction to a tragedy in another state, raising concerns about its relevance and effectiveness in addressing New York's unique crime dynamics. Similarly, after the 2018 Parkland, Florida, school shooting, California passed additional gun control laws, including raising the minimum age for purchasing rifles and expanding red flag laws—despite already having some of the nation's strictest firearm regulations.

Critics argue that such legislative actions are more about political posturing than addressing the root causes of gun violence. The phrase "Never let a crisis go to waste" aptly describes how tragedies are leveraged to push controversial laws that might not withstand scrutiny in calmer times. Emotional urgency often overrides rational policymaking, leading to broad, ill-fitting measures rather than targeted solutions.

Gun violence is not a one-size-fits-all issue. Each state has distinct demographics, crime patterns, and cultural attitudes toward firearms. Rural communities with strong hunting traditions and low crime rates often see sweeping gun restrictions as unnecessary and intrusive. Mass shootings in schools and urban gang violence stem from different causes and require different solutions. Reactionary policies frequently ignore these distinctions, prioritizing blanket restrictions over strategies tailored to actual risk factors.

While public safety is a legitimate concern, enacting broad, knee-jerk gun control laws in response to out-of-state incidents fosters political opportunism rather than genuine solutions. This approach not only alienates responsible gun owners but also diverts attention from more effective, evidence-based measures that could actually reduce crime and violence.

## Anti-Gun Executive Actions: Dictates from the Executive Branch

Executive orders are intended to help the executive branch carry out its duties within constitutional boundaries, but they have increasingly been misused as a way for presidents to bypass the legislative process and impose policies by decree. While many executive orders are lawful and fall within the president's authority, others, particularly those concerning Second Amendment rights, represent clear overreach. Because executive orders are enacted by the executive branch, they can also be repealed by a future president—meaning that while one administration may impose unconstitutional restrictions, another can just as easily revoke them. However, this back-and-forth power struggle does not justify using executive orders to infringe on fundamental rights in the first place.

Throughout history, presidents have used executive orders to push policies that would never pass through Congress, particularly when it comes to gun control. Bill Clinton, for example, banned the importation of certain semi-automatic firearms via executive order in 1993, a move designed to impose gun restrictions without legislative approval. Barack Obama followed suit after the 2012 Sandy Hook shooting, issuing executive orders that expanded background checks and attempted to limit access to firearms under the guise of public safety. These actions set a dangerous precedent, allowing presidents to chip away at the Second Amendment without debate or due process.

Joe Biden took this executive overreach to new heights, signing many unconstitutional executive orders targeting gun rights. In April 2021, he issued orders restricting "ghost guns" and expanding red flag laws, which allow firearms to be confiscated without due process. These measures were widely criticized as undermining both the Second Amendment and the legal rights of gun owners. The increasing reliance on executive orders to implement gun control is a troubling trend, signaling a shift away from democratic lawmaking and toward rule by fiat.

While the courts have occasionally stepped in to block executive overreach, as seen when federal judges overturned parts of Clinton's and Biden's anti-gun orders, the problem persists. Executive orders were never meant to create laws, yet they are now being wielded as weapons against constitutional rights. This issue became even more apparent during Kamala Harris's campaign and tenure as vice president, where she openly stated her willingness to bypass Congress and impose gun control through executive action. Her stance exemplified the authoritarian mindset of the anti-gun left, where constitutional constraints are ignored in pursuit of an agenda. Thankfully, the American people dodged a bullet with Kamala Harris's decisive defeat to Donald Trump in the 2024 presidential election. Her loss has thwarted—for now—plans to enact more unconstitutional restrictions on legal firearm ownership.

Since assuming office on January 20, 2025, President Donald Trump quickly surpassed the record for the most executive orders issued on the first day and first week of a presidential term. However, unlike the unconstitutional overreach of his predecessor, the vast majority of these actions fell well within the legal authority of the executive branch. Many of Trump's executive orders were aimed at repealing unlawful mandates and regulations imposed by the previous administration, restoring constitutional governance rather than circumventing it. Additionally, a significant portion of these orders served to clarify existing federal law, ensuring that agencies enforced policies in accordance with congressional intent rather than political activism. While critics may attempt to equate Trump's use of executive orders with past abuses, the key distinction lies in their purpose:

restoring constitutional limits rather than expanding executive power beyond its rightful scope.

On February 7, 2025, President Trump signed an executive order titled "Protecting Second Amendment Rights," which aims to halt federal policies enacted between January 2021 and January 2025 that infringe upon Americans' constitutional right to bear arms. This order directed the attorney general to review all existing orders, regulations, and actions from the previous administration that may violate Second Amendment protections and to propose a plan to eliminate such infringements. By mandating this comprehensive review, the executive order sought to reverse unconstitutional restrictions, ensuring that law-abiding citizens can exercise their right to self-defense without undue governmental interference.

As defenders of the Second Amendment, we must remain vigilant, ensuring that the gains made under this administration are not only preserved but expanded. The forces seeking to erode our freedoms are persistent, and history has shown that they will regroup and continue their efforts at every opportunity. Every law, every regulation, and every attempt to circumvent the Constitution must be met with the same resolve and determination. Our work is far from over, and we must stay engaged, hold our leaders accountable, and continue to fight for the liberties that define us as Americans.

\*\*\*

All the different gun control laws previously discussed at both the state and federal levels have painted a bleak picture for Second Amendment advocates in recent years. From restrictive firearm bans to bureaucratic red tape designed to make gun ownership increasingly difficult, the erosion of gun rights has often felt like an unstoppable tide. Anti-gun politicians continue to push their agendas, using fearmongering and misinformation to justify unconstitutional measures, while activist judges and overreaching federal agencies attempt to chip away at the very foundation of our rights.

However, despite the doom and gloom of this ongoing assault on the Second Amendment, there is a shift taking place—one that offers hope for the future. Across the country, pro-gun states are pushing back with bold new legislation, a Second Amendment–friendly federal government is in power, and courts are beginning to strike down unconstitutional gun control measures at an unprecedented rate. The battle is far from over, but momentum is finally swinging in the right direction.

Court rulings, legislative actions, and executive orders are continually reshaping the legal framework surrounding gun ownership, making it nearly impossible to keep up with every update. By the time this book is published, some of the laws discussed may already be obsolete or overturned. However, the principles at stake remain the same. Even outdated restrictions serve as valuable lessons, highlighting the ongoing battle between individual liberty and government overreach.

The following sections present a handful of encouraging developments—laws, court rulings, and political shifts—that signal a potential sea change in the fight for the Second Amendment. From acts of civil disobedience against unconstitutional gun laws to courts striking down restrictive measures, and the rise of pro-2A administrations and legislators, there is reason for optimism. However, this is no time for complacency. Victories today do not guarantee the same outcome tomorrow, and the political and cultural landscape can shift quickly. The fight to preserve our gun rights is ongoing, and without constant vigilance, the progress made could just as easily be undone.

## The Rise of Constitutional Carry

Amidst all the doom and gloom and unconstitutional gun control legislation being passed in several states, a substantial development has emerged: the rise of constitutional carry. This movement, now adopted by most states, allows law-abiding citizens to carry firearms without a permit. This trend reflects a growing recognition of Second Amendment rights and is a positive counterbalance to the extensive gun control efforts at the federal level and in a handful of other states.

The movement towards constitutional carry gained substantial momentum over the past decade. States like Texas, Arizona, and Wyoming have been longtime proponents of constitutional carry, reinforcing their commitment to minimal restrictions on the right to bear arms. Other states, such as South Carolina and Tennessee, have also joined this list in recent years, following meaningful legislative efforts and advocacy from gun rights groups like the NRA and local grassroots organizations. Notable recent milestones include the passage of such laws in Florida and Nebraska in 2023, and in Louisiana in 2024.

By 2024, 29 states had enacted permitless or constitutional carry laws, reflecting a major shift towards expanded gun rights across the United States in recent years.

The laws typically stipulate minimum age requirements, usually 18 or 21, and some states include specific provisions for military personnel, allowing them to carry at a younger age. For instance, Georgia and Oklahoma permit 18-year-olds in the military to carry without a permit, while the general public must be 21.

However, the push for constitutional carry has not been without controversy. Critics argue that permitless carry could lead to increased gun violence and public safety concerns, as it removes the checks and balances provided by background checks and training requirements associated with concealed carry permits. Proponents, however, assert that these laws uphold the Second Amendment and enhance personal freedom by reducing governmental oversight.

Despite most states not requiring a permit to carry, many states do not honor permits obtained in other states or allow permit holders to cross state lines with their firearms. This creates widespread confusion for individuals traveling armed for self-protection or hunting trips. This inconsistency underscores the need for nationwide recognition of firearm permits, also known as national reciprocity.

## Gun Control Measures Overturned

In recent years, courts across the country have struck down federal and state gun control laws as unconstitutional, signaling a shift in a more pro-gun direction. Supreme Court rulings have reaffirmed that the right to bear arms cannot be arbitrarily restricted, leading to the overturning of restrictive concealed carry laws, magazine bans, and other excessive regulations. The rejection of these laws highlights a growing judicial pushback against government overreach and a renewed commitment to protecting Second Amendment rights.

For example, a federal court struck down the longstanding federal ban on handgun sales to adults under the age of 21 on January 30, 2025. The ruling effectively nullified restrictions that had previously prevented federally licensed firearm dealers (FFLs) from selling handguns to law-abiding adults aged 18 to 20. This decision marks a consequential victory for Second Amendment advocates, reinforcing the principle that constitutional rights should not be arbitrarily restricted based on age.

The federal ban, first enacted as part of the Gun Control Act of 1968, prohibited licensed gun dealers from selling handguns to individuals under 21, while still allowing them to purchase rifles and shotguns. This inconsistency had long been criticized as illogical and unconstitutional, given that 18-year-olds are legally recognized as adults for nearly all other rights and responsibilities, including voting, serving in the military, signing contracts, and getting married. The ruling emphasized that the Second Amendment does not impose age-based restrictions and that young adults have the same fundamental right to self-defense as any other law-abiding American.

The court's decision cited Supreme Court precedents such as *Bruen* and *Heller*, reinforcing that any firearm restriction must align with the historical understanding of the Second Amendment. The judge ruled that there is no historical tradition of banning young adults from owning or purchasing handguns, making the federal prohibition unconstitutional under the *Bruen* test, which requires modern gun laws to be deeply rooted in historical tradition.

The decision was met with strong support from Second Amendment groups, who hailed it as a crucial step toward restoring gun rights for all law-abiding Americans. Many pointed out that young adults are among the most vulnerable demographics when it comes to violent crime and should not be denied their right to self-defense. Critics of the ban had long argued that it unfairly targeted responsible gun owners while doing nothing to curb crime, as criminals do not obtain their weapons through legal dealers. While gun control advocates voiced concerns over increased access to handguns among young adults, the ruling does not eliminate background checks or other existing federal regulations on firearm sales. Instead, it simply ensures that legal adults between 18 and 20 can exercise their Second Amendment rights without unnecessary government interference.

Other recent court rulings continue to signal a shift in favor of Second Amendment rights. For example, on January 14, 2025, the US Court of Appeals for the Third Circuit struck down Pennsylvania's restrictions preventing 18- to 20-year-olds from carrying firearms in public during a state of emergency, reaffirming that such laws violate the Second Amendment. Less than a month later, on February 11, 2025, an Illinois circuit court ruled that the state's Firearm Owner's Identification (FOID) card requirement is unconstitutional, stating that forcing residents to obtain government approval just to possess firearms in their own homes places an undue burden on their rights. These rulings align with a growing legal trend of rejecting excessive firearm regulations, reinforcing that states cannot impose arbitrary restrictions without clear historical precedent. As challenges to restrictive gun laws continue, these victories highlight a renewed judicial commitment to upholding constitutional firearm protections.

## National Reciprocity

National reciprocity for gun rights refers to a legislative framework that would allow individuals with a valid concealed carry permit from one state to legally carry a concealed firearm in any other state where concealed carry is legal. This concept aims to create a standardized recognition of concealed carry permits across state lines, similar to how driver's licenses are recognized nationwide. The idea is rooted in the belief that the Second Amendment rights of Americans should not be hindered by the varying and often complex state laws regarding firearm possession and carry. By implementing national reciprocity, gun owners would be able to travel more freely and confidently across state borders without the risk of inadvertently violating local laws, thereby ensuring that their right to self-defense is uniformly protected throughout the country. This proposal underscores the principle that the constitutional right to bear arms is a fundamental right that should be respected and upheld consistently across all states.

Consider the case where New York issues a concealed carry permit to a resident after a thorough vetting process. This individual has been deemed responsible and without a violent crime history, making them eligible to carry a firearm in New York. Under national reciprocity, the state of Massachusetts, for instance, would be required to honor this permit. Such recognition would not only simplify travel for gun owners but also uphold the principle that an individual's rights should not be arbitrarily restricted by crossing state borders. It ensures that a person's Second Amendment rights are respected uniformly across the nation.

One of the principal arguments for national reciprocity is the inconsistency and complexity of state gun laws, which create a patchwork of regulations that can be difficult for gun owners to navigate. A person legally carrying a firearm in their home state may unknowingly become a criminal by crossing into another state with stricter laws, placing an undue burden on responsible gun owners who must decipher each state's unique restrictions to avoid prosecution. National reciprocity would eliminate this legal minefield, ensuring that a permit issued in one state is recognized nationwide, protecting citizens from unnecessary legal risks. This principle is further reinforced by the Full Faith and Credit Clause of the US Constitution, which requires states to honor the public acts, records, and judicial proceedings of others. Just as marriage licenses and driver's licenses are recognized across state lines, concealed carry permits should be no different. If a state has determined that an individual meets the necessary criteria, including background checks and training, other states should respect that decision, reinforcing trust in state-level vetting processes and ensuring Second Amendment rights are upheld uniformly.

Proponents of national reciprocity argue that it enhances public safety by allowing law-abiding citizens to protect themselves regardless of location and potentially deterring crime by making it uncertain who is armed. A traveler from a high-crime state to a stricter state could still exercise their right to self-defense, ensuring consistent personal security. Opponents, however, worry that varying permit standards among states could undermine stricter regulations. A balanced approach, incorporating minimum national standards for issuing concealed carry permits, could address these concerns while still preserving the benefits of reciprocity.

The argument for states' rights to regulate firearms as they see fit often centers on the principle of federalism, which allows states to exercise considerable control over their own affairs. The Second Amendment explicitly protects the right to keep and bear arms, and any state laws that infringe upon this right must be reconciled with the Constitution; the right to bear arms should not be hindered by inconsistent state regulations.

The Constitution's Supremacy Clause, found in Article VI, establishes that federal law takes precedence over state laws. This clause ensures that the rights enshrined in the Constitution, including the Second Amendment, are uniformly applied across all states, superseding any conflicting state legislation. Therefore, the implementation of national reciprocity for concealed carry permits would mandate that all states honor permits issued by other states. This approach respects the constitutional right to bear arms, ensuring that lawful gun owners can exercise this right without being subjected to a patchwork of state laws.

Under national reciprocity legislation, the refusal of a state to recognize another state's concealed carry permits would be nullified, as it would conflict with the Second Amendment's protection of the right to bear arms. This legislative framework would create a consistent standard across the country, reducing the legal uncertainties faced by gun owners who travel between states. States would no longer be able to selectively disregard the rights granted to citizens by other states, aligning all jurisdictions with the constitutional mandate.

Conversely, any federal law that attempts to ban states from recognizing other states' firearms permits would inherently violate the Second Amendment. Such legislation would undermine the constitutional right to bear arms and could be challenged as unconstitutional. States have a duty to protect the constitutional rights of their citizens, including the right to keep and bear arms. If federal laws infringe upon these rights, states are within their rights to defy or refuse to enforce such unconstitutional laws, as they would be acting in defense of the Constitution.

Moreover, the argument for national reciprocity is reinforced by the need for a coherent and consistent legal framework for firearm ownership and use. The current system, with its myriad state laws and regulations, creates confusion and legal pitfalls for responsible gun owners. National reciprocity would simplify this landscape, ensuring that the constitutional rights of gun owners are respected regardless of the state they are in. This consistency is essential for upholding the Second Amendment for all Americans.

Donald Trump's decisive 2024 election victory, paired with Republican control of both the House and Senate, reignited the possibility of national reciprocity becoming law. Trump made his stance crystal clear during his campaign, declaring, "My administration will push for national reciprocity, so your Second Amendment rights do not end at your state line." This pledge resonated with millions of Americans who are tired of seeing their constitutional rights treated as second-class privileges depending on the state they travel to.

Several bills, including the Concealed Carry Reciprocity Act, were introduced in Congress in 2025 to establish national reciprocity for gun permits, allowing permit holders to legally carry across state lines while adhering to local laws. Despite vigorous support, these efforts faced opposition and stalled. With a pro-Second Amendment administration and Congress in power, the opportunity to pass national reciprocity is now within reach. This legislation is not just about convenience but about ensuring the Second Amendment is upheld as a national standard, rather than a patchwork of conflicting state laws. As President Trump stated, "It's time to make concealed carry permits valid across all 50 states, just like a driver's license." Now is the time to hold elected officials accountable and push for this long-overdue victory for gun owners and constitutional rights.

## Pro-Gun Legislation

Beyond constitutional carry, numerous states have passed proactive pro-gun legislation in recent years, further solidifying the nation's shift towards supporting gun rights. These laws include measures to expand stand-your-ground protections, enhance reciprocity for concealed carry permits, and reduce restrictions on where firearms can be carried.

For example, in 2021, Texas passed a law allowing residents to carry handguns without a permit. Tennessee enacted a law allowing permitless carry for adults over 21. States like Iowa and Montana have also adopted similar measures, broadening the ability for law-abiding citizens to exercise their Second Amendment rights without the need for state-issued permits.

Additionally, many states have introduced laws to protect gun owners from potential federal overreach. Missouri passed the Second Amendment Preservation Act (discussed in detail below) in 2021, which prohibits state and local law enforcement from enforcing federal gun laws that infringe on the Second Amendment. Similarly, Arkansas passed a law declaring federal gun regulations that violate the Second Amendment to be null and void within the state, signaling a firm stance against potential federal interventions.

Another notable example is the expansion of stand-your-ground laws. In Florida, the landmark 2005 law allows individuals to use force, including deadly force, if they believe they are in imminent danger, without the duty to retreat. Many other states have adopted similar legislation; Georgia and Alabama, for instance, have strengthened their stand-your-ground laws to provide greater legal protections for individuals defending themselves against threats.

States have also taken steps to enhance reciprocity for concealed carry permits. In 2021, Ohio passed a law ensuring that concealed carry permits from other states are recognized. This move aims to simplify the legal landscape for gun owners who frequently travel, reducing the risk of inadvertently violating state laws. Similarly, Utah has enacted legislation to make it easier for out-of-state permit holders to carry concealed firearms within its borders, fostering greater cooperation and recognition among states.

States are also reducing restrictions on *where* firearms can be carried. In 2020, Oklahoma passed a law allowing individuals to carry firearms in places of worship, provided they have permission from the property owner. This legislative trend reflects a broader acceptance of firearms in public spaces and acknowledges the rights of individuals to protect themselves in various environments. Similarly, Kentucky passed a law allowing permit holders to carry firearms in previously restricted areas, such as certain government buildings and public parks.

The recent wave of pro-gun legislation across the United States highlights a significant change towards reinforcing Second Amendment rights. By expanding constitutional carry, protecting against federal overreach, broadening self-defense laws, enhancing reciprocity, and making it easier to carry firearms in public spaces, states are responding to the growing public demand for greater gun rights and protections. These legislative actions demonstrate a robust commitment to upholding the constitutional freedoms of gun owners while addressing the evolving landscape of gun rights in America.

## The Second Amendment Preservation Act (SAPA)

In recent years, a coalition of states has formed a pact known as the Second Amendment Company (also known as the Second Amendment Interpact). This agreement, established in 2021, was born out of a growing frustration with federal gun control legislation. The member states assert that many of these federal laws infringe upon the constitutional right to bear arms as protected by the Second Amendment. The states involved—primarily Missouri, Alabama, Arkansas, Oklahoma, West Virginia, Mississippi, Georgia, Texas, and Tennessee—came together to create a unified stance against what they perceive as federal overreach. There are several other pro-Second Amendment states that have adopted their own version of SAPA, such as Arizona, Alaska, Kansas, and Wyoming.

SAPA can be traced back to a series of contentious debates over gun control measures proposed in Congress. In the wake of several high-profile mass shootings, federal lawmakers sought to implement more stringent background checks, assault weapon bans, and restrictions on magazine capacities. These proposed laws sparked intense debates across the country, but nowhere was the opposition more vocal than in the South. State legislatures, backed by strong pro-Second Amendment advocacy groups, began passing resolutions condemning these federal initiatives. This grassroots movement culminated in a formal agreement among the participating states to resist any federal gun control measures that they deemed unconstitutional.

The agreement itself is a detailed document that outlines the specific actions each member state will take to nullify federal gun control laws. Key provisions include a commitment to non-compliance with federal regulations, meaning that member states will not enforce any federal gun control laws, mandates, or executive orders. State and local law enforcement agencies are explicitly prohibited from cooperating with federal authorities in the enforcement of these laws. Additionally, the pact provides for comprehensive legal support for citizens, ensuring that any state resident prosecuted under federal gun laws receives funding for legal defense and state-level protections against federal actions. All member states are designated as Second Amendment Sanctuaries, offering safe harbor for firearm owners against federal prosecution. Moreover, the states agree to support each other both legally and politically, sharing resources, coordinating legal strategies, and providing mutual assistance in legal battles with the federal government. This interstate cooperation solidifies their united front against federal encroachments on Second Amendment rights.

SAPA has had a notable impact on the political landscape. The member states have successfully blocked several federal initiatives through both legislative and judicial means. Legal battles have been fought in various courts, with mixed outcomes. Some federal courts have upheld the states' rights to refuse enforcement of federal gun laws, while others have sided with the federal government, arguing that federal law supersedes state law.

SAPA has sparked considerable debate and controversy. Critics argue that it undermines the rule of law and sets a dangerous precedent for states to selectively adhere to federal laws. Supporters, however, view it as a necessary defense of constitutional rights and a check against federal overreach. Whether SAPA will ultimately be upheld or dismantled by the courts remains to be seen, but its existence underscores the ongoing struggle over the right to bear arms in the United States. Despite legal challenges, the Interpact remains a powerful symbol of resistance against federal gun control measures. The coalition continues to grow, with other states expressing interest in joining the pact. This movement has also influenced national politics, with politicians from these states using the Interpact as a platform to campaign for broader Second Amendment protections.

The increasing gun ownership rates, shifting public opinion, and widespread adoption of pro-gun legislation indicate that the United States is becoming more pro-gun and pro-Second Amendment. Despite efforts by some states to impose stricter gun control measures, the overall trend across the country reflects a strong support for gun rights and individual freedoms. The rise of constitutional carry laws and the passage of other pro-gun legislation demonstrate a solid majority of states and their populations favoring the Second Amendment and opposing more restrictive gun control measures. As this trend continues, it is likely that support for the Second Amendment will remain a defining feature of American society and politics.

## Civil Disobedience

Further evidence of growing public support for the Second Amendment is the widespread refusal to comply with blatantly unconstitutional gun control measures. Refusing to compromise on your Second Amendment rights is a stance grounded in the principle that these rights are fundamental and non-negotiable. Compromising on these rights or complying with unconstitutional gun control laws undermines this fundamental liberty and sets a dangerous precedent for the erosion of other constitutional rights.

Statistical examples of mass defiance against gun control laws underscore the widespread resistance to unconstitutional regulations. For instance, the New York SAFE Act previously discussed required the registration of certain firearms and the banning of others. However, compliance has been remarkably low, highlighting citizens' refusal to accept laws they perceive as infringing on their constitutional rights. According to estimates, fewer than 1 percent of the gun owners affected in New York complied with the registration requirement.

Similar patterns of defiance are observed in other states. In Connecticut, following the passage of stricter gun control measures in the wake of the Sandy Hook Elementary School shooting, thousands of gun owners failed to register their firearms as required by the new laws.

Moreover, numerous sheriffs and law enforcement officers across the country have publicly declared their refusal to enforce laws that they view as clear violations of the Second Amendment. For example, in Washington State, following the passage of Initiative 1639, which imposed strict gun control measures, several sheriffs announced they would not enforce the law. Similarly, in Virginia, over 90 percent of the state's counties declared themselves Second Amendment sanctuaries, with many sheriffs pledging not to enforce new gun control measures proposed by the state legislature.

The concept of Second Amendment sanctuary cities or counties has gained much traction in recent years. These jurisdictions pass resolutions or ordinances declaring that they will not enforce certain gun control laws that they deem unconstitutional. This movement is a form of civil disobedience that emphasizes the importance of constitutional rights and the role of local governments in protecting those rights. For instance, Effingham County in Illinois passed a resolution in 2018 declaring a sanctuary for gun owners, refusing to enforce new state gun control measures. Similar declarations have been made in states such as Colorado, New Mexico, and Kentucky, where numerous counties have adopted sanctuary resolutions.

The resistance to unconstitutional gun control laws is rooted in a deep-seated belief that the right to bear arms is essential to maintaining personal freedom and security. Historical and contemporary examples demonstrate that when governments have disarmed their populations, it has often led to tyranny and oppression. The disarmament of citizens in Nazi Germany, Soviet Russia, and Maoist China are stark reminders of the dangers of allowing the government to strip away the means of self-defense.

Furthermore, the argument for defying unconstitutional gun control laws is supported by the principle of civil disobedience. From the Civil Rights Movement led by Martin Luther King Jr. to the anti-apartheid struggle in South Africa, acts of civil disobedience have been instrumental in challenging unjust laws and policies. Similarly, refusing to comply with unconstitutional gun control laws is an act of civil disobedience aimed at preserving fundamental liberties.

The notion that gun owners should never give up their firearms is also supported by practical considerations. In times of crisis or societal collapse, the ability to defend oneself becomes even more critical. Natural disasters, civil unrest, and other emergencies can quickly overwhelm law enforcement and government resources. In such scenarios, an armed citizenry can provide essential security and stability. The right to bear arms ensures that individuals are not entirely dependent on the government for their protection and can take responsibility for their own safety.

Additionally, the presence of an armed populace serves as a deterrent to potential aggressors, both foreign and domestic. The knowledge that citizens are armed and capable of defending themselves can discourage criminal activity and deter governmental overreach. This deterrent effect is a fundamental aspect of the Second Amendment, which envisions a well-armed citizenry as a check against tyranny.

The refusal to compromise on Second Amendment rights is further justified by the reality that gun control laws often fail to achieve their intended goals.

Criminals, by definition, do not obey laws, and stringent gun control measures often leave law-abiding citizens vulnerable. Instead of preventing crime, these laws can create a false sense of security while disarming the very people who could act in defense of themselves and others. Studies and statistics consistently show that areas with strict gun control laws do not necessarily experience lower rates of violent crime. In fact, some of the cities with the highest rates of gun violence, such as Chicago and Baltimore, also have some of the strictest gun control measures in the country.

Moreover, the selective enforcement of gun control laws often targets marginalized communities and exacerbates existing social inequalities. This selective enforcement undermines the principle of equal protection under the law and contributes to a sense of injustice and mistrust in the legal system. By resisting unconstitutional gun control measures, citizens are also standing against policies that disproportionately impact vulnerable populations.

Another situation that we can use to our advantage is that law enforcement officers across the United States are overwhelmingly pro-Second Amendment and support gun rights. This strong support stems from their daily experiences on the front lines of crime prevention and public safety, where they see firsthand the crucial role that responsible gun ownership plays in deterring crime and protecting individuals. Furthermore, many in law enforcement understand that the foundational principle of the Second Amendment serves as a vital check against tyranny, ensuring a free and secure society.

One of the primary reasons law enforcement officers support the Second Amendment is their intimate understanding of the practical aspects of self-defense. Police officers recognize that they cannot be everywhere at once and that response times, even in the best scenarios, are often minutes away when seconds count. As such, they appreciate the importance of citizens being able to protect themselves and their families. Sheriff Richard Mack, a former sheriff of Graham County, Arizona, and a prominent advocate for gun rights, once stated, "The only thing that stops a bad guy with a gun is a good guy with a gun."

Those who pursue careers in law enforcement also tend to value self-reliance, personal responsibility, and the principles of liberty enshrined in the Constitution. These values naturally align with the ethos of the Second Amendment.

Many officers grew up in communities where firearms are a part of daily life, used for hunting, sport shooting, and self-defense. This cultural background fosters a deep respect for the right to bear arms and a recognition of its importance in maintaining a free society.

A significant portion of law enforcement officers are also veterans who have served in the military, where they developed a strong sense of duty to uphold and defend the Constitution. This experience reinforces their commitment to protecting all constitutional rights, including the Second Amendment. They understand that disarming law-abiding citizens does not make society safer; instead, it leaves them vulnerable to criminal elements who do not obey laws.

The practical experiences of law enforcement officers further underscore their support for the Second Amendment. Many officers have encountered situations where armed citizens have successfully defended themselves and others from criminal threats. These real-life examples reinforce the belief that an armed populace contributes to overall public safety. Former Detroit Police Chief James Craig is a notable advocate for armed self-defense, having publicly encouraged citizens to arm themselves in response to rising crime rates. Craig stated, "Good Americans with concealed weapons permits translates into crime reduction. I'm absolutely for it."

The commitment of law enforcement to upholding the Second Amendment is also evident in their training and education efforts. Many law enforcement agencies offer or support firearms training programs for civilians, emphasizing safe and responsible gun ownership. These programs help bridge the gap between law enforcement and the community, fostering mutual respect and understanding.

Law enforcement officers' opposition to unreasonable gun control laws is well documented. Many sheriffs and police chiefs have publicly declared their refusal to enforce laws they believe infringe on constitutional rights. In 2013, over 340 sheriffs and 14 state sheriff associations signed a pledge to uphold the Second Amendment and resist unconstitutional gun control measures proposed at the federal level. Sheriff Mike Lewis of Wicomico County, Maryland, stated, "As long as I'm sheriff in this county, I will not allow the federal government to come in here and strip my citizens of their rights to bear arms."

In Colorado, following the passage of stringent gun control laws in 2013, a group of sheriffs filed a lawsuit challenging the constitutionality of the new regulations. Weld County Sheriff John Cooke, one of the leading figures in the lawsuit, argued that the laws were unenforceable and infringed on the rights of law-abiding citizens. "These bills do absolutely nothing to make Colorado a safer place. Nothing to do with reducing violence," Cooke said.

The pro-Second Amendment stance of law enforcement is further evidenced by the proliferation of Second Amendment sanctuary counties and cities across the nation. These jurisdictions pass resolutions or ordinances declaring that they will not enforce certain state or federal gun control measures that they deem unconstitutional. For example, in Virginia, over 90% of counties have declared themselves Second Amendment sanctuaries in response to proposed gun control legislation by the state government. Sheriff Scott Jenkins of Culpeper County, Virginia, stated, "I've always pledged my unwavering support to uphold the Constitution and serve the people, and that includes standing against any unconstitutional laws."

Press releases and statements from various law enforcement organizations also reflect their support for the Second Amendment. The National Sheriffs' Association, representing thousands of sheriffs nationwide, has consistently advocated for the protection of gun rights. In a 2018 statement, the association emphasized, "The National Sheriffs' Association supports the right of law-abiding citizens to keep and bear arms as guaranteed by the Second Amendment of the Constitution."

Similarly, the Fraternal Order of Police (FOP), the largest organization of sworn law enforcement officers in the United States, has voiced its support for the Second Amendment. The FOP has argued that law-abiding citizens should not be penalized for the actions of criminals and that responsible gun ownership is a critical component of public safety. In a letter to Congress in 2019, FOP National President Chuck Canterbury wrote, "We believe in enforcing existing laws to keep firearms out of the hands of criminals while respecting the rights of law-abiding citizens to own and use firearms responsibly."

This alignment between law enforcement and responsible gun owners demonstrates a broader truth—support for the Second Amendment runs deep across

American society, even among those tasked with upholding the law. And while anti-gun activists may fantasize about sweeping bans or constitutional repeals, the reality is far more complicated.

## The Repeal of the Second Amendment Is Unlikely

The good news for Second Amendment supporters is that the prospect of repealing this fundamental right is not only unlikely but almost impossible under our constitutional framework. Anti-gun politicians may suggest that the Second Amendment should be removed from the Bill of Rights entirely, but the reality is that changing the Constitution is an incredibly arduous process—one that overwhelmingly favors the preservation of our rights.

To repeal the Second Amendment, a new amendment must be proposed and pass with a two-thirds majority in both the House of Representatives and the Senate. Given the current political landscape, where neither party consistently holds a supermajority in either chamber, reaching such an agreement is exceedingly improbable. The Second Amendment enjoys strong support across various constituencies, making it highly unlikely that such a proposal could garner the necessary backing from legislators.

But even if anti-gun politicians were somehow able to overcome this first hurdle, the battle would be far from over. Any amendment to repeal the Second Amendment would then need to be ratified by three-fourths of the states, meaning 38 states would have to agree to this drastic measure. This is where the idea of repealing the Second Amendment hits an insurmountable wall. The United States is deeply divided on this issue, and the majority of states, particularly those with strong gun rights traditions, would never consent to stripping away such a crucial element of the Bill of Rights. The federalist structure of our government is designed to ensure that no single region or group can impose its will on the entire country, especially when it comes to fundamental rights.

Anti-gun politicians are aware of these constitutional safeguards, which is why they often resort to more insidious methods—chipping away at our rights bit by bit. They push for restrictive legislation and executive actions that, while not outright repealing the Second Amendment, seek to erode it gradually.

While the idea of repealing the Second Amendment may be floated by some, the reality is that our constitutional system makes it nearly impossible for such an effort to succeed. The formidable process of amending the Constitution acts as a safeguard, ensuring that our rights cannot be easily stripped away. This is a testament to the enduring strength of the Second Amendment and the wisdom of the Founding Fathers in designing a system that protects our fundamental freedoms from transient political pressures.

It's clear that despite a growing pro-gun sentiment across much of the population, authoritarian politicians continue to push efforts to disarm the American public. The battle for gun rights is far from over, and the future of these rights increasingly hinges on where you live in the United States, which administration holds power, and the makeup of the Supreme Court. This reality calls for relentless advocacy and vigilance by gun rights supporters.

The stakes are high, as those who seek to disarm us do so not for public safety, but to consolidate power over the citizenry. It's not about reducing crime; it's about exerting control. As gun rights advocates and patriots, we must continue to put pressure on elected officials to oppose all gun control legislation. Our freedom depends on our ability to resist these encroachments, and we cannot afford to become complacent. The preservation of the Second Amendment is crucial to maintaining our autonomy and liberty, and it's up to the people to ensure these rights are protected for future generations.

# Chapter 7

## Myths, Absurdities, and Fallacies

*The right of the citizen to keep and bear arms must not be infringed if liberty in America is to survive.*

—Ronald Reagan

*The key fallacy of so-called gun control laws is that such laws do not in fact control guns. They simply disarm law-abiding citizens.*

—Thomas Sowell

*The modern liberal is a crybaby with a superiority complex—desperate to control others, but offended when anyone pushes back.*

—Dennis Prager

The discourse surrounding guns, gun control, and the Second Amendment is fraught with misconceptions and deliberate distortions, often propagated to shape public perception and influence policy. Debunking the myths, absurdities, and fallacies perpetuated by the media, gun control advocates, and political elites is an easy task when armed with historical facts, statistics, and reasoned arguments.

One of the most pervasive issues in the gun control debate is the manipulation of statistics to support a predetermined narrative. Whether it's the selective reporting of gun-related incidents or the broadening of definitions to inflate numbers, tactics are employed to create a sense of urgency and crisis. By examining how statistics are twisted, manipulated, and sometimes outright invented, we can reveal the deceptive strategies used to mislead the public.

Furthermore, the various untruths and fallacies that underpin many gun control arguments are evident. From the mythical "gun show loophole" to the exaggerated dangers of so-called assault weapons, these claims lack veracity. The elitist attitudes that often characterize the gun control movement highlight the disconnect between the views of political and cultural elites and the general public. Statistics indicate that public opinion toward gun rights and the Second Amendment has become more favorable over the past few decades, contrary to what the media often portrays. Through rigorous analysis and fact-checking, this chapter takes a scalpel and dissects the flawed arguments used to justify restrictive gun control measures. By exposing the myths and falsehoods, fostering a more informed and rational discussion about gun rights and public safety becomes achievable. The following sections target the heart of anti-gun rhetoric with facts and confront the misinformation head-on.

The myths, rhetorical fallacies, and absurd arguments propagated by the anti-Second Amendment and anti-gun crowd have unfortunately become so ingrained in mainstream society that they now dominate the prevailing narratives of our time. These narratives deserve thorough scrutiny and reexamination. It is crucial to recognize the often irrational and sometimes hysterical reactions of many cultural institutions to anything resembling a firearm, which is emblematic of the illogical and overly sensitive cultural shift that the Western world has witnessed over the past few decades. This shift reflects an infantilization of societal attitudes towards firearms, warranting a return to more reasoned and factual discussions.

To understand the broader strategy behind the rhetoric, narratives, and misinformation presented by the media, academics, and politicians, it is insightful to examine the four-stage process used by elites to push their agendas. First theorized by Thomas Sowell, a renowned economist, historian, and social theorist, this framework provides a clear lens through which we can analyze the methods employed by anti-gun and gun control advocates to manipulate public perception and legislative action.

## The Four-Stage Process to Gun Control

In his book *The Vision of the Anointed*, Thomas Sowell describes the four-stage process used by elites to push their agendas. This process—comprising the crisis, the solution, the results, and the response—highlights how problems are often exaggerated or fabricated, solutions are proposed that fail to address the issues effectively, blame is then shifted, or success is redefined when those solutions fail, and the narrative is continually adjusted to fit a predetermined agenda. Sowell's theory remains remarkably relevant in contemporary discussions, particularly when examining the issue of gun control in the United States. The process he describes can be observed in how gun control advocates present their case, propose legislation, and react to the outcomes. Here's how this four-stage process plays out.

Stage 1: The Crisis: Gun violence, particularly mass shootings, is presented as a crisis that demands immediate and sweeping legislative action. The elites, often through mainstream media and political platforms, amplify the perception that gun violence is the leading cause of death among children and that the existence of so-called assault weapons significantly contributes to these tragedies. Following tragic mass shootings, media outlets, and politicians frequently claim that assault weapons are a major cause of gun violence, despite statistics showing that rifles account for a tiny percentage of overall gun-related deaths.

Stage 2: The Solution: To address this perceived crisis, strict gun control measures such as banning assault weapons, mandating universal background checks, and introducing red flag laws are posited as necessary actions to curb gun violence and save lives. An example of this is the 1994 Federal Assault Weapons Ban, which was often cited as a solution to reduce mass shootings and gun violence. However, studies have shown that the ban had little to no impact on overall crime rates, partly because assault weapons were rarely used in crimes to begin with.

Stage 3: The Results: When these gun control measures do not lead to a significant decrease in gun violence or mass shootings, the elites shift the blame to other factors or claim that the measures were not comprehensive enough. After the Assault Weapons Ban expired, proponents claimed that the ban failed not because of its inherent flaws but because it was not strict enough or did not cover enough firearms. Despite this, data from the FBI and other sources indicated no clear reduction in gun violence during the ban's enforcement.

Stage 4: The Response: To maintain their agenda, proponents of gun control often redefine the criteria for success or focus on new narratives. They might shift their focus to advocating for expanded background checks, gun buyback programs, or even more restrictive measures. When the initial measures fail to produce the desired results, the elites advocate for more extensive restrictions, arguing that the only reason gun violence persists is because of the lack of even more stringent laws. They may also highlight selective data or isolated incidents to bolster their claims, rather than addressing the broader, more complex reality of gun violence.

This four-stage process highlights the systematic approach used by gun control elites to manipulate public perception and drive policy changes. By understanding this process, we can see how gun control advocates construct and maintain narratives that often rely on exaggerated or misleading information. The focus on high-profile mass shootings, while ignoring the broader context of gun violence statistics, perpetuates the dangerous push for increasingly restrictive laws, regardless of their actual effectiveness in addressing the purported crisis.

## Rhetorical Tactics

Anti-gun and gun control advocates frequently employ a range of rhetorical tactics designed to discredit gun rights and those who defend them. These tactics are often manipulative, aimed at shifting the narrative and undermining legitimate arguments in favor of the Second Amendment. Among the most common are *do-somethingisms, whataboutisms, presentism, feelgoodism, strawman arguments,* and the use of *false premises* and *false equivalences* to frame questions and statements. Each of these tactics serves to distort the debate, making it easier to dismiss or vilify pro-gun perspectives without engaging with the core issues. Let's explore these tactics to understand how they are used and how they can be effectively countered.

## Do-Somethingisms

Gun control advocates, politicians, and elites often engage in what can be termed "do-somethingism," a phenomenon where immediate, reactionary measures are taken in response to high-profile events, without fully considering the efficacy or potential negative consequences of these actions. This approach is largely driven by irrational emotion and hysteria, and the need to appear proactive and responsive, rather than by a thorough analysis of the problem and its underlying causes. The result is a series of policies that frequently fail to address the core issues and, in many cases, exacerbate the situation, disproportionately harming law-abiding citizens.

One notable example of do-somethingism is the push for stringent gun control measures following mass shootings. Politicians often rush to propose bans on certain types of firearms, such as so-called assault weapons, despite evidence that these measures do not effectively reduce gun violence. For instance, the 1994 Federal Assault Weapons Ban, which expired in 2004, had a negligible impact on overall gun violence and mass shootings, according to studies conducted by the Department of Justice and the Centers for Disease Control and Prevention. Despite this, calls for similar bans resurface after each tragic event, focusing on optics rather than solutions.

Another instance of a do-somethingism is the implementation of gun-free zones in the wake of school shootings. While these zones are established to create safe spaces free from the threat of gun violence, they often have the opposite effect. Criminals, knowing that these areas are populated by unarmed individuals, see them as soft targets. The tragic shooting at Sandy Hook Elementary School in 2012 is an example where the perpetrator targeted a gun-free zone, leading to devastating consequences. This policy does not deter criminals. Rather, it leaves law-abiding citizens vulnerable.

Background checks are also frequently touted as a solution to gun violence. While general background checks can indeed be a useful tool in preventing firearms from falling into the wrong hands, the way they are sometimes implemented can be problematic. The push for universal background checks often fails to address the significant issue of illegal firearms obtained through black markets or theft. Universal background checks also often lead to intrusive tactics, including government monitoring and surveillance of social media posts, political activities, and other personal behaviors. This level of scrutiny not only invades individual privacy but also sets a dangerous precedent for government overreach and control over lawful gun ownership.

The case of California's strict gun control laws illustrates the unintended consequences of do-somethingism. Despite having some of the toughest gun laws in the country, California has not seen a commensurate decrease in gun violence compared to states with more relaxed regulations. This discrepancy points to the complexity of gun violence and the failure of simplistic, reactionary policies to address the multifaceted nature of the problem. Instead of making communities safer, these laws often criminalize ordinary citizens who unintentionally violate complicated and ever-changing regulations.

Reactionary policies often serve as political theater rather than genuine attempts to solve problems. Politicians and elites frequently use high-profile events to push for legislation that aligns with their broader agendas, regardless of whether those measures actually improve public safety. This approach prioritizes appearances over substance, allowing these figures to claim they have "done something" without having to address the reality of the situation or debate contrary viewpoints.

In essence, do-somethingism is a flawed approach to policymaking elites, particularly in the realm of gun control. It is driven by a desire for immediate action and positive optics rather than by careful consideration of what will genuinely enhance public safety. This approach leads to policies that punish law-abiding citizens while failing to deter or address criminal behavior. As such, policymakers must resist the urge for quick fixes and instead focus on comprehensive, evidence-based strategies that address the underlying issues of gun violence in America.

## Whataboutisms

Anti-gun advocates also often engage in another rhetorical tactic known as "whataboutism" to deflect from the arguments at hand and shift the burden of proof back onto their opponents. This method involves responding to criticism or opposition by raising an unrelated issue or invoking an emotional appeal to sidestep addressing the efficacy and potential flaws of their proposals. This approach can muddle the discourse and prevent a focused, fact-based discussion on the merits and drawbacks of specific gun control measures.

For instance, when a gun control proposal faces criticism for its potential ineffectiveness or its infringement on constitutional rights, proponents often redirect the conversation. A common phrase is "What about the children?" used to evoke a strong emotional reaction and imply that any opposition to the proposal equates to indifference toward child safety. This tactic is frequently seen in media coverage and political debates, where the emphasis is placed on the emotional appeal rather than the substantive issues of the proposal.

This can be seen in the aftermath of school shootings. After these tragic events, media outlets and politicians frequently call for stricter gun control laws, citing the need to protect children in schools. However, when these proposals are scrutinized and found lacking in effectiveness or feasibility, the discussion often shifts to emotional appeals rather than addressing the critiques. During debates on proposed assault weapon bans, the focus often moves away from statistical evidence and historical context to dramatic imagery and stories of young victims. While these narratives are powerful and important, they can be used to shut down critical analysis and debate over the proposed legislation's actual impact on gun violence.

Politicians also engage in whataboutism to counter opposition to gun control measures. When faced with arguments that highlight the failure of certain gun control laws to reduce crime or prevent mass shootings, they pivot the conversation to broader social issues without directly addressing the critique. For example, if opponents of a proposed gun control law argue that it would not have prevented a specific mass shooting due to the perpetrator's method of obtaining the firearm, gun control advocates might respond by saying, "What about the need to do something to protect our communities?" This shift avoids engaging with the specifics of the argument and instead places the emotional burden on the opponents to prove they are not indifferent to community safety.

Media coverage often amplifies this tactic by framing the gun control debate in terms of moral urgency rather than policy efficacy. Headlines and soundbites frequently highlight the emotional stakes, focusing on the fear and sorrow surrounding gun violence, particularly involving children. By prioritizing emotional appeals, the media and politicians can sideline substantive debates about the actual effectiveness of proposed gun control measures and the broader implications for constitutional rights and individual freedoms. This framing can pressure policymakers and the public to support measures based on emotional reactions rather than thorough evaluations of potential outcomes.

Whataboutism in the gun control debate serves to deflect from legitimate criticisms and redirect the conversation toward emotional and moral high grounds. This tactic can undermine a constructive dialogue that seeks to balance the need for public safety with the preservation of individual rights. By recognizing and addressing these rhetorical strategies, it is possible to foster a more informed and rational discussion about gun control, grounded in facts and a comprehensive understanding of the issues at hand.

## Presentism

Presentism involves interpreting and judging past events, figures, and documents through the lens of contemporary values, attitudes, and knowledge. Anti-Second Amendment gun controllers often employ presentism by applying today's standards and changing language and definitions to reinterpret the original meaning of historical texts, including the Second Amendment. This practice not only distorts the true intent of the Framers but also risks rewriting history to conform to the current zeitgeist.

The language used in the late 18th century carries specific connotations and meanings that reflected the priorities and concerns of the time. The Second Amendment, as written in the Bill of Rights, states that "A well regulated Militia, being necessary to the security of a free State, the right of the people to keep and bear Arms, shall not be infringed." The words "well regulated" referred to the proper functioning and readiness of the militia, "Militia" encompassed all able-bodied men capable of bearing arms, and "the people" clearly denoted individual citizens. The term "infringed" meant "encroached upon or violated." The concept of a "free State" implied a community where liberty was preserved by an armed populace capable of resisting oppression.

Furthermore, the Second Amendment's sentence structure implies that the right of the people to keep and bear arms is not dependent on the necessity of a militia for the security of a free state. The amendment's construction—with its prefatory clause ("A well regulated Militia, being necessary to the security of a free State") followed by the operative clause ("the right of the people to keep and bear Arms, shall not be infringed")—indicates that while the militia is important, the right to bear arms is an independent and inherent right of the people that exists regardless of the state of the militia.

Gun control advocates often attempt to dissect the grammar of the Second Amendment, focusing on the placement of commas to support their interpretation that the right to bear arms is solely linked to militia service. This argument centers on the punctuation, suggesting that the Framers intended the right to be collective rather than individual. However, historical context and contemporary writings from the Framers and their peers consistently indicate that the right was understood to be an individual one, necessary for personal defense and the preservation of liberty.

Presentism, by imposing contemporary interpretations on historical texts, obscures these original meanings and intentions. It disregards the Framers' clear understanding and deliberate use of language to protect the natural right of self-defense and ensure a free society. The focus on evolving definitions and modern grammatical interpretations serves to distort the Second Amendment's purpose, rather than clarify it.

The Framers of the Constitution and the Bill of Rights chose their words carefully to protect individual liberties and ensure a balance of power between the government and the citizens. Understanding and preserving this original meaning is critical in safeguarding the liberties enshrined in the Second Amendment.

It is essential to resist the temptation of presentism and instead strive to understand historical documents within their original context. This approach ensures that the principles of liberty and justice continue to be upheld, protecting the rights envisioned by the founding generation against the shifting sands of contemporary political agendas.

## Feelgoodism: The Illusion of Progress

In the realm of gun control, another pervasive phenomenon can be observed: what might be called "feelgoodism." Gun control advocates and politicians push for laws and regulations that, while making them feel virtuous and enlightened, do little or nothing to actually reduce crime or enhance public safety. Instead, these measures often result in infringing on the rights of law-abiding citizens, all while allowing those who pass such laws to bask in the glow of self-righteousness. Unlike the related concept of do-somethingism, which is driven by a desperate need to act in the face of tragedy, feelgoodism is more about vanity and emotional gratification, with a focus on appearances rather than effectiveness.

Feelgoodism is particularly prevalent among political elites who are more interested in signaling their moral superiority than in crafting legislation that addresses the root causes of violence. By pushing for restrictive gun laws, these individuals can publicly align themselves with what they perceive as the "right side" of history, portraying themselves as champions of public safety and social progress. However, this posturing often comes at the expense of real-world solutions and can exacerbate the very problems they claim to be solving.

One prominent example of feelgoodism in action is the push for universal background checks. Advocates for this policy argue that expanding background checks to include private sales and transfers will help prevent guns from falling into the wrong hands. While the idea sounds reasonable on the surface and provides a sense of accomplishment for those who support it, the reality is far more complex. Studies have shown that criminals obtain firearms primarily through illegal means, such as theft or black-market purchases, rather than through legal channels. Expanding background checks won't stop them from doing so, but it will create additional burdens for law-abiding gun owners, potentially turning them into criminals for engaging in otherwise lawful transactions.

Another classic case of feelgoodism is the so-called assault weapons ban. Politicians who advocate for banning firearms based on cosmetic features—such as adjustable stocks, pistol grips, or flash suppressors—often do so with great fanfare, claiming that these measures will make communities safer by removing "military-style" weapons from the streets. However, this approach ignores the fact that these cosmetic features have little to do with a firearm's lethality. Furthermore, rifles of any kind, including those labeled as "assault weapons," are used in a small fraction of gun-related crimes. The Federal Assault Weapons Ban, in place from 1994 to 2004, brought no significant reduction in overall gun violence. Yet, despite the evidence, the push for such bans persists, driven by the emotional appeal of "doing something" rather than the effectiveness of the policy.

In addition to these legislative efforts, feelgoodism is often fueled by high-profile individuals who use their platforms to advocate for gun control while enjoying the benefits of armed security for themselves. Celebrities and politicians who push for restrictive gun laws often do so from a position of personal safety that is not afforded to the average citizen. Their advocacy is less about addressing the realities of crime and more about reinforcing their own image as caring and progressive, regardless of the practical consequences of their policies.

One notable example is former New York City Mayor Michael Bloomberg, who has spent millions of dollars advocating for stricter gun control laws through his organization, Everytown for Gun Safety. Bloomberg's push for measures such as bans on "high-capacity" magazines and mandatory waiting periods is often framed as a moral imperative, yet these policies do little to address the underlying issues of crime and violence. Meanwhile, Bloomberg himself is protected by armed security, illustrating the disconnect between the elites' pursuit of feelgood legislation and the realities faced by ordinary citizens.

The consequences of feelgoodism in gun control are not just limited to ineffective policies; they also contribute to the erosion of trust between the government and the people. When citizens see their rights being chipped away by laws that serve more to stroke the egos of politicians than to enhance public safety, it fosters resentment and a sense of alienation. Law-abiding gun owners often feel targeted by policies that seem more focused on controlling their behavior than on addressing criminal activity. This dynamic can lead to increased polarization and a growing divide between the governed and those who govern.

The allure of feelgoodism is strong, but its consequences are real and often counterproductive. It is essential to move beyond the superficial appeal of such measures and focus on policies that are grounded, respect constitutional rights, and are truly effective in making our communities safer.

## Strawman Arguments and False Premises

Anti-gun advocates often resort to strawman arguments and false premises to paint pro-gun advocates as unreasonable, unhinged, and even dangerous. A strawman argument is a common tactic where someone distorts or oversimplifies their opponent's position, making it easier to attack or discredit. By setting up these false representations, anti-gun activists create a misleading narrative that serves their agenda while avoiding a direct confrontation with the actual arguments in favor of gun rights.

One of the most prevalent strawman arguments is the claim that pro-gun advocates believe everyone should have unrestricted access to any kind of weapon, including military-grade firearms. This caricature suggests that those who support the Second Amendment want to see guns in every home, school, and public space, with no regulations whatsoever. This is not only a gross misrepresentation but also a deliberate attempt to stoke fear and hysteria. The reality is that most pro-gun advocates support reasonable regulations, such as background checks and measures to prevent criminals and the mentally ill from obtaining firearms. The actual argument is about preserving the right of law-abiding citizens to defend themselves and their families, not about arming everyone to the teeth without any oversight.

Another common strawman is the portrayal of pro-gun advocates as paranoid, conspiracy-driven individuals who believe that any form of gun control is a step toward total government tyranny. While it is true that a significant portion of these people are wary of government overreach, this concern is often rooted in historical precedent and legitimate fears about the erosion of constitutional rights. The Founding Fathers themselves included the Second Amendment as a safeguard against tyranny, recognizing the importance of an armed citizenry in maintaining a balance of power. By reducing this argument to mere paranoia, anti-gun advocates ignore the valid concerns of millions of Americans who understand that freedom is fragile and must be protected.

Anti-gun activists also frequently use false premises to advance their agenda, one of the most egregious being the notion that more guns lead to more violence. This premise is often supported by selective statistics and studies that ignore broader context. They may cite the fact that the United States has a higher rate of gun ownership than other developed nations, and then point to the higher rates of gun-related deaths in the US. However, this argument fails to account for the fact that most gun-related deaths in the US are suicides, not homicides, and that violent crime rates overall have been declining for decades, even as gun ownership has increased. Studies have shown that areas with higher rates of legal gun ownership often have lower rates of violent crime, as criminals are deterred by the prospect of encountering armed resistance.

Another false premise is the argument that gun control laws in other countries, such as Australia or the United Kingdom, have been overwhelmingly successful and should be replicated in the United States. While it is true that these countries have implemented strict gun control measures, the comparison is flawed for several reasons. First, the cultural, historical, and legal contexts of these countries are vastly different from those in the United States. Second, the impact of gun control measures in these countries is often exaggerated or misrepresented.

A specific example of a strawman argument is the way anti-gun advocates often respond to the idea of arming teachers or allowing concealed carry in schools as a means of protecting students. They frequently characterize this proposal as advocating for turning schools into war zones or suggesting that every teacher should be forced to carry a firearm. In reality, the argument is about giving teachers and school staff the option, with proper training, to defend themselves and their students in the event of an active shooter situation. It's about providing a last line of defense, not about militarizing schools. The suggestion that armed teachers would create chaos is a strawman designed to scare people away from considering reasonable measures for enhancing school safety.

Another common false premise is the idea that gun ownership is inherently linked to racism or white supremacy. This narrative has been pushed by certain anti-gun activists who argue that the Second Amendment was historically used to suppress minorities or that modern gun rights advocates are motivated by racial animus. Given their attempts to rewrite history, anti-gun activists work to portray modern gun owners as relics of a racist past, painting them as violent, armed white supremacists eagerly waiting to massacre minorities and stage an insurrection at any moment. This argument not only distorts history but also ignores the fact that the right to bear arms has been a valuable tool for self-defense among minority communities. During the Civil Rights Movement, many African Americans exercised their Second Amendment rights to protect themselves against violent attacks by the Ku Klux Klan and other racist groups. The Deacons for Defense and Justice, an armed African American self-defense group, played a significant role in protecting civil rights activists from violence in the 1960s. The false premise that gun rights are racially motivated overlooks this important history and misrepresents the motivations of millions of law-abiding gun owners of all races.

In addition to these specific examples, anti-gun advocates often use emotional appeals and loaded language to distract from the real issues. They may refer to "common-sense gun laws" or "gun safety measures," framing their proposals as inherently reasonable and portraying any opposition as irrational or dangerous. However, these terms are often used to describe sweeping restrictions that would significantly infringe on the rights of law-abiding citizens. By framing the debate in these terms, anti-gun advocates create a false dichotomy where their position is the only reasonable one, and any disagreement is cast as extreme.

To counter these strawman arguments and false premises, it is essential to engage with the actual facts and context surrounding the Second Amendment and gun rights. The right to bear arms is not about promoting violence or enabling chaos; it is about protecting individual freedom and ensuring that citizens have the means to defend themselves against threats, whether from criminals or from a tyrannical government. The arguments in favor of gun rights are rooted in a deep understanding of history, constitutional law, and the practical realities of self-defense. By exposing the distortions and misrepresentations used by anti-gun advocates, we can have a more honest and informed debate about the role of guns in American society.

The use of strawman arguments and false premises by anti-gun advocates is a deliberate attempt to mischaracterize the pro-gun position and marginalize those who support the Second Amendment. By setting up these distorted representations, they avoid engaging with the real issues and instead create a narrative that serves their agenda. It is important to recognize and debunk these tactics, exposing the truth about gun rights and defending the fundamental liberties that are essential to a free and secure society.

## False Equivalences

Anti-gun advocates frequently use the false equivalence of equating gun ownership with owning other dangerous items, such as illegal drugs or explosives, to make gun rights seem extreme or reckless. The tactic of false equivalence is designed to create fear and confusion, suggesting that if the government can ban one dangerous item, it should be able to ban guns as well. Some argue that just as the government has the authority to ban or heavily regulate substances like narcotics, cigarettes, or explosives to protect public safety, it should similarly restrict or even ban firearms. However, this comparison disregards the fundamental differences between these items and firearms, particularly in their legal, historical, and constitutional contexts.

Firearms (including ammunition) are explicitly protected by the Second Amendment as a core right integral to the security of a free state, whereas illegal drugs and explosives (i.e., bombs) are not mentioned in the Constitution and are subject to prohibition and regulation (on a state level) for their inherent dangers to public safety. Using this false equivalence ignores the legitimate, constitutionally enshrined reasons for gun ownership, such as self-defense, hunting, and protection against tyranny. By equating firearms with items that are inherently illegal or subject to complete prohibition, anti-gun advocates attempt to paint gun ownership as inherently dangerous and undesirable, even though responsible gun ownership is a legal and constitutionally protected right.

By exposing these false equivalences for what they are—flawed comparisons that distort the debate—we can better defend the Second Amendment and ensure that the conversation remains focused on the real issues at hand. More examples of false equivalences will be discussed in greater detail later.

## The Myth of the "Gun Lobby"

The concept of the "gun lobby" is a myth perpetuated by anti-gun advocates to delegitimize the support for the Second Amendment and its defenders. The term is often used to suggest a shadowy, monolithic entity exerting undue influence over politicians and public policy. However, no such entity exists in the way it is portrayed. What does exist are gun rights organizations—like the National Rifle Association (NRA) and Gun Owners of America (GOA) (see chapter 13)—that represent millions of law-abiding Americans who cherish their constitutional right to keep and bear arms. These groups advocate for the protection of gun rights, but they are neither taxpayer-funded nor wield disproportionate power through unethical means.

Unlike certain left-wing special interest groups or the well-funded abortion lobby, gun rights organizations rely entirely on voluntary donations, memberships, and grassroots support. No public tax dollars are funneled into these organizations, and they operate on the strength of their supporters' passion and commitment to preserving the Second Amendment. This stands in stark contrast to some advocacy groups on the left that have benefited from taxpayer-funded grants or government partnerships to advance their agendas.

The idea that pro-gun politicians are "beholden" to a so-called gun lobby is equally misleading. Politicians who support gun rights do so because they reflect the will of their constituents, many of whom are members of these organizations or share their values. Whether a politician donates their personal money to a gun rights group is irrelevant—it is a personal choice made with private funds. Accusations of undue influence ignore the fundamental truth that pro-gun policies have widespread grassroots support among millions of Americans who vote, donate, and advocate for their beliefs.

To illustrate, consider the massive mobilization of gun owners in Virginia in 2020, when proposed gun control measures sparked protests and resistance across the state. This wasn't the work of a mythical "gun lobby." Rather, it was sparked by ordinary citizens banding together to defend their rights. Similarly, organizations like the NRA have been instrumental in educating gun owners, promoting safety, and providing training—not merely lobbying for policy. These efforts are a far cry from the caricature of backroom deals and undue influence painted by anti-gun advocates.

It's important to clarify that organizations like the NRA do not manufacture, sell, or distribute firearms. The NRA is a nonprofit organization dedicated to advocating gun rights, providing firearms training, and promoting safety education. A significant aspect of their mission involves legal advocacy; the NRA employs attorneys who actively challenge unconstitutional gun control measures, striving to protect the rights of everyday Americans. This legal work is funded through membership dues and private donations, not taxpayer dollars. Therefore, labeling the NRA as a "gun lobby" in the sense of a profit-driven entity is a mischaracterization of its true role and functions.

Even if a "gun lobby" did exist, it would hardly resemble the caricature often painted by anti-gun advocates. Firearms and gun ownership are enshrined in the Constitution through the Second Amendment, making such a lobby inherently tied to a protected constitutional right. If this hypothetical lobby avoided corruption, refrained from coercive practices, and did not supply arms to adversaries or anti-American forces, its existence would align with the principles of liberty and transparency.

If a gun lobby were to emerge, it would be far less likely to stoop to the deceitful and divisive tactics frequently seen in many left-wing organizations. We hold ourselves to a higher standard of decency, respect for the law, and ethical principles, and would not tolerate unethical or corrupt behavior. Unlike the left-wing approach, where wrongdoing by their interest groups is often ignored or justified under the mantra of "by any means necessary," our community values accountability and integrity. Our commitment to principled advocacy and personal responsibility sets us apart.

Furthermore, the irony of anti-gun advocates accusing pro-Second Amendment supporters of being "beholden to the gun lobby" and responsible for gun deaths, including tragic school shootings, is almost too thick to fathom. They go so far as to claim that organizations like the NRA and law-abiding gun owners "have blood on their hands." Yet, these very same individuals and groups actively promote and finance the abortion industry, a multibillion-dollar enterprise that is heavily subsidized by taxpayer dollars and directly results in the termination of millions of unborn children. The hypocrisy is staggering. It would be laughable if it weren't so grotesque. The irony truly writes itself.

Ultimately, the narrative of the "gun lobby" is a rhetorical tool designed to vilify those who support the Second Amendment and distract from the fact that gun rights have deep roots in American culture and constitutional law. By fixating on this imagined bogeyman, critics marginalize the genuine grassroots movement of millions of people defending their rights. The reality is simple: Gun rights organizations reflect the people they represent, not a nefarious force pulling strings behind the scenes.

## The "Assault Weapons" Myth

Modern sporting rifles, such as the AR-15, AK-47, and their variants, are often misunderstood and deliberately misrepresented in the media and by gun control advocates. These firearms are frequently labeled as "assault weapons," a misleading term loaded with emotional connotations designed to evoke fear. Examining their features, functionality, and how they are used by responsible gun owners reveals that they are *not* assault weapons.

First and foremost, the term "AR" in AR-15 does not stand for "assault rifle." AR stands for "ArmaLite Rifle," named after the company that developed it in the 1950s. The AR-15 is a semi-automatic rifle, meaning it fires one round per trigger pull. This is fundamentally different from an assault rifle, which is capable of fully automatic fire, allowing multiple rounds to be fired with a single trigger pull. True assault rifles, such as the military's M16, are highly regulated and not readily available to the public.

The term "assault weapon" is a politically charged and media-driven term designed to provoke an emotional response. It has no precise technical definition and is often applied to firearms based on cosmetic features rather than their actual functionality. Features such as pistol grips, flash suppressors, and collapsible stocks are often cited as defining characteristics of assault weapons. However, these features do not impact the rifle's lethality or functionality.

The demonization of these firearms is largely driven by their tactical look, which can appear intimidating to those unfamiliar with firearms. However, this perception is based on aesthetics rather than the rifle's capability. Many firearms with similar or even greater firepower are not subjected to the same scrutiny, simply because they lack these cosmetic features.

The Supreme Court's decision in *District of Columbia v. Heller* (2008) affirmed that the Second Amendment protects an individual's right to possess firearms commonly used for lawful purposes, such as self-defense. Given the prevalence of AR-15s and similar rifles in civilian hands, they clearly fall into the category of firearms in common use, thereby enjoying constitutional protection. Modern sporting rifles like the AR-15 and AK-47 function similarly to many other semi-automatic firearms. They are popular among civilians for a variety of legitimate purposes, including sport shooting, hunting, and home defense.

According to recent statistics, the reported number of AR-15s owned by civilians as of 2024 in the United States was approximately 24.4 million, while the number of AK-47s and similar rifles was around 7 million. However, these figures are conservative estimates and do not fully capture the total number of these firearms in civilian hands. Many gun owners do not publicly disclose their firearms, and the estimates are based on data from registrations, permits, and manufacturing reports. Consequently, the actual number of AR-15s, AK-47s, and similar firearms could be much higher; there could be between 50 to 80 million such firearms in civilian possession.

Despite their widespread ownership, these firearms are used in a minuscule fraction of gun crimes. The FBI's Uniform Crime Reporting (UCR) data consistently shows that rifles of any kind, including AR-15s, are used in less than 3 percent of all gun-related homicides. Handguns, not rifles, are mostly used in crimes.

This stark contrast between perception and reality highlights the misinformation often spread about these rifles.

On a personal note, my first gun was an AR-15. My experience with this rifle has been overwhelmingly positive. It functions flawlessly, has numerous safety features, and is highly customizable to meet the needs of any user. The AR-15's versatility makes it an excellent choice for home defense. Its accuracy, ease of use, and effectiveness in defensive scenarios make it an ideal tool for protecting my home and family. Knowing that I have the means to defend myself against multiple intruders, should the need arise, gives me peace of mind. With the rise in home invasions and break-ins in my area caused by recent policies that have led to increased numbers of illegal aliens and squatters, having a reliable firearm for protection is more important than ever.

The media's portrayal of AR-15s and other modern sporting rifles often reveals a lack of understanding about firearms. Journalists and politicians frequently misuse terminology and misrepresent the capabilities of these guns, leading to widespread misinformation. For example, many incorrectly claim that AR-15s are "weapons of war" when, in reality, they lack the fully automatic capability of actual military rifles.

Misconceptions about modern sporting rifles contribute significantly to the heated debate on gun control. The media frequently amplifies the perceived danger of these firearms, despite statistical evidence showing that they account for a small percentage of gun-related crimes. The term "assault weapon" is a propaganda tool designed to evoke fear and support for gun control measures that are based on aesthetics rather than functionality. Modern sporting rifles like the AR-15 and AK-47 are *not* assault weapons. They are versatile, reliable firearms used by millions of Americans for lawful purposes. These rifles are constitution- ally protected and play a vital role in home defense and personal safety. Given the rising crime rates and social unrest, the importance of the Second Amendment and the right to keep and bear arms has never been clearer. Countless Americans believe it's essential to own a firearm capable not just of stopping a threat, but also as a symbol—reminding overreaching politicians that the Constitution still has teeth.

## False Equivalence: Guns vs. Other Weapons

Another tactic commonly employed is the creation of false equivalence be-tween modern firearms and vastly more destructive weapons, such as nuclear bombs. This strategy aims to evoke fear and urgency, further distorting public understanding of firearms and their role in society. Gun control advocates often pose the question, "Should we be able to own nuclear weapons?" to challenge the argument that the Second Amendment protects the right to own modern firearms like the AR-15. This comparison is not only misleading but also misrepresents the scope and intent of the Second Amendment.

The term "arms" has historically referred to personal firearms and other individual weapons used for self-defense, hunting, and militia service. The Founding Fathers, influenced by their experiences in the Revolutionary War and their understanding of natural rights, recognized the importance of an armed citizenry in deterring tyranny and ensuring personal and communal security. They anticipated technological progress and deliberately chose broad language to encompass future advancements in weaponry.

Modern rifles like the AR-15 are designed for individual use and function similarly to other firearms protected under the Second Amendment. Equating these firearms with nuclear bombs, which are state-level armaments designed for mass destruction, is a disingenuous argument that seeks to blur the lines between personal defense and military capabilities. Nuclear weapons are *not* analogous to personal firearms. They are classified as "arms" in the context of international treaties and state-level military capabilities, not individual rights.

In addition, the cost of a nuclear weapon is astronomical, billions of dollars, far beyond the reach of private citizens. Furthermore, nuclear weapons are heavily regulated by international law, including the Treaty on the Non-Pro-liferation of Nuclear Weapons (NPT), and are not owned by private indi-viduals. The suggestion that private citizens should have the right to own nuclear weapons ignores the practical and logistical impossibilities associated with such ownership.

The concept of "arms" has always been understood to cover personal firearms, not a nuclear bomb. At the time of the founding, "arms" referred to weapons that individuals could reasonably possess and use, including muskets, pistols, and swords—arms that were accessible to private citizens and essential for self-defense and militia service.

The historical and legal context of the Second Amendment clearly indicates that it was intended to protect the individual's right to bear arms for self-defense and resistance to tyranny. Modern sporting rifles like the AR-15, which are widely owned and used for lawful purposes, fall within this protection. The argument that civilians should not own these firearms because they are somehow equivalent to nuclear weapons is not only fallacious but also an attempt to undermine a fundamental constitutional right. When gun control advocates suggest that the Second Amendment implies a right to own nuclear weapons, they engage in a rhetorical tactic that distorts the public's understanding of gun rights. This misrepresentation serves to advance an anti-gun agenda by exploiting the fear and absurdity associated with weapons of mass destruction. This is just one of many tactics used to manipulate public perception, which will be explored further in later sections.

## Empty Rhetoric

Advocates of gun control often argue for banning certain firearms and imposing strict regulations, asserting that this would reduce gun violence and save lives. They say, "Even if we save only one life by banning guns, then it was worth it!" However, this perspective overlooks a critical historical lesson: Disarming civilians has often preceded some of the most horrific tyrannies and genocides in modern history. When the state possesses a monopoly on force, it becomes far easier to oppress, subjugate, and, ultimately, commit atrocities against its people.

Historical examples abound to illustrate this point. As previously discussed in chapter 4, but again worth noting, before the Nazi regime orchestrated the Holocaust, it systematically disarmed the German population, leaving them defenseless against government-led persecution. The Armenian Genocide, Soviet purges, Mao's Great Leap Forward, and the Cambodian Killing Fields similarly followed the disarmament of citizens. In each case, millions were slaughtered by their governments, underscoring the crucial role that an armed populace can play as a deterrent to tyranny. The combined death toll from these genocides is estimated to be in the hundreds of millions, a staggering figure that dwarfs the annual firearm-related deaths in the United States.

In the United States, there are approximately 40,000 firearm-related deaths each year. However, suicides account for about 60 percent of all gun-related deaths. When suicides are excluded, the number of gun deaths attributable to criminal activity significantly decreases. In 2020, for example, out of approximately 43,000 firearm-related deaths, around 24,000 were suicides and 19,000 were homicides, accidents, and other causes. While each death is undeniably tragic, these figures pale in comparison to the catastrophic death toll suffered by disarmed citizens at the hands of their governments. If one were to total all annual gun deaths in the United States since the adoption of the Second Amendment in 1791, even counting suicides, the resulting figure would represent only a minuscule fraction of the deaths caused by systematic genocides in the 20th century alone. This comparison underscores the severe consequences of civilian disarmament and highlights the protective intent behind the right to bear arms. The number of gun deaths in the United States is a small price to pay for the deterrence of the possibility of having a Holocaust of our own.

To draw a parallel, consider the societal acceptance of deaths caused by automobile accidents. In the United States, between 40,000 and 60,000 people die annually in car accidents, with a significant number of these deaths caused by drunk driving and negligence. Despite these tragic figures, society generally agrees that the benefits of widespread car ownership and the freedom it provides outweigh the associated risks. The ability to travel freely and the economic advantages of personal transportation are deemed worth the cost in human lives, tragic as they are.

Similarly, cell phone use while driving has been identified as a significant cause of car-related accidents and deaths. Despite the widespread recognition of this danger and the enactment of laws in many states making it illegal to use a cell phone while driving, this risky behavior persists. The convenience and utility of cell phones, which facilitate instant communication and access to information, are seen as outweighing the potential risks. Society does not call for a ban on cell phones because of their misuse, just as it does not call for a ban on cars or alcohol despite their associated risks. The needless deaths caused by drunk driving or distracted driving, which statistically exceed gun-related fatalities, are overlooked in favor of targeting firearms. This disparity in advocacy reveals a possible inconsistency in their approach to preventing avoidable deaths, influenced more by personal preferences than by a uniform standard of harm reduction.

The right to bear arms, as protected by the Second Amendment, should be seen in the same light. The freedom to own and carry firearms provides not only personal protection and a means for self-defense but also a critical check against potential government tyranny. The occasional misuse of firearms by criminals should not overshadow their critical role in maintaining the balance of power between the state and its citizens. Just as we do not ban cars despite the deaths they cause, we should not curtail the right to bear arms. This right remains a potent deterrent against tyranny and a guarantee of the freedoms that define the American way of life.

## Inanimate Objects

The argument that guns should be treated differently from cars because they were specifically made for killing people, while cars were made for transportation, is flawed and lacks relevance in the broader discussion of public safety and personal responsibility. The focus on a product's intended design overlooks the more important issue of misuse and improper use.

Yes, guns were designed to inflict lethal force, which is essential for their primary purposes: self-defense, law enforcement, and military use. In situations where individuals need to protect themselves or others, the ability to inflict pain or death, if necessary, is a critical function. To expect guns to shoot anything other than potentially lethal projectiles, like marshmallows or fairy dust, is to misunderstand their role in ensuring personal and public safety. The capacity for lethal force is what makes firearms effective tools for self-defense.

On the other hand, cars were made as a means of transportation, designed to facilitate the movement of people and goods efficiently. However, when misused or used improperly, cars can cause significant harm, including pain, injury, and death. Statistics show that automobile-related incidents result in a high number of fatalities each year, often surpassing those caused by firearms. This misuse can stem from various factors such as drunk driving, reckless driving, or simply accidents. And cars are not exempt from being used as weapons. Many individuals have deliberately used vehicles to inflict harm and kill multiple people, proving that the intended purpose of a product does not prevent it from being used lethally. In the US alone, the November 21, 2021, Waukesha Christmas parade attack, which killed six and injured 62 with an SUV, and the January 1, 2025, New Orleans terrorist attack, further highlight this point.

Similarly, knives and baseball bats were not designed to kill but are commonly used as weapons in violent crimes. A knife, typically intended for cooking or utility purposes, can inflict serious injury or death when wielded by someone with malicious intent. Baseball bats, meant for sports and recreation, can become deadly weapons in the hands of an aggressor. The intended use of these objects does not diminish the fact that they can cause significant harm when misused.

The core issue lies in the improper use of these tools, rather than their intended design. Both guns and cars require responsible handling and regulation to prevent misuse. The fact that cars, knives, and baseball bats were not specifically designed to kill does not diminish the need for stringent laws and responsible behavior to mitigate their potential for causing harm. Similarly, the intended lethal capacity of firearms necessitates responsible ownership, handling, and use to ensure they are used appropriately for self-defense and other legitimate purposes. The effect of a gun on people lies solely with the user, not the gun itself.

By focusing solely on the intended purpose of guns versus cars, knives, or baseball bats, this argument ignores the broader context of how all these items can be misused with deadly consequences. It is not the design but the behavior and choices of individuals that determine the potential for harm. Thus, treating guns differently from other tools based on their intended use is a spurious argument that fails to address the real issue of improper use and the need for responsible handling and use of all potentially dangerous objects.

## Fentanyl and Obesity: Deadlier Than Guns

Cars, knives, and baseball bats are just a few of the many objects that can—and do—kill people, but there are countless other indirect threats to life that gun control advocates conveniently ignore. While gun control advocates fixate on firearm-related deaths, they remain conspicuously silent on far deadlier (preventable) crises. Fentanyl poisoning alone kills tens of thousands of Americans each year—far exceeding total gun-related deaths—yet the same politicians pushing gun bans show little concern for open-border policies that fuel drug trafficking and cartel-driven fentanyl warfare. Illicit fentanyl is deliberately laced into pills and other substances, killing unsuspecting users, yet this ongoing mass poisoning is met with far less urgency than firearm restrictions. Similarly, obesity-related diseases, including heart disease and diabetes, claim hundreds of thousands of lives annually, with most Americans now classified as overweight or obese. But rather than addressing these preventable deaths, the same voices screaming about gun violence ignore the far more significant health crisis that affects millions. The selective outrage reveals that the real agenda isn't about saving lives—it's about controlling certain narratives while conveniently ignoring others that don't fit their political objectives.

## Rifle Murder Statistics

It is imperative to distinguish between "gun deaths" and "gun-related murders," as they encompass different aspects of firearm-related incidents. "Gun deaths" is a comprehensive term that includes all fatalities involving firearms, covering a wide range of circumstances, such as violent crimes, murders, accidents, suicides, and cases of self-defense. In contrast, "gun-related murders" refer specifically to gun deaths that are classified as homicides, where one individual intentionally kills another. While the broader category of gun deaths provides an overall picture of firearm-related fatalities, focusing on gun-related murders narrows the scope to those incidents where firearms are used explicitly to take another person's life through criminal intent. Understanding this distinction is essential for accurately discussing and analyzing the impact of firearms in society.

Also, to illustrate the points in this section, we will use 2019 as a baseline for our analysis. The events and conditions of 2020 and beyond, including widespread unrest, the pandemic, and the invasion across our southern border, significantly raised crime rates and altered societal behaviors, making 2019 a more stable and accurate reference point for understanding typical trends in gun-related and other types of homicides. However, despite these unique circumstances, the relative statistics between different methods of homicide have remained relatively consistent in the years since, reinforcing the broader trends observed.

While the debate over gun control often centers on the dangers posed by semi-automatic rifles, statistics show that murders caused by means other than these types of guns are often much greater than those committed with semi-automatic rifles.

According to the FBI's Uniform Crime Reporting (UCR) program, in 2019, there were 16,425 total homicides in the United States. In 2019, rifles of all types were involved in only 364 homicides in the United States, representing just 2.2 percent of all homicides that year. Despite being a frequent target of gun control advocates, who often focus on banning so-called assault rifles like AR-15s and AK-47s, the use of rifles in homicides remains relatively low when compared to other methods.

When breaking down the rifle-related homicides further, of the 364 homicides committed with rifles, only a fraction involved so-called assault rifles like AR-15s or AK-47s. Estimates suggest that these types of rifles were used in fewer than 100 of those 364 cases, making up less than 0.6 percent of all homicides nationwide. This starkly contrasts with the perception that such rifles are responsible for a significant portion of gun violence, highlighting how gun control efforts targeting these specific firearms are often based more on fear and emotion than on statistical reality.

Beyond 2019, as of the most recent data, rifles were again involved in only a small percentage of total homicides in the United States for the years 2021, 2022, and 2023. In 2021, rifles of all types were used in 447 homicides, accounting for roughly 2 percent of all homicides. In 2022, rifles were involved in approximately 470 homicides, about 2.2 percent of the total. For 2023, rifles were used in approximately 490 homicides out of 21,000, again representing around 2.3 percent of all homicides.

So-called assault weapons like AR-15s and similar firearms represent an even smaller percentage of total homicides for these years. In 2021, approximately 447 homicides involved rifles, and of those, only about 90 to 112, or 20–25 percent, were likely committed with these types of firearms. This amounts to 0.4–0.5 percent of all homicides that year. The trend continued in 2022, with an estimated 94 to 118 out of 470 rifle homicides involving so-called assault weapons, again making up just 0.4–0.6 percent of total homicides. In 2023, preliminary data suggests that out of approximately 490 rifle-related homicides, between 98 and 123 involved these firearms, reflecting a similar 20–25 percent of rifle homicides, or about 0.5–0.6 percent of total homicides.

These figures highlight that, despite the focus on rifles in gun control debates, their involvement in overall homicides remains consistently low. Also, despite the unprecedented challenges of 2020 and beyond—marked by rising crime rates, widespread lawlessness, and riots—rifles were still involved in only a small fraction of all homicides.

To put this more into perspective, examining other methods of murder in 2019, the statistics reveal that other forms of homicide are notably more common. For instance, stabbings and other murders involving knives or cutting instruments accounted for 1,476 homicides, making up 9 percent of the total. Blunt force objects, such as clubs, hammers, and similar instruments, were responsible for 397 homicides, or 2.4 percent of the total. Even personal weapons, which include hands, fists, and feet, led to 600 homicides, representing 3.7 percent of all murders.

The general trends from 2020 through 2023 indicate that methods of murder involving blunt force objects, stabbings, strangulation, and personal weapons continued to be more common than those involving rifles.

- 2020: Stabbings and other knife-related homicides accounted for approximately 1,700 homicides, or around 8 percent of the total. Blunt force objects were used in about 400 homicides (2 percent), and personal weapons, including hands, fists, and feet, were responsible for roughly 700 homicides, making up around 3.3 percent.

- 2021: Similar trends were observed, with knife-related homicides reaching approximately 1,800, constituting about 8.5 percent of the total. Blunt force object homicides remained steady at around 430 (2.1 percent), while personal weapons led to about 720 homicides, accounting for 3.4 percent.

- 2022: The year saw knife-related homicides at approximately 1,750, or 8 percent of all homicides. Blunt force objects were involved in around 410 homicides (2 percent), and personal weapons resulted in about 730 homicides, making up 3.5 percent of the total.

- 2023: Preliminary data suggests that knife-related homicides remained high, with around 1,760 cases (8.2 percent); blunt force objects accounted for about 420 homicides (2 percent); and personal weapons were responsible for roughly 740 homicides, or 3.5 percent of the total.

Furthermore, when considering total gun deaths in general, the majority are suicides. According to the Centers for Disease Control and Prevention (CDC), in 2019, out of the 39,707 total gun-related deaths, 23,941 were suicides, which is over 60 percent of the total gun deaths. The numbers from 2020 through 2023 show similar results (60–65 percent).

The statistics are clear: Murders by means other than guns, such as stabbings and physical assaults, are much greater than those committed with semi-automatic rifles. Gun deaths in general, including suicides, are a significant portion of the total, indicating a complex issue that requires more examination rather than just banning certain types of firearms. If gun control advocates argue for the banning of semi-automatic rifles based on their rare use in overall murders, why not advocate for the banning of other instruments that are more commonly used in homicides, such as knives, blunt objects, or even hands and feet? This rhetorical question highlights the inconsistency and misguided focus of gun control efforts. Putting an emphasis on banning certain types of firearms, despite their relatively lower use in homicides, suggests a symbolic rather than a pragmatic approach to reducing violence.

## The Urban–Rural Fallacy

Proponents of gun control often argue that states with high gun ownership rates, typically rural and low-population states, naturally have lower crime rates due to their rural nature rather than their gun laws. While rural areas generally experience lower crime rates, this argument overlooks critical exceptions. Texas, with a population of 32 million, and Florida, with 24 million residents, both have urban centers and diverse populations comparable to California and New York. Despite their large populations, both states exhibit lower crime rates per capita and overall compared to their counterparts with stricter gun laws.

Texas has embraced permissive gun laws, including open carry and concealed carry with minimal restrictions. Despite this, the state maintains relatively stable crime rates, and in some instances, lower crime rates than highly regulated states like California. Similarly, Florida's policies on gun ownership and carry laws have not led to an increase in crime. Instead, the state has reported lower rates of violent crime compared to New York, which has some of the most stringent gun control measures in the country.

One critical aspect often overlooked by gun control proponents is the crime rates within urban centers of these populous states. Some cities, like Houston, Dallas, and Miami, have adopted policies that align with their states' pro-gun stance, yet their crime rates do not surpass those of cities with strict gun control measures. Houston and Dallas have maintained crime rates comparable to or lower than those in Los Angeles and New York City, which are subject to strict gun laws.

When comparing crime rates, one must consider both the overall crime rate and violent crime rate per capita. According to the FBI's Uniform Crime Reporting (UCR) Program, Texas and Florida consistently report lower violent crime rates per capita than California and New York. This trend challenges the narrative that higher gun ownership inevitably leads to higher crime rates. Instead, it suggests that other factors, such as law enforcement policies, economic conditions, and community engagement, play significant roles in determining crime rates.

The experiences of Texas and Florida suggest that permissive gun policies can coexist with low crime rates. The presence of armed citizens can act as a deterrent to criminal activity, as potential offenders may be less likely to commit crimes if they believe they might encounter armed resistance. This deterrent effect is less likely to be present in states with strict gun control laws, where criminals can operate with greater confidence that their victims are unarmed.

By examining the crime rates in populous states with permissive gun laws, it becomes clear that other factors play significant roles in determining crime rates.

The consistent trend of lower or average crime rates in high populated states with high gun ownership suggests that an armed populace may contribute to public safety, challenging the narrative promoted by gun control advocates. This analysis highlights the need for a nuanced understanding of the relationship between gun ownership and crime rates, one that considers a broad range of factors beyond simple population density.

## Blue Cities in Red States Inflate the Crime Numbers

One of the most pervasive fallacies perpetuated by gun control advocates is that several of the most violent cities in America are in "red states" (i.e., conservative-leaning states) with supposedly "lax" gun laws. They point to states like Louisiana, Missouri, or Tennessee and declare that permissive gun laws must fuel these higher-than-average crime rates. Although some red states do have a violent crime rate that exceeds the national average, this assertion falls apart under scrutiny, particularly when one considers the distinct urban–rural divide within these states.

The truth is a huge majority of these violent crime statistics are concentrated in large urban centers—cities like New Orleans, St. Louis, Memphis, or Atlanta—not the rural and suburban regions where gun ownership is far more culturally embedded and firearm carry is both common and normalized. What these cities all have in common isn't a culture of gun-toting rural conservatives, but rather progressive urban populations with politics and policies that trend heavily to the left.

Even though state law allows for lawful firearm carry, including concealed and open carry, the reality on the ground in these cities tells a different story. Most urban residents, by and large, do not embrace gun culture. Despite having the *option* under state preemption laws to carry legally, city dwellers often choose not to. Why? It's a combination of anti-gun attitudes, local ordinances, and a social stigma that discourages gun ownership. Cities in many red states are still overwhelmingly blue in their political leanings, and this translates to a population that is far less likely to own, carry, or be proficient with firearms, even when state laws allow them to.

In other words, while state laws may provide the legal framework for lawful carry, it is personal choice, cultural dynamics, and political ideology that drive actual gun ownership behavior. The violent crime rates in these urban areas cannot be simplistically chalked up to the fact that the state has "lax" gun laws, because most of these city residents simply aren't part of the gun-owning demographic in the first place. In fact, many of these cities have their own restrictions, public messaging campaigns, and unwritten social norms that actively discourage law-abiding citizens from carrying firearms.

So when gun control advocates claim that "red state gun laws" are responsible for urban violence, they conveniently ignore the fact that these cities are not bastions of Second Amendment enthusiasm. Quite the opposite—they are islands of anti-gun sentiment within states that otherwise support individual gun rights. Realistically, the violence plaguing these cities has much more to do with other factors such as poverty, gang activity, broken criminal justice policies, and systemic urban dysfunction—not a proliferation of legal gun carriers exercising their rights.

Blaming rural voters and red state gun laws for urban crime is a lazy argument that glosses over the reality of who actually carries guns—and who doesn't—in America's most violent cities.

## "Need" vs. Rights

Gun-control advocates often argue that civilians do not need automatic or semi-automatic weapons, framing the debate as if they are parental figures dictating what is necessary for public safety. This perspective is condescending and controlling, suggesting that an elite class knows better than the average citizen what they should and should not have. It overlooks the foundational principle of the Second Amendment, which is not predicated on the concept of need but on the inherent right to self-defense and the preservation of liberty. The Bill of Rights enshrines fundamental freedoms that do not require justification or permission from the government. Just as the First Amendment does not require one to justify their need for free speech or freedom of religion, the Second Amendment does not require individuals to justify their need for a particular type of firearm.

The Framers of the Constitution recognized that the ability to bear arms was essential for maintaining a free state and deterring tyranny. Semi-automatic weapons, which are commonly used for self-defense, hunting, and sport shooting, fall within the scope of this right. By suggesting that the government can determine what firearms individuals need, gun-control advocates inadvertently support a paternalistic approach that undermines the autonomy and rights of citizens. The Second Amendment is about preserving the balance of power between the government and the people, ensuring that citizens have the means to protect their freedoms and resist oppression.

This paternalistic view extends beyond firearms, reflecting a broader attitude that the general populace needs to be managed and directed by a more enlightened elite. Such a perspective treats adults as children who require constant supervision and guidance. This is not only disrespectful but also undermines the concept of individual liberty and self-determination.

Moreover, this attitude ignores the practical realities of self-defense and the diverse needs of American citizens. The ability to choose the most effective means of self-defense should not be restricted by arbitrary judgments about what is deemed necessary. Everyone's circumstances and needs are unique, and blanket restrictions fail to account for these nuances.

The Second Amendment's importance lies in its role as a safeguard against tyranny. The Framers understood that an armed populace was crucial for preventing the rise of oppressive governments. This principle remains relevant today, as the balance of power between the government and the people continues to be a vital component of American democracy. By imposing strict limitations on firearm ownership, the government risks eroding this balance and diminishing the ability of citizens to protect their freedoms.

The debate over gun control should not be framed around the concept of need. The Second Amendment guarantees the right to bear arms, not because of what individuals might need, but because it is a fundamental right integral to the preservation of liberty and the prevention of tyranny. The Bill of Rights exists to protect individual freedoms, and any effort to curtail these rights must be viewed with scrutiny and skepticism.

## Bans on Cosmetic Features

The efforts to ban certain firearms based solely on their cosmetic features highlight the absurdity and futility of many gun control measures. These bans often focus on superficial characteristics that have no bearing on the gun's lethality or function. It's akin to banning cars based on how they look, rather than their engine size or safety features.

One of the most ludicrous aspects of these efforts is the focus on features like pistol grips, flash suppressors, and collapsible stocks. These components are often targeted because they make a firearm look more "military" or "scary," but in reality, they do nothing to alter the fundamental operation of the gun. A pistol grip, for instance, provides a more ergonomic way to hold the firearm but does not increase its rate of fire or its capacity to inflict harm. Banning such a feature is like banning ergonomic office chairs to reduce office-related injuries: It misses the mark entirely.

Flash suppressors, another commonly targeted feature, serve to reduce the visible flash of the gunpowder igniting when the gun is fired. This helps preserve the shooter's night vision but does not make the gun any more deadly. Proposals to ban flash suppressors are based more on the dramatic effect they have in movies than on any real understanding of their function. It's as if lawmakers are trying to legislate away Hollywood special effects rather than addressing actual public safety concerns.

Then there's the issue of collapsible or folding stocks, which allow a firearm to be more easily stored or carried. Critics argue that such features make guns more concealable, but this argument falls apart upon closer examination. A firearm's lethality is not determined by how easily it can be stored but by its caliber and rate of fire. Banning collapsible stocks is like banning adjustable car seats: It does nothing to address the core issue but makes the item less user-friendly.

Consider the case of the infamous "shoulder thing that goes up," a term used by a former US representative who was clearly out of her depth when discussing firearm mechanics. This phrase, referring to a barrel shroud, highlights the ignorance often displayed by those crafting these laws. A barrel shroud is simply a piece of plastic or metal that encases the barrel to prevent the user from burning their hands after prolonged shooting. It does not make the firearm any more powerful or deadly, yet it's frequently included in bans. It's like trying to ban oven mitts because they might be used to handle hot objects—the logic simply does not hold.

Another example is the obsession with the AR-15 and its "military-style" appearance. Despite looking like military rifles, the civilian AR-15 operates only in semi-automatic mode, firing one round per trigger pull. Its appearance has led to it being labeled an "assault weapon," a term with no consistent legal definition but plenty of emotional weight. This focus on aesthetics over function is akin to banning sports cars because they look fast, regardless of their actual engine performance.

Moreover, some proposals have sought to ban bayonet lugs, which are mounts for attaching bayonets to rifles. The idea that removing these mounts would prevent mass shootings is laughable; there has not been a single documented case of a bayonet charge in any recent crime. Banning bayonet lugs is the legislative equivalent of banning toasters with bagel settings because someone thinks they make toast too quickly.

These cosmetic bans do not make society safer; they merely provide a false sense of accomplishment for those who advocate for them. Efforts to ban firearms based on cosmetic features are as nonsensical as they are ineffective. They reflect a lack of understanding of firearm mechanics and a misguided attempt to legislate based on appearances rather than facts.

It is possible that by restricting a firearm's cosmetic features to the point of making them unappealing, unattractive, more difficult or uncomfortable to operate, or framing them as mere vanity items, gun control advocates may hope to diminish public interest and dismiss the need for ownership. This gradual erosion of individual liberties conditions people to accept ever-tightening restrictions, chipping away at their rights under the guise of irrelevance.

If lawmakers are serious about reducing gun violence, they need to address the deeper, more complex issues at the heart of this problem, like mental illness or the breakdown of the family unit. By focusing on superficial aspects, these bans distract from more substantive and effective measures that could genuinely enhance public safety. Once again, instead of confronting reality, many politicians have shifted their focus to banning the very components that allow firearms to function safely and reliably.

## High-Capacity Magazines

A magazine is a cartridge used to store ammunition and feed it into the chamber of a firearm. It is an essential component for both semi-automatic and fully automatic firearms, allowing them to fire multiple rounds without the need to manually reload after each shot. Magazines come in various capacities, commonly referred to as the number of rounds they hold. The most standard- capacity sizes for magazines vary depending on the firearm, but for popular rifles like the AR-15 and AK-47, the standard size is typically 30 rounds. This means that a magazine holding 30 rounds is considered the baseline or standard for these firearms.

However, there is a significant fallacy in labeling these standard-capacity magazines as "high-capacity." Anti-gun proponents often argue that any magazine holding more than 10 rounds constitutes a high-capacity magazine, leading to legislative efforts in many states to limit magazine sizes to 10 rounds or fewer. This redefinition effectively bans standard-capacity magazines and misrepresents them as excessive or unusual. In reality, reducing magazine capacity below the standard 30 rounds imposes arbitrary restrictions that do not align with the design and intended functionality of these firearms.

The argument that so-called high-capacity magazines contribute to more deaths and shootings is often used by gun control advocates. They claim that limiting magazine size will reduce the potential for mass casualties in shootings. However, this perspective overlooks several critical factors. First, a well-trained individual can reload smaller magazines quickly, minimizing the practical impact of magazine capacity limits.

Moreover, focusing on magazine capacity as a primary factor in gun violence is misleading. Research and statistics have shown that the presence of high-capacity magazines does not necessarily correlate with higher rates of gun violence. For example, many incidents of gun violence involve firearms with standard-sized or smaller-capacity magazines. The root causes of violence are complex and multifaceted, involving socioeconomic factors, mental health issues, and the illegal acquisition of firearms, among others. By demonizing standard-capacity magazines and enacting laws that restrict them, policymakers may divert attention from more effective measures that address the underlying causes of gun violence.

Further, true high-capacity magazines, such as those holding 40, 50, or even 60 rounds, do exist and are used by a niche group of shooters. These magazines are often favored in specific scenarios, such as competitive shooting sports, tactical training exercises, or by certain enthusiasts who enjoy the challenge and novelty of high-volume shooting. However, these magazines are impractical for the average gun owner. One of the primary reasons is the increased weight they add to the firearm. A fully loaded 40- or 50-round magazine is harder to maneuver and operate effectively. This added weight can lead to shooter fatigue, particularly during extended use or in situations requiring high mobility. In addition, due to their weight and spring tension, these high-capacity magazines often fail and cause malfunctions such as misfeeds, double feeds, or jams.

The added bulk of high-capacity magazines can also interfere with the balance and handling of the firearm, which can affect accuracy and control. The additional rounds stored in the magazine make the firearm more cumbersome, reducing the shooter's ability to quickly and effectively engage targets. This is important for defensive scenarios where maneuverability and quick response times are needed. Most gun owners find that standard magazines, typically holding 30 rounds for rifles like the AR-15, provide the best balance between capacity and practicality. These standard magazines are easier to carry, reload, and manage during shooting, offering a more reliable and user-friendly experience for the average shooter. While high-capacity magazines have their place in specific contexts, they are rarely used by the general gun-owning population due to their impracticality in everyday use.

As excessive as true high-capacity magazines may seem, they're still something to be admired and marveled at—and let's be honest, they just look cool. Besides, they're a far better option than slapping a "government-approved" low-capacity magazine into an AR-15, which is about as satisfying as a tax seminar on a Saturday night.

The portrayal of standard-sized magazines as "high-capacity" is a tactic used by anti-gun advocates to advance their agenda. It reflects a misunderstanding or deliberate misrepresentation of firearm mechanics and usage. Effective gun control measures should be based on accurate information and a comprehensive understanding of the factors contributing to gun violence, rather than focusing on arbitrary definitions and restrictions that fail to address the real issues at hand.

## Mass Shootings Redefined

When most people think of mass shootings, they recall horrific events like Columbine, the Charleston church massacre, the Pulse Nightclub attack, the Las Vegas concert shooting, Newtown, Parkland, and Uvalde—horrific incidents where an attacker deliberately targeted and killed many victims. However, the definition of mass shootings has evolved over time, significantly shaping the perception and statistical reporting of these tragic events. Traditionally, a mass shooting was defined by the Federal Bureau of Investigation (FBI) as an incident in which four or more people were killed in a single event, excluding the perpetrator. This definition focused on the lethality and severity of the attack, emphasizing incidents that resulted in multiple fatalities.

However, in recent years, the definition has been broadened by various organizations and researchers to include incidents where four or more people are injured, regardless of whether there are fatalities. This change significantly increases the number of incidents classified as mass shootings, as it encompasses a wider range of events, including those with fewer fatalities or none at all. This expanded definition is used by the Gun Violence Archive (GVA) and other advocacy groups, leading to a dramatic increase in the reported number of mass shootings. Using this broader definition is dishonest and manipulative, as it includes events that are markedly different from high-profile mass shootings that typically capture national attention, such as school shootings or attacks in public spaces with high casualties.

Using the broader definition, the GVA reported over 600 mass shootings in the United States in 2022. Many of these incidents involved gang violence, domestic disputes, or other criminal activities that, while serious, do not fit the traditional image of a mass shooting intended to cause widespread terror or chaos. Critics argue that this broader definition is misleading and inflates the perceived frequency of mass shootings, creating a distorted picture that fuels the push for more restrictive gun control measures.

One notable example is an incident in New York City in 2021, where a shooting at a block party resulted in four injuries but no deaths. Under the broader definition, this incident was classified as a mass shooting, despite the lack of fatalities.

By conflating these types of events, advocates for stricter gun control present a narrative that suggests mass shootings are more common than they might be under the traditional definition. This can lead to public fear and support for policies that might not effectively address the specific nature of more deadly mass shootings.

The change in definition also complicates efforts to understand and address the root causes of different types of gun violence. Gang-related shootings, domestic violence incidents, and random public attacks all have distinct underlying factors and require different preventative measures. By categorizing all these incidents as mass shootings, policymakers might overlook the specific strategies needed to address each type effectively.

The redefinition of mass shootings to include incidents with fewer or no fatalities has significantly increased the reported number of these events, influencing public perception and policy discussions. While the broader definition aims to capture the broader impact of gun violence, it can be misleading and obscure the differences between various types of shootings. This, in turn, can hinder the development of targeted, effective solutions to reduce gun violence and prevent the deadliest mass shooting incidents.

## The Myth That the Second Amendment Doesn't Apply to the States

In addition to manipulating the language and redefining terms, gun control advocates often argue that the Second Amendment applies solely to the federal government and not to the states, thereby asserting that states have the right to regulate firearms as they see fit. The claim rests on an outdated interpretation that ignores the Fourteenth Amendment's incorporation doctrine. The incorporation doctrine, developed through a series of Supreme Court rulings, asserts that the rights guaranteed by the Bill of Rights are fundamental liberties that cannot be infringed by state governments.

The Fourteenth Amendment, ratified in 1868, was a transformative addition to the Constitution. It explicitly guarantees that "No state shall make or enforce any law which shall abridge the privileges or immunities of citizens of the United States; nor shall any state deprive any person of life, liberty, or property, without due process of law." This amendment was intended to protect individual rights from state encroachment, forever altering the relationship between the federal government, states, and individual liberties.

Historically, certain states have attempted to deprive people of their rights, including the right to bear arms. However, these actions have often contradicted the spirit and letter of the Constitution. If states are allowed to nullify the freedoms guaranteed by the Bill of Rights, it would effectively render the Constitution meaningless, as each state could strip away fundamental rights at will.

The Supreme Court's monumental decision in *McDonald v. City of Chicago* (2010) reaffirmed the applicability of the Second Amendment to the states. The Court held that the right to keep and bear arms is a fundamental right deeply rooted in the nation's history and tradition and is therefore protected against state infringement through the Fourteenth Amendment. This ruling emphasizes that individual rights, including the right to self-defense, must be uniformly protected across the entire nation, not subject to the whims of individual states.

The Tenth Amendment, which reserves powers not delegated to the federal government to the states and the people, does not grant states the authority to infringe upon rights explicitly protected by the Constitution. The right to bear arms, as enshrined in the Second Amendment, is a constitutional guarantee, not an extra-constitutional issue. Therefore, it is not within the states' purview to deny this right to their citizens.

The Framers of the Constitution and the Bill of Rights intended these documents to serve as enduring safeguards of individual liberties against any form of governmental overreach. Allowing states to circumvent the Second Amendment would betray the fundamental principles of American governance and individual freedom. The incorporation of the Second Amendment through the Fourteenth

Amendment ensures that all citizens, regardless of their state of residence, enjoy the same protection against the infringement of their right to bear arms. In essence, the argument that the Second Amendment does not apply to the states is not only legally flawed but also contrary to the foundational ideals of the Constitution.

## The Myth That Machine Guns Aren't Protected Under the Second Amendment

Fully automatic weapons, commonly known as machine guns, are federally regulated and effectively banned for civilian use by the National Firearms Act (NFA) of 1934. A machine gun is defined as a firearm capable of firing multiple rounds with a single pull of the trigger, continuing to fire if the trigger is held down, allowing for rapid discharge of ammunition. Because of their high rate of fire, machine guns are often associated with military use rather than civilian applications.

The National Firearms Act was enacted in response to the widespread violence associated with Prohibition-era gangsters and the increasing use of automatic weapons in crimes. The NFA imposes stringent regulations on the manufacture, transfer, and possession of machine guns. As part of the Gun Control Act of 1968, and more definitively with the Firearm Owners' Protection Act of 1986, the sale and civilian possession of new machine guns were further restricted. Under current federal law, no new machine guns can be registered for civilian use, making the transfer and ownership of existing registered machine guns subject to rigorous oversight and approval processes.

Although the general civilian ownership of machine guns is largely banned and/or heavily restricted, it is still possible under federal law for civilians to own machine guns if they obtain a Federal Firearms License (FFL) and a tax stamp from the Bureau of Alcohol, Tobacco, Firearms and Explosives (ATF). This process is arduous and highly regulated. The tax stamp, costing $200, is part of the National Firearms Act (NFA) requirements, and the application process involves extensive background checks, fingerprinting, and compliance with stringent regulations. Only machine guns registered before May 19, 1986, are eligible for civilian ownership under the Firearm Owners' Protection Act, making such firearms rare and often prohibitively expensive. This ensures that only individuals who pass rigorous vetting can legally possess these weapons, adding an extra layer of oversight and control.

Despite these restrictions, there is a compelling argument that machine guns should be protected under the Second Amendment of the United States Constitution. There are historical precedents for the successful and responsible civilian use of machine guns. Prior to the 1986 ban, civilians legally owned and used machine guns for recreational shooting and historical reenactments and as part of private collections. The relative rarity of crimes committed with legally owned machine guns during this period supports the argument that responsible ownership is feasible.

The case against civilian possession of machine guns rests on flawed arguments and commonly perpetuated myths used by gun control advocates to support the federal prohibition. One common fallacy is the belief that machine guns are uniquely dangerous and inherently lead to higher crime rates. However, data does not support this assertion; legally owned machine guns are rarely used in crimes because of the stringent regulations already in place. Gun control advocates also claim that machine guns serve no legitimate purpose for civilians, ignoring the historical and legal context of the Second Amendment, which encompasses the right to own arms suitable for militia use. Notably, the Supreme Court's interpretation in cases like *Heller* supports the notion that arms in common use for lawful purposes are protected. Although machine guns may not be commonly used by civilians in contemporary society, millions of military personnel wield rifles with fully automatic capabilities as part of their service. And tens of thousands of Federal Firearm Licensees (FFLs) across the country are legally permitted to own such weapons. The Second Amendment does not limit the right to bear arms to military personnel. Given that members of the military are civilians and part of the general population, it stands to reason that machine guns, when owned by FFLs and military personnel which represent millions of United States citizens, could be considered "in common use." Therefore, these weapons should arguably be protected under the Second Amendment, reflecting the amendment's broader intent to allow civilians to bear arms suitable for lawful purposes.

In addition, there is a compelling argument that machine guns, as a category of arms, are protected under the Second Amendment, as they can be relevant for both large-scale self-defense and community-defense actions and to counter potential tyranny, which is a foundational premise of the right to bear arms. While the theoretical arguments for the Second Amendment protection of machine guns are strong, practical considerations often drive the debate. Opponents of civilian machine gun ownership cite the potential for increased violence and the difficulty of regulating such powerful weapons. However, these concerns must be balanced against the constitutional rights of citizens.

The Second Amendment explicitly references the need for a "well regulated Militia" as essential to the security of a free state. In the 18th century, militias were composed of ordinary citizens who provided their own weapons. Today, the concept of a militia implies that citizens should have access to the same level of firepower as the military to fulfill this role effectively. This perspective supports the notion that civilians should be allowed to own machine guns, as they represent the modern equivalent of the military arms available during the founding era. When the Second Amendment was drafted, the term "arms" encompassed all contemporary military-grade weapons. The Framers of the Constitution understood the importance of an armed populace capable of resisting not only foreign invaders but also domestic tyranny. At the time, there was no distinction between the arms held by the military and those owned by civilians. Given this historical context, modern military firearms, including machine guns, one could argue, fall within the scope of the Second Amendment's protection.

Critics often argue that the Framers could not have envisioned the technological advancements in firearms. However, as discussed in previous chapters, the Framers anticipated future developments and drafted the Bill of Rights in broad terms to encompass unforeseen advancements. Thus, the principles of the Second Amendment should logically extend to modern firearms, including machine guns.

Advocates argue that responsible gun ownership and rigorous training can mitigate the risks associated with machine guns. The existing regulatory framework for firearms can be adapted to include comprehensive background checks, mandatory training, and secure storage requirements for machine guns, ensuring that only qualified individuals possess them. Switzerland, for example, has a high rate of gun ownership, including military-grade firearms, yet maintains low levels of gun violence. This suggests that cultural factors, rather than the mere presence of firearms, play a significant role in determining the impact on public safety.

The debate over machine guns and the Second Amendment is complex and multifaceted. While current federal law imposes strict regulations on machine guns, there is a compelling constitutional argument that these firearms should be protected under the Second Amendment. Historical context, the principle of self-defense, and legal precedents all support the notion that citizens have the right to own and bear arms equivalent to those used by the military.

## Growing Support for the Second Amendment

As we have briefly touched upon in the sections above, a clever tactic used by the legacy media and gun controllers involves the manipulation of public opinion polls to yield results that support their narrative. By carefully framing questions or selectively reporting poll results, the media and gun control advocates create the illusion of broad public support for restrictive gun measures.

However, despite these efforts, public opinion for the Second Amendment has been steadily rising over the decades, while support for gun control measures has been waning. This change is evident in various statistics, polls, and legislative actions that highlight the increasing support for gun rights and the diminishing enthusiasm for restrictive gun control measures.

In the following subsections, we will explore the legislative developments that collectively indicate a more pro-gun and pro-Second Amendment stance across the nation, as well as discuss how statistical and polling manipulations occur and examine the true trends in public opinion.

## Increasing Gun Ownership

One of the most telling indicators of America's growing pro-gun sentiment is the rise in gun ownership. Data from the Small Arms Survey shows that the number of civilian-owned firearms in the United States has been steadily increasing. In 1993, there were approximately 192 million privately owned guns in the country.

By 2017, that number had surged to over 393 million, surpassing the total US population. In 2024, there were over 400 million privately owned guns in the United States, and that number is still growing. This trend reflects a broader cultural shift towards embracing gun ownership for self-defense, hunting, and sporting purposes.

The spike in gun sales in recent years further proves this point. The FBI's National Instant Criminal Background Check System (NICS) reported a record number of background checks for gun purchases in 2020, with over 39.7 million conducted, compared to 28.4 million in 2019. This surge continued into 2021 and 2022, reflecting ongoing concerns about personal safety and civil unrest.

## Public Opinion Trends

Polling data from the past few decades also shows a notable shift in public opinion towards supporting gun rights. Gallup polls in the early 1990s illustrate that support for stricter gun control laws was relatively high, with 78 percent of Americans favoring more stringent regulations in 1990, although by 2021, that number had dropped to 57 percent, indicating a significant decrease in support for gun control. However, a more in-depth study conducted by the Pew Research Center in 2021 found that 53 percent of Americans believe gun laws should be less strict or kept as they are, while only 47 percent support making gun laws more stringent. While both examples highlight a growing support for gun rights over the decades, the discrepancy between the 2021 Gallup poll and the results of the Pew Research Center's study highlights how polling questions are phrased and presented to respondents and can yield very different results. Nonetheless, the results represent a significant shift from past decades, where stricter gun control measures enjoyed broader support.

## Manipulated Public Opinion Statistics

Although statistics show that support for gun control has been waning in favor of a more pro-gun stance, as outlined above, it is important to scrutinize the methodologies and question phrasing used by polling organizations and media outlets. Often, the way questions are phrased can significantly influence the results, artificially boosting support for gun control. This tactic skews public perception and misrepresents the true sentiments of the American people.

One common strategy is to use loaded questions that lead respondents toward a particular answer. For instance, a survey might ask, "Do you support common-sense gun control measures to prevent gun violence?" The term "common-sense" implies that the measures are reasonable and universally agreeable, influencing respondents to answer affirmatively. Similarly, a question like, "Do you support measures to prevent dangerous individuals from obtaining firearms?" frames the issue in a way that most people would naturally support, regardless of their overall stance on gun control.

Polling organizations also frequently employ questions that conflate different types of gun control measures, making it difficult to discern the specific policies respondents support. For example, a question might ask, "Do you support stricter background checks and banning assault weapons?" Respondents might agree with stricter background checks but not with banning so-called assault weapons, yet their affirmative response is recorded as supporting both measures.

A notable example comes from a Gallup poll in October 2021, which found that 57 percent of Americans supported stricter gun laws. However, the same poll revealed that only 42 percent supported a ban on the manufacture, sale, and possession of semi-automatic rifles such as the AR-15. This discrepancy highlights how the phrasing of questions about "stricter gun laws" versus specific types of gun control can yield different results.

Historical data further illustrates this point. In the early 1990s, support for gun control was reportedly high, with over 70 percent of Americans favoring stricter laws according to Gallup. However, during this period, questions were often phrased in the context of high-profile mass shootings and urban crime waves, influencing public opinion. When questions are asked more neutrally, such as simply inquiring about support for more or less gun control without additional context or leading language, the results show less support for increased regulations.

Moreover, media outlets often highlight polls with favorable results for gun control while ignoring or downplaying those that do not fit their narrative. For example, in 2018, the Pew Research Center found that while 57 percent of Americans favored stricter gun laws, only 37 percent believed that banning handguns would reduce the number of homicides. Yet, the headline used by many media outlets was "Majority of Americans Support Stricter Gun Laws," omitting the nuances of the public's views on specific regulations.

Another recent example is the way media reports on support for "universal background checks." While surveys often show high support for this measure, the actual implementation and enforcement of such checks, along with their impact on gun rights, are rarely discussed in detail. This selective reporting leads to a skewed understanding of public opinion.

Additionally, anti-gun organizations and politicians often use these skewed statistics to push for more restrictive laws, claiming broad public support that may not exist when the questions are framed differently. For instance, during the 2020 US presidential campaign, numerous candidates cited polls showing support for "common-sense gun reforms" without addressing the varied and complex views Americans have on specific gun control measures.

The way questions about gun rights and gun control are phrased in polls can significantly influence the results, often boosting apparent support for gun control. By using loaded language, conflating different measures, and selectively reporting results, polling organizations and media outlets can misrepresent public sentiment. This manipulation underscores the importance of critically examining poll questions and understanding the nuances behind the statistics.

## Common Anti-Gun Myths Debunked

Gun control debates are rife with misconceptions and myths perpetuated by the media, politicians, and advocacy groups. Here, we aim to debunk 20 common myths with facts, historical context, and statistical evidence to provide a clearer understanding of the Second Amendment and gun ownership in America. This section will address the fallacies often presented by gun control advocates, who argue for stricter regulations and limitations on firearm ownership.

Many of the points we will discuss have been touched upon earlier and will be elaborated on further in subsequent chapters. But by revisiting these issues from various perspectives, as we do in this book, we can better appreciate the complexity of the debate and reinforce the core arguments that support the right to bear arms.

In subsequent chapters, we will delve deeper into these themes, providing a broader context and additional insights into the relationship between firearms and society. Our goal is to equip readers with the knowledge needed to engage in meaningful discussions about gun rights and public safety.

## Myth 1: "Gun violence is the number one killer of children."

This claim is frequently repeated by gun control advocates and often cited in media reports. However, it is misleading because it typically includes adolescents up to the age of 19, conflating child gun deaths with those involving older teens and young adults who are more likely to be involved in gang violence or criminal activities. By doing so, the statistics paint a distorted picture of the true nature of gun-related fatalities among younger children.

According to the Centers for Disease Control and Prevention (CDC), the leading causes of death for children aged one to 14 are drowning, car accidents, and congenital anomalies, not gun violence. The CDC's data indicates that for children under the age of 15, firearm-related deaths are significantly less common compared to older teens.

To boost the numbers and create a more alarming narrative, gun control advocates often include adolescents and young adults in their statistics. This group, which includes 18- and 19-year-olds, is more likely to be involved in violent crime and gang activity, significantly contributing to the number of firearm-related deaths. The inclusion of these older teens skews the data, making it appear as though gun violence is a more pervasive threat to young children than it actually is.

Moreover, these statistics typically exclude children under the age of four, as the number of deaths due to guns in this age group is statistically insignificant. Including toddlers or infants would lower the overall statistics, which is why they are often omitted. This selective categorization of what constitutes "children" is misleading and does not provide an accurate representation of gun-related fatalities among various age groups.

Media outlets like CNN often highlight the issue of gun violence among children, but their reports sometimes fail to distinguish between different age groups. By lumping together young children with older teens and legal adults, these reports create a generalized and misleading narrative. This can lead to emotional responses from the public and policymakers, driving policy decisions that may not be based on accurate data analysis or address the root causes of gun violence.

Additionally, the inclusion of older adolescents in these statistics often ignores the broader social and economic factors that contribute to youth violence. Factors such as poverty, lack of education, and limited access to mental health resources play significant roles in the prevalence of gang activity and criminal behavior among teenagers. Addressing these underlying issues requires targeted interventions and policies that go beyond general gun control measures.

By understanding and accurately representing the data, we can create more effective policies that address the specific needs and risks associated with different age groups. For instance, enhancing safety measures and education around firearms in homes where young children are present can help reduce accidental shootings. At the same time, community programs aimed at providing opportunities and support for at-risk teens can help mitigate the factors that lead to gang involvement and violent crime.

Accurate representation of the data is crucial for developing effective policies that address the real issues of gun violence, tailored to the specific circumstances of different age groups. By debunking these myths, we can foster a more informed and rational discussion about gun control and the Second Amendment, grounded in facts and historical context rather than misconceptions and fear.

## Myth 2: "The Second Amendment only applies to a well-regulated militia."

The term "militia," as understood by the Founding Fathers, referred to the general populace capable of bearing arms. The notion that the Second Amendment's right to bear arms is conditional upon service in a government-regulated militia is a common misconception. The Supreme Court's landmark decision in *Heller* clarified that the Second Amendment protects an individual's right to possess firearms unconnected with service in a militia and to use them for traditionally lawful purposes, such as self-defense within the home.

Justice Antonin Scalia, writing for the majority in *Heller*, emphasized that the phrase "the right of the people to keep and bear Arms" provides an individual right to firearm ownership. This interpretation is deeply rooted in the historical context of the Second Amendment, which was designed to protect individual liberties against potential government tyranny. Scalia noted that "the people" referred to the same class of individuals mentioned in other parts of the Bill of Rights, such as in the First and Fourth Amendments, which protect individual rights.

The *Heller* decision also undertook a linguistic analysis of the Second Amendment, highlighting the distinction between the prefatory clause ("A well regulated Militia, being necessary to the security of a free State") and the operative clause ("the right of the people to keep and bear Arms, shall not be infringed"). The Court determined that while the prefatory clause explains the purpose of the amendment, it does not limit or condition the operative clause. The operative clause stands as a distinct guarantee of the right to bear arms, independent of militia service. This clarification debunks the argument that the right to bear arms is solely tied to organized militia groups.

Despite this clear ruling, many politicians and media personalities continue to argue that the Second Amendment only applies to organized militia groups. *The New York Times* has published op-eds asserting that the amendment's intent was collective rather than individual, often ignoring the Supreme Court's interpretation and historical evidence. These arguments typically stem from a selective reading of the amendment's text, which overlooks the broader historical and linguistic context in which the Framers operated.

Historical documents and writings from the Founding Fathers further illustrate that the militia was intended to be a body of the people, distinct from a standing army. In The Federalist No. 29, Alexander Hamilton described the militia as "the body of the people, trained to arms." He argued that this citizen militia was necessary to prevent the government from becoming tyrannical, as it provided a counterbalance to a standing army. Similarly, James Madison, in The Federalist No. 46, emphasized that an armed populace was a necessary defense against government overreach, highlighting that Americans possessed a unique advantage because of their widespread gun ownership.

The Founding Fathers were wary of standing armies and sought to ensure that the general populace retained the means to defend their freedoms. This sentiment was echoed in various state constitutions and legal commentaries of the time, which recognized the right to bear arms as an individual right essential for self-defense and the preservation of liberty.

In contemporary times, the relevance of the Second Amendment remains significant. The principles enshrined in the amendment are evident in the checks it provides against potential government overreach and its role in ensuring personal security. The right to bear arms continues to serve as a critical component of American liberty, allowing individuals to defend themselves, their families, and their property.

## Myth 3: "Since each state has its own National Guard units, the need for a militia has been filled, making the right to bear arms null and void."

The term "militia," as understood by the Founding Fathers, referred to the general populace capable of bearing arms. This definition is key in understanding the original intent behind the Second Amendment. The modern National Guard, while an essential component of national defense, does not replace the traditional concept of a militia comprising ordinary citizens. This distinction is evident in historical documents and the writings of the Founding Fathers, who envisioned a militia as a safeguard against tyranny and an essential element of a free state.

Historical documents and writings from the Founding Fathers provide a clear insight into their understanding of the militia. In The Federalist No. 29, Alexander Hamilton described the militia as "the body of the people, trained to arms." He emphasized that a well-regulated militia was necessary for the security of a free state and distinct from a standing army, which he viewed with suspicion due to its potential for abuse by the government. Hamilton argued that the militia, composed of ordinary citizens, would act as a counterbalance to the power of a professional military force and prevent any potential usurpation of power.

Similarly, James Madison, in The Federalist No. 46, reinforced the idea that the militia was meant to be a body of armed citizens. Madison noted that the advantage of being armed—an advantage that was almost exclusive to Americans—was a primary means of preserving liberty. He argued that a federal standing army would be opposed by a militia made up of a large portion of the population, ensuring that the government could not easily overpower the populace. This view highlights the importance of an armed citizenry in the preservation of freedom and the prevention of tyranny.

The Supreme Court's decision in *Heller* further clarified the individual right to bear arms as protected by the Second Amendment. Justice Antonin Scalia, writing for the majority, affirmed that the Second Amendment protects an individual's right to possess a firearm, unconnected with service in a militia, and to use that arm for traditionally lawful purposes, such as self-defense within the home. The Court's interpretation emphasized that the right to bear arms was an individual right, rooted in the historical context of self-defense and resistance to oppression.

The misunderstanding of the term "militia" often arises from a lack of appreciation for the historical context and the specific language used by the Framers of the Constitution. As detailed in chapter 2, the Founding Fathers were deeply influenced by their experiences with British colonial rule and the oppressive use of a standing army against the colonists. Their intent was to ensure that the newly formed government of the United States would never have the means to disarm its citizens and impose tyrannical rule. This historical perspective is critical in interpreting the Second Amendment and understanding the importance of an armed populace.

Contemporary examples further illustrate the relevance of the Founders' vision. In various instances where governments have attempted to disarm their citizens, the absence of an armed populace has often led to increased governmental control and reduced individual freedoms. The historical examples of Nazi Germany, Soviet Russia, and more recently, Venezuela, where disarmament preceded widespread oppression, serve as stark reminders of the dangers of a disarmed citizenry, as discussed in chapter 4.

To put this issue to rest, the term "militia" in the context of the Second Amendment refers to the general populace capable of bearing arms, a concept that remains vital to the preservation of liberty and the prevention of tyranny. The writings of the Founding Fathers and the Supreme Court's interpretation in the *Heller* decision affirm that the right to bear arms is an individual right, integral to the defense against oppression. By understanding this historical context, we can better appreciate the enduring significance of the Second Amendment in protecting individual freedoms.

## Myth 4: "Civilians don't need 'assault weapons.'"

We touched upon this point above in the section "'Need' vs. Rights," but, as noted several times previously, the term "assault weapon" is often used to describe semi-automatic firearms that share cosmetic features with military rifles but do not function the same. True assault rifles, capable of fully automatic fire, are already heavily regulated and restricted under the National Firearms Act of 1934 and the Firearm Owners Protection Act of 1986.

Semi-automatic firearms often deliberately mislabeled as "assault weapons," function differently from their military counterparts. They fire one round per trigger pull, unlike fully automatic weapons that continue to fire if the trigger is held down. The use of the term "assault weapon" by media and politicians is a deliberate attempt to conflate these distinct types of firearms to generate public support for bans on these weapons.

Politicians like the late Senator Dianne Feinstein have repeatedly called for bans on "assault weapons," using emotionally charged language to describe these firearms without addressing their functional differences from actual military weapons. This rhetoric aims to create fear and misunderstanding about the capabilities and use of these firearms by law-abiding citizens.

## Myth 5: "Gun control laws prevent crime."

We have explored this topic in previous chapters, but it is nonetheless a notable argument to include on this list. As previously discussed, studies have shown that stricter gun control laws do not necessarily correlate with lower crime rates.

For example, cities with stringent gun control laws like Chicago and Baltimore continue to experience high rates of gun violence compared to cities with more permissive laws, underscoring the limitations of gun control measures in addressing deeper societal problems.

A comprehensive study by the National Research Council in 2004 found no clear link between gun control laws and crime rates. Instead, the study suggested that factors such as socioeconomic conditions, law enforcement practices, and community engagement play more significant roles in influencing crime rates.

Politicians and media outlets frequently tout gun control as a solution to gun violence yet fail to address the complex socioeconomic issues that contribute to crime.

## Myth 6: "The majority of crimes are committed with assault weapons."

FBI crime statistics consistently show that handguns are used in most firearm-related crimes. Rifles, including those often labeled as "assault weapons," account for a small fraction of gun crimes. This distinction is crucial for informed discussions on gun control policies and the effectiveness of proposed legislation.

According to the FBI's Uniform Crime Reporting (UCR) data, handguns are the predominant type of firearm used in crimes. The UCR data reveals that in recent years, handguns were involved in approximately 90 percent of all firearm-related homicides. In contrast, rifles and shotguns, which include those often referred to as "assault weapons," represent a much smaller percentage of these crimes. This significant disparity is frequently overlooked or misrepresented by those advocating for bans on "assault weapons," leading to policies that may not effectively address the most common sources of gun violence.

During debates on gun control legislation, media coverage often emphasizes mass shootings involving semi-automatic rifles. While these tragic events receive extensive attention and are undeniably horrific, they are statistically rare compared to crimes committed with handguns. The hyperfocus on mass shootings involving rifles creates a skewed perception of firearm violence and can lead to misinformed policy decisions. For example, in 2019, out of the 10,258 gun-related homicides reported by the FBI, only 364 were committed with rifles (all rifles). By contrast, the number of homicides committed with handguns numbered over 6,368. Subsequent years show comparable statistical ratios.

Selective reporting on high-profile mass shootings can also distort public perception, overshadowing the fact that handguns are more frequently used in everyday crimes. This selective emphasis can lead to calls for "assault weapon" bans, despite the limited role these firearms play in overall gun violence. Consequently, policy discussions may become overly focused on banning certain types of rifles, rather than addressing the broader and more pressing issue of handgun violence.

Moreover, legislative efforts to ban "assault weapons" often ignore the adaptability of criminals. Even if such bans were effective in reducing crimes committed with semi-automatic rifles, individuals intent on committing violence would still have access to handguns, which are more concealable and easier to obtain. This proves the need for comprehensive strategies that address all forms of gun violence, rather than targeting specific types of firearms.

In addition to the FBI's UCR data, research by criminologists supports the finding that handguns are the primary weapons used in firearm-related crimes. Studies have shown that the vast majority of firearm assaults, robberies, and homicides are committed with handguns. These findings suggest that policy measures aimed exclusively at banning "assault weapons" would likely have a minimal impact on overall gun violence.

Furthermore, focusing on the type of firearm rather than the underlying causes of gun violence can lead to ineffective solutions. Factors such as socioeconomic conditions, mental health issues, and gang activity play significant roles in firearm-related crimes. Addressing these root causes through targeted interventions, community programs, and mental health support can be more effective in reducing gun violence than banning specific types of firearms.

In conclusion, the FBI's crime statistics and extensive research consistently show that handguns are the most used firearms in crimes, while rifles, including those labeled as "assault weapons," are involved in a much smaller fraction of incidents. The media's focus on mass shootings involving semi-automatic rifles skews public perception and policy discussions, leading to calls for bans that would not effectively address the most common sources of gun violence.

## Myth 7: "Gun control laws would have prevented the mass shootings."

Many mass shooters obtained their firearms legally, often passing background checks. This fact challenges the effectiveness of current gun control measures and highlights the need to address deeper societal issues. That the shooters in Newtown, Las Vegas, and Parkland legally acquired firearms despite evident warning signs calls attention to the limitations of relying solely on legislative restrictions to prevent such tragedies.

In the case of the Sandy Hook Elementary School shooting in Newtown, Connecticut, the shooter used firearms legally purchased by his mother. Despite his known mental health issues, there were no legal barriers preventing his access to these weapons. This shows that even stringent background checks may not be sufficient if firearms are accessible within the home, emphasizing the importance of secure storage and responsible gun ownership.

The Las Vegas shooter, responsible for the deadliest mass shooting in modern US history, also legally acquired his extensive arsenal. Despite purchasing numerous firearms and large quantities of ammunition over a short period, these transactions did not trigger any alerts or preventive measures. This case illustrates the limitations of background checks in identifying and preventing individuals with malicious intent from obtaining firearms.

Similarly, the shooter in the Parkland, Florida, massacre legally purchased his firearm after passing a background check, despite exhibiting troubling behavior and despite the existence of multiple reports to the FBI and local authorities about his potential for violence. These warnings did not prevent him from acquiring a firearm legally. This tragic event highlights significant gaps in the system where red flags are not adequately addressed and necessary interventions are not implemented.

These examples accentuate the limitations of gun control laws in preventing mass shootings. While background checks and other regulatory measures are important, they often fail to address the underlying issues, such as mental health and societal factors, that contribute to such tragedies. Mental health issues are a significant factor in many mass shootings, yet they are often neglected in the broader conversation about gun control.

Addressing mental health requires a multifaceted approach, including better access to mental health care, early intervention programs, and improved mental health education. Ensuring that individuals with serious mental health issues receive the treatment and support they need can help prevent potential acts of violence. Additionally, implementing effective reporting systems that allow for timely interventions when individuals exhibit warning signs is very important.

Improving community and school safety measures is another essential component often overlooked in the push for more restrictive gun laws. Enhanced security protocols, such as controlled entry points, on-site security personnel, and emergency response plans, can significantly reduce the risk of mass shootings. Programs that foster a positive school environment and address bullying and other social issues can also play a vital role in preventing violence.

Furthermore, initiatives that promote responsible gun ownership, including safe storage practices and education on the risks of firearm access for individuals with mental health issues, are vital. Encouraging gun owners to secure their firearms properly can prevent unauthorized access and reduce the likelihood of firearms being used in crimes or accidental shootings.

While gun control laws such as background checks are important, they are not foolproof solutions to preventing mass shootings. The examples of Newtown, Las Vegas, and Parkland and highlight the limitations of these laws and the need for a more comprehensive approach. Addressing mental health issues, improving community and school safety measures, and promoting responsible gun ownership are crucial components of an effective strategy to prevent mass shootings.

## Myth 8: "Australia's gun buyback program is a model for the US."

After Australia's mandatory gun buyback in 1996, there was a significant reduction in gun ownership, but the impact on overall crime rates remains a topic of debate. The program, implemented in the wake of the Port Arthur massacre, involved the government purchasing and destroying over 600,000 firearms from private owners. While some studies (including one by the Australian Institute of Criminology) suggest a decline in gun suicides, there is no clear evidence that the program significantly reduced gun homicides or overall crime rates.

Critics of the Australian model argue that cultural and societal differences between Australia and the United States make such a program impractical and potentially ineffective in America. Australia's population is significantly smaller and more homogenous than that of the United States, and the country does not have a constitutional right to bear arms. What worked in Australia may not be applicable or successful in the US context.

Proponents of the Australian model often note that the buyback led to a reduction in the number of guns in circulation but fail to acknowledge the broader context and the mixed results of the program. It did not address the underlying issues that contribute to violent crime, such as socioeconomic factors, mental health issues, and gang violence. In fact, some studies suggest that the decline in gun-related deaths was part of a broader trend that was already occurring and cannot be solely attributed to the buyback program.

Additionally, the political and cultural landscape in the US poses significant challenges to implementing similar measures. The Second Amendment of the US Constitution guarantees the right to bear arms, a deeply ingrained aspect of American culture and identity. Any attempt to implement a mandatory gun buyback program would face strong opposition from gun rights advocates, legal challenges, and significant political hurdles. The US also has a far larger and more diverse population, with varying attitudes towards gun ownership across different states and regions.

While Australia's buyback program is often highlighted as a successful model, it is essential to consider the broader impact on crime rates. Some researchers have found that gun homicides did not decline as much as expected and that other forms of violent crime did not see a corresponding decrease either. In fact, the overall crime rate in Australia remained relatively stable, suggesting that factors other than gun availability play significant roles in determining crime levels.

The period following the buyback saw fluctuations in various types of crime unrelated to firearms. Property crimes, assaults, and other violent offenses showed no clear pattern of decline that could be directly linked to the reduction in gun ownership. This indicates that comprehensive crime prevention strategies must address a wide range of issues beyond just the availability of firearms.

Furthermore, the impact on gun suicides, while significant, highlights the need for a nuanced approach to gun control. Simply removing firearms from the equation does not address the underlying causes of suicide, such as mental illness, depression, and social isolation. Effective gun control policies should therefore be part of a broader strategy that include focuses on mental health care, tough on crime policies, and community support.

More importantly, the United States has a fundamentally different relationship with firearms, enshrined in constitutional rights and deeply rooted in its history, culture, and self-reliance. A government-mandated confiscation scheme in a small, isolated nation with no Second Amendment cannot simply be copy-pasted onto a country with tens of millions of legal gun owners who view firearm ownership as an essential liberty. Adopting such a policy without recognizing these key differences ignores the realities of American society and the consequences of stripping law-abiding citizens of their right to self-defense.

## Myth 9: "Good guys with guns don't stop bad guys with guns."

Numerous instances highlight how armed civilians have prevented or mitigated mass shootings and other crimes. The Clackamas Town Center shooting in Oregon (discussed in chapter 3) is one such example, where an armed civilian confronted the shooter, potentially preventing further casualties. Media coverage often ignores or downplays stories of armed civilians stopping crimes, as these events contradict the narrative that civilian gun ownership is ineffective in preventing crime.

In addition, a study by the Crime Prevention Research Center found that 94 percent of mass shootings occur in gun-free zones, where civilians are typically disarmed. This statistic suggests that areas where civilians can legally carry firearms may deter potential attackers.

## Myth 10: "The US has the highest gun violence rate because of gun ownership."

The first rule of statistics—correlation is not causation. The second rule of statistics—figures don't lie, but liars figure. The high gun ownership rate is not the cause of gun violence in the US. Once again, an absurd myth, mindlessly echoed by equally absurd people, falls apart the moment it's exposed to basic research and a shred of common sense.

While the US has a high rate of gun ownership, it does not lead the world in gun violence. Countries with strict gun laws, such as Mexico and Brazil, experience higher rates of gun violence. This suggests that cultural, economic, and law enforcement factors play significant roles in influencing gun violence, which cannot be mitigated solely through the enactment of strict gun control laws.

According to the World Population Review, the US ranks lower than several countries with stricter gun control laws regarding gun violence rates. Its 2022 statistics have the United States ranked 54th out of 207 countries for murder rates, placing it in the middle tier despite being number one in gun ownership. This ranking is artificially high because most US murders are concentrated in large cities with stringent gun control. Nearly all nations with the strictest gun control measures—such as Jamaica, Haiti, Venezuela, El Salvador, and Honduras—have much higher murder rates than the United States and have high rates of poverty, rampant corruption, and ineffective law enforcement. This discrepancy highlights the complex interplay of various factors that contribute to gun violence beyond the mere presence of firearms in a society.

Another example is that Mexico's strict gun laws have not prevented it from having one of the highest rates of gun violence in the world. Civilian gun ownership is heavily restricted in Mexico, with the country maintaining only one legal gun store, run by the military and requiring extensive background checks and documentation for firearm purchases. Despite these measures, Mexico suffers from a high rate of homicides, largely driven by drug cartel violence and organized crime. The government's inability to control these criminal elements and the widespread corruption within its institutions undermine the effectiveness of gun control laws.

Similarly, Brazil has stringent gun regulations, including requirements for background checks, psychological evaluations, and extensive documentation for firearm ownership. However, these laws have failed to curb Brazil's high homicide rates, which remain among the highest in the world. The prevalence of gang violence, political instability, and socioeconomic disparities contribute significantly to the high levels of gun violence in Brazil. This demonstrates that even comprehensive gun control measures cannot adequately address the root causes of violence if broader systemic issues remain unaddressed.

Further illustrating this point is Venezuela, where strict gun control laws have been implemented to reduce violence. Despite these regulations, Venezuela has one of the highest murder rates globally. The rampant crime and violence in Venezuela is exacerbated by severe economic distress, political turmoil, and law enforcement inefficacy. The correlation between strict gun laws and high rates of violence in these countries suggests that simply enacting such laws is not sufficient to reduce violence.

In contrast, some countries with high rates of gun ownership have relatively low rates of gun violence. Switzerland and Finland, where gun ownership is common due to mandatory military service and a strong tradition of hunting, respectively, experience low levels of gun-related crime. These countries benefit from strong social cohesion, effective law enforcement, and comprehensive mental health care, which contribute to maintaining low violence rates despite widespread firearm ownership.

The United States' experience demonstrates the complexity of the issue. While the US does have a significant gun violence problem, particularly in certain urban areas, it also has regions with high gun ownership and low crime rates. States like Vermont and New Hampshire, which have high rates of gun ownership, report some of the lowest crime rates in the nation. These examples indicate that gun violence in the US is not uniform and is influenced by a range of factors, including economic conditions, cultural attitudes towards guns, and the effectiveness of local law enforcement.

The examples of Mexico, Brazil, and Venezuela illustrate that strict gun control laws alone are not a panacea for reducing gun violence. These countries' experiences highlight the importance of addressing broader societal issues, such as corruption, economic inequality, and ineffective law enforcement, to achieve meaningful reductions in violence. By considering the broader context and the multifaceted nature of gun violence, policymakers can develop more effective strategies that go beyond simple legislative fixes.

## Myth 11: "Gun shows are a major source of illegal firearms."

It is commonly claimed that gun shows are a significant source of illegal firearms and that they contribute heavily to gun violence. However, this assertion does not align with the available data. Studies, including those conducted by the Bureau of Justice Statistics, show that most firearms used in crimes are obtained through theft, black market transactions, or straw purchases, not from gun shows.

A study by the Department of Justice found that only about 2 percent of criminals acquired their firearms from gun shows. The vast majority, around 80 percent, obtained guns through illegal means or from family and friends. This data contradicts the narrative often promoted by gun control advocates and some media outlets.

## Myth 12: "Background checks prevent all gun violence."

While background checks are a helpful tool for preventing firearms from falling into the wrong hands, they are not foolproof. Criminals and individuals with malicious intent often find ways to circumvent these checks, such as through straw purchases, theft, or acquiring firearms on the black market. The National Institute of Justice reports that despite federal background checks, many guns used in crimes are obtained illegally. For example, the shooter in the Charleston church shooting passed a background check because of a clerical error, highlighting the system's limitations.

Furthermore, studies show that a significant proportion of firearms used in criminal activities are acquired through means that bypass legal scrutiny entirely. This includes gun trafficking networks and unregulated private sales that occur outside the purview of background checks. While improving the efficiency and scope of background checks can certainly help reduce some instances of gun violence, it is not a comprehensive solution. Addressing the broader issues of illegal gun markets and enhancing law enforcement efforts to combat gun trafficking are also essential components in tackling the problem of gun violence.

## Myth 13: "Gun-free zones keep people safe."

The concept of gun-free zones, introduced by the Gun-Free School Zones Act of 1990, particularly around schools and other public areas, often borders on the absurd. The intention behind these zones is to create safe environments for children by prohibiting firearms within a designated radius, usually about half a mile from schools. However, these laws often have the unintended consequence of criminalizing law-abiding gun owners who happen to live near these zones, effectively making them lawbreakers without their knowledge. This not only undermines the rights of responsible gun owners but also highlights the inefficacy of such zones in preventing crime.

One of the most glaring issues with gun-free zones is their assumption that posting a sign will deter criminals or shooters from entering the premises with ill intent. This is flawed logic, as individuals who are determined to commit acts of violence are unlikely to be swayed by a sign prohibiting firearms. The mere presence of a Gun-Free Zone sign does little to enhance the safety of those within the designated area. The notion that gun-free zones protect people from gun violence is naïve at best. According to data from the Crime Prevention Research Center, 94 percent of mass shootings in the United States occur in gun-free zones.

Research has shown that Gun-Free Zones do not significantly deter crime. Instead, they may even invite it. Criminals are aware that these areas are populated by unarmed individuals, making them soft targets. The tragic school shootings in Columbine, Sandy Hook, and Parkland all occurred in gun-free zones, underscoring the fact that such measures do not prevent determined attackers from carrying out their plans. In fact, these zones may give a false sense of security while actually increasing vulnerability.

Moreover, the broad radius of these zones can inadvertently ensnare law-abiding citizens who live or work nearby. For example, a gun owner living within half a mile of a school may find themselves unknowingly breaking the law simply by possessing a firearm in their home. This broad-brush approach does not take into account the context of responsible gun ownership and unnecessarily criminalizes individuals who have no intention of bringing harm to a school or its occupants.

In addition, these zones fail to consider the protective benefits of responsible armed individuals. In instances where armed citizens have intervened, potential mass shootings have been thwarted.

Gun-free zones around schools and other sensitive areas are based on a well-intentioned but faulty and naïve premise. They fail to deter criminals, potentially increasing vulnerability by ensuring that law-abiding citizens are unarmed and criminalize those who inadvertently fall within their expansive boundaries. Instead of creating these zones, a more nuanced approach that respects the rights of responsible gun owners while focusing on effective, evidence-based measures to enhance public safety is needed. This includes better mental health support, more comprehensive background checks, and community-based interventions that address the root causes of violence rather than relying on symbolic but ineffective signs.

The 2015 shooting at Umpqua Community College in Oregon is an example where the presence of a gun-free zone may have contributed to the tragedy. Shooters often target these areas because they expect little to no armed resistance. The continued occurrence of mass shootings in gun-free zones suggests that these policies may not provide the safety they intend to. As the saying goes, "The road to hell is paved with good intentions," and gun-free zones, despite their well-meaning premise, create soft targets that leave law-abiding citizens defenseless while doing nothing to deter criminals who have no regard for the law—often with fatal consequences.

## Myth 14: "Gun ownership increases the risk of homicide and suicide."

The myth that increased gun ownership correlates directly with higher rates of homicide and suicide is often perpetuated by selectively citing studies that fail to account for a multitude of other influencing factors. While it is true that some studies, such as those by the National Research Council and the Harvard Injury Control Research Center, suggest a link between gun prevalence and violent outcomes, these studies frequently overlook critical variables like socioeconomic conditions, mental health issues, and cultural influences.

Switzerland and Finland are often cited in the gun control debate. Both countries have high rates of gun ownership due to mandatory military service and a strong tradition of hunting, respectively. Despite this, they maintain relatively low homicide rates. Switzerland has a homicide rate of about 0.5 per 100,000 people, significantly lower than many countries with strict gun control laws. This suggests that other factors, such as a well-regulated militia system in Switzerland and a strong social cohesion in Finland, play important roles in mitigating violence.

In the United States, a similar pattern is observed in states like Vermont and New Hampshire. These states boast high rates of gun ownership yet report some of the lowest homicide rates in the country. Vermont has a gun ownership rate of 42 percent but has a homicide rate of about 1.8 per 100,000 people. New Hampshire has a gun ownership rate of about 41.1 percent, but the homicide rate is approximately 1.3 per 100,000. These figures are well below the national homicide average of about ±5.0 per 100,000 people, illustrating that high gun ownership does not necessarily equate to higher crime rates. Factors such as lower poverty rates, higher levels of education, and robust community networks contribute significantly to these outcomes.

Moreover, it is imperative to distinguish between correlation and causation. The presence of guns alone does not cause violence; rather, violence is a complex phenomenon influenced by a myriad of factors. Socioeconomic disparities, lack of mental health support, substance abuse, and cultural attitudes towards violence all play pivotal roles. For example, Japan, which has some of the strictest gun control laws in the world, also has a high suicide rate, indicating that factors beyond gun availability contribute to these tragic outcomes.

Studies that fail to consider these broader contexts often present a skewed picture. The United States, with its diverse population and significant regional variations, cannot be effectively analyzed with broad-brush statistics that ignore local nuances. Comprehensive studies that include variables such as income inequality, education levels, and mental health services provide a more accurate understanding of the relationship between gun ownership and violence.

Additionally, cultural attitudes towards guns and self-defense play a significant role. In much of rural America, guns are integral to the lifestyle and are used for hunting and protection. This cultural respect for firearms, combined with responsible ownership and safety training, helps maintain low crime rates despite high gun prevalence. Conversely, urban areas with strict gun control laws often see higher crime rates, which may be attributed to factors such as gang violence and economic hardship, rather than gun ownership alone.

The simplistic argument that more guns lead to more violence fails to consider the multifaceted nature of human behavior and societal structures. Comprehensive, multifactorial analyses are essential to understand the true dynamics at play. Effective policies should focus not solely on gun control but also on addressing the root causes of violence, including socioeconomic inequality, mental health issues, and cultural attitudes towards violence. By acknowledging and addressing these underlying factors, we can create safer communities without infringing on the rights of responsible gun owners.

## Myth 15: "You are more likely to have your gun used against you by an intruder."

Gun control advocates often assert that having a firearm for self-defense increases the likelihood that the gun will be used against the owner during an intrusion. This claim is frequently cited in arguments for stricter gun control measures.

Extensive research conducted by criminologists like Gary Kleck challenges this narrative, demonstrating that defensive gun use (DGU) is both common and effective in preventing crimes. Kleck, a well-respected Florida State University professor, has conducted in-depth studies on the frequency and efficacy of defensive gun use. His research estimates that guns are used defensively by Americans between 500,000 and 3 million times annually. These figures are derived from various national surveys, including the National Crime Victimization Survey (NCVS), which consistently show significant instances of firearms being used to deter or stop criminal activity.

The data clearly shows that armed citizens successfully defend themselves without their firearms being turned against them. Studies reveal that in most defensive gun use cases, merely brandishing a firearm or firing a warning shot is enough to deter a criminal. Similarly, research from the Cato Institute has documented numerous instances of defensive gun use, from preventing home invasions to stopping armed robberies and assaults. The National Research Council found that a firearm frequently defuses situations without a single shot being fired. These findings reinforce that for many Americans—especially in high-crime areas—firearms play an important role in personal safety.

In contrast to the claim that firearms in the home increase the risk of injury to the owner, evidence suggests that responsible gun ownership, combined with proper training and safe storage practices, significantly reduces such risks and ensures that firearms are available for defensive use when needed.

The argument that having a gun for self-defense is more likely to result in the firearm being used against the owner does not hold up against empirical evidence. Defensive gun use is a common and effective means of preventing crime. The data supports the view that responsible gun ownership enhances personal safety and can play a vital role in protecting individuals and communities from criminal threats.

## Myth 16: "High-capacity magazines are unnecessary and only useful for mass shootings."

As we have already discussed in previous sections, high-capacity magazines are often targeted by gun control laws under the assumption that they are only useful for committing mass shootings. However, they also serve legitimate purposes for self-defense, especially in situations where multiple assailants are involved.

During the 1992 Los Angeles riots, business owners used firearms with high-capacity magazines to defend their properties from looters and violent mobs. This capability can be crucial for effective self-defense in scenarios where multiple threats are present. In addition, the definition of high-capacity magazines is arbitrary, as standard-capacity magazines for many firearms are incorrectly lumped into this category.

If standard-capacity magazines are effectively banned, then limiting civilians to low-capacity "state compliant" magazines not only increase the risk of running out of ammunition during a multi-threat encounter—such as a home invasion—but also introduces the danger of malfunctions, as these government-approved magazines are often poorly designed or incompatible with specific firearms, potentially rendering them unreliable when it matters most.

## Myth 17: "More guns means more crime."

We have already touched upon this topic in previous sections and chapters, but the assertion that more guns in circulation lead to higher crime rates is not supported by empirical evidence. In fact, research from the National Research Council and data from the FBI show that increased gun ownership has coincided with a decrease in violent crime over the past two decades. This counterintuitive trend challenges the simplistic narrative that more guns inevitably results in more violence.

States with high gun ownership rates, such as Wyoming and Montana, consistently report some of the lowest crime rates in the country. Wyoming, with a gun ownership rate of around 60 percent, has a violent crime rate of 200 incidents per 100,000 people, far lower than the national average of ±379 incidents per 100,000 people. Montana, where about 66.3 percent of households own guns, has a violent crime rate of 327 per 100,000; lower than the national average, and lower than heavily gun-controlled states like California and New York, which report significantly higher rates despite their low gun ownership rate. These statistics suggest that high gun ownership does not correlate with increased violence and may even contribute to lower crime rates through deterrence.

Another compelling example is the state of Maine. With a gun ownership rate of around 47 percent, Maine has one of the lowest violent crime rates in the country, at approximately 120 incidents per 100,000 residents. This contrasts sharply with states like California, where strict gun laws coexist with higher violent crime rates. California, despite its rigorous gun control measures, had a violent crime rate of about 503 per 100,000 residents in 2023. These disparities highlight the importance of considering a broader range of factors beyond gun ownership when addressing crime.

Conversely, states with strict gun control policies and lower gun ownership rates—such as New York (14.5 percent), California (28.3 percent), Illinois (27.8 percent), and Maryland (30.2 percent)—often report higher violent crime rates, largely in large urban centers.

Maryland has a violent crime rate of nearly ±400 per 100,000 residents, and Illinois reports a rate of 425.9 per 100,000 residents. Similarly, cities with strict gun control measures, like Chicago and Baltimore, continue to struggle with high levels of gun violence. Chicago, despite having some of the strictest gun laws in the nation, recorded over 770 homicides in 2020, a sharp increase from previous years, and has led the country in total homicide numbers every year since 2012. This inconsistency suggests that factors other than gun ownership, such as socioeconomic conditions, gang activity, and law enforcement practices, play a more significant role in influencing crime rates.

International comparisons also highlight the complexity of the relationship between gun ownership and crime. Switzerland and Israel have high rates of gun ownership because of their compulsory military service. Despite this, both countries have low rates of gun-related homicides. Switzerland has a homicide rate of 0.5 per 100,000 people, while Israel's rate is approximately 1.4 per 100,000. These examples further evidence that high gun ownership does not necessarily result in higher crime rates and that cultural, social, and legal factors are critical in understanding violence.

Moreover, studies examining the impact of gun control laws on crime often reveal mixed results. Some research suggests that certain measures, such as background checks and restrictions on high-capacity magazines, can reduce specific types of gun violence. However, other studies find little to no effect of these laws on overall crime rates. This variability emphasizes the need for a nuanced approach to gun policy, one that considers the diverse factors influencing crime rather than relying solely on restrictive measures.

The simplistic argument that more guns means more crime does not hold up against empirical evidence. The data from various states and countries suggest that other factors, including socioeconomic conditions, law enforcement practices, and cultural attitudes towards violence, play more significant roles in shaping crime rates. A comprehensive approach to reducing violence should address these underlying issues rather than focusing exclusively on gun ownership.

## Myth 18: "The 'gun show loophole' is a major source of firearms for criminals."

The term "gun show loophole" is often used to describe the belief that individuals can purchase firearms at gun shows without undergoing background checks. This assertion is misleading and does not accurately reflect the legal requirements in place. In reality, federal law mandates that licensed firearm dealers conduct background checks on all gun sales, including those at gun shows. This requirement is enforced under the Brady Handgun Violence Prevention Act, which obligates all federally licensed firearm dealers to perform background checks through the National Instant Criminal Background Check System (NICS) before completing any sale.

While private sales between individuals who are not licensed dealers are not subject to federal background check requirements, these transactions represent a small fraction of overall gun sales at gun shows. Most sellers at gun shows are licensed dealers who must comply with federal laws. Many states have also enacted their own laws requiring background checks for private sales, including those conducted at gun shows. California, Colorado, and New York mandate background checks for all firearm sales, closing any potential loopholes at the state level.

Empirical data supports the claim that firearms acquired at gun shows are rarely used in crimes. The Bureau of Justice Statistics conducted a survey that found less than 1 percent of prison inmates who used a firearm during their crime obtained it from a gun show. This finding is corroborated by other studies, such as those by the Department of Justice, which consistently show that most firearms used in criminal activities are acquired through illegal means, rather than legal purchases at gun shows. For instance, the firearms used in the infamous 1999 Columbine High School massacre were obtained through straw purchases and not from gun shows. This case, among others, illustrates that criminals often bypass legal purchasing channels altogether, relying instead on illegal methods to acquire firearms.

Efforts to close the so-called gun show loophole often distract from more pressing issues related to illegal firearm acquisition. Focusing on gun shows diverts attention from the need to address more significant sources of firearms used in crimes, such as black-market transactions and thefts from legal owners. Comprehensive strategies that target these sources would be more effective in reducing gun violence.

Additionally, the emphasis on gun shows overlooks the effectiveness of current regulations and enforcement mechanisms. Licensed dealers, who comprise the majority of gun show vendors, are already subject to strict federal regulations, including mandatory background checks. Enhancing the enforcement of existing laws and improving the NICS database can further ensure that individuals prohibited from owning firearms cannot bypass the system.

The "gun show loophole" is largely a myth. Federal and state laws already require background checks for most firearm sales at gun shows, and the data shows that firearms purchased at these events are rarely used in crimes. Addressing the real sources of illegal firearms, such as theft and black-market sales, should be the focus of efforts to reduce gun violence. By debunking the myths surrounding gun shows and concentrating on more impactful solutions, policymakers can make meaningful progress in enhancing public safety.

## Myth 19: "Armed citizens are not effective in stopping crime."

Contrary to the belief that civilian gun ownership is inherently dangerous and contributes to higher crime rates, there are numerous documented cases where armed citizens have successfully stopped crimes and saved lives. Defensive gun use (DGU) is far more common than often acknowledged, with many incidents going unreported by the media. A study by the Cato Institute supports this view, revealing that incidents of DGU occur frequently and play a critical role in public safety.

Defensive gun use encompasses a range of scenarios, from thwarting home invasions to stopping public shootings. The often-cited example of the 2012

Clackamas Town Center shooting illustrates the potential impact of an armed citizen in a crisis situation. During this incident, an armed civilian, Nick Meli, confronted the shooter, causing the assailant to retreat and ultimately take his own life, thus preventing further casualties. This case, along with many others, demonstrates that armed citizens can and do play a critical role in stopping crime and minimizing harm.

The effectiveness of DGU is further substantiated by studies conducted by various researchers and institutions. Citing a statistic we have mentioned before, criminologist Gary Kleck's research estimates that guns are used defensively by Americans between 500,000 and 3 million times annually. In many instances, simply brandishing a weapon or firing a warning shot is usually sufficient to de-escalate a potentially violent situation.

Moreover, data from the National Crime Victimization Survey (NCVS), as mentioned earlier, supports the prevalence of DGU. The survey indicates that firearms are used by victims in self-defense in hundreds of thousands of incidents each year. This aligns with findings from the Centers for Disease Control and Prevention (CDC), which also acknowledges the defensive use of firearms as a significant factor in preventing crime. Despite the substantial number of DGUs, these incidents receive limited media coverage and are often overshadowed by stories that fit a more sensational narrative.

The role of armed citizens extends beyond personal defense to protecting others in public spaces. Real-world examples further underscore the effectiveness of firearms in self-defense. One prominent case is the 2017 church shooting in Sutherland Springs, Texas. Stephen Willeford, a nearby resident and former NRA instructor, used his AR-15 rifle to confront and shoot the gunman, ultimately stopping the massacre. Willeford's intervention was critical in ending the rampage and has been highlighted in discussions about the importance of armed civilians in emergency situations.

In a similar incident in 2019, also in Texas, an armed civilian, Jack Wilson, intervened and stopped the attacker before more lives could be lost. Wilson, who was part of the church's volunteer security team, acted swiftly, demonstrating how trained and armed citizens can effectively neutralize threats. This incident received widespread media coverage and was cited as a clear example of the life-saving potential of defensive gun use.

Additionally, studies have shown that states with higher rates of concealed carry permits often experience lower rates of violent crime. Further research from John Lott, an economist and gun rights advocate, supports this view. In his book *More Guns, Less Crime*, Lott argues that right-to-carry laws, which allow citizens to carry concealed weapons, are associated with reductions in violent crime. His analysis indicates that states that have implemented these laws have seen declines in murder, rape, and aggravated assault rates compared to states with more restrictive gun policies. However, despite Lott's findings, major cities within these states often implement their own strict gun control measures or establish gun-free zones, creating pockets of higher violent crime. As a result, these gun-controlled cities contribute disproportionately to the overall crime rate of their respective states, artificially inflating statewide crime statistics and misleadingly painting an inaccurate picture of the effectiveness of pro-gun policies.

The presence of armed citizens serves as a deterrent to would-be criminals, who are aware that their potential victims might be armed and capable of defending themselves. This deterrent effect is a key argument in favor of concealed carry laws and broader firearm ownership rights.

Critics of civilian gun ownership frequently overlook these positive outcomes, focusing instead on the potential for misuse or accidents. While these concerns are valid, they represent a small fraction of gun-related incidents. The broader picture, supported by empirical evidence, shows that responsible gun ownership and the right to self-defense play vital roles in public safety and individual protection.

Even if you believe that armed citizens or good Samaritans rarely make a difference (contrary to the facts), wouldn't you still want the chance—however slim—to defend yourself or your loved ones if your life was on the line? Because when the threat is real and seconds count, having that option can mean the difference between being a victim and having a fighting chance.

The argument that civilian gun ownership is more harmful than beneficial fails to consider the substantial evidence of defensive gun use. By recognizing and understanding the importance of DGU, we can foster a more balanced and informed discussion about gun control and the Second Amendment, grounded in facts and historical context rather than misconceptions and fear.

## Myth 20: "The Second Amendment is outdated and irrelevant in modern society."

Some argue that the Second Amendment, written in the 18th century, is no longer applicable in today's world. However, this view overlooks the amendment's fundamental purpose: to protect individual liberties and provide a check against government tyranny. The principles enshrined in the Second Amendment remain as relevant today as they were over two centuries ago, primarily because the potential for government overreach and the need for individual self-defense are timeless concerns.

The Second Amendment was crafted with a deep understanding of human nature and the historical context of the times. The Founding Fathers, having fought against a tyrannical British regime, recognized the necessity of an armed populace as a safeguard against oppression. As previously discussed in chapter 4, this historical lesson is highlighted by numerous examples from the 20th and 21st centuries, such as Nazi Germany, Soviet Russia, Maoist China, and many others, where disarmament has preceded authoritarian control and widespread human rights abuses.

The United States has also seen instances where an armed populace has acted as a check against tyranny and protected individual rights. The Civil Rights Movement in the 1960s provides an example where armed self-defense played a role in protecting activists from violent opposition. Groups like the Deacons for Defense and Justice, an armed African American organization, defended civil rights workers from attacks by the Ku Klux Klan and other violent groups. This protection was crucial in allowing the movement to continue its efforts towards achieving equality and justice.

In addition to historical and contemporary examples, the argument for the Second Amendment's continued relevance is supported by the enduring potential for government overreach. While the United States is a democratic nation with checks and balances, the concentration of power and the potential for abuse remain concerns. The Second Amendment provides a form of insurance against this potential, ensuring that citizens have the means to defend their rights should the need arise.

The right to bear arms is not solely about resistance to tyranny; it also encompasses the fundamental right to self-defense. In a world where threats to personal safety can come from various sources, including criminals and other violent actors, the ability to own and carry firearms for protection remains a critical aspect of individual liberty. This right is particularly important in areas where law enforcement response times are slow, and individuals must rely on themselves for immediate protection.

The Second Amendment's relevance endures because its foundational principles are timeless. Historical and contemporary examples of disarmament leading to oppression, along with the ever-present potential for government overreach and the fundamental need for self-defense, illuminate the importance of maintaining the right to bear arms. As long as these threats exist, the protections provided by the Second Amendment will remain essential to preserving individual liberties and preventing tyranny.

The arguments against the Second Amendment and advocating for stricter gun control measures often rest on misconceptions and selective interpretations of data that fail to account for the complexity of gun ownership and its effects on crime and safety. Historical and contemporary evidence clearly demonstrates the importance of the Second Amendment in safeguarding individual liberties and providing a check against potential government overreach. By debunking these myths, we can foster a more informed and rational discussion about gun control and the Second Amendment, grounded in facts and historical context rather than misconceptions and fear.

## Nostalgia for Normalcy

I remember the days when kids could spend summer afternoons playing with water pistols, dashing around with Super Soakers, and engaging in imaginative games like cowboys and Indians with cap guns. We would play cops and robbers, using toy guns to pretend to shoot each other, and no one thought twice about it. People thought of these activities as innocent child's play, a normal part of growing up. There were no hysterics about toy guns or water pistols; instead, these were cherished memories of fun and camaraderie. Back then, no one worried that such innocuous play would lead to violent behavior, and indeed, mass shootings were not a societal issue.

Today, however, society's tendency to coddle children has led to an atmosphere of hysteria and overreaction. Children are no longer allowed to engage in the same carefree play without fear of severe repercussions. This shift has made kids neurotic, overly sensitive, and ill-prepared for the real world. It seems that in trying to protect children from every conceivable harm, we've instead made them more vulnerable. Overprotective parenting has contributed to a generation of adult children who lack resilience. The difference between then and now highlights how much societal attitudes have changed, not always for the better.

Back in the '70s and '80s, it was common to see rifle racks in the back of trucks, even in high school parking lots, where students would bring their rifles to school after a morning of hunting with their fathers and leave them in their vehicles, with no one thinking twice about it. Many schools had recreational shooting sports programs and even shooting ranges in their basements. This normalization of firearms in educational settings coexisted with an era when school shootings were virtually nonexistent.

Back then, the presence of guns was never a problem; they were once a respected and integral part of many communities and households. Yet today, despite stricter regulations and more barriers to legal gun ownership, an irrational, hysterical climate of fear surrounds firearms. This shift reveals that the real issue isn't the guns themselves but rather a broader cultural and societal decline—a breakdown of moral codes, community values, and personal responsibility. Over time, the corruption of our society created a culture where violence, lawlessness, anti-Americanism, and moral relativism replaced rugged individualism, personal accountability, and respect for life. The fundamental change wasn't the availability of firearms; it was the decay of a society that once understood the responsibility that came with them. As that cultural decay took root, each new generation became more coddled, more sheltered from reality, and more clueless about the very freedoms that protect them. It's no surprise, then, that so many now fear the tools of liberty rather than the erosion of liberty itself.

## Coddled and Clueless

Nowadays, even the mere photograph of a gun or something vaguely resembling the shape of a gun can send some people into a panic, causing them to hyperventilate and launch into hysterics. This kind of neurosis has infiltrated the upper echelons of many of our cultural and educational institutions and, unfortunately, within segments of the general population. For example, there have been several instances where children were severely punished for bringing toy guns to school or playing with them outside, reflecting the extreme measures adopted by educational and social institutions. These actions highlight the irrational responses to what used to be considered normal childhood behavior.

One notable example, which occurred in 2019, involves a second-grade boy named Josh Welch, who was suspended from Park Elementary School in Baltimore, Maryland, for chewing a Pop-Tart into the general shape of a gun and playfully pretending to shoot his classmates. This incident, which many would view as innocent childhood behavior, resulted in a two-day suspension and sparked significant controversy. Josh later explained that he was trying to shape the Pop-Tart into a mountain, not a gun, but the school administration interpreted his actions as a violation of their zero-tolerance policy on weapons, even imaginary ones.

The reaction to this event highlights the extreme measures some institutions have adopted in their efforts to enforce safety policies. Critics argue that such responses are absurd and reflect a broader societal hysteria about the mere sight or suggestion of a gun.

The suspension of Josh Welch was upheld by the Maryland State Board of Education, despite efforts by his family to have it removed from his permanent record. This kind of response highlights the inflexible application of zero-tolerance policies with little room for discretion or common sense that often fail to consider the context and intent behind a child's actions. Ultimately, Josh's case demonstrates how mainstream society's heightened sensitivity and hysteria regarding guns can lead to disproportionate and irrational reactions.

Another notable incident involved Josiah Green, a seven-year-old boy who was suspended for 10 days after bringing a water gun and a Nerf gun to Douglass Park Elementary School in Portsmouth, Virginia. The school's strict zero-tolerance policy led to severe disciplinary action despite the harmless nature of the toys. The school initially considered expulsion but later withdrew the recommendation, illustrating the absurd lengths to which institutions will go to enforce these policies.

In another case, a 10-year-old boy in Alexandria, Virginia, was arrested and charged with brandishing a weapon after bringing a plastic toy gun to school. The toy had a bright orange cap on the end of the barrel, clearly identifying it as a nonlethal item. Despite not threatening or pointing it at anyone, the boy now has a criminal record, a consequence that will follow him throughout his life.

Similarly, in Anne Arundel County, Maryland, two students were criminally charged in connection with separate incidents involving toy guns at school. One involved a 17-year-old student seen with a "gel blaster" type toy gun inside a school building.

A more subtle example of the infantilization of our society is the replacement of the revolver emoji on smartphones and social media platforms with a water pistol, a decision made by major tech companies between 2016 and 2018, and is emblematic of a society that has become increasingly hysterical and hypersensitive toward firearms. Framed as an effort to reduce online threats, this change did nothing to address real-world violence but instead reflected a broader cultural shift—one that infantilizes serious issues and equates the mere depiction of a gun with actual harm. Rather than confronting the root causes of violence, society now obsesses over symbols, treating even harmless representations as dangerous. This reaction highlights the deeper trend of overreaction, where gun control advocates and corporations seek to erase firearms from public consciousness as if doing so will magically erase their existence. This is just another superficial gesture that ignores the larger societal decline—a breakdown of values, responsibility, and rational discourse in favor of performative outrage and fear-driven policies.

These examples reveal how mainstream institutions have become neurotic and hysterical over innocent childhood behaviors. The overreaction to toy guns reflects a broader cultural shift towards an irrational fear of anything resembling a firearm. As children, many of us played with toy guns and cap guns without incident, yet today's hypervigilant policies can turn harmless play into serious disciplinary matters. This climate of fear and overreach not only disrupts the lives of the children involved but also sends a message that institutions lack the ability to distinguish between genuine threats and innocent play.

## Arm Yourself with the Facts

A nuanced approach, informed by empirical evidence and respectful of constitutional rights, is essential for developing effective policies that genuinely enhance public safety while preserving the freedoms that are fundamental to American society. In this chapter, we have meticulously demonstrated that debunking the myths, absurdities, and fallacies perpetuated by the media, gun control advocates, and political elites is not only achievable but relatively simple when approached with historical facts, accurate statistics, and reasoned arguments. The anti-gun narratives that frequently dominate public discourse are little more than a house of cards, easily toppled by the weight of truth. By dissecting the manipulation of statistics and the propagation of unfounded claims, we've shown how these tactics are used to create a false sense of urgency and crisis, distorting public perception and influencing policy in ways that are not rooted in reality.

The various untruths and fallacies that underlie most gun control arguments crumble under scrutiny. The "gun show loophole," the exaggerated dangers of "assault weapons," and the elitist attitudes that dismiss the views of ordinary citizens in favor of political and cultural agendas are all exposed as hollow. The disconnect between the mainstream media's portrayal of gun rights and the actual sentiments of the American public is stark, with public opinion increasingly favoring Second Amendment rights despite the relentless barrage of anti-gun rhetoric.

Ultimately, while the narratives pushed by the media and gun control proponents may shift to align with the latest cultural trends or political agendas, this chapter serves as a comprehensive debunking of the anti-gun and gun control nonsense from every conceivable angle. By confronting misinformation with facts and reason, we pave the way for a more informed and rational discussion about gun rights, public safety, and the enduring importance of the Second Amendment in American life. The challenge now is not just to refute these falsehoods but to ensure that the truth remains at the forefront of the national conversation on this critical issue.

It's crucial to arm yourself with the facts so that when you're debunking anti-gun nonsense with your uninformed, anti-gun friends, you can effortlessly lay out indisputable truths and watch them stammer in response. By studying the arguments and facts we've covered, you'll be prepared to counter the misguided opinions of those who act like they know what they're talking about but are utterly clueless. Knowledge is your best weapon in this debate, and with it, you can turn any conversation into an opportunity to set the record straight.

# Chapter 8

## American Pravda: Media Narratives and Propaganda

*Lay not that flattering unction to your soul, that not your trespass but my madness speaks.*

—William Shakespeare

*In the flaring parks, in the speakeasies, in the hushed academies, your murmur will applaud the wisdom of a thousand quacks. For theirs is the kingdom.*

—Kenneth Fearing

T he mainstream media in the United States has increasingly mirrored the characteristics of *Pravda*, the state-controlled newspaper of the Soviet Union, which was known for disseminating government propaganda. This devolution into a sort of American *Pravda* has resulted in a press that overwhelmingly cheerleads for one political side while demonizing those who oppose the prevailing narrative. By selectively reporting and often distorting facts, the mainstream media acts not as an impartial watchdog but instead as a tool for political advocacy and control, much like *Pravda* in its heyday.

The media's transformation into an activist wing of the far left is a phenomenon deeply rooted in ideological strategies and historical precedents. This shift aligns with directives outlined in *The Communist Manifesto* and subsequent strategies espoused by communist and socialist thinkers. One such strategy is the "long march through the institutions," which advocates for infiltrating influential societal structures—like the media—and gradually transforming cultural and political landscapes from within. This has been a crucial tactic for promoting anti-gun rhetoric and viewpoints as a means to sway public opinion towards socialist, and ultimately, communist goals.

Historically, the Communist Party recognized the power of media to shape public discourse and influence political outcomes. Documents and directives from the early 20th century highlighted the need for sympathizers to gain positions of influence within the media. The goal was to create a cultural shift that would pave the way for socialist policies. This strategy has borne fruit over the decades, with many media outlets now espousing left-leaning ideologies and promoting narratives that align with socialist objectives.

The erosion of support for the Second Amendment is a significant part of this agenda. An armed population presents a formidable barrier to the implementation of socialist and communist policies. The Founding Fathers of the United States enshrined the right to bear arms in the Constitution, recognizing that an armed citizenry is a safeguard against tyranny. Therefore, to dismantle this constitutional protection, the media employs a variety of propaganda techniques.

The motivations behind this anti-gun propaganda are multifaceted. At one level, it reflects the ideological commitment of many media professionals to leftist causes. However, there is also a deeper, more insidious aspect. The drive to disarm the population is part of a broader agenda to undermine individual freedoms and pave the way for greater state control. An unarmed populace is less capable of resisting authoritarian policies and more reliant on the state for protection and security.

Some individuals within this movement may genuinely believe that disarming the public will lead to a safer society. However, most others are driven by a desire for power and control. These control freaks, who often occupy positions of influence, are genetically predisposed to seek dominance over others. Their bad ideas, rooted in a desire to impose their will and eradicate dissent, pose a grave danger to freedom and democracy.

In recent years, the mainstream media has played a significant role in shaping public perception and policy decisions regarding the Second Amendment and the gun-owning community. Through selective framing of narratives, omission of critical information, and amplification of specific incidents, the media has demonstrated a clear bias and disdain for the rights enshrined in the Second Amendment. This bias often manifests in the portrayal of gun owners as reckless or dangerous individuals, rather than law-abiding citizens exercising their constitutional rights.

One of the most egregious tactics employed by the media is the selective presentation of information. Stories involving gun violence or mass shootings are often given extensive coverage, while instances of defensive gun use, where firearms are used to prevent crimes and save lives, receive minimal attention. This selective reporting creates a skewed narrative that guns are primarily a source of danger rather than a means of protection. Additionally, media outlets frequently leave out context, such as the legal status of firearms used in crimes or the existing laws that failed to prevent those crimes, thereby misleading the public about the effectiveness of current gun regulations.

The mainstream media's portrayal of the common everyday American gun owner is often colored by a sense of moral and intellectual superiority. Journalists and commentators who are far removed from the realities of rural or suburban life, where gun ownership is more prevalent, project their biases onto their reporting. This condescension fosters a divide between urban and rural populations and perpetuates stereotypes that do not reflect the responsible and diverse community of gun owners across the country.

Moreover, the media's influence extends beyond public perception to influence politicians and policy decisions. By controlling the gun control narrative, the media puts pressure on lawmakers to enact more restrictive measures, regardless of their effectiveness or constitutionality. This influence is evident in the way certain high-profile shootings lead to immediate calls for gun control legislation, often before all the facts are known. Politicians, eager to appear responsive and proactive, often propose or support legislation that aligns with the media-driven narrative, further entrenching the bias.

Unfortunately, many Americans are susceptible to this propaganda, accepting media portrayals and narratives at face value without seeking out alternative perspectives. This gullibility is partly due to the media's pervasive reach and the trust that people place in familiar news sources. The mainstream media has devolved into a Soviet-style entity that reports events through a partisan lens, demonizing, silencing, and even outright censoring opposing views, not just on the Second Amendment, but on a wide range of issues.

A consequential factor in this biased landscape is the cohesive, partisan alignment of most mainstream media outlets with the Democratic Party. With some notable exceptions, these media organizations operate almost as the audiovisual department of the Democratic Party, shaping narratives to solely support the party's agenda. This alignment is evident in the consistent framing of gun control debates, where pro-Second Amendment arguments are marginalized or ridiculed, and anti-gun viewpoints are given prominence and legitimacy.

Even media outlets that occasionally present alternative viewpoints often tread lightly, fearing backlash and potential cancellation by the powers that be. This dynamic results in a controlled opposition, where dissenting voices are allowed only within narrowly defined parameters, ensuring that the dominant narrative remains unchallenged. True unbiased reporting is rare, and even those outlets that strive for balance must navigate a media environment heavily skewed against them.

The influence of this biased reporting extends into the digital realm, with search engines like Google manipulating algorithms to suppress pro-Second Amendment content. When users search for information about guns and the Second Amendment, they are often presented with negative news stories and anti-gun perspectives at the top of the search results. Positive or neutral information, as well as expert opinions supporting gun rights, are buried several pages deep, knowing that most people do not go past the first page of search results. This manipulation ensures that most users are exposed primarily to the media's preferred narrative.

Similarly, platforms like YouTube engage in shadow banning, demonetizing, and removing content from influencers and creators who discuss firearms and advocate for the Second Amendment. This censorship stifles open discussion and prevents a balanced exchange of ideas, further entrenching the biased narrative. Other search engines yield similar results, contributing to a broader effort to control the flow of information and shape public opinion in favor of more restrictive gun laws.

The media and pop culture often glorify guns in movies, TV shows, and video games, despite many pop culture figures such as actors, TV stars, producers, directors, and animators harboring anti-Second Amendment views. These movies are popular with the public because the use of guns for entertainment value provides thrill and excitement, making the content more engaging. Pop culture and media elites will capitalize on the general public's acceptance and positive view of guns as tools of self-defense and excitement to make money. This demonstrates a profound hypocrisy, as the media and those in pop culture are willing to endorse the portrayal of guns when it benefits them financially, even as they advocate gun ownership in their personal and public lives.

## Media Narratives

Anti-gun rhetoric often comes from politicians, media figures, and cultural influencers who use misleading information to push their agenda. These individuals deliberately manipulate statistics and distort facts to create a narrative that supports their views on gun control. By playing on public fears and emotions, they aim to gain support for restrictive policies that may not be based on reality. There are numerous examples, but here we will highlight a few notable ones, illustrating how these arguments often fail to stand up to scrutiny.

*USA Today*'s infamous "chainsaw bayonet" graphic in 2017 following the Texas church shooting is a glaring example. By depicting an unrealistic and exaggerated firearm accessory, *USA Today* sensationalized the incident, fostering unnecessary fear and confusion about gun modifications. This was an overt attempt to amplify the narrative that guns and their accessories are excessively dangerous, even when such modifications are impractical and virtually nonexistent in real-life scenarios.

Similarly, CNN has consistently pushed misleading narratives around gun violence. After the Sandy Hook shooting, CNN reported an inflated number of mass shootings based on a broad and inconsistent definition, which included many incidents where no one was killed. Specifically, CNN's Jim Acosta made numerous statements promoting anti-gun views, often citing inflated numbers of mass shootings. For example, he claimed there have been over 1,500 mass shootings since the Sandy Hook massacre, using data from the Gun Violence Archive, which includes incidents that do not meet the traditional definition of a mass shooting. This selective use of statistics creates a misleading picture of the frequency and severity of gun violence, aiming to garner support for more restrictive laws. This misrepresentation was not just an oversight but part of a broader pattern to shape public opinion against gun ownership by making it seem that mass shootings are far more common than they actually are.

Michael Moore's 2002 film *Bowling for Columbine* is a well-known piece of anti-gun propaganda that seeks to paint a grim picture of America's gun culture. One of the most notable segments in the film is when Moore walks into a bank that offers a free gun as a promotional gift for opening a new account. The film depicts Moore walking out of the bank with a rifle, implying that acquiring a firearm in the United States is alarmingly easy and unregulated. However, this portrayal was highly misleading. Moore did not simply walk out of the bank with a gun. The process involved extensive background checks and compliance with all legal requirements before he could take possession of the firearm. The scene was staged to make it appear as though Moore received the gun immediately after opening the account, which was not the case. This manipulation was intended to underscore the film's message about the supposed dangers of easy access to firearms, but it did so at the expense of truth and transparency. This example is emblematic of the broader tactics used by anti-gun advocates and filmmakers like Moore. By presenting a skewed version of reality, they aim to foster fear and misinformation among the public.

In 2018, former President Barack Obama often spoke out against gun violence, calling for stricter gun control measures. During his presidency, he often cited misleading statistics, such as the claim that 40 percent of gun sales occurred without background checks. This statistic was based on outdated and flawed studies, yet it was repeatedly used to justify universal background checks. Obama's rhetoric often framed the debate as a battle between common sense and extremism, disregarding the legitimate concerns of Second Amendment advocates. The hypocrisy lies in the fact that while advocating for gun control, he was protected by heavily armed Secret Service agents.

Another example is former New York City Mayor Michael Bloomberg, a vocal advocate for gun control who has spent millions of dollars through his organization, Everytown for Gun Safety, to push for restrictive gun laws. Bloomberg has claimed that the majority of Americans support stricter gun control measures, yet his assertion is based on biased polling methods. And Bloomberg's private security detail is armed, highlighting the double standard where elites protect themselves with firearms while advocating to disarm ordinary citizens.

The late Senator Dianne Feinstein (D-CA) was a longtime advocate for banning so-called assault weapons, frequently stating that these firearms are responsible for a substantial portion of gun violence. However, FBI data consistently shows that rifles, including those labeled as assault weapons, are used in a tiny percentage of gun crimes. Feinstein's arguments often ignored this data, instead focusing on the emotional impact of high-profile shootings to push for legislation that would have little effect on overall gun violence.

And then there's filmmaker and activist Spike Lee, who has used his platform to advocate for stricter gun control, often blaming the NRA for gun violence in America. In interviews, Lee has suggested that the availability of guns is the primary cause of violence, yet he overlooks the role of illegal firearms and the failure of existing laws to prevent crime. Spike Lee is just one of many high-profile individuals whose rhetoric contributes to the demonization of lawful gun owners and ignores the complexities of gun violence.

These examples show how anti-gun rhetoric often relies on misleading information, emotional manipulation, and double standards. The narratives pushed by these figures do not stand up to scrutiny and fail to address the root causes of violence, instead focusing on the simplistic solution of restricting gun rights. This approach not only misleads the public but also undermines legitimate efforts to find effective solutions to gun violence.

Given that nearly every major institution—from legacy media and entertainment to the education system, corporate America, and cultural elites—relentlessly peddles far-left, anti-gun propaganda, it is no wonder these narratives saturate the culture, with millions absorbing them without question. This creates a dangerous herd mentality, where people blindly follow trends or prevailing sentiment—what psychologists call *social proof*—even when it runs counter to their own values, logic, or lived experience.

### *Extraordinary Popular Delusions* and Anti-Gun Sentiment

In the mid-19th century, Scottish journalist Charles Mackay penned a seminal work titled *Extraordinary Popular Delusions and the Madness of Crowds*, a book that has since become a classic in the study of mass psychology. The book explores the phenomena of collective illusions, irrational behaviors, and societal crazes that sweep through populations, often leading to destructive consequences. Mackay chronicles a variety of historical examples where entire populations, driven by emotion rather than reason, fell victim to mass delusions—from the infamous Tulip Mania in the Netherlands to the South Sea Bubble in England. The underlying theme of Mackay's work is that humans are highly susceptible to herd mentality, where logic and reason are overshadowed by the overwhelming force of collective emotion.

When we apply the insights from Mackay's work to contemporary gun control narratives and anti-gun sentiment, we can see striking parallels. Just as the crowds of the past were gripped by economic or social delusions, today's gun control zealots exhibit similar behaviors, driven by fear, misinformation, and emotional rhetoric rather than by rational discourse or a solid understanding of the issues at hand. The push for more restrictive gun laws, often in response to high-profile but statistically rare events, reflects a modern-day version of the madness of crowds that Mackay so vividly described.

One of the key features of Mackay's analysis is the idea that popular delusions are often fueled by misinformation and a lack of understanding. In the context of gun control, this is evident in the widespread misconceptions about firearms and their role in society. For example, many gun control advocates fixate on so-called assault weapons, driven by the erroneous belief that these firearms are responsible for the majority of gun-related deaths in the United States. However, as discussed earlier in this book, FBI crime statistics consistently show that rifles of any kind, including those labeled as "assault weapons," are used in a small fraction of homicides compared to handguns. Yet, despite the data, the push to ban these firearms persists, driven not by facts but by the emotional response to their appearance and the fear they evoke.

The phenomenon of scapegoating, another common theme in Mackay's book, is also prevalent in the anti-gun movement. Throughout history, when societies have faced crises or sought to explain complex problems, they have often looked for a simple target to blame. In the case of gun control, firearms themselves—and by extension, law-abiding gun owners—have become the scapegoat for broader social issues such as crime and violence. This oversimplification ignores the root causes of these problems, such as poverty, lack of education, mental health issues, and the breakdown of the family unit. Instead, the focus is placed on the tool used in a minority of these crimes, leading to policies that do little to address the underlying issues but provide the illusion of action.

Historical examples abound where societies, gripped by collective delusions, have enacted policies that were later recognized as misguided or harmful. The Prohibition era in the United States is a classic case of a well-intentioned but ultimately disastrous policy driven by popular sentiment. The movement to ban alcohol was fueled by a genuine desire to reduce social problems associated with drinking, but it ignored the complexities of human behavior and the demand for alcohol. The result was the rise of organized crime, widespread corruption, and a general disregard for the law. Similarly, modern gun control efforts, while often motivated by a desire to reduce violence, risk repeating the mistakes of Prohibition by focusing on banning objects rather than addressing behaviors.

More recent examples of the madness of crowds in the gun control debate can be seen in the aftermath of mass shootings, where the emotional response to these tragedies often leads to calls for sweeping and immediate changes to gun laws. Following the tragic events at Sandy Hook in 2012, there was an intense push for new federal gun control measures, including the renewal of the assault weapons ban and the implementation of universal background checks. While the horror of the event was undeniable, the legislative proposals that followed were largely based on emotion rather than a careful analysis of what would prevent such incidents. The emotional fervor of the moment led to proposals that ignored the complex factors contributing to gun violence and instead focused on visible but largely ineffective solutions.

Mackay's work also touches on the cyclical nature of these popular delusions, noting that they tend to rise and fall as public opinion shifts. In the case of gun control, we can see a similar pattern. After each major incident involving firearms, there is a surge in anti-gun sentiment, driven by media coverage and emotional appeals from political leaders. Yet, over time, as the initial shock fades and more rational voices emerge, public support for extreme measures often wanes. This cycle of panic and calm mirrors the booms and busts of the economic bubbles Mackay described, where the initial excitement gives way to a more sober assessment of reality.

One of the most striking aspects of Mackay's analysis is how quickly reason can be abandoned in favor of collective emotion. In the realm of gun control, this is evident in the rush to pass legislation in the wake of tragedies, often without careful consideration of the implications. The 1994 Assault Weapons Ban, for example, was passed as part of a broader crime bill in response to rising concerns about gun violence. However, subsequent studies, including those by the Department of Justice, found that the ban had little effect on overall crime rates. Despite this, the emotional appeal of "doing something" in response to gun violence continues to drive similar proposals, demonstrating the enduring power of popular delusions.

Mackay also discusses how those who resist the tide of popular sentiment are often marginalized or dismissed. When it comes to gun control, proponents of the Second Amendment and gun rights are often portrayed as extremists or out of touch with modern society. This marginalization serves to silence dissenting voices and reinforces the dominant narrative, even when that narrative is based on flawed premises. The result is a narrowing of the debate, where only certain perspectives are considered legitimate, further entrenching the delusion.

The parallels between Mackay's analysis of historical delusions and the modern gun control debate are clear. Just as past societies have fallen victim to the madness of crowds, today's gun control movement is driven by emotional appeals, misinformation, and a desire to appear virtuous rather than by a careful consideration of facts and consequences. The result is a series of policies that, while providing a sense of accomplishment for their proponents, do little to address the real issues at hand and often infringe on the rights of law-abiding citizens.

## Doxxing

Gun control and anti-gun initiatives manifest not only through media propaganda and legislative actions but also through the more insidious practice of doxxing. Doxxing, the act of publicly revealing private or personal information about an individual without their consent, is used as a tactic to intimidate and harass gun owners, gun store owners, and Second Amendment advocacy groups. One gun control advocacy group submitted a Freedom of Information Act (FOIA) request to the state of New York, seeking the names and addresses of individuals who possess firearms licenses and own firearms. This group, driven by a desire to expose and doxx gun owners, published the obtained information online, making the private details of these individuals publicly accessible. The motivations behind such tactics are rooted in a desire to stigmatize and intimidate gun owners, portraying them as a danger to society and hoping to deter others from exercising their Second Amendment rights.

This tactic was infamously employed by Gawker in 2012, when they published the names of gun permit holders in New York City. Similarly, *The Journal News*, serving Westchester and Rockland counties, published an interactive map in 2012 showing the names and addresses of gun owners based on government records they obtained. These publications sparked outrage, as they blatantly disregarded the privacy and safety of law-abiding citizens. By releasing this information, these media outlets aimed to create an environment of fear, making gun owners reluctant to acquire firearms or renew their permits. This strategy not only violates the privacy rights of gun owners but also endangers their safety. The data made publicly available can be used by criminals to target homes for firearm thefts, putting both the gun owners and their families at risk.

Publishing such information is not just a theoretical danger. Following *The Journal News*' publication, there were burglary attempts on the homes of listed gun owners, highlighting the real-world consequences of such irresponsible actions. This doxxing can also lead to harassment and threats from anti-gun activists, further endangering the lives of those whose information was exposed.

The actions of these media outlets reflect a broader trend of using fear and intimidation to advance their agenda. They aim to create a chilling effect that discourages people from exercising their Second Amendment rights. This strategy sets a dangerous precedent for how personal information can be weaponized against individuals with opposing views, infringing on their constitutional rights and privacy. As such, the need for stronger protection against the misuse of FOIA requests and the need to safeguard the privacy of individuals who are lawfully exercising their constitutional rights is paramount. This incident shows the lengths to which some groups will go to push their agenda, regardless of the potential harm to innocent individuals.

## Bias in Media Reporting of Mass Shootings

In contemporary media, a distinct bias often surfaces in the coverage of gun crimes and mass shootings, revealing an elitist tendency to protect certain groups and individuals while demonizing others. This bias is particularly evident in the narratives constructed around the identities and motives of the perpetrators and victims. The media's selective reporting practices serve to uphold certain ideological agendas while undermining the complexity and nuance of real-world events.

One striking example of this bias is the tendency to quickly push narratives that depict shooters as white individuals targeting racial minority groups, even when such details are not substantiated by evidence. For instance, in the aftermath of the Boulder, Colorado, supermarket shooting in March 2021, initial reports and social media commentary quickly assumed that the shooter was a white male motivated by racial hatred. This narrative persisted until it was revealed that the perpetrator was actually of Syrian descent. Despite this correction, the initial false narrative had already shaped public perception, illustrating the media's readiness to fit incidents into a preconceived framework of white aggression.

Conversely, when the perpetrators belong to protected or minority groups, the media often downplays or omits critical details about their motives or demographics. The 2019 Dayton, Ohio, shooting serves as an example. The shooter was found to have expressed leftist political views and was involved in left-wing extremist groups, yet these aspects received scant attention compared to the immediate coverage and scrutiny applied to other incidents involving perpetrators with more conservative affiliations. Similarly, in the case of the 2020 Kenosha unrest shooting, while significant attention was given to Kyle Rittenhouse's background and motives, less emphasis was placed on the criminal records and actions of those involved in the altercation with him, who did not fit the preferred narrative of right-wing violence.

Another instance is the media's handling of the 2021 Atlanta spa shootings. Initially, the media widely reported the shootings as racially motivated hate crimes against Asian Americans, framing the incident within the broader context of rising anti-Asian sentiment. However, further investigations revealed that the shooter's motives were more likely tied to issues of sexual addiction and personal turmoil. Despite this, the initial racial narrative continued to dominate public discourse, showcasing the media's inclination to prioritize certain storylines over complex, multifaceted truths.

Another striking instance is the 2016 Orlando nightclub shooting, which was initially reported as an anti-gay hate crime. The shooter targeted the Pulse nightclub, a known LGBTQ+ venue, killing 49 people and injuring many others. While the media emphasized the anti-gay nature of the attack, they often downplayed the shooter's background as a radical Islamic extremist who had pledged allegiance to ISIS. Additionally, reports emerged that he might have been gay, adding complexity to his motivations, but this aspect received minimal attention compared to the predominant hate crime narrative.

This selective reporting extends to the reluctance or outright refusal to highlight the demographics of shooters who are black, gay, or transgender. In cases where black individuals have committed mass shootings or major gun crimes, media coverage often avoids discussing racial motives or societal issues that may have contributed to the violence. This trend can be seen in the coverage of the 2019 Virginia Beach shooting, where the shooter, a black man, killed 12 people. Media outlets largely avoided discussing his race or potential racial motivations, instead focusing on other aspects of the incident.

The reluctance to scrutinize certain groups also manifests in the handling of shootings involving LGBTQ+ individuals. When a transgender person was implicated in the 2018 Denver school shooting, media coverage was notably muted regarding the shooter's identity and potential influences. Another notable example is the 2023 shooting in Louisville, Kentucky, committed by a transgender individual. The shooter, who left behind a manifesto, targeted a Christian school, and killed several people. Despite the clear indications of motive and identity, the media coverage was notably restrained, avoiding in-depth discussion about the perpetrator's background, anti-Christian sentiments, and potential influences. This selective reporting stands in stark contrast to the intense scrutiny typically applied to other shooters who fit a different profile. This selective silence stands in contrast to the intense media focus and speculation that often accompanies shootings involving other demographics.

These patterns of selective reporting and narrative construction reveal a broader agenda among the media elite, who often exhibit contemptuous attitudes toward rural white gun owners. By disproportionately focusing on white perpetrators and framing them as embodiments of a broader cultural and racial threat, the media perpetuates a stereotype of rural gun owners as violent and backward. This narrative not only misrepresents the reality of gun crime, which is often more prevalent in urban settings and involves a diverse array of perpetrators, but also stigmatizes a large portion of the American population. In media coverage, when shooters do not fit the preferred narrative of white, so-called right-wing extremism, their backgrounds and motivations are often downplayed or omitted. This selective reporting serves to protect certain groups while demonizing others, particularly rural white gun owners, who are unfairly portrayed as the primary source of gun violence despite statistical evidence to the contrary.

The implications of this media bias are profound. By shaping public perception through selective coverage, the media influences policy debates and societal attitudes towards gun ownership and regulation. The portrayal of rural white gun owners as the primary source of gun violence distracts from a more nuanced understanding of the issue and prevents constructive dialogue on effective solutions. Furthermore, the protection and downplaying of crimes committed by individuals from certain demographic groups undermines the principle of equal accountability and contributes to a sense of injustice and mistrust among the public.

In addition to the biased media coverage of gun crimes, another troubling trend has emerged involving transgender individuals who exhibit threatening behavior online yet face little to no scrutiny from authorities. This disparity is drastic when compared to the treatment of YouTube influencers and other pro-gun individuals who merely discuss their shooting hobby, gun safety, and recreational shooting.

One notable example is a transgender individual who posted a social media video showing themselves loading ammunition into an AR-15, while issuing threats to kill anyone who opposed their access to women's spaces and restrooms. This video, which clearly demonstrated both a capability and intent to commit violence, was widely circulated and discussed within online communities. Despite clear threats, the FBI and other law enforcement took no meaningful action, exposing a troubling double standard in how violent threats are handled depending on who makes them. In contrast, YouTube influencers who focus on gun safety, gun use, and recreational shooting are often subject to intense scrutiny and prosecution. Popular gun safety channels have faced demonetization, shadow banning, and even legal action for merely discussing firearm use in a responsible manner. Influencers like Hickok45 and AK Operators Union, who educate millions on safe gun handling and legal use, have encountered various forms of censorship and pressure from social media platforms and regulatory bodies.

Another example is the case of InRange TV, a channel that focuses on historical firearms and responsible gun ownership. The creators of InRange TV have repeatedly faced restrictions and penalties from social media platforms, despite their content being educational and aimed at promoting safe gun practices. These channels are often targeted under the guise of community standards or public safety concerns, even though their content does not promote violence or illegal activity.

This contrast in treatment reveals yet another example of how the media, social media platforms, and the powers that be protect certain classes of people, even when they exhibit threatening and violent behavior. The leniency shown towards individuals who fit certain protected categories, such as the transgender individual making explicit threats, stands in sharp contrast to the harsh measures taken against those promoting lawful and safe gun use.

The implications of this selective enforcement are substantial. By failing to address explicit threats of violence from certain individuals, authorities effectively signal that such behavior is acceptable or at least will be overlooked. This undermines public trust in law enforcement and contributes to a sense of injustice among those who are targeted for far less egregious behavior. Moreover, it perpetuates a narrative that certain classes of people are above scrutiny, while others, particularly those advocating gun rights and safety, are unfairly vilified. The protective stance towards certain groups, even when they pose clear threats, reflects broader societal biases that prioritize ideological alignment over objective assessment of risk. This approach not only endangers public safety but also erodes the principles of equal accountability and justice. By selectively enforcing laws and regulations, authorities and media outlets further polarize public discourse and deepen societal divides.

Another tactic used by the mainstream media and network news is the pronounced tendency to trumpet only high-profile mass shootings, such as school shootings or incidents in public places, while hardly addressing the much more prevalent gun and gang violence in inner cities across America. The rampant killings in these inner cities surpass the number of people killed in so-called mass shootings by orders of magnitude, yet the media's focus remains disproportionately on the latter.

Cities like Chicago, Memphis, and St. Louis experience gun violence at alarming rates, with hundreds of shootings occurring every year. According to the *Chicago Tribune*, in 2021 alone, Chicago saw over 770 homicides, the highest ever, the majority of which were gun related. Similarly, Democrat-controlled Memphis and St. Louis, due to demographic shifts and local governance, experienced some of the highest violent crime rates per capita during that time. These numbers are staggering compared to the fatalities from high-profile mass shootings. However, the media's spotlight seldom shines on these daily tragedies, choosing instead to focus on events that involve a larger number of victims at once, often in suburban or more affluent areas.

When mass shootings do occur, the type of firearm used becomes a focal point, particularly if it fits the narrative of so-called assault weapons. If an AR-15 or a similar rifle is used, it dominates the headlines, and there is an immediate outcry for bans on these specific types of firearms. However, if the incident involves handguns or other less politically charged firearms, the media often glosses over the specifics, simply referring to "guns" in a generic sense. This selective reporting can mislead the public, making it seem as if the problem lies primarily with certain types of firearms rather than addressing the broader issues of gun violence.

Moreover, the extensive coverage of mass shootings provides a perverse form of legitimacy and inspiration for other would-be shooters. By saturating the airwaves with every detail of the tragedy, the media inadvertently glorifies the shooter, giving them the notoriety they sought. This phenomenon, known as the "media contagion effect," has been discussed by various psychologists and criminologists. Dr. Sherry Towers, a professor at Arizona State University, has pointed out that mass shootings can inspire copycat attacks, with extensive media coverage playing a significant role. The Columbine shooters, for example, have been cited as inspirations in several subsequent mass shootings, showing how the media's handling of these events can perpetuate a cycle of violence. The intense focus on mass shooters, often delving into their backgrounds and motives, serves as a blueprint for other potential shooters who crave the same infamy.

Additionally, the media's coverage can skew public perception of gun violence. By focusing almost exclusively on mass shootings, the media creates the impression that these incidents are the most common and pressing form of gun violence. This ignores the daily reality of gang violence and other forms of gun-related crime that devastate inner-city communities. As a result, public policy and gun control debates are often shaped by the fear of mass shootings, rather than the more pervasive and persistent problem of urban gun violence.

The mainstream media's selective focus on gun violence is closely tied to its broader ideological leanings. By downplaying the chronic violence plaguing inner cities—often governed by long-standing Democratic policies that have contributed to poverty and despair—the media avoids exposing the failures of those in power. Instead, it preserves the status quo, ensuring these urban populations remain dependent on Democratic leadership. To advance a broader liberal agenda, the media prioritizes mass shootings, especially when they occur in rural, suburban, or affluent areas, framing them as a national crisis to justify calls for stricter gun control. This focus shifts attention away from the daily violence in cities, which would require confronting complex socioeconomic issues tied to failed governance. By spotlighting mass shootings, the media bolsters support for policies like banning so-called assault weapons while sidestepping the deeper reforms needed to address the root causes of inner-city violence.

Also, the elites in the media often deliberately focus on mass shootings involving AR-15s, despite the rarity of such events, to demonize gun owners, particularly those in rural areas who use these firearms for self-defense and recreational purposes. This skewed reporting stems from a deep-seated disdain for individuals living outside of large cities, portraying them as paranoid and violent hillbillies. The media's emphasis on the AR-15 serves as a tool to paint rural gun owners in a negative light, suggesting that they are inherently dangerous and untrustworthy.

This attitude and prejudice displayed by these elitists are ironic considering the very elites who accuse everyone of being racists or bigots are the ones exhibiting hatred toward a group of people. By focusing on these rare kinds of shootings, the media attempts to sway public perception against rural residents, cultivating a narrative that these individuals are the root of the gun violence problem in America. This narrative not only distorts the true nature of gun violence but also fuels resentment and deepens the divide between urban and rural communities.

The portrayal of rural gun owners as paranoid and violent is an oversimplification and mischaracterization. Many rural residents view firearms as essential tools for self-defense, hunting, and sport shooting. They often have a deep respect for gun safety and responsible ownership. The media's selective focus on mass shootings involving AR-15s ignores the broader context of gun ownership in rural areas and fails to acknowledge the legitimate reasons why these firearms are valued by millions of Americans.

Rather than fostering a nuanced and informed debate, the media's biased reporting fuels misconceptions and prejudice, making it harder to address the actual causes of gun violence in a constructive and inclusive manner. In doing so, they do not just mislead the public—they actively poison the national conversation, turning a constitutional right into a cultural battleground where truth is the first casualty.

## Media Bias for and Against Certain Movements

Another glaring example of the media's bias against the Second Amendment can be seen in their broadcasting of the March for Our Lives rally in Washington, DC, a radical cause with a deliberately vague, feel-good name designed to be unassailable—masking the true intentions behind a facade of virtue. The media heralded this movement as a significant and laudable effort to influence public opinion toward accepting more gun control measures. Organized by survivors of the 2018 Marjory Stoneman Douglas High School shooting, March for Our Lives called for stricter gun laws, including bans on certain types of firearms. The media provided extensive coverage of the event, showcasing impassioned speeches and widespread support, portraying it as a pivotal moment in the fight for gun control. Commentators and journalists alike used their platforms to pontificate how banning guns would save lives, framing the movement as a moral imperative.

In contrast, the media's treatment of the March for Life, an annual rally advocating for the right to life and opposing abortion, is markedly different and reveals a profound hypocrisy. Instead of being celebrated, this movement and its participants are demonized and mocked by the media. This paradox is striking, given that the March for Life's stance on protecting unborn children directly aligns with the objective of saving lives.

The contradiction in media coverage would be almost humorous if it were not for the sobering reality that abortion results in the death of nearly a million unborn children each year in the United States, a number far surpassing all gun-related deaths combined. If the goal were genuinely to protect life, one would expect the media to support the March for Life with the same fervor as they do gun control initiatives.

But the media's bias against guns is not truly about saving lives. Rather, it is about advancing an anti-gun agenda and demonizing gun owners. By promoting the March for Our Lives and denigrating the March for Life, the media demonstrates that its stance on gun control is more about promoting a particular narrative than it is about the consistent application of principles regarding the value of life.

Another example of an anti-Second Amendment organization propped up by the media is Moms Demand Action, an organization that has become a leading voice in the movement to implement stricter gun control laws in the United States. Founded in the wake of the Sandy Hook Elementary School shooting in 2012 by Shannon Watts, Moms Demand Action positions itself as a grassroots movement advocating for "common-sense" gun reforms. However, their agenda often extends beyond reasonable regulations to advocate for extensive gun bans and measures that infringe upon the Second Amendment rights of law-abiding citizens.

Moms Demand Action employs a range of lobbying and advocacy tactics to push for their anti-gun agenda, often partnering with politicians and activist groups to promote legislation aimed at disarming Americans. Through financial contributions and behind-the-scenes influence, they help shape public policy in ways many argue infringe on constitutional rights. They rely on emotional appeals and tragic events to rally support, often at the expense of factual accuracy and a deeper understanding of the root causes of gun violence—such as gang activity, drug trafficking, illegal firearms, and mental health crises. Rather than addressing these complex issues, they advocate for sweeping gun bans that primarily impact law-abiding citizens, while ignoring the reality that most gun violence stems from illegally obtained weapons.

Additionally, the organization is frequently accused of using unethical lobbying tactics, orchestrating media campaigns, and applying pressure on lawmakers, often framing their opposition as indifferent or complicit in violence. Their polarizing rhetoric stifles meaningful debate and diverts attention from more effective, nuanced strategies to reduce crime. Despite these tactics, Moms Demand Action enjoys consistent and favorable media coverage, positioning them as champions of public safety while gun rights advocates are often vilified or silenced. This selective support reveals a broader agenda—one less concerned with genuinely saving lives and more focused on advancing an ideological goal of disarming the populace.

Through relentless propaganda, anti-gun lies, and the demonization of gun owners and non-urban lifestyles, the media has shown a deep-seated disdain for anything that deviates from radical leftist ideologies. They propagate false narratives, vilify law-abiding citizens who exercise their Second Amendment rights, and mock the values held by millions of Americans living outside of urban centers. Apart from a few outlets and publications, the mainstream media appears to harbor a palpable contempt for the American people, seeking to manipulate public opinion and erode the foundational principles that define our nation. This biased and adversarial stance undermines trust and divides our society; the media's agenda is often at odds with the interests of the very people it is supposed to inform and serve.

## Firearms in Pop Culture

The portrayal of firearms in pop culture has long shaped public perception and fueled the gun rights debate. From movies and television to video games and literature, guns are prominently featured, with depictions often straddling the line between glamorizing their power and highlighting their potential for violence. Music, too—whether through the gritty narratives of gangsta rap or the aggressive themes of heavy metal—frequently references shooting, murder, and gun violence. These cultural depictions not only influence how society views firearms but also expose the contradictions within a media landscape that profits from violent imagery while simultaneously pushing anti-gun narratives.

In movies, firearms are ubiquitous, often serving as critical plot devices or character-defining tools. From classic Westerns like *The Good, the Bad, and the Ugly* to modern action franchises like *John Wick*, guns are depicted as essential to heroism and justice. These films frequently portray protagonists who are highly skilled with firearms, using them to overcome evil and protect the innocent. This romanticized view can instill a sense of respect and admiration for gun ownership and skill, suggesting that firearms are tools for good in the hands of responsible individuals.

Television shows have similarly contributed to the cultural landscape of firearms. Series such as *The Walking Dead* and *Breaking Bad* showcase characters navigating dangerous worlds where guns are necessary for survival and protection. These portrayals emphasize the utility of firearms in desperate situations, reinforcing the idea that owning a gun can be crucial for self-defense. However, television also depicts the darker side of gun use, often highlighting the consequences of violence and the moral complexities faced by characters who wield guns.

Video games, particularly those with first-person shooters like *Call of Duty* and *Fortnite*, have a profound impact on youth culture and their perceptions of firearms. These games often glamorize gunplay, presenting it as exciting and heroic. The interactive nature of video games allows players to immerse themselves in scenarios where firearms are central, potentially fostering a familiarity and comfort with guns. This popularity among younger audiences indicates a generally positive view of firearms, despite ongoing debates about the influence of violent video games on real-world behavior.

Gun violence in music lyrics and videos has become a cultural staple, particularly in genres like rap and heavy metal, where artists often glorify guns, shootings, and murder. Yet, many of these same performers hypocritically promote anti-gun political views when stepping off the stage or out of character. Take Snoop Dogg, for instance, who pointed a gun at a clown dressed as Donald Trump in his "Lavender" music video, an image that sparked controversy while he simultaneously champions gun control in public appearances. Similarly, Marilyn Manson's violent music video for the song "We Know Where You F-----g Live" features graphic scenes of gun violence and home invasions, yet Manson and others like him often advocate for more restrictive gun laws. This hypocrisy runs deep throughout the industry, where artists routinely profit from violent, gun-laden imagery while lecturing the public on the dangers of firearms. The contradiction is glaring: profiting off fictionalized violence while pushing policies that would strip law-abiding citizens of their right to self-defense. These artists are happy to sell records and concert tickets with gun-centric themes, but when the cameras stop rolling, they join the chorus calling for disarmament.

Literature has also played a large role in the cultural portrayal of firearms. Classic works like *For Whom the Bell Tolls* by Ernest Hemingway and contemporary novels like *No Country for Old Men* by Cormac McCarthy explore the nuanced and often grim realities of gun use. These stories delve into the psychological and emotional impacts of wielding firearms, offering a more introspective view of the consequences of violence. While literature tends to provide a more balanced perspective, it still contributes to the broader cultural narrative that guns are integral to certain aspects of life and conflict.

Hollywood's hypocrisy on gun control is glaring when you consider the movies that consistently dominate the box office. Audiences flock to see action films where the hero, often armed with an array of firearms, takes on the villains, drives fast cars, and rescues the beautiful damsel in distress. These are the movies that generate massive profits, not films about pacifists discussing gun control. The public craves excitement, and Hollywood delivers, despite its stars publicly advocating for gun control or pushing their unpopular political views during interviews. This reveals a stark contradiction. When faced with the choice between adhering to their anti-gun rhetoric or cashing in on what the public actually wants to see, Hollywood chooses profit every time. This contradiction exposes the reality that many in Hollywood don't truly believe in the gun control positions they preach; if they did, their principles would outweigh their desire for blockbuster success.

Despite the efforts of elites to demonize firearms, the persistent popularity of guns in pop culture suggests a more nuanced public perception. Movies, television shows, video games, and literature that feature firearms remain commercially successful because they resonate with audiences. This popularity indicates that, on some level, people recognize the value and necessity of firearms, whether for self-defense, heroism, or survival. Moreover, the blockbuster success of action-packed films featuring firearms serves as anecdotal evidence that the public generally views guns in a necessary and positive light, even if primarily for entertainment. This popularity suggests that most people have an inherently favorable perception of firearms or at least acknowledge their appeal in certain contexts. If the public were overwhelmingly anti-gun, these movies wouldn't enjoy such widespread support. Instead, their success indicates that firearms hold a valued place in popular culture for various reasons, whether for self-defense, empowerment, or simply thrilling entertainment.

For example, the *John Wick* series has gained a massive following not only for its high-octane action scenes but also for its meticulous depiction of gun handling and tactics. The protagonist's expertise with firearms is portrayed with a level of respect and authenticity that appeals to both enthusiasts and casual viewers. This positive portrayal contrasts sharply with the negative rhetoric from anti-gun advocates, highlighting a disconnect between elite narratives and popular culture.

Moreover, the portrayal of firearms in media often emphasizes their role in empowerment and protection. In *The Walking Dead*, characters like Rick Grimes rely on guns to safeguard their community against both human and zombie threats. This depiction aligns with the real-world argument that firearms are essential tools for self-defense, reinforcing the belief that responsible gun ownership is a legitimate and necessary aspect of personal security. However, pop culture also highlights the potential for misuse and the consequences of gun violence. Television shows like *Breaking Bad* and movies like *Taxi Driver* explore the destructive paths of characters who misuse firearms, offering a cautionary perspective. These narratives acknowledge the potential dangers of guns while also emphasizing the importance of responsible use and the moral implications of violence.

In movies, firearms are often depicted as easy to use, with characters effortlessly picking up a gun and instantly demonstrating expert marksmanship. This portrayal is far from reality. The process of becoming proficient with a firearm involves extensive training, practice, and a deep understanding of gun safety and mechanics. In many action films, we see protagonists and even ordinary characters suddenly wielding firearms with remarkable accuracy and control, as if using a gun requires no more skill than wielding a kitchen knife. This simplification can lead to broad misconceptions about the ease and safety of handling firearms.

Take, for example, the character of Jason Bourne in the *Bourne* series or John McClane in *Die Hard*. These characters often find themselves in situations where they have to use unfamiliar firearms under extreme stress. Despite this, they consistently hit their targets and operate the weapons flawlessly. This cinematic trope can give the false impression that anyone can pick up a gun and use it effectively without any prior experience or training. Proper training includes learning how to handle a gun safely, understanding the mechanics of different firearms, and practicing shooting techniques under controlled conditions. These skills are developed over time and cannot be acquired instantly, as movies often suggest.

The ease of access to firearms in movies is another area where fiction diverges from reality. Characters often find guns conveniently placed or quickly improvise to obtain one, reinforcing the notion that firearms are readily accessible and easy to use in moments of crisis. This portrayal can mislead viewers into believing that guns are ubiquitous and simple to procure, which is not the case in many real-world scenarios where strict regulations and safety measures govern firearm access.

The fictional ease of gun use also contributes to a distorted view of violence. By making it appear as if anyone can effortlessly pick up a gun and use it to deadly effect, movies can inadvertently glamorize and simplify the act of taking a life. The reality is that the psychological and physical aspects of using a firearm, especially in self-defense or combat situations, are complex and fraught with challenges. The decision to use a gun, the precision required to hit a target accurately, and the aftermath of such an action are all factors that are rarely explored in depth in popular media.

Furthermore, this cinematic portrayal can influence public perception, especially among youth who consume large amounts of media. When video games, movies, and television shows depict guns as easy-to-use tools for solving problems, it can create unrealistic expectations and a casual attitude towards firearms. This can be dangerous, as it underestimates the responsibility and skill required to handle guns safely and effectively.

Responsible gun owners spend considerable time and effort learning how to use their firearms correctly. This includes regular practice at shooting ranges, taking safety courses, and staying informed about the laws and regulations surrounding gun ownership. The skills required to handle a firearm proficiently involve both mental and physical discipline, much like any other sport or specialized activity.

Movies often fail to capture the seriousness and dedication involved in responsible gun ownership, opting instead for sensationalism and ease. This discrepancy between fiction and reality is consequential and highlights the need for better public education on the responsible use of firearms. By understanding the complexities and responsibilities of gun ownership, individuals can appreciate the serious nature of handling firearms and the importance of proper training and safety measures.

The dichotomy in media and pop culture—where firearms are both glorified and scrutinized at the same time—mirrors the broader societal debate on gun rights. While elites and media outlets often focus on the negative aspects of gun ownership, pop culture continues to reflect a more complex and sometimes positive view of firearms. This ongoing portrayal in popular media suggests that the public's perception of guns is multifaceted and influenced by a variety of narratives. Ultimately, the persistent presence of firearms in pop culture highlights their significance in American society. Despite efforts to demonize them, the widespread depiction of guns in movies, television, video games, and literature indicates a deep-seated recognition of their role in protection, empowerment, and conflict resolution. This cultural portrayal plays a critical role in shaping public perception and will continue to influence the gun rights debate for years to come.

## Hollywood Hysteria

While there is considerable overlap between pop culture at large and Hollywood, the film industry stands out as especially brazen, hypocritical, and unapologetic in its gun control posturing. Nowhere is the disconnect between anti-gun rhetoric and glorified on-screen gun violence more blatant than in Hollywood's own productions and public statements.

Hollywood is a cesspool of double standards, hypocrisy, and sheer stupidity, particularly when it comes to its stance on the Second Amendment. Many of the industry's most outspoken critics of gun rights are the very same individuals and studios that churn out films glorifying gun violence and heroic self-defense. This blatant contradiction is as glaring as it is infuriating, highlighting the disingenuous nature of Hollywood's elite who are more than willing to profit off the very thing they publicly denounce.

Take, for instance, the endless array of action movies that Hollywood produces each year. These films often center on themes of revenge, justice, and heroism, with protagonists wielding firearms to protect themselves and others. The very imagery of guns and their usage in dramatic, high-stakes situations is what drives the success of these movies. Despite this, many of Hollywood's leading figures, who star in or produce these films, are quick to jump on the anti-gun bandwagon when the cameras stop rolling. They speak out vehemently against the private ownership of firearms, often supporting stringent gun control measures that would strip law-abiding citizens of their right to self-defense.

Think about some of the most popular and highest-grossing action films in recent years and the glaring contradictions behind them. Consider, for example, the case of Matt Damon, star of the *Bourne* series, whose character dispatches enemies with firearms in nearly every film. Despite profiting from gun-laden blockbusters, Damon has publicly voiced support for stricter gun control, a position that seems disconnected from the very imagery that built his on-screen persona.

After the Virginia Tech shooting, actor Kevin Costner, who has starred in numerous films featuring firearms used in both offensive and defensive roles, stated, "I think there should be a lot of gun laws," illustrating another case of Hollywood preaching one thing while selling another.

The hypocrisy extends beyond actors to directors and producers as well. Quentin Tarantino, known for his hyper-violent films like *Pulp Fiction* and *Django Unchained*, has publicly criticized American gun culture. These films, renowned for their graphic depiction of gun violence, have achieved cult status and generated immense revenue. Tarantino's stance against gun rights, while simultaneously profiting from films that glorify such violence, is a stark example of Hollywood's double standards.

Hollywood's penchant for anti-gun rhetoric, juxtaposed with its relentless production of gun-centric films, underscores a profound disconnect. It reveals an industry eager to capitalize on the allure and excitement of firearms while simultaneously condemning their private ownership. This hypocrisy is not only intellectually dishonest but also insulting to the intelligence of the movie-going public. This double standard not only exposes Hollywood's inherent stupidity but also its contempt for the everyday citizen's right to self-defense. It's no wonder no one watches their awards shows anymore—bloated spectacles where out-of-touch millionaires pat themselves on the back, preach from a podium while clutching a golden statue, and spew political sermons under the protection of armed security wielding the very firearms they claim the rest of us shouldn't have.

## Social Media Censorship

In recent years, social media platforms have increasingly wielded their power to shadow ban, demonetize, or outright take down channels, often citing vague community guidelines without providing clear explanations or warnings. This practice has had devastating effects on the livelihood and reach of many firearms and Second Amendment social media influencers, who find themselves disproportionately targeted by these censorship tactics.

Shadow banning is a stealthy form of censorship where a user's content is hidden or suppressed without their knowledge. This means that while the user can still post content, it is significantly less visible to their followers and the broader audience, drastically reducing engagement and reach. Demonetizing, on the other hand, involves removing a creator's ability to earn revenue from their content through ads or sponsorships. This not only affects the creator financially but also discourages them from producing more content.

Decisions to censor or penalize gun-related content are often made whimsically by social media companies. These platforms have shown a clear bias against anything related to firearms, while other disturbing and often violent or threatening content unrelated to firearms remains untouched. This selective enforcement of community guidelines reveals a hostile stance toward gun-related content and a broader ideological agenda.

Several notable examples highlight the impact of these censorship practices. YouTube channels like Colion Noir, Demolition Ranch, and Hickok45 (see chapter 13) have faced demonetization or video removals despite their content adhering to legal standards and often being educational or entertaining. In some cases, these influencers were able to resolve issues through public outcry or by appealing to the platform, but the process is often opaque and inconsistent. For many, the damage to their reach and income remains crushing and unresolved.

This censorship is a form of modern-day tyranny, disproportionately targeting guntubers and other Second Amendment advocates. Social media companies' community guidelines are notoriously vague, allowing them to arbitrarily enforce rules and censor content without accountability. This lack of transparency and consistency further erodes trust and highlights the platforms' bias.

Social media platforms, by default, have evolved into the modern public square, where the free exchange of ideas and information should be protected under the First Amendment. However, these companies often operate as monopolies, controlling vast amounts of online discourse. By editorializing which videos to censor and which to promote, they act more like publishers than as mere carriers of content. Publishers are subject to regulation and antitrust laws, which they currently circumvent by claiming neutrality as platforms.

The editorial decisions made by these social media giants violate antitrust laws, as they are effectively acting as gatekeepers of information and expression. By suppressing certain viewpoints, particularly those related to firearms and Second Amendment rights, they stifle free speech and manipulate public perception. This not only undermines the principles of a free society but also threatens the very foundation of democratic discourse.

The actions of big social media companies reflect a broader agenda to control and influence public opinion by silencing dissenting voices. This practice of censorship, especially when it targets specific political views or educational content related to firearms, is an affront to the constitutional rights of users. It is imperative that these platforms be held accountable and subject to regulations that protect free speech and ensure a fair and open public square for all.

Big social media companies also play a big role in shaping political landscapes by contributing to political campaigns and causes that undermine the Second Amendment and advocate for strict gun control. These companies often align with progressive ideologies and use their substantial financial resources to support candidates and initiatives that favor restrictive gun policies. Executives and employees of companies like Facebook, Twitter, and Google have historically donated millions of dollars to Democratic candidates and gun control advocacy groups such as Everytown for Gun Safety and Moms Demand Action.

In the 2020 election cycle, tech giants funneled substantial donations to campaigns and political action committees (PACs) that prioritized gun control measures. Facebook CEO Mark Zuckerberg and his wife Priscilla Chan, for instance, donated $300 million to election organizations in battleground states, a move that raised concerns about undue influence on electoral processes and the advancement of specific political agendas. Additionally, Google's Political Action Committee, NetPAC, has supported candidates who champion gun control legislation, further indicating the tech industry's bias against the Second Amendment.

These contributions are not just monetary; they also include in-kind support such as advertising credits, technology tools, and data analytics, which can significantly enhance a campaign's outreach and effectiveness. By supporting candidates and causes that advocate for gun control, social media companies not only influence the political discourse but also help shape legislation that could infringe upon the rights of law-abiding gun owners. This alignment between big tech and anti-gun advocacy highlights a concerted effort to sway public opinion and policy in favor of stricter gun regulations, undermining the constitutional right to bear arms.

## International Media Bias

Guns and gun owners in the US aren't just misrepresented at home—they're also targeted and distorted by voices from beyond our borders. The British Broadcasting Corporation (BBC) has long been a mouthpiece for leftist elitist agendas, and its coverage of gun rights and the Second Amendment in the United States is no exception. Through a combination of half-truths, false narratives, and outright deception, the BBC has worked tirelessly to paint a distorted picture of the role of guns in American society. This international network, steeped in snobbery and arrogance, exemplifies the meddling of global elites in American affairs, attempting to sway public opinion against our Constitution and the fundamental rights it enshrines.

The BBC's bias is not a new phenomenon. In 2002, the network aired a program titled *Panorama: The Gun Industry's Lethal Profit*, which claimed that the US firearms industry was knowingly fueling gun violence for profit. The program relied on cherry-picked statistics and sensationalist rhetoric to demonize gun manufacturers and portray them as morally bankrupt. The documentary failed to acknowledge the legal and ethical responsibilities that gun manufacturers adhere to, as well as the historical importance of the American firearms industry and the protection of individual rights. Instead, it sought to vilify the industry and, by extension, the millions of Americans who support it.

One of the most glaring examples of the BBC's anti-gun bias was its coverage of the so-called gun culture in the United States following the tragic mass shooting in Las Vegas in 2017. In a documentary segment, the BBC selectively interviewed only Americans who supported gun control or who lamented the widespread availability of firearms. This narrow portrayal ignored the vast majority of responsible gun owners who cherish their Second Amendment rights and use firearms safely for self-defense, hunting, and sport. The segment used sensationalist imagery and emotional appeals rather than presenting a balanced view of the issues surrounding gun ownership in the US, ultimately leaving viewers with the impression that America's relationship with guns is entirely toxic and irrational.

Another recent example can be found in the BBC's reporting on the rise in gun sales during the COVID-19 pandemic in 2020 and 2021. Rather than exploring the legitimate concerns of millions of Americans who purchased firearms for personal protection during uncertain times, the BBC chose to focus on fearmongering about the dangers of increased gun ownership. The network repeatedly implied that more guns would inevitably lead to more violence, ignoring data that shows responsible gun owners are not the ones committing crimes. This narrative is not only misleading but also reflects the BBC's deep-seated disdain for the American ethos of self-reliance and personal responsibility.

Moreover, when discussing American gun rights, the BBC has often employed condescending language, reflecting the network's underlying elitism. Articles and segments frequently refer to American gun owners as "gun enthusiasts" or "pro-gun lobbyists," terms that carry a dismissive and negative connotation. This language is designed to marginalize and belittle those who exercise their Second Amendment rights, casting them as fringe extremists rather than mainstream Americans.

The BBC's coverage is emblematic of a broader trend among international elites who believe they have the right to dictate American policy and public opinion from afar. This meddling is not only unwelcome but deeply hypocritical, given that the BBC operates in a country with its own history of government overreach and restrictions on individual freedoms. The network's attempts to sway American public opinion against the Second Amendment reflect a fundamental misunderstanding of American values and a disregard for the rights that have defined our nation since its founding.

The BBC's anti-gun propaganda is not just a case of poor journalism; it is a deliberate effort to undermine the Second Amendment and weaken the fabric of American society. By spreading false narratives and engaging in deceptive reporting, the BBC seeks to erode public support for the right to bear arms and to promote a globalist agenda that is at odds with the principles of freedom and self-determination.

## So, What Now?

The future of the mainstream media's stance on the Second Amendment appears poised to continue its current trajectory of anti-gun bias, at least in the short to medium term. The entrenchment of progressive ideologies within major media organizations has created an environment where narratives opposing gun ownership and advocating for stricter gun control are prevalent. This bias is reinforced by the alignment of media executives and journalists with political figures and advocacy groups that share their views on firearms regulation. It seems unlikely that the mainstream media will experience a substantial shift in its editorial stance on the Second Amendment in the immediate future.

However, societal attitudes toward gun rights have been evolving, with a notable increase in public support for the Second Amendment and gun ownership. This shift is partly driven by rising concerns over personal safety, civil unrest, and a perceived decline in the effectiveness of law enforcement. As more Americans, including demographics traditionally less associated with gun ownership, embrace their right to bear arms, there is potential for a cultural shift that could influence media narratives. If public sentiment continues to move in a pro-gun direction, media organizations may eventually be compelled to recalibrate their coverage to better reflect the prevailing attitudes of their audience.

Social media platforms, on the other hand, present a more complex and dynamic landscape. There is growing recognition of the critical role these platforms play in public discourse and increasing pressure to uphold genuine free speech principles. Recent controversies over censorship, shadow banning, and demonetization have sparked a widespread backlash, leading to calls for regulatory reforms and the emergence of alternative platforms that promote free speech. If mainstream social media platforms face heightened scrutiny and regulatory pressure, they may be incentivized to reverse course on targeting Second Amendment content and adopt more balanced approaches.

In the long run, the increasing pro-gun stance among the general population and the push for greater accountability in social media governance could foster a more favorable environment for Second Amendment advocacy. Media outlets and social media platforms that adapt to these changing dynamics, by providing more nuanced and diverse perspectives on gun rights, may find themselves better positioned to maintain relevance and credibility. While a complete sea change in media culture is not a foregone conclusion, the convergence of public opinion, regulatory developments, and the rise of new media voices holds the potential to reshape the landscape in ways that more accurately represent the diverse views of American society on gun ownership and the Second Amendment.

# Chapter 9

## The Elites vs. the Unwashed Masses

*I don't care if you want to hunt, I don't care if you think it's your right. I say 'Sorry.' It's 1999. We have had enough as a nation. You are not allowed to own a gun, and if you do own a gun, I think you should go to prison.*

—Rosie O'Donnell

*I actually hate guns.*

—Matt Damon

In the discourse surrounding gun rights and the Second Amendment, a distinct divide often emerges between the coastal elites and the everyday citizens, particularly those in rural areas or so-called red states.

The elites, encompassing influential politicians, Big Tech CEOs, celebrities, and media figures, frequently express a condescending attitude towards gun owners. This disdain is readily apparent when discussing rural areas or conservative-leaning states. The narrative perpetuated by these elites often paints gun owners as uneducated, violent rednecks—a gross mischaracterization that ignores the diverse and responsible nature of the gun-owning community. The portrayal of rural Americans as backward and dangerous serves to marginalize and stigmatize a substantial portion of the population that values the right to bear arms.

Moreover, the hypocrisy of the elites regarding gun control is striking. Many of these individuals vocally support stringent gun regulations while simultaneously benefiting from armed security for their protection. This double standard is particularly evident in Hollywood and among high-profile media personalities.

This chapter delves into the complex dynamics of how elites perceive and treat gun owners and Second Amendment advocates with disdain, revealing their blatant hypocrisy. We will explore numerous instances where elites have used their political or celebrity status to evade the consequences of their own gun crimes or negligence, further highlighting the disparity in accountability.

The media plays a crucial role in shaping public perception, often talking down to the gun community and rural Americans. News outlets and entertainment media frequently depict gun owners in a negative light, contributing to a culture of scorn and misunderstanding. This portrayal not only alienates gun owners but also reinforces the elitist view that those who advocate for the Second Amendment are somehow lesser or morally inferior.

There are several specific examples of how elites have maneuvered their way out of legal repercussions for gun-related incidents. These cases demonstrate the privilege and immunity afforded to those with social and political capital, contrasting sharply with the experiences of ordinary citizens who face severe penalties for similar actions. This chapter illuminates the broader societal implications of such hypocrisy and the impact it has on public trust and the justice system.

The coastal elites, especially those entrenched in Hollywood and the media, often depict gun owners as the antithesis of civilized society. This depiction not only misrepresents the gun community but also serves to justify the elites' push for restrictive gun laws that they themselves frequently circumvent. The irony is palpable: While advocating for disarmament, they ensure their own security through the very means they seek to deny others.

Elites are always eager to dictate what we should do and think. They are, to use a term coined by Nassim Nicholas Taleb, "intellectual-yet-idiots." These individuals, insulated by their privileged positions, lack real-world experience and the consequences of their policies. They push for stringent gun control measures without understanding the practical implications for everyday citizens who rely on firearms for self-defense and sport. These elites never pay the real-world price for being wrong. Whether it's in areas like gun control, economic policies, or social engineering, their positions allow them to remain untouched by the adverse effects of their ideas, while ordinary people bear the brunt of their misguided policies. This disconnect results in policies that are out of touch with reality, showcasing a profound misunderstanding of the issues they claim to address.

There is a subset of society that loathes the gun-owning community, despite relying on armed protection for themselves. This disdain is not just about policy but reflects a deeper cultural and ideological divide. By examining the attitudes and actions of these elites, we can better understand the broader challenges facing the Second Amendment and the individuals who cherish it. Through this exploration, we hope to reveal the layers of bias and privilege that influence the gun control debate, encouraging a more informed perspective.

## Luxury Beliefs: The Status Symbols of the Elite

Luxury beliefs are the ideological equivalent of designer handbags—expensive in cost but ultimately useless in function. Coined by sociologist Rob Henderson, the term describes elitist viewpoints held primarily by wealthy or upper-middle-class liberals who fixate on issues that the average working-class person cannot afford to worry about. These beliefs, often detached from reality, serve as a form of social currency, allowing individuals to signal their moral superiority to their peers rather than addressing tangible concerns affecting everyday Americans.

The purpose of luxury beliefs is not to solve problems but to project an image of virtue. Holding and expressing these views serves as a form of social peacocking—virtue signaling designed to impress their elite peers while alienating the average American. They are not solutions but status symbols, used to elevate oneself above those who still concern themselves with basic realities like putting food on the table, protecting their families, or maintaining law and order.

Gun control is one of the most glaring examples of a luxury belief. The well-to-do elite sneer at the Second Amendment, claiming it is unnecessary in a "modern society," while ignoring the fact that those most affected by violent crime—the working class—often have no other means of protection. Their disdain for firearms is not based on lived experience but on an ideological posture meant to distinguish themselves from the "less enlightened" who still believe in self-defense.

At its core, luxury beliefs are a form of detached elitism, a way for the privileged to indulge in self-righteousness while remaining blissfully unaware—or willfully ignorant—of the real struggles faced by everyday Americans. Luxury beliefs allow those in ivory towers to feel morally superior while dictating policies that they will never have to suffer the consequences of.

## The "Anointed" Elite

The cultural elite and political left's support for and imposition of more gun control on the population can be understood through several key perspectives, often revealing a deep-seated hypocrisy and a huge disconnect between their public advocacy and personal practices. One major factor is that gun control is frequently a "luxury belief" held by liberal elites, who can afford to espouse these views precisely because they live in secure environments. Many prominent gun control advocates live in gated communities, are protected by private armed security, and enjoy a level of safety that ordinary citizens do not. This discrepancy highlights a fundamental hypocrisy.

The notion that gun control advocates do not genuinely oppose gun ownership *per se*, but rather do not want *you* to own guns, underscores a deeper intention to maintain control. This perspective is especially evident in the attitudes and actions of the "self-anointed elite," a term coined by economist and social theorist Thomas Sowell. These people often view themselves as intellectually and morally superior, believing they possess the wisdom and insight necessary to guide society. Their push for gun control can be seen as an effort to impose their will on a populace that might otherwise resist their unpopular and often impractical ideas.

Historically, the right to bear arms has been a powerful equalizer, allowing ordinary citizens to defend themselves against threats and to resist potential tyranny. The Second Amendment acts as a safeguard against the imposition of unpopular policies by force, ensuring that the government cannot easily overstep its bounds. For the political left, which seeks to expand governmental control and implement sweeping social reforms, the widespread ownership of firearms represents a significant obstacle. The persistence of the Second Amendment means that any attempt to enforce unpopular policies must contend with a potentially armed and resistant population.

The left's advocacy for gun control is an attempt to neutralize this resistance. By disarming the populace, they reduce the potential for opposition to their policies. This is particularly relevant, given that many of the left's policy proposals, such as increased taxation, wealth redistribution, and expansive government programs, are met with skepticism and resistance from large segments of the American public. The presence of an armed citizenry ensures that any government overreach must be carefully considered, as the potential for armed resistance acts as a powerful deterrent.

Moreover, the hypocrisy of gun control advocates is highlighted by their own practices. Politicians, celebrities, and other prominent figures who champion strict gun laws frequently rely on armed security for their personal safety. This double standard suggests that their opposition to gun ownership is not based on a principled stance against firearms but rather on a desire to control who has access to them. It reflects a belief that they are entitled to protection, but ordinary citizens are not.

In practice, this approach to gun control has severe implications for public safety and individual rights. By advocating for disarmament while ensuring their own protection, the elites effectively create a two-tiered system of security. Ordinary citizens, especially those in high-crime areas, are left vulnerable to threats that the elite never have to face.

The ongoing debate over gun control is not merely about public safety but also about the fundamental balance of power in society. The hypocrisy and double standards of the left in this debate reveal their true intentions: not to eliminate guns, but to ensure that they alone control who is allowed to possess them.

## The Vocabulary of the Elite

It's crucial to understand the constantly evolving vocabulary and definitions concocted by those who consider themselves our moral superiors. The vocabulary of the anti-gun elite is meticulously crafted to evoke emotional responses and shape public perception. They employ a repertoire of buzzwords and phrases designed to tug at heartstrings and paint a grim picture of gun ownership. Terms like "assault weapon," "high-capacity magazine," and "gun violence epidemic" are not just descriptions but carefully selected labels intended to elicit fear and urgency. These words are loaded with connotations that shift the debate away from a rational discussion of rights and responsibilities to an emotional plea for drastic measures.

By redefining guns and gun parts, the anti-gun elite manipulates the narrative. "Assault weapon," for example, is a term often used to describe semi-automatic firearms that share cosmetic features with military-grade weapons, despite being functionally different. This redefinition blurs the lines between what is legally owned by civilians and what is used in warfare, creating a misleading impression. Similarly, "high-capacity magazine" is a term used to describe *standard* magazines for many firearms, yet it is framed as an excessive and dangerous feature. This linguistic strategy distorts the facts, making everyday gun accessories seem like tools of mass destruction.

Statistics and definitions of shootings are also manipulated to support the anti-gun agenda. The term "mass shooting" has been broadened to include incidents that traditionally wouldn't meet the criteria, inflating the numbers and heightening the sense of crisis. This tactic shifts the debate from specific incidents and their causes to a generalized fear of widespread violence.

The anti-gun elite also uses highly emotional phrases to shift the debate. Phrases like "gun violence epidemic" and "public health crisis" are designed to frame gun ownership as a disease that needs to be eradicated. This rebranding steers the discussion away from constitutional rights and individual responsibility to a moral imperative to save lives at any cost. The use of these emotionally charged terms shifts the focus from the complexity of the issue to a simplistic good-versus-evil narrative, where guns and their owners are cast as the villains.

This vocabulary also serves to delegitimize opposing viewpoints. Terms like "common-sense gun laws" imply that any resistance to proposed regulations is irrational or malicious. By framing their positions as common sense, the anti-gun elite positions themselves as the rational and moral authority, while casting their opponents as unreasonable and dangerous. This linguistic strategy is not about fostering debate but about silencing dissent and marginalizing those who support gun rights.

In essence, the vocabulary of the anti-gun elite is a powerful tool for shaping public opinion and driving policy. By redefining terms, manipulating statistics, and using highly emotional language, they shift the debate away from factual and constitutional considerations to an emotional and moral battleground. This tactic not only distorts the reality of gun ownership but also undermines the principles of open and honest discourse, replacing it with a narrative designed to achieve specific policy goals regardless of the truth.

## Urban vs. Rural Attitudes

The divide between urban and rural attitudes towards the Second Amendment and gun control is a complex issue that highlights the vast cultural differences across America. This divide is not merely about differing opinions on firearms but also encompasses broader social and political tensions, reflecting a fundamental clash between urban elites and rural residents. The disdain, disrespect, and often outright disgust that urban elites express towards country folk fuels a deep seeded resentment among non-urban populations. This cultural and political rift has profound implications for how Second Amendment rights are perceived, legislated, and defended across the nation.

Urban elites often view rural America through a lens of condescension and moral superiority. This attitude manifests in various ways, from media portrayals to political rhetoric. Rural residents are depicted as backward, uneducated, and clinging to outdated traditions, with their attachment to firearms seen as a symbol of their supposed primitiveness. This portrayal is not only inaccurate but also deeply insulting to those who take pride in their heritage and lifestyle.

Quotes from influential urban figures and media outlets often underscore this disdain. For instance, former President Barack Obama, during his 2008 campaign, famously remarked that rural Americans "cling to guns or religion" out of bitterness over economic hardships. This comment epitomizes the urban elite's perception of rural culture as irrational and regressive. Such statements fuel the narrative that urban areas are centers of enlightenment and progress, while rural areas are bastions of ignorance and stubbornness.

The media plays a significant role in perpetuating these stereotypes. They often depict rural gun owners as dangerous extremists or ignorant rednecks, rather than law-abiding citizens exercising their constitutional rights. This biased portrayal contributes to a broader cultural disdain that many urban elites hold towards rural lifestyles. It also ignores the historical and practical reasons why firearms are integral to rural life, including hunting, protection from wildlife, and self-defense in areas where police response times can be much longer.

The condescension and disrespect from urban elites ignite sharp resentment among rural residents. This resentment is not just about cultural misunderstandings but also about political power and representation. Rural Americans feel that their voices are drowned out by the political and cultural dominance of urban areas. Urban areas, with their dense populations, often have the political clout to dictate statewide policies, including those related to gun control. This dynamic leads to a paradox where urban voters, who experience higher rates of crime and violence, vote for stricter gun control measures, which in turn restrict the rights of rural residents who use firearms primarily for lawful purposes.

Urban areas, paradoxically, are often the epicenters of crime and violence, yet city voters frequently support policies that make their cities more dangerous by disarming law-abiding citizens. Cities like Chicago, New York, and Washington, DC, have some of the strictest gun control laws in the country, yet they also experience some of the highest rates of gun violence.

Despite the crime and violence in their communities, urban voters often support candidates and policies that further restrict gun rights. This trend highlights a disconnect between the perceived solutions offered by gun control measures and the actual on-the-ground realities of urban crime. Instead of addressing the more common causes of violence such as mental illness, breakdown of family units, homelessness, and soft-on-crime policies, the focus remains on restricting access to firearms, often to the detriment of law-abiding citizens who seek to protect themselves.

The arrogance of many urban voters in voting away the rights of more rural residents displays a troubling moral superiority complex. Urban elites express a pervasive "we know what's best for you" attitude, which translates into a self-righteousness that seeks to impose their values and policies on the rest of the population. This imposition is particularly evident in the realm of gun control, but it extends to broader political and cultural issues. Urban elites often advocate for policies that reflect their values and lifestyle choices, with little regard for how these policies impact rural communities. This dynamic deepens the divide and the growing resentment between urban and rural populations. Rural Americans feel marginalized and disrespected, leading to a broader distrust of urban-dominated government and media institutions.

The political power imbalance means that one or two densely populated urban counties can effectively control the entire state's policy direction. This situation is especially problematic in states with large rural populations, where the needs and values of rural residents are vastly different from those of urban dwellers. For instance, in states like New York and California, urban areas like New York City and Los Angeles wield substantial political influence, often leading to statewide policies that do not reflect the interests of the rest of the state.

The arrogance of many urban voters in imposing their values on the rest of the state not only undermines the Second Amendment rights of rural residents but also deepens the divide between urban and rural America. Addressing this divide requires a more nuanced and respectful approach to policymaking—one that considers the diverse needs and values of all Americans, ensuring that the rights enshrined in the Constitution are protected for everyone, regardless of where they live.

## Security for Me but Not for Thee

The debate over gun control often reveals a striking hypocrisy among some of its most vocal proponents: celebrities and politicians who advocate for stringent gun laws while relying on armed security to protect themselves and their families. This duality underscores a fundamental disconnect between their public stance on gun ownership and their private reliance on firearms for personal safety. By examining specific examples, quotes, and public reactions, we can illuminate how these elites often perceive themselves as superior and more deserving of protection than the general populace.

One prominent example is actress and activist Alyssa Milano. Milano has been an outspoken advocate for gun control, frequently using her platform to call for stricter regulations. In a 2018 tweet, she stated, "The NRA & gun lobby are tearing our country apart. We need gun control NOW!" However, in 2019, it was revealed that Milano employed armed security guards to protect her home during a protest she attended against the National Rifle Association (NRA). When confronted about this apparent hypocrisy, Milano responded by saying, "I have a right to protect myself and my family. We shouldn't have to worry about being attacked at a protest." This statement highlights a belief in a personal right to protection that she seemingly denies others through her advocacy for restrictive gun laws.

Another high-profile example involves actress and activist Kim Kardashian. Kardashian has publicly supported various gun control measures and called for legislative action to curb gun violence. Despite her advocacy, she employs armed security to protect herself and her family. In 2016, following a robbery in Paris, Kardashian greatly increased her security detail, including armed guards. Her actions point to a reliance on firearms for protection, even as she supports measures that would restrict others' access to similar means of defense.

In 2016, nearly 200 artists and entertainment industry executives, including Barbra Streisand, Billy Joel, and Madonna, signed Billboard's Open Letter on Gun Violence, urging Congress to enact universal background checks and other gun control measures. While these artists publicly support stricter gun laws, they often rely on armed security for personal protection, highlighting a perceived disparity between their advocacy and personal practices. Similarly, country music artists Tim McGraw, Faith Hill, and pop artist Taylor Swift have expressed support for gun control initiatives. Despite their public stance on gun regulation, these celebrities typically maintain armed security personnel to ensure their safety, both at home and while on tour.

In February 2023, during an *American Idol* audition, contestant Trey Louis—a survivor of the 2018 Santa Fe High School shooting—shared his harrowing experience, prompting pop star and *American Idol* judge Katy Perry to become visibly emotional. Overcome with tears, Perry exclaimed, "Our country has f-----g failed us!" highlighting her distress over the ongoing issue of gun violence in schools. Katy Perry, a vocal advocate for strict gun control, employs armed security to protect her $15 million mansion in Montecito, California, and frequently retreats to her heavily guarded $11 million penthouse in West Hollywood's exclusive Sierra Towers.

Politicians, too, often exhibit this double standard. Former New York City Mayor Michael Bloomberg is a notable example. Bloomberg has been a major proponent of gun control through his organization, Everytown for Gun Safety, and has spent millions advocating for stricter gun laws. Despite this, Bloomberg is protected by a team of armed security guards. When questioned about this contradiction, Bloomberg's response was telling: "I have a security detail. I pay for it all myself. And you know, they're all retired police officers who are very well-trained in firearms." Bloomberg's acknowledgment of his reliance on trained armed security while advocating disarmament for the average citizen highlights a clear divide between his personal safety provisions and his public policy positions.

Joe Biden has also been a vocal advocate for gun control. Throughout his political career, Biden has pushed for measures such as the assault weapons ban and universal background checks. However, as vice president and then as president, Biden has been surrounded by armed Secret Service agents. This reliance on armed protection for personal safety stands in stark contrast to his advocacy for reducing the availability of firearms to the general public. When pressed about this apparent inconsistency, Biden has often emphasized the need for professional security for high-profile individuals, inadvertently underscoring the perceived need for armed defense that he seeks to limit for ordinary citizens.

These examples illustrate a broader trend among some celebrities and politicians: advocacy for strict gun control measures while simultaneously relying on armed security for personal protection. This dual approach reveals a belief that their safety and the safety of their families justify the use of firearms, even as they seek to limit the same rights for others. This hypocrisy not only undermines their arguments but also exposes a fundamental elitism, where their security needs are deemed more important than those of ordinary citizens.

## The Privilege of Armed Security for High-Profile Individuals

The argument that high-profile individuals should have more privileges when it comes to armed security is elitist and undermines the principle of equal protection under the law. This view suggests that the lives of celebrities, politicians, and other public figures are somehow more valuable and more important than those of ordinary citizens. In a society that values equality, no individual's right to safety should be deemed more important than another's based on their social status or public profile. The Second Amendment guarantees every American the right to self-defense—not just the wealthy elite who can afford private security.

The President of the United States, as well as other high-profile politicians, should indeed be subject to the same gun control measures they advocate for the general populace. When these leaders push for strict gun regulations while maintaining their own armed security, they create a double standard that erodes public trust and undermines the legitimacy of their arguments. If the proposed gun control measures are genuinely effective and necessary for public safety, then those advocating for them should be willing to abide by the same rules.

This double standard is especially problematic when considering the realities faced by ordinary citizens. Many individuals live in high-crime areas where the threat of violence is a daily concern. For these people, the ability to legally own and carry firearms for self-defense is a crucial aspect of their personal security. Denying them this right while allowing high-profile individuals to enjoy armed protection creates a dangerous disparity. It suggests that the safety of ordinary citizens is a lower priority, which is both unjust and counterproductive to the goal of reducing violence.

Moreover, the argument that high-profile individuals require more protection due to their visibility and potential threats ignores the fact that many ordinary people also face significant risks. Small business owners in crime-ridden neighborhoods, victims of domestic violence, and individuals living in rural areas far from law enforcement are all groups who might benefit greatly from the ability to protect themselves with firearms. These individuals are no less deserving of protection than any celebrity or politician.

The notion that armed security is a necessity for high-profile individuals but not for ordinary citizens also fails to recognize the broader implications for society. When leaders and public figures advocate for disarmament while relying on armed guards, they foster a sense of helplessness among the general populace. This can lead to increased fear and anxiety, as well as a diminished sense of personal agency and responsibility. Empowering citizens to take charge of their own safety through responsible gun ownership can enhance community resilience and reduce reliance on state protection.

Furthermore, the effectiveness of armed security in preventing violence has been well-documented. Instances where armed individuals have thwarted crimes, including mass shootings, highlight the potential benefits of allowing responsible citizens to carry firearms. If armed protection is deemed necessary for high-profile individuals to deter threats, it stands to reason that the same logic applies to the general public. The presence of armed, law-abiding citizens can serve as a deterrent to criminals and enhance overall public safety.

The problem with the "only trained security should have guns" attitude is that it creates a two-tier system: protection for the privileged, vulnerability for everyone else. The argument that high-profile individuals should have more privileges regarding armed security is inherently elitist and undermines the principle of equality. It's not only blatantly unfair and hypocritical; it's also flat-out unconstitutional. The value of human life and the right to self-defense should not be determined by social status or public visibility. The Second Amendment guarantees every American—not just the wealthy or connected—the right to defend themselves and their families.

If gun control measures are truly intended to enhance public safety, like our moral betters claim, they should apply equally to everyone, including those who advocate for them.

## The "I Don't, So You Shouldn't Either" Mentality

A recurring theme among anti-gun elites and gun control advocates is a peculiar sense of grievance rooted in personal choice. Some of these individuals openly express the view that it is somehow unjust or unfair that others choose to exercise their Second Amendment rights when they themselves have voluntarily opted out.

It often sounds like this: "I don't own a gun, I don't want to own a gun, so no one else should either." Or worse, "If I am unwilling or incapable of defending myself with a firearm, then no one else should be allowed to either—because that gives you an 'unfair advantage.'"

At the heart of this logic, there is a dangerous conflation between personal preference and public policy. These advocates frame lawful gun ownership as an injustice—not because it violates anyone's rights, but simply because it exists outside of their chosen worldview. They elevate their individual discomfort or disinterest into a justification for restricting the rights of others.

Beneath the surface of this argument lies something even more troubling: projection. Many of these individuals, out of fear, moral cowardice, or an unwillingness to confront the harsh realities of self-defense, have psychologically resigned themselves to dependency. For whatever reason—be it weak-mindedness, naivety, or fear—they are unwilling or unable to take responsibility for the defense of themselves or their loved ones. Instead of admitting to this shortcoming, they seek to impose it on everyone else.

Rather than acknowledging that their refusal to be their own first responder is a personal choice (or failing), they lash out at those who have chosen a different path. To them, gun owners possess a power they refuse to give themselves—a power that provides agency and self-reliance—and they resent it. This resentment reveals an implicit admission: They know firearms level the playing field. They understand that guns empower individuals—particularly those who may otherwise be at a physical disadvantage. But rather than taking personal responsibility for their own safety or acknowledging the prudence of lawful gun ownership, they attempt to pull everyone else down to their level of vulnerability.

It's not enough that they choose not to own a gun—they want to ensure you don't either, so no one has the "upper hand" in protecting themselves. It's a zero-sum mentality rooted in envy, fear, or misplaced moral superiority. It completely disregards the very nature of constitutional rights: that they are yours to exercise—or not—without infringing upon someone else's freedom to make a different choice.

This "I don't, so you shouldn't either" attitude has no place in a free society, where rights are individual and not subject to collective feelings of inadequacy, fear, or psychological surrender.

## Using Groups as Political Pawns

Politicians and celebrities who advocate for strict gun control measures often use the plight of poor and inner-city communities as a talking point to garner support and get elected. They highlight the high rates of gun violence in these areas to justify their calls for more regulations. However, once in office, the policies they enact often fail to address the root causes of violence, such as poverty, lack of education, and inadequate mental health care. Instead, these policies focus on restricting gun ownership, which disproportionately affects the very communities they claim to protect.

Many high-crime areas have seen the implementation of stringent gun control laws that require extensive background checks, waiting periods, and high fees for permits. These measures, while well-intentioned, often make it prohibitively expensive and difficult for low-income individuals to legally obtain firearms. As a result, law-abiding citizens in these communities are left without the means to defend themselves against violent criminals who do not adhere to gun laws.

Moreover, these policies fail to consider the unique challenges faced by residents of high-crime neighborhoods. In areas where police response times can be slow and law enforcement resources are stretched thin, the ability to own and carry a firearm for self-defense is crucial. By making it harder for residents to arm themselves, gun control advocates inadvertently create a power imbalance where criminals, who obtain firearms illegally, have the upper hand over unarmed citizens.

The impact of these policies is starkly evident in Chicago and Baltimore, where strict gun control measures have done little to curb gun violence. Instead, year after year, these cities continue to experience high rates of violent crime, and residents are left feeling increasingly unsafe. The restrictive laws prevent law-abiding citizens from protecting themselves, while criminals continue to exploit the black market for firearms.

Besides making communities less safe, restrictive gun control policies can also contribute to economic decline. High-crime rates and the perception of danger deter businesses from investing in these neighborhoods, leading to fewer job opportunities and perpetuating cycles of poverty. In recent years, a growing number of businesses have pulled out of high-crime neighborhoods across major US cities due to skyrocketing rates of violent crime, robberies, and looting. Retailers like Walgreens, Walmart, and Target have closed stores in areas such as San Francisco, Chicago, and Portland, citing persistent theft and unsafe working conditions for employees. In some neighborhoods, brazen daylight robberies and repeated smash-and-grab incidents have made it nearly impossible for businesses to remain profitable, or even safe. The situation has become so dire in some urban areas that stores are leaving behind entire communities, turning once-vibrant commercial corridors into economic wastelands plagued by shuttered storefronts and rising unemployment. When residents are unable to protect themselves or their property, it further discourages economic development and exacerbates social and economic disparities.

The push for more gun control also often ignores the potential benefits of responsible gun ownership in reducing crime. Numerous studies have shown that communities with higher rates of lawful gun ownership experience lower rates of violent crime. Responsible gun owners can act as a deterrent to criminal activity, and the presence of armed citizens can enhance community safety. By denying poor and inner-city residents the right to own firearms, gun control advocates undermine a potentially effective tool for crime prevention.

The persistent desire of liberal elites to disarm inner-city and poor communities—while doing little to actually address the violence within them—seems less like misguided policy and more like a deliberate strategy to keep these populations vulnerable, dependent, and politically compliant. After all, a disarmed, helpless community is far easier to control than an empowered one that no longer needs rescuing.

The push for stricter gun control by elites often hurts poor and inner-city communities the most. These policies, while supposedly intended to reduce gun violence, fail to address the underlying causes of crime and instead make it more difficult for law-abiding citizens to protect themselves. The result is a cycle of vulnerability and insecurity that perpetuates the very problems these policies aim to solve. To create safer communities, it is essential to focus on comprehensive approaches that address economic, social, and criminal justice issues while respecting the right of individuals to defend themselves.

## Gun Owner Stereotypes

The stereotype that gun owners and Second Amendment advocates are a bunch of racist, uneducated rednecks is not only inaccurate but also an example of the cultural and political elite's condescension and ignorance towards a diverse group of citizens. The narrative perpetuated by many in the progressive elite unfairly mocks gun owners as ignorant and backward, when they actually represent a broad cross section of American society who are deeply committed to their rights and freedoms.

First and foremost, the demographics of gun ownership in America are far more diverse than the stereotype suggests. According to the Pew Research Center, in 2017, approximately 42 percent of Americans live in a household with a gun. By 2022, that number rose to 45 percent. Gun owners come from all walks of life; this includes men and women, people of various racial and ethnic backgrounds, and individuals from different educational and economic statuses. The notion that gun owners are predominantly white, rural, uneducated males is outdated and inaccurate.

The progressive elite's efforts to paint gun owners as racists also fall flat when confronted with reality. Gun ownership crosses racial lines, with many African Americans, Hispanic Americans, and other minorities owning firearms. For several in these communities, guns are a means of protection against crime and a symbol of empowerment. The National African American Gun Association, for example, has seen substantial growth in membership, reflecting the increasing diversity within the gun-owning community. The most recent statistics from 2020 show that 45,000 members belong to this organization, and gun ownership among African Americans increased by 60 percent in 2020 alone.

The stereotype that gun owners are uneducated is also unfounded. Many gun owners are well-educated professionals, including doctors, lawyers, engineers, and educators, who value their Second Amendment rights. The decision to own a firearm is often based on a well-considered understanding of personal safety, constitutional rights, and a recognition of the importance of self-defense. The portrayal of gun owners as unthinking and uneducated is a deliberate attempt to marginalize and discredit a huge portion of the American population.

Figures in the media, academia, and politics often sneer at gun owners, portraying them as backward and violent. This contempt is not only unfair but also ignores the legitimate concerns and values of millions of Americans. Furthermore, the characterization of gun owners as "rednecks" is a cultural slur that disregards the values and traditions of rural America. Many rural Americans have a long history of responsible gun ownership, rooted in hunting, sport shooting, and self-reliance. These traditions are part of the cultural fabric of the country and deserve respect, not derision. The progressive elite's mockery of these traditions reveals a deep-seated disdain for the values and lifestyles of millions of Americans.

The contempt held by some progressives for gun owners also stems from a fundamental misunderstanding of the Second Amendment and its importance. The right to bear arms is not about hunting or sport shooting; it is about the fundamental right to self-defense and the preservation of liberty. Gun owners understand this, and their advocacy for Second Amendment rights is grounded in a commitment to safeguarding these principles. The elite's dismissal of these concerns as paranoid or reactionary ignores the historical and contemporary relevance of an armed populace in protecting freedom. It is essential to recognize and respect the diversity and legitimacy of gun ownership in America, rather than perpetuating divisive and unfounded stereotypes.

## Rules for Thee but Not for Me

As the following eight examples demonstrate, the debate over gun control in the United States is often marked by a complex interplay of advocacy, legislation, and personal conduct, revealing a dichotomy and hypocrisy among those who champion stricter regulations.

This dichotomy is starkly illustrated with Hunter Biden, son of former President Joe Biden, a prominent advocate for stringent gun control measures. The actions and subsequent defense of Hunter Biden provide a vivid example of the inconsistencies and contradictions that can arise within the gun control debate.

Hunter Biden's case is controversial due to his alleged violations of existing gun control laws, which his father and other gun control advocates have staunchly supported. In 2018, Hunter Biden purchased a firearm, during which he allegedly lied on the required background check form by not disclosing his illegal drug use. Federal law mandates that any person purchasing a firearm must truthfully answer questions regarding their drug use, and lying on this form is a felony offense. But that's not all. Hunter Biden reportedly handled the firearm while under the influence of drugs and alcohol, and later disposed of the gun in a trash can near a school, actions that are both illegal and highly irresponsible.

These actions directly contravene the very laws that gun control advocates, including Joe Biden, have promoted. Biden has consistently called for stricter gun laws, including more comprehensive background checks, measures to keep guns out of the hands of individuals with substance abuse issues, and safe storage requirements to prevent accidents and unauthorized access. The revelations about Hunter Biden's conduct starkly contrast with these advocacy efforts, highlighting a blatant hypocrisy.

The ramifications of Hunter Biden's actions extend beyond personal misconduct, raising broader questions about the integrity and consistency of gun control advocacy. When prominent figures and their families flout the laws they advocate for others, it undermines public trust in the legitimacy and fairness of these regulations. This hypocrisy fuels skepticism and resistance among those who already view gun control measures as infringements on their Second Amendment rights.

The case of Hunter Biden also brings into focus the broader issue of accountability. If high-profile individuals are not held to the same legal standards as ordinary citizens, it suggests that laws are only enforced selectively, based on social or political standing, rather than uniformly applied to all citizens. Such perceptions weaken the rule of law and diminish respect for legal processes.

The defense of Hunter Biden by some gun control advocates on grounds of his Second Amendment rights adds another layer of complexity and contradiction. The argument that Hunter Biden's rights should be protected despite his illegal actions stands in stark contrast to the typically stringent stance taken by gun control advocates who argue for the disqualification of individuals from gun ownership based on similar criteria. This selective application of principles undermines the consistent enforcement of laws that gun control efforts rely on.

In the big picture, the Hunter Biden controversy illustrates the inherent challenges and potential hypocrisies within the gun control debate. It emphasizes the need for consistency and fairness in the application of laws and highlights the importance of personal responsibility and accountability, regardless of one's status. The situation also underscores the tension between advocating for restrictive measures and respecting constitutional rights, a balance that is crucial for maintaining public trust and support for any legislative efforts.

The case of Hunter Biden presents a vivid example of the dichotomy and hypocrisy that can arise in the gun control debate. This situation serves as a reminder of the importance of upholding the principles of accountability and equal application of the law, especially when high-profile figures are involved, to ensure the integrity and effectiveness of gun control measures.

Hunter Biden's trial began amid rumors of his father, Joe Biden, pulling strings and engaging in witness tampering to influence the outcome. Regardless, Hunter Biden was ultimately convicted of federal gun charges, facing a potential prison sentence. Throughout his presidency, Joe Biden repeatedly claimed he would not intervene in his son's legal troubles. But in a final act of political hypocrisy, on his last day in office, President Biden quietly pardoned Hunter—using an autopen, no less—shielding him from the consequences of the very gun laws his administration so aggressively pushed on law-abiding citizens.

Some argue that this verdict indirectly sets a precedent that individuals with drug or alcohol problems could have their Second Amendment rights stripped from them, which they believe is unconstitutional. The question of their constitutionality can be addressed separately, as it is not relevant to this argument at this moment. What is relevant is that Hunter Biden violated gun laws. He should have faced the same consequences as any other citizen for breaking them. Baby Biden's case highlights the double standards and hypocrisy that often permeate political discussions around gun control and legal accountability.

Another example of rules for thee but not for me is highlighted in the accidental shooting incident involving Alec Baldwin on the set of the film *Rust* in October 2021, where he pointed a loaded gun at cinematographer Halyna Hutchins and pulled the trigger, resulting in her tragic death. This incident has brought to light several issues, including the hypocrisy surrounding the lack of criminal charges against Baldwin, the basic rules of gun safety, and the perceived privilege afforded to certain individuals due to their status and political affiliations.

On that fateful day, Baldwin was rehearsing a scene that involved him drawing a revolver. He pointed the gun at Hutchins and discharged it, fatally wounding her and injuring director Joel Souza. Despite Baldwin's claims that he did not know the prop gun was loaded with a live round, the fact remains that he pointed a firearm at another person and pulled the trigger. In any standard gun safety protocol, this act alone constitutes gross negligence. The fundamental rule of gun handling is to never point a gun at anyone unless you intend to shoot and always treat every firearm as if it is loaded with live rounds. Baldwin's actions violated these basic principles, yet he has not faced the same legal consequences that an ordinary individual likely would.

The responsibility for the handling and safety of firearms on a film set typically falls to the armorer and assistant director. However, as the person who pulled the trigger, Baldwin's responsibility cannot be entirely absolved. In the aftermath, much of the blame was directed towards the film's armorer and crew, with Baldwin maintaining his innocence. This deflection of responsibility underscores a troubling double standard. Regardless of whether Baldwin knew the gun was loaded, he ultimately pointed the gun at the victim and pulled the trigger, making him culpable. Yet, his status as a prominent actor seems to have shielded him from accountability.

This incident exemplifies how the elite can avoid facing the consequences of their actions, even when those actions result in someone's death. The notion of "liberal privilege" has been cited by critics who argue that Baldwin's political affiliations and status have played a role in the lack of criminal charges. If a regular citizen had been involved in a similar incident, it is likely they would face severe legal repercussions. The disparity in how justice is applied highlights a two-tiered system where the influential and well-connected are treated differently than the average person.

The irony of this situation is further compounded by Baldwin's public stance on gun control. As a staunch supporter of stricter gun regulations, Baldwin has been vocal about the dangers of firearms and the need for more rigorous controls. Yet, his actions on the *Rust* set contradict his advocacy. The fact that he pointed a gun at someone, pulled the trigger, and then evaded substantial legal consequences is starkly hypocritical. It suggests that those who loudly champion gun control may not adhere to the very principles they advocate when it comes to their own conduct.

This incident also raises broader questions about the culture of accountability in Hollywood and among the elite. The entertainment industry showcases a reluctance to hold its own accountable. Baldwin's case is not an isolated one but rather part of a pattern where prominent individuals receive lenient treatment for serious offenses. Baldwin's ability to avoid severe repercussions, despite clear negligence, highlights the disparities in accountability based on status and political connections, reinforcing the perception of a two-tiered justice system. This perpetuates a sense of injustice and undermines public trust.

The hypocrisy of elites advocating for stringent gun control laws while flouting these same regulations without any consequences is also illustrated by the Fast and Furious scandal. Operation Fast and Furious was a controversial program initiated by the Bureau of Alcohol, Tobacco, Firearms and Explosives (ATF) largely under the Obama administration. The operation, which ran from 2006 to 2011, aimed to track the flow of firearms from the United States to Mexican drug cartels. However, the strategy involved allowing suspected straw purchasers to buy firearms and transport them across the border, hoping to trace these weapons to high-ranking cartel members.

During the operation, approximately 2,000 firearms, including AK-47 and .50 caliber rifles, were sold to suspected gun traffickers with the knowledge and oversight of the ATF. These firearms, which the government sought to prohibit civilians from owning under various gun control proposals, ended up in the hands of violent criminal organizations. The flawed execution of the operation led to disastrous consequences, including the death of US Border Patrol agent Brian Terry, who was killed in 2010 by one of the trafficked weapons.

Despite the magnitude of the scandal, which saw thousands of guns end up in the hands of dangerous criminals, there were ultimately no serious consequences for the government officials responsible for Operation Fast and Furious. Key figures, including then–Attorney General Eric Holder, faced minimal repercussions. Holder was held in contempt of Congress for refusing to release documents related to the operation, but he retained his position and suffered no significant legal penalties.

The mainstream media and political elites swept the scandal under the rug, minimizing coverage and downplaying the severity of the government's actions. This response exemplifies the two-tiered justice system, where elected officials and high-ranking bureaucrats evade the consequences that ordinary citizens would undoubtedly face for similar actions. While civilians face stringent regulations and potential prosecution for gun-related offenses, the same standards do not apply to those in power who orchestrated a program that directly contradicted the principles they publicly championed.

The scandal once again highlighted a discrepancy between the actions of government officials and the laws they enforce on ordinary citizens. While the government sought to impose stricter gun control measures on the populace, it simultaneously facilitated the illegal trafficking of firearms to foreign nations and criminal organizations. This blatant criminality and hypocrisy were met with little to no accountability for the officials involved.

Another glaring example of this two-tiered justice system occurred in 2012, when David Gregory, then-host of NBC's *Meet the Press*, found himself at the center of a controversy that further exemplifies the double standards often afforded to media elites. During a segment discussing gun control in the aftermath of the Sandy Hook Elementary School shooting, Gregory displayed a 30-round magazine on air. At the time, possessing such a magazine was illegal in Washington, DC, where the show was filmed. This act was a clear violation of DC law, which bans the possession of any magazine capable of holding more than 10 rounds of ammunition.

Gregory's on-air demonstration was intended to support his argument for stricter gun control measures, ironically showcasing an item that the very laws he advocated for deemed illegal. The incident quickly garnered attention, sparking a debate not only about the content of the discussion but also about the apparent hypocrisy and potential legal consequences.

Despite the clear-cut nature of the violation, the District of Columbia attorney general, Irvin Nathan, decided not to prosecute Gregory. In a letter explaining the decision, Nathan cited prosecutorial discretion and argued that pursuing charges would not serve public safety interests. He acknowledged that while Gregory had technically broken the law, there was no intent to commit a criminal act, and Gregory's actions were part of an effort to inform the public on an important issue.

This decision sparked outrage among gun rights advocates and many members of the public, who saw it as a glaring example of a double standard. Ordinary citizens who inadvertently violate similar gun laws often face strict legal consequences, including fines and potential jail time. The decision not to prosecute Gregory reinforced the perception that media elites and public figures are treated differently under the law, afforded leniency that would not be extended to average citizens.

Furthermore, the incident served as a stark reminder of the power of media figures in shaping public discourse. Gregory's use of an illegal magazine on national television was intended to underscore the dangers of high-capacity magazines and the need for stricter regulations. However, the legal repercussions—or lack thereof—drew attention away from the intended message and focused it instead on the inequities in how gun laws are applied. In the end, the David Gregory incident became a case study in the broader debate over gun control and media influence. It illustrated how high-profile figures inadvertently undermine their advocacy by failing to adhere to the laws they support and how the selective enforcement of these laws can fuel public distrust and skepticism.

The late Senator Dianne Feinstein, who was a longtime advocate for strict gun control measures, played a large role in the push for tighter firearm regulations in the United States. Representing California, Feinstein was instrumental in crafting and supporting legislation aimed at restricting access to firearms, including the Assault Weapons Ban of 1994. Her advocacy was often characterized by strong rhetoric, including her infamous statement, "Mr. and Mrs. America, turn them all in," referring to a national gun confiscation proposal. This stance made her a hero among gun control advocates and a prominent adversary for Second Amendment supporters.

However, Feinstein's credibility on the issue of gun control was seriously undermined by revelations about her own personal firearm use. In the past, Feinstein had admitted during a Senate hearing that she carried a concealed weapon for personal protection after receiving threats. She explained her rationale for carrying a firearm, stating, "I know the urge to arm yourself because that's what I did. I was trained in firearms. I carried a concealed weapon. I made the determination that if somebody was going to try to take me out, I was going to take them with me."

While Feinstein's actions were not illegal, the disclosure struck many as profoundly hypocritical. As a senator with influence over gun legislation, her personal choice to carry a concealed weapon for protection starkly contrasted with her public advocacy for disarming law-abiding citizens. This contradiction fueled accusations of elitism and double standards, suggesting that Feinstein believed in one set of rules for herself and another for the general public and highlighting a perceived disconnect between the ruling class and the everyday American.

The criticism against Feinstein was not merely about personal choices but about the significant impact of her legislative efforts. As a powerful senator, Feinstein pushed for measures that many argued infringed upon constitutional rights. Her ability to influence and enact laws that could potentially disarm millions of Americans, while she herself took measures to ensure her personal safety through firearm use, struck at the heart of the debate over gun control.

Feinstein's high-profile advocacy and her actions raised important questions about fairness, representation, and the true intentions behind legislative efforts to restrict firearms. The juxtaposition of Feinstein's public positions and private actions served as a powerful illustration of why many Americans remained skeptical of gun control advocates and their motives.

The most recent example of the elite violating laws they impose on the rest of us is the case of Judge Cylenthia LaToye Miller. On June 8, 2024, Judge Miller, a juvenile judge for Wayne County, Michigan, was caught with a loaded .380

caliber Smith & Wesson in her purse at Detroit Metro Airport. TSA agents discovered the firearm during a security screening. Despite having a concealed pistol license, the firearm was unregistered, and its serial number was scratched off, which alone would be a felony for an average citizen. Additionally, Miller claimed that her brother gave her the gun, another action that could lead to severe legal consequences for most people.

Judge Miller broke four notable gun laws in Michigan: failing to register the firearm, possessing a gun with a scratched-off serial number, bringing a loaded gun into an airport, and conducting an illegal private sale transfer. Despite these serious infractions, she was only charged with a misdemeanor for carrying a dangerous weapon in an airport, which would have carried a penalty of up to one year in jail and a $1,000 fine. Judge Miller pled no contest to the misdemeanor charge, paid a $1,400 fine, and walked away with a clean slate—her record expunged just 90 days later. For most Americans, that kind of legal leniency isn't just rare—it's unthinkable. As of March 2025, there were no further updates available regarding the resolution of the remaining charges.

If an average citizen had committed the same offense, they would likely face severe penalties, including potential years in prison, and be vilified by the media as a terrorist or attacker. The contrasting treatment of Judge Miller compared to ordinary citizens highlights the hypocrisy and disparity in how laws are applied and exemplifies how the elite can flout regulations with minimal consequences while enforcing strict compliance on the general populace.

Although a bit different from these other cases, the arrest of Patrick Burke, armed bodyguard to loudmouth anti-gun crusader Michael Moore, is a textbook case of elitist hypocrisy. While Moore campaigns to disarm law-abiding Americans, he has no problem hiring someone with a gun to protect him. In January 2005, Burke was arrested at JFK International Airport for violating New York's infamous gun laws after declaring his firearm—something responsible gun owners are supposed to do. Yet in New York, where anti-gun laws trip up travelers like booby traps, Burke found himself in handcuffs, a felon in the eyes of the state. Moore, from behind the safety of his armed entourage, couldn't have cared less.

Meanwhile, Moore got to walk away unscathed while Burke took the fall. This is the elitist double standard in action—protection for them, restrictions for you. It's the classic "guns for me but not for thee" mentality, straight from the Hollywood playbook, where their lives somehow matter more than yours.

As a final example, in 2013, a significant incident involving former New York City Mayor Michael Bloomberg's armed security detail highlighted the perceived double standards and hypocrisy in the enforcement of gun laws.

Bloomberg, a staunch advocate for gun control and the founder of Everytown for Gun Safety, has consistently pushed for stricter firearm regulations, including bans on certain types of firearms and high-capacity magazines. Despite his public stance on gun control, Bloomberg's personal security detail included armed bodyguards, highlighting a disconnect between his advocacy and his actions.

The incident in question occurred at New York's LaGuardia Airport, where one of Bloomberg's bodyguards was arrested for attempting to board a flight with an unloaded handgun in his luggage. This act was a clear violation of federal laws regulating the transportation of firearms on commercial flights, which require specific procedures to be followed, including declaring the firearm to the airline and ensuring it is properly secured and inaccessible during the flight.

Despite the clear violation, the bodyguard faced minimal consequences compared to what an ordinary citizen might experience in similar circumstances. The Transportation Security Administration (TSA) and law enforcement typically enforce strict penalties for such infractions, including substantial fines and potential criminal charges. In this case, however, because of who he was working for, the bodyguard avoided the severe repercussions that would likely have been imposed on a regular traveler. The perception that Bloomberg's bodyguard received special treatment only fueled existing frustrations over the unequal enforcement of gun laws. Critics quickly pointed out the irony: While Bloomberg campaigns for stricter gun control and fights against concealed carry for everyday Americans, his own safety depends on armed protection.

The incident exposed the glaring double standard behind many gun control policies—rules that burden law-abiding citizens but make exceptions for the elite. Bloomberg's reliance on armed security while advocating to disarm the public highlights a worldview where the safety of the privileged matters more than the rights of ordinary Americans.

## Speak Up

The hypocrisy and elitism surrounding the gun control debate are not just flaws to be acknowledged but battles to be fought head-on. These so-called elites, who advocate disarmament while ensuring their own protection with armed security, must be challenged at every turn. Their disdain for everyday citizens, especially those in rural or conservative areas, is rooted in ignorance and a fundamental disconnect from the real-world implications of their policies.

The manipulation of language, the twisting of statistics, and the blatant double standards they employ are tactics designed to undermine the rights of law-abiding Americans. This is not just a debate about policy—it's a fight for the very principles of equality and fairness. These elites deserve to be mocked, ridiculed, and exposed for the hypocrites they are, just as they have attempted to belittle and marginalize those who stand for their Second Amendment rights. It is essential to confront their arrogance with truth, and to ensure that the voices of everyday citizens are not only heard but respected in this critical national conversation.

We must speak up and refuse to be silenced by those who seek to cancel and erase our voices from the conversation. These hypocrites and snobs fear the power of our voice because it is our most potent weapon against their elitist agendas. They know that when we stand up, challenge their narratives, and call them out for the double standards they perpetuate, we expose the truth they work so hard to suppress. This is why they use their influence to try to silence us, to push us out of the public square, and to stifle open debate. But we must not be intimidated or back down. Our voice is crucial in defending our rights and holding these elites accountable. By speaking out boldly and unapologetically, we ensure that the truth prevails and that the principles of freedom and equality remain strong in the face of their condescension and hypocrisy.

# Chapter 10

## International Busybodies

*The right of self-defense is the first law of nature; in most governments, it has been the study of rulers to confine this right within the narrowest limits possible.*

—John Adams

*To disarm the people is the best and most effectual way to enslave them.*

—George Mason

The Second Amendment of the United States Constitution has long been a point of contention not only within America but also on the international stage. Various nations and international organizations have attempted to meddle in US gun rights through treaties, propaganda, and criticism.

Disinformation aimed at undermining American gun rights is not a new phenomenon. For decades, foreign adversaries have sought to exploit the United States' Second Amendment debates to sow discord and weaken American society from within. These influence operations have ranged from Cold War propaganda to sophisticated social media campaigns in recent years.

One of the most notable examples of international interference comes from the United Nations. The UN has repeatedly pushed for arms control treaties that would lead to the imposition of international regulations on domestic firearm ownership, undermining US sovereignty and the constitutional rights of American citizens. The Arms Trade Treaty (ATT), is one such subject of controversy and concern among gun rights advocates.

Additionally, international criticism often targets America's unique gun culture. European nations, in particular, view the US stance on firearms with a sense of snobbery and disdain. Countries with strict gun control laws, like the United Kingdom and Australia, frequently boast of their own policies as models for reducing gun violence and criticize the United States for not following suit. This criticism often ignores the significant cultural and historical differences that underpin America's relationship with firearms. US gun culture is deeply rooted in the nation's history of independence and self-reliance, making simplistic comparisons with other countries both unhelpful and misleading.

Furthermore, countries like China have found more insidious ways to influence American attitudes toward guns. By leveraging their economic power, China has increasingly gained control over Hollywood, subtly influencing the content of movies and media to align with their propaganda goals. This includes shaping narratives around gun ownership and violence, often portraying firearms in a negative light to sway public opinion. Social media platforms, many of which have ties to foreign interests, also play a large role in spreading anti-gun rhetoric and shaping public discourse.

In this chapter, we explore historical and contemporary cases—from Russian "active measures" to Chinese propaganda—detailing how foreign actors have targeted the Second Amendment, what strategies they've used, and the impact on public perception, policy debates, and media narratives. The evidence reveals an evolving playbook of deception that raises serious implications for American sovereignty and constitutional rights.

Ironically, while these international entities criticize and seek to change America's gun laws, they often rely on US military and financial support to protect foreign borders and intervene in international conflicts, underscoring the paradox of foreign interference in domestic policy. This hypocrisy highlights the complex and often contradictory nature of international relations when it comes to gun rights and national sovereignty.

The international community's attempts to influence American gun laws and culture are multifaceted and persistent. From treaties proposed by the United Nations to the subtle propaganda efforts of foreign governments, these external pressures underscore the global significance of the Second Amendment. As we explore these influences, it becomes clear that the defense of the right to bear arms is not just a domestic issue but a crucial aspect of maintaining national sovereignty and individual liberty in the face of international meddling.

## UN Meddling

The international effort to regulate firearms in the United States through the United Nations (UN) and international arms treaties has been a contentious issue for years. Central to this effort is the Arms Trade Treaty (ATT), which aims to establish common standards for the international trade of conventional weapons to prevent and eradicate illicit trade and its resultant humanitarian consequences. The ATT, adopted by the UN General Assembly in 2013, is designed to promote responsibility and transparency in the arms trade. It requires countries to assess exports to ensure they are not used to violate human rights, commit acts of terrorism, or exacerbate armed conflicts.

The goals of the ATT on the surface are ostensibly noble. By setting international standards for the transfer of weapons, the treaty aims to reduce the proliferation of arms that can fuel violence and instability. Signatory nations are expected to implement rigorous checks and controls to ensure that arms exports do not contribute to these adverse outcomes. The treaty also encourages international cooperation and information sharing to tackle the illicit arms trade more effectively.

However, the ATT is perceived by many in the United States as a potential threat to the Second Amendment and American sovereignty, as the treaty could pave the way for international regulations that undermine the Second Amendment. One of the main points of contention is the ATT's provision for recordkeeping and reporting on arms transfers, which some Americans view as a precursor to an international gun registry. Critics argue that such measures could lead to increased surveillance and tracking of lawful gun owners in the United

States, infringing on their privacy and rights. The requirement for signatories to report on arms transfers could also pressure the US government to adopt stricter controls on the domestic firearms market to align with international norms, further infringing on the Second Amendment.

Opponents of the ATT also contend that the treaty's language is vague and open to interpretation, allowing for the possibility of overreach by international bodies. This could put pressure on the United States to conform to international standards that conflict with its own constitutional protections and legal traditions. The ATT's emphasis on preventing arms from being used to commit human rights abuses is seen by some as a backdoor approach to gun control, potentially leading to restrictions on the types of firearms and ammunition available to American citizens.

The debate over the ATT and its implications for American gun rights is also influenced by broader concerns about international influence on US policy. Many Americans are wary of ceding any level of control to international organizations, particularly on issues as deeply rooted in national identity and culture as the right to bear arms. This skepticism is amplified by the belief that the United States should remain vigilant in protecting its sovereignty against external pressures and maintaining its constitutional freedoms.

The potential impact of the ATT on American gun rights has led to widespread political opposition within the United States. The treaty was signed by the Obama administration in 2013 but has not been ratified by the US Senate. The Trump administration formally announced its intent to withdraw from the treaty in 2019, citing concerns about its potential to infringe on American sovereignty and the Second Amendment. This decision was supported by many gun rights advocates and organizations, who view the ATT as incompatible with US constitutional principles.

In addition to the ATT, the United Nations has made several other efforts to influence and potentially undermine the Second Amendment rights of American citizens through international resolutions and initiatives that, while ostensibly aimed at curbing global violence and illicit arms trade, raise concerns among US gun rights advocates about their implications for domestic firearm ownership.

One notable example is the UN Programme of Action to Prevent, Combat and Eradicate the Illicit Trade in Small Arms and Light Weapons in All Its Aspects, commonly known as the UN Programme of Action (PoA). Adopted in 2001, the PoA aims to tackle the global issue of illicit small arms trafficking. However, critics argue that the measures proposed under the PoA could lead to stricter regulations and control over civilian gun ownership. The implementation of the PoA includes calls for UN member states to adopt stringent measures on gun registration, marking, and tracing, which might infringe on the privacy and rights of lawful gun owners.

Another UN effort that has raised alarms is the International Small Arms Control Standards (ISACS) initiative. This framework seeks to provide guidelines for states to manage and regulate small arms and light weapons effectively. While ISACS is presented as a voluntary set of standards, some worry that it could pave the way for mandatory international regulations that might conflict with the Second Amendment. The standards emphasize stringent recordkeeping and reporting requirements that could burden legal firearm owners and infringe upon their rights.

The UN Office on Drugs and Crime (UNODC) has also been active in promoting international regulations that could affect domestic gun laws. The UNODC's Firearms Protocol, which is part of the UN Convention against Transnational Organized Crime, aims to promote international cooperation in combating the illicit manufacturing and trafficking of firearms. While this goal is widely supported, the broad and ambiguous language of the protocol has led to concerns that it could be used to justify far-reaching gun control measures that impact lawful gun owners.

Furthermore, the Sustainable Development Goals (SDGs), specifically Goal 16, which aims to "promote peaceful and inclusive societies," includes targets related to significantly reducing illicit arms flows and strengthening the recovery and return of stolen assets. Critics argue that the vague language of these targets could be interpreted to push for stricter gun control measures globally, including in the United States.

In addition to these specific initiatives, the broader discourse within various UN forums often reflects a bias against civilian firearm ownership. UN conferences and reports frequently highlight the negative impacts of small arms and light weapons, emphasizing the need for tighter controls without equally acknowledging the legitimate uses of firearms for self-defense, hunting, and sporting activities. This one-sided narrative can contribute to shaping international norms and expectations that are at odds with the Second Amendment.

Overall, the UN's various efforts to address the global challenges of illicit arms trade and violence often intersect with domestic debates over gun control in the United States. While the stated goals of these initiatives are to enhance global security, the implications for US gun rights are a grave concern for advocates of the Second Amendment. The potential for international agreements and standards to influence or dictate domestic firearm regulations underscores the importance of vigilance and advocacy in protecting constitutional rights against external pressures.

## Soviet and Russian Influence on US Gun Rights

Throughout history, Russia has often attempted to undermine the Second Amendment in the United States, employing various strategies ranging from propaganda campaigns to political and cultural influences. This effort can be traced back to the days of the Soviet Union, when leftist intellectuals and politicians in the US lauded Soviet gun control measures as a model for America. Despite the millions killed under Soviet rule, these figures ignored the dire consequences of civilian disarmament in favor of promoting strict gun regulations.

During the Cold War, the Soviet Union was notorious for its propaganda efforts aimed at destabilizing American society and sowing discord among its population, often highlighting America's perceived social problems—including violent crime and civil unrest—to discredit US democracy. Soviet propaganda outlets frequently pointed to incidents of gun violence and lawlessness in American cities to portray the US as a dangerous, chaotic society. While their primary messaging focused on issues like racism and economic inequality, these campaigns implicitly suggested that America's freedoms (such as the right to bear arms) led to societal turmoil.

By broadcasting stories of high murder rates and armed criminals, Moscow sought to undermine American moral authority and argue that Western freedoms—including gun rights—were a path to anarchy rather than prosperity. This early propaganda laid the groundwork for later disinformation efforts: Foreign actors learned that America's gun debate was a potent wedge issue, capable of stirring emotions and division. This narrative was picked up by sympathetic leftist intellectuals in the United States, who echoed these sentiments in their writings and political advocacy, calling for stricter gun control laws.

A prominent example of this influence can be seen in the writings of American intellectuals, such as Norman Cousins, editor of the *Saturday Review*, who praised the Soviet model of disarmament, often ignoring the brutal realities of Soviet oppression and the millions who were killed or imprisoned under the regime. This intellectual admiration for Soviet policies played a role in shaping the gun control debate in the United States, framing the issue as one of public safety and order rather than individual liberty and defense against tyranny.

In the 1970s and '80s, the Soviet state media often ran reports on gun-related violence in the US, using sensational headlines about "American carnage" to alarm their audiences. Though much of this content was factual, it was presented without context and with obvious schadenfreude—the message to the world (and to Soviet citizens) was that US constitutional freedoms made its people unsafe. By exaggerating the prevalence of shootings and framing US gun ownership as reckless, the Kremlin's propagandists aimed to undermine the Second Amendment's reputation abroad. These efforts were relatively overt propaganda rather than covert disinformation, but they established a narrative of American gun culture as a societal failure—a narrative that would resurface in more insidious ways in the 21st century.

In more recent times, Russia has continued its efforts to undermine American gun rights through cyber operations and disinformation campaigns. Russian operatives have used social media platforms to spread divisive messages and stoke fear and confusion among the American populace. These efforts have included spreading misinformation about gun control policies, exaggerating the risks associated with gun ownership, and pitting gun rights advocates against gun control supporters. In the mid-2010s, Russia launched an expansive influence campaign targeting numerous hot-button issues in the US—and gun rights were front and center. The Kremlin's strategy, carried out largely by the Internet Research Agency (IRA) "troll farm," was not to take one side, but to inflame both sides of the gun debate. By doing so, Russian operatives hoped to deepen American polarization and weaken trust in democratic institutions.

For example, the IRA sought to sway public opinion in favor of anti-gun political candidates who supported strict gun control policies. During the 2016 US presidential election, the IRA strategically targeted American voters with ads and posts that highlighted gun violence and portrayed pro-gun rights politicians negatively. This manipulation was designed to erode public support for the Second Amendment. The IRA also engaged in online discussions and forums, posing as concerned citizens to influence public perception and spark debates that favored gun control policies and anti-gun political candidates. These efforts were part of a broader strategy to deepen societal divisions and weaken trust in democratic institutions by polarizing the gun control debate.

Another stark illustration of Russia's tactics came in February 2018, after the tragic mass shooting at Marjory Stoneman Douglas High School in Parkland, Florida. As Americans mourned the 17 lives lost and students mobilized for gun reform, Russian disinformation crews saw an opportunity. Within hours of the shooting, automated bot accounts with suspected ties to Russia began pumping out false or inflammatory tweets using hashtags like #Parkland, #guncontrol, and #guncontrolnow. They hijacked the conversation to amplify hyper-partisan rhetoric. Some of these fake personas attempted to inflame both sides of the debate, quoting National Rifle Association arguments and talking points that the solution was arming teachers. Others pushed far-left slogans demanding immediate gun bans and confiscation. The Alliance for Securing Democracy's Hamilton 68 dashboard, which tracks Russian-linked influence accounts, saw Parkland-related terms dominate its trending topics that day.

Observers noted a specific strategy at play: Troll factories would seize popular hashtags (like #ParklandShooting) and inject left-wing extremist spin into them. Simultaneously, they invented divisive new hashtags and waited for real Americans to pick them up, blurring the line between fake agitation and organic grassroots tweets. This feedback loop between bots and unwitting real users made the disinformation hard to stamp out. In the case of Parkland, Russian-linked accounts were soon pushing conspiracy theories as well—such as smearing the teenage survivors as "crisis actors" or alleging the shooting was staged by the government to justify gun confiscation. These falsehoods, though homegrown in US conspiracy circles, were amplified by foreign actors to maximize chaos. American officials quickly noticed the pattern. Senator James Lankford (R-OK) pointed out that Russian troll farms had taken "both sides of the argument . . . to raise the noise level in America." In an NBC interview, Lankford noted that during the Parkland aftermath, Kremlin bots were simultaneously pushing pro-gun rights messages and pro-gun control messages at the same time as a deliberate tactic. The intended outcome was not to achieve a policy change on guns per se, but to make an already passionate issue even more bitter and polarized.

Indeed, the immediate effect was a flood of vitriol and misinformation in social media feeds, which made it harder for legitimate voices to be heard without harassment or doubt. By playing arsonist in America's raging gun debate, Russia undermined constructive discourse and further eroded Americans' trust in what they were seeing online.

In addition to its widespread online disinformation efforts, Russia engaged in a more insidious campaign to tarnish the reputation of one of America's most respected gun rights organizations—the National Rifle Association (NRA). The Kremlin's goal wasn't to promote the NRA's values but rather to corrupt its image and manufacture a false narrative that the pro-gun movement was aligned with Russian interests. This manipulation was part of a broader left-wing strategy—rooted in classic communist subversion tactics—to discredit gun rights and paint them as part of an international conspiracy rather than an American tradition of freedom.

A prime example of this effort was Maria Butina, a Russian agent who infiltrated the NRA under the guise of being a gun-rights activist and student. In reality, she was working at the behest of Alexander Torshin, a Kremlin operative, in an attempt to gain access to influential figures in the pro-gun community. Between 2015 and 2016, Butina attended NRA conventions, arranged "friendship dinners" with conservative leaders, and even publicly questioned then-candidate Donald Trump about his stance on US–Russia relations. The real goal wasn't to foster legitimate ties but to set the stage for a disinformation campaign that would later be used to smear the NRA and gun-rights advocates as Kremlin operatives.

By embedding herself within pro-Second Amendment circles, Butina's presence created a false association between American gun rights advocates and the Russian government. The media, particularly left-leaning outlets, quickly seized on this manufactured link, amplifying claims that the NRA was cozying up to Russia. This was precisely what Moscow—and its ideological allies in the Western media—wanted: to create a perception that gun rights activists were either compromised or were extremists willing to align with foreign adversaries. Butina's "networking" was in fact a carefully orchestrated ploy to manufacture distrust in the NRA and the larger gun-rights movement, weaponizing public perception against the very people fighting to uphold constitutional freedoms.

The intended outcome was twofold. First, to delegitimize the NRA and gun-rights advocates by linking them to Russia, an easy sell to those already predisposed to view conservatives and libertarians as untrustworthy. Second, to distract from credible threats posed by gun control advocates and their own ties to leftist globalist movements, shifting focus away from those who seek to dismantle the Second Amendment.

In the following years, so-called photos of NRA executives supposedly meeting with Russian officials were widely circulated in the press, with no similar scrutiny placed on left-wing organizations meeting with foreign actors. The media and anti-Second Amendment advocates erupted in outrage over the NRA having a conversation with a Russian agent, yet they turned a blind eye to years of left-wing politicians directly aligning with Russian interests. Obama's missile defense concessions, Biden's approval of Nord Stream 2, and Hillary Clinton's role in the Uranium One deal—handing Russia control of 20 percent of US uranium while the Clinton Foundation raked in millions—were all conveniently dismissed. Meanwhile, Russian disinformation networks pushed gun control narratives after mass shootings, and leftist activists unknowingly amplified Kremlin propaganda. The hypocrisy is staggering: While Democrats and left wing officials actively shaped policies that benefited Russia, the media fixated on the NRA for simply being in the same room as a Russian agent. This selective outrage was a clear sign of orchestrated disinformation at work, as the media sought to convince the public that defending the right to bear arms was somehow an unpatriotic act.

This blurring of foreign subversion and domestic advocacy is a hallmark of modern leftist disinformation tactics—using agents like Butina to embed within conservative circles, only to later expose their involvement and claim that the entire movement is compromised. It was never about gun rights for Russia; it was about creating division, vilifying the Second Amendment movement, and giving anti-gun activists the ammunition they needed to frame the NRA as something it was not.

Russia's efforts to undermine the Second Amendment have evolved from Cold War propaganda to a more sophisticated, multipronged strategy that includes political infiltration, economic leverage, and cultural manipulation. By attempting to gain control over firearms production, influencing public perception through media, and amplifying divisive narratives, Russia exploits America's internal debates to weaken national unity. These tactics reflect a broader objective: to erode trust in American institutions and fuel polarization on key issues like gun rights. This serves as a stark warning for Americans: The enemies of freedom will not always attack directly—they will infiltrate, distort, and manipulate until their targets are destroyed from within. Recognizing and countering these efforts is crucial to preserving the integrity of the Second Amendment and preventing foreign actors from shaping the debate on American freedoms.

## Chinese Communist Party (CCP) Influences

China has also engaged in campaigns to sway American opinions on gun rights, though its methods differ from Russia's. The Chinese government uses state-controlled media, social media, and propaganda outlets to broadcast narratives about US gun violence, rather than covert troll farms, to infiltrate online communities (although that is slowly changing). Beijing's message is consistently aimed at undermining the image of the Second Amendment by highlighting the human cost of America's armed society.

For example, Chinese state news agency Xinhua and the Communist Party's mouthpieces routinely publish commentaries after major US mass shootings.

These articles emphasize the carnage and gridlock around gun policy in America, often concluding that the US should restrict firearms. In one 2024 series of propaganda essays timed for the US elections, Xinhua declared that violent crime was surging due to "gun violence" and noted that Americans own over 400 million guns—implying this is a national pathology.

The commentary bluntly stated that guns should be restricted, blaming "deep partisan divisions and influential lobbying groups, such as the National Rifle Association," for blocking needed reforms. By seizing on America's failure to prevent school shootings, the Chinese propaganda machine portrays US democracy as fundamentally broken. The intended outcome is twofold: to erode global and domestic faith in the American system, and to deflect criticisms of China's own human rights record by pointing out US hypocrisy (a classic "whataboutism" tactic).

Chinese propaganda often uses visual media as well. Political cartoons in outlets like the *Global Times* depict the US as a land where schoolchildren cower under the threat of gunfire while politicians do nothing. One Chinese cartoon (shared via a state-affiliated account, "Valiant Panda") mockingly called gun violence "the epitome of the American Dream," casting US freedom as a nightmare scenario. Unlike Russia's shadowy social media trolls, these Chinese efforts are overt—but they still qualify as disinformation when they employ exaggeration or selective facts to mislead. Beijing's propagandists cherry-pick statistics to make the US look uniquely dangerous (for instance, highlighting that more children died in American shootings than in any other wealthy nation), without acknowledging China's own issues or the nuances of American liberties. The broader implication is a narrative that American-style freedoms (like the right to bear arms) lead to chaos, whereas Chinese authoritarian governance leads to safety. This narrative is pushed not only to Chinese audiences but increasingly to English-speaking audiences worldwide, via expanding Chinese global media and social media presence.

On US social platforms, American officials have noted an uptick in Chinese influence accounts mimicking Russian tactics. The FBI reported that China has started creating fake social media personas to "push narratives and sow divisiveness" in the US, much as Russia has done.

While specific examples in the gun debate are less documented, it stands to reason that Chinese operatives see the same opportunity: exploit America's internal divisions to weaken its focus. As such, Chinese propaganda seized upon events like the 2020 George Floyd riots and the January 6, 2021, Capitol demonstration to paint a picture of an America on the brink—often mentioning armed militias or the proliferation of guns as factors in domestic instability. And in Chinese-language communities within the US, researchers have found disinformation targeted at immigrants, some of it promoting gun ownership by playing on fears of crime and even of the Chinese Communist Party itself. This illustrates that Chinese information operations are adaptive; in some contexts, they argue Americans have too many guns, in others they suggest you'd better arm yourself. The common thread is undermining social trust and pushing narratives beneficial to Beijing's interests—either by denigrating American governance or by encouraging factions within the US that Beijing deems favorable.

The influence of Chinese investments in Hollywood and its potential impact on American cultural and political landscapes, including the Second Amendment, is also a topic of growing concern. Over the past decade, China has exponentially increased its financial stakes in the American film industry, leveraging its economic power to shape the narratives presented in popular media. This strategic investment is seen by many as an attempt to subtly influence American public opinion on various issues, including gun control.

China's approach to gun control is drastically different from that of the United States. In China, private gun ownership is almost entirely prohibited, and the government maintains strict control over firearms. This policy aligns with the Chinese Communist Party's broader goals of maintaining social stability and minimizing potential threats to its authority. Given this context, it's not surprising that Chinese investors might support narratives that align with their domestic policies, including those that favor stringent gun control measures.

Hollywood, as a global cultural powerhouse, has become a key arena for China's soft power strategy. Chinese companies have invested billions of dollars in American entertainment, acquiring stakes in major studios, production companies, and cinema chains. This financial influence often comes with editorial leverage, enabling Chinese investors to push for content that aligns with their interests. This phenomenon has raised concerns about the subtle ways in which these investments might shape the content of movies and television shows, particularly regarding sensitive political issues like gun rights.

While most documented cases focus on issues like Taiwan, Tibet, or the portrayal of the Chinese government, this pattern shows a willingness by studios to adjust messaging on any issue that might conflict with the values or preferences of major investors—including gun rights. This sets a precedent: If avoiding gun-positive narratives helps maintain favor or business ties, it's a move studios may be willing to make. For example, China's Dalian Wanda Group, at one point, owned AMC Theatres and had significant stakes in Legendary Entertainment. Tencent, a massive Chinese conglomerate, invested in various American entertainment ventures, including co-financing blockbusters like *Wonder Woman* and *Top Gun: Maverick* (the latter originally edited to remove Taiwan's flag from Tom Cruise's jacket—but reinstated after criticism). While no overt anti-gun content has been directly tied to these deals, the broader editorial trend is one of cautious, sanitized storytelling to avoid controversy—including pro-gun themes that might clash with Chinese state ideology or the preferences of politically cautious investors.

In addition, recent years have seen a steady decline in sympathetic portrayals of armed civilians. Unlike action films of the '80s and '90s—*Die Hard*, *Lethal Weapon*, *The Terminator*—modern blockbusters often frame private gun ownership as reckless, dangerous, or linked to mental instability (*Joker*, *The Purge*, etc.). This tonal shift coincides with an era of growing Chinese influence in film financing and global market prioritization. As of 2022, in an era of substantial Chinese influence and money in Hollywood and US media, over 200 prominent writers, directors, and producers signed an open letter pledging to limit depictions of guns in movies and shows in an effort to appease Chinese sensibilities.

Given Hollywood's influence on public opinion, these portrayals can contribute to a broader cultural shift against the Second Amendment. By consistently presenting firearms in a negative light and emphasizing the need for gun control, Hollywood can influence public opinion and contribute to a climate that is more receptive to restrictive gun laws. This shift in cultural attitudes can have substantial political implications, potentially eroding support for the Second Amendment over time.

In addition to direct investments, China also exerts influence through its control over content distribution. The Chinese market is one of the largest and fastest growing for Hollywood films, making access to it a critical consideration for American studios. This economic leverage allows China to shape the types of stories that get told and the way sensitive issues are portrayed. The result is a form of indirect censorship, where the need to appease Chinese authorities and investors leads to content that aligns more closely with Chinese political and social values, including their stance on gun control.

China's efforts to undermine American Second Amendment rights extend beyond its influence through Hollywood films and delve into various strategic, economic, and political spheres. These multifaceted tactics aim not only to challenge US gun culture but also to weaken America's overall national security and sovereignty.

China's influence also permeates the political landscape in the United States. Through extensive lobbying efforts and strategic donations to political campaigns and organizations, China seeks to sway US politicians and policymakers. These activities often include pushing for stricter gun control measures. The subtle infiltration of Chinese interests into the American political system is part of a broader strategy to shape US policy in ways that benefit China while undermining American constitutional rights. China also deploys cyber operations and social media influence campaigns to spread disinformation and propaganda aimed at destabilizing American society and promoting internal divisions. These efforts are designed to weaken the social fabric of the United States, making it more susceptible to internal conflict and easier to manipulate on the world stage.

By supporting global gun control initiatives and international treaties that advocate for stricter firearm regulations, China aligns itself with efforts that could pressure the United States to conform to international norms. This approach not only aims to erode American sovereignty but also seeks to impose global standards that conflict with the Second Amendment. China's support for these initiatives is part of a broader strategy to challenge American exceptionalism and diminish its global influence.

Additionally, China's economic strategies, such as leveraging its massive manufacturing capabilities, play a role in influencing American gun policies. By dominating global supply chains and manufacturing sectors, including those related to firearms and ammunition, China can exert economic pressure on the US firearm industry. This control over critical supply chains allows China to manipulate market conditions and influence domestic policies indirectly. Disruptions in the supply of ammunition or firearm components can create shortages and drive up prices, contributing to the overall push for stricter gun control measures by making firearm ownership more challenging and costly for Americans.

Furthermore, China's long-term strategy involves cultivating relationships with influential American businesses and academic institutions. Through partnerships, investments, and collaborative projects, China gains access to influential platforms and networks that can be used to shape public discourse and policy decisions. By embedding itself within key sectors of American society, China enhances its ability to influence US policy from within, including efforts to undermine Second Amendment rights.

China's multifaceted approach to undermining American Second Amendment rights involves a combination of strategic land acquisitions, political influence, cyber operations, international alliances, economic leverage, and partnerships with influential American institutions. These efforts are part of a broader strategy to weaken American sovereignty, destabilize its social fabric, and diminish its global influence. The complexity and breadth of China's tactics highlight the need for vigilance and a robust response to protect American constitutional rights and national security.

## Iran, North Korea, Venezuela, and Cuba

In addition to the United Nations, Russia, and China, other hostile countries have actively sought to undermine American gun rights through propaganda and political or cultural means.

One such country is Iran, which has consistently portrayed the United States as a nation plagued by gun violence and instability. Iran, through its state-run media and online influence campaigns, frequently highlights mass shootings and gun-related crimes in the US to criticize American society and its constitutional right to bear arms. This portrayal is part of a broader strategy to depict the US as a dangerous and chaotic country, undermining its global image and influence. Iranian outlets like Press TV have frequently featured America's mass shootings and gun homicide rates in their coverage, using them as evidence of US moral decay. The tone is openly propagandistic: Press TV articles refer to the "US gun epidemic" and ask, "how many more lives would it take to jolt America awake?" Such coverage portrays the United States as unwilling or unable to protect its people.

Iranian media often highlight the political stalemate over gun control, suggesting that so-called corruption or extremist lobbies (like the NRA) have paralyzed American leaders. By harping on these false themes, Tehran's goal is to weaken America's image globally and to counter US criticism of Iran by pointing to American society's flaws.

There is also evidence that Iranian-linked trolls have tried to impersonate American activists online. In 2019 and 2020, US intelligence uncovered Iranian influence operations on social media which, like Russia's, sought to amplify divisive issues in the US—including racial tensions, anti-government sentiments, and likely the gun rights debate as well.

North Korea also engages in anti-American propaganda that includes attacks on the Second Amendment. The North Korean regime characterizes the United States as a violent and lawless society where gun ownership contributes to widespread crime and social decay. North Korea has mostly confined their commentary to official statements condemning American "gun culture" to criticizing US human rights, which is ironic. This narrative serves to justify North Korea's authoritarian control and lack of civil liberties by contrasting it with the supposed chaos of American freedom. Through state-run media, North Korea disseminates this propaganda to its citizens and attempts to influence international opinion against the US.

Venezuela, under the leadership of Nicolás Maduro and previously Hugo Chávez, has similarly criticized American gun culture as part of its anti-US rhetoric. The Venezuelan government has used state media to highlight gun violence in the United States, framing it as a symptom of broader societal problems caused by capitalism and American imperialism. This propaganda aims to bolster the regime's narrative that socialism is superior to the American model of democracy, while also distracting from its own human rights abuses and internal crises.

Cuba, with its long-standing animosity toward the United States, has also joined the chorus of nations condemning American gun rights. The Cuban government, through its tightly controlled media, frequently highlights incidents of gun violence in the US to portray it as a failing state. This narrative is part of a broader effort to undermine American influence in Latin America and globally, presenting Cuba's restrictive gun laws and government control as a preferable alternative.

These hostile countries leverage various platforms to disseminate their anti-gun propaganda, including state-run media, social media campaigns, and international forums. By consistently highlighting American gun violence and criticizing the Second Amendment, they aim to weaken US influence, promote their own political ideologies, and undermine American democracy. Some of the instances discussed above may be less directly tied to policy influence, but they nevertheless contribute to an echo chamber of foreign voices undermining the Second Amendment by depicting it as a dangerous anomaly. This concerted effort by multiple nations underscores the geopolitical significance of the Second Amendment and its role in the broader struggle between democratic and authoritarian values.

## International Influences on Higher Education

The negative and dangerous influences of hostile nations like China, Iran, and other anti-American countries on the United States' educational and university systems are profound and far-reaching. These nations strategically invest in American academic institutions, using their financial clout to spread propaganda, undermine American values, and indoctrinate generations of students with Marxist and anti-American ideologies. Their goal is to create a society of young revolutionaries who will support their agendas, including the erosion of Second Amendment rights.

China, in particular, has been highly effective in infiltrating American educational institutions through extensive funding and partnerships. The Confucius Institutes are one of the most well-known examples. Funded by the Chinese government and established on college campuses across the United States, they promote Chinese language and culture. But they also serve as platforms for spreading Chinese Communist Party propaganda, censoring discussions on topics like Tiananmen Square, Taiwan, and human rights abuses in China. The presence of Confucius Institutes has raised concerns about academic freedom and the potential for espionage.

In addition to Confucius Institutes, China has invested heavily in American universities through donations and partnerships. A notable example is the University of Pennsylvania, which received substantial donations from Chinese sources during Joe Biden's tenure as a professor and later as US vice president. These donations have raised questions about the influence of Chinese money on American academic institutions and their potential impact on US policy. Critics argue that such financial ties compromise the integrity of these institutions and make them susceptible to foreign influence.

Iran and other anti-American nations also exert influence on American educational institutions. Iran has funded Islamic studies programs that align with its religious and political agenda. These programs can spread anti-American sentiments and radical ideologies among students, further undermining American values and promoting hostility towards the United States.

One of the most concerning aspects of foreign influence in American education is the systematic undermining of the Second Amendment. By promoting anti-gun propaganda and Marxist ideologies, these nations aim to weaken the foundational principles of American society, including the right to bear arms. The Second Amendment is a threat to authoritarian regimes, as it empowers citizens to resist tyranny. Therefore, these foreign actors work to instill anti-gun sentiments in young Americans, hoping to erode support for the Second Amendment over time.

The influence of these hostile nations extends beyond funding and propaganda. They also dictate the terms of their financial support, often requiring academic institutions to adhere to specific agendas. This can include the appointment of faculty members who are sympathetic to their ideologies, the creation of curricula that promote their political views, and the suppression of dissenting opinions. Such practices undermine the integrity of American education and create an environment where academic freedom is compromised.

Moreover, the collaboration between American universities and foreign governments can lead to the transfer of sensitive technologies and intellectual property. This poses a big national security risk. For example, Chinese nationals working in American research institutions have been implicated in cases of intellectual property theft, raising concerns about the potential for espionage and the loss of critical technologies.

The infiltration of American educational institutions by hostile nations poses a considerable threat to the integrity of American society and the preservation of fundamental rights, including the Second Amendment. By spreading propaganda, funding academic programs, and dictating the terms of their financial support, these nations seek to undermine American values and create a generation of young revolutionaries who support their agendas. To safeguard national sovereignty and protect the rights of American citizens, the United States must take bold steps to counter foreign influence in its educational system and uphold the principles enshrined in the Constitution. To counter these threats, the United States must vote in political candidates that take decisive action to protect its educational system from foreign influence. This includes implementing stricter regulations on foreign donations and partnerships, enhancing transparency in funding sources, and promoting academic freedom. The US should also invest in its own educational institutions to reduce reliance on foreign money and ensure that American values are upheld.

## European and Australian Attitudes on US Gun Culture

In the global arena, a significant cultural clash exists between Europe and the United States, particularly regarding gun rights. Many Europeans look down on Americans for their robust defense of the Second Amendment, perceiving it as a primitive relic of a bygone era. This perception is deeply rooted in the contrasting historical and cultural developments of Europe and America, reflecting drastically different views on government, liberty, and self-reliance.

Historically, European societies have often depended on centralized governments to provide security and social welfare. Centuries of monarchies, empires, and state-centric governance have ingrained a reliance on the government to meet societal needs. This dependency has fostered a collective mindset where the state's role is paramount in ensuring public safety, often at the expense of individual liberties. Consequently, the concept of personal gun ownership as a means of self-defense and deterrence is foreign to many Europeans.

In contrast, the United States was born out of a revolution against oppressive government control. The American ethos is steeped in the ideals of independence and self-reliance. The right to bear arms is enshrined in the Second Amendment of the US Constitution, reflecting a deep-seated belief in the necessity of an armed citizenry to safeguard freedom and deter tyranny. This foundational difference has shaped American attitudes towards firearms, viewing them as symbols of liberty and self-sufficiency rather than instruments of violence.

Europeans often exhibit a form of snobbery towards American gun culture, considering themselves more enlightened and civilized. This attitude is partly a result of Europe's long history of intellectual movements, such as the Enlightenment, which emphasized reason, science, and the role of government in promoting societal progress. Europeans pride themselves on their advanced social policies and strict gun control measures, viewing these as hallmarks of a more evolved society.

However, this perspective overlooks the unique American context, where individual freedoms are paramount. The American spirit of entrepreneurship and innovation is closely linked to personal liberty, including the right to bear arms. Unlike Europe, where heavy regulation and a large welfare state are the norms, the US has historically emphasized minimal government interference, encouraging citizens to take responsibility for their own lives and safety.

The entrepreneurial spirit and work ethic of Americans are often cited as key drivers of the nation's success. This ethos is at odds with the European model, which places greater emphasis on social welfare and government support. While European countries boast extensive entitlement programs and safety nets, they often do so at the cost of personal initiative and economic dynamism. In the US, the right to bear arms is part of the broader framework of individual responsibility and self-reliance. Gun ownership is not merely about self-defense; it is also about preserving the freedom to shape one's destiny without undue dependence on the state. This mentality fosters a culture of innovation and resilience, which many Americans believe is critical to maintaining their nation's competitive edge.

Europeans often view Americans as brutes for their staunch defense of gun rights, failing to understand the underlying principles that drive this commitment. The stereotype of the gun-toting American as violent and uncivilized ignores the reality that responsible gun ownership is a deeply ingrained part of American culture. The majority of American gun owners are law-abiding citizens who view their firearms as tools for protection, hunting, and sport shooting.

Moreover, the belief that strict gun control leads to lower crime rates is not universally supported by evidence. Some European countries with stringent gun laws still experience high levels of violence, often through illegal means, just as several American states with permissive gun laws report lower crime rates, suggesting that an armed populace can serve as a deterrent to crime.

In sum, the American viewpoint, the right to bear arms is a fundamental aspect of liberty and a safeguard against government overreach. This belief stands in stark contrast to the European reliance on government control and regulation, highlighting the profound differences in how each culture views the role of the individual versus the state.

Likewise, Australians, having experienced a shift in their own gun laws following the Port Arthur massacre in 1996, tend to view America's staunch defense of the Second Amendment as both dangerous and anachronistic. This perspective is rooted in Australia's own historical and cultural experiences with firearms and government regulation, which differ markedly from those of the United States.

In 1996, Australia experienced one of its worst mass shootings when a gunman killed 35 people and wounded 23 others in Port Arthur, Tasmania. The tragedy shocked the nation and led to swift and decisive action from the Australian government. Within months, the government implemented the National Firearms Agreement (NFA), which introduced stringent gun control measures, including a mandatory buyback program for semi-automatic and automatic firearms, strict licensing requirements, and comprehensive background checks.

The NFA slashed the number of firearms in civilian hands and imposed strict controls on gun ownership. For many Australians, these measures have become a source of national pride, seen as a necessary and effective. The country's low rates of gun-related deaths and mass shootings since the implementation of the NFA are often cited as evidence of the success of these policies.

Australia's historical reliance on government regulation and welfare has fostered a cultural mindset that views state intervention as essential for public safety, in stark contrast to the American ethos of self-reliance and skepticism of government power. Rooted in its colonial heritage, Australia's long-standing reliance on government for social and economic security, rather than individual responsibility and self-reliance, likely contributed to this cultural mindset that sees self-preservation through firearm ownership as unnecessary and even foreign.

Australians often view Americans as reckless and irresponsible for their strong defense of gun rights. Like Europe, this perception is intertwined with a sense of snobbery and a belief in their own enlightened approach to public safety. Australians take pride in their strict gun laws and low rates of gun violence, seeing these as markers of a more civilized and rational society.

This attitude is reflected in public discourse and media representation, where American gun culture is portrayed as chaotic and dangerous. Australians often struggle to understand the deep-seated American belief in the Second Amendment and the cultural importance placed on firearms as symbols of liberty and self-defense.

In the context of gun culture, this difference in attitudes is stark. Americans view firearms as valuable tools for personal protection and symbols of independence, while Australians, accustomed to a more regulated environment, see them as unnecessary and potentially dangerous. The stereotype of the gun-toting American as violent and uncivilized ignores the nuanced reality that most American gun owners are responsible and law-abiding citizens. The complex legal framework and cultural significance of the Second Amendment are frequently overlooked in Australian critiques.

Moreover, the assumption that strict gun control universally leads to lower crime rates is not always supported by evidence. While Australia has seen a decline in gun-related deaths since implementing the NFA, the overall impact of gun control on crime rates is a subject of ongoing debate. In contrast, several American states with permissive gun laws report lower crime rates, suggesting that responsible gun ownership can coexist with public safety.

The cultural clash between Europe and Australia and the United States over gun rights reflects deeper historical and philosophical differences. While Australians may look down on American gun culture as reckless and outdated, they fail to grasp the foundational principles that underpin the American ethos of liberty and self-reliance. Americans, on the other hand, see their right to bear arms as an essential part of their identity and a bulwark against tyranny.

This firm commitment to the Second Amendment, despite international criticism, exemplifies the unique spirit of independence that defines the United States. It is a testament to the belief that true freedom comes from the ability to protect oneself and one's community, a principle that Americans hold dear. If this belief endures, the right to bear arms will remain a cornerstone of American life, standing as a symbol of the nation's dedication to liberty and individual rights.

## Combating Hostile or Negative International Influences

To combat international attempts to undermine our Second Amendment rights, the United States must adopt a multifaceted approach that involves policy changes, cultural initiatives, and legislative action. This strategy should focus on preserving national sovereignty, protecting cultural institutions, and curtailing foreign influences that seek to destabilize American values.

First, the United States should consider pulling out of international agreements and treaties that threaten Second Amendment rights. The Arms Trade Treaty (ATT), for instance, poses substantial risks by imposing international regulations on firearm transfers that could conflict with US constitutional rights. By withdrawing from such treaties, the US can maintain its sovereignty and ensure that domestic laws align with the Constitution rather than international mandates. Additionally, any future treaties that could infringe upon gun rights should be scrutinized, and the Senate should refuse to ratify agreements that infringe upon the Second Amendment.

Next, the US should implement policies to restrict foreign ownership of American land, resources, and cultural institutions. This includes passing legislation that prohibits entities from hostile nations, such as China and Iran, from purchasing farmland, real estate near military installations, or key infrastructure. The Committee on Foreign Investment in the United States (CFIUS) could be granted broader powers to review and block transactions that pose a threat to national security. By tightening these regulations, the US can prevent foreign adversaries from gaining strategic footholds within the country.

In higher education, bold steps must be taken to reduce the influence of foreign governments, particularly those with anti-American agendas. This can include prohibiting universities from accepting funding or establishing partnerships with institutions linked to authoritarian regimes, such as China and certain Middle Eastern countries. The Confucius Institutes, which promote Chinese government propaganda, should be closed down, and universities should be encouraged to seek alternative funding sources that do not compromise academic integrity or national security.

To address the threat of foreign influence in higher education, the US should implement stricter visa requirements for students and researchers from countries with hostile agendas. This can include enhanced background checks and monitoring to prevent espionage and the transfer of sensitive technologies or knowledge. Promoting academic exchange programs with allied nations can help foster positive international relationships without compromising national security.

Culturally, the US should invest in initiatives that promote American values and counteract foreign propaganda. This could involve funding media campaigns that highlight the importance of the Second Amendment and the historical context of gun rights in America. Supporting independent journalism and media outlets that provide balanced coverage on firearms and gun control can help counteract the biased narratives often pushed by foreign and domestic anti-gun groups.

Legislation aimed at prohibiting foreign entities from influencing US cultural institutions should also be considered. This can include restricting foreign ownership of media companies, film studios, and other entertainment entities that have the potential to shape public opinion. Preventing Chinese companies from owning significant stakes in Hollywood studios would reduce their ability to influence the portrayal of gun rights and American culture in movies and television.

Furthermore, the US should enhance its cybersecurity measures to protect against foreign interference in domestic affairs. This includes securing election systems, protecting critical infrastructure, and countering disinformation campaigns on social media. By strengthening these defenses, the US can ensure that foreign adversaries cannot easily manipulate public opinion or disrupt democratic processes.

Ultimately, combating international attempts to undermine Second Amendment rights requires a comprehensive approach that addresses multiple fronts. By pulling out of threatening international agreements, restricting foreign ownership and influence, promoting American values, and strengthening cybersecurity measures, the United States can protect its sovereignty and ensure the preservation of its constitutional rights. These bold measures, though controversial, are necessary to safeguard the nation's security and uphold the principles enshrined in the Constitution.

## International Gun Culture

Not all countries around the world are ignorant, hostile, or contemptuous of American gun culture. In fact, several countries have high rates of gun ownership and a robust gun culture of their own. While these nations may not have a Second Amendment enshrining the right to bear arms, their gun culture is deeply rooted in tradition and the belief in self-reliance. Switzerland, Serbia, and Finland, for example, boast considerable civilian gun ownership, often linked to compulsory military service and a strong emphasis on individual preparedness. These nations illustrate that the appreciation for firearms and the principles of self-defense and self-sufficiency can transcend borders, reflecting a shared value in personal responsibility and community security.

## Switzerland: A Unique Model of Gun Ownership and Militia Culture

Switzerland stands out as one of the most heavily armed countries in the world, yet it boasts a remarkably low rate of gun violence and has not been involved in a war for centuries. This unique situation provides a compelling case study on how gun ownership can coexist with societal stability and peace. Switzerland's approach to firearms is deeply rooted in its history, culture, and legal framework, offering a fascinating comparison to the United States.

Switzerland's history of gun ownership is closely tied to its tradition of militia service. The Swiss model of national defense is based on the concept of a well-armed citizenry, capable of mobilizing quickly in times of need. This tradition dates to the medieval era, when local militias were essential for defending the country's mountainous terrain against invaders. This policy has changed little, even though Switzerland evolved into a modern state.

Switzerland's gun culture is characterized by widespread firearm ownership, with a large portion of the population trained in the use of guns from a young age. Swiss men are required to undergo military training and serve in the militia, which includes maintaining their service rifles at home. This practice ensures that many citizens are proficient in handling firearms and prepared to defend the country if necessary.

According to recent statistics, Switzerland has one of the highest rates of gun ownership in the world, with approximately 28 guns per 100 people. While this figure is lower than that of the United States, where there are around 120 guns per 100 people, it is still remarkably high for a country with such low levels of gun violence.

The Federal Constitution of the Swiss Confederation does not explicitly mention the right to bear arms like the US Constitution, but the legal framework supports a well-regulated system of gun ownership. Firearms are regulated under the Federal Act on Arms, Arms Accessories, and Ammunition, which require background checks, registration of certain types of firearms, and a permit system for carrying guns in public. The law also mandates safe storage practices to prevent unauthorized access. However, the emphasis is on ensuring that responsible citizens can own and use firearms for legitimate purposes, such as defense, sport shooting, and hunting.

Despite its high rate of gun ownership, Switzerland has a low incidence of gun-related violence. The country's homicide rate is around 0.5 per 100,000 people, much lower than the United States, which has a rate of approximately 4.5 per 100,000.

This disparity is often attributed to several factors unique to Switzerland. Firstly, Swiss culture places a strong emphasis on responsibility and community. The mandatory military training instills discipline and a deep understanding of the serious nature of handling firearms. The societal attitude towards guns is one of respect and duty, rather than a means of personal power or status.

Secondly, Switzerland's comprehensive mental health care system and social support networks help address potential issues before they escalate into violence. The country's robust economy and low unemployment rate also contribute to social stability, reducing the factors that often lead to crime.

While both Switzerland and the United States have high rates of gun ownership, their approaches and the cultural context surrounding firearms are quite different. In the US, the right to bear arms is enshrined in the Second Amendment of the Constitution, reflecting a historical emphasis on individual liberty and self-defense against tyranny. American gun culture is diverse, encompassing self-defense, hunting, sport shooting, and a strong advocacy for personal freedoms. In contrast, Swiss gun culture is deeply integrated with the concept of national defense and communal responsibility. The focus is less on individual rights and more on collective security and preparedness. This communal approach is reinforced by the mandatory military service, which ensures that gun ownership is coupled with extensive training and a sense of duty.

Another key difference lies in the regulatory frameworks. While the US has a patchwork of state laws regulating firearms, leading to variations in gun control measures, Switzerland has a more uniform national system. The Swiss system is stringent in ensuring that gun owners are responsible and well-trained, with background checks and permits required for certain types of firearms.

While the Swiss Constitution does not explicitly mention the right to bear arms, it supports a well-regulated system of gun ownership through legislation that balances individual rights with public safety. This approach contrasts with the more absolutist interpretation of the Second Amendment in the United States, where any form of gun control is often met with strong resistance from certain advocacy groups.

One of the most striking aspects of Switzerland's history is its long-standing policy of neutrality. The country has not been involved in an international conflict since the early 19th century, despite being surrounded by countries that have experienced much turmoil. Switzerland's armed neutrality policy has enabled it to avoid the devastation of wars while maintaining a powerful defense posture. The Swiss model demonstrates that a well-armed populace, coupled with a strong sense of duty and discipline, can contribute to national security and stability without resorting to aggression.

While there are many differences between Switzerland and the United States, particularly in terms of cultural attitudes and legal provisions, the Swiss experience challenges the notion that high rates of gun ownership lead to increased violence and highlights the importance of a disciplined and responsible approach to firearms. For Americans, the Swiss tradition underscores the potential for a culture of responsible gun ownership that prioritizes training, community, and safety. It serves as a reminder that the right to bear arms comes with responsibilities, and that these responsibilities, when embraced, can contribute to a secure and stable society.

## Finland: They Love Their Guns Too

Another country that largely embraces firearms ownership is Finland, which has a higher rate of gun ownership than that of Switzerland, with over 32 guns per 100 people. Gun culture in Finland is deeply rooted in the country's history, traditions, and societal values. Finland's relationship with firearms dates to its time under Swedish and Russian rule, where hunting and military service played important roles in everyday life. After gaining independence in 1917, Finland maintained a strong connection to firearms, both for practical purposes and as a symbol of national defense.

Finland's gun laws are relatively permissive compared to other European countries, reflecting a balanced approach to gun rights and regulation by European standards. Finnish citizens are allowed to own firearms for hunting, sport shooting, and self-defense, provided they obtain the necessary licenses. The process involves background checks, psychological evaluations, and a demonstrated need for firearm ownership. Hunting is a popular activity in Finland, with vast forested areas and abundant wildlife providing ample opportunities for hunters. Consequently, hunting rifles and shotguns are among the most owned firearms by Finnish civilians.

The popularity of guns in Finland is also tied to the country's compulsory military service. Most Finnish men undergo military training, during which they become familiar with firearms. This training instills a sense of responsibility and respect for firearms, contributing to a culture where guns are known as tools for protection and recreation rather than instruments of violence. The prevalence of shooting sports further bolsters this cultural acceptance, with many Finns participating in competitive shooting events and recreational shooting clubs.

Common firearms owned by Finnish civilians include hunting rifles, shotguns, and various types of pistols used in sport shooting. The Sako TRG series, manufactured by the Finnish company Sako, is a popular choice for precision shooters and hunters alike. Additionally, various models of the Tikka T3 rifle are widely favored for their reliability and accuracy. Finnish gun owners also appreciate high-quality foreign-made firearms, with brands like Beretta, Glock, and Remington being commonly used.

The Finnish constitution does not explicitly guarantee the right to bear arms; instead, gun ownership is regulated by specific legislation. However, there is a degree of admiration for the American emphasis on individual rights and freedoms, including the Second Amendment, in which many Finns appreciate the US stance on gun rights as a reflection of personal liberty and self-reliance.

At the same time, Finland's approach to gun ownership is shaped by its own unique cultural and historical context, which differs drastically from that of the United States. Finnish gun laws prioritize public safety and responsible ownership, and there is a broad consensus on the necessity of regulation to prevent misuse. Overall, Finland's gun culture is characterized by a deep respect for firearms, rooted in historical traditions of hunting, military service, and sport shooting. While Finland does not have an equivalent to the Second Amendment, its balanced approach to gun rights and regulation reflects a commitment to preserving individual freedoms while ensuring public safety. This perspective allows Finland to appreciate aspects of American gun culture while maintaining its own distinct approach to firearms.

## Serbia: Locked, Loaded, and Balkan Proud

Gun culture in Serbia is deeply intertwined with the country's tumultuous history and cultural heritage. Serbia has a long-standing tradition of firearm ownership that dates back to its struggles for independence and various conflicts in the region. Firearms have historically played a crucial role in the defense of the nation and in the personal lives of its citizens, serving both as tools for protection and symbols of resistance and resilience.

Serbia's gun laws are relatively permissive compared to many other European countries. This is evident in the fact that Serbia boasts the highest rate of civilian gun ownership in Europe, with over 39 firearms per 100 people—reflecting a deeply rooted cultural acceptance of armed citizens. Citizens are allowed to own firearms for hunting, sport shooting, and self-defense, provided they obtain the necessary permits. The licensing process involves background checks, psychological evaluations, and safety training to ensure responsible ownership.

Guns are popular in Serbia for several reasons. Firstly, hunting, supported by the country's rich biodiversity and extensive rural areas, is a deeply rooted tradition, passed down through generations and widely practiced across the country. Secondly, Serbia's historical conflicts, including the Yugoslav Wars of the 1990s, have left a significant number of firearms in civilian hands, fostering a culture of familiarity and acceptance of guns. Thirdly, shooting sports are highly valued, with many Serbians participating in competitive shooting and recreational activities, further embedding firearms into the social fabric.

Common firearms owned by Serbian civilians include hunting rifles, shotguns, and various pistols. Serbian-made firearms, such as those produced by Zastava Arms, are popular. The Zastava M70 rifle, modeled after the AK-47, is widely used for hunting and sport shooting. Other common firearms include the CZ 75 pistol and various models of Beretta and Glock pistols, which are favored for their reliability and performance in sport shooting and self-defense.

Serbia's gun culture, like that of Finland, is characterized by a deep respect for firearms, rooted in historical traditions of hunting, military service, and sport shooting. The country's regulatory approach aims to balance individual freedoms with public safety, ensuring that firearms are used responsibly. While Serbia does not have a constitutional provision equivalent to the Second Amendment, many Serbians admire the American emphasis on individual liberties and the constitutional protection of the right to bear arms. This admiration is partly attributed to the shared cultural value placed on self-reliance and personal responsibility. The Serbian constitution and laws provide for the right to own firearms, subject to regulatory controls, reflecting an attempt to balance between individual rights and public safety.

Serbia's gun culture is a product of its historical experiences, cultural traditions, and legal frameworks. The country's permissive gun laws reflect a deep-seated familiarity and comfort with firearms, supported by traditions of hunting and sport shooting. While Serbia admires aspects of American gun culture, particularly the emphasis on individual rights, it maintains its own distinct approach, balancing the right to bear arms with necessary regulatory controls. This nuanced perspective allows Serbia to navigate the complexities of firearm ownership while ensuring the safety and well-being of its citizens.

## Switzerland, Finland, and Serbia: Key Takeaways

While Switzerland, Finland, and Serbia each embrace firearm ownership to varying degrees, their approaches are shaped by unique historical, cultural, and legal frameworks. Switzerland's gun culture is deeply entwined with national defense, emphasizing a well-trained citizenry and communal responsibility. Finland maintains a strong tradition of hunting and sport shooting, balancing individual gun rights with public safety through stringent licensing and regulation. Serbia's firearm culture, forged through a history of conflict and resilience, reflects a blend of self-reliance and national pride, with a regulatory system that seeks to preserve personal freedoms while ensuring responsible ownership. Despite their differences, all three nations demonstrate that widespread firearm ownership does not inherently lead to violence—rather, societal attitudes, training, and responsible regulation play crucial roles in maintaining a stable and secure gun culture. Their experiences challenge the notion that civilian gun ownership is inherently dangerous and highlight the importance of a balanced approach—one that respects individual rights while fostering a culture of responsibility. For Americans, these examples serve as a reminder that while the Second Amendment is uniquely rooted in the nation's identity, the principles of discipline, respect for firearms, and an informed, well-trained populace are essential in preserving both freedom and security.

***

The arrogance and hypocrisy of foreign elites and global institutions that lecture Americans on gun rights while enjoying the protection of armed security or enforcing draconian restrictions in their own countries cannot be overstated. Whether it's the UN pushing disarmament, foreign media painting American gun culture as barbaric, or international investors with anti-gun agendas, the pattern is clear: Elites love to meddle in our affairs while ignoring their own failings. However, Switzerland, Finland, and Serbia stand as exceptions, showing that robust gun cultures and relatively lax firearm laws can—and do—exist outside the United States. These nations demonstrate that high rates of gun ownership can coincide with responsible citizenship, national pride, and relatively low rates of gun crime. Their examples dismantle the tired narrative that more guns automatically lead to more violence and prove that cultural values, not just legislation, play a pivotal role in shaping firearm outcomes.

Ultimately, the Second Amendment wasn't written for global approval—it was written for American liberty. And no amount of foreign pressure or cultural condescension will ever override the constitutional right of the American people to keep and bear arms. Maybe one day the rest of the world will catch up to the United States when it comes to freedom, liberty, and the right to bear arms—so long as we don't lose our footing or surrender those rights ourselves.

# Chapter 11

---

# Arming the Economy

*The rifle on the wall of the laborer's cottage or the working-class flat is the symbol of democracy. It is our job to see that it stays there.*
—George Orwell

*The right to keep and bear arms is not just a constitutional guarantee—it is a pillar of American industry, providing jobs, innovation, and economic strength.*

—Unknown

The gun industry is an important pillar of the American economy, encompassing a wide range of activities, from manufacturing and retail to gun safety and training programs, as well as shooting sports. The financial impact of this industry is substantial, contributing billions of dollars annually and supporting countless jobs across the country. Companies that produce firearms, ammunition, and related accessories not only generate revenue but also play a crucial role in maintaining and advancing the technical expertise and innovation that keeps the industry thriving. Meanwhile, shooting ranges and training facilities offer vital services, ensuring that gun owners can safely and responsibly use their firearms, promoting a culture of safety and proficiency that benefits all.

In addition to its economic contributions, the gun industry also fosters a strong sense of community and shared values among enthusiasts and professionals alike. Events such as gun shows, competitions, and training seminars not only generate economic activity but also create opportunities for education, networking, and the celebration of Second Amendment rights. These gatherings serve as a platform for innovation, where new products and technologies are showcased and best practices in safety and training are disseminated. This communal aspect of the gun industry helps to strengthen the bonds between individuals and organizations, reinforcing a collective commitment to responsible gun ownership and the preservation of constitutional freedoms.

## The Firearms Economy

The economic impact of the firearms industry in the United States is massive, encompassing a wide range of activities, from manufacturing and retail to tourism. This sector contributes significantly to the national and local economies, providing jobs, generating tax revenue, and supporting various ancillary businesses.

Manufacturing is the cornerstone of the firearms industry, with numerous companies producing firearms, ammunition, and related accessories. Major manufacturers like Smith & Wesson, Ruger, and Remington employ thousands of workers and invest heavily in research and development to innovate and improve their products. These companies not only produce firearms for civilian use but also fulfill contracts for law enforcement and military agencies, further expanding their economic footprint. The biggest employer in gun manufacturing is Smith & Wesson, a company that has been a leading name in the industry for over a century. Originally based in Springfield, Massachusetts, from 1852 to 2023, Smith & Wesson is now headquartered in Maryville, Tennessee, where it continues to employ thousands of workers across its nationwide manufacturing operations, contributing largely to the industry's overall economic impact. The production of firearms involves a complex supply chain that includes raw material suppliers, parts manufacturers, and assembly plants, all contributing to economic activity.

From 2020 through 2024, the gun industry in the United States generated a lot of revenue, reflecting its robust market presence and consumer demand.

The industry saw an enormous increase in sales, particularly in 2020, driven by heightened concerns over personal safety and the political climate. Estimates suggest that the firearms and ammunition industry generated over $70 billion in total revenue in 2020 alone.

The retail sector also plays a crucial role in the economic impact of the firearms industry. Firearm retailers range from large chains like Cabela's and Bass Pro Shops to small, independent gun stores. These retailers provide jobs and contribute to local economies through sales tax revenues and community engagement. The firearms retail market is robust, driven by a consistent demand for hunting, sport shooting, and self-defense purposes. In addition to firearms and ammunition, retailers who sell guns often sell a variety of outdoor and sporting goods too, which broadens their economic contribution.

Tourism associated with the firearms industry is another important economic contributor. Shooting ranges, hunting lodges, and firearm-related events attract enthusiasts from across the country and even internationally. States like Texas, Colorado, and Alaska are popular destinations for hunting trips, which support local economies through lodging, food services, and guided tours. Shooting competitions, such as those organized by the National Rifle Association (NRA) or the International Defensive Pistol Association (IDPA), also draw participants and spectators, boosting local tourism and hospitality sectors.

Gun shows are another facet of firearm-related tourism and commerce, attracting thousands of attendees annually and generating abundant economic activity. These events provide a venue for enthusiasts to buy, sell, and trade firearms, accessories, and memorabilia. Gun shows attract significant foot traffic, benefiting local businesses such as hotels, restaurants, and transportation services. They also provide an opportunity for education and networking within the firearms community, further solidifying the cultural and economic importance of the industry. Some of the most popular and well-attended gun shows include the National Rifle Association (NRA) Annual Meetings & Exhibits, the NRA's Great American Outdoor Show, and the National Shooting Sports Foundation (NSSF) SHOT Show (Shooting, Hunting and Outdoor Trade Show). These events not only serve as marketplaces for firearms and related products but also as social and educational gatherings for gun enthusiasts.

The NRA's Annual Meetings & Exhibits, which has been held in various cities across the United States, draw tens of thousands of attendees. This event features over 800 exhibitors showcasing firearms, ammunition, hunting gear, and accessories. The economic impact of the NRA Annual Meeting is substantial, contributing millions of dollars to local economies through hotel bookings, restaurant visits, and other related expenses.

The Great American Outdoor Show, hosted in Harrisburg, Pennsylvania, is another major event that spans nine days and attracts over 200,000 attendees. This show features a wide range of firearms, hunting equipment, fishing gear, and outdoor apparel. It is known for its family-friendly atmosphere and educational seminars on topics such as gun safety and hunting techniques. The Great American Outdoor Show boosts the local economy, with attendees spending on lodging, food, and other services.

The SHOT Show, held annually in Las Vegas, Nevada, is one of the largest firearms trade shows in the world. It attracts over 60,000 industry professionals, including manufacturers, retailers, and media representatives. The SHOT Show is not open to the general public, but it plays a crucial role in setting industry trends and introducing new products to the market and generates much revenue for the local economy through convention-related activities and business transactions.

At these gun shows, a wide variety of firearms are sold, ranging from handguns and rifles to shotguns and antique firearms. The most popular firearms sold at gun shows often include semi-automatic handguns, such as Glock and Smith & Wesson models, AR-15 rifles, and popular hunting rifles like those made by Remington and Winchester. Shotguns for sporting and home defense, such as the Mossberg 500 and the Remington 870, are also in high demand.

In addition to firearms, gun shows also feature a broad array of accessories and related products. These include ammunition, scopes, holsters, gun safes, reloading equipment, and tactical gear. The variety of products available caters to a diverse audience, from casual gun owners and hobbyists to serious hunters and competitive shooters.

Gun shows generate several billion dollars in sales annually. In 2022, it is believed that gun shows contributed approximately $4 billion to $5 billion in direct sales. This includes the sale of firearms, ammunition, accessories, and other related products. In 2023, the trend continued, with gun shows maintaining a strong presence in the firearms market. The overall sales generated by gun shows in 2023 contributed another $4 billion to $5 billion in direct sales.

These figures highlight the important role that gun shows play in the broader firearms economy. They provide a vital marketplace for manufacturers, retailers, and consumers to interact, conduct business, and promote the latest products and innovations in the firearms industry. Additionally, the economic benefits of gun shows extend to the host communities. Local businesses see increased revenue from the influx of attendees, as these events also boost local economies through spending on lodging, dining, transportation, and other services.

The economic impact of the gun training industry, including training and safety classes and shooting ranges, is also notable in the broader firearms industry. This sector not only provides crucial education and safety services but also contributes enormously to the economy through various revenue streams. The gun training industry encompasses a wide array of services, from basic firearm safety courses to advanced tactical training. These classes are often conducted at shooting ranges, which serve as the hubs for training and recreational shooting activities. Shooting ranges, both indoor and outdoor, generate considerable revenue through membership fees, class fees, range time rentals, and sales of related products and services. For instance, modern shooting ranges have evolved to offer a variety of amenities, including dining options, retail shops, and social spaces, which attract a diverse clientele and encourage repeat visits.

According to industry reports, the economic contributions from hunting, target shooting, and associated activities are huge. The National Shooting Sports Foundation (NSSF) reported that the overall economic impact of hunting and shooting sports in the US is approximately $110 billion annually. This figure includes spending on firearms and ammunition, as well as expenditures on equipment, travel, and other related activities. Shooting ranges alone contribute billions to the economy and support thousands of jobs across the country.

The industry also supports a wide range of jobs, from range safety officers and instructors to retail employees and maintenance staff. The combined activities of hunting and target shooting support over 866,000 jobs in the US, making it a substantial employment sector. These jobs are often well-paying and contribute to the economic stability of many communities, particularly in rural areas where other employment opportunities may be limited.

The presence of shooting ranges and training facilities also has a notable impact on local economies. They attract visitors from outside the immediate area, leading to increased business for hotels, restaurants, and other local services. Special events, such as shooting competitions and training seminars, further boost local economies by drawing large numbers of participants and spectators.

However, the industry also faces challenges from regulatory changes. Stricter gun control measures threaten the operations of shooting ranges and training facilities, potentially reducing their profitability. For example, regulations that limit the types of firearms and ammunition that can be used or sold can affect the range of services offered. Plus, compliance with new safety standards or environmental regulations can incur steep costs for facility upgrades and staff training.

Despite these challenges, the gun training and shooting range industry remains a vibrant and growing part of the firearms economy. It promotes safe and responsible gun ownership while contributing to economic activity. As interest in recreational shooting and self-defense continues to grow, the demand for high-quality training and well-equipped shooting facilities is likely to remain strong, ensuring that this sector continues to thrive.

Gun regulations can also have profound negative effects on the economic factors associated with the firearms manufacturing industry. Stricter gun control measures, such as bans on certain types of firearms or high-capacity magazines, can hurt manufacturers by reducing the range of products they can legally produce and sell. This, in turn, can lead to decreased revenue and potential job losses within the industry. The 1994 Federal Assault Weapons Ban, for instance, led to a major downturn for manufacturers of affected firearms and accessories until its expiration in 2004.

A notable example of the consequences of strict gun control regulations on gun manufacturers and local economies is the closure of Remington Arms in upstate New York. In March 2024, Remington Arms, a storied name in the firearms industry, closed its manufacturing facility in Ilion, New York, ending a remarkable 195-year history. Established in 1816 by Eliphalet Remington, the plant had been a cornerstone of the local economy in the Mohawk Valley, providing steady employment and contributing largely to the community's economic stability. This closure marked the end of an era, leaving a profound impact on the region.

Several factors contributed to the shutdown of this historic Remington facility. One of the primary reasons was increasing regulatory pressures from both state and federal governments. New York State, in particular, had implemented a series of stringent gun control measures that hampered the operations of firearms manufacturers. These regulations included tighter restrictions on the types of firearms that could be produced and sold, as well as more rigorous compliance requirements. The financial burden of adhering to these regulations, coupled with the constant threat of further legislative changes, made it increasingly difficult for Remington to remain viable in New York.

Another critical factor was the shift in market dynamics and consumer preferences. With growing competition from manufacturers in states with more favorable regulatory environments and lower operational costs, Remington's Ilion facility struggled to maintain its market share. Additionally, advancements in manufacturing technology and production methods necessitated generous capital investments to modernize the plant, which was not financially feasible given the declining revenues and increasing costs.

The closure of the Remington facility had far-reaching consequences for the local economy. The plant had been one of the largest employers in the region, providing jobs to over 300 workers. These employees, many of whom had spent their entire careers at Remington, were suddenly left without employment, creating a ripple effect throughout the community. Local businesses that relied on the patronage of the plant's workers, from diners and retail stores to service providers, experienced a sharp decline in revenue, exacerbating the economic downturn.

Moreover, the facility's closure meant the loss of a significant source of tax revenue for the local government. This revenue had been essential for funding public services and infrastructure projects, and its absence created budget shortfalls that had to be addressed through cuts or increased taxes on remaining residents and businesses. The community also lost a part of its cultural heritage and identity, as Remington had been a symbol of industrial pride and resilience for generations.

The end of Remington's historic plant operations marked the loss of not only an economic engine but also a piece of the region's industrial legacy.

Retailers are also affected by gun regulations. Background check requirements, waiting periods, and restrictions on sales can create additional administrative burdens and reduce the volume of sales. Small retailers, in particular, may struggle with the costs associated with compliance, potentially leading to closures and reduced economic activity in their communities. Also, the uncertainty surrounding changing regulations can deter investment and innovation within the industry, stifling growth.

Tourism related to firearms can be indirectly affected by gun regulations too. Restrictions on hunting rifles, for example, can impact hunting tourism, reducing the number of visitors to popular hunting destinations. Similarly, stringent regulations on transporting firearms across state lines can deter participation in shooting competitions and gun shows, leading to lower attendance and economic contributions from these events.

The economic impact of the ammunition industry is extensive, playing a crucial role in the overall firearms industry. The sector includes the production, distribution, and retail of ammunition, which supports numerous jobs and generates a lot of revenue. According to the National Shooting Sports Foundation (NSSF), the total economic impact of the firearm and ammunition industry reached $80.73 billion in 2022, a marked increase from $19.1 billion in 2008. This growth highlights the importance of ammunition in the broader economic landscape of firearms.

However, the industry faces several challenges, particularly from regulatory pressures. Efforts to ban certain types of ammunition, such as lead-based bullets, and the federal government's large-scale purchases of ammunition, have led to scarcity and increased prices for civilian consumers. These regulatory actions create supply constraints that drive up costs for both recreational shooters and those who rely on ammunition for self-defense and hunting.

One major regulatory impact was the Biden administration's ban on the importation of Russian-made ammunition in 2021. This ban specifically targeted popular and affordable ammo types, most notably the 7.62×39mm steel-cased ammunition used in AK-47 rifles. Russian ammunition was a staple for many

American shooters due to its cost-effectiveness and reliability. The ban forced consumers to turn to more expensive alternatives, increasing the overall cost of shooting sports and self-defense training. This policy change had a ripple effect, driving up prices and reducing the availability of affordable ammunition, further straining the budgets of many gun owners.

The economic impact of these regulatory measures extends beyond just higher prices for consumers. It also affects the profitability of shooting ranges and training facilities that rely on affordable ammunition to attract and retain customers. Higher ammunition costs lead to decreased participation in shooting sports, driving down the revenue of these businesses and the associated economic activity in their communities.

Despite these challenges, the ammunition industry remains a significant economic driver. It supports thousands of jobs, contributes to local and federal tax revenues, and plays a vital role in wildlife conservation through excise taxes on ammunition sales. The industry's ability to adapt and innovate in response to regulatory pressures and market demands will be crucial for its continued economic contribution.

Just as gun control measures have the potential to adversely affect the economy and reduce revenue generated from gun ownership and activities, the firearms industry can also benefit from regulations that are supportive or favorable. For instance, legislation that promotes concealed carry permits or expands hunting seasons can lead to increased sales of firearms and accessories, boosting the manufacturing and retail sectors. Furthermore, educational and safety programs funded by gun taxes or fees can enhance the industry's reputation and encourage responsible ownership, fostering a positive economic environment.

## The Hunting Economy

The percentage of Americans who hunt has been on a steady decline since 1960, when 7.7 percent hunted, down to under 5 percent today. In the 1970s and 1980s, hunting was a common American pastime. In 1982 the US had about 16.7 million hunters—roughly 7.2 percent of the population at that time. By comparison, the number of hunters in 2022 was about 15.9 million, but due to population growth, this represented only 4.8 percent of Americans. In short, since 1960, hunting has declined in popularity as a share of the population. This decades-long decline prompted conservation agencies to launch R3 efforts (Recruit, Retain, Reactivate) to bolster hunting participation and license sales.

Hunting generates a lot of economic activity through license fees, equipment sales, travel, and related services. Each year, hunters collectively spend billions of dollars on firearms, ammunition, archery gear, clothing, vehicles, guide services, lodging, and more—supporting jobs and local businesses. In 2011 American hunters spent about $36.3 billion on hunting trips, gear, licenses, and other expenses. By 2016, during a dip in participation, hunter spending had declined to $25.6 billion. These expenditures include money spent on trip-related tourism (fuel, hotels, food), which increased in some categories even as overall spending fell in that period. Hunting also funnels money into conservation: Hunters contribute hundreds of millions of dollars annually through license fees and special taxes (via the Pittman–Robertson Act). Hunting license sales alone provide a major funding source for state wildlife agencies—on the order of hundreds of millions of dollars nationwide each year (for instance, Texas's hunting licenses bring in over $50 million annually). In addition, federal excise taxes on guns, ammo, and archery equipment earmark around $1 billion per year for wildlife conservation and habitat restoration. All told, hunters generate over $1.8 billion each year for wildlife conservation in the United States when combining license fees, excise taxes, and donations.

Over the last decade (from 2015 to 2025), the economic impact of hunting has shown notable shifts. Early in the 2010s, hunting participation and spending were in decline. Between 2011 and 2016, the number of hunters dropped by about 2 million and total spending fell nearly 30 percent. However, recent years have seen a resurgence. By 2022, hunters spent an estimated $45.2 billion on equipment, licenses, trips, and other hunting-related expenses. This was a drastic increase from mid-2010s levels. This rise in spending coincided with a stabilization or slight uptick in hunting participation. After hitting a low around 11 to 12 million hunters in 2016, numbers climbed back toward 15 million by 2020–2022. The COVID-19 pandemic likely played a role in this rebound, as more people turned to outdoor recreation, leading to a nearly 5 percent jump in hunting license sales in 2020. By 2022, hunting-related expenditures reached their highest levels in decades (in nominal terms), indicating renewed economic strength in the hunting sector. Despite these gains, today's hunting community still represents a smaller slice of American society than in the 1970s–1980s, suggesting that hunting as a lifestyle has declined in overall popularity over time even if recent interest has grown slightly.

Hunting's economic and cultural importance varies widely by state. In terms of prevalence, rural states in the Mountain West and Midwest have the highest participation rates—for example, roughly 23 percent of Wyoming's residents hold hunting licenses (the highest per capita rate in the nation). Other states with a strong hunting heritage include Montana (around 21 percent of residents) and South Dakota (approximately 23 percent per capita). These states see a large share of their population hunting, which injects considerable spending into local economies (gear shops, outfitters, meat processors, etc.). In absolute numbers, however, most hunters are found in more populous states. Texas leads the nation with over 1.1 million paid hunting license holders in recent years.

States like Pennsylvania, Wisconsin, Michigan, and Missouri each enroll hundreds of thousands of hunters annually, making them major contributors to hunting-related revenue. For example, Wisconsin sold roughly 670,000 hunting licenses in a recent year and in 2020, hunters spent about $2.9 billion on hunting-related activities and gear. Texas by itself accounted for about $2.7 billion in direct hunting-related sales in 2020, contributing an estimated $2.5 billion to state GDP and supporting nearly 38,000 jobs. Michigan and Wisconsin similarly see annual hunting expenditures in the $2–3 billion range each, thanks to large deer hunting communities and related industries. Meanwhile, states like Wyoming and Montana benefit from out-of-state hunters traveling for big-game hunts, bolstering tourism in those regions. This means that Texas, Pennsylvania, Wisconsin, Michigan, and Missouri lead in total hunters and economic output, while Wyoming, Montana, and South Dakota lead in per capita participation—together illustrating that hunting remains economically impactful, especially in states where it is most culturally rooted.

Over the past half century, the trend in US hunting showed a decline in relative popularity but a persistently strong economic footprint. The 1970s–1980s were a high-water mark for hunter participation, and although today's hunter numbers have nearly recovered to those levels, they have not kept pace with population growth. Recent data suggest that, in the last ten years, hunting participation has stabilized or even modestly increased, reversing earlier declines. Correspondingly, spending on hunting has climbed to new heights (exceeding $45 billion in 2022) as avid hunters invest in more gear and travel further for hunting experiences. Hunting continues to be a multibillion-dollar industry nationwide—supporting hundreds of thousands of jobs and generating tax revenue—even though a smaller fraction of Americans hunt now compared to 40–50 years ago. Even though hunting as a lifestyle has moderately waned in popularity over time, it remains an important economic contributor at both national and state levels. States with deep hunting traditions reap enormous benefits, and recent efforts to engage new hunters aim to sustain this economic and cultural cornerstone for the future.

## Brick-and-Mortar Retailers: The Frontlines of the Firearms Economy

As of 2024, the United States hosts approximately 17,361 brick-and-mortar gun and ammunition stores, reflecting a 3.7 percent increase from the previous year. These establishments represent a significant portion of the firearms retail sector, offering customers the opportunity to purchase firearms, ammunition, and related accessories in person.

In addition to these physical stores, the broader landscape of federally licensed firearms dealers encompasses various types of operations, including pawn shops and home-based businesses. As of 2024, there are approximately 129,000 active Federal Firearms Licensees (FFLs) operating across the United States. These licenses cover a wide range of categories, including firearm dealers, collectors of curios and relics, and manufacturers of firearms. Among these, the most common licenses are those held by traditional gun dealers, collectors, and firearm manufacturers. The five states with the highest number of FFLs are Texas, California, Florida, Pennsylvania, and North Carolina. Texas leads the country with roughly 11,000 FFLs, followed closely by California with around 10,000, Florida with about 7,000, Pennsylvania with over 6,000, and North Carolina with approximately 4,500.

The trend in the number of FFLs over the past several decades tells an interesting story about the evolution of gun commerce in America. In the early 1990s, there were close to 250,000 federal firearms dealers operating nationwide. At that time, obtaining an FFL was relatively easy and inexpensive, leading many individuals to obtain licenses simply to enhance their private collections or conduct occasional sales. However, in the mid-1990s, a wave of regulatory reforms under the Clinton administration imposed stricter requirements on license holders, including higher fees and compliance inspections. As a result, the number of FFLs was cut by more than half over the next decade. By 2020, the number had stabilized at around 53,000 active retail gun dealers. In recent years, the total number of FFLs has seen a modest uptick, driven primarily by growth in firearm manufacturers and specialty retailers rather than traditional storefront dealers.

This shift reflects the broader changes in the firearms industry, where small manufacturers, custom builders, and specialty shops have flourished alongside traditional retailers. Despite these changes, the network of FFLs remains a crucial backbone of the firearms economy, ensuring that lawful transactions are conducted under strict federal guidelines while also contributing billions of dollars to the American economy through taxes, wages, and commerce.

The concentration of these dealers varies significantly across states. For instance, states with deeply ingrained gun cultures and less restrictive firearm regulations tend to have a higher density of gun stores per capita. This distribution reflects regional differences in firearm ownership rates, cultural attitudes towards guns, and the regulatory environment governing firearm sales.

It's important to note that while the number of licensed dealers provides insight into the availability of firearms, it doesn't directly correlate with the volume of firearm sales, as some dealers may conduct higher transaction volumes than others. Nonetheless, the presence of these establishments plays a crucial role in the economic landscape of the firearms industry, contributing to employment and generating significant revenue within local communities.

When it comes to the economic impact of firearms, brick-and-mortar retailers are a driving force behind the numbers. According to the National Shooting

Sports Foundation (NSSF), the total economic impact of the firearms and ammunition industry in the United States was over $80 billion in both 2022 and 2023—an increase of $10 billion since 2020. Retail gun stores—both major chains and independent shops—account for a significant portion of that figure. Beyond the raw sales, these businesses generate tens of thousands of jobs, contribute billions in federal and state taxes, and fuel local economies through wages, tourism, and related industries.

At the national level, few names are as dominant as Bass Pro Shops and Cabela's. Together, they form an outdoor retail empire, offering an expansive selection of firearms, ammunition, and shooting accessories across hundreds of locations nationwide. Their merger in 2017 created one of the largest sporting goods operations in the country. Bass Pro and Cabela's stores aren't just retail centers; they're often tourist attractions themselves, drawing millions of visitors annually, many of whom spend money in surrounding hotels, restaurants, and local businesses, providing an important economic ripple effect far beyond the checkout counter.

Academy Sports + Outdoors, with over 250 stores primarily in the South and Midwest, has also become a key player. Academy offers a wide range of handguns, rifles, shotguns, and related gear, and is known for making firearms more accessible to everyday Americans with competitive pricing. Sportsman's Warehouse, heavily concentrated in the West, and Scheels, a growing force in the Midwest, continue to expand their reach, combining an extensive selection of firearms and outdoor gear with an emphasis on customer service and education.

However, the heart and soul of the gun retail economy still belongs to the independent local gun shops—small businesses that serve communities across the country. These are the businesses where customer relationships matter, where employees know their customers by name, and where the Second Amendment is treated with the reverence it deserves. Shops like Smoke Wagon Firearms in Pine Bush, New York, and Wallkill River Small Arms in nearby Wallkill, are prime examples. These businesses offer everything from firearms and ammunition to expert advice and gunsmithing services, playing a crucial role not just in commerce, but in building a culture of responsible gun ownership.

In Walden, New York, Thruway Sporting Goods has long been a staple for sportsmen and gun owners alike, offering a wide range of firearms, accessories, hunting equipment, apparel and many other firearms-related inventory. Heading south, Benton Shooter's Supply in Benton, Tennessee, and Gun Works in Cleveland, Tennessee, both represent the strength of the independent gun store model in the southern United States. Benton Shooter's Supply, in particular, is one of the largest independently owned gun stores in the region, with a massive selection that attracts buyers from neighboring Georgia and western North Carolina. These businesses not only serve local residents but also attract tourists and non-local customers passing through the area, sometimes traveling from hundreds of miles away. In doing so, they contribute meaningfully to regional economies and highlight the enduring importance of rural and suburban commerce.

Collectively, local gun shops and national retailers account for over 170,000 jobs directly tied to the firearms and ammunition industry, according to NSSF data. These jobs generate more than $8.4 billion in wages and support countless related industries, from shipping and logistics to marketing, tourism, and hospitality.

Whether massive or modest, every firearms retailer contributes to an economic ecosystem that supports American livelihoods, strengthens communities, and keeps the constitutional right to bear arms alive and well at the grassroots level. These aren't just businesses—they are the economic and cultural lifeblood of the Second Amendment.

## Online Retailers: The New Frontier of the Firearms Economy

As technology has reshaped retail across all industries, the firearms world has adapted and thrived in the digital marketplace. Online gun and ammunition retailers have exploded in popularity over the past decade, offering customers convenience, competitive pricing, and vast selection that traditional brick-and-mortar stores sometimes cannot match. The digital shift has not only made it easier for Americans to exercise their Second Amendment rights, but it has also created a booming sector of the firearms economy worth billions.

One of the most significant players in the online space is Bud's Gun Shop, based in Lexington, Kentucky. Bud's operates both a physical store and a massive online business, offering thousands of firearms, ammunition, optics, and accessories. Known for competitive pricing and frequent promotions, Bud's is often one of the first stops for online gun buyers. Their easy-to-use website, vast inventory, and solid reputation for customer service have made them a trusted name among gun owners nationwide.

Another giant in the online firearms economy is GunBroker.com, often described as the "eBay of the gun world." GunBroker is not a retailer in the traditional sense—it is an online auction site where individuals, licensed dealers, and wholesalers can list firearms, ammunition, and accessories for sale to the public. Users can bid on items or use "Buy Now" options, and once the auction concludes, the seller ships the firearm to the buyer's local FFL dealer for legal transfer and background check. With millions of listings annually, GunBroker has revolutionized how firearms are bought and sold between private parties, opening up a competitive national marketplace where buyers have access to products they might never find locally. GunBroker alone is estimated to generate hundreds of millions of dollars in transactions each year, underscoring its massive impact on the economy.

Brownells is another cornerstone of the online gun world. Founded in 1939 and based in Grinnell, Iowa, Brownells specializes not just in selling firearms, but also in gunsmithing tools, AR-15 parts, custom build kits, and hard-to-find components. Brownells has positioned itself as the go-to site for serious hobbyists and professional armorers alike, combining a strong retail presence with educational content and DIY support. They have earned a stellar reputation for quality and service, particularly among those interested in building or modifying firearms.

MidwayUSA is another major player, offering an expansive catalog of hunting, shooting, and outdoor gear. Based in Columbia, Missouri, MidwayUSA was founded by Larry Potterfield in 1977 and transitioned early into e-commerce. Today, they offer thousands of firearms, parts, ammunition, and reloading supplies. Their dedication to customer service and fast shipping times has made them a favorite among both casual shooters and serious competitors.

When it comes to ammunition, Outdoor Limited, based in North Carolina, has emerged as a major online source for competitive pricing and bulk buying options. They specialize in popular calibers for rifles, pistols, and shotguns, often offering hard-to-find brands and loads. Outdoor Limited caters to high-volume shooters and ranges that need large quantities of ammo at fair prices. Sites like AmmoSeek.com have also transformed how people shop for ammunition by operating as comparison search engines—allowing users to find the best prices across dozens of online retailers in real time.

Palmetto State Armory (PSA) deserves a special mention. Originally focused on affordable AR-15 parts and kits, PSA has grown into a full-fledged firearm and ammunition retailer, manufacturing their own branded rifles, pistols, and even AK-47 variants. Palmetto State Armory's mission has been to make owning quality firearms affordable for every American, and they have successfully dominated a large segment of the online market by offering unbeatable deals on everything from complete firearms to build kits and tactical gear.

Primary Arms, based out of Texas, has also become a go-to for budget-conscious shooters looking for optics, accessories, and firearms. They are particularly well known for their in-house line of optics, which offer excellent performance at a fraction of the cost of some of the bigger European brands.

Collectively, the online firearms and ammunition marketplace accounts for billions of dollars in annual sales, providing tens of thousands of jobs in distribution, shipping, warehousing, customer service, and tech support. Online sales have also given rise to an entirely new class of entrepreneurs—from small businesses specializing in niche products to large warehouses moving high volumes of inventory across the country.

Online retailers have not only made firearms and ammunition more accessible but have also democratized the market, giving Americans in restrictive states or remote rural areas access to products that local stores may not carry. This new frontier of the firearms economy represents freedom of choice, convenience, and competitive free market capitalism at its best.

The online firearms and ammunition economy is not without its challenges, however, as it faces a constant minefield of evolving regulations, shipping restrictions, and political pressure from anti-gun states and financial institutions alike.

In recent years, online firearms and ammunition retailers have been increasingly targeted by control-heavy states like New York to limit access to gun-related products through backdoor restrictions. As early as 2020, New York gun owners routinely ordered ammunition online, enjoying better prices, wider selection, and the convenience of home delivery. But that changed when the state passed laws prohibiting the direct shipment of ammunition and certain accessories to private residences. Many online retailers, under pressure to comply, began outright refusing to ship to New York addresses—effectively deputizing themselves as enforcers of state policy and treating law-abiding customers as if they could not be trusted to follow the law without supervision.

## The Retail Exodus: How Major Chains Abandoned Firearms Sales

Despite the gun industry's robust contributions to the United States economy, it has faced many challenges. For decades, firearms and ammunition were a staple in American retail. Walking into a Walmart, Kmart, or even a department store like Sears, it was normal to see rifles and shotguns displayed in glass cases with stacks of ammunition nearby. It was not unusual to pick up a new hunting rifle or a box of .22 LR while grabbing groceries. Gun ownership was widely accepted, and firearms were seen as just another part of American life. But times have changed. Over the past two decades, major retailers have systematically retreated from the firearms business, whether because of political pressure, corporate virtue signaling, or outright cowardice in the face of anti-gun activism. Walmart, Dick's Sporting Goods, Kmart, and even grocery chains like Kroger have all either pulled certain firearms from their shelves, restricted ammunition sales, or exited the gun business entirely.

This shift has had significant consequences, not necessarily in terms of gun availability—since firearms remain widely accessible through specialized gun stores and sporting retailers—but in the normalization of firearm ownership. By removing guns from their shelves, these companies contribute to the very stigma that anti-gun activists want to create: the idea that firearms are dangerous, fringe, and should not be easily accessible to the average citizen. It is not just about lost sales; it's about erasing the visibility of lawful gun ownership from everyday American life, making firearms seem more controversial than they really are.

Walmart, once one of the largest firearm and ammunition retailers in the country, has spent the last three decades steadily chipping away at its own gun sales. In 1993, Walmart stopped selling handguns in all stores except in Alaska. In 2015, they discontinued sales of AR-15s and similar semi-automatic rifles, citing declining customer demand, though the decision coincided with increasing political pressure against modern sporting rifles. In 2018, following the Parkland school shooting, Walmart raised the minimum age to purchase any firearm or ammunition to 21 years old, regardless of state law. A year later, after mass shootings at Walmart locations in El Paso, Texas, and Southaven, Mississippi, the company announced it would no longer sell handgun am-munition or rifle calibers like .223 and 5.56 NATO—the very rounds used in the most popular rifles in America. They also ended handgun sales in Alaska, removing pistols from their stores entirely. That same year, Walmart CEO Doug McMillon publicly requested that customers no longer open-carry in their stores, even in states where it was perfectly legal. Before these policy shifts, Walmart held roughly 20 percent of the ammunition market in the US; after their decision to stop selling certain calibers, their market share dropped to around 6–9 percent. Today, while Walmart still sells traditional hunting rifles and shotguns in some locations, it has firmly distanced itself from the modern firearms market.

While Walmart's retreat from gun sales was slow and calculated, Dick's Sport-ing Goods took a much more aggressive approach, openly attacking the Second Amendment community. After the Sandy Hook shooting in 2012, Dick's an-nounced that it would no longer sell "assault-style" rifles in its stores—though this only applied to Dick's-branded locations, as its Field & Stream stores con-tinued selling AR-15s and similar firearms. However, after the Parkland shooting in 2018, CEO Edward Stack decided to go further, permanently removing all AR-15s and semi-automatic rifles from Field & Stream locations as well. At the same time, Dick's raised the minimum age for all firearm and ammunition purchases to 21, regardless of state law, and stopped selling high-capacity mag-azines. To make its anti-gun stance crystal clear, the company did not return its unsold rifle inventory to manufacturers but instead had them destroyed—nearly $5 million worth of firearms.

By 2020, Dick's had removed the hunting and firearms department from over 440 stores, nearly eliminating gun sales entirely. These decisions had serious financial consequences. Dick's estimated it lost around $250 million in revenue. Gun owners boycotted the company, and firearms manufacturers cut ties. The National Shooting Sports Foundation (NSSF) even expelled Dick's from its membership, citing the company's "conduct detrimental" to the firearm industry. Despite the financial losses and backlash, Edward Stack remained unapologetic, making it clear that Dick's had no intention of returning to the firearms business.

Other major retailers soon followed suit. Kmart, once a consequential firearm retailer, stopped selling handguns in the 1970s but continued carrying rifles and ammunition for years. However, after the Columbine shooting in 1999, anti-gun activists, including filmmaker Michael Moore, pressured Kmart to phase out handgun ammunition. By 2001, Kmart had completely removed all handgun ammo from its stores. Kroger, through its Fred Meyer brand, also exited the firearms market in 2018, citing "softening consumer demand," though the decision was widely seen as political posturing following the Parkland shooting. Outdoor retailer L.L.Bean, which only sold firearms at its flagship store in Maine, stopped selling guns to anyone under 21. In addition, REI announced it will resume orders from brands like Giro, Bell, and CamelBak now that their parent company, Vista Outdoor, has sold off its firearms manufacturer, Savage Arms. REI had suspended orders in 2018 after Vista declined to engage in the national gun safety debate following the Parkland shooting, emphasizing that while REI doesn't sell firearms, it expects companies profiting from guns to take civic responsibility in such discussions.

The slow but deliberate retreat of big-box retailers from gun sales has less to do with financial practicality and more to do with ideological positioning. These corporations, many of which once served hunters, sport shooters, and Second Amendment advocates, are now aligning themselves with the anti-gun establishment. By refusing to sell guns, they reinforce the narrative that firearms are dangerous, controversial, and something to be kept out of the hands of everyday citizens. This is part of a broader effort to erode gun culture—not by banning guns outright, but by slowly making them harder to see, harder to buy, and harder to normalize in American life.

But despite this corporate virtue signaling, Americans have found other ways to exercise their Second Amendment rights. Gun stores, online retailers, and dedicated sporting goods chains like Bass Pro Shops, Cabela's, and Academy Sports continue to thrive, stepping in to fill the void left by companies that abandoned their pro-gun customers. The retreat of major retailers has not slowed gun sales in America—if anything, it has further strengthened independent firearm businesses and made gun owners more intentional about where they spend their money.

The message for gun owners is clear: Corporations that abandon firearms are making a choice, and so can we. They don't deserve our business. If a company decides that it no longer wants to serve the law-abiding gun community, then gun owners should respond in kind by refusing to support them. The free market works both ways. If they don't stand with us, we have no reason to stand with them.

## Panic Buying

Political climate, social unrest, and a sense of economic insecurity within the population can lead to the mass purchasing and hoarding of guns and ammunition. In 2020, the United States witnessed an unprecedented surge in the purchase of firearms and ammunition, driven by a combination of factors, including the COVID-19 pandemic, civil unrest, and political uncertainty. This phenomenon, often referred to as "panic buying," led to gun stores across the country being flooded with customers. Lines stretched out the door and down the block as people scrambled to purchase guns and ammunition, fearing potential shortages or increased regulations. This sudden spike in demand had a big impact on prices. The cost of ammunition saw a dramatic increase. Supply chains were strained, and manufacturers struggled to keep up with the heightened demand. As a result, prices soared, and certain calibers of ammunition became scarce, creating a secondary market where prices were even higher.

While the initial wave of panic buying subsided, prices for firearms and ammunition remain relatively high. Ongoing debates about gun control and potential new regulations keep demand high. Economic uncertainty, including inflation and supply chain disruptions, continues to affect prices. And concerns about rising crime rates and border security issues contribute to the sustained demand for firearms and ammunition.

Given these factors, the future of firearms and ammunition prices remains uncertain. However, there are a few key points to consider. Firearms and ammunition are often seen as good investments. Unlike cars, which depreciate the moment they are driven off the lot, guns tend to retain their value, and limited edition models, historical firearms, and those from renowned manufacturers can even appreciate over time. As long as there are concerns about regulations, economic instability, and personal safety, the demand for firearms and ammunition is likely to remain strong, supporting higher prices. The firearms market has shown resilience in the face of economic fluctuations, and this stability makes firearms and ammunition attractive to investors who are looking for tangible assets that are less volatile than stocks or real estate.

While prices have moderated somewhat, they remain high due to ongoing political, economic, and social factors. For those looking to invest, firearms and ammunition present a unique opportunity, offering the potential for appreciation and value retention. As the market continues to evolve, it will be important to monitor these trends and adjust investment strategies accordingly.

## Lawfare Against Gun Manufacturers

In recent years, gun control advocates and certain legislative bodies have pushed for laws that would allow victims of gun violence to sue gun manufacturers and their products, rather than holding the actual shooter accountable. This approach is not only absurd and ridiculous but also economically detrimental to both gun manufacturers and consumers.

One of the most contentious aspects of this legal strategy is its deviation from the principle of holding individuals accountable for their actions. In any other industry, it would be inconceivable to sue the manufacturer of a product used improperly or criminally by an end-user. For instance, no one would consider suing a car manufacturer because a drunk driver caused an accident. Yet, with firearms, there is a concerted effort to shift blame from the individual who committed the crime to the companies that produced the weapon.

One notable example is the lawsuit filed against Remington Arms Company by the families of victims of the Sandy Hook Elementary School shooting. In 2014, the families sued Remington, arguing that the company was negligent in its marketing of the AR-15 rifle used in the massacre. They claimed that Remington's marketing tactics were designed to appeal to younger, at-risk males, contributing to the misuse of the firearm. In 2022, Remington agreed to a $73 million settlement, marking a significant moment in the legal battles against gun manufacturers.

Smith & Wesson has also faced several high-profile lawsuits tied to shootings involving its firearms, each testing the limits of legal accountability in an industry largely protected by federal law. After the 2015 terrorist attack in San Bernardino, victims' families sued the company, claiming it was negligent in how its weapons were distributed. That case was dismissed in 2016 under the Protection of Lawful Commerce in Arms Act, which shields gun manufacturers from liability when their products are used unlawfully. In 2018, a man was fatally shot by Kansas City police, prompting his parents to file a 2020 lawsuit against Smith & Wesson, alleging a design defect caused the gun to discharge accidentally. Most recently, following the 2022 Highland Park Fourth of July parade shooting, victims and their families sued the company, accusing it of irresponsibly marketing AR-15-style rifles to young, at-risk males. While these cases vary in scope and outcome, they illustrate a broader effort to use the courts as a battleground for gun control policy—placing manufacturers like Smith & Wesson in the legal and cultural crosshairs.

It's not just Smith & Wesson that has been dragged into emotionally charged, baseless lawsuits—many other firearm manufacturers have found themselves in the crosshairs of activists looking to assign blame where it doesn't belong. Following the tragic mass shooting at the Route 91 Harvest Festival in Las Vegas, the family of victim Carrie Parsons filed a wrongful death lawsuit against Colt and other gun manufacturers. The lawsuit alleged that the design of AR-15-style rifles, including those produced by Colt, allowed them to be easily modified with bump stocks to function similarly to automatic weapons. However, in 2021, the Nevada Supreme Court ruled that state law immunizes gun manufacturers from civil actions unless the weapon malfunctions, effectively siding with the manufacturers in this case.

That same year, in 2021, the Mexican government filed a $10 billion lawsuit against Colt and other US firearm manufacturers, accusing them of negligent business practices that facilitated the trafficking of guns to Mexican drug cartels, contributing to violence in Mexico. While initially dismissed by a federal court citing the Protection of Lawful Commerce in Arms Act (PLCAA), the case was later revived by the First US Circuit Court of Appeals under an exception to the PLCAA. In early 2025, the US Supreme Court agreed to hear arguments in this case.

The real motivation behind these lawsuits appears to be less about justice for victims and more about punishing gun manufacturers. By inundating these companies with legal challenges, the aim is to financially cripple them, making it increasingly difficult for them to operate. If such laws gain traction, the legal costs alone could be staggering, potentially bankrupting smaller manufacturers and severely affecting larger ones.

The economic implications of this strategy are pronounced. According to the National Shooting Sports Foundation (NSSF), the firearms industry contributes tens of billions of dollars to the US economy annually and supports hundreds of thousands of jobs. Legal attacks on gun manufacturers threaten this abundant economic contribution. Should these companies face an unmanageable volume of lawsuits, the ripple effects could lead to factory closures, job losses, and a decline in related industries, such as ammunition production and retail sales of firearms and accessories.

For consumers, the impact would be equally dire. The increased legal risks and associated costs for manufacturers would inevitably lead to higher prices for firearms and ammunition. This would make these items less accessible to law-abiding citizens, particularly those of lower economic means who may rely on firearms for personal protection. The artificially inflated prices could also drive a black market for guns, exacerbating the very issues gun control advocates claim to address.

Furthermore, the precedent set by allowing such lawsuits could extend to other industries, fostering a litigious environment that stifles innovation and economic growth. If manufacturers can be held liable for the criminal misuse of their products, the door opens for similar claims against makers of knives, cars, and other tools that can be used harmfully. This broader economic impact would stifle entrepreneurship and innovation, as companies would be forced to divert resources from development and production to legal defense.

Ultimately, the strategy to allow victims of gun violence to sue manufacturers is a thinly veiled attempt to dismantle the firearms industry through economic attrition. It shifts accountability away from the perpetrators of violence and places an undue burden on companies that operate within the bounds of the law. The economic fallout from such measures would not only harm the manufacturers but also consumers and the broader economy, leading to higher prices, job losses, and a potential decline in economic productivity.

## Operation Choke Point

One of the more underhanded assaults on the Second Amendment didn't come through flashy legislation or a high-profile Supreme Court case. It came quietly, under the banner of a little-known government program called Operation Choke Point. Launched by the Obama administration's Department of Justice (DOJ) in 2013, Operation Choke Point was marketed to the public as a noble effort to fight fraud. In reality, it was a weaponized campaign to financially strangle lawful industries that the left didn't like—with gun dealers placed squarely in the crosshairs.

Operation Choke Point's official goal was to pressure banks and financial institutions to cut ties with businesses that were supposedly "at high risk for fraud." Working with federal agencies like the Federal Deposit Insurance Corporation (FDIC) and the Consumer Financial Protection Bureau (CFPB), the DOJ leaned on banks with a not-so-subtle message: If you continue to do business with these "risky" industries, you might just invite federal scrutiny. Unsurprisingly, the list of high-risk businesses included payday lenders, coin dealers, fireworks retailers, dating services, and—of course—firearms dealers.

The government didn't have to ban guns or even regulate them directly. They simply had to choke off the financial lifeline of lawful gun dealers, ammunition suppliers, and firearm-related businesses. No cash flow meant no business. Problem solved without the inconvenience of having to deal with the Constitution.

Although Operation Choke Point was framed as an anti-fraud initiative, its real-world impact landed heavily on law-abiding gun shops and online firearm retailers. Banks began closing the accounts of gun shops without warning. Credit card processors started refusing to process transactions related to firearms or ammunition. Businesses that had operated cleanly for decades were suddenly branded as too "risky" to insure, finance, or partner with. It was nothing less than financial blacklisting—and it didn't require a single act of Congress. All it needed was a few backroom conversations and a lot of government pressure applied quietly but firmly behind the scenes.

Operation Choke Point officially ended in 2017 under the Trump administration after enormous backlash from members of Congress, government watchdog groups, and pro-Second Amendment advocates. The DOJ eventually issued a statement announcing the end of the program. The FDIC issued new guidance instructing banks not to cut ties with legal businesses solely based on "reputation risk." Lawsuits followed, with several gun dealers and affected businesses successfully settling with the government for the damage done.

However, anyone who thinks the story ends there would do well to think again. Although Operation Choke Point as an official program is dead, its spirit is very much alive today, just operating under different names and methods. Financial discrimination against the firearms industry continues, only now it comes in the form of "corporate policy" rather than explicit government orders.

Major banks like Citibank, Bank of America, and JPMorgan Chase have instituted internal rules refusing to lend money or provide services to gun manufacturers and dealers unless they meet specific "social responsibility" standards. Translation: Disarm yourself, or we're cutting you off. Payment processors like PayPal, Square, and Stripe have long banned transactions involving firearms and ammunition, making it even harder for gun-related businesses to operate online.

And now, the rise of Environmental, Social, and Governance (ESG) scoring gives corporations a new weapon to pressure businesses based on political virtue-signaling, with firearms companies inevitably scoring dead last.

The takeaway is simple: Operation Choke Point never really ended—it just evolved. Instead of direct government pressure, we now have a cozy dance between woke corporations and bureaucratic regulators, all quietly working to sideline industries they find politically inconvenient.

Operation Choke Point proved that the government doesn't have to pass new laws to attack gun rights. By weaponizing the financial system, they can kill gun culture quietly—one closed bank account at a time. And if they can do it to gun dealers, they can do it to anyone who steps out of line next. Defending the Second Amendment isn't just about fighting new legislation anymore. It's about keeping an eye on every front, including the financial front, where the attack is often invisible until it's too late.

## Credit Card Tyranny

In addition to Operation Choke Point and its offshoots, the anti-gun lobby's quiet war against the Second Amendment continued to intrude into the financial realm, through efforts to track gun and ammunition purchases made with credit cards. The idea was simple: If you couldn't outright ban gun ownership, you could at least make it feel dangerous, stigmatized, and heavily monitored.

In 2022, under heavy political pressure from gun control activists and state officials like those in New York and California, the major credit card companies—Visa, Mastercard, and American Express—were urged to adopt a new merchant category code (MCC) specifically for firearm and ammunition retailers. Previously, gun stores were lumped into broader categories like "sporting goods." By creating a specific MCC for firearms, activists and some lawmakers hoped to flag, track, and potentially even block purchases they deemed suspicious.

Supporters of the move claimed it would help detect and prevent mass shootings or gun trafficking. Realistically, it was a clear attempt to create a private-sector gun registry by financial proxy. With a specific code attached to every firearm and ammo transaction, it would become burdensome for financial institutions—and by extension, the government—to build databases of who was buying guns, how many, and how much ammunition they were purchasing. It was surveillance by another name, and it had nothing to do with stopping crime. Criminals, after all, aren't known for buying their weapons at Bass Pro Shops with a Visa card.

The backlash was swift and fierce. Gun rights groups, free speech advocates, and even financial privacy organizations slammed the proposal as a blatant violation of constitutional rights and an abuse of the financial system. Lawsuits and legislative pushback followed. In response, several states, including Florida, Texas, and Montana, passed laws explicitly banning the use of merchant category codes to track firearms purchases. By 2023, under mounting legal and political pressure, Visa, Mastercard, and American Express announced they would pause the implementation of the firearm-specific tracking codes. For a moment, it seemed like the threat had been beaten back.

However, gun control advocates and hostile state governments were not about to give up. In June 2024, New York State passed legislation requiring credit card companies to adopt merchant category codes for firearm and ammunition retailers. Then, in April 2025, New York doubled down when Governor Hochul signed into law a package of three new gun control measures that expanded these efforts even further. One of the new laws mandates that credit card companies use specific merchant category codes to track all purchases at gun and ammunition retailers. Even more chillingly, the law requires these companies to report "suspicious activity" to the government, although what exactly qualifies as suspicious is left deliberately vague. In effect, New York has turned financial institutions into government informants, tasked with monitoring and flagging the lawful purchase of a constitutionally protected product.

The implications are enormous. By forcing credit card companies to track and report gun and ammo purchases, New York is sidestepping the traditional protections built into the Second Amendment. It's backdoor gun control by way of financial surveillance, and it creates a chilling effect on gun owners who now have to wonder if buying a box of ammunition could land them on a government watch list. Worse yet, if other blue states follow New York's lead, a patchwork of financial spying laws could emerge, putting lawful gun owners at constant risk of being flagged simply for exercising their rights.

The legal fallout is already beginning. Several gun rights organizations and privacy advocacy groups have announced plans to challenge New York's new laws in court, arguing that they violate not only the Second Amendment but also the Fourth Amendment protections against unreasonable searches and seizures. Cases are expected to wind their way through the court system in the coming months, and it's likely the issue will ultimately end up in front of the US Supreme Court.

In the meantime, the situation serves as yet another reminder that the attacks on gun rights are no longer limited to traditional bans and restrictions. Financial warfare—whether through Operation Choke Point, ESG pressure, or mandatory tracking of lawful purchases—has become the new frontline. The goal is the same as it has always been: to chill, stigmatize, and ultimately discourage Americans from exercising their constitutional rights, all while pretending it's about public safety. If Americans don't remain vigilant, today's backdoor tracking could become tomorrow's de facto national gun registry—created not by legislation, but by bureaucratic bullying and corporate compliance.

The real lesson here—and a bit of advice: Use cash to buy anything firearms-related, if possible.

***

The firearms industry is not just a cornerstone of American freedom—it is a powerhouse of economic activity, supporting jobs, businesses, and local economies across the country. From manufacturing and retail sales to hunting, sport shooting, and self-defense training, firearms contribute billions to the US economy every year. However, this industry faces constant threats from multiple fronts. Activist retailers who abandon gun sales for political reasons, anti-gun legislators pushing restrictive policies, and an increasingly hostile social climate all pose significant challenges. The political landscape can shift rapidly, as seen in 2020, when civil unrest, economic uncertainty, and calls for stricter gun control caused a massive surge in firearms and ammunition sales, leading to nationwide shortages and skyrocketing prices. The lesson is clear: When political or social instability arises, demand for guns and ammo surges, often overwhelming supply chains.

This underscores the importance of a resilient and independent firearms industry, free from government overreach and corporate virtue signaling. The right to keep and bear arms is not just a constitutional guarantee; it is also an economic force, one that must be protected from those who seek to erode both our freedoms and the financial backbone that supports them.

# Chapter 12

# Mind Over Matter: Navigating Mental Health & Gun Rights

*It's not the guns that kill, it's the maladjusted kids.*

—Charlton Heston

*Mental illness and hatred pull the trigger, not the gun.*

—Donald J. Trump

*The will to survive is not as important as the will to prevail . . . the answer to criminal aggression is retaliation.*

—Jeff Cooper

There's something *off* about modern America. You can feel it in the air—like a low hum of anxiety pulsing through the culture. More people today are being diagnosed with some form of mental illness than at any point in our nation's history. Depression, anxiety, ADHD, PTSD—pick your acronym. Kids can't sit still in class, adults can't handle the stress of everyday life, and somehow, the answer to all of it seems to be stuffing everyone with pills. Psychotropic medication has become so common it's practically a food group.

Basic human emotions, it seems, have been pathologized. Stress after a long day of work? That's not just stress anymore—that's burnout syndrome, anxiety disorder, or some other label that needs a prescription and a week off. Sad about a breakup? That's not heartbreak, that's clinical depression. Kids acting like kids? Better slap a label on them and dope them up with Adderall. And the kicker? The more comfortable society becomes, the more fragile people become. When the wolf is far from the door, even a paper cut becomes a crisis.

Not to get too political (but let's be honest, it's impossible not to)—studies have consistently shown that people who identify as liberal report being more unhappy than their conservative or independent counterparts. And it's not hard to see why. Conservative-leaning individuals are more likely to value faith, build families, and engage with their communities. These aren't just lifestyle choices—they're mental anchors. When life gets hard, they don't scream at the sky—they pray, work, and vote. On the other hand, the activist left seems to live in a constant state of meltdown.

Now, why does this matter? It matters because we need to explore what mental health *actually* has to do with gun ownership. Because this chapter isn't just about mental health in general—it's about mental health and gun rights. There is a very real and very important conversation to be had about how we distinguish between *real* mental illness, the kind that leads to genuine danger, and this growing cultural tendency to treat every unpleasant feeling as a diagnosable disorder. In an age where people are medicated into compliance and rioters act out with impunity, the question must be asked: Who decides who is mentally fit to own a firearm?

Because here's the double standard: When an angry mob attacks police officers, vandalizes property, and sets things on fire over political grievances, that's a violent, public display of instability. These people are showing the world they are unwell. That's not just a red flag—that's a screaming siren. Yet when a peaceful, responsible gun owner is flagged for something as mild as depression or ADHD, suddenly their Second Amendment rights are under threat. That's where we have a problem.

So, in this chapter, we're going to dive headfirst into this thorny issue: the line between real mental illness, subjective interpretation, and flat-out cultural invention. Because if we're going to talk about rights—especially the right to keep and bear arms—then we'd better get serious about who is truly a danger to themselves or others, and who is simply being labeled as such because they don't fit into the soft, overmedicated mold of modern fragility.

## What Constitutes a Mental Health Condition?

The intersection of gun rights and mental health is a complex and contentious issue that poses significant challenges for ensuring public safety while respecting Second Amendment rights. On one hand, there is a clear need to prevent individuals with severe mental health issues from accessing firearms, as this could mitigate the risk of tragic events involving gun violence. On the other hand, there is a legitimate concern that mental health criteria may be misused or weaponized to unjustly deny law-abiding citizens their constitutional rights.

One of the primary challenges is defining what constitutes a mental health condition severe enough to restrict someone from owning a firearm. Mental health encompasses a wide range of conditions, from temporary states of anxiety and depression to more severe and persistent disorders. Many individuals seek therapy for manageable issues like depression or anxiety and use medication to maintain their mental health. These individuals, despite their conditions, often live productive lives without posing any danger to society. Therefore, blanket restrictions based on mental health diagnoses could unfairly penalize those who are managing their conditions responsibly. Stripping an individual of their Second Amendment rights based solely on speculation or a gut feeling, without solid evidence, raises serious legal and ethical concerns.

The slippery slope of using mental health as a criterion for gun ownership becomes particularly concerning when considering the potential for definitions and classifications to be expanded or reinterpreted. If mental health standards are reworked to classify broader behaviors or beliefs as indicators of unfitness, it could lead to a significant erosion of Second Amendment rights. If certain political beliefs or dissenting opinions were labeled as signs of mental instability, an entire class of people could be unjustly deemed unfit to own firearms. This would represent a dangerous precedent, where subjective criteria are used to infringe upon fundamental rights.

## Avoiding the Slippery Slope

Moreover, mental health diagnoses could be weaponized for political or ideological purposes. If psychologists or mental health professionals were influenced by prevailing political biases, they might classify individuals with opposing views as mentally unfit. This scenario could lead to widespread disenfranchisement and the erosion of civil liberties, creating a society where dissent is equated with mental illness and punished by the loss of constitutional rights.

To address these challenges and avoid the potential slippery slope, several measures could be implemented:

1. Clear and Objective Criteria: Establish clear, objective criteria for determining mental unfitness for gun ownership. These criteria should be based on empirical evidence and expert consensus, focusing on conditions that are directly associated with a demonstrable threat of harm to oneself or others.

2. Due Process Protections: Ensure that any process for denying firearms based on mental health includes robust due process protection. Individuals should have the right to challenge and appeal decisions, with access to legal representation and an impartial hearing.

3. Privacy Safeguards: Protect the privacy of individuals seeking mental health treatment. Fear of losing gun rights should not deter individuals from seeking the help they need. Confidentiality must be maintained, and mental health records should not be easily accessible without due cause.

4. Regular Review and Oversight: Implement regular review and oversight of the criteria and processes used to determine mental unfitness. This will help prevent abuse and ensure that the system remains fair and just.

5. Public and Professional Input: Involve mental health professionals, legal experts, and the public in the development of policies and criteria. This

collaborative approach can help balance the need for safety with the protection of constitutional rights.

By taking these steps, it is possible to address the intersection of gun rights and mental health in a way that enhances public safety without infringing on the rights of responsible, law-abiding citizens.

## Who Gets To Decide?

The question of whether someone with a legitimate mental health issue but no history of violent behavior or criminal activity should be denied their right to own firearms is a deeply nuanced and complex issue. The potential risk posed by individuals with certain mental health conditions cannot be ignored. However, most people with common mental health issues, including conditions like depression, anxiety, or PTSD, do not pose a threat to themselves or others. Many of these individuals lead productive, responsible lives and use their firearms for lawful purposes such as self-defense, hunting, or sport shooting.

The National Institute of Mental Health (NIMH) reports that nearly one in five US adults lives with a mental illness, translating to approximately 51.5 million people in 2019. Despite these high numbers, the connection between mental illness and violence is often exaggerated in public discourse and media portrayals. According to the American Psychiatric Association, only about 3 to 5 percent of violent acts can be attributed to individuals living with a serious mental illness. In contrast, people with severe mental illnesses are more likely to be victims rather than perpetrators of violence.

Additionally, the use of psychotropic drugs is widespread. Data from the Centers for Disease Control and Prevention (CDC) indicates that about one in six US adults reported taking some form of antidepressants, antipsychotics, or anxiolytics. This statistic reflects the high prevalence of mental health treatment in the country, yet it also underscores the fact that most of these individuals manage their conditions responsibly without posing a threat to society.

Denying these individuals their Second Amendment rights solely based on a mental health diagnosis is an unjust and discriminatory practice. It fails to consider the individual's overall behavior, personal history, and the specific nature of their condition. For example, veterans who have served their country and have PTSD often use firearms responsibly and see them as a means of protecting themselves and their families. Automatically stripping them of their gun rights not only disregards their service and sacrifices but also their need for self-defense in potentially dangerous situations.

Moreover, implementing such blanket restrictions can deter individuals from seeking the mental health treatment they need out of fear that they will lose their constitutional rights. This could lead to a worsening of mental health issues and potentially increase the risk of untreated conditions. Instead of blanket bans, a more individualized approach should be considered, where mental health evaluations are used to assess an individual's specific risk factors and history of behavior. This would allow for a fairer determination that respects both public safety and the individual's rights. A balanced, case-by-case approach that considers the totality of an individual's circumstances is necessary to protect both public safety and personal freedoms.

Addressing the mental health crisis does not mean diagnosing the entire country with a blanket mental illness and disarming the population (or large swaths of it); rather, it requires an honest and nuanced examination of the societal trends and commonalities that mass shooters and criminals share. While mental illness is a common denominator among many perpetrators of violence, it is crucial to identify the specific factors that contribute to these individuals' descent into criminal behavior. Studies and statistics often reveal that many mass shooters and violent criminals are troubled boys who lack a father figure or stable family environment. These individuals frequently experience feelings of isolation, rejection, and anger, which are compounded by other issues such as substance abuse, bullying, and a lack of access to mental health care. Understanding these underlying factors and demographics is essential for developing targeted interventions and support systems that address the root causes of violence, rather than imposing broad and ineffective measures that infringe on the rights of law-abiding citizens. By focusing on these common threads, society can better prevent violence and support those who are most at risk, without resorting to overgeneralization or stigmatization of mental health conditions.

## Is It Trendy to Have Something Wrong with You?

In contemporary culture, there is a troubling trend where having a mental health issue is sometimes seen as desirable or even fashionable. This phenomenon is partly driven by a societal shift that emphasizes victimhood over personal responsibility. The narrative that it is "cool" to be a victim can detract from genuine efforts to address mental health issues and promote resilience and accountability. Therapists and psychologists, whose livelihoods depend on diagnosing and treating mental health conditions, may inadvertently contribute to this trend by overdiagnosing or pathologizing normal human experiences and behaviors.

The self-diagnosis of mental illnesses, often influenced by social media and pop psychology, can lead to the trivialization of serious conditions. People may claim mental health labels without proper medical evaluation, using these labels as a scapegoat for personal shortcomings or to garner sympathy. This not only diminishes the experiences of those with legitimate mental health struggles but also fosters a culture where personal accountability is overshadowed by a perpetual state of victimhood.

The culture of self-diagnosis and the tendency among psychologists to overdiagnose have contributed to an artificial inflation of mental illness statistics. Everyday stresses and the normal ups and downs of life are increasingly perceived as abnormal, leading many to seek medical intervention for issues that might otherwise be resolved on their own. This phenomenon is exacerbated by the pervasive influence of social media, which often promotes a toxic environment and heightens feelings of inadequacy and anxiety. As a result, what might be a temporary emotional state or a rough day is quickly labeled as a mental health disorder requiring medication. That one in six adults in the US takes psychotropic medication suggests that the numbers of diagnosed mental illnesses are suspiciously high. While some genuinely benefit from these medications, it is plausible that many are being treated for conditions that have been overmedicalized or misdiagnosed.

The inflated numbers of mental health diagnoses pose a significant threat to gun rights. When normal experiences and behaviors are mistaken for mental illnesses, it becomes alarmingly easy to justify stripping individuals of their right to bear arms. Loose standards for diagnosing mental health conditions could be weaponized to disarm large swaths of the population under the guise of public safety. This slippery slope leads to a scenario where almost everyone could be deemed ineligible to own a gun, which appears to align with the goal of some gun control advocates. Broadening the criteria for mental unfitness can undermine the Second Amendment and disempower citizens, infringing upon their ability to protect themselves and their families.

Further, depriving someone of their Second Amendment rights based on something someone thinks they might do based on a hunch, without concrete evidence, poses a major legal and ethical dilemma. Just as one cannot be arrested for a crime they have not committed, it is problematic to revoke constitutional rights without tangible evidence of a clear and present danger. Such actions could lead to a slippery slope where subjective judgments and fears override individual freedoms.

## Mental Illness on Display

While it is crucial to protect Second Amendment rights, there are certain mental health conditions that may justifiably warrant the restriction of an individual's ability to own firearms, primarily when these conditions pose a grave and direct threat to public safety. Severe mental illnesses that involve psychosis, delusional thinking, or uncontrollable violent tendencies are such examples. Conditions such as schizophrenia with active psychotic symptoms, severe bipolar disorder during manic episodes with aggressive behavior, or severe major depressive disorder with suicidal ideation can impair judgment and increase the risk of harm to oneself or others. In these cases, it is reasonable to impose restrictions on firearm ownership as a precautionary measure to prevent potential tragedies.

Individuals who have a documented history of violent behavior or credible threats, particularly in conjunction with a diagnosed mental health condition, are often considered for restrictions on their right to own firearms. If implemented properly and fairly, this can be a common-sense approach that aims to prioritize public safety without stigmatizing everyone with a mental health diagnosis. It recognizes a critical truth: Not all mental illnesses carry the same risks, and most people with mental health conditions are not violent. However, when violent behavior is paired with instability, society has both the moral obligation and constitutional challenge to determine how to act—swiftly, but justly.

Unfortunately, there is a growing and visible segment of the population, often tied to far-left political activism, that engages in open, documented acts of violence and threats—and yet rarely get scrutinized through this lens. We've seen this across the country. During the George Floyd riots of 2020, cities were burned, businesses were looted, and police officers were assaulted—all under the banner of "justice." According to a study from Princeton University, over 500 of these so-called protests involved violence, arson, or destruction of property. In Portland alone, Antifa members and radical activists rioted for over 100 consecutive nights, throwing Molotov cocktails, shining lasers into officers' eyes to blind them, and even attempting to set federal buildings on fire with people inside.

Many of the people involved in these acts were later identified as having prior criminal records, mental health histories, or both. Yet rarely were these individuals flagged for firearm restrictions—in fact, many were released the next day without charges, thanks to soft-on-crime DAs and politically motivated prosecutors. So we have to ask ourselves: If we can't even acknowledge when someone is *actively rioting in public* as a sign of instability or violent intent, how are we supposed to prevent the next tragedy?

And that brings us to the uncomfortable but important question: *But can it go fast enough to stop a tragedy?* The answer? Not usually—and that's the problem. The process to remove firearms from someone who is *truly* dangerous is often so bogged down in red tape, politics, or a fear of being labeled "insensitive" that by the time anything is done, it's too late. In the case of the Parkland shooter, there were dozens of red flags—police visits, threats, disturbing online posts—and yet no meaningful intervention happened in time.

Also, there are often obvious telltale signs of an impending tragedy due to mental illness that go unaddressed, indicating negligence by authorities, parents, peers, or teachers. Mass shooters often exhibit severe, disturbing, or bizarre behaviors prior to their acts of violence, which in hindsight can be seen as telltale signs of their dangerous and unstable mental states. These behaviors frequently include expressions of extreme anger, detailed planning of violent acts, fascination with previous mass shootings, abusing or torturing animals, and clear threats made to peers or authorities.

For example, the Columbine shooters exhibited several alarming behaviors and signs prior to the massacre on April 20, 1999. One of them was known to keep a detailed journal where he documented his hatred towards society and his plans for the attack. He also created violent and disturbing content on his website, including threats against students and teachers at Columbine High School. They both wrote about their depression and anger in personal journals, expressing a deep sense of hopelessness and desire for revenge. Both boys were fascinated by previous acts of violence and had a growing obsession with death and destruction.

Their behaviors included making threats, engaging in violent fantasies, and amassing a significant arsenal of weapons and explosives. They recorded videos, known as the "Basement Tapes," where they spoke openly about their plans, demonstrating their meticulous preparation and intent to cause mass casualties. Despite these glaring warnings, their actions were not sufficiently reported or addressed by authorities in time to prevent the tragedy. At the time, there were no red flag laws in place, or they were only in the earliest stages of implementation in a few states. However, this is not a case where red flag laws would have made a difference. These individuals were minors, still under the custody and supervision of their parents—who, astonishingly, were completely unaware of their children's activities and the elaborate and violent plans being hatched right under their own roofs. This wasn't a legislative failure. It was a *parental* failure. Red flag laws are designed to flag dangerous behavior among legal adults—typically gun owners—not to intervene in households where teenagers are secretly constructing bombs and filming kill lists in the basement. The responsibility to monitor children falls squarely on the shoulders of the parents and, to a lesser extent, the schools and other adults charged with overseeing them. In this case, both sets of parents failed to see or ignored the signs, and the school system—despite complaints, warning signs, and behavioral issues—failed to act decisively. This was not a failure of policy; it was a failure of *awareness, accountability,* and *adult responsibility*.

Other notable mass shooters have exhibited similar alarming behaviors. The Virginia Tech shooter showed signs of severe mental illness long before the 2007 massacre. He was known for his bizarre and threatening behavior, including stalking female students, writing violent and macabre plays, and expressing intense anger and paranoia. He had been previously diagnosed with severe anxiety disorder and was ordered to undergo psychiatric treatment, but he fell through the cracks of the mental health system.

The Sandy Hook Elementary School shooter also exhibited deeply troubling behaviors. He was diagnosed with Asperger's syndrome and had a history of social isolation, extreme anxiety, and obsessive-compulsive behaviors. He developed an obsession with mass shootings and compiled detailed research on previous incidents. His deteriorating mental state, coupled with his fascination with violence, should have been noticed.

These examples highlight the critical importance of recognizing and *acting on* dangerous behaviors exhibited by individuals struggling with mental instability. In many mass shooting incidents, there were clear, documented warning signs long before the first shot was fired: online manifestos, explicit threats, detailed planning, stalking behavior, or a disturbing obsession with previous mass shooters. These are not subtle hints—they are neon signs flashing *DANGER*. And yet time and again, the system shrugs, families look the other way, or worse, society chalks it up to "just venting."

So, what kind of intervention is needed? Let's stop being vague. The most effective form of intervention starts with the people closest to the individual—*family, friends, teachers, co-workers,* and even *neighbors.* These are the folks who see the red flags early, but are often unsure of what to do, or scared to speak up. That has to change. We need to foster a culture where it's not only *acceptable* but *expected* to sound the alarm when someone you care about is spiraling into obsession, rage, or nihilism. That doesn't mean canceling or condemning people for edgy opinions or quirky behavior—it means knowing the difference between a troubled personality and a ticking time bomb.

If your adult son is holed up in his room watching Columbine documentaries on repeat and talking about how "people will remember him someday," that's not the time to worry about offending him. That's the time to intervene. Parents need to stop being afraid of their own kids and start parenting again. This may mean checking their social media, reporting threats, or working with a mental health professional. It might mean temporarily removing them from an environment where they could harm others. If a teenager is writing in detail about how they'd carry out a school attack, that's not therapy material—that's criminal intent.

Law enforcement and school officials also need to be more empowered—and obligated—to act on credible threats. Too often, they're hamstrung by red tape or the fear of political backlash. *We saw something but couldn't do anything* has become a tired refrain. If someone, whether they're a minor or an adult, posts a video saying they're going to shoot up a school or maps out an attack online, that's not protected speech—that's evidence of premeditation.

Community-level programs that allow concerned individuals to report serious warning signs—without automatically invoking a SWAT team or triggering an unconstitutional gun grab—can make a difference. This isn't about throwing people in padded rooms. It's about creating a channel for early intervention, follow-up, and monitoring that doesn't require someone to commit a crime *before* the system acts.

And perhaps most importantly, we need to overhaul how mental health professionals approach threat assessments. It's time to prioritize *risk* over feelings. If a patient exhibits violent ideation, detailed planning, or clear threats against others, confidentiality cannot be a shield. Mandatory reporting laws must be clear, firm, and followed—with legal consequences for willful negligence.

Preventing tragedy doesn't mean stripping rights away from everyone. It means targeting the people *who have already demonstrated*, through words or actions, that they pose a real threat. If we want to respect the Second Amendment—and we should—we also must respect the responsibility that comes with it: to act decisively when someone shows signs that they intend to abuse that right.

This isn't about punishing mental illness. It's about protecting the public from individuals who have crossed the line from disturbed to dangerous—and making sure we're brave enough to call it what it is *before* innocent lives are lost.

## Downplaying Mental Illness

Even though the vast majority of these publicized mass shooters exhibited severe mental illness, various psychological organizations, including the American Psychiatric Association (APA), acknowledge that mental illness can be a factor in mass shootings but claim it is not the predominant cause. APA research indicates that less than one third of mass shooters had a "confirmed diagnosis" of a serious mental illness. However, the term "confirmed diagnosis" is key here. It suggests that many of these individuals likely suffered from undiagnosed or untreated mental health issues. In many cases, these conditions went unnoticed or were ignored, making the statistics presented by the APA somewhat unreliable. A deeper psychological analysis of the vast majority, if not all mass shooters, would likely reveal underlying untreated or mismanaged mental illnesses. The very act of committing such a horrific crime suggests a departure from mental stability. It is difficult to argue that someone who engages in a mass shooting is mentally stable or properly treated. Furthermore, studies that downplay mental illness as the primary factor in mass shootings often conform to the ever-changing definitions of "mass shooting," including gun crimes and murders that don't fit the traditional profile. This approach skews the statistics in an effort to destigmatize most mental illnesses, treating them as a protected class while potentially overlooking the critical role severe mental health issues play in such tragedies.

Tying this into the Second Amendment, it is crucial to recognize that individuals managing mild forms of mental illness, such as depression or anxiety, with medication, should not be automatically denied their Second Amendment rights. Most of these individuals use their medications responsibly and do not pose a threat to society. Denying them the right to own firearms based solely on their mental health treatment would be unjust and discriminatory.

However, there is a case to be made that people with severe mental illness, who exhibit psychotic or dangerous behaviors, should perhaps be subject to more scrutiny, provided that such measures include fair due process under the legal system.

On the flip side, when the government does act quickly, it often acts too broadly and without due process. Enter red flag laws—policies that allow authorities to seize someone's firearms based on suspicion alone, often without a hearing or conviction. While the intention behind these laws is to prevent harm, they are ripe for abuse and lack consistent standards. A bitter ex, an angry neighbor, or a political opponent could potentially use these laws as a weapon, putting innocent gun owners at risk of being disarmed without ever having committed a crime.

That's why any restrictions on the Second Amendment must involve a high bar of proof, clear evidence of violent behavior or threats, and real due process. A psychiatrist's opinion alone shouldn't be enough. One vague comment online shouldn't trigger a SWAT raid. And simply being prescribed medication for anxiety or depression shouldn't disqualify someone from owning a firearm. Liberty means risk—but it also means fairness.

So when it comes to mental illness and gun rights, we need a policy that moves fast *enough* to stop real threats, but not so fast that it steamrolls the innocent. The focus should be on *actions*, not just *conditions*. If someone is attacking cops, lighting cars on fire, or threatening someone's life, we don't need a PhD in psychology to recognize they've disqualified themselves from responsible gun ownership.

## Medicated Madness: The Role of Psychotropic Drugs and Big Pharma in Mass Shootings

The relationship between psychotropic drugs and violent behavior is one of the most overlooked—and perhaps deliberately avoided—angles in the national debate on mass shootings. Whenever tragedy strikes, the mainstream narrative zeroes in on the firearm used, the type of ammunition, or the make and model of the rifle. Cue the talking heads, the emotional appeals, and the same tired calls for more gun control. But almost no one asks the most obvious question: *What medications was the shooter on?*

There is growing evidence suggesting that certain antidepressants, SSRIs (selective serotonin reuptake inhibitors), antipsychotics, and other psychotropic medications may be linked to an increased risk of violent, impulsive, or psychotic behavior in a subset of individuals. While Big Pharma insists that these medications are safe and effective, there is a laundry list of cases where individuals engaged in horrific acts of violence while under the influence of these drugs—often after recently starting them, adjusting their dosage, or discontinuing them abruptly.

Let's talk about some of the patterns. One of the Columbine shooters was on Luvox, an SSRI. The Virginia Tech shooter had a history of mental illness and was reported to be on antidepressants, though exact prescriptions were never fully disclosed. The Aurora theater shooter was reportedly on sertraline (Zoloft) and clonazepam, both psychotropic medications known for potential behavioral side effects. The list goes on. In case after case, we find the same disturbing common denominator: the presence of powerful, mood-altering prescription drugs.

These are not isolated anecdotes. In 2010, a study published in the journal *PLOS ONE* found that 31 of the top 100 drugs most frequently associated with violent behavior included 11 antidepressants, 6 sedative/hypnotics, and 3 drugs for ADHD. In other words, some of the very same medications being handed out like candy are showing up time and time again in connection with unprovoked, unpredictable outbursts of violence.

And let's not kid ourselves—Big Pharma is a multibillion-dollar juggernaut with a vested interest in making sure this angle stays buried. There is little appetite among media outlets (many of which are sponsored by pharmaceutical companies) to investigate or report on these connections. The narrative is easier when it's just about the gun. Guns don't have billion-dollar lobbying firms. Pharmaceutical companies do. The idea that one of these "FDA-approved" drugs could have pushed a person over the edge threatens the entire house of cards.

Here's where things get especially dangerous: Many of these drugs include black-box warnings about suicidal thoughts and tendencies, particularly in young people. But those same neurological effects—mood instability, disassociation, emotional numbing—can just as easily flip outward as inward. Some users report feeling detached from reality, not recognizing their own emotions, or feeling like they're watching their life through a screen. That kind of mental dissociation can be a breeding ground for violent ideation, especially in individuals already dealing with rage, depression, or unresolved trauma.

So what do we do when someone becomes a danger to themselves or others on these medications? We prescribe them more medications. Uppers, downers, tranquilizers, sleeping pills—a toxic cocktail of chemicals that masks symptoms instead of treating causes. We don't ask what happened in their life. We don't offer real support. We just write a prescription and send them on their way.

We have a medicated society that's growing increasingly disconnected, unstable, and numb. Our young people are being raised in a culture that pathologizes every negative feeling and then attempts to chemically suppress it. And when the side effects manifest in violence, the gun becomes the scapegoat. No mention of the prescriptions. No scrutiny of the system that pumped their brain full of SSRIs and benzos. No questions asked.

When we talk about mass shootings, we can't just talk about guns. We must talk about what's going on inside the heads of these individuals. What they've been told. What they've been fed—literally and chemically. And we must shine a spotlight on the pharmaceutical–industrial complex that's become America's unofficial mental health provider. Because if we don't, we'll keep disarming innocent people while ignoring the ticking time bombs our medical system is quietly creating.

***

It's worth pausing here for a moment to address an uncomfortable yet glaringly obvious truth: The hysterical reactions we often see from those who advocate gun control highlight a much larger issue: a deep-seated mental health crisis that has gripped America and much of the West. Scroll through any social media platform after a pro-Second Amendment statement or legal victory, and you'll witness a parade of unhinged outbursts. Screaming diatribes, threats of violence, and all-caps rants accusing gun owners of every imaginable evil are disturbingly common, and they lay bare a troubling reality: There are a lot of unstable people out there. Following Donald Trump's landslide victory in the November 2024 presidential election, many of the same individuals who advocate for restricting gun rights were the ones taking to social media and mainstream outlets to unleash unhinged emotional meltdowns and openly spew violent rhetoric toward the winning side. It's ironic, then, that these same individuals, some who (surprisingly) own guns and (unsurprisingly) post death threats on social media, often champion the idea of mental health screenings for gun ownership. One wonders if they ever stop to consider how their own behavior—issuing death threats, public temper tantrums, violent rhetoric, and emotional volatility—might place them at the top of the list for disqualification. If such screenings were ever seriously implemented (a questionable idea for many reasons), these self-styled anti-gun crusaders would likely face more scrutiny than the law-abiding gun owners they vilify.

This kind of instability also underscores why so many sane, responsible Americans feel the need to own firearms. When unpredictable, emotionally unbalanced individuals are not only walking the streets but actively threatening others online and on television for all to see, the case for self-defense becomes painfully clear. No matter what kind of weapons they own, they remain fully capable of threatening public safety and private property. It's a sobering reminder that the Second Amendment isn't just about the right to bear arms in theory—it's a practical necessity in a world where chaos and unpredictability are increasingly visible.

While this is merely a side note in the larger discussion, it highlights the stark contrast between those who exercise their rights responsibly and those whose actions serve as a reminder of why those rights matter. The mental health crisis in America is real, and addressing it is vital.

However, the intersection of mental health and gun rights is a complex and often manipulated topic—one that gun control advocates routinely mishandle or outright ignore in their efforts to limit the availability of guns to civilians. Instead of addressing the real causes of violence—untreated or improperly treated mental illness, the role of psychotropic medications, parental negligence, and the cultural glorification of rage—they reflexively blame the inanimate object: the gun. Gun control advocates rarely, if ever, offer serious solutions to mental health-related violence beyond generic soundbites and virtue-signaling legislation. Red flag laws, often touted as a common-sense fix, have proven ripe for abuse—allowing individuals to be stripped of their constitutional rights based on accusations, without a crime being committed, without the right to face their accuser, and in many cases, without any real evidence of danger. Worse yet, these laws are inconsistently applied, frequently skipping over actual threats in favor of politically convenient targets.

Meanwhile, the fear of offending certain groups or being accused of profiling has handcuffed law enforcement and educators alike, allowing real warning signs to slip through the cracks under the guise of political correctness. The hard truth is this: If we are going to prevent violence while preserving liberty, we must be honest about where the real problems lie. That means holding parents and schools accountable, questioning the overmedication of our population, and crafting interventions that are targeted, fair, and rooted in due process—not emotion, politics, or fear. Protecting public safety should never come at the expense of punishing the innocent, and defending our rights should never mean ignoring the obvious.

However, until we confront the cultural and systemic factors fueling such instability, the need for law-abiding citizens to protect themselves with firearms will remain more relevant than ever.

# Chapter 13

## Taproot to Grassroots

*The Second Amendment isn't just about hunting or sport shooting—it's about ensuring that the people have the means to defend themselves against any form of oppression. In America, the power lies with the people, and the Second Amendment ensures it stays that way.*

—Rob Ski, AKOU

*Your home is your sanctuary and the people in it are priceless. Don't guard it with your life; guard it with a gun.*

—Colion Noir

A ll across America, the fight to preserve the Second Amendment is carried out not just by individual patriots, but by a vast network of advocates, organizations, and communities—both large and small. From law enforcement officers, veterans, and ranchers in the heartland to online influencers engaging millions of followers, the defense of this fundamental right reflects a shared commitment to liberty, self-reliance, and the principles that define our nation.

Among the loudest voices in this fight are Second Amendment rights groups and organizations that span the spectrum, from household names like the National Rifle Association (NRA) and Gun Owners of America (GOA) to grassroots coalitions and state-level organizations with fiercely dedicated memberships. Each plays a vital role in the fight to safeguard gun rights—lobbying policymakers, educating the public, and rallying their communities to stand firm against encroachments on freedom.

Equally significant are the individuals and smaller, lesser-known groups that amplify the message and ensure it resonates beyond traditional platforms. Guntubers, bloggers, and advocates on social media bring the Second Amendment into living rooms and mobile devices, creating an informed and engaged populace ready to take action. These modern-day champions provide everything from firearm safety education to legal analysis and real-time updates on legislative threats, ensuring that no infringement goes unnoticed.

The strength of this movement lies in its diversity and grassroots nature. It's powered by everyday Americans—mothers, fathers, tradespeople, and professionals—who recognize that the Second Amendment isn't just about firearms; it's about ensuring the balance of power between the government and its citizens. It's about the unshakable belief that liberty must be defended, whether in Congress, on the airwaves, or in the homes and hearts of Americans. The collective efforts of these organizations, their members, and individual advocates work tirelessly to protect our gun rights. By examining the breadth and depth of their contributions, we uncover the unifying spirit of a movement that spans every corner of the nation, reminding us that the fight for the Second Amendment is a fight for the soul of America itself.

Below, we will highlight some of the most influential, informative, and engaging social media platforms created by individuals who are passionate about freedom and the Second Amendment. These talented and driven creators use their channels to educate, entertain, and advocate for gun rights, reaching millions of viewers worldwide. I have personally learned a great deal from their content—everything from responsible gun ownership and self-defense tactics to understanding the legal landscape and staying informed on the latest threats to our Second Amendment rights.

In addition to showcasing these influential voices, this chapter also explores organizations—both large and small—that have been instrumental in defending the Second Amendment. From national advocacy groups shaping policy to grassroots organizations fighting restrictive gun laws at the state level, these efforts collectively play a crucial role in preserving America's gun rights for future generations.

## Colion Noir

Colion Noir, whose real name is Collins Iyare Idehen Jr., is a prominent attorney, Second Amendment advocate, urban gun enthusiast, and influential guntuber known for his articulate and passionate defense of gun rights. With a background in law and a keen understanding of firearms, Colion Noir has carved out a niche in the online world, blending legal expertise with practical gun knowledge. His dynamic approach to advocacy has earned him a massive following, making him one of the most respected voices in the gun rights community.

Colion became a key supporter of gun rights through his work with the National Rifle Association (NRA). As a featured commentator and host for NRA TV, Noir brought a fresh and dynamic voice to the organization's media efforts. He produced and starred in numerous videos and series, providing insightful commentary on gun rights, firearm laws, and the cultural significance of the Second Amendment. His presentations helped to engage a younger and more diverse audience, expanding the reach of the NRA's message. Through his work with the NRA, Noir became a key figure in the gun rights movement, using his platform to advocate for responsible gun ownership and to challenge misconceptions about firearms and gun owners.

Noir's YouTube channel, which boasts over three million subscribers, is a treasure trove of content covering a wide range of topics related to firearms and the Second Amendment. His videos feature thorough reviews of the latest guns and gear, insightful commentary on gun laws and legislation, and engaging discussions about the cultural and societal aspects of gun ownership. You can easily find his YouTube channel at https://www.youtube.com/MrColionNoir.

In addition to his YouTube presence, Colion Noir maintains a comprehensive website, https://www.mrcolionnoir.com, where he shares articles, videos, and updates on Second Amendment issues. His advocacy extends beyond digital platforms, as he frequently participates in speaking engagements and collaborates with other prominent figures in the gun rights movement.

Through his informative and thought-provoking content, Colion Noir continues to educate, inspire, and mobilize a growing community of gun owners and advocates. Noir's ability to connect with a diverse audience and his unwavering commitment to defending the right to bear arms have made him a vital resource in the ongoing fight for Second Amendment freedoms. Noir provides a wealth of information and advocacy resources, making him a pivotal figure in the gun rights community.

## Demolition Ranch

Demolition Ranch is a wildly popular YouTube channel created and hosted by Matt Carriker, a veterinarian by profession and a firearms enthusiast at heart. With nearly 12 million followers, the channel became a staple for gun lovers and those who enjoy high-energy, entertaining content centered around firearms. Matt's charismatic personality and innovative approach to creating engaging videos made Demolition Ranch a go-to source for both fun and educational content in the gun community.

The channel features a wide array of content, primarily focusing on testing and showcasing different firearms, ammunition, and related gear. One of the hallmarks of Demolition Ranch is Matt's creative and often humorous approach to firearms demonstrations. He frequently conducts entertaining and unconventional experiments, pushing the limits of what various guns and ammo can do. For example, the popular "Will It Stop a Bullet?" series tests the bullet-stopping capabilities of everyday items, from household appliances to bizarre objects like stacks of paper or watermelons, with surprising results that highlight the power of different firearms.

In his videos, Matt also compared different types of guns, from handguns and rifles to shotguns and exotic firearms, offering viewers a detailed look at the performance, accuracy, and overall capabilities of each weapon. True to the channel's name, many videos involved blowing things up. Whether testing the explosive power of certain ammunition or setting up elaborate targets that detonate on impact, these videos were a hit with viewers who enjoy a bit of pyrotechnics. Additionally, Matt sometimes collaborated with other popular guntubers, gunsmiths, and other experts to create custom firearms or modify existing ones, delving into the process of enhancing and personalizing guns.

Demolition Ranch can be found on YouTube at https://www.youtube.com/ @DemolitionRanch. Although Matt Carriker announced he would be stepping away from creating new Demolition Ranch content, citing to personal reasons, stricter YouTube policies on gun content, shadow banning, and a decline in viewership, his videos remain available and continue to be relevant and valuable to firearm enthusiasts today. However, be sure to check back for new content—videos continued to be uploaded even after he officially announced his retirement from the channel.

## Kentucky Ballistics

One of my favorite YouTube gun channels, Kentucky Ballistics, hosted by Scott DeShields Jr., is another immensely popular YouTube channel in the firearms community. With over five million subscribers, Scott's channel stands out for its engaging and often thrilling content that explores the capabilities of various firearms and ammunition in creative and entertaining ways. With a growing number of followers, Kentucky Ballistics has become a favorite destination for gun enthusiasts who appreciate a mix of education, fun, and high-octane action.

Scott's videos often feature extreme tests and experiments that push firearms and ammunition to their limits. One of the channel's popular series involves testing the power of different calibers against a variety of targets. For example, in the video ".50 BMG vs. Body Armor," Scott tests the legendary .50 BMG round against multiple layers of body armor, showcasing the impressive power and penetration capabilities of this massive cartridge. These tests provide viewers with a visual and practical understanding of the performance differences between various calibers and types of ammunition.

Another notable video, "World's Largest Handgun vs. Ballistic Gel," features Scott firing an enormous revolver, the Magnum Research BFR, chambered in .45-70 Government. This video is both educational and entertaining, as Scott demonstrates the devastating impact of the powerful handgun round on ballistic gel, a substance used to simulate human tissue. The dramatic visual effects and

Scott's informative commentary make it a standout piece of content on his channel.

In addition to extreme tests, Scott often engages in more lighthearted and fun experiments. Videos like "Shooting a Steel Target at 200 Yards with a Slingshot" and "Shooting Giant Jawbreakers with a .500 Magnum" highlight the playful side of Kentucky Ballistics. These videos mix humor with impressive marksmanship and creative target choices, offering viewers a unique blend of entertainment and skill demonstration.

Scott also provides detailed reviews and comparisons of various firearms and accessories, helping his audience make informed decisions about their purchases. His approachable and down-to-earth style makes complex information accessible, ensuring that both novice and experienced gun owners can benefit from his insights.

Kentucky Ballistics can be found on YouTube at https://www.youtube .com/@KentuckyBallistics. Through his dynamic and entertaining content, Scott has established himself as a beloved figure in the firearms community, continually drawing in viewers with his unique blend of education, fun, and explosive action.

## Hickock45

Hickok45 is a legendary YouTube channel in the firearms community, boasting nearly eight million followers. Hosted by Greg Kinman, a retired middle school English teacher and former law enforcement officer, Hickok45 has become a cornerstone for gun enthusiasts seeking detailed reviews, historical insights, and engaging shooting demonstrations. Greg's calm demeanor, deep voice, and extensive knowledge make his videos both entertaining and educational.

One of the most distinctive features of the Hickok45 channel is its relaxed and informal style. Filmed on a picturesque shooting range nestled in the Tennessee woods, the videos often feel like a casual yet informative conversation with a knowledgeable friend. Greg, along with his son John, who assists with filming and occasionally co-hosts, covers a wide range of topics, from modern firearms to historical weapons, always providing thorough and honest reviews.

Hickok45's content includes a variety of shooting demonstrations where Greg tests the accuracy, reliability, and handling of different firearms. Whether he's shooting pistols, rifles, or shotguns, his skill and expertise are evident as he takes aim at a diverse array of targets, including steel plates, soda bottles, and various other reactive targets that add an element of fun to his videos.

In addition to reviews and shooting demonstrations, the channel offers educational content on firearm safety, maintenance, and the history of various guns. Greg's background as an educator shine through in these segments, as he breaks down complex information into easily understandable lessons that appeal to both novice shooters and experienced gun owners.

Another popular feature of Hickok45 is the "Shooting the Breeze" series, where Greg discusses current events, gun culture, and personal anecdotes in a more laid-back format. These videos provide viewers with a deeper connection to Greg and his perspectives on various topics, further enriching the channel's content.

Through his engaging and informative videos, Greg Kinman has built a massive following and continues to be a trusted and beloved figure in the firearms community. His commitment to providing high-quality content and fostering a respectful and informed approach to gun ownership makes Hickok45 a must-watch for anyone interested in firearms. Hickok45 can be found at https://www.youtube.com/@hickok45.

## Brandon Herrera

Brandon Herrera, better known as "The AK Guy," has taken the YouTube firearms community by storm with his charismatic presence and deep knowledge of guns, especially the AK-47 platform. His channel, simply named Brandon Herrera, is a treasure trove for gun enthusiasts, combining technical expertise, humor, and a healthy dose of personality. With a subscriber base of nearly four million, Herrera's content is both highly educational and thoroughly entertaining, making him one of the most influential figures in the gun rights community today.

Brandon's passion for the AK-47 is evident in every video. From detailed tutorials on building and modifying AK rifles to historical deep dives into the weapon's origins, his channel covers it all. His "Gun Meme Review" series has become particularly popular, where he hilariously critiques internet memes about firearms, blending comedy with insightful commentary on gun culture and politics. These videos not only entertain but also educate viewers on the intricacies and ongoing debates surrounding firearm ownership and use.

Beyond YouTube, Brandon made headlines in 2024 with his primary run for Texas's 23rd District Congress seat. His campaign was driven by a strong commitment to defending Second Amendment rights and addressing the concerns of gun owners across the state. While his bid was marked by the same straightforward and unapologetic style that defines his online presence, it also showcased his serious dedication to political activism and the protection of individual liberties.

Brandon's impact extends beyond his own channel; he frequently collaborates with other prominent figures in the firearms community, expanding his reach and influence. His work with companies and appearances at industry events further cement his status as a key player in the world of gun advocacy.

Whether he's disassembling an AK-47, sharing a laugh over gun memes, or discussing serious political issues, Brandon Herrera's content remains fresh and engaging. His YouTube channel, https://www.youtube.com/@BrandonHerrera, continues to grow, bringing in new viewers who appreciate his unique blend of expertise and entertainment. As he balances his roles as a content creator and political activist, Brandon Herrera remains a powerful voice for the Second Amendment and a beloved figure in the firearms community.

## Awaken with JP

Awaken with JP is a widely recognized YouTube channel hosted by JP Sears, a comedian and life coach known for his satirical and insightful commentary on a variety of social and political issues. While not exclusively a gun channel, JP is one of the leading voices on YouTube promoting and championing freedom, truth, and constitutional rights, including the Second Amendment.

JP Sears has built a substantial following of over three million followers through his unique blend of humor and thought-provoking content. His videos often tackle controversial topics with a mix of satire and sincerity, providing a refreshing perspective that resonates with viewers seeking honest and unfiltered discussions. Through his comedic lens, JP addresses issues such as government overreach, censorship, and the importance of individual liberties.

A notable aspect of JP's content is his staunch defense of the Second Amendment. He frequently discusses the importance of the right to bear arms as a fundamental pillar of American freedom. JP emphasizes that the ability to defend oneself and resist tyranny is crucial to maintaining a free society. His videos often highlight the absurdities and contradictions in arguments against gun ownership, using humor to underscore the seriousness of the issue.

In his video "Why Guns Must Be Banned Now," JP employs his trademark humor to mock the extreme arguments made by gun control advocates. Through exaggerated and ironic statements, he exposes the logical flaws and emotional rhetoric often used in the anti-gun debate. This video not only entertains but also encourages viewers to critically assess the arguments surrounding gun control.

Another impactful video, "Why I Was Wrong About Guns," showcases JP's ability to blend personal reflection with advocacy. In this video, he shares his own journey from being skeptical about gun rights to becoming a strong supporter of the Second Amendment. By openly discussing his change of heart, JP provides a relatable narrative that resonates with viewers who may be on a similar path. His transparency and authenticity in addressing his evolving views make the video both compelling and persuasive.

In addition to his YouTube channel, JP engages with his audience through live events, social media, and his website, https://awakenwithjp.com where he offers additional content and merchandise. His ability to connect with viewers on a personal level and inspire them to advocate for their rights has made Awaken with JP a powerful platform for promoting freedom and truth.

Awaken with JP can be found on YouTube at https://www.youtube.com/@AwakenWithJP. Through his entertaining and thought-provoking videos, JP Sears continues to champion the values of freedom, individual rights, and the importance of the Second Amendment. His unique blend of comedy and advocacy makes him a compelling voice in the ongoing conversation about preserving liberty in America.

## Tom Grieve

Tom Grieve is a renowned gun rights attorney with a deep passion for protecting gun rights who has become a respected figure among firearm enthusiasts and constitutional advocates alike. As a founding partner of Grieve Law, a criminal defense firm based in Wisconsin, he has dedicated his career to defending the rights of gun owners and ensuring that the Second Amendment is upheld in the face of legal challenges.

Grieve's expertise extends beyond the courtroom, as he is also a prolific content creator. Through his YouTube channel, Tom Grieve, and other social media platforms, Grieve educates his audience on a variety of legal issues related to gun ownership, self-defense, and firearm laws. His videos break down complex legal concepts into easily understandable segments, providing valuable information to both novice gun owners and seasoned enthusiasts.

In addition to his online presence, Tom Grieve is a sought-after speaker and commentator on gun rights issues. He frequently participates in seminars, workshops, and media appearances, sharing his insights on the importance of the Second Amendment and the legal challenges that gun owners face.

Tom Grieve's law firm website can be found at https://www.grievelaw .com. This site provides information about his legal services, insights into gun laws, and resources for gun owners. Through this platform, Grieve continues to educate and support individuals in navigating the complexities of firearm-related legal issues. His dedication to education and advocacy has earned him a loyal following and a reputation as a leading voice in the gun rights community.

## Heavy Duty Country

Heavy Duty Country is a popular YouTube channel hosted by Dan Swick, a passionate advocate for the Second Amendment and rural American culture. Dan's channel has garnered over 750,000 followers through his straightforward and no-nonsense approach to discussing firearms, gun rights, self-defense, and the everyday challenges and rewards of country living.

Dan's videos cover a wide range of topics, including honest reviews of guns and gear, practical tips for self-reliance, and in-depth discussions on the importance of preserving Second Amendment rights. His content often includes hands-on demonstrations and real-world applications, making it both educational and engaging for his audience.

In addition to focusing on firearms, Dan frequently addresses current events and political issues that impact the rights and freedoms of Americans. He isn't afraid to voice his opinions on controversial topics, and his candid style resonates with viewers who appreciate his authenticity and dedication to speaking the truth as he sees it. A recurring theme in many of Dan's videos is his reporting on the abuses of the Bureau of Alcohol, Tobacco, Firearms and Explosives (ATF). For example, Dan has highlighted instances where the ATF has aggressively pursued gun owners and small firearms businesses over minor technicalities, often leading to devastating consequences for those targeted. One such video details a case where the ATF conducted a raid on a family-owned gun shop, allegedly over paperwork errors, resulting in significant financial and emotional stress for the owners.

## Yoki Stirrup

Yoki Stirrup, who I brand as the "most armed woman in America," is quickly becoming a powerhouse in the firearms community, bringing a unique blend of passion, expertise, and authenticity to her growing audience. Known for her engaging presence and relatable content, Yoki has carved out a niche on YouTube, where she shares her love for guns and the Second Amendment with viewers from all walks of life.

What sets Yoki apart is her deep appreciation for the AK rifle platform. Self-professed as the "AK-Queen," her videos often feature this iconic firearm, showcasing her extensive knowledge and hands-on experience. Whether she's breaking down the intricacies of the AK-47, offering maintenance tips, or demonstrating its capabilities on the range, Yoki's content is both informative and captivating. Her enthusiasm for these rifles resonates strongly with viewers, many of whom share her admiration for this robust and reliable weapon.

Yoki's firearms collection is nothing short of impressive. With hundreds of guns spanning various makes and models, her videos provide a comprehensive look at the world of firearms. From handguns to rifles to shotguns, Yoki offers detailed reviews and comparisons, helping her audience make informed decisions about their own firearms purchases. Her extensive arsenal not only highlights her dedication to the craft but also provides a rich source of content that keeps viewers coming back for more.

A significant aspect of Yoki's channel is her frequent trips to the shooting range, where she provides live gun reviews and demonstrations. These range sessions offer viewers a firsthand look at how different firearms perform in real-world conditions. Her husband, who acts as the cameraman, captures these moments with precision, ensuring that the audience gets an immersive and detailed view of each firearm in action. This dynamic duo's teamwork adds a personal touch to the videos, making the content even more engaging.

Yoki's YouTube channel, boasting over 1.5 million followers, can be found at https://www.youtube.com/@YokiSturrup305, where her videos continue to inspire and educate a diverse audience. Her commitment to promoting responsible gun ownership and her ability to connect with viewers on a personal level make her a standout figure in the firearms community. As she breaks down barriers and challenges stereotypes, Yoki Stirrup remains a powerful advocate for the Second Amendment and a beloved presence in the world of firearms.

## Valor Ridge

Valor Ridge is a renowned tactical firearms training facility in the picturesque hills of Tennessee. Founded and hosted by Reid Henrichs, a former Marine Corps Infantryman and Army sniper, Valor Ridge offers a comprehensive training experience designed to enhance the skills and confidence of gun owners of all levels. Reid brings his extensive military background and a deep passion for the Second Amendment to his teaching, making Valor Ridge a premier destination for those seeking to improve their proficiency with firearms.

The Valor Ridge YouTube channel, also hosted by Reid Henrichs, is an extension of the facility's training philosophy and serves as a valuable resource for firearms enthusiasts. The channel features a variety of content aimed at educating viewers on shooting techniques, tactical skills, firearms safety, and the principles of self-defense. Reid's approach is thorough and methodical, ensuring that viewers gain a clear understanding of each topic covered.

In addition to instructional videos, the Valor Ridge YouTube channel frequently posts content related to the philosophy and mindset necessary for effective self-defense. Reid discusses the importance of situational awareness, mental preparation, and the ethical considerations of using force in defensive situations. These discussions provide a holistic view of what it means to be a responsible and prepared gun owner.

Reid also uses the channel to address current events and legislative issues affecting the Second Amendment. His informed and passionate commentary helps viewers stay up to date with the latest developments in gun laws and rights. By blending practical training with philosophical insights and current affairs, Valor Ridge offers a well-rounded and engaging viewing experience.

The Valor Ridge website can be found at https://valorridge.com, and the YouTube channel can be found by a simple search. Through his informative and thought-provoking content, Reid Henrichs continues to educate and inspire a growing community of responsible gun owners dedicated to mastering their skills and understanding the broader implications of firearm ownership.

## American Gun Chic

Brickell Clark, known to her fans as American Gun Chic, has become a standout figure in the firearms community. With a blend of enthusiasm, expertise, and a touch of fun, Brickell has made a lasting impact on the world of guntubers, appealing to a broad audience with her engaging content and genuine passion for firearms.

Brickell's journey into the firearms world is both inspiring and relatable. She didn't just stumble into this field; she embraced it with a commitment to learning and sharing her experiences. Her channel is a dynamic mix of in-depth gun reviews, training sessions, and personal insights, all presented with a keen eye for detail and a genuine enthusiasm that draws viewers in.

One of the highlights of American Gun Chic's content is her dedication to firearm education and safety. Brickell takes her viewers along as she participates in various training programs, emphasizing the importance of proper technique and responsible gun ownership. Her videos often showcase her progress and learning experiences, making her channel a valuable resource for both novice shooters and seasoned firearms enthusiasts.

Brickell's focus on empowering women in the shooting sports is particularly noteworthy. Through her "Girls Just Wanna Have Guns" series, she highlights female shooters from diverse backgrounds, celebrating their achievements and encouraging more women to get involved in the firearms community. This series not only provides practical shooting advice but also fosters a supportive environment for women to learn and grow.

Her content isn't just informative; it's also engaging and entertaining, whether she's conducting a high-octane shooting drill, reviewing the latest gear, or sharing a humorous anecdote from her time at the range. Brickell shares her deer hunting adventures, offering viewers insights into preparation, skill, and technique. Her content highlights her versatility and deep knowledge of firearms and the outdoors. This blend of professionalism and personality makes her channel both enjoyable and educational.

Brickell extends her influence beyond YouTube. Through her website and social media platforms, she connects with her audience on a deeper level, offering exclusive content, merchandise, and training programs. This multifaceted approach helps foster a vibrant community of fans who share her passion for firearms and personal defense. American Gun Chic's YouTube channel can be found at https://www.youtube.com/@AmericanGunChic.

## Classic Firearms

Classic Firearms is a popular YouTube channel dedicated to firearms enthusiasts and collectors. The channel is hosted by Clint Morgan, who is known for his engaging and informative presentation style. Classic Firearms covers a wide range of topics related to firearms, including reviews of various guns, ammunition, and accessories, as well as in-depth looks at both historical pieces and modern-day firearms. It also provides educational content on firearm safety, maintenance, and shooting techniques. Clint Morgan, along with occasional guest hosts, brings a wealth of knowledge and enthusiasm to the channel, making it a favorite among gun enthusiasts.

Classic Firearms came about as an extension of Classic Firearms, a retail business specializing in firearms, ammunition, and related accessories. Their goal was to create an online presence that could reach a wider audience and provide valuable content to both novice and experienced gun owners. Over time, the channel's high-quality videos and engaging content helped it grow in popularity.

Classic Firearms' YouTube channel can be found at https://www.youtube.com/@ClassicFirearms. Today, Classic Firearms has over 1.6 million subscribers, a testament to its strong following and the value it provides to the firearms community. The channel's success is also supported by their retail website, https://www.classicfirearms.com, where viewers can browse and purchase a wide variety of firearms and accessories featured on the channel. The combination of informative content and a robust online store has solidified Classic Firearms' reputation as a trusted source for firearms information and products.

***

While YouTube and social media have played a crucial role in promoting the Second Amendment, providing education, training, and firearm reviews to millions, these platforms can sometimes create a sense of distance between influencers and their audiences. Watching videos and reading posts is informative, but it doesn't always capture the full depth of the people behind the content—their motivations, experiences, and personal connections to gun rights. To bridge that gap, I spoke directly with a few Second Amendment advocates, firearms trainers, and reviewers who have built business or successful platforms. Through these conversations, I aimed to humanize the voices of gun rights advocacy, exploring not just their work but the personal stories that fuel their passion for the right to keep and bear arms.

## AK Operators Union, Local 47-74

Rob Ski, the owner and operator of AK Operators Union, is a leading figure in the firearms community and a strong advocate for the Second Amendment. His life story embodies the American dream—one built on determination, resilience, and an unwavering belief in freedom.

Rob was born and raised in Poland. "In Poland, we lived under the shadow of communism," Rob has often said. "The government controlled every aspect of our lives, and the people had no means to resist." His early fascination with firearms, particularly the AK rifle, took root in childhood and deepened through his military service in Poland, where he honed his skills and developed a firm understanding of the importance of being armed. "The military taught me discipline, tactical skills, and the vital role of being armed in protecting one's freedoms," Rob reflects. "I was exposed to AK rifles at a very early age. AKs were always around me. I even remember when I was seven years old, my grandfather gave me a beautiful AK toy rifle." Rob recalls. "This left a mark on my soul for the rest of my life. And after I finished my military service in Poland, I wanted to own my very own AK."

After the fall of communism, Rob seized the opportunity to immigrate to the United States, eager to escape government overreach and experience true freedom. The stark contrast between life in Poland and America was immediately clear. Here, citizens had the right to own firearms and defend themselves. "After [the] fall of communism, Poland was quickly integrating with the Western world. At that time, because of my family, I was presented with an offer to immigrate to the USA. I didn't hesitate for a minute." His newfound liberty cemented his passion for the Second Amendment, which he saw not as a privilege but as a safeguard against oppression. "When I first came to America, I was amazed at the freedom and opportunities available," he shared. "It was a stark contrast to what I had experienced in Poland. Here, people had the right to own firearms and defend themselves. It was liberating."

Determined to give back to his new country, Rob joined the US Army, serving as an Infantryman and paratrooper. His time in the military reinforced his belief that an armed citizenry is essential to maintaining freedom. He also became a firm believer in personal responsibility, stressing that individuals, not the government, are ultimately responsible for their own safety. "Serving in the US military reinforced my belief in the importance of the Second Amendment," Rob explains. "It's what keeps us free. It's a fundamental part of what makes America great." He continues, "I don't think you can really trust the government to protect you 24/7. You must be responsible for your own safety and the safety of your family."

Rob's deep immersion in American gun culture led to the creation of AK Operators Union, an organization dedicated to educating and advocating for responsible firearm ownership, focusing specifically on the AK rifle platform. Through his YouTube channel and social media platforms, he provides detailed firearm reviews, instructional videos, and survival training, amassing over 350,000 subscribers. The Union serves as both an educational resource and a strong voice for Second Amendment advocacy, warning against the creeping influence of gun control measures. Drawing from his personal experiences and the history of firearm restrictions in Eastern Europe, he consistently emphasizes that the erosion of gun rights happens gradually—and that vigilance is necessary to prevent it.

Rob's stance on the Second Amendment is uncompromising: Every law-abiding citizen should have access to the same firearms as the government. His story serves as a powerful reminder of the value of freedom and the importance of protecting individual rights. Rob Ski is not only an excellent source of information on the AK platform, but also a living example of the dangers of socialism and communism—having lived through it firsthand—making his perspective invaluable to anyone naïve enough to believe socialism would be a good idea for America. Through AK Operators Union, he continues to educate, advocate, and inspire a growing community of responsible gun owners. As he often says, "In America, the power lies with the people, and the Second Amendment ensures it stays that way."

Those interested in learning more or following Rob Ski's work can visit the AK Operators Union website at https://www.akoperatorsunionlocal4774.com or check out his videos on YouTube at https://www.youtube.com/@AkOperatorsUnion. Through these platforms, Rob Ski continues to educate, advocate, and inspire a growing community of responsible gun owners dedicated to preserving their constitutional rights.

## Apex Security Consultants

Ryan Sloan, a veteran and firearms trainer (and a friend of mine), has a deep-rooted connection to guns that began in his early childhood. Growing up in a household where firearms were ever-present, he learned basic gun safety from his father at a young age. "We always had guns in the house. My father taught me basic gun safety at a very young age. I bought my first gun at 18 and applied for my pistol permit the day I turned 21, so you could say the interest was always there," Ryan recalled, emphasizing his lifelong passion for firearms. Before joining the US Army in 2017, he already owned several guns, including an AR-15, which proved beneficial when he enlisted.

As an infantryman, Ryan's military service from 2017 to 2021 honed his marksmanship and deepened his appreciation for the Second Amendment. He explained his views:

> *From a veteran's perspective, I firmly believe in the right to bear arms. Not only do I support this right, but I also believe we should all have equal gun rights. My experience, training, or background should not grant me more rights than you. We are all Americans and should have equal access.*

Ryan's stance is clear: The right to bear arms should not be contingent on one's background or training. He highlighted the disparity in firearm access between law enforcement and ordinary citizens, including veterans, in states like New York: "In New York, law enforcement officers have greater access to firearms, even when off duty, than the average citizen, including veterans and those who have served. In my view, all citizens should have equal access."

Ryan's views on the Second Amendment are shaped by his interactions with fellow service members. When asked if military personnel universally advocate for gun rights and the Second Amendment or if opinions are mixed, he responded:

"There are many different roles in the military, so opinions can vary depending on who you ask and what their job was. However, in my field, the overwhelming majority strongly support the Second Amendment. I believe this sentiment is likely true for other fields as well."

After his military service, Ryan founded Apex Security Consultants LLC, initially aiming to provide security consulting. He described the origin and evolution of his company:

> *When I started this business, the initial goal was to provide security consulting. I aimed to help individuals and businesses identify security flaws to make themselves and their families safer. However, people tend to be more reactive than proactive, so that aspect wasn't very successful. While setting up that part of the business, I thought, 'Why not help people learn to shoot?' Now, I teach people how to shoot and have helped many people both in and out of the Army. I love guns and embrace the learning and teaching aspects, especially as I am currently a full-time teacher at West Point.*

Navigating New York's stringent gun laws has been a challenge for Ryan:

> *Navigating the rules has always been challenging and continues to be. They change frequently, and we must stay informed. No one informs us directly, so we often find out the same way you do. Regardless, it's crucial for us to learn quickly so we can pass the information along to people as soon as possible.*

Despite these hurdles, he emphasizes the importance of personal responsibility in gun ownership:

> *Believe it or not, I am not in favor of the new rules or longer classes. In my class, we discuss rights versus responsibilities. Do I believe you should have the right to own a gun without mandatory training?*

*Yes. But is it your responsibility to seek further training? Absolutely. Guns are the only things Americans buy and instantly believe they are proficient with. They purchase a shotgun or rifle and assume their family and home are safe because they own a gun. Possession does not equal proficiency. You wouldn't buy a guitar and expect to play for Nirvana or buy running shoes and sign up for the New York City Marathon without training. Unfortunately, this unrealistic expectation is often applied to guns.*

Ryan is skeptical about the future of the Second Amendment, noting the continuous battle against the "disarmament regime." When asked if he felt gun laws will become more pro-Second Amendment or see more restrictions in the future, he responded:

*Unfortunately, I believe we will face a continuous battle with those pushing for disarmament. They will always try to take what is ours and attempt to justify it in different ways. A major issue is that politicians can enact extremely unconstitutional laws with the stroke of a pen, which then take effect overnight, as we saw with the SAFE Act. The real challenge comes when we try to fight these laws—it takes years and millions of dollars. As taxpayers, we end up funding both sides through taxes and contributions to organizations like the NRA, GOA, and FPC. While I think we will see a few significant victories, like the* Bruen *case, politicians will likely respond by enacting similar unconstitutional and vengeful laws, just as they did with the CCIA in response to* Bruen.

His advice to those uncertain about guns or the Second Amendment is straightforward:

*One piece of advice I'd give is to simply give it a shot—pun intended. But don't just pick up a gun with a friend or relative. Set yourself up for success with a reputable company such as mine. Try it out, listen to our stories about why we carry, hear what we have experienced and seen, and experience firearms in a safe, controlled environment.*

Ryan Sloan's journey from a childhood surrounded by guns, through military service, to becoming a firearms instructor, illustrates a deep-seated belief in the Second Amendment. His story highlights the importance of education, responsibility, and equal access to firearms for all Americans. To sign up for one of his training courses, visit Apex Security Consultants at https://www.apexsecurityc onsultants.com.

## Double Eagle Brass

Mark H. Smith, hailing from Louisville, Nebraska, is a passionate Second Amendment advocate who owns and operates Double Eagle Brass, a reputable gun store and custom rifle builder known for its high-quality custom firearms. Mark has a lifelong connection to firearms that began in his childhood in Fullerton and Dana Point, California. Growing up, Mark was deeply influenced by his father, who was passionate about guns. Reflecting on those early years, Mark recalls, "My father was into guns all his life. I was exposed all my life, starting as a toddler." His father's preference for bolt-action rifles over pistols set the tone for Mark's early experiences with firearms. As a true gunsmith, his father built rifles from scratch for customers and was a pioneer in glass-bedding techniques. Mark spent countless hours at the range, hunted small game, and absorbing the skills and values that would shape his future.

Mark's exposure to firearms through his father laid a solid foundation for his views on the Second Amendment, but his journey into the world of custom firearms began somewhat unexpectedly. Originally, Mark started a business focused on brass processing, but when that venture struggled, he decided to pivot and become a Federal Firearms Licensee (FFL), expanding into building AR-15s. "Building ARs is simple," Mark explains, adding that once you grasp a few basics, the process becomes straightforward. He credits the internet, particularly YouTube, as offering valuable resources in mastering these skills.

Mark has been running his gun shop for about eight years, but he candidly admits that the business has not been as successful as he had hoped. "I wish I'd never opened the brass business and gun business," he reflects, acknowledging that his challenges in marketing have hindered the shop's success. "I'd be way ahead financially if I'd just stayed with construction," he adds.

Mark Smith's exceptional craftsmanship and dedication to quality in his custom firearms are evident in the two custom rifles he built for me. Each rifle stands as a testament to his skill and passion for firearms. The first rifle, an AR-10 chambered in .308 Winchester, is a masterpiece of precision engineering. "Every detail in this AR-10 was meticulously crafted," Mark explained. "From the match-grade barrel to the high-performance trigger, everything is designed for accuracy and reliability." This rifle is not only a powerful tool for long-range shooting but also a work of art, with a sleek, customized finish and top-tier components that ensure optimal performance.

The second firearm, a custom replica version of the "Honey Badger" AR-style pistol that Mark named "Corn Husker" chambered in 5.56 NATO, showcases Mark's innovative approach to firearm design. "The Corn Husker was built for versatility and compactness without sacrificing performance," he said. This custom AR-style pistol features a unique, integrated suppressor and a pistol brace that can be used to shoulder the pistol, making it perfect for both tactical applications and recreational shooting. The attention to detail and quality craftsmanship makes this firearm stand out, with a smooth action and impeccable balance.

Mark's dedication to producing high-quality firearms is evident in every aspect of these rifles. "I want every firearm that leaves my shop to be something the owner can rely on and be proud of," he shared. The AR-10 and Corn Husker are not just tools for shooting; they are embodiments of Mark's commitment to excellence and the Second Amendment. Each rifle, built to the highest standard, reflects his belief that owning a firearm is a fundamental right and a deeply personal experience.

When it comes to the Second Amendment, Mark's views are clear and uncompromising. "The Second Amendment guarantees us the right to bear arms. Period," he states firmly. He believes that there should be no restrictions on any type of weapon, whether it's a machine gun, grenade launcher, or even a tank.

However, Mark also recognizes the complexity of the issue, particularly when it comes to individuals who may pose a danger to themselves or others. "For me, the big question here is who should decide if a person is fit to own weapons? Certainly not the government, as they are corrupt and will take weapons away from political opponents. But then who?" This question underscores the tension between the need for safety and the protection of individual rights, a balance that Mark grapples with.

Looking to the future, Mark sees the nation at a crossroads regarding gun rights. He observes two distinct factions: those who want to preserve gun ownership and those who want to restrict it. "Neither side will budge," he notes, acknowledging the deep divisions in the country. Despite this, Mark is optimistic about the direction in which the country is heading concerning gun rights. He points out that many states have passed more favorable gun laws and that the Supreme Court has upheld these laws. "As a whole, I think we're becoming more pro-gun," Mark concludes, seeing a trend towards greater protection of Second Amendment rights nationwide.

Through his experiences and reflections, Mark Smith provides a compelling perspective on the importance of the Second Amendment, the challenges of running a gun-related business, and the ongoing battle over gun rights in America. His story is one of deep-rooted beliefs shaped by a lifetime of exposure to firearms, a commitment to individual liberty, and a clear-eyed view of the challenges that lie ahead

Mark Smith has indicated that he is retiring from Double Eagle Brass soon to enjoy the rest of his days shooting, hunting, and spending time with family. However, his story and contributions to my Second Amendment journey (and firearms collection) will always be appreciated.

***

While individual YouTubers and social media influencers have been instrumental in spreading awareness and education about the Second Amendment, they are just one part of the broader gun rights movement. Beyond these independent voices, larger organizations—both national and statewide—play a critical role in shaping policy, challenging restrictive gun laws, and mobilizing grassroots activism. These organizations provide legal support, political advocacy, and educational outreach, ensuring that the fight to preserve gun rights extends beyond online platforms and into the courts, legislatures, and local communities. Understanding their influence is essential to seeing the full scope of Second Amendment advocacy and the collective effort to protect firearm freedoms across the country.

## The National Rifle Association

The National Rifle Association (NRA) has a long and storied history as an organization dedicated to the protection and promotion of gun rights and responsible gun use in the United States. Founded in 1871 by Union veterans Colonel William C. Church and General George Wingate, the NRA was initially established to improve marksmanship among American citizens. Recognizing the poor shooting skills of many soldiers during the Civil War, the NRA's founders aimed to create an organization that would provide training and education in the safe and effective use of firearms.

The NRA has a commendable yet often overlooked history as one of the earliest civil rights organizations in the United States. After the Civil War, in a time when African Americans faced pervasive threats from terror groups such as the Ku Klux Klan (KKK), the ability to defend themselves and their families became paramount. The NRA provided essential support and training, helping these individuals embrace their newfound freedom and protect themselves from violent intimidation and persecution. This early commitment to civil rights highlights the NRA's broader mission to ensure that all Americans, regardless of race, have the means to defend their lives and liberties.

Over time, the NRA's mission expanded to include the defense of the Second Amendment rights of all Americans. As the leading organization advocating gun rights, the NRA has played a crucial role in shaping public policy and protecting the rights of gun owners. The NRA has consistently informed the public about the ever-changing gun rights landscape across the country, providing resources and support for responsible gun ownership and self-defense.

Despite its positive impact, the NRA has faced relentless demonization from the media and political classes. Critics often portray the organization as extremist and out of touch with mainstream America. However, these characterizations are unfounded. The average NRA member is much more law-abiding than the average citizen, and there has never been a mass shooter who was a member of the NRA. The organization's diverse membership includes individuals from all walks of life, united by their commitment to preserving the right to bear arms.

One of the most pervasive myths about the NRA is that it is solely responsible for the gun violence in America. This narrative ignores the complex social, economic, and cultural factors that contribute to crime and violence. The NRA promotes responsible gun ownership and has long been involved in firearms safety education, hunter education, and training programs for law enforcement and civilians. These efforts have undoubtedly contributed to the safe and lawful use of firearms by millions of Americans.

Additionally, the NRA is a nonprofit organization that operates solely on membership dues, donations, and revenue from merchandise sales, receiving no taxpayer funds or government subsidies. This financial independence underscores the grassroots support the organization enjoys among its millions of members. Contrary to a widely believed myth propagated by its critics, the NRA is also not involved in the business of dealing firearms or ammunition. Its primary focus remains on advocating for Second Amendment rights, providing firearms education and safety training, and supporting responsible gun ownership. This distinction is crucial in understanding the true nature and mission of the NRA.

The NRA's commitment to civil rights extends beyond just gun rights. Throughout its history, the organization has supported various legal challenges to protect individual liberties. For example, the NRA was instrumental in the landmark Supreme Court cases *District of Columbia v. Heller* and *McDonald v. City of Chicago*, which affirmed the individual's right to keep and bear arms as protected by the Second Amendment.

However, the NRA is not without controversy. Allegations of misuse of funds have plagued the organization in recent years, raising concerns about financial mismanagement and ethical lapses. These issues have tarnished the NRA's reputation and sparked internal conflicts, leading to calls for reform and greater transparency within the organization.

Additionally, the NRA has supported some gun control measures, which has led to criticism from staunch Second Amendment advocates. The organization's backing of the 1934 National Firearms Act and the 1968 Gun Control Act, as well as more recent support for "red flag" laws in certain contexts, has been seen by some as a betrayal of its mission to protect gun rights. These actions have created a rift among gun rights supporters, some of whom feel that the NRA has compromised too much in its efforts to navigate the political landscape.

Despite being stereotyped by elites as an organization of "hillbillies" and "rednecks," the National Rifle Association (NRA) boasts a diverse membership spanning all backgrounds, professions, and political affiliations. Its supporters include law-abiding citizens from urban and rural communities alike, as well as military veterans, law enforcement officers, competitive shooters, and everyday gun owners who value their Second Amendment rights. As a matter of fact, many high-profile figures have publicly supported or been members of the NRA. These include actor Tom Selleck, basketball Hall of Famer Karl Malone, former NRA president Oliver North, and the late Congressman Don Young. Other well-known supporters include rock musician Ted Nugent, actor and martial artist Chuck Norris, country music star Charlie Daniels, and firearms expert Colion Noir. Additionally, prominent politicians such as Senator John Kennedy (R-LA) and former Vice President Mike Pence have voiced strong support for the NRA and its mission.

Far from the media's caricature, the NRA represents millions of responsible gun owners who believe in preserving the right to self-defense, responsible firearm ownership, and protecting constitutional freedoms.

The NRA remains a powerful force in American politics and a steadfast defender of the Second Amendment. Through its educational programs, advocacy efforts, and legal battles, it has played a crucial role in preserving gun rights in the United States. By providing a platform for millions of gun owners, the organization ensures their voices are heard in the national debate over gun control. Despite facing both internal challenges and external opposition, the NRA's legacy as a champion of gun rights continues to resonate with Americans who value their constitutional freedoms. Its diverse membership, commitment to public education, and dedication to defending civil liberties underscore its significance in the ongoing fight to protect the right to bear arms. While not without controversy or financial struggles, the NRA remains a valuable resource for those who wish to stay informed on Second Amendment issues, making it worth considering for membership.

## Gun Owners of America

Gun Owners of America (GOA) is a prominent national gun rights organization dedicated to preserving and defending the Second Amendment rights of American citizens. Founded in 1976 by H. L. "Bill" Richardson, a California state senator, GOA is supported by a robust membership base of over two million people.

The primary mission of GOA is to protect and restore the constitutional rights of Americans to keep and bear arms. This is pursued through a combination of legislative advocacy, legal action, and public education. GOA maintains a strong presence in Washington, DC, and state capitals across the country, lobbying lawmakers to oppose restrictive gun control measures and support pro-gun legislation. They provide detailed legislative alerts, helping their members stay informed about pending laws and encouraging grassroots activism.

GOA also engages in litigation to challenge unconstitutional gun laws and regulations on behalf of gun owners to ensure that their rights are protected in the courts, often filing amicus briefs in significant Second Amendment cases and supporting legal challenges to anti-gun laws.

In addition to legislative and legal efforts, GOA hosts events and training programs aimed at promoting responsible gun ownership and activism. These include educational seminars, grassroots training sessions, and public rallies.

GOA publishes a range of materials to keep its members informed, including newsletters, action alerts, and in-depth analysis of gun-related issues. Their communication efforts are geared towards mobilizing their base and encouraging active participation in the defense of the Second Amendment.

One of the hallmarks of GOA's approach is its uncompromising stance on gun rights. Unlike some other organizations, GOA is known for its refusal to support any form of gun control, arguing that any infringement on the right to bear arms is unacceptable. This principled position has garnered a loyal following among gun owners who believe in the absolute protection of their constitutional rights.

Overall, Gun Owners of America remains a vital force in the American gun rights movement. Through relentless advocacy, legal action, and public education, GOA continues to fight for the preservation of the Second Amendment and the protection of individual freedoms for all Americans.

## Local and Lesser-Known Grassroots Organizations

Grassroots gun rights organizations play a pivotal role in advocating for Second Amendment rights at the local and state levels. These smaller, often volunteer-driven groups focus on mobilizing local communities, influencing legislation, and providing a voice for gun owners. Their strategies and successes have helped to defend gun rights across the United States.

Firearms Policy Coalition (FPC): The Firearms Policy Coalition (FPC) is an influential advocacy group that fights for the preservation and expansion of Second Amendment rights. Although they are based in Sacramento, California, their influence is nationwide. Founded in 2015, FPC is known for its aggressive and proactive approach to defending gun rights through litigation, legislation, public education, and grassroots activism. The organization works to challenge unconstitutional gun laws and regulations across the United States, often filing lawsuits against federal, state, and local governments. FPC also engages in legislative advocacy, working to influence policy decisions and support pro-gun legislation. Their commitment to grassroots activism is evident in their efforts to mobilize gun owners and Second Amendment supporters, encouraging them to participate in the political process and advocate for their rights. FPC's influence is notable, as they have successfully challenged numerous restrictive gun laws and continue to be a powerful voice in the fight for gun rights. For example, FPC has been successful in challenging restrictive gun laws in court, including a recent victory in Pennsylvania, where they blocked a handgun carry ban. Through their multifaceted approach, FPC ensures that the rights of gun owners are vigorously defended and advanced. Their litigation efforts are complemented by grassroots campaigns that mobilize gun owners to contact their legislators and oppose anti-gun bills.

Second Amendment Foundation (SAF): The Second Amendment Foundation (SAF), headquartered in Bellevue, Washington, is a prominent nonprofit organization dedicated to promoting a better understanding of the constitutional right to own and bear arms. Founded in 1974 by Alan Gottlieb, SAF engages in legal action, education, and research to protect and restore gun rights in the United States. The organization is known for its involvement in high-profile court cases that challenge restrictive gun laws, often achieving significant victories that uphold Second Amendment rights. One of their landmark successes was the *McDonald v. City of Chicago* case in 2010, where the Supreme Court ruled that the Second Amendment applies to state and local governments, effectively incorporating the right to bear arms under the Fourteenth Amendment. SAF's influence extends beyond the courtroom, as they also conduct educational programs and publish materials to inform the public about their rights and the importance of the Second Amendment. Through their persistent legal and educational efforts, SAF continues to play a crucial role in the ongoing battle for gun rights in America.

The New York State Rifle and Pistol Association (NYSRPA) is another prime example of a grassroots organization with substantial influence. Established in 1871, NYSRPA is affiliated with the National Rifle Association (NRA) and serves as the state's primary advocate for gun rights. The organization has been instrumental in challenging restrictive gun laws in New York. One of their notable successes was the case of *New York State Rifle & Pistol Association Inc. v. City of New York*, which reached the US Supreme Court. This case challenged the city's regulations on transporting legally owned firearms and resulted in a ruling that emphasized the protection of gun owners' rights under the Second Amendment.

Gun Owners of Maine is an all-volunteer organization dedicated to preserving and promoting gun rights in the state. Based in Augusta, this group tracks legislative developments, provides analysis, and mobilizes gun owners to act against anti-gun legislation. Their grassroots efforts have successfully opposed several restrictive bills in the Maine legislature, ensuring that the state remains gun friendly. By engaging directly with the community and maintaining a strong presence in local media, they have built a robust network of supporters who are ready to defend their rights at a moment's notice.

Florida Gun Owners (FLGO) is another grassroots organization that operates with a no-compromise stance on gun rights. Based in Tallahassee, FLGO mobilizes residents across the state to take legislative action, equipping them with tools and information to lobby for their firearm freedoms. They have been instrumental in pushing for legislation that supports open carry and opposing bills that seek to restrict gun rights. Their aggressive advocacy and extensive use of technology to organize and communicate have made them a formidable force in Florida politics.

A Girl & A Gun Women's Shooting League is a nationwide organization that empowers women through firearms training and education. Founded in 2011, this organization provides a supportive environment for women to learn about gun safety, improve their shooting skills, and connect with other female gun enthusiasts. They offer classes, events, and competitions tailored to women, helping to demystify firearms and promote responsible gun ownership. Their success is evident in the rapid growth of their chapters and the positive impact on women's confidence and competence in handling firearms.

The DC Project: Women for Gun Rights is another significant grassroots group focused on women's advocacy for the Second Amendment. Founded by Dianna Muller, a former law enforcement officer, the DC Project brings women from all 50 states to Washington, DC, to meet with legislators and discuss the importance of gun rights. Their personal stories and diverse backgrounds provide powerful testimonies that influence policymakers. The DC Project's advocacy has helped to counteract anti-gun narratives and demonstrate that gun rights are a critical issue for women across the country.

Another organization, Operation Blazing Sword, provides firearms training and education to gay and lesbian individuals. Founded in response to the Pulse nightclub shooting in Orlando, Florida, this organization connects gun-friendly trainers with LGBTQ+ people who want to learn about firearms. Their mission is to ensure that gay individuals have the knowledge and skills to defend themselves if necessary. Operation Blazing Sword has been effective in fostering a sense of security and self-reliance within the gay community.

These grassroots organizations achieve success through a combination of direct action, legal challenges, and public education. They often rely on passionate volunteers who are deeply committed to the cause of gun rights. By focusing on local and state issues, they can mobilize their communities more effectively than larger, national organizations. This localized approach allows them to respond quickly to legislative threats and take advantage of opportunities to advance pro-gun legislation.

The impact of these organizations extends beyond state borders. Their victories often set precedents that influence gun rights nationally. For example, court decisions influenced by FPC's activism can affect how other states interpret similar laws. The mobilization strategies developed by groups like Gun Owners of Maine and FLGO can be replicated in other states, amplifying their impact.

Several other statewide grassroots gun organizations may not be as widely recognized but still play important roles in advocating for gun rights, providing valuable contributions to the broader Second Amendment movement. Here are some notable examples:

Calguns Foundation (CGF): Based in California, the Calguns Foundation focuses on the protection and advancement of Second Amendment rights through strategic litigation, education, and outreach. They work closely with other organizations to challenge restrictive gun laws in California and provide resources for gun owners to understand their rights.

Vermont Federation of Sportsmen's Clubs (VFSC): This organization is the oldest statewide conservation and sportsmen's organization in Vermont. They advocate for gun rights, hunting, and conservation issues, working to ensure that sportsmen and gun owners have a voice in the legislative process.

Virginia Citizens Defense League (VCDL): Known for its no-compromise stance on gun rights, VCDL is a powerful grassroots organization in Virginia. They organize lobbying efforts, public demonstrations, and educational campaigns to protect and expand Second Amendment rights in the state.

Buckeye Firearms Association (BFA): Operating in Ohio, the Buckeye Firearms Association focuses on grassroots activism to influence legislation and public policy in favor of gun rights. They provide educational resources, support pro-gun candidates, and engage in legal actions to protect gun owners' rights.

Texas State Rifle Association (TSRA): The TSRA is a key player in Texas gun rights advocacy. They work on legislation, provide training and education, and support shooting sports. Their efforts have significantly influenced pro-gun legislation in Texas.

Maryland Shall Issue (MSI): This organization advocates for the right to bear arms in Maryland. They focus on legal action, public education, and lobbying efforts to combat restrictive gun laws in the state.

Iowa Firearms Coalition (IFC): The IFC works to protect and advance the rights of Iowa gun owners through legislative action, public education, and community engagement. Their efforts have led to the passage of pro-gun legislation in the state.

Minnesota Gun Owners Caucus (MNGOC): This grassroots organization advocates for Second Amendment rights in Minnesota. They focus on legislative efforts, community outreach, and public education to ensure that gun owners' voices are heard.

Nevada Firearms Coalition (NVFAC): The NVFAC is dedicated to protecting the rights of Nevada gun owners. They engage in lobbying, education, and legal action to fight against restrictive gun laws and promote responsible gun ownership.

Tennessee Firearms Association (TFA): The TFA advocates gun rights in Tennessee through legislative efforts, public education, and community outreach. They work to ensure that state laws protect the rights of gun owners and promote a pro-gun culture.

Arizona Citizens Defense League (AzCDL): The AzCDL is a grassroots organization focused on protecting and restoring the right to bear arms in Arizona. They engage in legislative lobbying, public education, and grassroots activism to advance pro-gun policies.

These organizations, while perhaps not as well-known as larger national groups, play critical roles in their respective states. They work tirelessly to protect and advance gun rights through a combination of legal action, lobbying, education, and grassroots activism. By focusing on local and state issues, they ensure that the voices of gun owners are heard and that their rights are defended against restrictive legislation.

There are countless grassroots organizations across the country doing incredible work to defend the Second Amendment, far too many to name individually. But I strongly encourage anyone passionate about preserving their rights to do a little digging—connect with local gun owners, visit nearby ranges, and get involved with state-level advocacy groups or firearms clubs that share your values.

# Chapter 14

## Building Confidence

*A firearm in untrained hands is a liability; in disciplined hands. It is a shield. Confidence, skill, and preparation turn a tool into a lifeline, ensuring that in the face of danger, you are not a victim—you are your own first responder.*

—J. P. Rothe

*In close quarters fighting, the man who can shoot the fastest with the greatest accuracy is the man who will survive.*

—William E. Fairbairn

B uilding confidence with the idea of owning and properly using a firearm begins with education and training. For many, the thought of handling a firearm can be intimidating, especially for those who have never done so before. However, understanding the fundamentals of gun safety and operation can ease these fears and build a strong foundation of confidence. This starts with enrolling in a reputable firearms training course where certified instructors provide hands-on experience and teach the basics of gun handling, shooting techniques, and safety protocols.

Proper training is a must for anyone looking to own a gun. Training sessions often cover critical topics such as how to load and unload a firearm safely, how to aim and shoot accurately, and how to maintain and store the firearm properly.

These courses also emphasize the importance of situational awareness and decision-making under pressure. Regular practice at a shooting range can further enhance these skills, ensuring that gun owners are comfortable and proficient with their firearms. Consistent practice helps to develop muscle memory, which is crucial for responding effectively in high-stress situations.

Safety is important when it comes to owning and using a firearm. Adhering to the basic safety rules—such as treating every gun as if it is loaded, never pointing the gun at anything you do not intend to shoot, keeping your finger off the trigger until ready to fire, and being aware of your target and what is beyond it—can prevent accidents and ensure responsible gun ownership. Additionally, understanding and practicing safe storage methods, such as using gun safes and locks, can prevent unauthorized access and misuse, particularly in homes with children.

Handling emergency or dangerous situations with a firearm requires not only technical skills but also mental preparedness. It is vital to have a clear plan and remain as calm as possible in such scenarios. Training courses often simulate real-life situations to help individuals develop the ability to think critically and act decisively under stress. Learning how to assess threats, determine the appropriate level of force, and communicate effectively with law enforcement are all part of comprehensive firearms training. By building these skills, gun owners can increase their confidence and readiness to protect themselves and their loved ones when necessary.

Ultimately, confidence in gun ownership stems from a commitment to on-going education and practice. By prioritizing training, safety, and preparedness, individuals can transform their initial nervousness into a sense of responsibility and assurance. This confidence is not only empowering; it is imperative for the safe and effective use of firearms. This chapter explores the steps for becoming familiar with firearms, gaining comfort and proficiency in their use, and building the confidence to handle them effectively in various emergency situations. It provides a comprehensive guide to mastering firearm skills through detailed, step-by-step analysis of different scenarios you might encounter. By addressing these key areas, the chapter aims to equip you with the basic knowledge and skills necessary to respond confidently and competently when faced with potentially dangerous situations.

Choosing the right firearm to suit your specific needs can be a daunting task, given the wide array of options available on the market. Firearms come in various types, including pistols, revolvers, rifles, and shotguns, each with its own set of characteristics and variations. The selection process should consider factors such as intended use, personal comfort, stopping power, and practicality. Whether you're looking for a firearm for self-defense, hunting, sport shooting, or any other purpose, it's important to understand the basic differences between these categories. With hundreds of models and variants to choose from, finding the one that best fits your unique situation requires thorough research and understanding. Here is a basic description of the different kinds of firearms you can choose from.

Disclaimer: The discussions below are not intended to provide expert tactical training or legal advice. I am not a lawyer, nor do I claim to be a trained expert in self-defense situations. The information presented is based on my personal research and/or general knowledge commonly known among gun enthusiasts and law enforcement. Seek professional training from certified instructors for tactical guidance and consult with qualified attorneys for any legal advice or concerns related to firearms and self-defense. Always prioritize safety and legal compliance by relying on professionals in these fields.

## Pistols

A pistol is a handgun that is designed to be operated with one hand, making it a convenient and versatile option for many users. Pistols are popular for self-defense due to their compact size, ease of use, and concealability, allowing individuals to carry a firearm without it being easily noticeable, which is recommended for personal protection in everyday situations. Modern pistols come with a variety of features, such as semi-automatic firing mechanisms, high-capacity magazines, and ergonomic designs, all of which contribute to their widespread popularity among those seeking reliable self-defense options. Semi-automatic pistols have become a cornerstone of personal defense, law enforcement, and recreational shooting.

These handguns are characterized by their ability to fire one round per trigger pull, automatically chambering the next round from the magazine.

Semi-automatic pistols have evolved significantly since the introduction of early models like the Borchardt C-93 and the Colt M1911. The M1911, with its .45 ACP chambering and single-action trigger, became a standard-issue sidearm for the US military and remains popular for its stopping power and reliability. Post–World War II innovations, such as the Walther P38's double-action/single-action mechanism and the high-capacity CZ 75, further advanced pistol design. Modern standouts include the Glock series, known for its polymer frame and striker-fired mechanism, and the Sig Sauer P320, praised for its modular design and adopted by the US military as the M17. The Smith & Wesson M&P series, particularly the compact M&P Shield, is favored for concealed carry due to its ergonomic design and reliability. Common calibers for semi-automatic pistols include the versatile 9mm Parabellum, the powerful .40 S&W and .45 ACP, and the compact .380 ACP. A semi-automatic pistol can fire as many rounds as its magazine capacity allows, plus one in the chamber. Magazine capacity varies depending on the model, but most standard semi-auto pistols hold between 10 to 17 rounds, with the average being around 15. Some extended magazines can increase capacity, holding up to 30 rounds or more.

The muzzle velocity of a pistol ranges anywhere from 700 feet per second (fps) to 1,800 feet per second. Muzzle velocity refers to the speed at which a bullet exits the barrel of a firearm, playing a crucial role in its trajectory, range, and impact energy. A higher muzzle velocity typically results in a flatter trajectory, extended range, and greater stopping power. However, several factors influence these variations, including caliber, ammunition type, the composition and amount of gunpowder, and the specific firearm being used. Understanding these elements is essential for selecting the right firearm and ammunition combination for a specific purpose, whether it be precision shooting, self-defense, or hunting.

The customization options for semi-automatic pistols are vast, allowing users to tailor their firearms to specific needs and preferences. Common upgrades include night sights or red dot optics for improved accuracy, extended magazines for increased capacity, and custom grips for better control and comfort. Additionally, many pistols can be fitted with tactical accessories such as lights and lasers, enhancing their utility for self-defense and tactical applications.

Despite their widespread popularity and versatility, semi-automatic pistols are not without controversy. They are frequently at the center of debates over gun control because of their use in most gun crimes and gang activity. Proponents argue that these firearms are important for personal defense and law enforcement, while opponents call for stricter regulations to prevent misuse. As technology and legislation evolve, the role of semi-automatic pistols in personal defense, law enforcement, and recreational shooting will undoubtedly continue to be a topic of great interest and discussion.

## Revolvers

A revolver is a type of handgun that uses a rotating cylinder to hold and fire cartridges. Unlike semi-automatic pistols, which rely on the energy from a fired cartridge to cycle the action and load the next round, revolvers are mechanically simpler. Each pull of the trigger or cocking of the hammer rotates the cylinder to align a new cartridge with the barrel. This design, while older, offers reliability and ease of use, as it is less prone to jamming compared to semi-automatic pistols.

Revolvers differ from pistols in several ways. The most noticeable difference is the cylinder versus the magazine. Revolvers typically hold fewer rounds, usually between five and seven, compared to the higher capacity of semi-automatic pistols. However, revolvers are appreciated for their simplicity and robustness. They can fire a variety of ammunition types, including some powerful calibers not typically used in semi-automatics.

The history of revolvers dates to the early 19th century, with Samuel Colt's 1836 patent for a revolving-cylinder pistol revolutionizing firearms design and leading to iconic models like the Colt Paterson and Colt Single Action Army. These early revolvers played major roles in American history, especially during westward expansion and the Civil War. Notable models include the Smith & Wesson Model 10, widely used by police departments, and the Colt Python, prized for its smooth trigger pull and craftsmanship. The Ruger GP100 is favored for its durability and versatility. Common calibers include .38 Special and .357

Magnum, known for their balance of recoil and stopping power, with larger calibers like .44 Magnum offering significant stopping power for hunting and defense. Revolvers also offer customization options, such as different grips and sights, to enhance comfort and accuracy.

In terms of firepower, the Smith & Wesson Model 500 is often hailed as the most powerful production revolver in the world. Introduced in 2003, it was designed to be the ultimate handgun for hunting large game. Chambered in .500 S&W Magnum, this revolver weighs 4.5 pounds and features an 8.38-inch barrel with an overall length of 15 inches. The .500 S&W Magnum cartridge was specifically developed to generate maximum power, with bullet weights ranging from 275 to 700 grains and energy levels exceeding 3,000 foot-pounds. The Model 500's muzzle velocity can reach up to 2,075 feet per second, and it has an effective range of 200 meters. This revolver is designed for hunting the largest game animals, including bears, moose, and even African big game, ensuring deep penetration and massive tissue damage. Its formidable recoil and weight make it less suitable for self-defense or concealed carry but highly regarded among handgun enthusiasts and hunters.

Despite being based on older technology, revolvers remain popular for self-defense. Their straightforward operation makes them an excellent choice for those who may not have the time or inclination for extensive firearm training. In high-stress situations, the simplicity of a revolver can be a great advantage. Revolvers are available in compact models that are highly concealable, making them ideal for everyday carry. Their reliability, ease of maintenance, and ability to function without the need for magazines ensure that revolvers continue to be a trusted option for personal protection.

## Rifles

A rifle is a long-barreled firearm designed for precision shooting, typically used with both hands and shouldered for stability. Rifles are known for their accuracy and range, making them popular for a variety of applications, including self-defense, hunting, and sport shooting. The rifling in the barrel, which consists of helical grooves, imparts a spin to the bullet, stabilizing it in flight and enhancing accuracy. Rifles are a preferred choice for self-defense in scenarios where stopping power and accuracy are paramount, particularly in rural areas or situations requiring defense over longer distances.

Rifles offer significant stopping power due to their higher-velocity cartridges and larger calibers. The variety of calibers available for rifles is extensive, ranging from small, high-speed rounds like the .223 Remington and 5.56 NATO, commonly used in AR-15 style rifles, to larger, more powerful rounds like the .308 Winchester and .30-06 Springfield, which are popular for hunting and long-range shooting. This wide range of calibers allows rifle owners to choose the ammunition appropriate for their specific needs, whether it's for self-defense, hunting large game, or competitive shooting. The muzzle velocity of rifles can be subsonic, meaning the bullet leaves the barrel at 1,125 feet per second (fps) or less, or supersonic, where it exceeds the speed of sound, creating a distinct sonic boom. Most rifles fire supersonic rounds, with muzzle velocities commonly ranging from 2,500 to 3,500 fps, thanks to their high-pressure cartridges and longer barrels, which maximize speed and energy transfer.

There are several types of rifles, each with its own operating mechanism. Fully automatic rifles can continuously fire rounds as long as the trigger is held, but they are highly regulated and largely unavailable to the general public. Semi-automatic rifles, on the other hand, fire one round per trigger pull and are widely popular for their balance of rapid fire and control. Lever-action rifles, which require the shooter to manually cycle the action using a lever located around the trigger guard, offer reliability and have a nostalgic appeal; they're often associated with the American West. Pump-action rifles, like pump-action shotguns, require the shooter to manually cycle the action by moving a pump handle back and forth. Single-shot rifles, which require the shooter to manually load each round, are valued for their simplicity and precision and are often used in long-range shooting competitions and by hunters who prioritize accuracy over rate of fire.

One of the most popular semi-automatic rifles available to the civilian market is, of course, the AR-15, developed by Eugene Stoner in the late 1950s, and it is one of the most iconic and debated firearms in modern history. Originally designed as a lightweight military rifle, it utilized advanced materials like aluminum and synthetic composites, departing from the traditional wood and steel designs of the time. After Armalite sold the rights to Colt, the US military adopted a modified version, the M16, which saw extensive use during the Vietnam War. The civilian market saw the introduction of a semi-automatic version in the 1960s, which gained popularity due to its modular design, ease of customization, low recoil, and lightweight. By the 1980s and 1990s, the AR-15 became a symbol of the gun rights movement and a staple in American gun culture.

The AR-15's modularity allows for extensive customization, with options to replace sights, barrels, handguards, triggers, stocks, grips, and muzzle devices. It is commonly chambered in calibers like 5.56 NATO/.223 Remington, and .300 Blackout, catering to a variety of shooting needs. The AR-10, a larger version designed for more powerful calibers like 7.62 NATO/.308 Winchester, offers greater power and range, suitable for hunting large game and precision shooting. Both platforms highlight the AR-15's adaptability and enduring popularity in the civilian firearms market, despite ongoing legal and political battles.

The AK-47, another popular semi-automatic rifle used by civilians, was developed by Mikhail Kalashnikov in 1947 and is one of the most iconic firearms in history. Designed for the Soviet military, its reliability, simplicity, and ease of mass production made it ideal for battlefield conditions. Officially adopted by the Soviet Armed Forces in 1949, the AK-47's gas-operated, rotating bolt mechanism and long-stroke piston system ensured durability and effectiveness in harsh environments. Over the decades, numerous variants, such as the AKM, AK-74, AK-103, and AK-12, have been developed, each with specific improvements like lighter receivers, improved recoil reduction, and enhanced ergonomics.

The AK-47's ruggedness and reliability have made it a favorite worldwide among militaries and insurgent groups. Its ability to function with minimal maintenance in adverse conditions is legendary. Variants like the AKM with a stamped steel receiver, the AK-74 with a smaller, high-velocity cartridge, and the modernized AK-12 highlight its evolution. The rifle's customization options, such as adding optics, upgrading stocks and handguards, and installing muzzle devices, further increase its versatility. Despite its age, the AK-47 continues to be a widely used and influential firearm, symbolizing resistance and reliability.

Belt-fed rifles are a category of firearm designed to feed ammunition from a continuous belt, allowing for sustained fire without frequent reloading. These rifles are often associated with military use due to their high rate of fire and capacity for extended engagements. However, they also have applications in civilian contexts, primarily for recreational shooting, historical reenactments, and firearms collections. One of the most iconic belt-fed rifles is the M60, famously used in the *Rambo* films. The M60 is a 7.62×51mm NATO belt-fed, air-cooled, gas-operated machine gun that has been a staple of the US military since the late 1950s. Designed for sustained fire, it features a quick-change barrel system to prevent overheating and is typically fed by linked ammunition belts. Another example is the M240, a modernized belt-fed machine gun also chambered in 7.62×51mm NATO, widely used by US armed forces and allied militaries. Both firearms are built for suppressive fire in combat situations, again, making them vastly different from civilian semi-automatic rifles often mislabeled as "assault weapons" by gun control advocates.

Federally, fully automatic belt-fed rifles are legal to own, provided they comply with the National Firearms Act (NFA) of 1934 and other relevant regulations. This means that fully automatic belt-fed rifles, or machine guns, are heavily regulated and require the owner to obtain a specific license, complete a background check, and pay a $200 tax. Additionally, the manufacture of new machine guns for civilian use has been banned since 1986 under the Hughes Amendment to the Firearm Owners Protection Act, limiting civilian ownership to pre-1986 registered machine guns.

For semi-automatic belt-fed rifles, which fire one round per trigger pull, the regulatory landscape is less stringent but still subject to varying state laws. In states with more permissive gun laws, such as Texas, Florida, and Arizona, semi-automatic belt-fed rifles are legal to own and use. These states often have fewer restrictions on firearm ownership and do not impose additional bans on specific types of firearms beyond federal regulations.

Conversely, in states with stricter gun control measures, such as California, New York, and New Jersey, belt-fed rifles, particularly those with certain features or configurations, may be outright banned or heavily restricted. California's assault weapons ban includes provisions that prohibit firearms with large-capacity magazines and certain military-style features, which can encompass belt-fed rifles.

In these states, owning a belt-fed rifle could require navigating complex legal requirements or may be entirely prohibited.

Belt-fed rifles are used for a variety of purposes in civilian contexts. Enthusiasts often use them for recreational shooting, taking advantage of their high capacity and sustained fire capabilities for target practice and competition. Historical reenactors and collectors value belt-fed rifles for their authenticity and historical significance, often using them to recreate battles or display in private collections. Some firearms training facilities and private ranges offer experiences with belt-fed rifles, providing individuals with the opportunity to handle and shoot these unique firearms in a controlled environment.

The Barrett M82, also known as the Barrett .50 cal or M107, is widely regarded as one of the most powerful rifles in the world. Designed by Barrett Firearms Manufacturing, this semi-automatic, anti-materiel rifle has seen extensive use by military and law enforcement agencies worldwide. The Barrett M82 is chambered in .50 BMG (Browning Machine Gun), a caliber known for its incredible power and long-range capabilities. Weighing approximately 30 pounds with a 29-inch barrel and an overall length of 57 inches, the M82 can achieve a muzzle velocity of 2,800 feet per second and has an effective range of 1,800 meters. The rifle's 10-round magazine capacity allows for sustained fire without frequent reloading. The .50 BMG round is capable of penetrating armored vehicles, concrete barriers, and even light tanks, making it highly effective in disabling enemy equipment and providing long-range sniping capabilities.

Rifles continue to be a versatile and powerful choice for many firearm enthusiasts. Whether used for self-defense, sport, or hunting, their range, accuracy, and stopping power make them a reliable option. The variety of calibers and types of rifles available allows individuals to select the firearm that best suits their needs and preferences, ensuring that they are well-equipped for any situation.

## Shotguns

A shotgun is a type of long-barreled firearm designed to fire a spread of shot or a single slug, making it highly versatile for various applications. Unlike rifles, which are designed for precision shooting with a single projectile, shotguns are typically used for shooting moving targets at close to medium range. This makes them effective for hunting birds and small game, as well as for home defense.

Shotguns differ from rifles primarily in the type of ammunition they use. While rifles fire bullets—single projectiles designed for long-range accuracy—shotguns fire shells that can contain multiple small pellets (birdshot), a single large projectile (slug), or specialized loads, such as buckshot, which fires multiple larger pellets. This spread pattern of shot allows for a greater chance of hitting a target without needing pinpoint accuracy, which is especially useful in dynamic and unpredictable situations, such as self-defense scenarios or hunting game in flight. The versatility of shotgun ammunition makes it adaptable to a variety of tasks, from bird hunting to breaching doors in tactical operations.

Shotgun ammunition typically has a slower muzzle velocity than rifle rounds and many handgun rounds due to the larger, heavier projectiles and lower-pressure loads designed for short-range effectiveness rather than the high-speed penetration of rifles and some handguns. Birdshot and buckshot typically travel between 1,100 and 1,600 fps, while slugs range from 1,200 to 1,800 fps, with some high-velocity slugs reaching up to 2,000 fps. Shotguns prioritize stopping power over speed, relying on large, heavy projectiles that deliver devastating energy transfer at close range rather than high-speed penetration.

Shotguns, like rifles, come in a variety of styles and types, each suited to different needs and preferences. Semi-automatic shotguns automatically cycle a new shell into the chamber with each pull of the trigger, allowing for rapid follow-up shots. Pump-action shotguns require the shooter to manually cycle the action by pumping the fore-end back and forth, offering reliability and control. Lever-action shotguns, while less common, provide a unique blend of speed and nostalgia, operating similarly to lever-action rifles. Single-shot and double-barreled shotguns, including side-by-side and over-and-under configurations, are often used in hunting and sport shooting for their simplicity and traditional design.

The popularity of shotguns for self-defense is due to their stopping power and ease of use. In home defense situations, a shotgun's wide shot spread can cover more area and increase the likelihood of hitting an intruder. The intimidating and distinctive sound of a shotgun being racked can also act as a deterrent. For hunting, shotguns are favored for their ability to effectively take down game at varying distances and their adaptability to different hunting environments. The choice of ammunition can be tailored to the specific game being hunted, whether it's birds, deer, or other animals.

There are several popular models of shotguns widely in use. The Remington 870, known for its ruggedness and reliability since its introduction in 1950, is favored by hunters and law enforcement and for home defense. Similarly, the Mossberg 500, introduced in 1960, is renowned for its reliability, ease of use, and affordability, making it popular among law enforcement and civilian shooters. The Benelli M4, a semi-automatic shotgun, is highly regarded for its durability and performance in tactical applications, while the Beretta 1301 is praised for its fast cycling and ergonomics, making it ideal for tactical and competitive shooting. Classic models like the Winchester Model 1897 and the modern Winchester Model 1300 are appreciated for their distinctive designs and reliability. The Browning A5, with its unique "humpback" receiver, is favored for its inertia-driven system and versatility in hunting and sporting. The Mossberg 590, a tactical variant of the 500, is preferred by military and law enforcement for its robust design. The CZ-USA CZ Drake is a popular over-and-under shotgun known for its quality and affordability, ideal for upland game hunting and clay shooting. These shotguns are renowned for their reliability, versatility, and suitability for a wide range of shooting activities.

The T-Rex 12-Gauge Shotgun is one of the most powerful shotguns available, delivering massive firepower with high-power loads. Weighing around 8 pounds with a 24-inch barrel and an overall length of 44 inches, this shotgun can fire various types of ammunition, including birdshot, buckshot, and slugs. High-power slugs and buckshot loads can deliver incredible stopping power, with muzzle velocities typically around 1,600 feet per second. T-Rex's 12-gauge shotgun is designed for big game hunting, home defense, and tactical use, capable of delivering powerful slugs that can penetrate body armor and dense materials. This shotgun's versatility and power make it a favorite among hunters and tactical operators who need a reliable and devastating firearm.

The shotgun's versatility, ease of use, and adaptability make it a popular choice for both self-defense and hunting. Its versatility in ammunition and operating mechanisms allows it to adapt to different tasks and shooter preferences. Whether used for protecting a home or pursuing game in the field, the shotgun remains an indispensable tool for many firearms enthusiasts.

Ultimately, deciding which type of firearm suits you best requires proper training and hands-on experience with various models. Be sure to understand the differences between pistols, revolvers, rifles, and shotguns and test out different options to see what feels most comfortable and meets your needs. Factors such as ease of use, recoil, purpose, weight, and comfort play important roles in determining the right fit. For instance, women and older adults often prefer handguns and rifles with less recoil and lighter weight for easier handling. By learning how to use each type of firearm and evaluating different models, you can make an informed decision that ensures both effectiveness and personal comfort.

## Ammunition

Ammunition, often referred to as a round or cartridge, is composed of four main components: the case, primer, gunpowder, and projectile. The case, typically made of brass, steel, or aluminum, houses the other elements and holds everything together. At the base of the case is the primer, a small metal cup containing a chemical compound that ignites when struck by the firearm's firing pin. This ignition sets off the gunpowder inside the case, creating expanding gases that propel the projectile—the bullet—down the barrel and toward the target.

Caliber refers to the diameter of the bullet and is measured either in inches, such as .45, or in millimeters, like 9mm. Caliber size is one of the primary factors in determining a round's intended use, level of recoil, and terminal performance. For instance, .22 LR is a small, low-recoil round widely used for target shooting, small game hunting, and training beginners. In contrast, 9mm strikes a balance between recoil and stopping power, making it one of the most popular calibers for self-defense and law enforcement. Stepping up in power, .40 S&W and .45 ACP both deliver heavier recoil but also increased bullet weight and impact, preferred by shooters seeking more punch from their handguns.

Rifle cartridges like 5.56 NATO, commonly used in AR-15s, offer light recoil and high velocity, making them versatile for both home defense and sporting purposes. The 7.62×51mm 39mm, the standard round for the AK-47 platform, hits harder and performs well at intermediate ranges. For larger game or long-range shooting, .308 Winchester (7.62 NATO) is a classic choice, producing noticeably more recoil in exchange for greater power and reach. On the shotgun side, 12-gauge shells are the most common and can be loaded with birdshot, buckshot, or slugs, making them highly versatile but also known for significant recoil.

Casing material also plays a role in performance and reusability. Brass casings are the most popular due to their durability and ease of reloading. Steel casings are less expensive and non-reloadable, often found in imported or surplus ammunition, while aluminum casings are lightweight and used primarily for low-cost target shooting.

The world of ammunition is vast, with calibers ranging from ultra-light rounds like .17 HMR to heavy-hitting .50 BMG cartridges capable of penetrating armor and disabling vehicles. Mid-range cartridges like 6.5 Creedmoor are prized by long-range marksmen for their accuracy and manageable recoil, while rounds such as .300 Blackout are favored in short-barreled rifles and suppressed firearms. From plinking to precision shooting to dangerous game hunting, there is a caliber for nearly every purpose—and each choice brings trade-offs between recoil, velocity, range, and terminal effectiveness.

Choosing the right ammunition caliber comes down to understanding the purpose behind the firearm. A caliber suited for home defense may not be ideal for small game hunting or precision shooting, and vice versa. If your focus is self-defense, particularly in a concealed carry scenario, 9mm is a popular choice given its manageable recoil, good stopping power, and higher magazine capacity compared to larger calibers like .45 ACP or .40 S&W. Those seeking additional knockdown power in a defensive handgun might opt for the heavier .45 ACP, though it comes with more recoil and lower capacity.

For home defense with a rifle, the 5.56 NATO/.223 Remington shines as a lightweight, fast round, with low recoil and solid terminal performance at typical home defense distances. If you prefer a shotgun for home defense, a 12-gauge loaded with buckshot is a proven, devastating choice, though it comes with considerable recoil—especially in lighter or shorter shotguns.

Hunters have a different set of priorities. A .22 LR is excellent for small game like rabbits and squirrels but is insufficient for larger animals. For deer hunting, calibers like .308 Winchester or even 6.5 Creedmoor are commonly used for their accuracy and stopping power at longer distances. Meanwhile, those venturing into bear country or hunting larger game often step up to magnum calibers like .300 Winchester Magnum or .45-70 Government for the added punch and penetration.

Sport shooters and hobbyists may lean toward calibers like .22 LR for cost-effective practice or competition rounds like 9mm and .223, which are affordable, widely available, and produce minimal recoil. Long-range shooters often gravitate toward precision-focused calibers such as 6.5 Creedmoor, .308 Winchester, or .300 PRC, depending on how far they plan to reach out.

In short, no single caliber is perfect for every application. Factors like recoil tolerance, firearm platform, cost of ammunition, terminal ballistics, and the legal considerations in your state all play into what caliber is best suited for your needs. Ultimately, it's about finding the right tool for your mission, whether that's protecting your home, plinking at the range, putting meat on the table, or hitting steel targets at 1,000 yards.

## Ammunition Ballistics

Ballistics is the science of how projectiles behave before, during, and after being fired. When discussing common calibers like .22 LR, 9mm, .45 ACP, 5.56 NATO, 7.62×39mm, or .308 Winchester, each round brings unique ballistic characteristics that affect its accuracy, terminal performance, and overall effectiveness. For instance, lighter rounds like .22 LR and 5.56 NATO are known for high velocity and flat trajectories over short to medium distances. The .22 LR, while traveling at relatively lower velocities (around 1,100 to 1,300 feet per second), is often subsonic or right at the edge of the speed of sound. As mentioned earlier, a subsonic round is one that travels below the speed of sound (approximately 1,125 feet per second at sea level), avoiding the sonic "crack" associated with faster rounds. This makes subsonic ammunition quieter, especially when paired with suppressors, but it generally has more bullet drop and less energy retention over distance. The .22 LR is highly accurate at shorter ranges but suffers from wind drift and energy drop-off beyond 100 yards due to its low mass and subsonic to near-supersonic speeds.

By contrast, the 5.56 NATO is firmly in the supersonic category, meaning it exceeds the speed of sound (typically traveling between 2,900 and 3,200 feet per second). Supersonic rounds are more aerodynamic and carry more energy over longer distances, but they generate a distinct sonic crack in flight. The 5.56 NATO's high velocity contributes to its flat trajectory and low recoil, offering excellent performance out to 300 to 500 yards and beyond, depending on the shooter's skill and environmental conditions.

Pistol rounds like 9mm, .40 S&W, and .45 ACP have lower velocities compared to most rifle cartridges, typically ranging from 900 to 1,200 feet per second, depending on bullet weight and powder charge. Standard pressure 9mm is often right around the supersonic threshold, while .45 ACP tends to remain subsonic, traveling around 850 to 950 feet per second. The subsonic nature of the .45 ACP makes it naturally compatible with suppressors and helps reduce its report. The 9mm is valued for its balanced velocity, recoil, and capacity, providing quick follow-up shots and less felt recoil under stress. The .40 S&W, while offering increased energy over 9mm, introduces sharper recoil. The .45 ACP delivers heavier recoil and more mass to the target, often resulting in larger wound channels but with greater bullet drop over distance.

Intermediate rifle rounds like 7.62×39mm, used in AK-pattern rifles, are heavier and slower than 5.56 NATO, typically traveling around 2,300 to 2,400 feet per second. While still supersonic, the round experiences more bullet drop at extended ranges and is more affected by wind due to its lower ballistic coefficient. However, at closer ranges, it transfers more energy on target compared to the lighter 5.56 round.

For larger game or precision shooting, .308 Winchester (7.62 NATO) is a full-power rifle cartridge traveling around 2,600 to 2,800 feet per second. It excels at maintaining velocity and energy out past 800 yards and is less prone to wind drift than intermediate rounds. Shooters seeking even better long-range performance often turn to calibers like 6.5 Creedmoor, which is engineered with a higher ballistic coefficient for flatter trajectories and superior performance in windy conditions.

External ballistics—the behavior of a projectile after it leaves the barrel—is influenced by several environmental factors, including gravity, air resistance, wind, altitude, and temperature. All projectiles, regardless of caliber, begin to lose velocity immediately after exiting the barrel. Gravity constantly pulls the round downward, creating bullet drop, while air resistance slows the bullet and can cause drift, especially at longer ranges. Supersonic rounds like 5.56 NATO and .308 Winchester resist wind and drop better than subsonic or heavy, slower rounds, but even they are affected by environmental conditions over distance.

Bullet design—such as full metal jacket (FMJ), hollow point (HP), soft point (SP), or match-grade open tip—further shapes external ballistics. Heavier, more aerodynamic bullets with streamlined profiles retain energy and resist wind drift more effectively, while flatter, blunter bullets lose speed faster and drop more quickly.

Understanding both internal and external ballistics gives shooters a clearer picture of how ammunition behaves in the real world, helping to inform caliber selection based on intended use, environment, and effective range.

## Basic Rules of Firearm Safety

Now that you've gotten a solid grasp of the different types of firearms and ammunition, it's time to move on to the most important part—learning how to handle a firearm safely and responsibly. Ensuring proper and responsible use of a firearm is essential for the safety of the shooter and those around them. Adhering to the fundamental rules of gun safety can prevent accidents and injuries. This manual outlines the most common and critical rules of gun safety.

First, treat every firearm as if it is loaded. Always assume that a firearm is loaded, even if you believe it to be unloaded. This mindset reduces the likelihood of negligent discharges and always encourages careful handling. Check the chamber, magazine, and action each time you pick up a firearm and never rely solely on the firearm's safety mechanism.

Second, keep your finger off the trigger until you are ready to shoot. Maintaining control over the trigger prevents accidental discharges. Rest your finger along the frame or trigger guard until you are prepared to fire, and practice this habit regularly.

Third, always point the muzzle in a safe direction. Control the direction of the firearm's muzzle to minimize the risk of injury or damage if an accidental discharge occurs. Never point a firearm at anything you do not intend to shoot, and always be aware of your surroundings.

Fourth, be sure of your target and what is beyond it. Identify your target with certainty and be aware of what lies beyond it to ensure you do not unintentionally shoot something or someone else. Use binoculars or a scope to positively identify your target and consider the range, surroundings, and backdrop before firing.

Fifth, store firearms securely to prevent unauthorized access. Proper storage of firearms is important to prevent unauthorized access, especially by children or untrained individuals. Use a gun safe, lockbox, or trigger lock to secure firearms and store ammunition separately.

Sixth, use the correct ammunition. Using the correct ammunition for your firearm is vital for safe operation. Check the firearm's barrel and chamber markings to verify the correct ammunition type and read ammunition packaging to ensure it matches the firearm specifications.

Seventh, wear appropriate eye and ear protection. Firearms produce noise and debris that can damage your eyes and hearing. Always use shooting glasses or goggles and earplugs or earmuffs when shooting.

Eighth, know how to operate your firearm safely. Familiarize yourself with the specific operation, safety features, and maintenance requirements of your firearm. Read the owner's manual and take a firearm safety course to gain hands-on experience.

Ninth, never use alcohol or drugs before or while shooting. Substances that impair your judgment and coordination should never be consumed before or during firearm handling.

Lastly, handle firearms with respect and care. Treat firearms with the respect they deserve to reduce the likelihood of negligent behavior and accidents. Always follow safety rules, set a positive example for others, and educate others on the importance of firearm safety and responsible use.

By adhering to these gun safety rules, you can ensure that your use of firearms is both responsible and safe. Safety is the most critical aspect of firearm ownership and use. Prioritizing these principles helps prevent accidents and promotes a culture of respect and responsibility within the shooting community.

## Basic Training

Once you've chosen your firearm and familiarized yourself with the basic gun safety rules, it's time to head to the range for some practical training. Getting comfortable with your firearm and developing your shooting skills requires consistent practice and the right techniques. For beginners, starting with the basics and progressively building up to more advanced drills is ideal.

Before you begin shooting, you need to properly sight in your firearm. This process ensures that your sights are accurately aligned with the point of impact of your bullets. Start by setting up a target at a relatively close distance, around 10 to 15 yards. Use a stable shooting position, such as a bench rest, to minimize movement and ensure accuracy. Fire a few rounds, then check the target to see where the bullets are hitting relative to your aiming point. Adjust the sights accordingly until the point of impact matches the point of aim. This step is vital for ensuring that your shots are accurate and consistent.

Once your firearm is sighted in, it's time to begin basic drills. One of the fundamental drills for beginners is the slow-fire drill. Start by setting up a target at a distance of 5 to 7 yards. Focus on the core principles of shooting: stance, grip, sight alignment, sight picture, breath control, and trigger control. Take your time to aim carefully and squeeze the trigger smoothly. This drill helps you develop the muscle memory and discipline needed for accurate shooting.

After mastering the slow-fire drill, you can move on to controlled pair drills. This involves firing two shots in quick succession while maintaining accuracy. Start with the target at 5 to 7 yards and gradually increase the distance as you become more comfortable. The controlled pair drill teaches you to manage recoil and reacquire your sights quickly, which is essential for defensive shooting scenarios.

Another useful drill is the draw-and-fire drill. This drill helps you practice drawing your firearm from its holster and firing a shot accurately under time pressure. Begin with an unloaded firearm to practice the draw motion safely. Once you're comfortable with the motion, you can move on to live fire. Start with the target at a close distance and focus on smooth, deliberate movements. Speed will come with practice, so prioritize safety and accuracy initially.

Engaging multiple targets is another important skill for defensive shooting. Set up two or more targets at varying distances and practice transitioning between them smoothly. This drill helps you develop situational awareness and the ability to engage multiple threats efficiently. Start slowly to ensure accurate shots and gradually increase your speed as your skills improve.

Shooting from different positions develops versatility and adaptability. Practice shooting from standing, kneeling, and prone positions. Each position presents unique challenges, and becoming proficient in all of them will make you a more effective shooter. Additionally, practice shooting while moving, as real-life scenarios often require you to engage threats while on the move.

It's highly recommended to go to the range with someone who is familiar with firearms and shooting techniques. An experienced shooter can provide valuable guidance, correct any mistakes, and offer tips to improve your performance. Many ranges also offer training courses or have on-site instructors who can provide professional instruction.

For beginners, consistency and repetition are key. Regular practice will help reinforce the fundamentals and build confidence in your abilities. As you progress, you can incorporate more advanced drills and techniques into your training regimen. Remember to always prioritize safety and never hesitate to seek guidance from more experienced shooters or professional instructors. With consistent practice and a focus on safety, you'll develop the skills needed to handle your firearm effectively and responsibly.

Once you have had some practice and basic training under your belt, you will be better prepared to defend yourself in the event of a break-in or home invasion, scenarios that have unfortunately become increasingly more common in modern times. With your newfound skills and familiarity with your firearm, you possess the advantage of being able to protect yourself and your loved ones effectively. Remain vigilant and ready, understanding that your training has equipped you to handle these dangerous situations with confidence and composure.

## Practice Concealed Carry

Practicing concealed carry can be an intimidating and stressful venture for many, as it completely changes one's awareness and demeanor. Carrying a firearm can be burdensome on both a comfort level and a stress level. However, with the right approach and gradual practice, it can become a manageable and even second-nature aspect of personal safety. Once you obtain your concealed carry license, however, avoid starting to carry your firearm in public without proper training and practice.

Begin by familiarizing yourself with carrying the firearm at home. Start by carrying your unloaded firearm with the magazine detached. This initial step allows you to get used to the feel of the firearm on your person without the added weight or concern of a loaded gun. Wear the firearm as you would in public, ensuring it is properly holstered. You will become acutely aware of the gun's presence, and this awareness is an important part of the acclimation process.

After you are comfortable carrying an unloaded firearm, progress to inserting an unloaded magazine into the firearm. Continue to carry the gun around your house and property, walking up and down your driveway and yard. This step simulates the added weight and balance of a loaded firearm without the actual risk, helping you adjust further to the feel of carrying a gun.

The next phase involves carrying the firearm with a loaded magazine but without a round in the chamber. This means the firearm is technically loaded, but it is not ready to fire since there is no round in the chamber. Always keep the safety on during this practice. Carry the firearm around your property, getting used to the idea of carrying a loaded gun in a safe manner.

Finally, once you feel comfortable and confident, you can carry the firearm around your property with a round in the chamber, fully loaded and ready to fire. Ensure it is securely holstered and that the safety is engaged. This technique allows you to become thoroughly familiar with your firearm and the experience of carrying it, which is crucial for safely carrying in public.

This step-by-step method will help you get to know your firearm intimately, making the transition to carrying in public much smoother. By practicing in a controlled environment, you reduce the stress and intimidation factor, building the necessary confidence and comfort to carry your firearm responsibly and effectively.

## Concealed Carry in Public

Carrying a concealed firearm in public places is a deeply rooted aspect of the Second Amendment, encompassing the right to not only keep arms but also to bear them on one's person wherever one goes. The ability to carry concealed weapons in various public settings—such as concerts, bars, sporting events, stores, restaurants, and shopping centers—reflects the fundamental principle that self-defense is a personal responsibility, especially in times when public safety is increasingly under threat.

In public venues like concerts, bars, and sporting events, the presence of concealed firearms can be a contentious issue. While some argue that these environments are too volatile for firearms, proponents of concealed carry assert that these are precisely the places where law-abiding citizens might need to defend themselves. There will always be some level of risk involved in carrying firearms in public spaces. However, in an era where criminals are often released back into communities, law enforcement agencies face defunding and demoralization, and the judicial system sometimes fails to uphold public safety effectively, the argument for personal protection becomes even more compelling. When elected officials and judges are not fulfilling their duties to protect citizens, individuals must be prepared to defend themselves and their loved ones.

Conversely, when it comes to stores, restaurants, and shopping centers, the right to bear arms in these commercial spaces is equally important. These are everyday locations where individuals should feel safe, and carrying a concealed firearm provides an additional layer of protection. The recent rise in public shootings and violent crimes underscores the necessity for citizens to have the means to always protect themselves. Concealed carry in these environments ensures that responsible gun owners can respond swiftly and effectively to threats, potentially saving lives.

Many people do not realize that commercial properties and retail spaces, despite being accessible to the public, are still private properties. This means that store owners and proprietors can implement rules regarding firearms on their premises based on their preferences and policies. While public property, such as parks and government buildings, must adhere to constitutional protections that prevent the infringement of Second Amendment rights, private business owners have the discretion to create environments they deem safest for their customers and staff. Business owners have the authority to decide whether they want to allow firearms on their property, and this right must be respected, as it aligns with the broader principle of private property rights.

The balance between respecting private property rights and ensuring public safety through the Second Amendment is a delicate one. As society navigates these complexities, it is vital to understand and respect the distinctions between public and private spaces while advocating for the right to self-defense in an increasingly unpredictable world.

## Ambient Risk

The concept of ambient risk represents the baseline level of risk that exists in a particular situation, which can change based on activities or environmental factors. For example, the ambient risk of simply sitting at home is relatively low. However, this risk increases when you get into a car, as driving inherently carries more risk than being stationary at home. Similarly, walking through a high-crime inner-city neighborhood carries a higher ambient risk compared to strolling through a safe small rural town.

Everyday activities can also alter the ambient risk level. When you pick up a knife to chop onions, the ambient risk increases because handling a sharp object introduces a potential for injury that wasn't present when you were simply standing in the kitchen. Likewise, the presence of a gun in a room elevates the ambient risk due to the inherent dangers associated with firearms. Picking up and handling a loaded gun further increases this risk, as the potential for accidental discharge or mishandling becomes a factor.

However, an increase in ambient risk does not necessarily mean that something bad will happen. It merely indicates that the background concentration of risk has changed because new elements or activities have been introduced. Just as getting into a car does not guarantee a crash, having a gun in a room does not ensure that an accident or violent incident will occur. The concept of ambient risk helps to contextualize the potential dangers present in various situations and underscores the importance of being aware of these risks.

In discussions about gun ownership and safety, recognizing the concept of ambient risk can provide a balanced perspective. While the presence of a firearm does elevate the background risk, this risk can be managed through proper training, responsible handling, and adherence to safety protocols. Just as drivers mitigate the risks of the road through careful driving and adherence to traffic laws, gun owners can manage the ambient risks associated with firearms through education, safe storage, and responsible use.

The concept of ambient risk illustrates that while carrying a concealed firearm does increase the background level of risk, this increase is justified when considering the potential to neutralize even greater threats. In scenarios where a violent crime is unfolding, the ambient risk dramatically increases beyond the normal background level. For example, a robbery in progress or a mugging dramatically escalates the potential for harm, injury, or even death. In such situations, the presence of a concealed firearm in the hands of a responsible gun owner can drastically alter the outcome. In a world where law enforcement cannot be omnipresent and response times can be delayed, individuals must take personal responsibility for their safety. The ability to defend oneself and others against immediate threats can neutralize the heightened ambient risk posed by criminals. This capability transforms the individual from a potential victim into someone who can effectively mitigate the danger.

Moreover, the presence of armed, law-abiding citizens can serve as a deterrent to crime. Criminals are less likely to target individuals or locations where there is a higher probability of encountering armed resistance. This deterrent effect contributes to an overall reduction in the ambient risk for the community. By carrying a concealed firearm, individuals not only protect themselves but also contribute to a broader sense of security.

While the act of carrying a concealed firearm does increase the ambient risk, this increase is outweighed by the potential benefits. The ability to defend oneself and others against violent crime, deter criminal activity, and contribute to a safer community justifies the elevated background risk. In the face of escalating threats, violent criminals who do not adhere to laws or moral codes, and the inherent unpredictability of life, the increased ambient risk of carrying a firearm is a prudent and necessary measure for ensuring personal safety and protecting the lives of others. The right to self-defense is a fundamental aspect of the Second Amendment, and carrying a concealed firearm is a practical exercise of that right.

## Open Carry

Open carry refers to the practice of visibly carrying a firearm in public, typically in a holster. Unlike concealed carry, where the firearm is hidden from view, open carry allows the firearm to be seen by others. This practice is governed by state laws, which vary across the United States. Most states permit some form of open carry, including Arizona, Texas, Virginia, and Nevada, where residents can openly carry a firearm without a permit. This widespread acceptance is rooted in the belief that visible firearms serve as a deterrent to crime and that carrying a gun is a constitutional right under the Second Amendment.

Open carry is common in rural areas, small towns, and some suburban regions, where it is often viewed as a normal and acceptable practice closely tied to traditions of hunting, self-defense, and personal freedom. It is common to see individuals openly carrying firearms in local stores and restaurants and at public events. Conversely, open carry is less common in densely populated urban areas, where stricter regulations and different attitudes toward firearms prevail.

The types of firearms commonly open carried include handguns, which are the most prevalent, and occasionally long guns such as rifles and shotguns. Handguns are typically carried in holsters on the hip, thigh, or chest, making them easily accessible yet securely fastened. Long guns are less frequently seen in open carry scenarios, primarily because they are larger and less convenient to carry in public settings.

Many states do not require a permit for open carry, unlike concealed carry, which often demands a rigorous permitting process. The rationale behind this difference lies in the visibility of the firearm. Lawmakers in states that allow open carry without a permit argue that the visible presence of a firearm does not pose the same perceived threat as a concealed weapon, which could potentially be drawn and used without prior notice. They believe that open carry maintains transparency and deters crime by signaling that the individual is armed. However, some states, such as Oklahoma, Tennessee, and Georgia, do impose permit requirements for open carry in certain locations or under specific conditions. These permits often involve background checks, firearms training, and other qualifications to ensure that those openly carrying firearms are responsible and law-abiding citizens.

The responsibilities that come with open carry are momentous. Openly carrying a firearm in public means being constantly aware of the weapon's presence and ensuring it is handled safely and responsibly at all times. There are inherent risks associated with open carry, including the potential for the firearm to be taken by someone else or to escalate a situation unnecessarily. However, there are also benefits, such as the deterrent effect it can have on potential criminals who may be less likely to target someone who is visibly armed.

Open carry can be seen as a symbol of freedom and self-reliance, and it is particularly encouraged in certain places. For example, Congresswoman Lauren Boebert owned Shooters Grill, a gun-themed restaurant in Colorado where firearms were an integral part of the experience. The menu featured firearm-inspired items like the Double Barrel Cookie and the Swiss & Wesson burger, while both staff and customers were encouraged to open carry. Employees openly carried firearms, including semi-automatic handguns, reinforcing the idea that personal protection is a shared responsibility and that firearms are a normal part of everyday life. Unfortunately, the restaurant closed in 2022.

Between open carry and concealed carry, the latter tends to be more popular among gun owners because it is more discreet and offers the element of surprise in a defensive situation. However, open carry remains an essential aspect of gun rights and culture in the United States. Whether a state requires a permit for open carry or not, the underlying principle remains the same: The right to visibly and openly carry a firearm in public places is a freedom that must be balanced with personal good judgement and responsibility.

## Firearms Transport

Carrying firearms in your vehicle involves understanding and adhering to various transportation laws, which can differ dramatically from state to state and even within jurisdictions. When transporting a firearm in your vehicle, you must know the specific regulations in the areas you are traveling through, as well as best practices for ensuring safety and compliance with the law. Many states allow individuals to carry firearms in their vehicles, but the specifics can vary. Some states require that firearms be unloaded and stored in a locked container or the trunk of the vehicle. Others may permit loaded firearms in the vehicle, particularly if you have a concealed carry permit. Check the local laws of the states you will be traveling through to ensure compliance.

If you are pulled over by law enforcement while carrying a firearm in your vehicle, your best approach can depend on the state and your legal obligations. In some states, you are required by law to disclose to the officer that you have a firearm in the vehicle. This is often the case if you have a concealed carry permit and are carrying a concealed firearm. In other states, you are not obligated to disclose this information unless directly asked by the officer.

Regardless of the legal requirements, it is advisable to be polite and cooperative during any traffic stop. If you choose to disclose that you have a firearm, do so calmly and clearly. You might say something like, "Officer, I want to let you know that I have a legally owned firearm in the vehicle. It is located [specific location]." Keep your hands visible and avoid making sudden movements. Following the officer's instructions carefully can help ensure a smooth interaction.

When transporting a firearm from one place to another, the safest and most legally compliant method is often to keep the firearm unloaded and stored in a locked container or in the trunk. Ammunition should be stored separately from the firearm. This approach minimizes the risk of accidental discharge and aligns with the laws of many states, which require firearms to be transported in a manner that prevents immediate access. Even in states where it is legal to carry a loaded firearm in your vehicle, consider the risks and ensure you have proper training and understanding of safe handling procedures.

If you plan on going on a trip out of state and bringing your firearms, always aim to travel through states that are friendly to gun owners, as this will minimize the risk of legal complications. However, if you are landlocked between gun-hostile states, thoroughly research the specific laws of each state you will be passing through. Understand the requirements for transporting firearms, such as whether they need to be unloaded and stored in a locked container. This knowledge will help you stay compliant with the law and ensure your safety and the safety of others. Additionally, consider contacting law enforcement agencies in those states to get clear and accurate information about their regulations for traveling with firearms. Being well-informed and prepared can help you navigate these jurisdictions safely and legally, ensuring a smooth trip without unexpected legal issues.

## Break-Ins and Home Invasions

If you find yourself faced with the terrifying reality of a break-in or home invasion, you need to have a clear plan and remain as calm as possible. The following steps outline how to handle such a situation, from contacting authorities to potentially defending your life with a firearm.

If you become aware that your home is being broken into, the most important thing is to stay calm. Your immediate reaction might be panic, but maintaining a clear head will help you think and act more effectively. Assess the situation quickly but thoroughly. If you can do so safely, find a secure place to hide or fortify yourself and your family.

Once you have a moment, the next step is to contact the police. Dial 911 and provide them with as much information as possible: your address, the nature of the emergency, the number of intruders if known, and any details about their appearance or behavior. Stay on the phone if possible, so the dispatcher can hear what is happening and provide guidance.

While waiting for the police to arrive, if you are in a secure location, stay put. Do not attempt to confront the intruders unless it is absolutely necessary. Your primary goal is to ensure the safety of yourself and your family. If you have children, instruct them to remain quiet and stay hidden with you.

If the intruders find you or if it becomes clear that they intend to cause harm, you may need to defend yourself. This is where having a firearm and being trained in its use becomes critical. If you decide to use a firearm, remember the fundamentals: Know your target and what is beyond it, keep your finger off the trigger until you are ready to shoot, and only use lethal force if you are in imminent danger of death or serious bodily harm.

In the case of a home invasion with several armed assailants, the situation escalates exponentially. If you see that your house is about to be invaded by multiple armed individuals, immediate action is required. Firstly, secure yourself and your family in a safe room if you have one. This room should ideally be fortified and have a solid door with a lock. It should also have a phone or a way to communicate with the authorities.

Call 911 immediately and inform them of the situation, emphasizing that there are multiple armed intruders. Provide any details you can observe without compromising your safety, such as the number of assailants, their appearance, and any weapons they have.

While in the safe room, arm yourself if you have a firearm. Position yourself in a way that gives you a clear view of the entrance without exposing yourself unnecessarily. If the intruders attempt to break into the safe room, warn them loudly that you are armed and have called the police. This may deter them, but be prepared to defend yourself if they proceed to breach the room.

Throughout this ordeal, maintaining communication with the police dispatcher is vital. They can provide real-time advice and update you on the arrival of law enforcement. Once the police arrive, follow their instructions carefully. Do not leave your safe room until you are certain that law enforcement is at your door. They may need you to identify yourself or provide other information to ensure they can safely enter and secure the premises.

After the immediate threat is neutralized, there are still important steps to take. Cooperate fully with law enforcement officers as they investigate the scene.

Provide them with all the information you have about the intruders and what transpired. This will aid in their investigation and increase the likelihood of capturing the perpetrators.

On the other hand, if retreating doesn't work and you find yourself in the terrifying situation of being threatened or attacked by intruders while armed, it is essential to know how to defend yourself effectively and responsibly. Here are the steps you should take, how to decide when to use lethal force versus incapacitating an attacker, and the possible legal fallout of such an incident.

Your primary goal should always be to avoid confrontation if possible. If the intruders are attacking you and you have no other option but to defend yourself, your firearm becomes a critical tool for your survival. Position yourself in a secure location where you have a clear line of sight to the entry points. This allows you to control the situation as best as possible and avoid being caught off guard.

When defending yourself, keep a firm grip on your firearm and maintain a steady aim. If you have time, take a deep breath to steady your nerves. Aim for the center mass of the intruder, which is the torso area, as it is the largest target and increases the likelihood of stopping the threat effectively. If the intruder continues to pose a direct threat to your life or the lives of others, you may need to use lethal force.

The decision to use lethal force should not be taken lightly. You are justified in using lethal force if you genuinely believe that you or others are in imminent danger of death or serious bodily harm. This standard is critical and is typically recognized in self-defense laws across many jurisdictions. Shooting to incapacitate, such as aiming for limbs, is not advisable, because it is less effective in stopping the threat and introduces both practical and legal complications. Practically speaking, limbs are smaller, faster-moving targets, hard to hit under the stress of a life-threatening situation. A miss could endanger bystanders or give the assailant more time to harm you. Legally, it can suggest that you had the time, control, and clarity of mind to shoot with precision, which may undercut your self-defense claim by implying the threat wasn't imminent or severe. Worse yet, if the attacker survives and claims excessive force, you could face civil liability—even if the shooting was justified. In contrast, aiming for center mass is the standard taught in self-defense training because it maximizes your chance to stop the threat quickly and shows that your intent was to survive, not to maim. The intent of using a firearm in self-defense is to neutralize the threat, not to harm more than necessary.

After the immediate danger has passed, secure your firearm and ensure that the intruder is no longer a threat. Do not tamper with the crime scene; instead, contact law enforcement immediately if you haven't already. When the police arrive, identify yourself and follow their instructions carefully. Inform them that you are the homeowner and explain the situation calmly. It is recommended to be cooperative and transparent during this process.

After using a firearm in self-defense, there are several legal and emotional considerations to address. You should expect to be thoroughly investigated by law enforcement. They will need to determine whether the use of force was justified under the circumstances. You may be taken in for questioning, and your firearm might be confiscated as evidence. Contact a lawyer as soon as possible to guide you through the legal process and ensure your rights are protected.

The legal fallout of a self-defense shooting can vary substantially depending on the jurisdiction and the specific circumstances of the incident. If the investigation determines that your actions were justified, you may not face any charges. However, there is always the possibility of civil lawsuits from the intruder or their family, even if no criminal charges are filed. This is another reason why having legal representation is crucial.

Emotionally, the aftermath of a self-defense incident can be challenging. Taking a life or causing serious injury, even in defense of your own life, is a traumatic experience. It is important to seek support from family, friends, or professional counselors to help cope with any emotional or psychological impact. Processing the event and its aftermath healthily is important for your well-being.

If you are attacked by intruders while armed, act decisively and responsibly to defend yourself using the steps outlined above. Use lethal force only when you believe there is an imminent threat to your life or the lives of others. After the incident, cooperate with law enforcement, seek legal counsel if necessary, and address any emotional aftermath to ensure you navigate the situation effectively and legally.

## Self-Defense in Public Places

Finding yourself in a public place, such as a store, during a robbery or attack is a highly stressful and dangerous situation. If you are carrying a concealed firearm, you must have a clear understanding of how to respond effectively and responsibly.

First and foremost, assess the situation as calmly and quickly as possible. Note the assailant's position, their weapon, and their behavior. If the assailant has everyone at gunpoint and is demanding money or valuables, the immediate priority should be to avoid escalating the situation. Do not draw attention to yourself or make any sudden movements. Comply with the assailant's demands to the best of your ability while you evaluate the best course of action.

If the assailant's focus is not directly on you and you can safely do so, discreetly position yourself in a spot where you have cover and a clear view of the assailant. This could be behind a display, a counter, or another object that offers protection. The goal is to find a spot where you can observe the situation without being seen or putting yourself in immediate danger.

Drawing your firearm should be a last resort, reserved for when there is an imminent threat to your life or the lives of others. If the assailant begins to act violently or if it becomes clear that their intent is to harm, you may have to take action. Before drawing your firearm, ensure that you have a clear line of sight and are not endangering other innocent bystanders. The decision to use your firearm must be made with the utmost consideration of the potential consequences.

When you decide that it is necessary to act, do so swiftly and decisively. Draw your firearm and issue a clear, loud command for the assailant to drop their weapon and get on the ground. This can sometimes deter them and avoid the need to fire. However, be prepared to use lethal force if the assailant does not comply and poses a direct threat to your life or the lives of others. Aim for the center mass to maximize the chances of stopping the threat effectively.

After neutralizing the threat, secure the scene to the best of your ability. Keep your firearm drawn but pointed in a safe direction. Check on the safety of others around you and instruct them to remain calm and stay where they are. Call 911 immediately to report the incident, providing them with all necessary information, including your location, the nature of the threat, and the fact that you are armed.

When law enforcement arrives, follow their instructions meticulously. Holster your firearm and raise your hands to show that you are not a threat. Identify yourself as the person who neutralized the threat and explain the situation calmly. Expect to be questioned thoroughly by the police and understand that your firearm will likely be confiscated as part of their investigation.

In the aftermath of such an event, legal and emotional considerations will arise. Seek legal counsel as soon as possible to navigate the investigation and protect your rights. Using a firearm in public, even in self-defense, will be subject to intense scrutiny. Legal representation is crucial in ensuring that your actions are appropriately understood and justified.

Emotionally, such an incident can be deeply traumatic. Even if you acted correctly and saved lives, the gravity of taking a life or seriously injuring another person can be profound. It is important to seek support from mental health professionals, as well as from family and friends, to process the event and its impact on your life.

Being in a public place during a robbery or attack requires calm assessment, strategic positioning, and decisive action only when absolutely necessary. The primary goal should always be to avoid escalation and protect lives. If forced to use a concealed firearm, do so with a clear understanding of the legal and emotional aftermath that will follow.

## Stand Your Ground Laws (Castle Doctrine)

In many states across the United States, stand your ground laws provide home-owners with the legal right to use deadly force against an intruder without the duty to retreat. These laws assert that if someone breaks into your home, you are legally justified in defending yourself with a firearm, even before the intruder physically attacks or aims a weapon at you. The rationale behind these laws is rooted in the fundamental principle that a person's home is their sanctuary, and any uninvited intrusion is considered a dangerous and imminent threat to the safety and well-being of the occupants.

Stand your ground laws recognize that when an intruder breaks down your door, the act itself is a clear and immediate danger. The law presumes that anyone forcibly entering your home has malicious intent, and thus, you are justified in using lethal force to protect yourself and your family. This principle is often referred to as the "castle doctrine," which derives from the old English common law notion that "a man's home is his castle."

If an intruder kicks in your door and enters your home, you do not need to wait for them to draw a weapon or make an explicit threat before you act. The mere act of breaking into your home is considered enough of a threat to justify the use of deadly force. Waiting for further aggression could put you and your loved ones at greater risk.

In states with stand your ground laws, the legal system generally supports the right of homeowners to defend their homes without fear of legal repercussions. If you shoot an intruder under these circumstances, the law typically provides you with immunity from criminal prosecution and civil lawsuits. However, be sure to understand the specific provisions of the stand your ground laws in your state, as they can vary slightly from one jurisdiction to another.

These laws are not without controversy. Critics argue that they can lead to unnecessary violence and misuse of deadly force. However, proponents maintain that they are a necessary protection for law-abiding citizens who find themselves in life-threatening situations. No one should be forced to flee from their own home in the face of an intruder; instead, they have the right to stand their ground and defend themselves.

It is important for homeowners to be fully aware of their rights and responsibilities with respect to stand your ground laws. While these laws provide significant protection, they also come with the responsibility of ensuring that the use of force is truly justified. Homeowners should take self-defense courses and understand the legal ramifications of using a firearm in self-defense. Additionally, it is wise to have a plan in place for such emergencies, including safe places to retreat to within the home if possible, and steps to take immediately after an incident, such as calling law enforcement.

Stand your ground laws serve as a strong deterrent to potential criminals, reinforcing the idea that homeowners have the right and the means to defend their property and their lives. Knowing that these laws exist can give homeowners peace of mind, allowing them to feel more secure in their own homes. However, the goal should always be to avoid violence whenever possible, using deadly force only as a last resort when faced with an imminent threat.

When it comes to self-defense *outside the home*, stand your ground laws also play an important role in defining your legal right to protect yourself without the obligation to retreat. Unlike traditional self-defense laws that may require you to attempt escape or avoid confrontation if safely possible, stand your ground laws remove that duty. If you are in a place where you are lawfully present—whether that's a parking lot, sidewalk, store, or public park—and you reasonably believe you are in imminent danger of death or great bodily harm, you are legally justified in using force, including deadly force, to stop the threat.

Consider situations like being stalked in a dimly lit parking lot or ambushed while shopping. In states with stand your ground protections, you do not have to flee or attempt to hide before defending yourself. If someone charges at you with a weapon or behaves in a way that any reasonable person would perceive as a deadly threat, the law is on your side—assuming your response is proportionate and you weren't the aggressor. This legal doctrine reinforces the idea that your right to self-defense doesn't end at your front door. It affirms that law-abiding citizens have the right to defend their lives anywhere they have a legal right to be. However, it's still crucial to understand the laws in your specific state, as interpretations and applications can vary, and prosecutors may scrutinize claims of self-defense carefully, especially in high-profile cases.

As an example, the 2012 George Zimmerman case, which remains one of the most controversial self-defense cases in modern American history, involved Zimmerman, a neighborhood watch volunteer in Sanford, Florida, who encountered 17-year-old Trayvon Martin, who was walking through a gated community. After a confrontation, Martin physically assaulted Zimmerman, knocking him to the ground and slamming his head into the pavement. Fearing for his life and unable to escape, Zimmerman drew his legally owned firearm and fatally shot Martin.

Despite the media firestorm and political pressure surrounding the case, the facts presented in court showed that Zimmerman was brutally attacked and had every reason to believe he was in imminent danger of serious bodily harm or death. Under Florida law, he had no duty to retreat. The state's stand your ground law made it clear: If you are lawfully present and facing a deadly threat, you are not required to flee. You have the right to defend yourself.

Zimmerman was charged with second-degree murder and manslaughter, but in 2013, a jury unanimously found him not guilty. The verdict affirmed that, based on the evidence and Florida's self-defense laws, Zimmerman acted within his legal rights. While the case became a political lightning rod, the legal outcome reflected a fundamental principle of self-defense: The right to defend one's life, especially when violently attacked, is not a privilege granted by public opinion—it's a right enshrined in law.

Ultimately, understanding and respecting the power that comes with the right to self-defense is necessary. While stand your ground laws provide robust protections, they must be exercised with caution, awareness, and a deep respect for the serious consequences that come with using a firearm. These laws affirm the right to protect oneself and one's home, reflecting a fundamental aspect of personal liberty and security.

## States Without Stand Your Ground Laws

In contrast to states *with* stand your ground laws, there are several states and locales where the legal framework is markedly different, often favoring the assailant over the person defending themselves. As of April 2025, there are 13 states that have some form of duty to retreat laws. These states are Connecticut, Delaware, Hawaii, Maine, Maryland, Massachusetts, Minnesota, Nebraska, New Jersey, New York, North Dakota, Rhode Island, and Wisconsin. In these jurisdictions, individuals who defend themselves against attackers, even within their own homes, can face serious legal repercussions. This approach is often rooted in a Marxist-inspired belief that society, rather than the individual, bears the ultimate responsibility for criminal behavior. This ideology posits that societal inequities and injustices drive individuals to commit crimes, and therefore, holding criminals fully accountable is deemed unjust. This way of thinking shifts responsibility away from individuals and undermines the rule of law. It fails to address the root causes of crime and instead punishes those who seek to protect themselves. This approach is not only ineffective but also dangerous, as it creates an environment where criminals feel empowered to act with impunity, knowing that their victims are legally constrained from defending themselves effectively.

In states without stand your ground laws, the legal doctrine typically requires individuals to retreat from a threat if it is safe to do so. This principle is known as the duty to retreat. If someone uses deadly force in self-defense without first attempting to retreat, they can be prosecuted for assault or even homicide. This legal stance can create absurd and dangerous situations where law-abiding citizens are forced to weigh the risk of being attacked against the risk of legal prosecution for defending themselves.

One notable example is New York State, which follows the duty to retreat principle. In 2018, in the city of Rochester, 64-year-old Willie King faced prosecution after shooting an intruder in his home. King, who had previously been a burglary victim, encountered a man breaking into his residence through a window. Fearing for his life, he fired his legally owned handgun, wounding the intruder. Despite the apparent justification, authorities charged King with first-degree assault, arguing that he failed to retreat from the threat as mandated by state law. This case ignited debates over self-defense rights and the obligations imposed by duty-to-retreat statutes. Ultimately, after public outcry and legal proceedings, the charges against King were dropped. However, the incident underscored the complexities and potential pitfalls homeowners face when defending themselves in jurisdictions without stand-your-ground protections.

A more recent example is the conviction of 78-year-old Robert Fisher Jr. on March 7, 2025, for manslaughter, a glaring miscarriage of justice and a stark example of how self-defense is being undermined by so-called "duty to retreat" laws. In this case, which took place in Connecticut, a physically frail senior citizen was ambushed in his own vehicle by a violent, intoxicated aggressor—more than 30 years his junior—who yanked open his car door, punched him in the face, spat on him, and explicitly threatened to kill him. Fisher, fearing for his life, exercised his fundamental right to self-defense by using a legally owned firearm. Yet, instead of the aggressor facing the consequences, Fisher was punished.

In the *Fisher* case, Prosecutor David Shannon's argument that "you can't bring a gun to a fistfight" is not only legally flawed but outright dangerous. By that logic, a woman being strangled by a 250-pound man should be expected to fight back with her fists rather than use a firearm to save her own life. Similarly, if an attacker armed with a knife charges, the victim should apparently be required to arm themselves with an equally "fair" weapon rather than take decisive action to survive. The notion that victims must match their defense to an attacker's chosen method of violence defies both logic and justice. When an assailant explicitly states their intent to kill and follows through with an assault, it is not only reasonable but necessary to take them at their word. Expecting an old man to "retreat" from a life-threatening attack rather than defend himself is beyond outrageous—it is a complete failure of the justice system.

Even in states without stand your ground laws where a self-defense shooting is ultimately deemed justified, there are documented cases where prosecutors still pursue alternative charges—highlighting a clear anti-gun bias and a determination to punish gun ownership itself rather than the actual circumstances of the incident.

For example, in 2019, Ronald Stolarczyk of Oneida County, New York, was attacked by two armed intruders who broke into his home. Stolarczyk feared for his life—not only because his own home had been broken into before, but also because he knew of recent home invasions in which homeowners had been killed. Stolarczyk first yelled at the burglars to leave. But they were undeterred and continued to advance at him. Fearing for his life, Degenhart retrieved his late father's .38 caliber revolver and shot the intruders, killing them both.

Although the Oneida County district attorney agreed the shooting was justified and declined to charge Stolarczyk with murder, he was still prosecuted for using his late father's legally owned revolver. Because he hadn't obtained his own pistol permit or registered the firearm in his name, he faced a Class E felony—punishable by up to four years in prison and the permanent loss of his Second Amendment rights. To make matters worse, local authorities seized his home for alleged housing code violations, citing a lack of utilities and a clutter of old electronics. All of this happened simply because Stolarczyk, a financially struggling man who couldn't even afford a basic phone plan, failed to navigate the bureaucratic maze required just to legally defend himself in his own home. The legal battle that ensued placed immense stress on Degenhart and highlighted the precarious position of individuals trying to defend themselves in such jurisdictions.

These cases underscore the absurdity of a legal system that prioritizes the rights of the assailant over those of the victim. The belief that society is to blame for criminal behavior, and thus criminals should be treated leniently, undermines the God-given right of individuals to protect themselves and their families. This approach not only endangers law-abiding citizens but also emboldens criminals who know they are less likely to face meaningful consequences for their actions.

In addition to legal ramifications, the emotional and financial toll on individuals who defend themselves in such states can be devastating. Legal battles can drain savings, cause loss of employment, and lead to severe psychological stress. The case of the bodega clerk in New York City illustrates the potential consequences. In July 2022, a 61-year-old New York City bodega clerk named Jose Alba was jailed and charged with murder after fatally stabbing a man who had cornered and attacked him behind the store's counter. Alba insisted he acted in self-defense, but New York's restrictive laws—including a duty to retreat and a rule that deadly force is justified only against an imminent deadly threat—meant authorities initially treated his actions as criminal. The widely criticized case put Alba at serious risk of prosecution despite his self-defense claim, demonstrating how ambiguous, stringent self-defense statutes can jeopardize people who protect themselves in such confrontations.

In locales with these restrictive self-defense laws, individuals must navigate a complex legal landscape that often leaves them vulnerable to prosecution. The duty to retreat can place victims in life-threatening situations where they must choose between defending themselves and facing potential legal consequences. This is not only impractical but also deeply unjust, as it fails to recognize the inherent right of individuals to protect themselves from harm.

The legal ramifications in such states are severe. Individuals who defend themselves can face charges ranging from assault to homicide, some of which carry harsh mandatory minimum sentences. They may also be subjected to civil lawsuits from the assailant or their family, leading to further financial and emotional burdens. The legal system's focus on retreating rather than defending can deter individuals from taking necessary actions to protect themselves, ultimately compromising public safety.

Ultimately, the unjust nature of these laws becomes evident when considering the right to self-defense. In a just society, individuals should not be forced to retreat from their own homes or be punished for protecting themselves and their loved ones. The right to self-defense is a cornerstone of personal liberty and security, and any legal framework that undermines this right is inherently unjust and counterproductive.

Nevertheless, it is crucial to familiarize yourself with your state's laws regarding how to react to a burglary, break-in, or home invasion. Knowing the legal guidelines will help you proceed appropriately. However, if you or your loved ones face an immediate threat of death or serious injury, use your firearm in self-defense and address the legal ramifications later. It is better to save your life and the lives of your family than to let tragedy occur out of fear of prosecution under questionable laws.

## Swatting

Swatting is a malicious and highly dangerous tactic where someone falsely reports a serious crime, such as an armed hostage situation or active shooter scenario, to law enforcement to provoke a heavily armed SWAT team response to an unsuspecting victim's home or place of business. In recent years, this egregious practice has been weaponized by radical activists, particularly against conservative commentators, Republican lawmakers, and even everyday citizens who happen to express viewpoints the far-left disapproves of. The purpose behind swatting is clear: to harass, intimidate, and, in some cases, put political opponents in mortal danger. When SWAT teams respond to these calls, they are operating under the assumption that there is an immediate and lethal threat. In the confusion, chaos, and high-stress nature of these situations, innocent people have been hurt or killed.

Imagine this scenario: It's late evening, you're at home relaxing or spending time with family when suddenly floodlights illuminate your windows, and you hear the unmistakable sound of officers shouting commands. You are startled, unsure of what is happening, but any sudden movement could be perceived as a threat by officers outside, who believe they're responding to a violent situation. In such moments, the wrong gesture—a cell phone mistaken for a weapon, a movement misinterpreted—can lead to deadly consequences. The horror of this tactic lies in its unpredictability and the immediate danger it presents to innocent people caught in the crosshairs of political vendettas or ideological warfare.

For those of us who have any form of public presence—whether as a social media influencer, YouTuber, political figure, or even as an author—it is increasingly necessary to be proactive. The first step is to contact your local law enforcement agency. Inform them that, due to your public profile or controversial opinions, you could be a potential target of swatting. Many police departments are familiar with this tactic and can place a note in their system alerting responding officers to verify any high-risk calls involving your address before storming in guns drawn. This won't guarantee your safety, but it significantly reduces the chance of escalation.

It is also important to brief family members or roommates on how to respond calmly and compliantly should law enforcement arrive unexpectedly. Make sure everyone understands the importance of following commands without question in such situations, no matter how confusing or unjust it may seem in the moment. Having a security camera system with external and internal coverage can also provide context to law enforcement and help protect you legally if things go sideways.

The unsettling reality is that swatting has moved from being an internet prank to a form of psychological warfare aimed at silencing or punishing ideological dissent. Awareness and preparation are your best defense against this cowardly tactic. While the goal of swatting is to instill fear, those in the crosshairs must remain vigilant, prepared, and unshaken.

## Carjackings

Being carjacked is a terrifying and potentially life-threatening situation. If you have a gun in the car, knowing how to respond effectively is pivotal. Your first priority should always be to assess the immediate threat to your life and the lives of any passengers. If the carjacker is armed or presents a clear and imminent threat, drawing your firearm to defend yourself may be necessary. Many states recognize the concept of the car as an extension of someone's private domain under the castle doctrine and allows self-defense from an intruder or aggressor within their vehicle.

The castle doctrine typically provides legal protection for using force in self-defense when an intruder unlawfully enters your home or car. If you are in a state that upholds this doctrine for vehicles, you have a legal right to defend yourself against a carjacker. It is vital to understand the specific laws and nuances of self-defense in your state; some states may have different thresholds for what constitutes a lawful use of force in a vehicle.

Being carjacked is one of the most frightening experiences one can face, especially when the carjacker is armed and makes demands for you to drive. In such a high-stress scenario, having a clear understanding of how to protect yourself can save your life. If you have access to your gun, the priority is to remain as calm and composed as possible to evaluate the situation and identify any opportunities to safely neutralize the threat.

Firstly, assess the immediate threat level. The carjacker's weapon, demeanor, and specific demands will influence your response. If the carjacker is agitated or erratic, making sudden movements or showing signs of imminent violence, your response must be swift and decisive. However, if the carjacker appears to be focused on taking your vehicle without immediate harm, you might have more time to carefully consider your actions.

If you are ordered to drive, comply initially to buy yourself some time and to avoid escalating the situation prematurely. Keep your hands visible and follow the carjacker's instructions while continuously scanning for an opportunity to access your firearm safely. As you drive, subtly adjust your body position if possible, making sure that your gun is within reach. The key is to move naturally and avoid drawing attention to your intentions.

An opportunity to neutralize the situation might arise if the carjacker becomes momentarily distracted or if you reach a location where you feel it is safer to act. If the carjacker looks away or shifts their focus, you might have a brief window to draw your firearm. The action must be swift and confident to minimize the risk of the carjacker reacting violently. Aim to disarm and neutralize the threat as quickly as possible.

When you decide to draw your firearm, ensure that you maintain control of the situation. Command the carjacker to drop their weapon and cease any aggressive actions. Your tone should be authoritative and unwavering, signaling that you are serious and in control. If the carjacker complies, keep them at gunpoint and call for law enforcement assistance immediately. If they do not comply and continue to pose a threat, you may have to use your firearm to protect yourself.

The decision to use lethal force must be based on the immediate threat to your life. Many states' self-defense laws will support your right to protect yourself if you are in imminent danger.

Throughout this ordeal, your primary goal is to survive and protect yourself. Remember that engaging with an armed carjacker is extremely dangerous, and the best course of action might sometimes be to de-escalate the situation without using your firearm. Complying with demands, such as handing over your vehicle, might be the safest option if you judge that immediate resistance could result in greater harm.

In situations involving rioters or protesters blocking the road and attacking your car, the scenario becomes even more complex. If individuals are hitting your car, attempting to break in, or smashing the glass, it poses an imminent threat to your safety and that of your passengers. In many states, you would be justified in using your firearm to defend yourself if you genuinely believe your life is in imminent danger. The justification for using force in these situations often hinges on the perceived threat level and the immediacy of the danger.

However, in states where the use of force in such scenarios is heavily restricted, the decision becomes morally and legally complicated, especially if you have children in the car. The instinct to protect your children and ensure their safety can outweigh legal considerations in the heat of the moment. In these cases, your moral obligation to safeguard your loved ones may conflict with state laws that do not recognize the castle doctrine in vehicles or restrict the use of force in self-defense.

The consequences of using your firearm in these situations can be severe, particularly in states with stringent self-defense laws. You may face legal repercussions, including criminal charges, if your actions are deemed excessive or unjustified under state law. Despite this, many would argue that the immediate threat to your life and the lives of your children justifies taking action, even if it means facing legal consequences later. The moral imperative to protect your family can often drive decisions in high-stress, dangerous situations.

Ultimately, the decision to use a firearm in self-defense during a carjacking or while under attack by rioters is deeply personal and situational. It requires a clear understanding of your state's laws, a calm assessment of the threat level, and a willingness to face the potential legal consequences. The moral and self-defense aspects of such a decision often intertwine, creating a challenging landscape where the safety of yourself and your loved ones must be carefully balanced against the legal framework of the state, county, or city in which you live.

## Drive-by Shootings

Although one of the least likely situations for the average citizen, drive-by shootings are a terrifying and chaotic situation, typically occurring in urban areas and often associated with gang violence or targeted attacks. If you find yourself caught in the crossfire of a drive-by shooting, your primary objective should be to protect yourself and others around you by taking immediate action to minimize the risk of injury or death.

The first step in such a situation is to take cover. Look for the nearest solid barrier, such as a wall, a car engine block, or any other substantial object that can provide protection from bullets. Quickly move to this cover and stay low to the ground to reduce your exposure to gunfire. Encourage others around you to do the same, using clear and urgent instructions to help them understand the gravity of the situation.

If you are armed, the decision to draw your firearm and engage the shooters is complex and fraught with risks. In the chaos of a drive-by shooting, accurately identifying the shooters and ensuring that your return fire does not harm innocent bystanders is extremely challenging. Engaging in a firefight with moving vehicles increases the likelihood of stray bullets causing unintended injuries or fatalities.

Given these considerations, the best course of action is typically to take cover and not engage the shooters unless absolutely necessary. The primary goal should be to survive the immediate threat and avoid escalating the situation further. Only consider drawing your firearm if the shooters exit their vehicle and directly threaten you or others in your immediate vicinity, making it clear that there is no alternative to defending yourself.

Even if you are trained and confident in your ability to use your firearm, the unpredictable nature of a drive-by shooting means that taking cover and waiting for the danger to pass is usually the safest and most prudent option. After the initial threat has subsided, assess the situation carefully before making any further decisions.

Once it is safe to do so, call law enforcement to report the incident and provide any relevant information about the shooters, their vehicle, and the direction they were heading. Your priority should be to assist the authorities in apprehending the perpetrators and ensuring that medical help arrives for any injured individuals.

Being caught in the crossfire of a drive-by shooting is a rare but extremely dangerous situation. Taking cover and protecting yourself and others should be your immediate focus. Engaging the shooters should be a last resort, reserved for situations where there is no other option to ensure your survival. By prioritizing safety and providing information to law enforcement, you can help mitigate the dangers and contribute to the apprehension of those responsible.

## Firearms Education and Training for Youth

Adults are not the only ones who should know how to handle a potentially dangerous situation. If an adult is not around, or if an adult is injured or incapacitated, children should have the knowledge and confidence to respond appropriately—especially in an emergency involving firearms. Educating children about gun safety from an early age instills respect, not fear, and helps prevent tragic accidents. They should understand the difference between responsible gun handling and reckless behavior, knowing never to touch a firearm unsupervised unless it is absolutely necessary to save a life.

The role of firearms education and training for youth is crucial in developing a responsible gun culture in the next generation. Youth firearms training, when done properly, teaches children discipline, responsibility, and critical thinking under pressure. Programs like hunter safety courses and junior marksmanship leagues demonstrate that children can learn to handle firearms safely and competently. Programs designed to teach gun safety to children and teenagers focus on instilling respect, knowledge, and proper handling skills, which are essential for reducing firearm-related accidents and promoting safe usage. These programs emphasize that minors should always be accompanied by an experienced adult or parent when they use or handle firearms, ensuring supervision and adherence to safety protocols.

A well-informed child is far less likely to make a fatal mistake than one who has been sheltered from knowledge about firearms altogether. Instead of demonizing gun ownership, we should focus on fostering a culture where children respect firearms, understand their power, and, if the situation ever arises, know how to act decisively and safely.

Historically, firearms training among children and teenagers was more common, particularly in rural areas. As recently as the 1970s and 1980s, after-school extracurricular activities often included shooting sports and gun safety classes. These programs taught young people how to handle firearms safely, respect the power of guns, and understand the consequences of their misuse. Such training helped to demystify firearms and foster a culture of respect and responsibility.

Exposure to firearms at an early age, when done responsibly and under proper supervision, can sharply reduce the chances of accidents or mishandling. Children who are taught to respect firearms and understand their potential dangers are more likely to handle them safely throughout their lives. For example, in rural communities where hunting is a common activity, it is typical for children to be introduced to firearms early. These children learn from their parents and other adults about the importance of gun safety, the proper use of firearms, and the ethical considerations involved in hunting and shooting sports.

Moreover, early education helps to counteract the often-sensationalized portrayals of firearms in media and popular culture. By providing factual, hands-on experience with firearms, these programs can help children and teenagers develop a realistic understanding of guns, which is imperative for making informed decisions about their use and ownership.

One notable example of successful firearms education is the 4-H Shooting Sports program, which has been active for decades. This program provides structured, supervised training for youth in various shooting disciplines, including rifle, shotgun, and archery. Participants learn not only technical skills but also important values, such as discipline, focus, and respect for others. Case studies have shown that children who participate in the 4-H Shooting Sports program show a high level of safety consciousness and are less likely to be involved in firearm-related accidents.

Several organizations offer comprehensive firearms education programs targeted at youth. The NRA, for instance, has long championed the importance of gun safety education through its Eddie Eagle GunSafe® program, which teaches children what to do if they encounter a firearm: "Stop! Don't Touch. Run Away. Tell a Grown-Up." This program is designed for younger children to understand the basic principles of gun safety without needing to handle firearms. For teenagers, the NRA offers more advanced training courses that cover safe handling, shooting techniques, and the ethical responsibilities of gun ownership.

Scouting America (formerly known as the Boy Scouts of America) also incorporates firearms education into their activities, offering merit badges in shooting sports. These programs require participants to demonstrate their knowledge of gun safety, marksmanship, and respect for firearms under the guidance of trained instructors. By including these activities in their curriculum, Scouts aim to promote a culture of responsible gun use and respect among youth.

The importance of adult supervision cannot be overstated. Children and teenagers must learn to always obey adults and authorities when it comes to handling firearms. This ensures that they receive consistent, accurate information and that their behavior is monitored to prevent accidents. Experienced adults can provide practical demonstrations and correct any unsafe practices, reinforcing the lessons learned in formal training programs.

Overall, the role of firearms education and training for youth is vital for promoting a culture of safety and responsibility. By teaching young people to respect firearms and understand their proper use, we can reduce the likelihood of accidents and foster a generation that values the principles of responsible gun ownership.

***

Choosing the right firearm is only the beginning of responsible gun ownership. Understanding the different types of firearms and selecting one that suits your needs—whether for home defense, concealed carry, or sport shooting—is a critical first step. But owning a firearm is meaningless without proper training and familiarity with its operation. Regular practice at the range, defensive shooting courses, and scenario-based training will ensure you can use your firearm effectively and instinctively in a high-stress situation. Carrying concealed requires not just skill, but confidence, which comes through repetition, comfort with your holster setup, and developing situational awareness in your daily life. Equally important is knowing your state and local laws to avoid unnecessary legal trouble. Ignorance of the law is not a defense and understanding when and how you can legally use your firearm will prevent a justified self-defense situation from turning into a criminal prosecution. Finally, no one wants to be caught in an emergency where they must draw their firearm, but being mentally prepared for that possibility is just as crucial as physical training. Running through different scenarios, knowing how to react under pressure, and committing to always carrying where legally allowed can mean the difference between being a victim or surviving a deadly encounter. Owning a firearm is a responsibility that extends far beyond purchasing a gun—it's a commitment to being prepared, trained, and legally informed at all times.

# Chapter 15

## Thought Experiments and Hypothetical Scenarios

*A man's rights rest in three boxes: the ballot box, the jury box, and the cartridge box.*

—Frederick Douglass

In exploring the many facets of the Second Amendment and its significance in American society, it's essential to consider not only the current debates but also the broader implications of gun rights through various hypothetical scenarios. These thought experiments don't just stretch the imagination—they force us to confront uncomfortable possibilities and ask hard questions about what could happen if the balance between liberty and control were pushed to its breaking point.

What if the Second Amendment were repealed tomorrow—stripped from the Constitution with the stroke of a pen? Now flip the script: What if the Second Amendment were not just preserved, but supercharged—amended to void all federal and state gun control laws across the board? What if a future administration launched a full-blown disarmament campaign, threatening severe penalties for those who refused to hand over their firearms? These aren't just wild hypotheticals—they're the scenarios that define the true boundaries of liberty, power, and the people's willingness to fight for one over the other.

This chapter delves into a series of hypothetical situations, each designed to challenge and explore the boundaries of gun rights in America. Each thought experiment serves as a lens through which we can analyze the consequences of different approaches to gun control and gun rights. By considering the potential realities of these scenarios, we aim to strengthen the case for the Second Amendment, debunk anti-gun positions, and highlight the importance of maintaining this constitutional right in a variety of contexts.

Whether it's imagining a world where citizens are completely disarmed, contemplating the deterrent effect of an armed populace against government overreach, or envisioning how the Second Amendment might be interpreted in future societies, these thought experiments provide valuable insights into why the right to bear arms is crucial for preserving freedom, security, and individual autonomy. Through these explorations, we reaffirm the enduring relevance of the Second Amendment in an ever-changing world.

## Thought Experiment: The Repeal of All Gun Control Laws

Imagine a scenario where all restrictive gun control laws, aside from basic background checks to prevent violent criminals from obtaining firearms, were repealed. The National Firearms Act (NFA) is abolished, the ATF dismantled, and every law-abiding citizen is allowed to own and carry any firearm they choose. Citizens are legally permitted to carry concealed firearms anywhere in the country. Now, consider the potential impact if nearly every law-abiding American were to own and carry a gun, both at home and in public.

In such a society, crime rates would likely plummet due to the immense deterrent effect on potential criminals. When every potential victim is armed and capable of defending themselves, the risks associated with crimes like robbery, assault, or burglary would increase exponentially. Criminals, aware of the overwhelming likelihood that their targets could be armed, would be far less inclined to engage in illegal activity. Historical data supports this notion: States with higher per capita rates of legal gun ownership, such as Vermont and Maine, consistently report some of the lowest violent crime rates in the nation.

Law-abiding citizens would be empowered to take responsibility for their safety, reducing dependence on law enforcement, which cannot be everywhere at once. Vulnerable populations, including the elderly, women, and those in high-crime areas, would particularly benefit. The ability to carry a firearm fosters not only personal security but also a sense of confidence and collective safety for entire communities. The elimination of gun-free zones—areas often targeted by criminals due to the absence of armed resistance—would further enhance public safety by disrupting the ease with which criminals currently operate in "soft targets."

Widespread gun ownership would allow quicker, more decisive responses to criminal activity. Instead of waiting for law enforcement, citizens could protect themselves and others in real time, potentially reducing the severity and duration of crimes like mass shootings, muggings, or home invasions. Numerous examples exist where armed citizens have successfully intervened, such as the 2017 Sutherland Springs, Texas, church shooting, where an armed neighbor confronted the shooter and prevented further loss of life. Expanding such scenarios could make community-driven defensive action the rule rather than the exception.

Despite fears expressed by gun control advocates, this scenario would not devolve into chaos or a "Wild West" atmosphere. The vast majority of law-abiding gun owners consistently demonstrate responsible behavior and do not engage in reckless or violent actions. While isolated incidents might occur, the overall reduction in crime and increased deterrence would far outweigh these rare events. When many are armed, individuals think twice before engaging in aggression.

The notion that more armed citizens would lead to widespread disorder also fails to account for the proven safety and effectiveness of responsible gun ownership. Instead of escalating violence, a well-armed populace would likely foster greater respect and order, as the need for defensive firearm use diminishes over time in safer communities. A society that fully embraces the Second Amendment would uphold peace through mutual respect, safeguarding individuals' rights to defend themselves and their loved ones.

If all state and federal gun control laws were repealed, the economic impact could be substantial. A freer firearms market would likely spur a surge in new businesses—from manufacturers and gunsmiths to training centers, shooting ranges, and retail stores—creating jobs and stimulating local economies. Consumer spending on firearms, accessories, ammunition, and related services would increase dramatically, along with expanded demand for raw materials and logistics. The manufacturing sector would see notable growth, with small and mid-sized companies entering a previously over-regulated space.

Politically, such a sweeping repeal would be seismic. Pro-Second Amendment states and regions would likely celebrate the decision as a long-overdue restoration of constitutional rights. However, anti-gun jurisdictions would face public outcry, legal challenges, and potential civil disobedience. The polarization between pro- and anti-gun factions would intensify, with some states pushing back through alternative legislation or federal court appeals. Still, the move could also lead to a clearer reaffirmation of the Constitution's authority and provoke a nationwide reassessment of the role individual liberty plays in a functioning republic.

In this hypothetical scenario, crime rates would likely decline dramatically. The deterrent effect, coupled with the empowerment of citizens to take proactive roles in their own defense, would enhance public safety. The myth of lawlessness fails to recognize that responsible gun owners uphold the peace and stability of a community. A nation where the Second Amendment is fully realized would be one defined by respect, safety, and the protection of personal liberty, resulting in a stronger, more secure society.

## Hypothetical Scenario: Complete Disarmament

Imagine a scenario where the US government mandates the complete disarmament of civilians, confiscating firearms and imposing strict penalties for possession. While this might be promoted to create a safer society, the likely outcome would be the opposite.

Without armed citizens, criminals—who do not obey laws—would find themselves operating in a defenseless environment, emboldened by the absence of resistance. Historical examples, like the United Kingdom and Australia, demonstrate this reality. Following the UK's gun bans, gun-related crime initially rose as criminals took advantage of a disarmed populace. Similarly, Australia's gun buyback program after the 1996 Port Arthur massacre led to an increase in violent crimes like home invasions, as criminals exploited defenseless citizens. The black market for firearms persists in both nations, proving that disarmament does not eliminate gun violence.

Disarmament would also alter the relationship between citizens and the government. The Second Amendment is a safeguard against tyranny, ensuring that citizens retain the means to resist government overreach. As we outlined in previous chapters, history has shown that disarmed populations are vulnerable to oppressive regimes, as seen in Nazi Germany and the Soviet Union, where disarmament preceded widespread atrocities. A disarmed America would face similar risks, with no recourse against potential abuses of power.

Additionally, reliance on the government for protection undermines self-reliance, a core American value. In rural areas with long law enforcement response times, disarmament could leave citizens defenseless in life-threatening situations. Enforcing such a policy would likely provoke widespread resistance, strain government resources, and foster civil unrest, creating a police-state atmosphere that erodes civil liberties.

In this hypothetical scenario, complete disarmament of the American public would have devastating economic consequences. The firearms industry is a multibillion-dollar contributor to the US economy, supporting over 300,000 jobs and generating billions in wages, taxes, and local commerce. If all civilian gun ownership were outlawed and enforced, manufacturers, gun shops, shooting ranges, ammunition producers, and related businesses would be forced to shut down. Hunting, competitive shooting, and self-defense training—industries that fuel tourism and outdoor recreation—would disappear almost overnight. Small towns anchored by firearm-related commerce would suffer first, followed by widespread job losses, bankruptcies, and the collapse of an entire supply chain from raw materials to retail.

The economic fallout would be matched by volatile political consequences. While some anti-gun factions might hail such a move as a moral victory, the backlash from gun-owning Americans would be fierce and immediate. The repeal of Second Amendment protections and the launch of a nationwide disarmament effort would be seen not as legislation, but as tyranny. Many citizens—particularly in rural and traditionally pro-gun states—would refuse to comply, viewing such an order as a direct violation of their constitutional rights. Civil disobedience could quickly spiral into widespread unrest.

If the federal government were to initiate door-to-door confiscation campaigns, it could ignite violent confrontations. The very scenario the Founders feared—a government turning its power inward against its own people—could come to life. Shootouts between law enforcement and resistant citizens, bloodshed in once-quiet neighborhoods, and a divided military or law enforcement apparatus refusing to enforce unconstitutional orders are no longer far-fetched ideas—they become the logical conclusion of a forced disarmament policy. In this hypothetical, the loss isn't just economic or political—it's national cohesion itself, risking a fracture that could lead to the unthinkable: a second civil war on American soil.

Complete disarmament is not a path to safety but a gateway to vulnerability, crime, and authoritarianism. The Second Amendment is essential for preserving the balance of power between the government and its citizens and ensuring that individuals can protect themselves and their families. History has shown that disarmed societies are neither safer nor freer; they are simply at greater risk of exploitation and oppression.

## (Not So) Hypothetical Scenario: Government Overreach Rising

Let's face it: This has been happening for decades. But now, let's consider a scenario where the government begins to significantly overreach, infringing on various civil liberties beyond just gun rights.

In this scenario, imagine a government that begins to pass laws infringing on free speech, curtailing the right to assembly, and expanding surveillance on private citizens. As these measures become more draconian, the existence of a well-armed populace acts as a brake on the government's actions. Knowing that millions of citizens have the means to resist, the government is less likely to impose further authoritarian policies.

Historical examples abound where the presence or absence of an armed citizenry has influenced the trajectory of government power. In Switzerland, for instance, the tradition of widespread gun ownership has long been credited with preserving the country's independence and preventing both external invasions and internal tyranny. Conversely, in countries where the government successfully disarmed the population, such as in Venezuela, the government has been able to implement increasingly authoritarian measures with little resistance from the people.

One might argue that the presence of an armed populace could lead to violent resistance or even civil war. However, this is a misunderstanding of the deterrent effect of widespread gun ownership. The mere fact that the government knows the people are armed can be enough to prevent it from taking actions that would provoke such resistance. The Second Amendment creates a balance of power where both the government and the people understand the limits of their actions, fostering a situation where civil liberties are more likely to be respected.

Anti-gun advocates often dismiss the idea that firearms could serve as a check against government overreach, arguing that modern governments are too powerful for armed citizens to pose a meaningful threat. However, this argument overlooks the fact that successful resistance does not necessarily require a direct military confrontation. The threat of armed resistance can be enough to force a government to reconsider its policies, especially in a democratic society where public opinion and legitimacy are crucial.

Additionally, the concept of "government overreach" is not limited to scenarios of outright tyranny. It can also include more subtle forms of encroachment, such as excessive regulation, the erosion of privacy rights, or the militarization of law enforcement. In each of these cases, the knowledge that the population is armed can serve as a deterrent, encouraging the government to seek more balanced and less coercive solutions. However, recent events since 2020 have severely tested this theory, revealing the government's unprecedented abuse of power. In turn, the realities of the 2020s have shown that the American people's tolerance and restraint for such overreach is remarkably high.

## Hypothetical Scenario: Technological Advances in Firearms

Now, imagine a future where technological advances have drastically improved the capabilities and safety of firearms. This includes smart guns that only respond to their owners, nonlethal options that are as effective as traditional guns, or firearms equipped with advanced tracking and identification systems. How would these innovations impact the debate around gun rights and gun control?

In such a scenario, these technological advancements would likely lead to a shift in the arguments for and against gun ownership. On one hand, proponents of gun rights could argue that these technologies make firearms safer than ever before, addressing many of the concerns that anti-gun advocates raise. Smart guns, for example, would reduce the likelihood of accidents or misuse by ensuring that only the registered owner can fire the weapon. This could prevent tragedies such as accidental shootings by children or the use of stolen firearms in crimes. However, smart guns would have its share of problems and risks.

Nonlethal options can often be an effective choice for self-defense. The Byrna SD and similar Nonlethal self-defense weapons offer an alternative for those who want protection without carrying a traditional firearm. These $CO_2$-powered launchers fire pepper spray, tear gas, or kinetic rounds, incapacitating threats without causing permanent harm. Marketed as legal in most states without a permit, they provide an option for self-defense in areas with strict gun laws. However, despite their nonlethal nature, cities like New York City still ban them, proving that even innocuous self-defense tools are subject to excessive government overreach. This raises an important question: If individuals are restricted from defending themselves even with nonlethal means, what real options do they have? However, these kinds of weapons could address the concern that firearms are inherently dangerous and could be used for self-defense without the risk of causing fatal harm, making them more acceptable to those who are uncomfortable with lethal force. This could lead to a broader acceptance of firearms ownership, as the debate shifts from the risks of gun ownership to the benefits of self-defense technologies.

Advanced tracking and identification systems could also have a significant impact on the gun control debate. These technologies would allow for more precise regulation and tracking of firearms, ensuring that guns are not used for illegal purposes. For example, a gun equipped with a tracking system could alert law enforcement if it is stolen or used in a crime, making it easier to recover and prevent further misuse. This could address the concern that guns are often used in crimes or fall into the wrong hands. However, these technologies would not be without controversy. Privacy advocates might raise concerns about the potential for government surveillance and control over firearms. The tracking systems could be seen as an infringement on the right to privacy and the freedom to bear arms without government oversight. These technologies could be unreliable and susceptible to glitches, malfunctions, hacking, or misuse by bad actors or rogue governments.

Moreover, the introduction of these technologies could lead to new forms of regulation and control, as the government might seek to mandate their use or restrict access to traditional firearms. This could lead to a new front in the gun rights debate, as proponents argue that the government should not have the power to dictate the terms of gun ownership. These concerns are valid. To prevent government overreach and protect gun owners' privacy, a potential solution could be that smart gun technology could be designed with an optional tracking service rather than a mandatory one. Gun owners could opt in to a subscription-based service that allows tracking for personal security—helping to locate a stolen firearm, monitor for malfunctions, or report criminal misuse—without granting government agencies unchecked access. Alternatively, smart gun technology could include a self-monitoring feature, enabling owners to track their own firearm through an integrated chip, allowing them to report its location to police only if necessary. This approach would provide the benefits of advanced security while ensuring that gun owners maintain full control over their data and privacy.

Despite these potential challenges, technological advancements in firearms could ultimately strengthen the case for the Second Amendment. By making guns safer and more controlled to the user, these innovations could address many of the concerns that fuel the push for gun control. At the same time, they could enhance the ability of individuals to protect themselves and their families, reinforcing the importance of the right to bear arms in a modern society.

In defending the Second Amendment in this scenario, it is important to emphasize that technological advancements can make firearms ownership safer and more responsible, but they should not be used for registration, surveillance, or as a pretext for further regulation or control on traditional firearms. Instead, these advancements should be embraced as more options *in addition to* traditional firearms that can strengthen the Second Amendment and ensure that it remains relevant in the 21st century.

## A Hypothetical Gun-Free World

Let's explore a hypothetical scenario in which the entire world agrees to disarm, and all countries enact strict gun control laws that effectively eliminate civilian ownership of firearms. The idea behind this scenario is that without guns, there would be less violence and the world would be a safer place. However, this utopian vision overlooks the complexities of human nature, power dynamics, and the role that firearms play in maintaining security and deterring aggression.

In a world where only governments and militaries possess firearms, the balance of power shifts dramatically. Civilians, now completely disarmed, would have no means of defending themselves against criminal elements, oppressive regimes, or even foreign invaders. History has shown that governments with a monopoly on the use of force often become tyrannical, suppressing dissent and violating human rights with impunity. The absence of an armed citizenry removes the primary check on government power, leaving populations vulnerable to exploitation and abuse.

Moreover, the notion that disarming the populace would lead to peace fails to account for the realities of human conflict. Violence is not solely a product of firearm availability; it results from deeper social, economic, and political factors. In countries or cities with strict gun control laws, such as China or the United Kingdom, violent crime still occurs, often involving other weapons or methods. In fact, disarming civilians could lead to an increase in other forms of violence, as criminals exploit the knowledge that their victims are defenseless.

China has some of the strictest gun laws in the world, yet it has suffered multiple mass stabbings and knife slashings in schools, where attackers have brutally targeted children. Meanwhile, the United Kingdom has seen a surge in knife-related crimes, particularly in London, where stabbings and slashings have skyrocketed despite the country's near-total civilian gun ban. The situation became so extreme that London Mayor Sadiq Khan proposed knife control legislation, including bans on carrying knives without a "good reason" and restrictions on home deliveries of sharp blades. If it weren't so real, one might laugh at the absurdity of trying to legislate away human violence by controlling cutlery. Even in the United States, where guns are heavily restricted in certain areas, violent crime persists. New York City has seen a rise in slashings and stabbings, particularly in its subway system, where innocent commuters have been attacked with knives and razors in broad daylight. These crimes underscore the reality that criminals will always find weapons—whether legal or not—while law-abiding citizens remain vulnerable under restrictive self-defense laws.

The black market for firearms would also likely thrive in a gun-free world. Criminal organizations and terrorist groups would continue to find ways to arm themselves, using smuggled or illegally manufactured weapons such as 3-D printed guns or "ghost guns." This would create a stark divide between the law-abiding majority, who are unarmed, and the criminal minority, who have access to illegal firearms. The average person would be less safe, not more.

Internationally, the absence of civilian firearms would not necessarily lead to greater peace between nations. Governments and militaries would still possess weapons, and the threat of war or aggression would remain. In fact, the lack of an armed populace could embolden aggressive states, knowing that their potential adversaries are weaker and less capable of resistance. The deterrent effect of widespread firearm ownership, both domestically and internationally, cannot be underestimated. In a world without civilian firearms, the balance of power would tip in favor of those who already possess it—governments, militaries, and criminal organizations.

This scenario also overlooks the cultural and constitutional significance of the Second Amendment in the United States. The right to bear arms is not just about personal defense; it is about maintaining the principles of freedom, independence, and self-reliance. If these rights are taken away, the very fabric of American society would be altered. Individual liberty and responsibility, values which are central to the American identity, would be eroded, replaced by a reliance on the state for security and protection.

In debunking the anti-gun position that a gun-free world would be a safer world, it is essential to highlight the unintended consequences of disarmament.

Violence and conflict would not disappear; they would simply take different forms. The disarmament of civilians would lead to greater vulnerability, increased government control, and a more dangerous world overall.

## A Hypothetical Future Scenario: The Collapse of Civil Order

Imagine a scenario where a significant national disaster or series of catastrophic events—such as a prolonged blackout, economic collapse, or a severe natural disaster—leads to the breakdown of civil order. In such a situation, the presence or absence of widespread firearm ownership would have a profound impact on the ability of communities to protect themselves, maintain order, and survive.

In the chaos that follows the collapse of civil order, the traditional structures of law enforcement and government would likely be overwhelmed or even nonexistent. In such a scenario, the responsibility for security would fall to individual citizens and local communities. Those who are armed would have the means to protect themselves, their families, and their property from looters, gangs, and other criminal elements that often emerge in times of crisis. The presence of firearms would act as a deterrent to criminal activity, as potential wrongdoers would know that they are likely to face armed resistance. Instances of civil disorder have shown that armed citizens are often the first line of defense in protecting their communities. As discussed in previous chapters, numerous examples illustrate this point.

In rural areas, where law enforcement response times are often longer even in normal circumstances, the ability to defend oneself becomes even more critical. In the absence of a functioning government, rural communities would rely on their own resources for survival, including the ability to hunt for food, protect against wildlife, and defend against human threats. Firearms would be essential in ensuring the safety and well-being of these communities.

The absence of widespread firearm ownership in such a scenario would lead to a vastly different outcome. Unarmed citizens would be at the mercy of criminals and gangs, who would exploit the lack of resistance to impose their will. The breakdown of civil order would lead to widespread violence, theft, and lawlessness, as those who are armed would prey on those who are not. The government's inability to protect its citizens in such a scenario would be starkly apparent, and the reliance on firearms for self-defense would become a matter of survival.

Anti-gun advocates might argue that the presence of firearms in such a situation would lead to increased violence, as armed citizens engage in shootouts or take the law into their own hands. However, this argument overlooks the fact that responsible gun owners do not seek out violence but rather use their firearms as a last resort in defense of themselves and their communities. The deterrent effect of widespread firearm ownership would likely prevent many crimes from occurring in the first place, as criminals would be less willing to risk confrontation with armed citizens.

Furthermore, the breakdown of civil order would reveal the fallacy of the anti-gun position that relies on government protection as the sole means of ensuring safety. In times of crisis, when government services are stretched thin or are completely unavailable, the ability to protect oneself becomes paramount. The Second Amendment ensures that citizens are not left defenseless in such situations, providing a critical safeguard against the worst outcomes of civil disorder.

In times of crisis, when traditional structures of law and government fail, the responsibility for security falls to individual citizens and local communities. Widespread firearm ownership would enable these communities to protect themselves, maintain order, and survive in the face of adversity. The absence of firearms, on the other hand, would lead to vulnerability, lawlessness, and increased violence. The Second Amendment is a vital protection that ensures citizens are not left defenseless in times of need.

## Dystopian Scenario: Gun Control Utopia

Imagine a hypothetical future where gun control advocates have achieved their vision of a utopia—a society where extremely strict gun laws are in place, near-total bans on civilian ownership of firearms are enforced, and extensive government surveillance is used to ensure compliance. In this scenario, the promise of safety and security is held up as the ultimate goal, but what are the real consequences of such a world?

In this gun control utopia, the government would have unprecedented power over the lives of its citizens. With the population disarmed, the state would face little resistance in implementing and enforcing its policies, regardless of how intrusive or authoritarian they might be. The lack of firearms in civilian hands would embolden the government to push its agenda without fear of pushback, leading to a society where individual freedoms are severely curtailed.

One of the most immediate consequences of this scenario would be the loss of personal autonomy and self-reliance. In a gun-free society, citizens would be completely dependent on the government for their safety and protection. This reliance would extend beyond firearms to other areas of life, as the state imposes its will on a population that has no means of resistance. The result would be a society where individuals are powerless to defend their rights, their property, or their way of life.

Furthermore, the implementation of such strict gun control measures would likely require extensive government surveillance and monitoring. To enforce a near-total ban on firearms, the government would need to monitor its citizens closely, tracking their movements, communications, and activities to ensure compliance. This level of surveillance would erode privacy and civil liberties, creating a society where the government knows everything about its citizens, while the citizens know little about the workings of their own government. This imbalance of power is the hallmark of an authoritarian regime, not a free society.

The promise of safety in this gun control utopia would also prove to be illusory. The disarmament of the population would not eliminate violence; it would simply change the nature of it. Criminals, who are often undeterred by laws, would continue to find ways to arm themselves, creating a black market for firearms that is outside the control of the government. Meanwhile, law-abiding citizens would be left defenseless, unable to protect themselves from criminal elements that do not adhere to the laws of the utopian society.

Internationally, the disarmament of the populace could have even more dire consequences. Without an armed citizenry, the nation as a whole would be more vulnerable to external threats, whether from hostile nations or terrorist organizations. The deterrent effect of a well-armed population would be lost, making the country a more attractive target for those who seek to do harm.

Anti-gun advocates might argue that this scenario is far-fetched and that the benefits of strict gun control—such as reduced gun violence—would outweigh the potential downsides. However, this argument overlooks the unintended consequences of disarmament and the loss of individual freedoms that would accompany it. The focus on reducing gun violence at any cost ignores the broader impact on society, including the erosion of civil liberties and the empowerment of the state at the expense of the individual. A society where the government holds all power is not a utopia; it is a dystopia where individual freedoms are sacrificed for the illusion of safety. The Second Amendment is a safeguard against this outcome, ensuring that citizens retain the means to defend themselves and their liberties.

The vision of a gun control utopia is a dangerous fantasy that ignores the realities of human nature, power dynamics, and the importance of individual freedoms. While the promise of safety may be appealing, the cost in terms of lost autonomy, privacy, and civil liberties is far too high. The defense of gun rights is ultimately a defense of a free and just society.

## Constitutional Convention: Redefining the Second Amendment

Now, consider a scenario where a new constitutional convention is convened specifically to address the Second Amendment. Imagine that this gathering is a response to increasing political pressure from anti-gun advocates who seek to either repeal or heavily modify the amendment. What might happen if a modern reexamination of gun rights was to take place? Would the right to bear arms be strengthened, weakened, or fundamentally changed?

In this hypothetical scenario, the constitutional convention would be a battleground of ideas, with fierce debates between those who seek to preserve the Second Amendment as it currently stands and those who wish to see it rewritten or repealed entirely. The stakes would be incredibly high, as the outcome would determine the future of gun rights in America. However, under Article V of the US Constitution, calling a convention requires a two-thirds majority vote in both the House and Senate, as well as applications from two-thirds of the state legislatures (34 out of 50). To ratify (i.e., officially pass) a new amendment to the US Constitution, three-fourths of the states (38 out of 50) must approve it—setting a deliberately high bar to ensure broad national consensus.

On one side of the debate would be those who argue that the Second Amendment is more relevant than ever in a world where government overreach, domestic terrorism, and personal safety are significant concerns. The right to bear arms, they would say, is not just about hunting or sport shooting, but about ensuring that citizens have the means to defend themselves and maintain a balance of power between the government and the governed. Historical precedents, such as the role of armed citizens in resisting tyranny and oppression, would be cited as evidence of the enduring importance of the Second Amendment.

On the other side would be those who argue that the Second Amendment is outdated and no longer necessary. They might propose modifications that limit the types of firearms that can be owned, impose stricter regulations on gun ownership, or even remove the right to bear arms from the Constitution altogether. Their arguments would likely focus on public safety concerns, pointing to incidents of gun violence as justification for restricting or eliminating gun rights.

If the pro-Second Amendment side were to prevail, the result could be a reaffirmation of gun rights, perhaps even with additional protections to prevent future erosion. This could include clarifying the language of the amendment to reinforce the individual right to bear arms, as well as adding provisions to protect against executive overreach or excessive regulation.

If the anti-gun side were to prevail, the result could be a significant weakening of the Second Amendment, with new restrictions that limit the types of firearms that can be owned, impose mandatory buybacks, or create barriers to gun ownership that effectively disarm the populace. In the worst-case scenario, the Second Amendment could be repealed entirely, leaving gun rights to be determined by individual states or future federal legislation.

The implications of such changes would be profound. A weakened or repealed Second Amendment would not only impact gun ownership but also shift the balance of power between the government and the people. Without the constitutional guarantee of the right to bear arms, citizens would be at the mercy of laws and regulations that could change with each new administration. The loss of this fundamental right could lead to an erosion of other civil liberties as the government becomes more emboldened to impose its will without fear of resistance.

Defending the Second Amendment in this scenario would require a robust and well-organized effort to educate the public and the delegates at the convention about the importance of preserving this right. The arguments in favor of the Second Amendment would need to be clear, concise, and backed by historical evidence and legal precedent. It would also be crucial to highlight the dangers of allowing the government to dictate the terms of gun ownership, as this could lead to a slippery slope where other rights are gradually eroded.

***

In considering these hypothetical scenarios, it becomes evident that the Second Amendment is more than just a legal provision—it is a fundamental safeguard of freedom, self-reliance, and balance of power. Whether imagining a completely armed society, total disarmament, government overreach, or a Constitutional Convention, each scenario highlights a critical truth: The right to bear arms is inextricably linked to personal liberty and national security. History and logic demonstrate that violence is not dependent on firearm availability, but on deeper societal factors, and that arming law-abiding citizens serves as both a deterrent and a means of protection.

As technology advances and political debates continue, the fight to preserve the Second Amendment remains not just relevant, but essential in ensuring that the power remains with the people, rather than solely in the hands of the state.

# Chapter 16

# Liberty's Last Line: Preserving the Second Amendment in Perilous Times

*There's no harm in hoping for the best as long as you're prepared for the worst.*

—Stephen King

*Hope for the best, but prepare for the worst.*
—Thomas Norton and Thomas Sackville

In the perilous and uncertain times we have been facing since at least 2020, there is a palpable sense of unease among the civilian population. Government overreach, political targeting of gun owners, overtaxation, international conflicts, an open southern border, and rising crime rates across the nation contribute to this growing anxiety. The disappearance of foreign nationals within the country only heightens this tension. The collective intuition of the populace suggests that something significant is bound to happen. Many feel as if a breaking point is imminent.

As government actions become increasingly intrusive and overbearing, and the rule of law deteriorates, the right to keep and bear arms serves as an important safeguard of individual liberty and collective security. It is a reminder that the ultimate power lies with the people, who must be prepared to defend their freedoms if necessary. The feeling of unease and readiness among the population today echoes the sentiments of past generations who understood the importance of maintaining their right to self-defense in the face of uncertain and perilous times. However, at what point does the Second Amendment transition from being a theoretical deterrent to justifying armed rebellion? This is a critical question that demands thoughtful consideration and thorough analysis from all of us.

## When Is Armed Resistance Justified?

The question of when the Second Amendment should be invoked to overthrow an overreaching or tyrannical government is complex and fraught with moral and legal considerations. The right to bear arms as a defense against tyranny is deeply rooted in the American ethos, but the point at which it becomes appropriate to use armed force against a government is subject to rigorous debate.

Historically, governments that have become tyrannical exhibit certain behaviors: They infringe upon basic civil liberties, disregard the rule of law, suppress free speech, and use force to maintain control. The American Revolution was sparked by such grievances, where the British Crown imposed taxes without representation, disbanded local governments, and used military force to suppress dissent.

The Declaration of Independence articulates a philosophy that governments derive their just powers from the consent of the governed and that it is the right of the people to alter or abolish any government that becomes destructive to these ends. This principle provides a foundation for understanding when armed resistance might be justified.

However, the threshold for using the Second Amendment in this way is high. It is not a tool for preemptive action based on potential signs of tyranny but a last resort when all other avenues of redress have been exhausted. Engaging in armed resistance prematurely, based on perceived rather than actual tyranny, risks chaos and the undermining of legitimate governance structures. The consequences of such actions are severe and often lead to widespread violence and instability.

That said, vigilance is crucial. Citizens should remain aware of their government's actions, particularly those that erode civil liberties and democratic processes. Warning signs of potential tyranny, such as the suppression of dissent, unwarranted surveillance, the concentration of power in a single branch of government, or the use of military force against civilians, should be met with strong civic resistance. This resistance should take the form of peaceful protest, legal challenges, and the use of political processes to demand accountability and change.

The Second Amendment becomes a necessary tool only when a government crosses the line into overt tyranny—when it begins to systematically violate the rights of its citizens, ignore the rule of law, and use force to maintain power. An example of such a scenario might be the rounding up of political dissidents into reeducation camps, a clear indicator of a regime that has abandoned democratic principles and the protection of individual rights.

While the Second Amendment provides for the possibility of armed resistance against tyranny, it is a measure of last resort. It requires a clear demonstration of overreach and the failure of all other methods of addressing grievances. It is a safeguard against the most extreme form of government oppression, to be used judiciously and with full awareness of its profound implications.

However, many people feel that the threshold for justified armed rebellion has been crossed long ago. After all, the American Revolution was started in response to government infractions that paled in comparison to the abuses of government today. In recent years, freedom of speech is increasingly under attack, with the government using social media and big business to silence and censor opposing political views. This trend has been seen in the deplatforming of dissenting voices and the suppression of information that conflicts with the prevailing narrative.

Moreover, the partisan use of the legal system to target political rivals has become alarmingly evident. High-profile cases where political figures are prosecuted under dubious circumstances suggest that the legal system is being weaponized to stifle opposition. This erosion of judicial impartiality undermines the rule of law and threatens the democratic process. When political opponents are prosecuted, jailed, and even, in some extreme cases, murdered or turned into political prisoners without due process, it signals a severe breakdown in the protections that should be afforded to all citizens.

The role of the media in these developments cannot be overlooked. The mainstream media has abandoned its duty as a watchdog of the government, instead becoming a protector of Democratic administrations, lawmakers, and activists covering up rampant corruption and ignoring abuses of power. By failing to hold those in power accountable, the media contributes to the growing tyranny and fosters an environment where dissent is not tolerated.

Furthermore, the use of government agencies such as the ATF, or the support of radical leftist organizations to intimidate and terrorize communities, has escalated tensions, further eroding the freedoms that the Second Amendment was designed to protect. The systematic targeting of those who speak out against Democrat policies demonstrates a blatant disregard for civil liberties and a move towards authoritarianism.

This politically motivated abuse is even more infuriating by the fact that the same anti-gun, anti-American faction of the Democrat Party that points the finger at law-abiding gun owners—accusing us of being violent, extremist vigilantes for merely preparing for the possibility of government tyranny—are the very ones imposing that tyranny in real time—even when they aren't in power. While we are vilified for advocating preparedness and self-defense, it's the radical left that throws violent tantrums, burns down cities, harasses political opponents, and commits acts of vandalism, arson, and even murder whenever they lose political ground. Ironically, the policies they riot over—border security, parental rights, energy independence—are hardly tyrannical; they are simply no longer in control, and that loss of power sends them into unhinged rage. If anything, their violent reaction to our constitutional victories is the real call to arms—not for aggression, but for vigilance, unity, and a renewed commitment to defending liberty by any means necessary.

Despite these provocations, the armed population has shown incredible restraint. This restraint is grounded in the hope that peaceful solutions can still be found through political and legal channels. The restraint shown thus far is a testament to the commitment of the American people to uphold the principles of democracy and the rule of law. However, there is a growing consensus that there will be a breaking point if these trends continue unchecked. Continued abuse of power and the suppression of fundamental rights will inevitably lead to a tipping point where the invocation of the Second Amendment may no longer be a theoretical discussion but a necessary course of action to preserve the Republic.

The potential for armed rebellion is not taken lightly by those who cherish their freedoms. It is seen as a necessary response only when all peaceful means of restoring justice and liberty have been exhausted. Armed rebellion against a tyrannical government has indeed occurred in recent history within the United States, when civilians felt compelled to take up arms to restore justice and dismantle rampant political corruption. This incident is famously known as the Battle of Athens and serves as an example of when the use of the Second Amendment to fend off tyranny and injustice is justified.

## The Battle of Athens (1948)

The Battle of Athens, also known as the McMinn County War, took place in 1946 in Athens, Tennessee. This dramatic event serves as a compelling historical example of citizens using their Second Amendment rights to fight back against government overreach and tyranny.

In the early to mid-1940s, McMinn County was plagued by a corrupt political machine led by Sheriff Paul Cantrell and his cronies. Cantrell's administration was notorious for manipulating elections, intimidating voters, and exploiting their positions for personal gain. They employed deputies who were little more than armed thugs to enforce their rule, often using violence and threats to maintain control. The citizens of McMinn County grew increasingly frustrated with the blatant corruption and abuses of power.

The situation reached a boiling point during the 1946 elections. In the lead-up to the election, Cantrell and his deputies engaged in widespread voter intimidation and fraud. They controlled the polling places, monitored the voting process, and ensured that ballots were counted in their favor. Many citizens were determined to restore democracy and integrity to their community. They formed a group called the GI Non-Partisan League, composed primarily of veterans who had fought for freedom abroad and were now determined to fight for it at home.

On August 1, 1946, the day of the election, tensions escalated. Poll watchers from the GI Non-Partisan League were denied access to the polling places, and there were numerous reports of voters being assaulted and intimidated by Cantrell's deputies. The veterans, realizing that the democratic process was being subverted, decided to act. Armed with rifles, shotguns, and pistols, they gathered at the Athens Armory and planned to confront the corrupt officials.

That evening, the veterans surrounded the jail where the ballot boxes had been taken for counting. They demanded that the ballot boxes be turned over to an impartial group for counting. The sheriff and his deputies refused, and a standoff ensued. As tensions mounted, shots were fired, and a fierce gun battle erupted between the veterans and the deputies. The veterans, well-trained and battle-hardened from their experiences in World War II, gained the upper hand.

The fighting continued into the night, and by early morning, the veterans had successfully overpowered the corrupt officials. They seized the ballot boxes and took control of the town. The ballots were counted, and it was confirmed that the GI Non-Partisan League had won the election. The corrupt regime of Sheriff Cantrell was dismantled, and democracy was restored to McMinn County.

The Battle of Athens is a powerful example of the Second Amendment in action. The right to keep and bear arms enabled the citizens of McMinn County to revolt against tyranny and reclaim their democratic rights. This event underscores the importance of the Second Amendment as a safeguard against government overreach and corruption. It shows that an armed citizenry can serve as a formidable check on power, ensuring that the government remains accountable to the people.

## The Farce of January 6th, 2021

The portrayal of the January 6th Capitol protest as an "insurrection" or " armed rebellion" is highly contested and, to most, appears grossly exaggerated. Many argue that the events of that day were a mostly peaceful protest apart from outside agitators consisting of corrupt federal agents, Antifa members, and other left-wing agitators dressed as Trump supporters causing some property damage in order to "create the evidence" for the narrative to come. This perspective is bolstered by video evidence that shows various provocateurs inciting violence, which casts doubt on the narrative that the event was an organized, armed insurrection.

Critics point out that none of the protesters were armed with guns or other traditional weapons. As a matter of fact, many hours of video footage from within the Capitol building showing people walking around and taking selfies. The only person who was killed that day was Ashli Babbitt, an unarmed woman murdered by a Capitol police officer. This singular fatality, along with the absence of firearms among the protesters, underscores the argument that labeling the event as a violent insurrection is laughable. Historically, insurrections involve armed conflict, yet the January 6th event lacked this critical element. The irony noted by critics is that this would be the worst insurrection in history since "everyone forgot their guns."

The prosecution of individuals who were present at the protest, many of whom committed no violent acts or crimes, were perceived by many as attempts to intimidate and suppress political dissent, highlighting a partisan legal system used to stifle opposition. The government's aggressive stance against these protesters has been cited as a potential justification for invoking the Second Amendment, which was designed to protect citizens from tyrannical government actions.

The media's portrayal of January 6th has largely been aligned with the Democrats' narrative, framing the protest as an insurrection and failing to critically examine the evidence of external agitators. This biased reporting further inflames the divide and perpetuates a one-sided view of the events. The lack of balanced coverage contributes to the perception of a hostile media environment that covered for the Biden administration while ignoring or downplaying its transgressions. However, the message to the population by the government and the media was quite clear: "Don't you dare ever challenge or question us, or we will come after you and throw you in prison."

The persecution of January 6th participants from 2021 until January 2025, coupled with the broader trend of silencing political dissent, almost pushed the nation toward a breaking point. Many Americans believe that government overreach and the suppression of political opposition could ignite an armed revolution reminiscent of the Civil War. Given that most gun owners align with the politically targeted group, there is almost no doubt about which side would emerge victoriously in such a conflict.

Amid ongoing and rapidly shifting political tides across the country, there remains a growing concern that radical elements on the left will escalate their efforts to persecute political opponents—pushing tensions to a boiling point that could one day ignite armed conflict. This fear is rooted in the belief that the current trajectory of political repression and media complicity could make an armed response not only justified, but inevitable. The restraint shown thus far by gun owners across America underscores their hope for peaceful resolution, but the increasing pressure could eventually force their hand.

## Armed Rebellion in the United States

So, if this were to happen, what would armed rebellion in the modern-day United States look like? An armed rebellion against tyranny or a civil war in the modern era would likely look very different from the American Revolution in the 1770s and the American Civil War of the 1860s. During those historical conflicts, there were clear geographic divides: The colonies were united against British rule in the Revolution, and the North and South were distinctly opposed in the Civil War, each with majority populations supporting their respective causes. Today, however, the divisions are primarily ideological, with supporters of various political beliefs dispersed throughout the country. This ideological fragmentation means that any potential conflict would be far more complex and fragmented, lacking the clear regional delineations that characterized earlier American conflicts. The absence of geographic unity would complicate efforts to organize and sustain large-scale military engagements, leading to a more decentralized and multifaceted struggle.

In today's context, an armed rebellion would probably not feature large-scale battles between two clearly defined armies. Instead, it might involve smaller, decentralized groups engaging in guerrilla warfare, sabotage, and other asymmetric tactics. These groups would likely form based on shared ideologies rather than geographic proximity, and their actions would be coordinated through modern communication technologies. The urban and suburban landscapes would become the primary theaters of conflict, with engagements occurring sporadically rather than on well-defined battlefields.

The mixed population throughout the country means that regions might not form cohesive blocs representing a single side or interest. Instead, there could be pockets of resistance in various areas, including cities and rural communities. These groups would be interspersed with those holding opposing views, leading to a highly unpredictable and volatile situation.

Warfare in this scenario would likely be characterized by a combination of conventional and unconventional tactics. The use of firearms, improvised explosive devices, and cyber warfare could become prevalent. Modern technology, including drones and encrypted communication, would play a significant role in both offensive and defensive operations. The conflict would involve not just physical confrontations but also battles for control over information and resources.

Given the ideological divisions, some states or regions could attempt to secede and form alliances with others that share their beliefs. However, this process would be far from straightforward, as internal divisions within states could complicate such efforts. The federal government's response to secession attempts would also be a critical factor, potentially leading to further escalation.

If large regions or factions were to no longer recognize the authority of the federal government, its ability to govern effectively would be severely compromised. This lack of recognition could manifest in various forms, such as refusal to pay federal taxes, noncompliance with federal laws, and the establishment of alternative governance structures. The fragmentation of federal authority could lead to different regions being governed by various factions. In such a situation, the federal government might struggle to maintain control over its institutions and resources, leading to a decline in its overall power and influence.

The federal government might also face the dilemma of choosing sides in the conflict. Aligning with one or more factions could alienate other groups, exacerbating divisions and further eroding the government's authority. Ultimately, the fragmentation of federal authority and the alignment of the government with specific factions could lead to a protracted and complex conflict. The weakened federal government would struggle to reassert its control, and the resulting power vacuum could lead to the rise of new political entities and alliances. This scenario underscores the importance of addressing the underlying causes of division and seeking peaceful solutions to prevent such a breakdown of governance.

## Lack of National Unity

Uniting the population against a tyrannical government in modern times presents an almost insurmountable challenge due to the deep divisions that exist within the country. In the past, the two sides of the aisle disagreed about policy but still shared a common love for America and a desire to make it better. Now, both sides are diametrically opposed on virtually every issue, making consensus on combating tyranny elusive. This polarization is not merely about differing opinions but encompasses fundamental disagreements on the nature of rights, governance, and justice. In such an environment, any action perceived as a fight against tyranny by one side could be seen as an act of insurrection or terrorism by the other.

The anti-Second Amendment segment of the population often perceives tyranny as merely having a different opinion from their own. This leads to hysterical and sometimes violent responses towards those who disagree with their worldview. For instance, opposition to free college education funded by taxpayers is seen by some as an act of tyranny, as they consider their entitlement to such benefits as a fundamental right. However, there is no constitutional right to free college, and not providing this entitlement does not constitute tyranny. This perspective illustrates an infantile and loose interpretation of what constitutes rights and tyranny, where hurt feelings are equated with oppression. The anti-2A left takes issue with the Constitution because it stands as an obstacle to their agenda, limiting their ability to impose sweeping restrictions, whereas Second Amendment proponents and right-leaning individuals view the Constitution as sacrosanct, recognizing it as the foundation that protects individual liberties from government overreach.

In contrast, supporters of the Second Amendment view tyranny in its literal form, as government overreach that infringes upon basic constitutional rights. For them, tyranny is manifested through actions that undermine freedoms explicitly protected by the Constitution, such as freedom of speech and the right to keep and bear arms. These individuals see policies and laws that erode these fundamental liberties as inherently tyrannical. This distinction highlights a significant divide in understanding between the two segments of the population. While one side equates the denial of desired commodities with tyranny, the other side focuses on the preservation of constitutionally enshrined rights as the true measure of freedom.

The calls for censorship and cancel culture from the anti-Second Amendment camp are often justified on the grounds of protecting their ideology and views of society. However, these actions can be seen as attempts to silence political opponents rather than engaging in constructive dialogue. The fervor with which they pursue these goals suggests a belief that dissenting opinions are not just wrong, but dangerous and deserving of suppression. This approach contrasts sharply with the values upheld by Second Amendment supporters, who argue that a truly free society must allow for diverse viewpoints and protect individual liberties against government overreach.

Ultimately, the disparity in how each group defines tyranny and rights further underscores the broader cultural and political divide in contemporary America. One glaring example of this division is the differing reactions to governmental overreach and perceived threats. Prominent political figures, such as Hillary Clinton, have suggested that those who disagree with her politics should be subjected to "reeducation"—a term that echoes the chilling practices of totalitarian regimes. This idea resonates with some who view dissent as a threat that must be neutralized, while others see it as an overt sign of tyranny. Such opposing views make it difficult to achieve unity, even when the threat to liberty is clear to one half of the population.

The state of New York's implementation of COVID-19 quarantine camps during the lockdowns further illustrates this divide. Quarantine facilities were ostensibly meant to protect public health, but many saw them as draconian measures reminiscent of authoritarian control. While a significant portion of the population supported these measures, believing them necessary for public safety, others perceived them as a grave overreach of governmental power, akin to tyranny. The stark difference in perceptions highlights how difficult it is to unite against a common enemy when the enemy is not universally recognized.

The celebration of tyrannical acts by parts of the population is not new. History provides ample examples of factions supporting oppressive regimes because they believed those regimes aligned with their interests or values. This historical precedent suggests that a large segment of today's population might similarly endorse or at least tolerate tyranny, especially if it is directed against political adversaries. This tolerance or even celebration of suppression creates an environment where uniting against genuine threats to life and liberty becomes nearly impossible.

Where does this leave us? In a nation where political and ideological divisions run so deep, the prospect of forming a united front against tyranny seems bleak. Efforts to resist oppression may be stymied by those who view such resistance as illegitimate. This polarization could lead to a situation where half the population is willing to tolerate, or even support, the suppression of the other half, thus undermining any concerted effort to defend freedoms and rights against government overreach.

Although the lack of national unity on most issues today presents significant challenges, it does not mean that fighting back against tyranny is unjustified simply because a large portion of the population might disagree. During the American Revolution, the revolutionaries themselves did not have majority support. Historical estimates suggest that about a third of the colonists supported independence, a third wanted to keep the peace and stay under British control, and a third were indifferent or neutral. This distribution of sentiment mirrors today's situation, although there is a substantial majority of the current population that supports Second Amendment rights and opposes collectivist tyranny.

Despite the divided opinions during the American Revolution, the commitment of the revolutionaries to their cause of independence and liberty was unwavering. They understood that the principles at stake were worth fighting for, regardless of the broader public consensus. Similarly, in today's context, the fundamental rights enshrined in the Second Amendment hold significant importance for many Americans. The defense of these rights is seen not just as a matter of personal security, but as a bulwark against government overreach and potential tyranny. Even if a sizeable portion of the population is apathetic or supports stricter gun control, it does not negate the justified resistance against efforts to erode these freedoms. In this way, the spirit of the revolutionaries endures, serving as a reminder that preserving liberty requires unwavering resolve, even in times of division. This very principle fuels the existence of organized and loosely organized citizen militias across the country, prepared to defend their freedom should the need ever arise.

## Forming Citizen Militias

Forming a citizen militia during trying times can serve as a crucial means of ensuring community security and resilience. Establishing an effective militia involves several important steps, each designed to foster organization, preparedness, and the ability to respond to threats. Forming a citizen militia requires careful planning, disciplined training, and a commitment to ethical conduct. By adhering to these principles and maintaining a state of readiness, a militia can effectively serve its community in times of crisis. The following several paragraphs provide a foundation for organizing and operating a citizen militia, emphasizing the importance of legality, preparedness, and the responsible use of force.

The first step in forming a citizen militia is to define its purpose and objectives, with common goals including community defense, emergency response, and the protection of civil liberties. Establishing a code of conduct and operational guidelines ensures the militia operates ethically and legally.

Recruitment and membership are the next critical steps. Identifying and recruiting individuals who share the militia's values and objectives is important, with a focus on those with relevant skills, such as former military personnel, first responders, and individuals with medical or logistical expertise. Conducting background checks helps ensure the integrity and reliability of members.

An organizational structure with clearly defined roles and responsibilities is vital for maintaining order and effectiveness. Key positions include a commander, who leads the militia and makes strategic decisions; a deputy commander, who assists the commander and steps in during their absence; a training officer, who oversees training programs; a logistics officer, who manages supplies; a communications officer, who handles internal and external communications; and a medical officer, who provides medical training and oversees medical supplies and emergency response procedures.

Regular training and drills are a must for ensuring all members are proficient in necessary skills. Training sessions should cover firearms proficiency, tactical maneuvers, first aid, and emergency response. Engaging in regular drills helps practice various scenarios, such as defending a position, evacuating civilians, or responding to natural disasters.

Legal considerations are also important. During times of peace, members must be familiar with local, state, and federal laws regarding militia activities and firearm possession. Ensuring the militia operates within legal boundaries helps avoid conflicts with law enforcement and other authorities.

Members of the militia have several responsibilities, including adherence to the established code of conduct to ensure ethical behavior and respect for human rights. Regular attendance at training sessions and drills is mandatory to maintain readiness and proficiency. Each member should contribute to the militia's resources, whether through financial support, equipment, or skills. Fostering positive relationships with the community is indispensable to show that the militia is there for protection and support, not intimidation. Members should also stay informed about potential threats and maintain a state of readiness to mobilize quickly.

When preparing for engagement, having the right weapons and equipment is crucial. Firearms such as rifles (AR-15s or AK-47s), shotguns, and handguns suitable for various combat scenarios should be acquired, along with sufficient quantities of ammunition for training and potential engagements. Personal protective equipment like body armor and helmets is also necessary. Effective communication is imperative, so radios, encrypted communication devices, and signal flares should be maintained. Medical supplies, including first aid kits and trauma kits, along with training in basic and advanced medical care, are also vital.

Strategic planning involves developing and rehearsing for different scenarios, including defensive operations, search and rescue missions, and evacuation procedures. Secure locations for meetings, training, and supply storage should be established. Clear rules of engagement that prioritize the safety of civilians and the ethical conduct of militia members should be defined, with all members understanding the legal implications of using force and the importance of de-escalation whenever possible.

Staying alert and prepared involves intelligence gathering, regular drills, and community involvement. Keeping abreast of local and national news, maintaining a network of reliable sources, and monitoring potential threats is important. Frequent drills ensure all members are familiar with protocols and can act swiftly in an emergency. Engaging with the community builds trust and helps gather information about local concerns and potential threats.

## The Legal Ramifications of Militia Membership

In the event militia servicemen and women are met with legal ramifications for the mere act of belonging to an organized militia, several actions and strategies should be considered to protect their rights and ensure their safety. The Second Amendment's first clause explicitly states that a "well regulated Militia" is necessary to the security of a free state. Historically, a militia consisted of ordinary citizens armed and ready to defend their communities and the state, independent of government control. "Well regulated" means well trained and ready for service, not regulated under government control.

Militia members should familiarize themselves with their constitutional rights, particularly the Second Amendment and related case law. The right to form and join a militia is a protected activity under the US Constitution, provided the militia operates within legal boundaries. Militia members need to have access to competent legal representation. Lawyers specializing in constitutional law, particularly Second Amendment rights, can provide invaluable assistance in navigating legal challenges. Legal defense funds and organizations such as the NRA-ILA (National Rifle Association Institute for Legislative Action) and the Second Amendment Foundation offer resources and support for individuals facing legal battles over gun rights and militia activities. Keeping detailed records of all activities, communications, and training sessions can be critical in legal defense. Documentation can help prove that the militia operates ethically, legally, and with a clear purpose in line with constitutional rights.

Raising public awareness about the importance and legality of citizen militias can help garner support and reduce stigma. Engaging with local media, writing opinion pieces, and participating in public forums can help educate the community about the constitutional basis and necessity of militias. If faced with immediate legal action, contact legal counsel immediately. Do not make statements to law enforcement or the media without legal advice. Inform fellow militia members about the situation and coordinate a collective response. Transparency and solidarity are crucial in these situations. Challenge any anti-militia laws or regulations in court. Citing the Second Amendment and relevant case law can form the basis of the legal argument. Cases like *District of Columbia v. Heller* and *McDonald v. Chicago* reaffirm the individual right to bear arms and can be leveraged in defense. Seek injunctions against enforcement of any laws that infringe on the right to form or join a militia. Courts can issue injunctions to halt enforcement until a final decision is made.

Engage with local and state legislators to advocate for the protection of militia rights. Building relationships with sympathetic lawmakers can lead to legislative changes that protect these rights. Mobilize community support through educational campaigns and public outreach. Demonstrating the positive role of militias in community safety and disaster response can shift public perception and build a support base. Several states have attempted to pass or have passed legislation aimed at restricting militia activities. New Jersey and New York have stringent laws regulating paramilitary activities and militias. These laws often frame militias as potential threats to public safety, despite their constitutional protection. In Virginia, there have been efforts to pass anti-militia legislation following political unrest and public demonstrations involving armed groups. These legislative efforts typically aim to limit the organization, training, and public demonstration of armed militias.

In the face of potential legal and political challenges, militia members must remain vigilant, informed, and proactive. Building strong legal defenses, fostering community relationships, and advocating for constitutional rights are critical components of this effort. The right to form and join a militia is deeply rooted in American history and protected by the Constitution. Ensuring this right remains intact requires dedication, strategic action, and unwavering commitment to the principles of liberty and security. Ultimately, in times of unrest or governmental overreach, the existence of well-regulated militias can serve as a crucial check against tyranny and a means of preserving the freedoms guaranteed by the Constitution. If militias operate within legal frameworks and adhere to ethical standards, they remain a vital part of the American tradition of self-defense and community resilience.

## Weapons Caches

In times of unrest, martial law, or potential civil conflict, the concept of weapons caches becomes particularly relevant for those concerned with preserving their right to keep and bear arms. A weapons cache is a hidden stockpile of firearms, ammunition, and other necessary supplies that can be accessed in times of emergency. The strategic placement and maintenance of these caches can ensure that a militia or individual is prepared to defend themselves or resist tyranny even if the government attempts to confiscate their weapons.

Creating a weapons cache requires careful planning and consideration. The first step is to determine what items are necessary to store. This typically includes a variety of firearms, ammunition, magazines, cleaning supplies, and perhaps even non-perishable food and medical supplies. The selection of firearms should consider versatility and reliability. For example, including both a semi-automatic rifle like an AR-15 and a reliable handgun would cover a broad range of defensive needs.

Once the contents are determined, the next step is to select locations for these caches that are both accessible and discreet. In the context of militia service, caches might be hidden in rural areas, buried in waterproof containers, or concealed within natural landmarks. Urban caches, on the other hand, might be hidden in basements, attics, or false walls. The key is to ensure that the location is secure from discovery by government forces or others who might seek to disarm you.

During the Civil War, arms caches played a critical role in supplying both Union and Confederate forces, as well as partisan fighters and militias. These caches were often strategically placed in barns, cellars, forests, and caves to avoid detection by enemy troops and to ensure a steady supply of arms and ammunition. Partisan fighters, especially in border states, used these hidden stock-piles to resupply during raids and skirmishes. Confederate guerrilla fighters like Quantrill's Raiders, for example, relied on these secret depots to maintain their operations. These caches not only included firearms and ammunition but also food, medical supplies, and other supplies, enabling sustained resistance and combat readiness despite the shifting tides of war. The strategic placement and use of these caches underscore the importance of logistical planning and resource management in wartime efforts.

Another example from history that illustrates the use of weapons caches is the resistance movements in occupied Europe during World War II. Partisans and resistance fighters often buried weapons in forests or concealed them in hidden compartments within buildings. These caches allowed them to continue their fight against occupying forces even when traditional supply lines were cut off.

In the event of unrest or martial law in the modern era, having multiple caches spread across different locations ensures that if one cache is discovered, others remain accessible. It's also advisable to place caches in locations that are not immediately associated with your primary residence or usual haunts. A cache might be hidden on a trusted friend's property or in a remote location where few would think to look.

Maintaining these caches is another critical aspect. Regular checks should be conducted to ensure that the contents remain in good condition. Ammunition should be stored in a way that prevents moisture damage, and firearms should be oiled and protected against rust. Updating the cache periodically to include newer or more effective items is also a good practice.

A somewhat humorous but often mentioned aspect in discussions about pre-serving firearms is the idea of "losing all your guns in a boating accident." This phrase is a tongue-in-cheek way of saying that one's firearms have been hidden or disposed of in a way that makes them inaccessible to government confiscation. While it's a comical notion, it underscores the seriousness with which some individuals view their right to bear arms and their willingness to go to great lengths to protect it.

Creating a weapons cache could have legal implications depending on your jurisdiction. Stay informed about local laws and regulations regarding the storage and possession of firearms and act within legal boundaries wherever possible. However, during times of unrest, emergency, or tyranny, local laws would likely be naturally suspended by the civic power, making adherence to weapons laws neither feasible nor enforceable at that point. In such scenarios, the primary concern would shift to immediate survival and defense, rather than legal compliance.

## Foreign Nationals and Terrorists

The Second Amendment holds particular relevance in the context of national security, especially when considering the potential threats posed by foreign nationals and potential terrorists crossing the border and launching attacks from within the United States. The vulnerability of critical infrastructure, such as the electrical grid and communications networks, underscores the importance of being prepared for a worst-case scenario.

The invasion at our southern border, where foreign nationals cross into the United States, poses significant security risks. These individuals may include not only those seeking better economic opportunities but also those with malicious intent, such as terrorists or agents of foreign governments. Should such individuals launch coordinated attacks on critical infrastructure, like the electrical grid or communications networks, it could lead to widespread paralysis and chaos. An attack on these systems would cripple essential services, disrupt supply chains, and create fertile ground for widespread violence and disorder.

In such a scenario, commonly referred to as a "SHTF" (s--t hits the fan) situation, the ability to defend oneself, one's family, and community becomes paramount. This is where the Second Amendment's provision for an armed citizenry becomes crucial. Being prepared means not only having a stockpile of ammunition and firearms but also ensuring that one is well-trained in their use and maintenance. Regular practice, participation in training courses, and familiarization with different types of firearms can enhance one's ability to respond effectively to threats.

Amid such chaos, distinguishing between those who pose a threat and those who are allies can be challenging. Trust becomes a scarce commodity, and in many cases, it may indeed feel like every man for himself. However, here are seven guidelines that can help navigate this uncertain terrain:

1. Assess both intentions and behavior. Those who seek to cause harm often exhibit suspicious traits such as aggression, dishonesty, or reluctance to share their background or intentions. In contrast, individuals genuinely in need of help may appear desperate but not aggressive and are typically more open about their circumstances.

2. Establish secure checkpoints. If you are involved in a community defense effort, establishing secure checkpoints is an effective way to vet individuals before granting them access to your safe zone. This process should include checking for weapons, questioning their intentions, and evaluating whether they pose a potential threat or genuinely need assistance.

3. Form alliances with trusted allies—in advance. Building a network of trusted allies before a crisis occurs can be invaluable, as strong relationships with neighbors, friends, and community members who share a commitment to mutual defense and support provide a critical safety net. Establishing these alliances in advance ensures that you have a reliable support system in place when chaos arises.

4. Identify trustworthy and skilled individuals. Identifying trustworthy individuals is crucial, and those who possess valuable skills—such as medical knowledge, mechanical abilities, or tactical expertise—can be strong allies. People who are willing to share resources, information, and support demonstrate reliability and a commitment to mutual aid.

5. Exhibit caution with strangers. In a SHTF scenario, it is imperative to exercise caution with strangers; trust should be earned rather than given freely. Assuming that unknown individuals could pose a threat until they prove otherwise is a safer approach to protect yourself and your community.

6. Develop a community defense plan. Developing a community defense plan with clear roles, communication protocols, and security measures

strengthens collective security. Regular drills and coordination help ensure that everyone understands their responsibilities and can respond effectively in an emergency.

7. <u>Respond strategically if armed strangers enter your property</u>. If armed strangers encroach on your property, the situation demands a measured response focused on safety, defense, and ethical responsibility. First, assess the threat using available security tools and fortify your home by securing entry points and establishing defensive positions. If confrontation becomes necessary, a loud verbal warning may deter intruders, but if they pose an imminent threat, be prepared to use force within the bounds of self-defense laws while maintaining cover and a tactical advantage. Afterward, secure the area, check for injuries, and assess any damage to supplies or property. If possible, document the incident, as this may be important should law and order later be restored. For a more detailed breakdown of handling armed intruders, refer to "Break-Ins and Home Invasions" in chapter 14.

The potential for widespread chaos, riots, violence, looting, and destruction, particularly in urban areas, means that resources will become scarce quickly. Preparedness involves not only stockpiling like food, water, and medical supplies but also having contingency plans for replenishing these resources. Bartering, foraging, and self-sufficiency skills become vital in a prolonged crisis.

In such a dystopian scenario, the Second Amendment's role in ensuring that citizens have the means to defend themselves and their communities cannot be overstated. It empowers individuals to take their security into their own hands when traditional law enforcement and military resources are overwhelmed or unavailable. While the hope is that such a dire situation will never occur, being prepared and understanding the importance of the right to bear arms is crucial for those who value their safety and liberty.

Understanding the potential risks and having a plan in place can mean the difference between survival and succumbing to chaos. The Second Amendment provides the foundation for this preparedness, ensuring that American citizens are not left defenseless in the face of unprecedented threats.

Maintaining community and continued defense is of utmost importance. If you haven't already, reach out to neighbors or nearby trusted individuals to form a mutual defense group. A coordinated effort can provide better security and resource sharing. Establish regular patrols and surveillance to monitor the area for further threats, rotating responsibilities among group members to ensure everyone stays rested and alert. Continue to manage and protect your resources carefully, bartering and trading with trusted individuals to replenish supplies.

In such a dire scenario, the absence of conventional law enforcement means you must rely on self-governance and community cooperation. While the use of deadly force should always be a last resort, protecting yourself, your family, and your resources in a lawless environment might require difficult decisions and decisive action. Ensuring that everyone in your group is trained, prepared, and understands the gravity of the situation can help maintain order and safety in an otherwise chaotic environment.

## Sniping

In SHTF scenarios, or during a societal breakdown or civil war, numerous situations may necessitate sniper marksmanship. Proactively safeguarding your private property or home from would-be trespassers may require positioning yourself in strategic locations, such as a hunting platform, a rooftop, or even from within the confines of your home. Understanding the role of a sniper in these scenarios is fundamental for effectively neutralizing armed threats and maintaining the security of your environment.

When faced with armed intruders attempting to breach your property, having a sniper position allows you to maintain a defensive posture and engage threats from a distance. The element of surprise and the ability to strike accurately from concealed positions provide a significant tactical advantage. One of the primary objectives of a sniper in these situations is to neutralize armed threats before they can reach your home or harm your family. This may involve taking out aggressors who are advancing toward your property or disabling vehicles that intruders might be using to penetrate your defenses. Large caliber ammunition is particularly effective in disabling vehicles, ensuring that potential threats are stopped before they can pose a direct danger.

Selecting the right firearm for sniper duties is crucial. Bolt-action rifles, such as the Remington 700, are known for their accuracy and reliability, making them a popular choice among snipers. Chambered in .308 Winchester or .300 Winchester Magnum, these rifles are ideal for long-range engagements. For situations requiring a higher rate of fire, semi-automatic sniper rifles like the AR-10 or the M1A offer a good balance of accuracy and firepower, making them versatile for various defensive scenarios. Anti-materiel rifles, such as the Barrett M82 or M107 chambered in .50 BMG, are highly effective for disabling vehicles or engaging targets at extreme distances. These larger-caliber rifles can penetrate vehicle engines and provide significant stopping power.

Effectively using sniper skills for home defense requires the mastery of certain fundamental techniques. The ability to remain unseen is paramount, requiring the use of natural or artificial cover to blend into your surroundings. This could involve using ghillie suits, camouflage netting, or simply positioning yourself in shadowed areas. Know the distance to your target and the ballistic performance of your ammunition. Use rangefinders or pre-measured markers to estimate distances accurately and familiarize yourself with the trajectory and impact of your rounds at various distances to make precise adjustments.

Maintaining steady breathing and smooth trigger control are necessary for accurate shooting. Practice the technique of taking a deep breath, exhaling halfway, and then holding your breath while gently squeezing the trigger to minimize movement and enhance shot accuracy. Being able to identify and prioritize threats quickly is crucial, focusing on the most immediate and dangerous threats first, such as armed individuals or vehicles attempting to breach your perimeter. Sniper roles require high-quality optics, so equip your rifle with a reliable scope that offers clear magnification and reticle adjustments. Night vision or thermal scopes can also be valuable for low-light conditions or for detecting hidden targets.

Maintain effective communication and coordination if you are part of a larger group or family defense team. Establish signals and protocols for alerting others to threats and coordinating defensive actions. In a SHTF situation, positioning yourself as a sniper can provide a significant defensive advantage. Occupy elevated positions such as rooftops or upper-story windows to gain a clear line of sight over your property. Establish multiple sniper nests to cover various approaches and ensure redundancy in case one position is compromised.

Monitor your property regularly and stay vigilant for signs of intrusion or suspicious activity. Use spotting scopes or binoculars to scan your surroundings and identify potential threats from a distance. Maintaining a proactive and defensive posture can deter aggressors and provide early warning of incoming dangers. By mastering sniper skills and selecting the appropriate firearms, you can safeguard your home and property against armed threats, ensuring the safety and security of your loved ones in times of societal upheaval.

## Be Prepared

Although the above scenarios may seem extreme or exaggerated, and the likelihood of the worst-case scenario may be remote, it is still wise to prepare for such possibilities. The principle of preparedness is about ensuring readiness for any potential threat, no matter how improbable it may seem. By being prepared for the worst, you can navigate lesser crises with greater confidence and capability.

As much as worst-case scenarios may appear unlikely, they are not impossible. In recent years, the possibility of such scenarios has increased as tensions rise, conflicts within and abroad flare, and the population feels more unsafe and uneasy. Social unrest, economic instability, and global uncertainties contribute to a growing sense of vulnerability. In this climate, being prepared for extreme events becomes not just a prudent choice but a necessary one. This approach ensures that you can protect yourself and your loved ones, maintain stability in times of crisis, and face unforeseen challenges with resilience and determination.

## Challenge Yourself

If you're on the fence about guns and Second Amendment rights, or perhaps even hold a negative view of gun ownership, I urge you to step out of your comfort zone and challenge your own assumptions. The discourse around firearms and the Second Amendment is often clouded by media narratives, political agendas, and societal biases. However, personal experience and open-minded exploration can significantly shift perspectives.

Consider getting to know people who are knowledgeable and experienced with firearms. Engage in conversations, ask questions, and genuinely listen to their perspectives. Many gun enthusiasts are passionate about safety, responsibility, and the constitutional right to bear arms. They can provide insights that you might not encounter in mainstream media. Also, it's statistically likely that someone you know or are close to owns a firearm. Consider asking them why they decided to become armed and what the process was like for them. Ask about their experiences, the steps they took to obtain their firearm, and how they ensure safety and responsibility in their gun ownership. This firsthand insight can provide valuable perspective and help demystify the realities of gun ownership.

Take a step further and visit a shooting range. Safe and supervised shooting events with seasoned shooters can be enlightening. The hands-on experience of handling a firearm under professional guidance can demystify guns and provide a practical understanding of their role in personal defense and recreation.

Let's put this into perspective with a hypothetical scenario. Imagine facing a home invasion—in that high-stress moment, your ability to defend yourself and your loved ones is paramount. Now, consider your firearm options: If confronted by two intruders, would you trust a revolver or an AR-15 to neutralize the threat? What if the number increased to five, eight, or even ten? The capacity and capability of your firearm become crucial as the threat level escalates. This isn't about paranoia—it's about preparedness and ensuring you have the right tools for worst-case scenarios. For a deeper discussion on firearm effectiveness in self-defense, refer to chapter 14.

Beyond the practical aspect of self-defense, exploring the world of the Second Amendment can be fulfilling, provide peace of mind, and even be enjoyable. Shooting sports, for example, are a popular and engaging hobby for many. They offer a combination of skill development, discipline, and camaraderie. Additionally, understanding the historical and constitutional significance of the Second Amendment can deepen your appreciation for this right. It's about recognizing the balance of power and the role that an armed populace plays in preserving liberty and deterring tyranny.

To further challenge your perspective, consider the mind game of situational preparedness. If you were in a rural area with a limited law enforcement presence, how would you protect yourself and your property? In urban environments with rising crime rates, what measures would you take to ensure your safety? These scenarios underscore the importance of being equipped and prepared, reinforcing the practical value of the Second Amendment.

Be sure to consider also the broader societal context. Countries with stringent gun control laws often experience different kinds of violence and crime rates. Exploring comparative studies and statistics can provide a nuanced understanding of how firearms impact safety and security. Engaging with diverse sources of information, including those that challenge your preconceptions, can lead to a more balanced and informed viewpoint.

Also, make it a priority to educate yourself on the gun laws in your state, city, or county, and compare them to those in other places you might visit or consider moving to. Connect with local gun owners, ask questions, and learn from their experiences—they're often the best source of real-world insight into how laws are enforced on the ground.

Approaching the topic of firearms and the Second Amendment with an open mind and a willingness to explore new experiences can lead to a deeper understanding and potentially a shift in perspective. The world of the Second Amendment is not just about the right to bear arms; it's about responsibility, safety, personal empowerment, and the preservation of liberty. So, step out of your comfort zone, challenge your assumptions, and explore the realities beyond the rhetoric. You might find that your views evolve in unexpected and meaningful ways.

## A Future Worth Fighting For

The Second Amendment is not negotiable. It isn't a relic to be reinterpreted to fit modern sensibilities. It is a promise that the right to bear arms shall not be infringed—a recognition that individual liberty depends on the ability of citizens to protect themselves from threats, whether they come from criminals or from tyrannical government overreach.

As we reach the conclusion of this extensive exploration of the Second Amendment, it is clear this right is not merely a relic of the past but a vital and dynamic part of the American identity. Throughout this book, we have journeyed through history, examined the philosophical foundations of self-defense, debunked myths, scrutinized media narratives, and highlighted the importance of responsible gun ownership. We have seen how the Second Amendment serves as a bulwark against tyranny, a guarantor of personal security, and a pillar of our national ethos.

The essence of the Second Amendment is the recognition of the inherent right to self-defense and the principle that a free society is one where its citizens are empowered to protect themselves and their communities. This right is not granted by the government; it is an inalienable right that predates the Constitution, one that the Framers included to protect against future encroachments.

However, the preservation of this right is not guaranteed. It requires vigilance, education, and active participation from every citizen. The responsibility now rests upon us to ensure that the Second Amendment is not eroded by ignorance, apathy, or political agendas. It is up to us to educate future generations, to foster a culture of responsible gun ownership, and to remain steadfast in our defense of this fundamental freedom.

As we reflect on the journey through this book, several philosophical questions arise: What kind of society do we want to leave for our children and grandchildren? Do we want a society where individuals are free and autonomous, capable of defending their rights and liberties? Or do we want a society where the government holds a monopoly on force, and citizens are rendered powerless and dependent?

The answer to these questions will shape the future of our nation. The Second Amendment is more than just a right to own firearms; it is a symbol of our autonomy and our resolve to stand against oppression. It embodies the spirit of independence that has defined America since its inception.

To preserve this right, we must be proactive. We must enable thoughtful discussions, advocate for sound policies, and hold our leaders accountable. We must support organizations that defend the Second Amendment and challenge those who seek to undermine it. We must pass on our knowledge and values to the next generation, ensuring that they understand the importance of this right and are prepared to defend it.

To those who seek to undermine the Second Amendment: You are mistaken if you believe Americans will surrender their right to bear arms. The Second Amendment is the backbone of liberty, and armed citizens are its steadfast guardians. Efforts to disarm law-abiding Americans, whether through legislation or rhetoric, will meet firm resistance, rooted in the principles that founded this nation.

It is ironic that those who advocate gun control often do so from places of privilege, protected by armed security while seeking to strip others of the same protection. Misleading statistics, fearmongering, and hollow arguments will not sway those who understand that the right to bear arms is not merely about firearms—it is about preserving freedom, protecting families, and ensuring security against tyranny.

Americans have a long tradition of defending liberty, and that resolve has not wavered. The Second Amendment is non-negotiable, a safeguard of the freedoms generations have fought and sacrificed to uphold. The choice before us is clear: Stand idly by as these rights are chipped away or take action to ensure their preservation. No politician, no matter how well-intentioned, is going to ride in on a white horse and save us. Preserving our Second Amendment rights and liberties has always been, and will always be, up to the people. The responsibility lies with all of us to protect the liberty that defines the American experience. Politicians and governments act as they do because, ultimately, we allow it. They only have power because we give it to them. The responsibility to protect our freedom lies squarely with us. It's up to you to stand up, take action, and do your part. Freedom is not a gift—it's a duty. So, get to work!

# Acknowledgments

I am deeply grateful to Carl—for everything, as well as my family and friends, for their unwavering belief in me and for surrounding me with love and encouragement every step of the way. I'm also grateful to the many inspirational voices in the Second Amendment community who continue to stand firm and fight for our rights. Your dedication made this work not only possible, but necessary. I would also like to thank the great State of Tennessee for blessing me with peace, serenity in the Smoky Mountains, and a true escape to freedom. A special thanks to my dog Zach, whose loyal companionship and quiet presence kept me grounded during the countless hours I spent writing—your unconditional love and company meant more than you'll ever know. Last but certainly not least, I thank God for guiding me through this journey and granting me the strength and clarity to see it through.

# Glossary

The following glossary provides definitions of key terms and concepts referenced throughout this book. It is intended to assist readers in understanding specialized language, technical terms, and commonly discussed topics related to firearms, the Second Amendment, and related political and legal debates. Whether you are new to the subject or seeking clarification on specific terminology, this section serves as a quick and reliable reference to enhance your reading experience. While most of these terms appear within the text of this book, some have been included additionally to provide further context and to assist readers who wish to deepen their understanding of related topics.

**2A.** Shorthand for the Second Amendment.

**2A Renegade.** A defiant supporter of the Second Amendment who refuses to bow to political pressure, media narratives, or anti-gun agendas. The term embodies an unapologetic, principled stance in defense of the right to keep and bear arms—someone who challenges mainstream gun control rhetoric and stands firm on constitutional freedoms, regardless of public opinion or cultural trends.

**active shooter.** A person actively engaged in killing or attempting to kill people in a populated area, typically with firearms, often indiscriminately.

**activist judge.** A judge who is viewed as making rulings based on personal beliefs, political ideology, or social agendas rather than a strict interpretation of the law or Constitution. *See also* judicial activism.

**AK-47.** A rugged, gas-operated rifle designed by Mikhail Kalashnikov. The civilian-legal versions available in the US are semi-automatic. Often demonized in gun control debates as a symbol of "military-style" weapons.

**ammo.** Short for ammunition. A general term for cartridges, shells, or rounds used in firearms.

**Antifa.** A violent, far-left extremist movement that uses intimidation, assault, and property destruction to silence political opponents under the banner of "anti-fascism." Antifa is widely criticized for suppressing free speech and promoting chaos while claiming to oppose authoritarianism.

**AR-15.** A lightweight, modular, semi-automatic rifle originally designed by Eugene Stoner. AR stands for "Armalite Rifle," not "assault rifle," despite common media misconceptions. One of the most popular civilian rifles in America.

**assault rifle.** A military firearm capable of selective fire (both semi-auto and full-auto), not readily available to the general public. Often misused by politicians and media to describe civilian semi-automatic rifles.

**ATF.** Abbreviation for Bureau of Alcohol, Tobacco, Firearms and Explosives. A federal agency under the DOJ tasked with enforcing federal gun laws. Criticized by many gun owners for regulatory overreach and controversial enforcement actions.

**ballistics.** The science of projectiles and their behavior in flight, from barrel exit to impact.

**ballistic coefficient.** A numerical value that measures a bullet's ability to overcome air resistance in flight. A higher BC means the bullet is more aerodynamic, retains velocity better, and is less affected by wind drift, making it ideal for long-range shooting.

**background check.** A review of an individual's criminal and legal history before purchasing a firearm. A common point of contention in gun control debates.

**barrel.** The long metal tube of a firearm through which a bullet travels when fired.

**bayonet lug.** A mounting point, typically found on military-style rifles, allowing the attachment of a bayonet. Often targeted in gun control legislation despite its limited modern use.

**belt-fed.** Describes a firearm, typically a machine gun, that is supplied with ammunition via a linked belt of cartridges rather than a traditional box or drum magazine.

**black powder.** The original gunpowder, composed of saltpeter (potassium nitrate), charcoal, and sulfur. Used in early firearms like muskets and cannons, it produces significant smoke and fouling compared to modern smokeless powder.

**Bill of Rights.** The first 10 amendments to the United States Constitution, ratified in 1791, designed to protect individual liberties and limit government power. The Bill of Rights guarantees fundamental rights such as freedom of speech, freedom of religion, due process, and the right to keep and bear arms, as outlined in the Second Amendment. It remains a cornerstone of American constitutional law and civil liberties.

**bolt.** The component of a firearm, typically in bolt-action and semi-automatic rifles, that moves forward to chamber a round and backward to extract and eject a spent casing. In bolt-action rifles, they are manually operated by the shooter using a handle. In semi-automatic firearms, the bolt is cycled automatically by gas pressure or recoil.

**bolt-action.** A type of firearm action operated manually by lifting and pulling back a bolt handle to chamber a round.

**bolt carrier group.** The assembly within certain semi-automatic and automatic firearms, such as the AR-15, that houses the bolt, firing pin, and related components. It is responsible for chambering rounds, extracting spent casings, and cycling the firearm during operation.

**bolt catch.** A mechanical component on certain semi-automatic firearms, such as the AR-15, that locks the bolt to the rear when the magazine is empty or when manually engaged. It allows the shooter to inspect or clear the chamber without the bolt closing.

**bolt release.** The portion of the bolt catch that, when pressed, releases the bolt to move forward and chamber a round. It allows for faster reloading and immediate readiness after inserting a fresh magazine.

**bullet.** The projectile component of a cartridge that is expelled from the barrel when a firearm is fired. Typically made of lead, copper, or other metals, bullets come in various shapes and designs, including full metal jacket (FMJ), hollow point (HP), and soft point (SP), each influencing how the bullet performs upon impact.

**bullet drop.** The downward trajectory of a bullet as it travels away from the firearm because of gravity.

**bump stock.** A device that uses recoil to increase the rate of fire of a semi-automatic rifle. Banned by ATF rule despite prior legality.

**Caliber.** The internal diameter of a firearm's barrel or the diameter of the bullet fired, typically measured in inches or millimeters.

**carbine.** A shorter-barreled rifle, often lighter and more maneuverable than standard-length rifles.

**casing.** The metal, brass, or steel shell that houses the primer, gunpowder, and bullet in a complete cartridge. After firing, the casing is ejected from the firearm, leaving the chamber ready for the next round. Casings are a critical component of modern ammunition and are often reusable in reloading.

**castle doctrine.** A legal principle allowing individuals to use force, including deadly force, to protect themselves in their home without a duty to retreat.

**chamber.** The part of a firearm's barrel or receiver where a cartridge is seated before being fired. When the action cycles, a fresh round is loaded into the chamber, ready to be ignited by the firing pin. The chamber is designed to contain the pressure from the expanding gases when the round is fired.

**charging handle.** A manually operated lever used to cycle the bolt of a firearm, typically to chamber the first round, clear malfunctions, or lock the bolt to the rear. Commonly found on rifles like the AR-15, it is essential for initial loading and clearing jams.

**civil war.** (1) A large-scale armed conflict between organized groups within the same country, typically fought over control of the government, territorial independence, or major political and ideological differences. (2) Refers specifically to the American Civil War (1861–1865), a conflict between the United States (Union) and the Confederate States of America over issues including states' rights, slavery, and the preservation of the Union. The war resulted in significant casualties and the eventual abolition of slavery in the United States.

**clip.** A device used to hold cartridges together for faster loading into a firearm or magazine. Often incorrectly used to describe a magazine.

**collectivism.** A political and economic system where the group takes priority over individual rights. Often linked to leftist ideologies such as socialism and communism.

**communism.** A political and economic ideology advocating for the abolition of private property and the establishment of a classless, stateless society where the means of production are owned collectively. In practice, communist regimes have historically centralized power under authoritarian governments, often suppressing individual freedoms and disarming the population to maintain control. Commonly associated with mass atrocities, genocide, forced collectivization, and totalitarian rule in countries such as the Soviet Union, China, and Cambodia.

compensator. A muzzle device attached to the end of a firearm's barrel that redirects gases upward to counteract muzzle rise during firing. By reducing the upward movement of the barrel (muzzle rise), compensators help improve follow-up shot speed and accuracy, especially in rapid-fire situations.

**concealed carry.** The practice of carrying a hidden firearm on one's person in public, legal under permit or constitutional carry in many states.

**conspiracy theorist.** A label often slapped onto anyone who presents facts, evidence, or uncomfortable questions that challenge the mainstream narrative—especially when those facts contradict leftist talking points or expose government overreach. In today's culture, it's less about tinfoil hats and more about daring to think critically in a world that punishes dissent.

**conspiracy theory.** Any explanation for events that involves collusion or hidden agendas—particularly when it challenges official narratives or exposes inconvenient truths. Once used to describe fringe ideas, the term is now routinely applied to shut down debate, dismiss dissent, or ridicule anyone presenting facts that make powerful people or institutions uncomfortable.

**constitution.** *See* US Constitution.

**constitutional carry.** The legal right to carry a firearm without a permit, based on the belief that the Second Amendment is all the permit a citizen needs.

**controlled opposition.** A term for individuals or organizations that appear to support a cause while working to undermine it from within.

**defensive gun use (DGU).** The act of using a firearm to deter or stop a threat. Often underreported in mainstream statistics on gun violence.

**Department of Justice (DOJ).** The federal agency that oversees the ATF and other law enforcement bodies.

**deterrence.** The prevention of criminal activity through the threat or presence of defensive force.

**disarm.** To take away or deprive an individual or group of weapons or means of defense. Often used in the context of military surrender or as a political objective in gun control efforts.

**disarmament.** The act or policy of reducing, restricting, or eliminating weapons, typically refers to government-led efforts to limit or abolish civilian or military armaments. In gun rights discussions, disarmament is viewed as a threat to personal liberty and self-defense.

**double-action.** A trigger mechanism that both cocks and releases the hammer when the trigger is pulled.

**double-barrel shotgun / rifle.** A firearm with two barrels, either side-by-side or over-and-under, common in hunting and sport shooting.

**drop safe.** A firearm that will not discharge when dropped from a certain height.

**dry fire.** The practice of pulling the trigger on a firearm without live ammunition present, often used for training or function testing.

**duty to retreat.** A legal principle requiring an individual to attempt to avoid confrontation or safely retreat from a threat, if possible, before using force in self-defense. The duty to retreat is applied in some states, while others have "stand your ground" laws that remove this obligation, allowing individuals to defend themselves without retreating if they are in a place where they have a legal right to be.

**effective range.** The maximum distance at which a firearm or specific cartridge can be expected to deliver accurate, lethal, or reliable performance. Effective range varies based on the type of weapon, ammunition, and shooter proficiency, and is distinct from a bullet's maximum travel distance, which may be much farther but less predictable or accurate.

**ejection port.** The opening on the side or top of a firearm's receiver through which spent casings are expelled after firing. The ejection port allows for the removal of empty cartridges and can also be used to clear malfunctions or inspect the chamber.

**elevation.** The vertical adjustment of a firearm's sights or optic to account for bullet drop over distance. Adjusting for elevation allows the shooter to raise or lower the point of aim to ensure accurate targeting at varying ranges.

**elitist / elite.** A person or group who views themselves as superior and is often disconnected from the realities of everyday citizens. In gun rights discussions, often refers to politicians, celebrities, or bureaucrats who advocate disarmament while enjoying personal protection.

**emergency powers.** Temporary legal authority granted during crises, often criticized when used to infringe on civil liberties, including gun rights.

**executive order.** A directive issued by the President. Frequently used to impose gun regulations without congressional approval.

**extracting.** The act of removing a spent cartridge casing from a firearm's chamber after firing.

**extended magazine.** A magazine with greater capacity than standard models, often targeted by gun control laws under the label "high-capacity."

**external ballistics.** The study of a bullet's behavior after it exits the barrel but before it hits the target. Influenced by factors like velocity, gravity, wind, and air resistance.

**fallacy.** A flaw or error in reasoning that weakens an argument. Frequently used to describe manipulative or illogical tactics in political discourse, including gun control debates.

**false flag.** A deceptive operation intended to blame one group for actions carried out by another, often discussed in conspiracy theories related to gun control events.

**fascism.** A totalitarian, nationalist, and Marxist ideology advocating for centralized control and suppression of dissent. Though historically left-wing, statist, and authoritarian, it is now often misused as a slur by leftists against anyone who disagrees with them politically.

**Fast and Furious (operation).** A failed ATF operation that allowed firearms to fall into cartel hands, resulting in deaths and scandal.

**Federal Firearms License (FFL).** A license issued by the ATF that allows the sale and manufacture of firearms.

**Fifth Amendment.** Protects individuals from self-incrimination. Often referenced when gun owners resist disclosing personal firearm details to authorities.

**firearm.** A portable, barreled weapon that uses an explosive charge (gunpowder) to propel a projectile. The legal term commonly used in US law to describe handguns, rifles, shotguns, and other guns regulated under federal and state statutes. Unlike air guns or other projectile devices, firearms rely on combustion to operate.

**firing pin.** A small metal rod or component within a firearm that strikes the primer of a cartridge when the trigger is pulled, igniting the gunpowder and firing the round.

**fixed magazine.** A non-detachable magazine that is permanently affixed to a firearm. Often referenced in laws aimed at limiting detachable magazines.

**flintlock musket.** A type of musket that uses a flintlock ignition system, where a piece of flint strikes a steel frizzen to create sparks that ignite the gunpowder in the pan, firing the weapon.

**foot-pound.** A unit of energy used to measure the force transferred by a bullet upon impact. One foot-pound is equal to the energy required to move one pound of mass one foot in distance. In firearms, higher foot-pound values generally indicate greater stopping power, penetration, or recoil, depending on the bullet's speed and mass.

**forward assist.** A device on some rifles, such as the AR-15, that allows the shooter to manually push the bolt carrier group fully into battery if it does not fully close on its own. Often used in situations where the firearm is dirty or when positive bolt closure is necessary.

**forward grip.** A grip mounted beneath the handguard of a rifle, providing shooters with additional control and stability, especially during rapid fire.

**Founding Fathers.** The American leaders who authored the Constitution and Bill of Rights, including the Second Amendment.

**fully automatic.** A firearm that continues to fire multiple rounds with a single pull of the trigger until released or the ammunition is exhausted. Strictly regulated under the National Firearms Act.

**genocide.** The deliberate and systematic extermination of a national, ethnic, racial, or religious group. Genocide is considered one of the gravest crimes against humanity, often carried out by authoritarian regimes or occupying powers to eliminate a targeted population. History has shown that disarmed populations are particularly vulnerable to such atrocities.

**ghost gun.** A term used by gun control advocates to describe privately made firearms without serial numbers. Typically built from kits or 80 percent lower receivers.

**Great Leap Forward.** A socioeconomic campaign led by Chinese Communist Party Chairman Mao Zedong from 1958 to 1962, aimed at rapidly transforming China from an agrarian society into an industrialized socialist state. The policy forced collectivization, industrialization, and agricultural reforms, which led to widespread famine, economic collapse, and the deaths of tens of millions. It is considered one of the deadliest manmade disasters in history.

**guerilla warfare.** A form of irregular warfare in which small, mobile groups of combatants use hit-and-run tactics, ambushes, sabotage, and unconventional strategies to fight a larger, traditional military force. Often employed by insurgent groups, militias, or resistance fighters, guerilla warfare relies on mobility, surprise, and intimate knowledge of the terrain.

**gun.** A general term for a device that launches a projectile through a barrel using rapidly expanding gases from a chemical reaction, typically involving gunpowder. Guns include a wide range of firearms, such as pistols, rifles, shotguns, and machine guns. The term is often used interchangeably with "firearm," though it can also apply to non-firearm devices like air guns or cannons depending on context.

**gunpowder.** The chemical propellant inside a cartridge case that, when ignited by the primer, rapidly burns and creates expanding gases to propel the bullet through the barrel. Modern firearms typically use smokeless powder, while older firearms used black powder.

**guntuber.** A slang term for a content creator who produces firearm-related videos on platforms like YouTube or similar sites. Guntubers often review firearms, discuss Second Amendment issues, demonstrate shooting techniques, and provide educational content for gun enthusiasts.

**gun control.** Laws aimed at regulating or restricting firearms, frequently criticized by Second Amendment supporters as infringing on fundamental rights.

**gun-free zone.** An area where firearms are legally prohibited, often criticized for leaving law-abiding citizens defenseless.

**gun show loophole.** A misleading term used to describe private firearm sales that do not require background checks under federal law.

**hammer.** A component of certain firearms that strikes the firing pin (or directly strikes the primer in some designs) to ignite the cartridge.

**handgun.** A firearm designed to be held and fired with one hand. Includes revolvers and semi-automatic pistols. Handguns are commonly used for self-defense, law enforcement, and concealed carry.

**high-capacity magazine.** A politically loaded term referring to magazines holding more rounds than arbitrary legal limits (e.g., 10 rounds). Gun owners typically refer to them as standard-capacity magazines.

**holographic sight.** A type of non-magnified optic that uses a laser and holographic reticle projected onto a viewing window, allowing for rapid target acquisition with a clear aiming point. Unlike red dot sights, the reticle in a holographic sight remains focused regardless of eye position, offering faster sight picture recovery and improved performance in dynamic shooting scenarios.

**holster.** A carrying case designed to securely hold a handgun, typically worn on the body for quick access and safe retention. Holsters come in various styles—inside-the-waistband (IWB), outside-the-waistband (OWB), shoulder, ankle, and more—and are essential for both concealed and open carry. A good holster balances accessibility, comfort, and firearm retention.

**hoplophobia.** An irrational fear of firearms, a term coined by firearms expert Jeff Cooper.

**hypothetical scenario.** A theoretical situation used to illustrate a point, argument, or concept. Common in debates to test the logic or consequences of a particular belief or policy.

**infringement.** Any action by the government that limits or restricts or violates constitutional rights, especially the Second Amendment.

**Intellectual Yet Idiot (IYI).** A term popularized by author Nassim Nicholas Taleb to describe individuals who are highly credentialed but lack practical wisdom, often disconnected from real-world consequences of the policies or theories they promote.

**internal ballistics.** The science of what happens inside the firearm from the moment the primer ignites until the bullet exits the barrel, including gas expansion and barrel pressure.

**iron sights.** Non-optical aiming devices found on most firearms, typically consisting of a front sight post and rear notch or aperture.

**judicial activism.** A term used to describe when judges are perceived to go beyond interpreting existing law and instead create new policy through court rulings. Often associated with decisions that reflect personal or political beliefs rather than strict adherence to the Constitution or legislative intent. Judicial activism undermines the separation of powers by allowing courts to function as unelected lawmakers.

**Justice Department.** *See* Department of Justice (DOJ).

**justifiable homicide.** A legally sanctioned killing in defense of oneself or others.

**Kalashnikov.** A reference to the AK-47 rifle platform, named after its designer, Mikhail Kalashnikov.

**Kevlar.** A strong synthetic fiber used in ballistic vests and body armor.

Khmer Rouge. The communist regime that ruled Cambodia from 1975 to 1979 under the leadership of Pol Pot. Implemented radical agrarian socialism and carried out genocide, mass executions, forced labor, and widespread purges.

**leftist**. A general term describing someone who aligns with progressive or far-left ideologies, often favoring increased government control, collectivism, and cultural shifts toward political correctness and centralized authority.

**lever-action.** A type of firearm action operated by a lever, commonly seen in rifles associated with the Old West.

**liberal elite.** A colloquial term for influential figures who advocate for gun control while enjoying personal armed security.

**live fire.** The use of a firearm with live ammunition during training, practice, or real-world scenarios.

**long gun.** A general term for firearms with a longer barrel designed to be fired from the shoulder, including rifles and shotguns. Distinguished from handguns, which are designed for one-handed use.

**lower receiver.** The serialized part of a firearm (especially in AR-15s) that houses the fire control group, magazine well, and buffer system. Legally considered the "firearm" under US law.

**luxury belief.** A term describing beliefs typically held by elites that signal status but often have little direct negative impact on them, while harming or burdening lower or middle-class individuals (e.g., promoting gun control while living in gated communities with private security).

**machine gun.** A firearm capable of fully automatic fire. Strictly regulated under the National Firearms Act.

**magazine.** A device that feeds ammunition into a firearm. Commonly confused with a clip.

**magazine release.** A button, lever, or catch on a firearm that, when activated, allows the shooter to eject or remove the magazine from the magazine well. Positioned for quick access, the magazine release is commonly found on pistols and rifles to facilitate fast reloads.

**magazine well.** The opening or cavity in a firearm's receiver or grip where a detachable magazine is inserted. The magazine well guides the magazine into proper alignment for reliable feeding of cartridges into the chamber.

**mass shooting.** A loosely defined term typically referring to an incident in which multiple people are shot in a single event. Definitions vary, but the FBI often considers four or more people shot and/or killed, excluding the shooter. The term is frequently politicized, with differing interpretations used to advance various narratives about gun violence and gun control. *See also* shooting.

**may-issue.** A type of firearm permitting system in which authorities have discretion to approve or deny concealed carry permits, even if the applicant meets all legal requirements. Often criticized for being subjective, inconsistent, and ripe for political or personal bias, may issue laws are seen by gun rights advocates as a bureaucratic obstacle to exercising a constitutional right. *See also* shall issue.

**militia.** The body of armed citizens capable of defense. Frequently misinterpreted in modern debates over the Second Amendment.

**Molon Labe.** Greek for "Come and take [them]," a popular pro-Second Amendment slogan symbolizing resistance to gun confiscation.

**musket.** A smoothbore, muzzle-loading long gun commonly used from the 16th to the 19th centuries. Firing spherical lead balls or shot, muskets lacked rifling and were less accurate than modern rifles. Often associated with early American history, including the Revolutionary War.

**muzzle.** The front end of a firearm's barrel.

**muzzleloader.** A firearm in which the projectile and powder charge are loaded from the open end of the barrel (the muzzle), rather than through a breech or chamber. Common in early firearms like muskets and still used today in traditional hunting or historical reenactments.

**muzzle blast.** The explosive burst of gas, heat, noise, and light that exits the muzzle of a firearm when it is fired. Caused by rapidly expanding gases from ignited gunpowder, muzzle blast contributes to the firearm's report (sound) and visible flash, especially in low-light conditions.

**muzzle brake.** A device attached to the muzzle to reduce recoil and muzzle rise.

**muzzle flash.** The visible burst of flame that appears at the muzzle of a firearm when it is fired, caused by hot gases and unburned powder igniting upon contact with outside air. Muzzle flash is more pronounced in low-light conditions and can temporarily affect a shooter's night vision.

**muzzle rise.** The upward movement of a firearm's barrel when a shot is fired, caused by the force of recoil. Also known as muzzle flip, this effect can reduce accuracy in rapid-fire shooting and is often mitigated by devices such as compensators or muzzle brakes.

**National Firearms Act (NFA).** A 1934 federal law heavily regulating certain firearms and accessories like suppressors and short-barreled rifles.

**NICS.** The FBI-run National Instant Criminal Background Check System used for most commercial firearm purchases.

**Naziism.** The ideology of the National Socialist German Workers' Party, characterized by extreme authoritarianism and mass atrocities. Frequently and inaccurately used by modern leftists to insult anyone with differing political views.

**noncompliance.** Refusal to obey laws viewed as unconstitutional or unjust, particularly regarding gun restrictions.

**open carry.** The act of visibly carrying a firearm in public.

**optic.** A general term for any sighting device mounted on a firearm, including red dots, holographic sights, magnified scopes, and prism sights. Optics enhance aiming precision and target identification.

**overreach.** When government agencies or lawmakers exceed their lawful authority.

**pistol.** A semi-automatic handgun designed for one-handed use.

**pistol grip.** A vertical grip on a firearm, allowing the shooter to hold it in a similar fashion to a handgun. Common on modern sporting rifles and tactical shotguns.

**plinking.** Informal, recreational target shooting.

**point of aim / point of impact (POA/POI).** The relationship between where a shooter aims and where the bullet actually strikes.

**polymer.** A synthetic material used in modern firearm construction.

*Pravda.* The official newspaper of the Soviet Communist Party, synonymous today with biased or state-controlled media spreading propaganda rather than objective reporting.

**preamble.** The opening statement of the US Constitution outlining its foundational principles.

**preemption.** Laws preventing local governments from enacting stricter gun control than what is allowed by state law.

**prepper.** A person who actively plans and prepares for emergencies, natural disasters, economic collapse, or other potential crises. Similar to a survivalist but often more focused on practical, everyday readiness, preppers stockpile food, water, medical supplies, and other essentials to ensure self-reliance in times of disruption.

**primer.** A small ignition component located at the base of a cartridge. When struck by the firing pin, it ignites the gunpowder inside the case, initiating the firing sequence. Primers can be centerfire (located in the center of the base) or rimfire (ignition compound located in the rim).

**propaganda.** Information, especially of a biased or misleading nature, used to promote or advance a particular political cause, ideology, or point of view. Designed to manipulate public opinion through emotional appeal, selective facts, or outright falsehoods. Commonly employed by governments, media outlets, and activist groups.

**pump-action.** A manually operated firearm action commonly found in shotguns.

**qualify.** To meet the minimum training or shooting requirements for a concealed carry permit or other firearm certification.

**radical left.** A term used to describe individuals or movements on the far-left end of the political spectrum who advocate for extreme progressive, socialist, or collectivist policies. The radical left often seeks sweeping societal changes, including expanded government control, wealth redistribution, and the erosion of traditional institutions, usually at the expense of individual rights and constitutional freedoms.

**radical.** A person who advocates for sweeping, fundamental changes to political, social, or economic systems, often rejecting traditional values or incremental reform. Radicals can exist on any point of the political spectrum, but the term is frequently used to describe those whose extreme views or actions threaten established freedoms and institutions.

**rangefinder.** A device that measures the distance between the shooter and the target. Used in both shooting sports and hunting to calculate accurate shot placement, especially at long ranges.

**recoil.** The backward force or "kick" a shooter feels when a firearm is discharged. Caused by the equal and opposite reaction to the bullet and expanding gases exiting the barrel, recoil varies based on caliber, firearm weight, and action type. Heavier calibers and lighter firearms generally produce stronger felt recoil.

**red dot.** A type of non-magnified optic that projects a red (or sometimes green) illuminated dot onto a lens, allowing for quick target acquisition and precise aiming. Popular on rifles, pistols, and shotguns due to their speed and simplicity.

**red flag law.** Laws allowing firearms to be confiscated from individuals deemed a risk, often criticized for bypassing due process.

**reloading.** (1) The process of assembling ammunition by manually combining components—casing, primer, gunpowder, and bullet—into a functional cartridge. Reloading is commonly practiced to save money, customize loads for specific shooting needs, or improve accuracy. (2) Refers to the act of refilling a firearm with fresh ammunition during use.

**renegade.** A person who rejects conventional norms, rules, or allegiances—often viewed as rebellious, defiant, or nonconformist. In the context of politics or culture, a renegade challenges the status quo, refuses to follow groupthink, and stands firm in personal convictions, even when unpopular. Often used as a badge of honor by those who prioritize principle over approval.

**repeal.** The act of rescinding a law, often referenced in efforts to overturn gun control measures.

**repeater.** A firearm that can fire multiple rounds without reloading after each shot.

**reticle.** The aiming pattern, often in the form of crosshairs, dots, or other shapes, visible through a scope or optic that helps the shooter align the firearm with the target. Reticles can be simple or complex, with advanced versions featuring range-finding or bullet drop compensation marks.

**Revolutionary War.** The conflict (1775–1783) in which the thirteen American colonies fought for and gained independence from British rule.

**revolver.** A type of handgun with a rotating cylinder that holds multiple cartridges, typically five to eight, which aligns each round with the barrel and firing pin as the cylinder turns.

**rifle.** A shoulder-fired firearm with a rifled barrel, meaning spiral grooves are cut inside the barrel to impart spin on the bullet for increased accuracy and stability. Rifles can be bolt-action, lever-action, pump-action, or semi-automatic, and are used for a variety of purposes including hunting, self-defense, sport shooting, and military applications.

**rifling.** The spiral grooves cut into the inside of a firearm's barrel that impart a spin to the bullet as it is fired. This spin stabilizes the projectile in flight, improving accuracy and range. Rifling is a defining characteristic of rifles and many handguns, differentiating them from smoothbore firearms like traditional shotguns and muskets.

**rounds.** Cartridges or bullets used as ammunition.

**SAFE Act.** The Secure Ammunition and Firearms Enforcement Act, a gun control law passed in New York State in 2013. Enacted swiftly after the Sandy Hook tragedy, the SAFE Act expanded background check requirements, banned "assault weapons" by redefining features, limited magazine capacity to 7 rounds (later struck down to 10), and mandated registration of certain firearms. Widely criticized by gun rights advocates as an unconstitutional overreach, the law is seen as a model for similar gun control proposals across the country.

**scope.** A magnified optic, typically a telescopic sight, used to improve accuracy at longer distances. Scopes come in variable or fixed magnifications and often include reticles for windage and elevation adjustments.

**Second Amendment.** The constitutional right guaranteeing Americans the ability to keep and bear arms, serving as a safeguard against tyranny.

**Second Amendment Sanctuary.** A locality that refuses to enforce certain gun control laws deemed unconstitutional.

**self-defense.** The act of protecting oneself from harm, often central to Second Amendment arguments.

**semi-automatic.** A firearm that fires one round per trigger pull and automatically chambers the next round.

**shall-issue.** A concealed carry permitting system where authorities must issue permits to qualified applicants.

**shooting.** (1) The act of discharging a firearm, resulting in the projectile being fired from the barrel. The term can apply to a wide range of contexts, including lawful activities like hunting and target practice, as well as unlawful incidents such as criminal assaults or homicides. (2) A violent act in which a firearm is used to intentionally wound or kill one or more individuals.

**short-barreled rifle.** A rifle with a barrel shorter than 16 inches or an overall length less than 26 inches, regulated under the National Firearms Act (NFA). Requires a tax stamp and ATF approval for civilian ownership.

**shotgun.** A firearm that fires shells containing multiple projectiles (shot) or a single slug.

**SHTF.** Acronym for "when the s--t hits the fan," a slang term used to describe a major crisis or disaster scenario where normal societal functions collapse. Common in survivalist and prepper circles, SHTF refers to situations requiring self-reliance, such as natural disasters, civil unrest, or government breakdowns.

**sidearm.** A secondary or backup weapon, usually a handgun, carried in addition to a primary weapon like a rifle. Traditionally used by military personnel, law enforcement, and security professionals.

**sight.** Aiming devices used on firearms, including iron sights, red dots, scopes, and other optics. "Sights" can refer to either non-optical aiming tools (iron sights) or optical devices.

**silencer.** A heavily regulated device attached to the muzzle of a firearm to reduce the noise and muzzle flash generated when the gun is fired. Commonly referred to as a suppressor within the firearms community, a silencer does not make a firearm "silent" but lowers the sound signature to safer or less detectable levels. *See also* suppressor.

**single-action.** A type of firearm mechanism in which the trigger performs only one function: releasing the hammer or striker to fire the weapon. The hammer must be manually cocked before each shot. Common in traditional revolvers and some semi-automatic pistols, single-action designs are valued for their light and crisp trigger pulls.

**small arms.** A military and law enforcement term referring to handheld firearms such as pistols, rifles, shotguns, and submachine guns. Typically defined as firearms designed to be carried and operated by a single individual.

**sniper.** A trained marksman who engages targets at long distances with precision and accuracy, typically using a specialized rifle equipped with optics. In military and law enforcement contexts, snipers are tasked with reconnaissance, overwatch, and eliminating high-value targets. In civilian usage, the term is often misapplied by media to describe any long-range shooter.

**socialism.** A collectivist left-wing ideology advocating for government ownership and control of industry and redistribution of wealth. Widely regarded by gun rights advocates as a threat to personal liberty.

**sonic crack.** The sharp, whip-like sound produced when a bullet travels faster than the speed of sound, creating a miniature sonic boom. This crack is distinct from the sound of the gunshot itself and is a telltale sign of supersonic ammunition in flight. Even with a suppressor, the sonic crack can still reveal a shooter's position.

**sporting rifle.** A non-military, civilian rifle designed for lawful activities such as hunting, target shooting, or competition. Often used as an alternative term by gun rights advocates to counter the misleading label of "assault weapon" frequently applied to semi-automatic rifles like the AR-15. Sporting rifles may include bolt-action, lever-action, or semi-automatic models.

**stand your ground laws.** *See* castle doctrine.

**stock.** The rear part of a rifle or shotgun that rests against the shooter's shoulder. An adjustable or telescoping stock can extend or collapse to accommodate different shooter preferences, improve portability, or adjust length of pull.

**subsonic.** Refers to a bullet traveling below the speed of sound, typically under 1,125 feet per second at sea level. Subsonic rounds are quieter, especially when used with suppressors, but generally have more bullet drop and less energy over long distances.

**supersonic.** Refers to a bullet traveling faster than the speed of sound, usually exceeding 1,125 feet per second. Supersonic rounds create a distinct sonic crack (i.e., sonic boom) in flight and are commonly used for long-range shooting due to their flatter trajectories and better energy retention.

**suppressor.** A device that reduces a firearm's sound and muzzle flash. Often misrepresented in media as making guns "silent." *See also* silencer.

**survivalist.** An individual who prepares for emergencies, disasters, or societal collapse by stockpiling supplies, developing self-sufficiency skills, and planning for long-term survival. Survivalists prioritize independence, resourcefulness, and personal defense, often viewing preparedness as a practical necessity rather than paranoia.

**swatting.** The act of making a false report to emergency services to provoke an aggressive law enforcement response, typically involving a SWAT team, to an unsuspecting victim's address. Often used as a harassment tactic, swatting is illegal and highly dangerous, sometimes resulting in injury or death.

**tactical.** Relating to strategies, equipment, or actions intended for combat, law enforcement, or self-defense scenarios. In firearms culture, it often refers to gear or firearms designed for practical and defensive applications, such as black finishes, optics, or modular attachments, as opposed to purely sporting or hunting use.

**terminal ballistics.** The study of what happens to a projectile when it strikes its target. Factors include bullet expansion, penetration, and energy transfer which are crucial in self-defense and hunting applications.

**threaded barrel.** A firearm barrel with external threads at the muzzle end, allowing the attachment of devices such as suppressors, compensators, or flash hiders. Threaded barrels are common on tactical or competition firearms and are regulated in some jurisdictions depending on the attached device.

**totalitarian.** Describes a system of government in which the ruling authority exercises absolute control over nearly every aspect of public and private life. Historically associated with authoritarian ideologies such as socialism, communism, fascism, and other collectivist movements. *See also* tyranny.

**trigger.** The lever on a firearm that the shooter presses to discharge a round. Pulling the trigger releases the hammer or striker, igniting the primer and firing the projectile. Trigger mechanisms can vary between single-action, double-action, and other specialized systems.

**trigger guard.** A loop, typically made of metal or polymer, that surrounds the trigger to prevent accidental discharge. The trigger guard protects the trigger from being pressed unintentionally by foreign objects or during handling.

**tyranny.** Oppressive government rule that violates basic freedoms. *See also* totalitarian.

**universal background checks.** A proposal to require background checks for all firearm transfers, including private sales. *See also* background check.

**unconstitutional.** A law or action that violates protections guaranteed by the US Constitution.

**upper receiver.** The top half of a modular firearm, like the AR-15, housing the barrel, bolt carrier group, and charging handle. Can be swapped out to change calibers or barrel lengths.

**US Constitution.** The supreme legal document of the United States, which establishes the framework for the federal government and outlines the rights and liberties of American citizens. The Constitution includes the Bill of Rights—the first 10 amendments—of which the Second Amendment secures the right to keep and bear arms. It serves as the highest legal authority in the country and is designed to limit governmental power.

**victim disarmament zone.** A sarcastic term used by gun rights advocates to describe gun-free zones.

**violent crime.** Criminal acts involving force or threat of force such as murder, robbery, or assault.

**virtue signaling.** The act of publicly expressing opinions or sentiments intended to demonstrate one's moral superiority or alignment with popular causes, often without taking meaningful action. Common in politics, social media, and corporate culture, virtue signaling is frequently criticized as performative or insincere.

**waiting period.** A mandatory delay between purchasing and receiving a firearm.

**well regulated.** A term from the Second Amendment historically meaning "properly functioning," "well-equipped," or "orderly and trained." In the 18th century, it did not imply heavy government control but rather described something operating effectively and in good working order—such as a militia capable of defending liberty. *See also* "well regulated Militia."

**"well regulated Militia."** Historically meant a properly functioning and well-trained militia, not one heavily controlled by government.

**weaponized bureaucracy.** The use of regulatory agencies to harass or restrict citizens, particularly gun owners.

**weapons cache.** A hidden or secured stockpile of firearms, ammunition, and related gear, often used in reference to military, survivalist, or criminal contexts.

**windage.** The horizontal adjustment of a firearm's sights or optic to compensate for the effect of wind or the natural drift of a projectile. Adjusting for windage helps ensure the bullet impacts the intended point of aim when crosswinds or other lateral forces are present during flight.

**x-ring.** The innermost scoring zone on a target used in competitive shooting.

**youth hunting license.** A permit allowing minors to hunt under adult supervision.

**zeroing.** The process of adjusting a firearm's sights or optic to align point of aim with point of impact.

**zoning laws.** Local regulations that sometimes restrict where firearm-related businesses can operate.

# Bibliography and Recommended Reading

2nd Amendment Daily News. "The Second Amendment Preservation Act—Gun Owners' Best Bet Against Federal Gun Control in 2021." 2nd Amendment Daily News, January 13,
2021. https://www.secondamendmentdaily.com/2021/01/second-amen
dment-protection-act-gun-owners-best-bet-against-federal-gun-control/.

ABC 7 News. "Armed Robber Flees in Panic When California Liquor Store
Owner Blasts Shotgun: 'He Shot My Arm Off!'" ABC 7 News, August 2,
2022. https://abc7news.com/norco-shooting-attempted-robbery-owner
-shoots-suspect/12093909/.

ABC News. "Okla. Mom Won't Face Charges, but Victim's Accomplice
Will." ABC News, January 6, 2012. https://abcnews.go.com/US/okla-m
om-face-charges-victims-accomplice/story?id=15304382.

Adams, Samuel. *The Writings of Samuel Adams*. Edited by Harry Alonzo
Cushing. G. P. Putnam's Sons, 1904–1908.

Ammoland Shooting Sports News. Tred Law. "Pennsylvania Cemetery
Shooting Death Ruled Justifiable Self Defense." *Ammoland*, April 26,
2023. https://www.ammoland.com/2023/04/pa-cemetery-shooting-dea
th-ruled-justifiable-self-defense-fafo/.

"Assize of Arms 1181." The British Library.

Bohbot, Amir, and Yaakov Katz. *The Weapon Wizards: How Israel Became a High-Tech Military Superpower.* St. Martin's Press, 2017.

Baus, Chad D. "Churchgoer with Concealed Carry Permit Stops Man with Shotgun." Buckeye Firearms Association, April 5, 2012. https://www.buc keyefirearms.org/churchgoer-concealed-carry-permit-stops-man-shotgun.

Bella, Rick. "Clackamas Town Center Shooting: Story of Armed Shopper Fuels National Debate." *The Oregonian*, May 2, 2013. https://www.oregonlive.co m/clackamascounty/2013/05/clackamas_town_center_shooting_84.html.

"Black Guns Matter: Maj Toure's Mission to Educate Urban Communities on Gun Rights." NRA News, October 15, 2016. https://www.nranews.com/series/spotlight/video/spotlight-black-guns-ma tter-maj-toures-mission-to-educate-urban-communities-on-gun-rights.

Bureau of Alcohol, Tobacco, Firearms and Explosives (ATF). "Minimum Age for Firearm Purchase and Possession." Accessed January 23, 2025. https:// www.atf.gov/firearms/firearms-statistics.

Bureau of Justice Statistics. "Guns Used in Crime." U.S. Department of Justice, July 1995. https://bjs.ojp.gov/content/pub/pdf/GUIC.PDF.

*Caetano v. Massachusetts, 577 U.S. 411* (2016). Legal Information Institute, Cornell Law School. https://www.law.cornell.edu/supremecourt/text/577 /411.

California Department of Justice. "Assault Weapons Law (Penal Code 30510-30530)." Accessed February 23, 2025. https://codes.findlaw.com/ca /penal-code/pen-sect-30510/.

Cato Institute. "Gun Buybacks: Ineffective and Expensive." Accessed November 23, 2025. https://www.cato.org/.

Cato Institute. "Red Flag Laws and DueProcess Concerns." Accessed January 3, 2025. https://www.cato.org/.

Centers for Disease Control and Prevention (CDC). "Firearm Mortality Data." Accessed December 1, 2025. https://www.cdc.gov/nchs/fastats/injury.htm.

Charles, Jeff. "Showdown at an Alabama Traffic Light: Good Guy With a Gun Stops Knife-Wielding Assailant." RedState, July 22, 2023. https://redstate.com/jeffc/2023/07/22/showdown-at-an-alabama-tr affic-light-good-guy-with-a-gun-stops-knife-wielding-assailant-n780561.

Courtois, Stéphane, et al. *The Black Book of Communism: Crimes, Terror, Repression*. Harvard University Press, 1999.

CSPOA. "Defend the Rights—an Interview With Sheriff Mack." August 12, 2024. https://cspoa.org/latest-news/defend-the-rights-an-interview-with-sheriff-mack/.

Dikötter, Frank. *Mao's Great Famine: The History of China's Most Devastating Catastrophe, 1958–1962*. Walker & Company, 2010.

*District of Columbia v. Heller, 554 U.S. 570* (2008). Legal Information Institute, Cornell Law School. https://www.law.cornell.edu/supremecourt/text/554/570.

*District of Columbia v. Heller, 554 U.S. 570* (2008). Supreme Court of the United States. https://www.supremecourt.gov/opinions/opinions.aspx.

Dobson, William J. *The Dictator's Learning Curve: Inside the Global Battle for Democracy*. Anchor Books, 2012.

Engels, Friedrich, and Karl Marx. *The Communist Manifesto*. Penguin Classics, 2002.

"English Bill of Rights 1689." Avalon Project, Yale Law School. https://avalon.law.yale.edu.

Federal Bureau of Investigation (FBI). "Crime Data Explorer." Accessed March 1, 2025. https://cde.ucr.cjis.gov/.

Federal Bureau of Investigation (FBI). "Crime in the United States." Uniform Crime Reporting Program. Annual reports.

Federal Bureau of Investigation (FBI). "Crime in the U.S." Accessed January 3, 2025. https://ucr.fbi.gov/crime-in-the-u.s/.

Federal Bureau of Investigation (FBI). "National Instant Criminal Background Check System (NICS)." Federal Bureau of Investigation. https://www.fbi.gov/services/cjis/nics.

Fox 12 Oregon. Paulina Aguilar. "Portland Business Owner Shoots Intruder Who Broke into Warehouse." Fox 12Oregon, March 8, 2023. https://www.kptv.com/2023/03/09/portland-business-owner-shoots-intruder-who-broke-into-warehouse/.

Fox 23 News. "Man Shot in Osage County Home Invasion Knew the Woman Inside." Fox 23 News, March 3, 2023. https://www.fox23.com/news/local/man-shot-in-osage-county-home-invasion-knew-the-woman-inside/article_4bf94e2e-b9d1-11ed-bf5e-e74301772775.html.

Fox 25. Callie Morris. "Man Drives Home After Being Shot in Face During Home Invasion, Deputies Say." Fox 25, March 3, 2023. https://okcfox.com/news/local/man-drives-home-after-being-shot-in-face-during-home-invasion-deputies-say.

Fox 29 Philadelphia. Ellen Kolodziej and Fox 29 Staff. "Woman Thwarts Home Invasion by Opening Fire on 4 Suspects in Germantown, Police Say." Fox 29 Philadelphia, July 16, 2023. https://www.fox29.com/news/woman-thwarts-home-invasion-by-opening-fire-on-3-suspects-in-germantown-police-say.

Fox News. "9 Killed in Shooting at Florida Nightclub in Possible Act of Islamic Terror." Fox News, June 12, 2016. https://www.foxnews.com/us/49-killed-in-shooting-at-florida-nightclub-in-possible-act-of-islamic-terror.

Fox News. Emma Colton. "Knife-Wielding Man Attacks Wife in Traffic but Armed Good Samaritan Steps In." Fox News, July 19, 2023. https://www.foxnews.com/us/knife-wielding-man-attacks-wife-traffic-armed-samaritan-steps-in.

Fox News. Stephen Sorace. "Armed Texas Store Owner Defends Self in Shootout with Would-Be Robbers, Video Shows." Fox News, November 8, 2023. https://www.foxnews.com/us/armed-texas-store-owner-defends-self-shootout-would-be-robbers-video.

Fox News. Andrea Vacchiano. "Pennsylvania Woman Foils Home Invasion by Shooting Burglary Suspects: Police." Fox News, July 16, 2023. https://www.foxnews.com/us/pennsylvania-woman-foils-home-invasion-shooting-burglary-suspects-police.

Galeano, Eduardo. The Collapse of Venezuela: The Rise and Fall of a Nation. Monthly Review Press, 2018.

Garland v. Cargill, No. 22-976, U.S. Supreme Court (2024). Supreme Court of the United States. https://www.supremecourt.gov.

Gast, Phil. "Oklahoma Mom Calling 911 Asks If Shooting an Intruder Is Allowed." CNN, January 4, 2012. https://www.cnn.com/2012/01/04/justice/oklahoma-intruder-shooting/index.html.

Giffords Law Center. "Extreme Risk Protection Orders." Accessed October 7, 2024. https://giffords.org/lawcenter/gun-laws/policy-areas/who-can-have-a-gun/extreme-risk-protection-orders/.

Gott, Richard. *Cuba: A New History.* Yale University Press, 2004.

Gourevitch, Philip. *We Wish to Inform You That Tomorrow We Will Be Killed with Our Families: Stories from Rwanda.* Farrar, Straus and Giroux, 1998.

Green, K. C. "This Is Fine." *Gunshow* (webcomic), 2013.

Griffin, Anna. "Clackamas Town Center Shooting: 22 Minutes of Chaos and Terror as a Gunman Meanders Through the Mall." *The Oregonian*, December 15, 2012. https://www.oregonlive.com/clackamascounty/2012/12/clackamas_town_center_shooting_61.html.

Gun Owners of America. "Gun Owners of America Official Website." Accessed July 13, 2024. https://www.gunowners.org/.

Gun Owners of America. "The Problems with Smart Guns." Accessed August 25, 2024. https://www.gunowners.org/.

Halbrook, Stephen P. Disarmed: *The Assault on Individual Rights in the Aftermath of Tyranny.* Independent Institute, 2008.

Hamilton, Alexander. "Federalist No. 29." In *We the People: Documents and Writings of the Founding Fathers*, 265–269. Sweet Water Press, 2014.

Harden, Blaine. *Escape from Camp 14: One Man's Remarkable Odyssey from North Korea to Freedom in the West.* Viking, 2012.

Haskins, Justin. "According to the Founders, All Federal Gun Restrictions Are Unconstitutional." The Hill, April 1, 2021. https://thehill.com/opinion/civil-rights/545847-according-to-the-founders-all-federal-gun-restrictions-are/.

Him, Chanrithy. *When Broken Glass Floats: Growing Up Under the Khmer Rouge.* W. W. Norton & Company, 2000.

Investors Business Daily. Editorial. "Lesson of Sandy Hook, Clackamas—Ban Gun-Free Zones." *Investors Business Daily*, December 17, 2012. https://www.investors.com/politics/editorials/sandy-hook-tragedy-prevented-at-clackamas/.

Jefferson, Thomas. Draft Virginia Constitution. 1776.

Jefferson, Thomas. Commonplace Book. 1774–1776.

Jews for the Preservation of Firearms Ownership (JPFO). *Innocents Betrayed*. Documentary film. Directed by Aaron Zelman, 2003.

Johns Hopkins Center for Gun Violence Solutions. "Gun Violence in the United States: Data and Trends." Accessed March 22, 2025. https://publichealth.jhu.edu/center-for-gun-violence-solutions/resear ch-reports/gun-violence-in-the-united-states.

Johnson, Nicholas. *Negroes and the Gun: The Black Tradition of Arms*. Prometheus Books, 2014.

KATU 1 ABC. KATU Staff. "Portland Business Owner Shoots, Injures Would-Be Burglar, Police Say." KATU 1 ABC, March 7, 2023. https://katu.com/news/local/portland-business-owner-shoots-injures -would-be-burglar-police-say.

Keeping, Julia. "Sarah McKinley Received Help 14 Minutes After Blanchard Home Invasion Call, 911 Records Reveal." *The Oklahoman*, January 5, 2012. https://www.oklahoman.com/story/news/crime/2012/01/22/sarah-mckinle y-received-help-14-minutes-after-blanchard-home-invasion-call-911-records-r eveal/61102725007/.

KGW8 News. KGW Staff. "Clackamas Mall Shooter Faced Man with Concealed Weapon." KGW8 News, December 16, 2013. https://www.kgw.com/article/news/clackamas-mall-shooter-faced-ma n-with-concealed-weapon/283-71624413.

King, Martin Luther, Jr. *Strength to Love*. Harper & Row, 1963.

Kuzio, Taras. *War and Peace in Ukraine*. E-International Relations, 2022.

Kyemba, Henry. *A State of Blood: The Inside Story of Idi Amin*. Grosset & Dunlap, 1977.

Lachut, Bradford J. "N.J.: Federal Court Puts a Hold on Insurance Mandate to Carry Firearms." Northeast News and Media, May 24, 2023. https://blog.pia.org/2023/05/24/n-j-federal-court-puts-a-hold-on-ins urance-mandate-to-carry-firearms/.

Lankov, Andrei. *The Real North Korea: Life and Politics in the Failed Stalinist Utopia*. Oxford University Press, 2013.

Lee, Richard Henry. *Letters from the Federal Farmer to the Republican*. T. Greenleaf, 1788.

Lehman, R. J. "Nation's First Gun-Insurance Mandates Take Effect. Will They Hold up in Court?" *Insurance Journal*, January 3, 2023. https://www.insurancejournal.com/blogs/law-and-economics/2023/01/03/701434.htm.

Levinson, Sanford. "The Embarrassing Second Amendment." *Yale Law Journal* 99, no. 3 (1989): 637–659.

Loesch, Dana. *Hands Off My Gun: Defeating the Plot to Disarm America*. Center Street, 2014.

Maass, Peter. *Love Thy Neighbor: A Story of War*. Vintage Books, 1997.

Machiavelli, Niccolò. *The Prince*. Translated by Peter E. Bondanella. Oxford University Press, 2005.

Madison, James. "Federalist No. 46." In *We the People: Documents and Writings of the Founding Fathers*, 365–370. Sweet Water Press, 2014.

Mammen, Neil. *The Weaponization of Fear: The Impact of COVID-19 and Lockdowns on American Freedom*. Published by the author, 2022.

Mason, George. Speech at the Virginia Ratifying Convention, 1788.

Mauser, Gary A. "Gun Control in Australia: A Model for America?" *Criminal Justice Policy Review* 29, no. 4 (2018): 418–439.

McArdle, Meghan. "Should People Be Forced to Buy Liability Insurance for Their Guns?" The Daily Beast, July 14, 2017. https://www.thedailybeast.com/should-people-be-forced-to-buy-liability-insurance-for-their-guns.

*McDonald v. City of Chicago*, 561 U.S. 742 (2010). Legal Information Institute, Cornell Law School. https://www.law.cornell.edu/supremecourt/text/561/742.

*McDonald v. City of Chicago*, 561 U.S. 742 (2010). Supreme Court of the United States. https://www.supremecourt.gov/opinions/opinions.aspx.

*Miller v. Texas*, 153 U.S. 535 (1894). Legal Information Institute, Cornell Law School. https://www.law.cornell.edu/supremecourt/text/153/535.

National Firearms Act (NFA) Handbook. Accessed December 7, 2024. https://www.atf.gov/firearms/national-firearms-act-handbook.

National Fraternal Order of Police. Canterbury, Chuck. Letter to Congress, 2019.

National Shooting Sports Foundation (NSSF). "Firearm Identification Cards: Barriers to Legal Gun Ownership." Accessed January 5, 2025. https://www.nssf.org/.

National Shooting Sports Foundation (NSSF). "The Flawed Technology of Microstamping." Accessed January 5, 2025. https://www.nssf.org/.

NBC News 4 New York. John Cádiz Klemack and Jonathan Lloyd. "Store Owner, 80, Fends Off Armed Robbers With Shotgun Blast: 'He Shot My Arm Off!'" NBC News 4 New York, August 3, 2022. https://www.nbcnewyork.com/news/national-international/armed-r obbers-norco-liquor-store-owner-shoots-robbery-suspect-gun/3805995/.

New Jersey Code of Criminal Justice, N.J.S.A. 2C:39-3(f).

New Jersey Legislature. "Smart Guns and the Law." Accessed February 2, 2025. https://www.njleg.state.nj.us/.

New York Secure Ammunition and Firearms Enforcement (SAFE) Act. 2013.

New York State Police. "Pistol Permit Information." New York State Police. https://troopers.ny.gov/Firearms.

*New York State Rifle & Pistol Association Inc. v. Bruen, 597 U.S. ___* (2022). Supreme Court of the United States. https://www.supremecourt.gov.

News 8 ABC. Matt Howerton. "Security Footage Shows Mesquite Jeweler Defending Himself in Shootout with Armed Robbers." News 8 ABC, November 7, 2023. https://www.wfaa.com/article/news/local/dallas-county/security-footage-me squite-jeweler-defending-himself-armed-robber-shootout/287-fa957c8f-384 b-4736-8dde-c73b4b8db60b.

News4. Ken Curtis. "Man Threatens Woman Stopped at Traffic Light with Knife in Domestic Dispute." News4, July 12, 2023. https://www.wtvy.com/2023/07/12/man-threatens-woman-stopped -traffic-light-with-knife-domestic-dispute/.

Ngo, Andy. *Unmasked: Inside Antifa's Radical Plan to Destroy Democracy*. Center Street, 2021.

Ngor, Haing and Roger Warner. *Survival in the Killing Fields*. Basic Books, 1987.

NPR. "The Surgeon General Declared Gun Violence a Public Health Crisis. What Does That Do?" June 25, 2024. https://www.npr.org/2024/06/25/nx-s1-5018625/surgeon-general-vivek-murthy-gun-violence-public-health-crisis.

NRA-ILA. "Ballistic Fingerprinting: Ineffective and Costly." Accessed [Date]June 3, 2024. https://www.nraila.org/.

NRA-ILA. "Comprehensive Information on State Gun Laws and Constitutional Carry." Accessed June 3, 2024. https://www.nraila.org/.

NRA-ILA. "Concealed Carry Reciprocity." NRA Institute for Legislative Action. Accessed June 3, 2024. https://www.nraila.org/.

NRA-ILA. "NRA-ILA Official Website." Accessed February 22, 2025. https://www.nraila.org/.

Oyewale, John. "Clerk Shoots Man Who Jumped Counter While Allegedly Robbing Gas Station: Nashville Police." Daily Caller, July 11, 2023. https://dailycaller.com/2023/07/11/clerk-shooting-decarlos-groves-gas-station-nashville/.

Palmer, R. R. Twelve Who Ruled: The Year of the Terror in the French Revolution. Princeton University Press, 1941.

Paul, Rand. "Speech on the Senate Floor." C-SPAN Senate Floor Speech Archive, February 2013.

Pew Research Center. "What the Data Says About Gun Deaths in the U.S." March 5, 2025. https://www.pewresearch.org/short-reads/2025/03/05/what-the-data-says-about-gun-deaths-in-the-us/.

Plato. Apology. Translated by Benjamin Jowett. Project Gutenberg. https://www.gutenberg.org/ebooks/1656.

Presser v. Illinois, 116 U.S. 252 (1886). Legal Information Institute, Cornell Law School. https://www.law.cornell.edu/supremecourt/text/116/252.

RAND Corporation. "The Effectiveness of Safe Storage Laws."

Reagan, Ronald. An American Life: Ronald Reagan. Simon & Schuster, 1990.

Reagan, Ronald. "NRA Speech." 1983. NRA Archives or Reagan Foundation.

"Red Flag Laws and Due Process Concerns." Accessed January 3, 2025. https://www.cato.org/.

"Safe Storage of Firearms." State of California Department of Justice. Accessed January 11, 2025. https://oag.ca.gov/firearms/tips.

Sanford, Carl T., ed. *The Second Amendment in Law and History: Historians and Constitutional Scholars on the Right to Bear Arms*. The New Press, 2000.

Schama, Simon. *Citizens: A Chronicle of the French Revolution*. Alfred A. Knopf, 1989.

Schanberg, Sydney. *The Killing Fields: The Facts Behind the Film*. Faber & Faber, 1984.

Scheeres, Julia. *A Thousand Lives: The Untold Story of Hope, Deception, and Survival at Jonestown*. Free Press, 2011.

Schiff, Stacy. *The Revolutionary: Samuel Adams*. Little, Brown and Company, 2022.

Second Amendment Foundation. "Second Amendment Foundation Official Website." Accessed May 22, 2024. https://www.saf.org/.

Second Amendment Foundation. "The Case Against Gun Purchase Limits." Accessed September 23, 2024. https://www.saf.org/.

Snyder, Timothy. *Bloodlands: Europe Between Hitler and Stalin*. Basic Books, 2010.

Solzhenitsyn, Aleksandr. *The Gulag Archipelago*. Harper & Row, 1973.

Sowell, Thomas. *The Vision of the Anointed*. Basic Books, 1995.

Statista. "Number of Murder Victims in the United States by Weapon Used, 2007–2021." Accessed March 22, 2025. https://www.statista.com/statistics/195325/murder-victims-in-the-us-by-weapon-used/.

"Statute of Winchester 1285." The National Archives. https://www.nationalarchives.gov.uk.

Stossel, John. "Black Guns Matter." Creators Syndicate, December 28, 2022. https://www.creators.com/read/john-stossel/12/22/black-guns-matter.

Supica, Jim, Doug Wicklund, and Philip Schreier. *An Illustrated History of Firearms*. Gun Digest Books, 2020.

Swearer, Amy. "11 Instances of Defensive Gun Use Dramatize Wisdom of Second Amendment." The Daily Signal, April 24, 2023. https://www.dailysignal.com/2023/04/24/second-amendment-still-about-armed-self-defense-as-these-11-examples-of-defensive-gun-use-show/.

Tactical Experts. "Stand Your Ground Law: All 50 States Reviewed." Tacti calGear.com, accessed April 3, 2025. https://tacticalgear.com/experts/st and-your-ground-law-all-50-states-reviewed.

Tomey, Ramon. "2A WORKS: Woman Shoots Four Would-Be Home Invaders in Philly's Germantown." Gun Sanctuaries, July 18, 2023. https://www.gunsanctuaries.com/2023-07-18-woman-stops-hom e-invasion-shoots-four-suspects.html.

TXGunRights.org. "Second Amendment Preservation Act." Accessed No- vember 2, 2025. https://txgunrights.org/second-amendment-preservati on-act/.

*United States v. Cruikshank, 92 U.S. 542*(1876). Legal Information Institute, Cornell Law School. https://www.law.cornell.edu/supremecourt/text/9 2/542.

*United States v. Michael Rahimi, No. 23-1055, U.S. Court of Appeals, 5th Cir.* (2024). PACER, Justia, or Reuters summaries available online.

*United States v. Miller, 307 U.S. 174* (1939). Legal Information Institute, Cornell Law School. https://www.law.cornell.edu/supremecourt/text/3 07/174.

UPI. "Man with Shotgun Arrested at S.C. Church." UPI, March 25, 2012. https://www.upi.com/Top_News/US/2012/03/25/Man-with-sh otgun-arrested-at-SC-church/35931332729850/.

Valladares, Armando. *Against All Hope: A Memoir of Life in Castro's Gulag.* Alfred A. Knopf, 1986.

WABE, NPR Network. "Political Breakfast Podcast: Georgia Sen. Raphael Warnock's Thoughts on a Possible Mandatory Gun Buyback Program." September 10, 2024. https://omny.fm/shows/political-breakfast-from-w abe/georgia-sen-raphael-warnocks-thoughts-on-a-possibl.

Waldman, Michael. *The Second Amendment: A Biography.* Simon & Schus- ter, 2014.

Washington, George. "A Free People Ought Not Only to Be Armed but Disciplined." First Annual Address to Congress, January 8, 1790.

Whittle, Bill. "Number One with a Bullet." Truth Revolt, January 23, 2015. https://youtu.be/pELwCqz2JfE?si=2DK2HmqlunAiMpqP.

Whittle Bill. "Worst Decision of Judge's Life: Gun Rights for Individual Americans." May 20, 2019. https://www.youtube.com/watch?v=P4BR_0IFSgk&list=PLobA-WQ_mD_dFZByYo4LNltA-fOy7FcVs.

Whittle, Bill. "Your Second Amendment." Truth Revolt, October 24, 2014. https://youtu.be/FOwy9OWfnAM?si=xRrLuBJMnld9n46t.

Wright, Mark Antonio. "Australia's 1996 Gun Confiscation Didn't Work—and It Wouldn't Work in America." *National Review*, October 2, 2015. https://www.nationalreview.com/2015/10/australia-gun-control-obama-america/.

WSMV4. Carmyn Gutierrez. "Police Investigate Self-Defense Claim After Fatal Shooting at Nashville Gas Station." WSMV4, July 8, 2023. https://www.wsmv.com/2023/07/08/police-investigate-self-defense-claim-after-fatal-shooting-nashville-gas-station/.

# About the Author

Joseph P. Rothe is an environmental project manager by profession with a master's degree in environmental chemistry. While his career has been rooted in science, his passion for American history and constitutional rights has made him an amateur historian and a dedicated Second Amendment advocate. His personal journey—from a cautious skeptic of firearms to a staunch defender of gun rights—was shaped by real-world experiences and a deep dive into the history, law, and cultural significance of the right to bear arms. When he's not writing or working, he can usually be found at home reading, hiking outdoors, shooting at the range, or cranking up some rock music somewhere off the beaten path.

www.ingramcontent.com/pod-product-compliance
Lightning Source LLC
Chambersburg PA
CBHW020414150626
46554CB00014B/1131